Plender and Usher's Cases and Materials on the Law of the European Communities

Second Edition

by

RICHARD PLENDER

QC, MA, LLB, LLM, PhD, JSD
Senior Member of Robinson College, Cambridge
Director of the Centre of European Law, King's College, London
Professeur associe a l'universite de Paris II

With a foreword by

Lord Mackenzie Stuart
Sometime President of the Court of Justice of the European Communities

United Kingdom	Butterworth & Co (Publishers) Ltd , 88 Kingsway , LONDON WC2B 6AB and 4 Hill Street , EDINBURGH EH2 3JZ
Australia	Butterworths Pty Ltd , SYDNEY , MELBOURNE , BRISBANE , ADELAIDE , PERTH , CANBERRA and HOBART
Canada	Butterworths Canada Ltd , TORONTO and VANCOUVER
Ireland	Butterworth (Ireland) Ltd , DUBLIN
New Zealand	Butterworths of New Zealand Ltd , WELLINGTON and AUCKLAND
Puerto Rico	Equity de Puerto Rico, Inc, HATO REY
Singapore	Malayan Law Journal Pte Ltd, SINGAPORE
USA	Butterworth Legal Publishers , AUSTIN , Texas ; BOSTON , Massachusetts; CLEARWATER , Florida (D & S Publishers); ORFORD, New Hampshire (Equity Publishing); ST PAUL , Minnesota ; and SEATTLE , Washington

A CIP Catalogue record for this book is available from the British Library .

ISBN 0 406 51146 2

Printed by Bookcraft (Bath) Ltd

Table of Contents

Foreword to the First Edition

In no field of legal study is descriptive writing a substitute for the basic texts. This is particularly so of Community law, which is for the most part a written law.

It is true that Advocate General M. Dutheillet de Lamothe has said of the fundamental principles of national legal systems that 'they contribute to forming that philosophical, political and legal substratum common to the Member States from which through the case-law an unwritten Community law emerges'. Increasingly, the importance of that unwritten Community law is being recognised.

None the less, all Community law by one route or another must find its roots and its authority in a written text, that of the Treaties themselves. The bulk of Community law, as the reported cases demonstrate, is concerned with the interpretation and validity of further written texts, Community 'acts' such as directives, regulations or decisions. Even in the case of unwritten Community law, as M. Dutheillet Lamothe has underlined, this can only be examined through the medium of the reported decisions of the Court.

Unfortunately, even the minimum library required by the student of Community law is formidable. The Official Journal (including, certainly, the Information volumes) from 1970 to 1976 alone runs to about 270 large volumes. Its bulk and cost make many librarians hesitate to take it.

Accordingly, the technique adopted by Dr Plender and Professor Usher has for the beginner everything to commend it. He has the actual text before his eyes; he is led to it by a series of short introductory chapters which, without in any way seeming to be overloaded, contain a surprising amount of information and comment, and he is guided by a carefully chosen list of further reading.

The reader who has mastered the contents of this book will have acquired a first-class base for further and more detailed research. Equally important, he will have learnt the right approach to his subject.

MACKENZIE STUART

Preface to the Second Edition

Since the publication of the first edition of this book European Community law has undergone a transformation. Significant changes have been brought about in the constitution of the Communities, particularly by the Single European Act; and there have been major developments in the case-law, especially in the field of competition.

To take account of these changes, it has been necessary to rewrite the book. The chapter dealing with the free movement of goods has been expanded so that it is several times the length of that in the first edition. In place of one chapter on competition, there are now three. A new chapter has been added on equal pay and treatment. In all of the remaining chapters, new material has been added.

The second edition is 100 pages longer than the first; but in order to keep the book within its present length I have found it necessary to amalgamate into a single chapter the two chapters in the first edition dealing with the origins and institutions of the Community; and to amalgamate the two chapters dealing with actions against Community institutions. Further, the material on external relations has been fitted into other parts of the book, instead of constituting a single chapter. The material drawn from the constitutions and laws of the Member States dealing with the reception of Community law into national legal systems has been deleted altogether.

I wish to express my appreciation of the outstanding assistance given by my research assistant, Mara Goldstein, particularly in respect of Chapter 6; and by Emily Driver for her help in proof-reading and in the compilation of the index. Finally, I have to thank Kathleen Fedouloff, who typeset the entire text ready for the publishers. This technically complicated and time-consuming task was discharged quickly, economically and cheerfully.

R.P.
The Temple
London EC4

May 1989

Table of Treaties

(Bold page numbers indicate that the text or a part of the text of the article is quoted in full. Italic page numbers indicate references to articles in editorial comment or case reports.)

Table of Decisions, Directives, Regulations and Other Acts

(Bold page numbers indicate that the text or a part of the text of the article referred to is quoted in full. Italic page numbers indicate other references in editorial comment or case reports.)

Table of Cases

(Bold page numbers indicate an extract from the case report)

1

THE ORIGINS AND INSTITUTIONS OF THE COMMUNITIES

I INTERNATIONAL AND SUPRANATIONAL ORGANISATIONS

By a treaty concluded in Paris on 18 April 1951 the heads of State of France, Italy, the Federal Republic of Germany and the Benelux countries established a European Coal and Steel Community (ECSC). This they did, in the words of the preamble of that Treaty, 'considering that world peace can be safeguarded only by creative efforts..., recognising that Europe can be built only by practical achievements' and resolving 'to create, by establishing an economic community, the basis for a broader and deeper community'. The association between the six ECSC States was broadened and deepened on 25 March 1957 when the same six States concluded in Rome two further treaties: one establishing the European Atomic Energy Community (Euratom) and the other establishing the European Economic Community (EEC).

The three Communities so created were part of a series of international organisations set up in western Europe after the Second World War with the object of forging a closer bond between the States or peoples of the region. At the Congress of Europe convened at The Hague in May 1948, with Sir Winston Churchill as President of Honour, delegates recorded by resolution their desire for 'a united Europe throughout whose area the free movement of persons, ideas and goods is restored'. The first organisation established to fulfil this desire was the Brussels Treaty Organisation (BTO), an arrangement made between the United Kingdom, France and the Benelux countries for their collective self-defence and also for collaboration on economic, social and cultural matters. The next step was the establishment of the Organisation for European Economic Cooperation, or OEEC (which was to be transformed in 1960 into the Organisation for Economic Cooperation and Development). The OEEC was designed to implement the

Marshall Plan. Its governing body, called the Council, soon established a hierarchy of legal acts, from 'recommendations' (which had only hortatory effect) through 'agreements' to 'decisions' (which were binding on Member States).

In May 1949 the ambassadors of the BTO States, together with those of Denmark, Ireland, Italy, Norway and Sweden, produced the draft statute of the Council of Europe. The object was to 'achieve a greater unity between its members for the purpose of safeguarding and realising the ideals and principles which are their common heritage and facilitating their economic and social progress'. Defence was excluded from the Council of Europe's mandate but economic, social, cultural, scientific, legal and administrative matters, together with the maintenance of human rights, were to fall within its province. The Council encompassed a Committee of Ministers, composed of the foreign ministers of the Member States or their deputies, and a Consultative Assembly consisting of representatives drawn from the several national parliaments in rough proportion to the national populations. The two chief organs were to collaborate via a joint committee served by a secretariat. By this machinery the Council of Europe sponsored a series of conventions, including the European Convention for the Protection of Human Rights and Fundamental Freedoms, whose enforcement called for the creation of an autonomous Commission and Court.

Following the blockade of Berlin and the coup in Czechoslovakia, the North Atlantic Treaty Organisation (NATO) was established, with a wider membership than the BTO and a separate identity. NATO's supreme organ is the North Atlantic Council, on which each Member State is represented, and which is served by a Secretary-General and secretariat.

When, therefore, the ECSC was created it joined a family of European organisations differing in their objects but characterised by a common acknowledgment of the need for regional collaboration, controlled by councils of foreign ministers and served by secretariats. Even so, the ECSC was a remarkable innovation. Its Assembly was to have powers greater than those of the Council of Europe: it was to be capable of overthrowing the executive. Its Court of Justice was to have jurisdiction of a different order from that of the European Court of Human Rights: it was to be charged not with the duty of securing observance of the Treaty, but with that of ensuring observance of *the law* in the interpretation *and application* of the Treaty. The ECSC Treaty itself purported not only to regulate the relationship between the Member States but also to produce direct effects within the territories of those States. The ECSC's permanent executive was to be a High Authority imbued with the 'supranational' power to take decisions binding on national enterprises without the intervention of any national parliament or government; the Council, consisting of representatives of Member States, was to have similar supranational powers.

An effort was soon made to apply the same formula to defence and to political union. On 27 May 1952 a treaty for the creation of a European Defence Community (EDC) was signed in Paris; and a treaty to set up a European Political Community was drafted. These ambitious projects were frustrated by the French National Assembly's failure to approve the EDC Treaty. This retarded but did not halt the development of supranational organisations in the region. When the European Organisation for Nuclear Research (CERN) was set up in 1953 its Council and Director were not given the power to bind national enterprises without national intervention; but limited supranational powers were conferred on the Council of a new organisation created in 1954 to replace the BTO. This was the Western European Union (WEU), a defensive union of the former BTO powers plus Italy and the Federal Republic of Germany. The Member States undertook to place certain of their forces under a supreme command (SACEUR) and in the case of Germany to refrain from the manufacture of certain weapons including atomic ones. The WEU was to have an Assembly fashioned after that of the Council of Europe and a Council authorised to make by majority vote certain decisions binding on the States to which they were addressed. In particular it could take such action in respect of a finding of a breach by Germany of its undertaking to refrain from manufacturing atomic weapons.

Only with the creation of the EEC and Euratom was there a genuine reappearance of supranational powers of the kind seen in the case of the ECSC. Indeed, the capacity of the institutions of those organisations to legislate without the intervention of national parliaments was one of the features that made them at the time unacceptable to west European States other than the six within the ECSC. In response to the creation of Euratom the OEEC Council in 1957 established a European Nuclear Energy Authority (ENEA) and a Convention on the Establishment of a Security Control in the Field of Nuclear Energy. In response to the creation of the EEC the United Kingdom, Denmark, Norway, Sweden, Austria, Switzerland and Portugal established in 1959 a European Free Trade Area (EFTA). These were timid institutions by comparison with Euratom and the EEC. The ENEA's Control Board was given powers of inspection and its Tribunal was enabled to adjudicate on questions of default, but unlike Euratom the ENEA was not entrusted with the ownership of special fissionable materials nor did it have the right of option over other nuclear materials produced or imported within the territory of its members. The institutional structure of EFTA was similar to that of the OEEC: it was governed by a Council which would normally act only on the basis of unanimity, and although the Council later agreed to present an Annual Report to the Council of Europe's Assembly, EFTA had no Assembly of its own with extensive supervisory powers such as was created for the several European Communities. EFTA was essentially to be a free trade zone in which Member States were to be at liberty to determine their external tariffs.

That the EEC is a supranational system has twofold significance: 1) rights and duties are created for individuals (see Case 26/62 *NV Algemene Transport - En Expeditie onderneming Van Gend en Loos* v *Nederlandse Administratie der Belastingen*, below p. 79) and 2) the EEC law prevails over national law in the event of a conflict.

Case 6/64 Flaminio Costa v ENEL

[1964] ECR 585; 10 *Recueil* (1964) 1141; [1964] 3 CMLR 425

By a law of 1962 and by subsequent decrees the Italian Republic nationalised the electricity industry and created the defendant company, Ente Nazionale per l'Energia Elettrica (ENEL), to which assets of private Italian electricity companies were transferred. Mr Costa, a lawyer, received a bill for 1950 lire (then about £1 or $2.80) from ENEL for electricity supplied to him by Edison Volta, one of the private companies affected by the nationalisation, and one in which Mr Costa was a shareholder. Mr Costa applied to the Milanese Giudice Conciliatore (local judge) for a declaration that he was not obliged to pay the sum. He alleged first that the law of 1962 infringed the Italian Constitution and secondly that it infringed certain provisions of the EEC Treaty including Article 37 (which deals with the progressive adjustment of State monopolies). At Mr Costa's request the giudice conciliatore referred the matter to the Court of Justice of the European Communities requesting an interpretation of the EEC Treaty and particularly of Article 37. The Italian Government intervened, objecting that the application for a ruling on the Treaty was absolutely inadmissible. The Government argued that a national court cannot refer a question to the Court of Justice of the European Communities when, for the purpose of deciding a dispute, it has only to apply a domestic law and not a provision of the Treaty. The Court ruled otherwise.

The Court

The Italian Government submits that the request of the Giudice Conciliatore is 'absolutely inadmissible', inasmuch as a national court which is obliged to apply a national law cannot avail itself of Article 177.

By contrast with ordinary international treaties, the Treaty has created its own legal systems which, on the entry into force of the Treaty, became an integral part of the legal systems of the Member States and which their courts are bound to apply.

By creating a Community of unlimited duration, having its own institutions, its own personality, its own legal capacity and capacity of representation on the international plane and, more particularly, real powers stemming from a limitation of sovereignty or a transfer of powers from the States to the Community, the Member States have limited their sovereign rights, albeit within limited fields, and have thus created a body of law which binds both their nationals and themselves.

The integration into the laws of each Member State of provisions, which derive from the Community, and more generally the terms and the spirit of the Treaty, make it impossible for the States, as a corollary, to accord precedence to a unilateral and subsequent measure over a legal system accepted by them on a basis of reciprocity. Such a measure cannot therefore be inconsistent with that legal system. The executive force of the Community law cannot vary from one State to another in deference to subsequent domestic laws, without jeopardising the attainment of the objectives of the Treaty set out in Article 5(2) and giving rise to the discrimination prohibited by Article 7.

The obligations undertaken under the Treaty establishing the Community would not be unconditional, but merely contingent, if they could be called in question by subsequent legislative acts of the signatories. Wherever the Treaty grants the States the right to act unilaterally, it does this by clear and precise provisions (for example Articles 15, 93(3), 223, 224 and 225). Applications by Member States for authority to derogate from the Treaty are subject to a special authorisation procedure (for example Articles 8(4), 17(4), 25, 26, 73, the third subparagraph of Article 93(2), and 226) which would lose their purpose if the Member States could renounce their obligation by means of ordinary law.

The precedence of Community law is confirmed by Article 189, whereby a regulation 'shall be binding' and 'directly applicable in all Member States'. This provision, which is subject to no reservation, would be quite meaningless if a State could unilaterally nullify by means of a legislative measure which could prevail over Community law.

It follows from all these observations that *the law stemming from the Treaty, an independent source of law, could not, because of its special and original nature, be overridden by domestic legal provisions, however framed, without being deprived of its character as Community law and without the legal basis of the Community itself being called into question.*

The transfer by the States from their domestic legal system to the Community legal system of the rights and obligations arising under the Treaty carries with it a permanent limitation of their sovereign rights, against which a subsequent unilateral act incompatible with the concept of the Community cannot prevail. Consequently Article 177 is to be applied regardless of any domestic law, whenever questions relating to the interpretation of the Treaty arise...

The Interpretation of Article 37

Article 37(1) provides that Member States shall progressively adjust any 'State monopolies of a commercial character' so as to ensure that no discrimination regarding the conditions under which goods are procured and marketed exists between nationals of Member States. By Article 37(2), the Member States are under an obligation to refrain from introducing any new measure which is contrary to the principles laid down in Article 37(1).

Thus, Member States have undertaken a dual obligation: in the first place, an active one to adjust State monopolies; in the second place, a passive one to avoid any new measures. The interpretation requested is of the second obligation together with any aspects of the first necessary for this interpretation.

Article 37(2) contains an absolute prohibition: not an obligation to do something but an obligation to refrain from doing something. This obligation is not accompanied by any reservation which might make its implementation subject to any positive act of national law. This prohibition is essentially one which is capable of producing direct effects on the legal relations between Member States and their nationals.

Such a clearly expressed prohibition which came into force with the Treaty throughout the Community, and so became an integral part of the legal system of the Member States, forms part of the law of those States and directly concerns their nationals, in whose favour it creates individual rights which national courts must protect. By reason of the complexity of the wording and the fact that Articles 37(1) and 37(2) overlap, the interpretation requested makes it necessary to examine them as a part of the Chapter in which they occur. This Chapter deals with the 'elimination of quantitative restrictions between Member States'. The object of the reference in Article 37(2) to 'the principles laid down in paragraph (1)' is thus to prevent the establishment of any new 'discrimination regarding the conditions under which goods are procured and marketed... between nationals of Member States'. Having specified the objective in this way, Article 37(1) sets out the ways in which this objective might be thwarted in order to prohibit them.

Thus, by the reference in Article 37(2), any new monopolies or bodies specified in Article 37(1) are prohibited in so far as they tend to introduce new cases of discrimination regarding the conditions under which goods are procured and marketed. It is therefore a matter for the court dealing with the main action first to examine whether this objective is being hampered, that is whether any new discrimination between nationals of Member States regarding the conditions under which goods are procured and marketed results from the disputed measure itself or will be the consequence thereof.

There remain to be considered the means envisaged by Article 37(1). It does not prohibit the creation of any State monopolies but merely those of a 'commercial character' and then only in so far as they tend to introduce the cases of discrimination referred to. To fall under this prohibition the State monopolies and bodies in question must, first, have as their object transactions regarding a commercial product capable of being the subject of competition and trade between Member States, and secondly must play an effective part in such trade.

It is a matter for the court dealing with the main action to assess in each case whether the economic activity under review relates to such a product which, by virtue of its nature and the technical or international conditions to which it is subject, is capable of playing an effective part in imports or exports between nationals of the Member States.

Exactly one year later the Italian Constitutional Court rejected Mr Costa's allegations of constitutional irregularity: [1964] 3 CMLR 425. The giudice conciliatore then decided that the law of 1962 and the subsequent decrees had no legal effect, as a result of Article 37 of the EEC Treaty, as interpreted by the European Court: [1968] CMLR 267 at 278. (His judgment goes further than the European Court's ruling, however, for whereas the European Court pointed out that Article 37(2) of the EEC Treaty prohibits the creation of new monopolies in so far as they tend to introduce new cases of 'discrimination' regarding the 'supply of goods', the giudice conciliatore ignored those two limitations. For this reason the giudice's final judgment is not generally accepted as reliable.)

EEC law prevails in those areas in which it applies, i.e. those areas in which the Member States have ceded sovereignty. In some areas defined by the Treaty it is beyond doubt that sovereignty has been ceded, but the European Court of Justice has not confined the supremacy of European law to areas in which the Treaty makes express provision. Rather it has held that the Member States have ceded sovereignty to the Communities by necessary implication whenever they have adopted a common policy to regulate a given matter.

Case 22/70 Commission of the European Communities v Council of the European Communities
[1971] ECR 263; [1971] CMLR 335

In 1962 five of the Member States of the EEC together with several other European States concluded, under the auspices of the United Nations Economic Commission for Europe (UNECE), the European Road Transport Agreement (ERTA or AETR). In 1967, before the Agreement had entered into force, negotiations began for its revision. These were protracted. They were conducted first in Paris and later, under the auspices of the UNECE, in Geneva.

The Commission of the European Communities was in the meantime engaged in drafting and making proposals for the implementation of the EEC's Common Transport Policy in pursuance of Article 75 of the EEC Treaty. In support of such a proposal the EEC Council made Regulation No 543/69 of 25 March 1969, governing the harmonisation of certain social provisions in the field of road transport.

At its meeting on 20 March 1970 the EEC Council discussed the attitude to be adopted by the six Member States of the EEC at the negotiations for the revision of ERTA, due to be held under the auspices of the UNECE from 1 to 3 April 1970. It was in accordance with the discussion of 20 March that the Member States of the EEC undertook and concluded negotiations at the subsequent meeting at the UNECE's premises in Geneva.

The EEC Commission took the view that the proceedings on 20 March 1970 amounted to an encroachment by the Council on the Commission's area of responsibility. It asked the Court of Justice of the European Communities to annul those proceedings.

The Court

By an application lodged on 19 May 1970 the Commission of the European Communities has requested the annulment of the Council's proceedings of 20 March 1970 regarding the negotiation and conclusion by the Member States of the Community, under the auspices of the United Nations Economic Commission for Europe, of the European Agreement concerning the work of crews of vehicles engaged in international road transport (AETR).

As a preliminary objection, the Council has submitted that the application is inadmissible on the ground that the proceedings in question are not an act the legality of which is open to review under the first paragraph of Article 173 of the Treaty.

To decide this point, it is first necessary to determine which authority was, at the relevant date, empowered to negotiate and conclude the AETR.

The legal effect of the proceedings differs according to whether they are regarded as constituting the exercise of powers conferred on the Community, or as acknowledging a coordination by the Member States of the exercise of powers which remained vested in them.

To decide on the objection of inadmissibility, therefore, it is necessary to determine first of all whether, at the date of the proceedings in question, power to negotiate and conclude the AETR was vested in the Community or in the Member States...

The Commission takes the view that Article 75 of the Treaty, which conferred on the Community powers defined in wide terms with a view to implementing the common transport policy, must apply to external relations just as much as to domestic measures in the sphere envisaged...

The Council, on the other hand, contends that since the Community only has such powers as have been conferred on it, authority to enter into agreements with third countries cannot be assumed in the absence of an express provision in the Treaty...

In the absence of specific provisions of the Treaty relating to the negotiation and conclusion of international agreements in the sphere of transport policy – a category into which, essentially, the AETR falls – one must turn to the general system of Community law in the sphere of relations with third countries.

Article 210 provides that 'The Community shall have legal personality'.

This provision, placed at the head of Part Six of the Treaty, devoted to 'General and Final Provisions', means that in its external relations the Community enjoys the capacity to establish contractual links with third countries over the whole field of objectives defined in Part One of the Treaty, which Part Six supplements.

To determine in a particular case the Community's authority to enter into international agreements, regard must be had to the whole scheme of the Treaty no less than to its substantive provisions.

Such authority arises not only from an express conferment by the Treaty – as is the case with Articles 113 and 114 for tariff and trade agreements and with Article 238 for association agreements – but may equally flow from other provisions of the Treaty and from measures adopted, within the framework of those provisions, by the Community institutions.

In particular, each time the Community, with a view to implementing a common policy envisaged by the Treaty, adopts provisions laying down common rules, whatever form these may take, the Member States no longer have the right, acting individually or even collectively, to undertake obligations with third countries which affect those rules.

As and when such common rules come into being, the Community alone is in a position to assume and carry out contractual obligations towards third countries affecting the whole sphere of application of the Community legal system.

With regard to the implementation of the provisions of the Treaty the system of internal Community measures may not therefore be separated from that of external relations...

Although it is true that Articles 74 and 75 do not expressly confer on the Community authority to enter into international agreements, nevertheless the bringing into force, on 25 March 1969, of Regulation No 543/69 of the Council on the harmonisation of certain social legislation relating to road transport (OJ L 77, p. 49) necessarily vested in the Community power to enter into any agreements with third countries relating to the subject-matter governed by that regulation.

This grant of power is moreover expressly recognised by Article 3 of the said regulation which prescribes that: 'The Community shall enter into any negotiations with third countries which may prove necessary for the purpose of implementing this regulation'.

Since the subject-matter of the AETR falls within the scope of Regulation No 543/69, the Community has been empowered to negotiate and conclude the agreement in question since the entry into force of the said regulation.

These Community powers exclude the possibility of concurrent powers on the part of Member States, since any steps taken outside the framework of the Community institutions would be incompatible with the unity of the Common Market and the uniform application of Community law.

This is the legal position in the light of which the question of admissibility has to be resolved.

The Court then analysed the discussion of 20 March 1970 and noted that it was designed to lay down a course of action binding on the institutions and on Member States and as such had definite legal effects. It also observed that the Commission has an incontrovertible interest in bringing the action. Thus it deduced that the measure impugned by the Commission was one that the Court could review, that the Commission had *locus standi*, and that the application was admissible. The Court continued as follows:

The Commission claims that in view of the powers vested in the Community under Article 75, the AETR should have been negotiated and concluded by the Community in accordance with the Community procedure defined by Article 228(1)...

In the absence of specific provisions in the Treaty applicable to the negotiation and implementation of the agreement under discussion, the appropriate rules must be inferred from the general tenor of those articles of the Treaty which relate to the negotiations undertaken on the AETR.

The distribution of powers between the Community institutions to negotiate and implement to the AETR must be determined with due regard both to the provisions relating to the common transport policy and to those governing the conclusion of agreements by the Community.

By the terms of Article 75(1), it is a matter for the Council, acting on a proposal from the Commission and after consulting the Economic and Social Committee and the Assembly, to lay down the appropriate provisions, whether by regulation or otherwise, for the purpose of implementing the common transport policy.

According to Article 228(1), where agreements have to be concluded with one or more third countries or an international organisation, such agreements are to be negotiated by the Commission and concluded by the Council, subject to any more extensive powers which may have been vested in the Commission...

If these various provisions are read in conjunction, it is clear that wherever a matter forms the subject of a common policy, the Member States are bound in every case to act jointly in defence of the interests of the Community.

This requirement of joint action was in fact respected by the proceedings of 20 March 1970, which cannot give rise to any criticism in this respect.

Moreover, it follows from these provisions taken as a whole, and particularly from Article 228(1), that the right to conclude the agreement was vested in the Council.

The Commission for its part was required to act in two ways, first by exercising its right to make proposals, which arises from Article 75(1) and the first paragraph of Article 116, and, secondly, in its capacity as negotiator by the terms of the first subparagraph of Article 228(1).

However, this distribution of powers between institutions would only have been required where negotiations were undertaken at a time when the vesting of powers in the

Community had taken effect, either by virtue of the Treaty itself or by virtue of measures taken by the institutions...

The stage of negotiations of which the proceedings in question formed part was not aimed at working out a new agreement, but simply at introducing into the version drawn up in 1962 such modifications as were necessary to enable all the contracting parties to ratify it.

The negotiations on the AETR are thus characterised by the fact that their origin and a considerable part of the work carried out under the auspices of the Economic Commission for Europe took place before powers were conferred on the Community as a result of Regulation No 543/69.

It appears therefore that on 20 March 1970 the Council acted in a situation where it no longer enjoyed complete freedom of action in its relations with the third countries taking part in the same negotiations.

At that stage of the negotiations, to have suggested to the third countries concerned that there was now a new distribution of powers within the Community might well have jeopardised the successful outcome of the negotiations, as was indeed recognised by the Commission's representative in the course of the Council's deliberations.

In such a situation it was for the two institutions whose powers were directly concerned, namely, the Council and the Commission, to reach agreement, in accordance with Article 15 of the Treaty in April 1965 establishing a Single Council and a Single Commission of the European Communities, on the appropriate methods of cooperation with a view to ensuring most effectively the defence of the interests of the Community.

It is clear from the minutes of the meeting of 20 March 1970 that the Commission made no formal use of the right to submit proposals open to it under Articles 75 and 116.

Nor did it demand the simple application of Article 228(1) in regard to its right of negotiation.

It may therefore be accepted that, in carrying on the negotiations and concluding the agreement simultaneously in the manner decided on by the Council, the Member States acted, and continue to act, in the interest and on behalf of the Community in accordance with their obligations under Article 5 of the Treaty.

Hence, in deciding in these circumstances on joint action by the Member States, the Council has not failed in its obligations arising from Articles 75 and 228.

II THE FOUNDING TREATIES

The original three Treaties concluded by the six Member States (Benelux, France, Italy and the Federal Republic of Germany) were accompanied by the Convention on Certain Institutions Common to the European Communities, which provided that the three Communities would be served by a single Assembly and a single Court of Justice. The basic Treaties were supplemented in May 1965 with a Merger Treaty, which, on its entry into force in July 1969, fused the three Councils of the Communities and amalgamated the High Authority of the ECSC with the Commissions of the EEC and Euratom.

On 22 January 1972 the six Member States of the Communities, together with Denmark, Ireland, Norway and the United Kingdom, signed at Brussels a Treaty of Accession. By this the last four States were to become members of the EEC and Euratom at the beginning of 1973 if they were able first to satisfy the requirements of their domestic constitutions. Their entry into those two Communities was conditional on their entering the ECSC. The Council of the Communities, on the same date, made two Decisions accepting the Danish, Irish, Norwegian and British applications to join the Communities and recording that they might accede to the ECSC Treaty. The Norwegian Constitution required that the proposal for Norway to ratify the Treaty of Accession should be subjected to a referendum. In the event the Norwegian electorate voted against entering the Communities. Denmark, Ireland and the United Kingdom were, however, able to satisfy their constitutional requirements and enter the Communities.

The Treaty of Accession for Denmark, Ireland and the United Kingdom was followed on 28 May 1979 and 12 June 1985 by similar Treaties of Accession, the first for Greece, and the second for Portugal and Spain.

ECSC Treaty

Article 1

By this Treaty, the High Contracting Parties establish among themselves a EUROPEAN COAL AND STEEL COMMUNITY, founded upon a Common Market, common objectives and common institutions.

Article 2

The European Coal and Steel Community shall have as its task to contribute, in harmony with the general economy of the Member States and through the establishment of a Common Market as provided in Article 4, to economic expansion, growth of employment and a rising standard of living in the Member States.

The Community shall progressively bring about conditions which will of themselves ensure the most rational distribution of production at the highest possible level of productivity, while safeguarding continuity of employment and taking care not to provoke fundamental and persistent disturbances in the economies of Member States.

Article 3

The institutions of the Community shall, within the limits of their respective powers, in the common interest:

(a) ensure an orderly supply to the Common Market, taking into account the needs of third countries;

(b) ensure that all comparably placed consumers in the Common Market have equal access to the sources of production;

(c) ensure the establishment of the lowest prices under such conditions that these prices do not result in higher prices charged by the same undertakings in other transactions or in a higher general price level at another time, while allowing necessary amortisation and normal return on invested capital;

(d) ensure the maintenance of conditions which will encourage undertakings to expand and improve their production potential and to promote a policy of using natural resources rationally and avoiding their unconsidered exhaustion;

(e) promote improved working conditions and an improved standard of living for the workers in each of the industries for which it is responsible, so as to make possible their harmonisation while the improvement is being maintained;

(f) promote the growth of international trade and ensure that equitable limits are observed in export pricing;

(g) promote the orderly expansion and modernisation of production, and the improvement of quality, with no protection against competing industries that is not justified by improper action on their part or in their favour.

Article 4

The following are recognised as incompatible with the Common Market for coal and steel and shall accordingly be abolished and prohibited within the community, as provided in this Treaty:

(a) import and export duties, or charges having equivalent effect, and quantitative restrictions on the movement of products;

(b) measures or practices which discriminate between producers, between purchasers or between consumers, especially in prices and delivery terms or transport rates and conditions, and measures or practices which interfere with the purchaser's free choice of supplier;

(c) subsidies or aids granted by States, or special charges imposed by States, in any form whatsoever;

(d) restrictive practices which tend towards the sharing or exploiting of markets.

Article 5

The Community shall carry out its task in accordance with this Treaty, with a limited measure of intervention.

To this end the Community shall:

- provide guidance and assistance for the parties concerned, by obtaining information, organising consultations and laying down general objectives;
- place financial resources at the disposal of undertakings for their investment and bear part of the cost of readaptation;
- ensure the establishment, maintenance and observance of normal competitive conditions and exert direct influence upon production or upon the market only when circumstances so require;
- publish the reasons for its actions and take the necessary measures to ensure the observance of the rules laid down in this Treaty.

The institutions of the Community shall carry out these activities with a minimum of administrative machinery and in close cooperation with the parties concerned.

...

Article 7

The institutions of the Community shall be:

a High Authority, assisted by a Consultative Committee;
a Common Assembly (hereinafter called the 'Assembly');
a Special Council of Ministers (hereinafter called the 'Council');

a Court of Justice (hereinafter called the 'Court').

Euratom Treaty

Article 1

By this Treaty the High Contracting Parties establish among themselves a EUROPEAN ATOMIC ENERGY COMMUNITY (EURATOM).

It shall be the task of the Community to contribute to the raising of the standard of living in the Member States and to the development of relations with the other countries by creating the conditions necessary for the speedy establishment and growth of nuclear industries.

Article 2

In order to perform its task, the Community shall, as provided in this Treaty:

(a) promote research and ensure the dissemination of technical information;

(b) establish uniform safety standards to protect the health of workers and of the general public and ensure that they are applied;

(c) facilitate investment and ensure, particularly by encouraging ventures on the part of undertakings, the establishment of the basic installations necessary for the development of nuclear energy in the Community;

(d) ensure that all users in the Community receive a regular and equitable supply of ores and nuclear fuels;

(e) make certain, by appropriate supervision, that nuclear materials are not diverted to purposes other than those for which they are intended;

(f) exercise the right of ownership conferred upon it with respect to special fissile materials;

(g) ensure wide commercial outlets and access to the best technical facilities by the creation of a Common Market in specialised materials and equipment, by the free movement of capital for investment in the field of nuclear energy and by freedom of employment for specialists within the Community;

(h) establish with other countries and international organisations such relations as will foster progress in the peaceful uses of nuclear energy.

Article 3

1. The tasks entrusted to the Community shall be carried out by the following institutions:

- an Assembly,
- a Council,
- a Commission,
- a Court of Justice.

Each institution shall act within the limits of the powers conferred upon it by this Treaty.

2. The Council and the Commission shall be assisted by an Economic and Social Committee acting in an advisory capacity.

EEC Treaty

Article 1

By this Treaty, the High Contracting Parties establish among themselves a EUROPEAN ECONOMIC COMMUNITY.

Article 2

The Community shall have as its task, by establishing a Common Market and progressively approximating the economic policies of Member States, to promote throughout the Community a harmonious development of economic activities, a continuous and balanced expansion, an increase in stability, an accelerated raising of the standard of living and closer relations between the States belonging to it.

Article 3

For the purposes set out in Article 2, the activities of the Community shall include, as provided in this Treaty and in accordance with the timetable set out therein:

(a) the elimination, as between Member States, of customs duties and of quantitative restrictions on the import and export of goods, and of all other measures having equivalent effect;

(b) the establishment of a common customs tariff and of a common commercial policy towards third countries;

(c) the abolition, as between Member States, of obstacles to freedom of movement for persons, services and capital;

(d) the adoption of a common policy in the sphere of agriculture;

(e) the adoption of a common policy in the sphere of transport;

(f) the institution of a system ensuring that competition in the Common Market is not distorted;

(g) the application of procedures by which the economic policies of Member States can be coordinated and disequilibria in their balances of payments remedied;

(h) the approximation of the laws of Member States to the extent required for the proper functioning of the Common Market;

(i) the creation of a European Social Fund in order to improve employment opportunities for workers and to contribute to the raising of their standard of living;

(j) the establishment of a European Investment Bank to facilitate the economic expansion of the Community by opening up fresh resources;

(k) the association of the overseas countries and territories in order to increase trade and to promote jointly economic and social development.

Article 4

1. The tasks entrusted to the Community shall be carried out by the following institutions:

an ASSEMBLY,
a COUNCIL,
a COMMISSION,
a COURT OF JUSTICE.

Each institution shall act within the limits of the powers conferred upon it by this Treaty.

2. The Council and the Commission shall be assisted by an Economic and Social Committee acting in an advisory capacity.

Article 7

Within the scope of application of this Treaty, and without prejudice to any special provisions contained therein, any discrimination on grounds of nationality shall be prohibited.

The Council may, on a proposal from the Commission and in cooperation with the European Parliament, adopt, by a qualified majority, rules designed to prohibit such discrimination.

Article 8

1. The Common Market shall be progressively established during a transitional period of twelve years.

This transitional period shall be divided into three stages of four years each; the length of each stage may be altered in accordance with the provisions set out below.

2. To each stage there shall be assigned a set of actions to be initiated and carried out concurrently...

Treaty of Accession

Article 1

1. The Kingdom of Denmark, Ireland, the Kingdom of Norway and the United Kingdom of Great Britain and Northern Ireland hereby become members of the European Economic Community and of the European Atomic Energy Community and Parties to the Treaties establishing these Communities as amended or supplemented.

2. The conditions of admission and the adjustments to the Treaties establishing the European Economic Community and the European Atomic Energy Community necessitated thereby are set out in the Act annexed to this Treaty. The provisions of that Act concerning the European Economic Community and the European Atomic Energy Community shall form an integral part of this Treaty.

3. The provisions concerning the rights and obligations of the Member States and the powers and jurisdiction of the institutions of the Communities as set out in the Treaties referred to in paragraph 1 shall apply in respect of this Treaty.

Article 2

This Treaty will be ratified by the High Contracting Parties in accordance with their respective constitutional requirements. The instruments of ratification will be deposited with the Government of the Italian Republic by 31 December 1972 at the latest.

This Treaty will enter into force on 1 January 1973, provided that all the instruments of ratification have been deposited before that date and that all the instruments of accession to the European Coal and Steel Community are deposited on that date.

If, however, the states referred to in Article 1(1) have not all deposited their instruments of ratification and accession in due time, the Treaty shall enter into force for those States which have deposited their instruments. In this case, the Council of the European Communities, acting unanimously, shall decide immediately upon such resulting adjustments as have become indispensable...

The Act mentioned in Article 1(2) of the Treaty of Accession contains 161 articles and has 11 annexes, 30 protocols and numerous declarations and other related instruments. It has been amended by a decision made by the Council under Article 2, paragraph 3 of the Treaty of Accession, as have the founding Treaties and various items of Community legislation.

Act of Accession

Article 1

[Amended by Adaptation Decision, Article 3.]

For the purposes of this Act:

– the expression 'original Treaties' means the Treaty establishing the European Coal and Steel Community, the Treaty establishing the European Economic Community and the Treaty establishing the European Atomic Energy Community, as supplemented or amended by treaties or other acts which entered into force before accession; the expressions 'ECSC Treaty', 'EEC Treaty' and 'Euratom Treaty' mean the relevant original Treaties thus supplemented or amended;

– the expression 'original Member States' means the Kingdom of Belgium, the Federal Republic of Germany, the French Republic, the Italian Republic, the Grand Duchy of Luxembourg and the Kingdom of the Netherlands;

– the expression 'new Member States' means the Kingdom of Denmark, Ireland and the United Kingdom of Great Britain and Northern Ireland.

Article 2

From the date of accession, the provisions of the original Treaties and the acts adopted by the institutions of the Communities shall be binding on the new Member States and shall apply in those States under the conditions laid down in those Treaties and in this Act.

Article 3

1. The new Member States accede by this Act to the decisions and agreements adopted by the Representatives of the Governments of the Member States meeting in Council. They undertake to accede from the date of accession to all other agreements concluded by the original Member States relating to the functioning of the Communities or connected with their activities.

2. The new Member States undertake to accede to the conventions provided for in Article 220 of the EEC Treaty, and to the protocols on the interpretation of those conventions by the Court of Justice, signed by the original Member States, and to this end they undertake to enter into negotiations with the original Member States in order to make the necessary adjustments thereto.

[Only two conventions and their protocols and annexes had been concluded under Article 220, at the time of conclusion of the Act of Accession. These were the Convention on the Mutual Recognition of Companies and Bodies Corporate and the Convention on Jurisdiction and the Enforcement of Civil and Commercial Judgments.]

3. The new Member States are in the same situation as the original Member States in respect of declarations or resolutions of, or other positions taken up by, the Council and in respect of those concerning the European Communities adopted by common agreement of the Member States; they will accordingly observe the principles and guidelines deriving from those declarations, resolutions or other positions and will take such measures as may be necessary to ensure their implementation.

Article 4

1. The agreements or conventions entered into by any of the Communities with one or more third States, with an international organisation or with a national of a third State, shall, under the conditions laid down in the original Treaties and in this Act, be binding on the new Member States.

2. The new Member States undertake to accede, under the conditions laid down in this Act, to agreements or conventions concluded by the original Member States and any of the Communities, acting jointly, and to agreements concluded by the original Member States which are related to those agreements or conventions. The Community and the original Member States shall assist the new Member States in this respect.

3. The new Member States accede by this Act and under the conditions laid down therein to the internal agreements concluded by the original Member States for the purpose of implementing the agreements or conventions referred to in paragraph 2.

4. The new Member States shall take appropriate measures, where necessary, to adjust their positions in relation to international organisations and international agreements to which one of the Communities or to which other Member States are also parties, to the rights and obligations arising from their accession to the Communities.

Political disagreements between the six original Member States led to the adoption in 1966 of an agreement known as the Luxembourg Accords. Controversy centred around Article 148 of the EEC Treaty which, as amended, provides for a system of voting by simple or qualified majority in the Council. At the insistence of General de Gaulle, it was agreed that in cases when important interests of a Member State were at stake, a rule of unanimity would be applied and this practice has continued to be followed within the enlarged Community despite the obscure and contentious nature of the document.

The Luxembourg Accords

...

(b) *Majority voting procedure*

I. Where, in the case of decisions which may be taken by majority vote on a proposal of the Commission, very important interests of one or more partners are at stake, the Members of the Council will endeavour, within a reasonable time, to reach solutions which can be adopted by all the Members of the Council while respecting their mutual interests and those of the Community, in accordance with Article 2 of the Treaty.

II. With regard to the preceding paragraph, the French delegation considers that where very important interests are at stake the discussion must be continued until unanimous agreement is reached.

III. The six delegations note that there is a divergence of views on what should be done in the event of a failure to reach complete agreement.

IV. The six delegations nevertheless consider that this divergence does not prevent the Community's work being resumed in accordance with the normal procedure.

The members of the Council agreed that decisions on the following should be by common consent:

(a) The financial regulation for agriculture;
(b) Extensions to the market organisation for fruit and vegetables;
(c) The regulation on the organisation of sugar markets;
(d) The regulation on the organisation of markets for oils and fats;
(e) The fixing of common prices for milk, beef and veal, rice, sugar, olive oil and oil seeds.

The relationship between the Council and the Commission is also dealt with.

The Luxembourg Accords

(a) Relations between the Commission and the Council

Close cooperation between the Council and the Commission is essential for the functioning and development of the Community.

In order to improve and strengthen this cooperation at every level, the Council considers that the following practical methods of cooperation should be applied, these methods to be adopted by joint agreement, on the basis of Article 162 of the EEC Treaty, without compromising the respective competences and powers of the two institutions.

1. Before adopting any particularly important proposal, it is desirable that the Commission should take up the appropriate contacts with the Governments of the Member States, through the Permanent Representatives, without this procedure compromising the right of initiative which the Commission derives from the Treaty.

2. Proposals and any other official acts which the Commission submits to the Council and to the Member States are not to be made public until the recipients have had formal notice of them and are in possession of the texts...

4. The Council and the Commission will inform each other rapidly and fully of any approaches relating to fundamental questions made to either institution by the representatives of non-Member States.

5. Within the scope of application of Article 162, the Council and the Commission will consult together on the advisability of, the procedure for, and the nature of any links which the Commission might establish with international organisations pursuant to Article 229 of the Treaty...

7. Within the framework of the financial regulations relating to the drawing up and execution of the Communities' budgets, the Council and the Commission will decide on means for more effective control over the commitment and expenditure of Community funds.

The effect of the Luxembourg Accords may be somewhat diminished with the ratification on 30 June 1987 of the Single European Act. Although this Treaty does not refer directly to the Accords, its principal objectives are to unblock the Community's decision-making process, largely through Article 8A of the EEC Treaty (see below p. 192), to increase the influence of the European Parliament which has played a less than satisfactory role since the first direct elections in 1979 (see Article 100A of the EEC Treaty – below p. 74) and to create a genuine single market by 1992 (see below p. 260). Article 30 of the SEA also provides a crystallisation of objectives in the sphere of EC foreign policy.

Single European Act

Article 1

The European Communities and European Political Cooperation shall have as their objective to contribute together to making concrete progress towards European unity.

The European Communities shall be founded on the Treaties establishing the European Coal and Steel Community, the European Economic Community, the European Atomic Energy Community and on the subsequent Treaties and Acts modifying or supplementing them.

Political Cooperation shall be governed by Title III. The provisions of that Title shall confirm and supplement the procedures agreed in the reports of Luxembourg (1970), Copenhagen (1973), London (1981), the Solemn Declaration on European Union (1983) and the practices gradually established among the Member States.

Article 2

The European Council shall bring together the Heads of State or of Government of the Member States and the President of the Commission of the European Communities. They shall be assisted by the Ministers for Foreign Affairs and by a Member of the Commission.

The European Council shall meet at least twice a year.

Article 3

1. The institutions of the European Communities, henceforth designated as referred to hereafter, shall exercise their powers and jurisdiction under the conditions and for the purposes provided for by the Treaties establishing the Communities and by the subsequent Treaties and Acts modifying or supplementing them and by the provisions of Title II.

2. The institutions and bodies responsible for European Political Cooperation shall exercise their powers and jurisdiction under the conditions and for the purposes laid down in Title III and the documents referred to in the third paragraph of Article 1.

...

Article 30

European Cooperation in the sphere of foreign policy shall be governed by the following provisions.

1. The High Contracting Parties, being members of the European Communities, shall endeavour jointly to formulate and implement a European foreign policy.

2. (a) The High Contracting Parties undertake to inform and consult each other on any foreign policy matters of general interest so as to ensure that their

combined influence is exercised as effectively as possible through coordination, the convergence of their positions and the implementation of joint action.

(b) Consultations shall take place before the High Contracting Parties decide on their final position.

(c) In adopting its positions and in its national measures each High Contracting Party shall take full account of the positions of the other partners and shall give due consideration to the desirability of adopting and implementing common European positions.

In order to increase their capacity for joint action in the foreign policy field, the High Contracting Parties shall ensure that common principles and objectives are gradually developed and defined.

The determination of common positions shall constitute a point of reference for the policies of the High Contracting Parties.

(d) The High Contracting Parties shall endeavour to avoid any action or position which impairs their effectiveness as a cohesive force in international relations or within international organisations.

3. (a) The Ministers for Foreign Affairs and a member of the Commission shall meet at least four times a year within the framework of European Political Cooperation. They may also discuss foreign policy matters within the framework of Political Cooperation on the occasion of meetings of the Council of the European Communities.

(b) The Commission shall be fully associated with the proceedings of European Political Cooperation.

(c) In order to ensure the swift adoption of common positions and the implementation of joint action, the High Contracting Parties shall, as far as possible, refrain from impeding the formation of consensus and the joint action which this could produce.

4. The High Contracting Parties shall ensure that the European Parliament is closely associated with European Political Cooperation. To that end the Presidency shall regularly inform the European Parliament of the foreign policy issues which are being examined within the framework of Political Cooperation and shall ensure that the views of the European Parliament are duly taken into consideration.

5. The external policies of the European Community and the policies agreed in European Political Cooperation must be consistent.

The Presidency and the Commission, each within its own sphere of competence, shall have special responsibility for ensuring that such consistency is sought and maintained.

6. (a) The High Contracting Parties consider that closer cooperation on questions of European security would contribute in an essential way to the development of a European identity in external policy matters. They are ready to coordinate their positions more closely on the political and economic aspects of security.

(b) The High Contracting Parties are determined to maintain the technological and industrial conditions necessary for their security. They shall work to that end both at national level and, where appropriate, within the framework of the competent institutions and bodies.

(c) Nothing in this Title shall impede closer cooperation in the field of security between certain of the High Contracting Parties within the framework of the Western European Union or the Atlantic Alliance.

7. (a) In international institutions and at international conferences which they attend, the High Contracting Parties shall endeavour to adopt common positions on the subjects covered by this Title.

(b) In international institutions and at international conferences in which not all the High Contracting Parties participate, those who do participate shall take full account of positions agreed in European Political Cooperation.

8. The High Contracting Parties shall organise a political dialogue with third countries and regional groupings whenever they deem it necessary.

9. The High Contracting Parties and the Commission, through mutual assistance and information, shall intensify cooperation between their representations accredited to third countries and to international organisations.

10. (a) The Presidency of European Political Cooperation shall be held by the High Contracting Party which holds the Presidency of the Council of the European Communities.

(b) The Presidency shall be responsible for initiating action and coordinating and representing the positions of the Member States in relations with third countries in respect of European Political Cooperation activities. It shall also be responsible for the management of Political Cooperation and in particular for drawing up the timetable of meetings and for convening and organising meetings.

(c) The Political Directors shall meet regularly in the Political Committee in order to give the necessary impetus, maintain the continuity of European Political Cooperation and prepare Ministers' discussions.

(d) The Political Committee or, if necessary, a ministerial meeting shall convene within forty-eight hours at the request of at least three Member States.

(e) The European Correspondents' Group shall be responsible, under the direction of the Political Committee, for monitoring the implementation of European Political Cooperation and for studying general organisation problems.

(f) Working Groups shall meet as directed by the Political Committee.

(g) A Secretariat based in Brussels shall assist the Presidency in preparing and implementing the activities of European Political Cooperation and in administrative matters. It shall carry out its duties under the authority of the Presidency.

11. As regards privileges and immunities, the members of the European Political Cooperation Secretariat shall be treated in the same way as members of the diplomatic missions of the High Contracting Parties based in the same place as the Secretariat.

12. Five years after the entry into force of this Act the High Contracting Parties shall examine whether any revision of Title III is required.

In principle, the Court has jurisdiction to interpret all of the founding Treaties and legislation made thereunder. But by Article 31 of the Single European Act, the Court has jurisdiction only in relation to Title II of that Act, which deals with the amendment of the founding Treaties, and in relation to Article 32. Moreover, it probably cannot interpret the Luxembourg Accords, which are not a treaty but a political compromise. The question arises from time to time whether the Court has jurisdiction to interpret other acts closely connected with the founding Treaties. The answer is that it does not. The Court's jurisdiction is one of attribution. It can interpret only those provisions for which it has been given explicit authority, although in interpreting them it may need to take account of the existence of those other measures.

Case 44/84 Derrick Guy Edmund Hurd v Kenneth Jones (Her Majesty's Inspector of Taxes) [1986] ECR 29

Mr Hurd, the headmaster at the European School in Culham, Oxfordshire, received a salary from the Department of Education and a supplement paid by the Member States (under rules laid down in the Statute of the European School). It was common ground that the salary was taxable in the United Kingdom. The point at issue was whether the supplement was taxable. In 1957 the Board of Governors of the European School in Luxembourg had decided in effect that the supplement paid to teachers there should be exempt from tax. The British Inspector of Taxes claimed that this decision was not binding on the United Kingdom, while Mr Hurd took the view that since the United Kingdom had acceded to the Statute of the European School by virtue of Article 3 of the Act of Accession (see p. 16), it had by implication accepted the 1957 decision as well.

The following question was amongst those referred to the Court by the Special Commissioners:

1. (a) Whether, in interpreting the provisions of Article 3 of the Act annexed to the Treaty of Accession to the European Economic Communities of 22 January 1972, the Court of Justice has jurisdiction to give a preliminary ruling on the question whether a particular matter falls within the meaning of the words 'all other agreements concluded by the original Member States relating to the functioning of the Communities or connected with their activities' (in paragraph 1 of the article) and the words 'declarations or resolutions... or other positions... concerning the European Communities adopted by common agreement of the Member States' (in paragraph 3 thereof)...

The Court

The Jurisdiction of the Court

Question 1(a) is essentially intended to establish whether the Court has jurisdiction to give a preliminary ruling under Article 177 of the EEC Treaty, and under Article 150 of the EAEC Treaty, on the interpretation of Article 3 of the Act of Accession with regard to the instruments concerning the European Schools and their teaching staff.

According to Article 1(3) of the Treaty of Accession the provisions concerning the powers and jurisdiction of the institutions as set out in the EEC and EAEC Treaties are to apply in respect of the Treaty of Accession, and the provisions of the Act of Accession which is annexed to that Treaty form a part of it. The powers and jurisdiction to which that provision refers include the jurisdiction of the Court to give a preliminary ruling under the first paragraph of Article 177 of the EEC Treaty and the first paragraph of Article 150 of the EAEC Treaty. The Court therefore has jurisdiction to give a preliminary ruling on the interpretation of Article 3 of the Act of Accession.

However, in the United Kingdom's view, the Court may not, in interpreting Article 3 of the Act of Accession, rule on the question whether instruments such as the Statute of the European School and the Protocol on the setting-up of European Schools and provisions adopted on the basis of those instruments are covered by that article; the Court does not have jurisdiction to interpret such instruments themselves and a reply to this question necessarily presupposes the interpretation thereof.

The Danish Government also takes the view that the jurisdiction of the Court may not be extended by means of interpretation of Article 3 of the Act of Accession to include the interpretation of instruments which are not covered by Article 177 of the EEC Treaty and Article 150 of the EAEC Treaty. However, it concedes that the Court may determine whether or not a particular agreement or provision falls within the categories of measures covered by Article 3 of the Act of Accession.

Ireland considers that the Court has jurisdiction to interpret Article 3 of the Act of Accession and that it may determine whether that provision covers a specific measure. It may not, however, rule on the legal effect produced by that measure with regard to the Member State concerned.

According to Mr Hurd and the Commission, the Court's jurisdiction to interpret Article 3 of the Act of Accession includes the power to determine the obligations which arise for the Member States under the measures which come under that provision. They argue that the functional, financial and organisational links between the European Schools and the Communities are so close that the Statute of the European School and the supplementary Protocol of 1962, together with the provisions of secondary law applicable to the European School, are part of 'complementary Community law' and, as such, fall within the jurisdiction of the Court.

In order to resolve this issue it should be stated in the first place that the European Schools were set up not on the basis of the Treaties establishing the European Communities or on the basis of measures adopted by the Community institutions, but on the basis of international agreements concluded by the Member States, namely the Statute of the European School and the Protocol on the setting-up of European Schools. Those agreements together with the instruments, measures and decisions of organs of the European Schools adopted on that basis do not fall within any of the categories of measures covered by Article 177 of the EEC Treaty and Article 150 of the EAEC Treaty. *The mere fact that those agreements are linked to the Community and to the functioning of its institutions does not mean that they must be regarded as an integral part of Community law, the uniform interpretation of which throughout the Community falls within the jurisdiction of the Court.* The Court therefore does not have jurisdiction to give a preliminary ruling, under Article 177 of the EEC Treaty and Article 150 of the EAEC Treaty, on the interpretation of such instruments.

However, in order to determine the scope of Article 3 of the Act of Accession with regard to such instruments, it may be necessary to define their legal status and, consequently, to subject them to such scrutiny as is necessary for that purpose. In performing that task the Court does not however acquire, on the basis of Article 3 of the Act of Accession, full and complete jurisdiction to interpret the instruments in question which it does not have under Article 177 of the EEC Treaty and Article 150 of the EAEC Treaty.

In reply to question 1(a) it must therefore be stated that the Court of Justice has jurisdiction to interpret Article 3 of the Act of Accession; by virtue of such jurisdiction it may interpret the measures covered by that provision only in order to determine its scope, and not for the purpose of defining Member States' obligations under such measures.

Further, a matter is not subject to Community law nor within the competence of the European Court by reason only of the fact that one of the parties places reliance on a Community Treaty. The factual situation must be such as to give rise to an element connecting the case with one of the situations envisaged by Community law.

Case 175/78 Regina v Vera Ann Saunders
[1979] ECR 1129; [1979] 2 CMLR 216

Miss Saunders was a British national who pleaded guilty to a charge of theft at Bristol Crown Court and was bound over in return for an undertaking to go to Northern Ireland and not return to England or Wales for three years. When the undertaking was broken, the question was raised whether such an Order was contrary to the EEC Treaty provisions on the free movement of workers.

The Court

The national court, on the basis that the accused was a worker within the meaning of Article 48 of the Treaty (see below, Chapter 7), wishes to know whether the rules of the Treaty on freedom of movement for workers prohibit measures in the nature of those by which the accused was bound.

For this purpose the national court asks whether 'the Order of this court made in the case of Vera Ann Saunders on 21 December 1977 may constitute a derogation from the right given to a worker under Article 48 of the Treaty establishing the European Economic Community, having regard in particular to the right specified in Article 48(b) of the said Treaty, and the fact that she appears to be an English national'.

This question asks in substance whether the principle of the freedom of movement for workers as laid down in Article 48 of the Treaty, in particular in so far as it entails the right for a worker, subject to limitations justified *inter alia* on grounds of public policy and public security, to move freely within the territory of Member States so as to accept offers of employment actually made and to stay there for the purpose of employment, may be relied upon by a national of a Member State residing in that Member State for the purpose of opposing the application of measures which restrict his freedom of movement within the territory of that Member State or his freedom to establish himself in that State in any place he chooses.

It therefore also concerns the question whether Article 48 of the Treaty confers rights upon a person in the same situation as Miss Saunders and, if the answer is in the affirmative, what the extent of those rights is.

The reply to that question depends, first, on the determination of the scope of that provision in conjunction in particular with the general principle expressed in Article 7 of the Treaty.

Under Article 7, any discrimination on grounds of nationality is prohibited within the scope of application of the Treaty and without prejudice to any special provisions contained therein.

In application of that general principle, Article 48 aims to abolish in the legislation of the Member States provisions as regards employment, remuneration and other conditions of work and employment – including the rights and freedoms which that freedom of movement involves pursuant to Article 48(3) – according to which a worker who is a national of another Member State is subject to more severe treatment or is placed in an unfavourable situation in law or in fact as compared with the situation of a national in the same circumstances.

Although the rights conferred upon workers by Article 48 may lead the Member States to amend their legislation, where necessary, even with respect to their own nationals, this provision does not however aim to restrict the power of the Member States to lay down restrictions, within their own territory, on the freedom of movement of all persons subject to their jurisdiction in implementation of domestic criminal law.

The provisions of the Treaty on freedom of movement for workers *cannot therefore be applied to situations which are wholly internal to a Member State, in other words, where there is no factor connecting them to any of the situations envisaged by Community law.*

The application by an authority or court of a Member State to a worker who is a national of that same State of measures which deprive or restrict the freedom of movement of that worker within the territory of that State as a penal measure provided for by national law by reason of acts committed within the territory of that State is a wholly domestic situation which falls outside the scope of the rules contained in the Treaty on freedom of movement for workers.

Consistently with this case, the Court ruled in Joined Cases 35 and 36/82 *Morson and Jhanjan* [1982] ECR 3723 that Community law does not prohibit a Member State from refusing to allow a relative of a worker employed within the territory of that State to enter and reside within its territory, where the worker has never exercised the right to freedom of movement within the Community.

III THE OBJECTS OF THE TREATIES

The Preamble to the EEC Treaty speaks of an ever closer union among the peoples of Europe. In principle, the Court will interpret the Treaties and subordinate legislation in the manner most likely to achieve this object. This principle of interpretation applies both in the assessment of the Court's jurisdiction and in the interpretation of provisions indisputably falling within its jurisdiction. In the *Johnston* case, the United Kingdom advanced the argument (among others) that matters of defence and national security fell outside the Treaty. The Court did not accept the argument.

Case 222/84 Marguerite Johnston v Chief Constable of the Royal Ulster Constabulary [1986] ECR 1651

The Chief Constable of the Royal Ulster Constabulary maintained a general policy of refraining from issuing firearms to female members of the force. Mrs Johnston, a reserve constable, maintained that this policy entailed unlawful discrimination on grounds of sex. The policy was defended by the Chief Constable on the ground, among others, that Article 53 of the Sex Discrimination (Northern Ireland) Order 1976 (SI 1976 No 1042 (NI 15)) permits sex discrimination for the purpose of 'safeguarding national security or of protecting public safety or public order'. Mrs Johnston claimed that Council Directive No 76/207 on equal treatment should take precedence over national law, even in matters concerning national security.

In order to be able to rule on the dispute, the Industrial Tribunal referred, among others, the following questions to the Court for a preliminary ruling:

(1) On the proper construction of Council Directive No 76/207 and in the circumstances of this case, can a Member State exclude from the directive's field of application acts of sex discrimination as regards access to employment done for the purpose of safeguarding national security or of protecting public safety or public order?

...

(6) Is the applicant entitled to rely upon the principle of equal treatment contained in the relevant provisions of the directive before the national courts and tribunals of Member States in the circumstances of the present case?

The Court

The Right to an Effective Judicial Remedy

It is necessary to examine in the first place the part of the sixth question which raises the point whether Community law, and more particularly Directive No 76/207, requires the Member States to ensure that their national courts and tribunals exercise effective control over compliance with the provisions of the directive and with the national legislation intended to put it into effect.

...

As far as this issue is concerned, it must be borne in mind first of all that Article 6 of the directive requires Member States to introduce into their internal legal systems such measures as are needed to enable all persons who consider themselves wronged by discrimination 'to pursue their claims by judicial process'. It follows from that provision that the Member States must take measures which are sufficiently effective to achieve the aim of the directive and that they must ensure that the rights thus conferred may be effectively relied upon before the national courts by the persons concerned.

The requirement of judicial control stipulated by that article reflects a general principle of law which underlies the constitutional traditions common to the Member States. That principle is also laid down in Articles 6 and 13 of the European Convention for the Protection of Human Rights and Fundamental Freedoms of 4 November 1950. As the European

Parliament, Council and Commission recognised in their Joint Declaration of 5 April 1977 (OJ C 103, p. 1) and as the Court has recognised in its decisions, the principles on which that Convention is based must be taken into consideration in Community law.

By virtue of Article 6 of Directive No 76/207, interpreted in the light of the general principle stated above, all persons have the right to obtain an effective remedy in a competent court against measures which they consider to be contrary to the principle of equal treatment for men and women laid down in the directive. It is for the Member States to ensure effective judicial control as regards compliance with the applicable provisions of Community law and of national legislation intended to give effect to the rights for which the directive provides.

A provision which, like Article 53(2) of the Sex Discrimination Order, requires a certificate such as the one in question in the present case to be treated as conclusive evidence that the conditions for derogating from the principle of equal treatment are fulfilled allows the competent authority to deprive an individual of the possibility of asserting by judicial process the rights conferred by the directive. Such a provision is therefore contrary to the principle of effective judicial control laid down in Article 6 of the Directive.

The answer to this part of the sixth question put by the Industrial Tribunal must therefore be that the principle of effective judicial control laid down in Article 6 of Council Directive No 76/207 of 9 February 1976 does not allow a certificate issued by a national authority stating that the conditions for derogating from the principle of equal treatment for men and women for the purpose of protecting public safety are satisfied to be treated as conclusive evidence so as to exclude the exercise of any power of review by the courts.

The Applicability of Directive No 76/207 to Measures taken to protect Public Safety

It is necessary to examine next the Industrial Tribunal's first question by which it seeks to ascertain whether, having regard to the fact that Directive No 76/207 contains no express provision concerning measures taken for the purpose of safeguarding national security or of protecting public order, and more particularly public safety, the directive is applicable to such measures.

...

It must be observed in this regard that the only articles in which the Treaty provides for derogations applicable in situations which may involve public safety are Articles 36, 48, 56, 223 and 224, which deal with exceptional and clearly defined cases. Because of their limited character those articles do not lend themselves to a wide interpretation and it is not possible to infer from them that there is inherent in the Treaty a general proviso covering all measures taken for reasons of public safety. If every provision of Community law were held to be subject to a general proviso, regardless of the specific requirements laid down by the provisions of the Treaty, this might impair the binding nature of Community law and its uniform application.

It follows that the application of the principle of equal treatment for men and women is not subject to any general reservation as regards measures taken on grounds of the protection of public safety, apart from the possible application of Article 224 of the Treaty which concerns a wholly exceptional situation... The facts which induced the competent authority to invoke the need to protect public safety must therefore if necessary be taken into consideration, in the first place, in the context of the application of the specific provisions of the directive.

The answer to the first question must therefore be that acts of sex discrimination done for reasons related to the protection of public safety must be examined in the light of the exceptions to the principle of equal treatment for men and women laid down in Directive No 76/207.

IV THE INSTITUTIONS OF THE EUROPEAN COMMUNITIES

1. THE EUROPEAN PARLIAMENT

In 1956, when the representatives of the six original members of the ECSC decided to begin to draft treaties establishing an economic and an atomic energy Community, they had before them a detailed report by M. Spaak on the feasibility of those plans. The Spaak report envisaged that the enlarged Common Assembly of the ECSC would act as the parliamentary body of both of the new institutions while continuing to serve the ECSC. This proposal was adopted. The EEC and Euratom Treaties, like the ECSC Treaty, specified the powers to be exercised by the Assembly within their respective fields; but Articles 1 and 2 of the Convention on Common Institutions provided that these powers should be exercised by a single Assembly. In March 1958 the Common Assembly took the name 'the European Parliamentary Assembly'. Since the entry into force of the Single European Act it has been known officially by the name previously used informally: 'the European Parliament'.

The European Parliament has more advisory and supervisory than legislative powers. The Commission is bound by Article 140 of the EEC Treaty to answer questions put to it by members of the European Parliament. It is obliged by Article 143 to submit to the Parliament for public debate an annual general report. It may be dismissed by a motion of censure carried by the Parliament in accordance with Article 144. The Council is not subjected by the Treaty to similar controls. For these reasons, it is sometimes claimed that the Parliament is not in a position to supervise the Council effectively, but has power only over the Commission. This assessment, however, is too often based on the letter of the Treaties, rather than on the political realities. The Council is usually represented at parliamentary debates, where it answers questions put to it by members; and every six months, at the beginning of its new Presidency, the Council makes a statement of policy to the Parliament. More significantly, as a result of an amendment to the founding Treaties signed by representatives of the nine Member States in July 1975, the Parliament exercises with the Council joint control of the Community's budget. The Council has the last word on 'obligatory' expenditure (defined as that 'necessarily resulting from [the Treaties] or from acts adopted in accordance therewith') and the Parliament has the last word on the remainder. It is, however, necessary for the Parliament and Council to achieve a wide measure of agreement on all major items of expenditure, and the Parliament can reject the budget as a whole.

The European Parliament is able to play an important part in the making of Community laws. Before the Commission or Council drafts legislation, members of the European Parliament are often able to affect its content by making representations either at Committee meetings attended by members of the Commission or in full parliamentary sessions. Once the proposed legislation is drafted it generally needs to be submitted to the European Parliament for its opinion before being adopted by the Council, although on this point the procedure varies according to the Treaty basis of the proposed measure. At this stage the proposed legislation is usually scrutinised by a parliamentary committee in the presence of members of the Commission, and sometimes of the Council. The Committee submits a report to the whole Parliament, which adopts a resolution and forwards this to the Council, along with the Commission's proposal.

EEC Treaty

Article 137

The Assembly, which shall consist of representatives of the peoples of the States brought together in the Community, shall exercise the advisory and supervisory powers which are conferred upon it by this Treaty.

Article 138

[Amended by Act of Accession, Article 10, and Adaptation Decision, Article 4.]

...

3. The Assembly shall draw up proposals for elections by direct universal suffrage in accordance with a uniform procedure in all Member States.

The Council shall, acting unanimously, lay down the appropriate provisions, which it shall recommend to Member States for adoption in accordance with their respective constitutional requirements.

Article 139

[Amended by Merger Treaty, Article 37.]

The Assembly shall hold an annual session. It shall meet, without requiring to be convened, on the second Tuesday in March.

The Assembly may meet in extraordinary session at the request of a majority of its members or at the request of the Council or of the Commission.

Article 140

The Assembly shall elect its President and its officers from among its members.

Members of the Commission may attend all meetings and shall, at their request, be heard on behalf of the Commission.

The Commission shall reply orally or in writing to questions put to it by the Assembly or by its members.

The Council shall be heard by the Assembly in accordance with the conditions laid down by the Council in its rules of procedure.

Article 141

Save as otherwise provided in this Treaty, the Assembly shall act by an absolute majority of the votes cast.

The rules of procedure shall determine the quorum.

Article 142

The Assembly shall adopt its rules of procedure, acting by a majority of its members.

The proceedings of the Assembly shall be published in the manner laid down in its rules of procedure.

Article 143

The Assembly shall discuss in open session the annual general report submitted to it by the Commission.

Article 144

If a motion of censure on the activities of the Commission is tabled before it, the Assembly shall not vote thereon until at least three days after the motion has been tabled and only by open vote.

If the motion of censure is carried by a two-thirds majority of the votes cast, representing a majority of the Members of the Assembly, the Members of the Commission shall resign as a body. They shall continue to deal with current business until they are replaced in accordance with Article 158.

Members of the European Parliament were at first designated by the national parliaments according to their several procedures. In the case of the United Kingdom, the 36 members were chosen by the whips of the political parties from members of those parties in numbers roughly proportionate to each party's representation in the House of Commons; but they were drawn from both Houses of Parliament (26 from the Commons and 10 from the Lords). Once in the European Parliament, delegates are seated and expected to vote in accordance with political, rather than national, groupings. In 1988 there were eight main political groupings, formed by alliances and coalitions of the national political groups. These were: Socialists (165), European People's Party (formerly Christian Democrats) (115), European Democratic Group (Conservatives and others) (66), Communists and affiliated (48), Liberal and Democratic Reformists (44), European and Democratic Alliance (29), Rainbow Group (20) and Group of the European Right (16). Additionally, there were 15 independents.

Although the EEC Treaty contemplated that members of the European Parliament would ultimately be elected by direct universal suffrage, and although as early as in 1960 the European Parliament adopted a 'resolution containing a Draft Convention introducing elections to the European Parliament by direct suffrage' and five complementary resolutions, the Council made no decision on the question for over twelve years. Following the enlargement of the Communities in 1973 the European Parliament decided to draw up a new report on direct elections. The report, known after the Rapporteur of the Committee as the 'Patijn Report', was submitted to the Parliament late in 1974 and amended in January 1975. Then the European Parliament adopted, on the basis of the Report, a further resolution containing a Draft Convention on direct elections. On 20 September 1976 the representatives of the Member States of the European Communities ratified an Act Concerning the Election by Direct Universal Suffrage of Members of the European Parliament. It was based on the Parliament's resolution of 1975, although it provided that the directly-elected Parliament would contain 410 members whereas the resolution had contemplated an assembly of only 355.

Act Concerning the Election of Representatives of the Assembly by Direct Universal Suffrage

Article 1

The representatives in the Assembly of the peoples of the States brought together in the Community shall be elected by direct universal suffrage.

Article 2

The number of representatives elected in each Member State shall be as follows:

Belgium	24
Denmark	16
Germany	81
Greece	24
Spain	60
France	81
Ireland	15
Italy	81
Luxembourg	6
Netherlands	25
Portugal	24
United Kingdom	81

Article 3

1. Representatives shall be elected for a term of five years.
2. This five-year period shall begin at the opening of the first session following each election.

It may be extended or curtailed pursuant to the second subparagraph of Article 10(2).

3. The term of office of each representative shall begin and end at the same time as the period referred to in paragraph 2.

Article 4

1. Representatives shall vote on an individual and personal basis. They shall not be bound by any instructions and shall not receive a binding mandate.

2. Representatives shall enjoy the privileges and immunities applicable to members of the Assembly by virtue of the Protocol on the Privileges and Immunities of the European Communities annexed to the Treaty establishing a single Council and a single Commission of the European Communities.

Article 5

The office of representative in the Assembly shall be compatible with membership of the Parliament of a Member State.

Article 6

1. The office of representative in the Assembly shall be incompatible with that of:
   - member of the Government of a Member State,
   - member of the Commission of the European Communities,
   - Judge, Advocate General or Registrar of the Court of Justice of the European Communities,
   - member of the Court of Auditors of the European Communities,
   - member of the Consultative Committee of the European Coal and Steel Community or member of the Economic and Social Committee of the European Economic Community and of the European Atomic Energy Community,
   - member of Committees or other bodies set up pursuant to the Treaties establishing the European Coal and Steel Community, the European Economic Community and the European Atomic Energy Community for the purpose of managing the Communities' funds or carrying out a permanent direct administrative task,
   - member of the Board of Directors, Management Committee or staff of the European Investment Bank,
   - active official or servant of the institutions of the European Communities or of the specialised bodies attached to them.

2. In addition, each Member State may, in the circumstances provided for in Article 7(2), lay down rules at national level relating to incompatibility.

3. Representatives in the Assembly to whom paragraphs 1 and 2 become applicable in the course of the five-year period referred to in Article 3 shall be replaced in accordance with Article 12.

Article 7

1. Pursuant to Article 21(3) of the Treaty establishing the European Coal and Steel Community, Article 138(3) of the Treaty establishing the European Economic Community and Article 108(3) of the Treaty establishing the European Atomic Energy Community, the Assembly shall draw up a proposal for a uniform electoral procedure.

2. Pending the entry into force of a uniform electoral procedure and subject to the other provisions of this Act, the electoral procedure shall be governed in each Member State by its national provisions.

Article 8

No one may vote more than once in any election of representatives to the Assembly.

Article 9

1. Elections to the Assembly shall be held on the date fixed by each Member State; for all Member States this date shall fall within the same period starting on a Thursday morning and ending on the following Sunday.

2. The counting of votes may not begin until after the close of polling in the Member State whose electors are the last to vote within the period referred to in paragraph 1.

3. If a Member State adopts a double ballot system for elections to the Assembly, the first ballot must take place during the period referred to in paragraph 1.

Article 10

1. The Council, acting unanimously after consulting the Assembly, shall determine the period referred to in Article 9(1) for the first elections...

The French Conseil constitutionnel has declared that this Act has the sole aim of requiring the representatives in the Assembly to be elected by universal suffrage; that it does not alter the respective powers of the Community and of the Member States; and that it contains for those reasons no clause contrary to the French Constitution: *Re Direct Elections to the European Assembly* [1977] 1 CMLR 121.

Two special problems have arisen in the case of the Parliament and its relationship with the Court:

1) Can the Parliament initiate proceedings in the European Court?

It is clear that the Parliament does not have *locus standi* to bring an action for review of the legality of acts of the Council or Commission under Article 173 of the EEC Treaty. That Article authorises the Court to review the legality of certain acts 'in actions brought by a Member State, the Council or the Commission'.

Case 302/87 Parliament v Council

27 September 1988 *(Editor's translation)*

The Court

By an application lodged at the Court Registry on 2 October 1987, the European Parliament brought an action under the first paragraph of Article 173 of the EEC Treaty for the annulment of Council Decision 87/373 of 13 July 1987 (OJ L 197/33) laying down the procedures for the exercise of the implementing powers conferred on the Commission.

...

The Council has raised a preliminary objection to the admissibility of the application on the basis of the first paragraph of Article 91 of the Rules of Procedure and has asked the Court to decide on this preliminary objection without dealing with the merit.

In support of its preliminary objection the Council submits that the first paragraph of Article 173 of the Treaty does not provide expressly that the Council can bring an action for annulment. Neither can such a capacity be recognised by applying an argument based on the necessity of ensuring the consistency of methods of judicial review. In fact, intervention and proceedings for failure to act, to which the Parliament has access ... are distinct from the action for annulment.

...

Article 173 distinguishes between actions initiated by institutions, which are governed by the first paragraph, and actions initiated by individuals (natural and legal persons), the conditions of which are governed by the second paragraph. The European Parliament, which is one of the institutions of the Community listed in Article 4 of the Treaty, is not a legal person.

Furthermore, it may be observed that the scheme of the second paragraph of Article 173 would in any event be unsuited to an action for annulment by the European Parliament. The applicants envisaged by the second paragraph of Article 173 must in fact be directly and individually concerned by the very content of the act that they are challenging. Now, it is not the content of the act which might affect the Parliament adversely, but a failure to respect the procedural provisions which require that it should be consulted. Moreover, the second paragraph of Article 173 only deals with one limited category of acts, namely acts which have their bearing only on individuals, whereas the European Parliament seeks to secure recognition of a right to secure the annulment of acts having a general application.

...

The Parliament has submitted that if it had no power to initiate an action for annulment, it would not be in a position to defend its own powers in relations with other institutions.

It is relevant to recall in this context that from its origin the Parliament has been invested with the power to participate on a consultative basis in the process of enacting legislative acts, but that it has not been thought right to go so far as to accord to it the power to bring an action for annulment. The powers of the Parliament have been increased by the Single European Act, which has conferred a power of co-decision on the Parliament as regards accession and association agreements and has instituted a cooperation procedure in certain specified cases without, however, the making of any amendments to Article 173 of the Treaty.

Apart from the rights ... accorded to the Parliament under Article 175, the Treaty provides a means of bringing before the Court acts of the Council taken in disregard of the powers of the Parliament. The first paragraph of Article 173 enables all Member States, in a general way, to bring an action for annulment against such acts; and Article 155 imposes more specifically on the Commission the duty to ensure respect for the powers of the Parliament to that end, and to bring an action for annulment when this appears necessary. Moreover, any natural or legal person may, in the case of disregard for the powers of the Parliament, invoke an infringement of an essential procedural requirement or infringement of the Treaty in order to secure the annulment of the act so adopted, or an incidental declaration of the inapplicability of that act on the basis of Article 184 of the Treaty. Furthermore, the illegality of an act, by reason of its inconsistency with the powers of the European Parliament, may be raised before a national court or tribunal, and the act in question may be made the subject of a reference for a preliminary ruling to enable the Court to decide upon its validity.

It follows from the foregoing that the present state of the relevant texts does not permit the Court to recognise a right on the part of the European Parliament to bring an action for annulment.

The preliminary objection must therefore be allowed and the application dismissed as inadmissible.

On the other hand, the Parliament can intervene in cases before the European Court under Article 37 of the latter's Statute (EEC), which provides expressly that 'Member States and institutions of the Community may intervene in cases before the Court'. Further, the Parliament may bring an action before the Court to establish that the Council or Commission has infringed the Treaty by failing to act.

Case 13/83 Parliament v Council
[1985] ECR 1513; [1986] 1 CMLR 138

For the facts of this case see below, Chapter 3 (p. 119).

The Council's first claim was that the Parliament lacked the capacity to bring proceedings at all.

The Court

The Council explains first of all that in its opinion the present action is to be seen as part of the Parliament's efforts to increase its influence in the decision-making process within the Community. Those efforts, although legitimate, should not seek to exploit the action for failure to act provided for by Article 175 since collaboration between the Community institutions is not governed by that provision. The political aims of the Parliament must be pursued by other means.

In the light of that the Council, while recognising that Article 175 gives a right of action in respect of omissions of the Council and Commission to Member States and 'the other institutions of the Community', enquires whether the right of review conferred on the Parliament by the Treaty is not exhausted by the powers provided for in Articles 137, 143 and 144 of the Treaty, which govern the ways in which the Parliament may exercise influence on the activities of the Commission and the Council. If so, the Parliament can have no right of review over the Council which may be exercised by means of an action for failure to act.

The Council adds that upon a systematic interpretation of the Treaty the Parliament has no capacity to bring proceedings. The Parliament has no right of action under Article 173, which enables a review of the legality of measures of the Council and Commission to be obtained by means of an action for annulment. In so far as the Treaty deprives the Parliament of the right to review the legality of measures of the two institutions it would be illogical to allow it a right of action in the case of unlawful failure by one of those institutions to act. Accordingly, only through an express attribution of powers would it have been possible to confer on the Parliament a right to bring an action for failure to act.

The European Parliament and the Commission contest that argument on the basis of the actual wording of Article 175, which in their view does not lend itself to any interpretation which would prevent the Parliament from bringing an action for failure to act. Both institutions also consider that recognition of such a power is in no way incompatible with the division of powers provided for by the Treaty.

The Court would emphasise that the first paragraph of Article 175, as the Council has recognised, expressly gives a right of action for failure to act against the Council and the Commission *inter alia* to 'the other institutions of the Community'. It thus gives the same right of action to all the Community institutions. It is not possible to restrict the exercise of that right by one of them without adversely affecting its status as an institution under the Treaty, in particular Article 4(1).

The fact that the European Parliament is at the same time the Community institution whose task is to exercise a political review of the activities of the Commission, and to a certain extent those of the Council, is not capable of affecting the interpretation of the provisions of the Treaty on the rights of action of the institutions.

Accordingly the first objection of inadmissibility must be rejected.

2) *Can the national courts or the European Court review the activities of the Parliament?*

The Court ruled in the *Lord Bruce of Donington* case that internal decisions of the Parliament relating to parliamentary procedure were not subject to review by national courts.

Case 208/80 Rt Hon. Lord Bruce of Donington v Eric Gordon Aspden [1981] ECR 2205; [1981] 3 CMLR 506

Parliament gave its members (including Lord Bruce of Donington) a 'travel and subsistence allowance' on a lump sum basis. Lord Bruce received an assessment for income tax under the Income and Corporation Taxes Act 1970 on the unexpended part of the allowance. He appealed to the Special Commissioners, who concluded that the outcome depended on a point of Community law. They referred to the Court the question whether Member States may tax any emoluments received by members of the European Parliament in respect of their parliamentary duties.

The Court

The United Kingdom Government, the French Government and the Commission maintained that in the absence of express provisions in the Protocol on the Privileges and Immunities of the European Communities conferring exemption from national taxes, there is nothing which precludes a Member State from charging such payments by the Parliament to national tax, since a tax exemption cannot be implied.

Lord Bruce takes the view that by virtue of the principle that the Parliament is sovereign in matters of procedure and in its internal relations with its Members, a principle enshrined in the first paragraph of Article 142 of the EEC Treaty, and by virtue of the first paragraph of Article 8 of the Protocol on the Privileges and Immunities of the European Communities which guarantees the free movement of Members of the Assembly, the authorities of the Member States are precluded from reviewing the performance by a Member of the European Parliament of his duties, his travel in connection with those duties and his related expenditure. The Member States may not therefore tax payments made by the Parliament in respect thereof. It would, moreover, be illogical if income tax were charged on these allowances whilst those paid to officials and servants of the Communities, including those employed by the Parliament, are exempt pursuant to Article 13 of the Protocol on the Privileges and Immunities of the European Communities and Article 3(1) of Regulation No 260/68 of the Council of 29 February 1968 laying down the conditions and procedure for applying the tax for the benefit of the European Communities (Official Journal, English Special Edition 1968 I, p. 37).

It is clear from the replies given by the European Parliament to the questions asked by the Court that the Parliament's view is that by virtue of the principle of the independence of the European Parliament with regard to provisions concerning the internal functioning of the institution embodied in the first paragraph of Article 142 of the EEC Treaty, the first paragraph of Article 112 of the EAEC Treaty and the first paragraph of Article 25 of the ECSC Treaty, an independence which the Member States are bound to respect under Article 5 of the EEC Treaty, the national tax provisions do not apply to Community payments which are necessary for the functioning of the institution. That also follows from the requirement that the Parliament must avoid treating differently Members coming from different Member States.

In reply to the question put by the national tribunal, it must first be observed, as the United Kingdom Government, the French Government and the Commission rightly pointed out during the procedure before the Court, that no provision of Community law confers exemption from national taxes on Members of the European Parliament.

In the absence of any provision conferring a tax exemption on Members of the European Parliament, the Member States are, in the present state of Community law, entitled to tax any emoluments derived by the Members of the Parliament from the exercise of their mandate. Consequently, the view cannot be taken that any payment made by the Parliament to its Members from Community funds is *ipso facto* exempt from national taxes.

Community law lays down certain limits, however, which the Member States must observe in the enactment of taxation laws applicable to Members of the Parliament. Those limits arise in particular from Article 5 of the EEC Treaty which provides that the Member States are bound to facilitate the achievement of the Communities' tasks and to abstain from any measure which could jeopardise the attainment of the objectives of the Treaty. That obligation includes the *duty not to take measures which are likely to interfere with the internal functioning of the institutions of the Community*. Furthermore, the effect of the first paragraph of Article 8 of the Protocol on the Privileges and Immunities of the European Communities is to prohibit Member States from imposing *inter alia* by their practices in matters of taxation administrative restrictions on the free movement of Members of the Parliament.

In this regard it must first be observed that the reimbursement of travel and subsistence expenses incurred by Members of the Parliament in the exercise of their mandates is a measure of internal organisation intended to ensure the proper functioning of the institution. It is essential that each Member of the Parliament should at all times be able to attend all the meetings and participate in all the activities of the Parliament and its organs without suffering financial loss, regardless of the Member's place of residence, the location of his constituency and his available financial means. Rules such as those adopted by the Parliament governing subsistence and travel expenses and allowances therefore fall within the scope of measures of internal organisation whose adoption is a matter for the Parliament pursuant to the first paragraph of Article 142 of the EEC Treaty, the first paragraph of Article 112 of the EAEC Treaty and the first paragraph of Article 25 of the ECSC Treaty.

If and so far as a national tax on the allowances received by Members of the Parliament were to be charged on the whole of the sums received, including the part which is in fact needed in order to cover their actual expenditure, it would form a financial obstacle to the movement of the Members of the Parliament who would then be obliged to bear personally a proportion of their travelling expenses. It should be mentioned that the United Kingdom

Government did not maintain that it was possible to tax the proportion of the allowances equal to the actual expenditure incurred.

It is a matter for the Parliament to decide which activities and travel of Members of the Parliament are necessary or useful for the performance of their duties and which expenses are necessary or useful in connection therewith. The autonomy granted to the Parliament in this matter in the interests of proper functioning also implies the authority to refund travel and subsistence expenses of its Members not upon production of vouchers for each individual item of expenditure but on the basis of a system of fixed lump-sum reimbursements. The choice of this system, as the Parliament indicated in its replies to the questions put by the Court, arises from concern to reduce the administrative costs and burdens inherent in a system involving the verification of each individual item of expense and therefore represents sound administration.

The appropriations available to the European Parliament for the lump-sum reimbursement of the travel and subsistence expenses of its Members appear in the annual Community budget and are subject to the budgetary procedures provided for by Community law. It is in the course of those procedures that the amount of the allowances must be considered in accordance with the applicable financial rules.

It is clear from the foregoing that the national authorities are bound to respect the decision taken by the European Parliament to refund travel and subsistence expenses to its Members on a lump-sum basis. *A review carried out in this area by the national revenue authorities, such as the one provided for by the United Kingdom legislation, constitutes an interference in the internal functioning of the Parliament resulting in a substitution by the national authorities of their appraisal of the system of allowances for the one undertaken by the Parliament in the exercise of its powers. It would therefore be likely to impair the effectiveness of the action of the Parliament and be incompatible with its autonomy.*

On the other hand, a decision by the Parliament to hold meetings in a particular place or places is not immune from challenge in the European Court at the instance of a Member State, at least if it bears upon the ECSC Treaty.

Case 230/81 Luxembourg v Parliament
[1983] ECR 255; [1983] 2 CMLR 726

When the European Communities were set up, the seats of the institutions were established in Strasbourg, Luxembourg and Brussels with the Parliament in Strasbourg, but its Secretariat located 'provisionally' in Luxembourg. After the election of the Parliament by direct universal suffrage, it adopted a resolution 'on the Seat of the European Parliament' calling on the Member States to put an end to the provisional arrangements and establish a single seat. The Heads of State and Government decided that a preservation of the status quo was the least problematic solution. The Parliament then adopted a resolution by which it decided, pending a final decision on the meeting place, to hold its part-sessions in Strasbourg and meetings of political groups generally in Brussels. Luxembourg challenged that resolution before the European Court.

The Court

Right of Action in respect of Measures of the Parliament

In the Parliament's view the action is inadmissible because neither Article 38 of the ECSC Treaty nor Article 173 of the EEC Treaty nor Article 136 of the EAEC Treaty gives a right of action in respect of the measures of the Parliament in the present case. As regards Article 38 of the ECSC Treaty that is so because in adopting the contested resolution the Parliament made a single and indivisible use of its powers under the three Treaties so that the resolution cannot be declared void solely in respect of the ECSC Treaty. The Parliament moreover referred to the principle of the separation of powers and emphasised that the contested solution was based on the sovereign power of the Parliament to organise the way in which it performs its tasks.

In the view of the Luxembourg Government recourse to Article 38 of the ECSC Treaty is excluded only in relation to measures relating specifically and exclusively to a field within the EEC or EAEC Treaties. Further, Article 173 of the EEC Treaty and Article 136 of the EAEC Treaty on which the application is based in the alternative should be given a wide interpretation in the light of the increased powers of the Parliament in order to avoid lacunae in the legal protection provided by the Court.

The first paragraph of Article 38 of the ECSC Treaty provides that 'the Court may, on application by a Member State or the High Authority, declare an act of the Assembly or of the Council to be void'. The power of the Member State to bring an action before the Court against measures of the Parliament relating to that Treaty is not therefore open to doubt. Nevertheless that power is restricted by the third paragraph of Article 38 of the ECSC Treaty to grounds based on lack of competence or infringement of an essential procedural requirement.

The first paragraph of Article 173 of the EEC Treaty and the first paragraph of Article 136 of the EAEC Treaty provide that the Court 'shall review the legality of acts of the Council and the Commission' and for that purpose it has jurisdiction in actions 'brought by a Member State, the Council or the Commission'. There is no express provision in those articles for active or passive participation of the Parliament in the proceedings before the Court.

Pursuant to the Convention on Certain Institutions Common to the European Communities of 25 March 1957 the powers and jurisdiction which the three Treaties confer upon the Parliament and the Court are to be exercised 'in accordance with those Treaties'. The differences existing in that respect in the various Treaties have thus not been erased by the creation of those common institutions.

Since the single Parliament is an institution common to the three Communities it necessarily acts in the field of the three Treaties, including that of the ECSC Treaty when it adopts a resolution relating to its operation as an institution and the organisation of its Secretariat. It follows that the jurisdiction of the Court and the proceedings provided by the first paragraph of Article 38 of the Treaty are applicable to measures such as the contested resolution which relate simultaneously and indivisibly to the spheres of the three Treaties.

Since the first paragraph of Article 38 of the ECSC Treaty applies in the present case, there is no need to consider the question whether the principles appertaining to observance of the law and review in that respect by the Court as embodied in Article 164 of the EEC Treaty and Article 136 of the EAEC Treaty require thatArticle 173 of the EEC Treaty and Article 146 of the EAEC Treaty be interpreted as meaning that the Parliament may be a party to proceedings before the Court.

That objection must therefore be dismissed.

...

The Legal Nature of the Contested Resolution

According to the Parliament the contested resolution is not an act within the meaning of Article 38 of the ECSC Treaty because it concerns only its internal organisation and that of its departments and therefore has no legal effect. It is alleged to be a measure arising from the Parliament's power to determine its own internal organisation, which moreover keeps completely within the limits outlined by the decisions of the Governments of the Member States.

In the view of the Luxembourg Government the Parliament intended by the contested resolution to substitute its own action for that of the Governments of the Member States in relation to the seat. It moreover denies that measures relating to internal organisation thereby escape review by the Court.

In that respect it must be observed that a determination of the legal effect of the contested resolution is inseparably associated with consideration of its content and observance of the rules on competence. It is therefore necessary to proceed to consideration of the substance of the case.

Substance

In support of its action the Luxembourg Government puts forward, in accordance with Article 38 of the ECSC Treaty, two submissions based on lack of competence and infringement of essential procedural requirements.

1. Lack of Competence

The Luxembourg Government observes in the first place that the Parliament has no power to take decisions in relation to the seat of the institution since that matter is reserved to the Member States. By reason both of its title and of its content the contested resolution relates to the seat of the Parliament, a matter which lies completely outside the powers of the Parliament independently of the existence and content of decisions of the Member States in the matter. Moreover the contested resolution infringes the decisions adopted by the Governments, in exercise of the powers reserved to them, in relation to the provisional places of work of the institutions. In abandoning the established practice of holding part-sessions in Luxembourg the Parliament infringed the decision confirming the *status quo* taken by the Heads of State and of Government of the Member States at Maastricht on 23 and 24 March 1981 and at the conference on the seat of the institutions of the Community on 30 June 1981. In providing for a change in the operation of the Secretariat and the departments of the Parliament on the basis of part-sessions in Strasbourg and meetings of the committees and political groups in Brussels the Parliament infringed Article 4 of the decision of 8 April 1965.

The Parliament contends that the Governments of the Member States have made no use of their power to fix the seat and there can therefore be no usurpation of that power. In any event the contested resolution constitutes on the one hand a request of a political nature addressed to the Governments of the Member States recommending them to adopt certain measures in relation to the seat and on the other hand a measure of organisation of its internal administration adopted in conformity with Article 142 of the EEC Treaty, Article 112 of the EAEC Treaty and Article 25 of the ECSC Treaty. That measure of internal organisation respects the decisions of the Governments of the Member States on the provisional places of work and in particular, as regards plenary sessions, the declarations of the Ministers for Foreign Affairs of 25 July 1952 and 7 January 1958. The holding of the meetings of committees and political groups in Brussels follows a practice established in an area which is not governed by any provisions in writing. In the contested resolution the Parliament took no decision on the location of the General Secretariat and dealt only with the proper functioning of the institution and the use of certain modern technology. Moreover this question does not concern the seat of the institution but the internal organisation of the Parliament in respect of which the Parliament is entitled and even required to adopt measures in accord with good administration.

In order to give a decision on this issue it is necessary first of all to consider the respective powers of the Governments of the Member States and the Parliament on the subject.

In that respect it is necessary to observe that according to Article 77 of the ECSC Treaty and also Article 216 of the EEC Treaty and Article 189 of the EAEC Treaty it is for the Governments of the Member States to determine the seat of the institutions. In giving the Member States power to determine the seat those provisions make them responsible for supplementing in that respect the system of institutional provisions provided for by the Treaties in order thus to ensure the working of the Communities. It follows that the Member States have not only the right but also the duty to exercise that power.

It is common ground that the Governments of the Member States have not yet discharged their obligation to determine the seat of the institutions in accordance with the provisions of the Treaties. Nevertheless, as is apparent from the above-mentioned facts, the Governments of the Member States have at different times taken decisions fixing the provisional places of work of the institutions on the basis of that same power and, as regards the decision of 8 April 1965, on the basis of the power expressly provided for in the aforesaid Article 37 of the Treaty establishing a Single Council and a Single Commission of the European Communities.

It must nevertheless be emphasised that when the Governments of the Member States make provisional decisions they must in accordance with the rule imposing on Member States and the Community institutions mutual duties of sincere cooperation, as embodied in particular in Article 5 of the EEC Treaty, have regard to the power of the Parliament to determine its internal organisation. They must ensure that such decisions do not impede the due functioning of the Parliament.

Furthermore the Parliament is authorised, pursuant to the power to determine its own internal organisation given to it by Article 25 of the ECSC Treaty, Article 142 of the EEC Treaty and Article 112 of the EAEC Treaty, to adopt appropriate measures to ensure the due functioning and conduct of its proceedings. However, in accordance with the above-mentioned mutual duties of sincere cooperation, the decisions of the Parliament in turn must have regard to the power of the Governments of the Member States to determine the seat of the institutions and to the provisional decisions taken in the meantime.

What is more, it must be emphasised that the powers of the Governments of the Member States in the matter do not affect the right inherent in the Parliament to discuss any question concerning the Communities, to adopt resolutions on such questions and to invite the Governments to act.

It follows that the Parliament cannot be considered to have exceeded its powers solely because it has adopted a resolution 'on the Seat of the Institutions of the European Community and in particular of the European Parliament' and dealing with the question of the place of work.

...

The submission of lack of competence is thus unfounded.

2. *Infringement of Essential Procedural Requirements*
The Luxembourg Government has further relied on infringement of essential procedural requirements inasmuch as the Governments of Member States have not given their assent to any decision on the subject of the seat nor did the Parliament consult its legal committee before adopting the contested resolution.

In that respect it suffices to observe that in the present case the Luxembourg Government has not established the infringement of any essential procedural requirements which must be observed by the Parliament before it adopts a resolution such as that in dispute.

That submission is therefore unfounded.

It follows from the foregoing that the application must be dismissed...

2. THE COUNCIL

Article 8 of the ECSC Treaty imposed on the High Authority the duty of securing the attainment of the objectives of that document. Article 145 of the EEC Treaty, however, entrusts to the Council the task of ensuring that the objectives set out in that Treaty are attained and to that end it empowers the Council to take decisions. (The Commission is given the more modest duties set out in Article 155.)

A single Council now operates in all of the three Communities. It consists of the representatives of the twelve Member States, each of which may be represented by its Foreign Minister or by its minister responsible for the specific field of government policy, such as agricultural policy, forming the subject of a particular meeting. In the absence of the Ministers the work of the Council is undertaken by a Committee of Permanent Representatives, which consists of the ambassadors of the Member States accredited to the Communities (or their deputies), who coordinate the work of various groups of experts.

The term 'European Council' is sometimes used to describe meetings of the Heads of Government of the Member States. Such meetings are wholly distinct from the Council of the European Communities and they were not envisaged in the founding Treaties but are now formalised under the Single European Act. Representatives of the Member States (other than Heads of Government) occasionally meet in the premises of the Council for the purpose of reaching decisions not authorised by the founding Treaties or subsequent agreements. These, like meetings of the 'European Council', are in principle governed by public international law and comity rather than by European Community law, but after the entry into force of the Single European Act such meetings may be even less frequent than in the past. In some exceptional instances, however, the founding Treaties require a decision to be made not by the Council but by the Member States (an example is the appointment of members of the Commission, governed by Article 11 of the Merger Treaty, replacing Article 158 of the EEC Treaty, below). In these exceptional cases the meetings of the representatives of the Member States are governed by the law of the European Communities.

EEC Treaty

Article 145

To ensure that the objectives set out in this Treaty are attained, the Council shall, in accordance with the provisions of this Treaty:

– ensure coordination of the general economic policies of the Member States;
– have power to take decisions;
– confer on the Commission, in the acts which the Council adopts, powers for the implementation of the rules which the Council lays down. The Council may impose certain requirements in respect of the exercise of these powers. The Council may also reserve the right, in specific cases, to exercise directly implementing powers itself. The procedures referred to above must be consonant with principles and rules to be laid down in advance by the Council, acting unanimously on a proposal from the Commission and after obtaining the opinion of the European Parliament.

Merger Treaty

Article 2

The Council shall consist of representatives of the Member States. Each Government shall delegate to it one of its members.

The office of President shall be held in turn by each Member State in the Council for a term of six months, in the following order of Member States:

– for a first cycle of six years: Belgium, Denmark, Germany, Greece, Spain, France, Ireland, Italy, Luxembourg, Netherlands, Portugal, United Kingdom.
– for the following cycle of six years: Denmark, Belgium, Greece, Germany, France, Spain, Italy, Ireland, Netherlands, Luxembourg, United Kingdom, Portugal.

Article 3

The Council shall meet when convened by its President on his own initiative or at the request of one of its members or of the Commission.

EEC Treaty

Article 148

[Amended by Act of Accession, Article 14, and Adaptation Decision, Article 8.]

1. Save as otherwise provided in this Treaty, the Council shall act by a majority of its members.

2. Where the Council is required to act by a qualified majority, the votes of its members shall be weighted as follows:

Belgium	5
Denmark	3
Germany	10
Greece	5
Spain	8
France	10

Ireland	3
Italy	10
Luxembourg	2
Netherlands	5
Portugal	5
United Kingdom	10

For their adoption, acts of the Council shall require at least:

54 votes in favour where this Treaty requires them to be adopted on a proposal from the Commission,

54 votes in favour, cast by at least eight members, in other cases.

3. Abstentions by members present in person or represented shall not prevent the adoption by the Council of acts which require unanimity.

Article 149

1. Where, in pursuance of this Treaty, the Council acts on a proposal from the Commission, unanimity shall be required for an act constituting an amendment to that proposal.

2. Where, in pursuance of this Treaty, the Council acts in cooperation with the European Parliament, the following procedure shall apply:

(a) The Council, acting by a qualified majority under the conditions of paragraph 1, on a proposal from the Commission and after obtaining the opinion of the European Parliament, shall adopt a common position.

(b) The Council's common position shall be communicated to the European Parliament. The Council and the Commission shall inform the European Parliament fully of the reasons which led the Council to adopt its common position and also of the Commission's position.

If, within three months of such communication, the European Parliament approves this common position or has not taken a decision within that period, the Council shall definitely adopt the act in question in accordance with the common position.

(c) The European Parliament may within the period of three months referred to in point (b), by an absolute majority of its component members, propose amendments to the Council's common position. The European Parliament may also, by the same majority, reject the Council's common position. The result of the proceedings shall be transmitted to the Council and the Commission.

If the European Parliament has rejected the Council's common position, unanimity shall be required for the Council to act on a second reading.

(d) The Commission shall, within a period of one month, re-examine the proposal on the basis of which the Council adopted its common position, by taking into account the amendments proposed by the European Parliament.

The Commission shall forward to the Council, at the same time as its re-examined proposal, the amendments of the European Parliament which it has not accepted, and shall express its opinion on them. The Council may adopt these amendments unanimously.

(e) The Council, acting by a qualified majority, shall adopt the proposal as re-examined by the Commission.

Unanimity shall be required for the Council to amend the proposal as re-examined by the Commission.

(f) In the cases referred to in points (c), (d) and (e), the Council shall be required to act within a period of three months. If no decision is taken within this period, the Commission's proposal shall be deemed not to have been adopted.

(g) The periods referred to in points (b) and (f) may be extended by a maximum of one month by common accord between the Council and the European Parliament.

3. As long as the Council has not acted, the Commission may alter its proposal at any time during the procedures mentioned in paragraphs 1 and 2.

Article 150

Where a vote is taken, any member of the Council may also act on behalf of not more than one other member.

Merger Treaty

Article 4

A committee consisting of the Permanent Representatives of the Member States shall be responsible for preparing the work of the Council and for carrying out the tasks assigned to it by the Council.

See also the Luxembourg Accords part (b) (p. 17 above).

3. THE COMMISSION

Whereas members of the Council represent the interests of several Member States, members of the Commission are bound to be completely independent in the performance of their duties.

The composition of the Commission is governed in part by Article 10 of the Merger Treaty which replaces Article 157 of the EEC Treaty, and was amended by the Adaptation Decisions taken in order to deal with the enlargement of the Communities by the accession of the United Kingdom, Denmark, Ireland, Greece, Spain and Portugal. For this reason the Article provided that the Commission should consist of 17 members – two for each of the five larger Member States and one for each of the others.

Two of the Commission's functions, set out in Article 155 of the EEC Treaty, are of special importance. The first of these is the task of securing observance of the Treaty and measures taken in pursuance of it. The second function is that of taking the initiative and participating in the shaping of measures of the Council. For the purpose of securing observance of the Treaty the Commission has the power to institute proceedings in the Court of Justice of the European Communities. This it may do, in the case of proceedings against Member States, in accordance with Articles 93 and 169 (below), and in the case of proceedings against other Community institutions, in accordance with Articles 173 and 175 (below). In order to secure observance by national or legal persons of the

Treaties and of implementing measures the Commission has a variety of powers including the capacity, in appropriate circumstances, to impose fines and to authorise Member States to take measures to terminate infringements (e.g. Articles 87(2) and 89, below).

EEC Treaty

Article 155

In order to ensure the proper functioning and development of the Common Market, the Commission shall:

- ensure that the provisions of this Treaty and the measures taken by the institutions pursuant thereto are applied;
- formulate recommendations or deliver opinions on matters dealt with in this Treaty, if it expressly so provides or if the Commission considers it necessary;
- have its own power of decision and participate in the shaping of measures taken by the Council and by the Assembly in the manner provided for in this Treaty;
- exercise the powers conferred on it by the Council for the implementation of the rules laid down by the latter.

Merger Treaty

Article 18

The Commission shall publish annually, not later than one month before the opening of the session of the Assembly, a general report on the activities of the Communities.

Article 10

1. The Commission shall consist of seventeen members, who shall be chosen on the grounds of their general competence and whose independence is beyond doubt.

The number of members of the Commission may be altered by the Council, acting unanimously.

Only nationals of Member States may be members of the Commission.

The Commission must include at least one national of each of the Member States, but may not include more than two members having the nationality of the same State.

2. The members of the Commission shall, in the general interest of the Communities, be completely independent in the performance of their duties.

In the performance of these duties, they shall neither seek nor take instructions from any Government or from any other body. They shall refrain from any action incompatible with their duties. Each Member State undertakes to respect this principle and not to seek to influence the members of the Commission in the performance of their tasks.

The members of the Commission may not, during their term of office, engage in any other occupation, whether gainful or not. When entering upon their duties they shall give a solemn undertaking that, both during and after their term of office, they will respect the obligations arising therefrom and in particular their duty to behave with integrity and discretion as regards the acceptance, after they have ceased to hold office, of certain appointments or benefits. In the event of any breach of these obligations, the Court of Justice may, on application by the Council or the Commission, rule that the member concerned be, according to the circumstances, either compulsorily retired in accordance with the provisions of Article 13 or deprived of his right to a pension or other benefits in its stead.

Article 11

The members of the Commission shall be appointed by common accord of the Governments of the Member States.

Their term of office shall be four years. It shall be renewable.

Article 12

Apart from normal replacement, or death, the duties of a member of the Commission shall end when he resigns or is compulsorily retired.

The vacancy thus caused shall be filled for the remainder of the member's term of office. The Council may, acting unanimously, decide that such a vacancy need not be filled.

Save in the case of compulsory retirement under the provisions of Article 13, members of the Commission shall remain in office until they have been replaced.

Article 13

If any member of the Commission no longer fulfils the conditions required for the performance of his duties or if he has been guilty of serious misconduct, the Court of Justice may, on application by the Council or the Commission, compulsorily retire him.

Article 14

The President and the five Vice-Presidents of the Commission shall be appointed from among its members for a term of two years in accordance with the same procedure as that laid down for the appointment of members of the Commission. Their appointments may be renewed.

Save where the entire Commission is replaced, such appointments shall be made after the Commission has been consulted.

In the event of retirement or death, the President and the Vice-Presidents shall be replaced for the remainder of their term of office in accordance with the preceding provisions.

Article 15

The Council and the Commission shall consult each other and shall settle by common accord their methods of cooperation.

...

Article 17

The Commission shall act by a majority of the number of members provided for in Article 10.

See also the Luxembourg Accords, part (a) (above, p.16).

4. THE COURT OF JUSTICE OF THE EUROPEAN COMMUNITIES

The ECSC, Euratom, and EEC Treaties make separate provision for the establishment of Courts of Justice to secure the observance of law in the interpretation and application of the several Treaties. Since, however, the Convention on Common Institutions established that the three Communities were to be served by a single Court, it has taken the name 'the Court of Justice of the European Communities'.

The Court consists of thirteen Judges and is assisted by six Advocates General. In practice, each Judge has been a national of a different Member State (the office of the thirteenth judge rotating between the larger Member States) and each of the five largest Member States has had one of its nationals among the six Advocates General (the office of the sixth Advocate General rotating between the smaller Member States). Apart from those occupying the rotating offices, the Judges and Advocates General are appointed for terms of six years, expiring at alternating intervals of three years, or for uncompleted terms of office of their precursors. The office is renewable (save in the case of rotating offices).

The role of the Advocates General is unique, although cognate with that of the *Commissaire du Gouvernement* at the French *Conseil d'Etat*. In each case before the Court one Advocate General delivers an impartial and reasoned opinion, after the conclusion of the arguments of the parties but before the judgment of the Court. The opinion is in fact the first part of the judicial process – the second being the judgment. The interposition of this stage in the process, between the arguments of the parties and the judgment of the Court, is commonly justified on the ground that the Court of Justice of the European Communities is in many cases a court of first and last instance. Advocates General's opinions are often cited as legal authority; although of course the judgment of thirteen Judges must outweigh the opinion of a single Advocate General, even though the new rules of procedure adopted in 1974 secured for Advocates General a status equal to that of Judges and even though Advocates General's opinions tend to be longer and more detailed than judgments of the Court.

EEC Treaty

Article 164

The Court of Justice shall ensure that in the interpretation and application of this Treaty the law is observed.

Article 165

The Court of Justice shall consist of thirteen Judges.

The Court of Justice shall sit in plenary session. It may, however, form chambers, each consisting of three or five Judges, either to undertake certain preparatory inquiries or to adjudicate on particular categories of cases in accordance with rules laid down for these purposes.

Whenever the Court of Justice hears cases brought before it by a Member State or by one of the institutions of the Community or, to the extent that the chambers of the court do not have the requisite jurisdiction under the Rules of Procedure, has to give preliminary rulings on questions submitted to it pursuant to Article 177, it shall sit in plenary session.

Should the Court of Justice so request, the Council may, acting unanimously, increase the number of Judges and make the necessary adjustments to the second and third paragraphs of this article and to the second paragraph of Article 167.

Article 166

The Court of Justice shall be assisted by six Advocates General.

It shall be the duty of the Advocate General, acting with complete impartiality and independence, to make, in open court, reasoned submissions on cases brought before the Court of Justice, in order to assist the Court in the performance of the task assigned to it in Article 164.

Should the Court of Justice so request, the Council may, acting unanimously, increase the number of Advocates General and make the necessary adjustments to the third paragraph of Article 167.

Article 167

The Judges and Advocates General shall be chosen from persons whose independence is beyond doubt and who possess the qualifications required for appointment to the highest judicial offices in their respective countries or who are jurisconsults of recognised competence; they shall be appointed by common accord of the Governments of the Member States for a term of six years. Every three years there shall be a partial replacement of the Judges. Seven and six Judges shall be replaced alternately.

Every three years there shall be a partial replacement of the Advocates General.

Two Advocates General shall be replaced on each occasion.

Retiring Judges and Advocates General shall be eligible for reappointment.

The Judges shall elect the President of the Court of Justice from among their number for a term of three years. He may be re-elected.

These Treaty rules are supplemented by three Protocols on the Statute of the Court – one for each of the Communities. The Protocols are similar. They deal not only with such matters as Judges' and Advocates General's oaths, immunities and tenures, but also with points of procedure.

Protocol on the Statute of the Court of Justice of the EEC

Article 17

The States and the institutions of the Community shall be represented before the Court by an agent appointed for each case; the agent may be assisted by an adviser or by a lawyer entitled to practise before a court of a Member State.

Other parties must be represented by a lawyer entitled to practise before a court of a Member State.

Such agents, advisers and lawyers shall, when they appear before the Court, enjoy the rights and immunities necessary to the independent exercise of their duties, under conditions laid down in the rules of procedure.

As regards such advisers and lawyers who appear before it, the Court shall have the powers normally accorded to courts of law, under conditions laid down in the rules of procedure.

University teachers being nationals of a Member State whose law accords them a right of audience shall have the same rights before the Court as are accorded by this article to lawyers entitled to practise before a court of a Member State.

Article 18

The procedure before the Court shall consist of two parts: written and oral.

The written procedure shall consist of the communication to the parties and to the institutions of the Community whose decisions are in dispute, of applications, statements of case, defences and observations, and of replies, if any, as well as of all papers and documents in support or of certified copies of them.

Communications shall be made by the Registrar in the order and within the time laid down in the rules of procedure.

The oral procedure shall consist of the reading of the report presented by a Judge acting as Rapporteur, the hearing by the Court of agents, advisers and lawyers entitled to practise before a court of a Member State and of the submissions of the Advocate General, as well as the hearing, if any, of witnesses and experts.

Article 19

A case shall be brought before the Court by a written application addressed to the Registrar. The application shall contain the applicant's name and permanent address and the description of the signatory, the name of the party against whom the application is made, the subject matter of the dispute, the submissions and a brief statement of the grounds on which the application is based.

The application will be accompanied, where appropriate, by the measure the annulment of which is sought or, in the circumstances referred to in Article 175 of this Treaty, by documentary evidence of the date on which an institution was, in accordance with that article, requested to act. If the documents are not submitted with the application, the Registrar shall ask the party concerned to produce them within a reasonable period, but in that event the rights of the party shall not lapse even if such documents are produced after the time limit for bringing proceedings.

Article 20

In the cases governed by Article 177 of this Treaty, the decision of the court or tribunal of a Member State which suspends its proceedings and refers a case to the Court shall be notified to the Court by the court or tribunal concerned. The decision shall then be notified by the Registrar of the Court to the parties, to the Member States and to the Commission, and also the Council if the act the validity or interpretation of which is in dispute originates from the Council.

Within two months of this notification, the parties, the Member States, the Commission and, where appropriate, the Council, shall be entitled to submit statements of case or written observations to the Court.

...

Article 37

Member States and institutions of the Community may intervene in cases before the Court.

The same right shall be open to any other person establishing an interest in the result of any case submitted to the Court, save in cases between Member States, between institutions of the Community or between Member States and institutions of the Community.

Submissions made in an application to intervene shall be limited to supporting the submissions of one of the parties.

The Court itself, in the exercise of powers conferred on it by the Treaties, has made rules of procedure. These deal not only with the conduct of written and oral proceedings but also with ancillary matters including the organisation of the Court and the provision of legal aid.

Rules of Procedure of the Court of Justice

OJ 1974 L 350/1

Article 7

1. The Judges shall, immediately after the partial replacement provided form him in Article 32 (b) of the ECSC Treaty, Article 167 of the EEC Treaty and Article 139 of the Euratom Treaty, elect one of their number as President of the Court for a term of three years.

2. If the office of the President of the Court falls vacant before the normal date of expiry thereof, the Court shall appoint a successor for the remainder of the term.

3. The elections provided for in this article shall be by secret ballot, the Judge obtaining an absolute majority being elected. If no Judge obtains an absolute majority, the second ballot shall be held and the Judge obtaining the most votes shall be elected. Where two or more Judges obtain an equal number of votes the oldest of them shall be deemed elected.

Article 8

The President shall direct the judicial business and the administration of the Court. He shall preside at hearings and at deliberations in the Deliberation Room.

Article 9

1. The Court shall set up two Chambers and shall decide which Judges and Advocates General shall be attached to them.

2. As soon as an application originating proceedings has been lodged, the President shall assign the case to one of the Chambers and designate from that Chamber a Judge to act as Rapporteur, and the Advocate General.

In cases which devolve directly on a Chamber by virtue of these rules the powers of the President of the Court shall be exercised by the President of the Chamber...

Article 10

The Court shall designate for a period of one year the Presidents of the Chambers and the first Advocate General.

The provisions of Article 7(2) and (3) shall apply in a corresponding manner.

...

Article 29

1. The language of a case shall be Danish, Dutch, English, French, German, Irish, Italian, Spanish, Portuguese or Greek.

2. The language of a case shall be chosen by the applicant, except that:

(a) where the application is made against a Member State or a natural or legal person having the nationality of a Member State, the language of the case shall be the official language of that State; where that State has more than one official language, the applicant may choose between them;

(b) at the joint request of the parties the Court may authorise another of the languages mentioned in paragraph (1) of this article to be used as the language of the case for all or part of the proceedings;

(c) at the request of one of the parties, and after the opposite party and the Advocate General have been heard, the Court may, by way of derogation from subparagraphs (a) and (b), authorise another of the languages mentioned in paragraph (1) of this article to be used as the language of the case for all or part of the proceedings; such a request may not be submitted by an institution of the European Communities.

Where Article 103 of these rules applies, the language of the case shall be the language of the national court or tribunal which refers the matter to the Court.

3. The language of the case shall in particular be used not only in parties' written statements and oral addresses to the Court and in supporting documents but also in the minutes and decisions of the Court.

Supporting documents expressed in any other language must be accompanied by a translation into the language of the case.

In the case of long documents translations may be confined to extracts. However, the Court or Chamber may, of its own motion or at the request of a party, at any time call for a complete or fuller translation.

4. Where a witness or expert states that he is unable adequately to express himself in one of the languages referred to in paragraph (1) of this article, the Court or Chamber may authorise him to give his evidence in another language. The Registrar shall arrange for translation into the language of the case.

5. The President of the Court and the Presidents of Chambers in conducting oral proceedings, the Judge Rapporteur both in his preliminary report and in his report at the hearing, Judges and Advocates General in putting questions and Advocates General in delivering their opinions may use a language referred to in paragraph (1) of this article other than the language of the case. The Registrar shall arrange for translation into the language of the case.

...

Article 37

1. The original of every pleading shall be signed by the party's agent or lawyer.

It shall be lodged together with two copies for the Court and a copy for every other party to the proceedings. Copies shall be certified by the party lodging them.

2. Institutions shall in addition produce, within time limits laid down by the Court, translations of all pleadings into the other languages provided for by Article 1 of Council Regulation 1. The second sub-paragraph of paragraph (1) of this article shall apply in a corresponding manner.

3. All pleadings shall bear a date. In the reckoning of time limits for taking steps in proceedings, the only relevant date shall be that of lodgment at the Registry.

4. To every pleading there shall be annexed a file containing all documents relied on in support of it, together with a schedule listing them.

5. Where in view of the length of a document only extracts from it are annexed to the pleading, the whole document or a full copy of it shall be lodged at the Registry.

Article 38

1. An application of the kind referred to in ... Article 19 of the EEC ... Statute shall state:

(a) the name and permanent residence of the applicant;
(b) the name of the party against whom the application is made;
(c) the subject-matter of the dispute and the grounds on which the application is based;
(d) the form of order sought by the applicant;
(e) the nature of any evidence founded upon by him.

2. For the purpose of the proceedings, the application shall state an address for service in the place where the Court has its seat. It shall also give the name of a person who is authorised and has expressed willingness to accept service.

3. The lawyer acting for a party must lodge at the Registry a certificate that he is entitled to practise before a court of a Member State...

7. If an application does not comply with the requirements, set out in paragraphs (2) to (6) of this article, the Registrar shall prescribe a reasonable period within which the applicant is to comply with them whether by putting the application itself in order or by producing any of the above-mentioned documents. If the applicant fails to put the application in order or to produce the required documents within the time prescribed, the Court shall, after hearing the Advocate General, decide whether to reject the application on the ground of want of form.

Article 39

The application shall be served on the defendant. In a case where Article 38(7) applies, service shall be effected as soon as the application has been put in order or the Court has declared it admissible notwithstanding the failure to observe the formal requirements set out in that article.

Article 40

1. Within one month after service on him of the application, the defendant shall lodge a defence, stating:

(a) the name and permanent residence of the defendant;
(b) the points of fact and law relied on;
(c) the form of order sought;
(d) the nature of any evidence founded upon by him.

The provisions of Article 38(2) to (5) of these rules shall apply in a corresponding manner to the defence.

2 The time limit laid down in paragraph (1) of this article may be extended by the President on a reasoned application by the defendant.

Article 41

1. The application originating the proceedings and the defence may be supplemented by a reply from the applicant and by a rejoinder from the defendant.

2 The President shall fix the time limits within which these pleadings are to be lodged.

Article 42

1. In reply or rejoinder a party may indicate further evidence. The party must, however, give reasons for the delay in indicating it.

2 No fresh issue may be raised in the course of proceedings unless it is based on matters of law or of fact which come to light in the course of the written procedure.

If in the course of the written procedure one of the parties raises a fresh issue which is so based, the President may, even after the expiry of the normal procedural time limits, acting on a report of the Judge Rapporteur and after hearing the Advocate General, allow the other party time to answer on that issue.

The decision on the admissibility of the issue shall be reserved for the final judgment.

Article 43

The Court may at any time, after hearing the parties and the Advocate General, order that for the purpose of the written or oral procedure or of its final judgment, a number of related cases concerning the same subject-matter shall be dealt with jointly. The decision to join the cases may subsequently be rescinded.

Article 44

1. After the rejoinder provided for in Article 41(1) of these rules has been lodged, the President shall fix a date on which the Judge Rapporteur is to present his preliminary report as to whether a preparatory inquiry is necessary. The Court shall decide the question after hearing the Advocate General. The same procedure shall apply:

(a) where no reply or no rejoinder has been lodged within the time limit fixed in accordance with Article 41(2) of these rules;

(b) where the party concerned waives his right to lodge a reply or rejoinder.

2 Where the Court orders a preparatory inquiry and does not undertake it itself, it shall assign the inquiry to the Chamber.

Where the Court decides to open the oral procedure without an inquiry, the President shall fix the opening date.

...

Article 56

1. The proceedings shall be opened and directed by the President, who shall be responsible for the proper conduct of the hearing.

2. The oral proceedings in cases which are heard *in camera* shall not be published.

Article 57

The President may in the course of the hearing put questions to the agents, advisers or lawyers of the parties.

The other Judges and the Advocate General may do likewise.

Article 58

A party may address the Court only through his agents, adviser or lawyer.

Article 59

1. The Advocate General shall deliver his opinion orally at the end of the oral procedure.

2. After the Advocate General has delivered his opinion, the President shall declare the oral procedure closed.

Article 60

The Court may at any time, after hearing the Advocate General, order any measure of inquiry to be taken or that a previous inquiry be repeated or expanded. The Court may direct the Chamber or the Judge Rapporteur to carry out the measures so ordered.

Article 61

The Court may after hearing the Advocate General order the reopening of the oral procedure.

Article 62

1. The Registrar shall draw up minutes of every hearing. The minutes shall be signed by the President and by the Registrar and shall constitute an official record.

2. The parties may inspect the minutes at the Registry and obtain copies at their own expense.

Article 63

The judgment shall contain:

- a statement that it is the judgment of the Court,
- the date of its delivery,
- the names of the President and of the Judges taking part in it,
- the name of the Advocate General,
- the name of the Registrar,
- the description of the parties,
- the names of the agents, advisers and lawyers of the parties,
- the submissions of the parties,
- a statement that the Advocate General has been heard,
- a summary of the facts,
- the grounds for the decision,
- the operative part of the judgment, including the decision as to costs.

...

Article 95

1. Cases referred for a preliminary ruling under Article 41 of the ECSC Treaty, Article 177 of the EEC Treaty and Article 150 of the Euratom Treaty may be assigned by

the Court to the Chambers. This provision shall apply to cases which are of an essentially technical nature or concern matters for which there is already an established body of case law.

The decision to assign shall be taken by the full Court following presentation by the Judge Rapporteur of his preparatory report and after the Advocate General has been heard.

A case may not be so assigned if, pursuant to Article 20 of the EEC Statute, or Article 21 of the Euratom Statute, a Member State has exercised its right to submit a statement of case or written observations, unless the State concerned has signified that it has no objection, or if an institution expressly requests in its observations that the case be decided in plenary session.

The Chamber to which a case is assigned pursuant to Article 9(2) of these rules shall have jurisdiction in the cases brought before it under this article.

2. Proceedings commenced by an official or other servant of an institution against the institution shall, with the exception of applications for the adoption of interim measures, be tried by a Chamber designated each year by the Court for that purpose.

3. The Chamber may refer to the Court the cases referred to in paragraphs (1) and (2) above.

Article 96

1. Where an application for the adoption of interim measures is made to the President in the course of proceedings under Article 95(3) of these rules but the President is absent or prevented from hearing the application, his place shall be taken by the President of the designated Chamber.

2. Without prejudice to his power of referral under Article 85 of these rules, the President may refer the application to the designated Chamber.

...

Article 102

1. An application for interpretation of a judgment shall be made in accordance with Articles 37 and 38 of these rules. In addition it shall specify:

(a) the judgment in question;

(b) the passages of which interpretation is sought.

The application must be made against all the parties to the case in which the judgment was given.

2. The Court shall give its decision in the form of a judgment after having given the parties an opportunity to submit their observations and after hearing the Advocate General.

The original of the interpreting judgment shall be annexed to the original of the judgment interpreted. A note of the interpreting judgment shall be made in the margin of the original of the judgment interpreted.

Article 103

1. In cases referred to in Article 20 of the EEC Statute...

...the provisions of Articles 44 *et seq.* of these rules shall apply in a corresponding manner after the written statements of case or written observations provided for in those Articles 20 and 21 have been lodged.

The same provisions shall apply even where such documents are not lodged within the time prescribed in those Articles 20 and 21, or where the parties to the main action, the

Member States, the Commission or, as the case may be, the Council declare an intention to dispense with them...

The reference in Article 96 of the rules of procedure to 'interim measures' contains an echo of Article 186 of the EEC Treaty (see Chapter 4, p. 146). This authorises the Court to prescribe interim measures in any case before it.

Although the competition rules of the EEC Treaty do not confer on the Commission a power to take interim measures similar to the power conferred on the Court by Article 96 of its rules of procedure, the Court has held that the Commission has an implied power 'to take interim measures which are indispensable for the effective exercise of its functions' under Regulation No 17. In reaching this decision, the Court extended to the Commission, by way of analogy, the power contained in Article 96.

Case 792/79R Camera Care Limited v Commission
[1980] ECR 119; [1980] 1 CMLR 334

The Court

Power of the Commission to adopt Interim Measures

The hesitation shown by the Commission stems from the fact that Regulation No 17 does not expressly confer upon the Commission, after receiving applications under Article 3 of the Regulation or when proceeding on its own initiative under the same provision, the power to adopt interim measures pending the time when it is in a position to adjudicate upon the substance of the case.

It is recalled that Article 3(1) of the regulation provides that: 'Where the Commission, upon application or upon its own initiative, finds that there is infringement of Article 85 or Article 86 of the Treaty, it may by decision require the undertakings ... concerned to bring such an infringement to an end'. Paragraph (3) of the same article adds that the Commission, before taking a decision under paragraph (1), may 'address to the undertakings ... concerned recommendations for termination of the infringement'.

It is obvious that in certain circumstances there may be a need to adopt interim protective measures when the practice of certain undertakings in competition matters has the effect of injuring the interests of some Member States, causing damage to other undertakings, or of unacceptably jeopardising the Community's competition policy. In such circumstances it is important to ensure that, whilst inquiries are being carried out, no irreparable damage is caused such as could not be remedied by any decision which the Commission might take at the conclusion of the administrative procedure.

Although it is true that, from the point of view of both the efficacy of competition law and the protection of the legitimate interests of the Member States or undertakings concerned, the adoption of protective measures may seem to be necessary in certain circumstances, the provisions of Regulation No 17 must nevertheless be examined to see whether they can accommodate this legal requirement.

It is as well to observe on this point that Article 3 of the regulation entitles the Commission to take two types of action in order to bring to an end any infringements that it finds: first, the Commission may take 'decisions' which, according to Article 189 of the Treaty, are binding upon those to whom they are addressed and which, according to

Articles 15 and 16 of Regulation No 17, may be accompanied by fines and periodic penalty payments; secondly, before taking a binding decision, the Commission is always entitled under Article 3(3) to address to the undertakings concerned 'recommendations for termination of the infringement'. The object of this last provision is to enable the Commission to inform the undertakings concerned of its assessment of the situation with regard to Community law in order to persuade them to comply with its point of view without immediately resorting to legal enforcement. It cannot, however, be construed as a limitation upon the practical ways in which the power to take a decision, which is the core of Article 3, may be exercised.

As regards the right to take decisions conferred upon the Commission by Article 3(1), it is essential that it should be exercised in the most efficacious manner best suited to the circumstances of each given situation. To this end the possibility cannot be excluded that the exercise of the right to take decisions conferred upon the Commission should comprise successive stages so that a decision finding that there is an infringement may be preceded by any preliminary measures which may appear necessary at any given moment.

From this point of view the Commission must also be able, within the bounds of its supervisory task conferred upon it in competition matters by the Treaty and Regulation No 17, to take protective measures to the extent to which they might appear indispensable in order to avoid the exercise of the power to make decisions given by Article 3 from becoming ineffectual or even illusory because of the action of certain undertakings. The powers which the Commission holds under Article 3(1) of Regulation No 17 therefore include the power to take interim measures which are indispensable for the effective exercise of its functions and, in particular, for ensuring the effectiveness of any decisions requiring undertakings to bring to an end infringements which it has found to exist.

However, the Commission could not take such measures without having regard to the legitimate interests of the undertaking concerned by them. For this reason it is essential that interim measures be taken only in cases proved to be urgent in order to avoid a situation likely to cause serious and irreparable damage to the party seeking their adoption, or which is intolerable for the public interest. A further requirement is that these measures be of a temporary and conservatory nature and restricted to what is required in the given situation. When adopting them the Commission is bound to maintain the essential safeguards guaranteed to the parties concerned by Regulation No 17, in particular by Article 19. Finally, the decisions must be made in such a form that an action may be brought upon them before the Court of Justice by any party who considers he has been injured.

As the President of the Court has indicated, in the context of the ECSC Treaty, in his interlocutory order of 22 October 1975 in Case 109/75R (*National Carbonising Company* [1975] ECR 1193), it is in accordance with the key principles of the Community that any interim measures which prove to be necessary should be taken by the Community institution which is given the task of receiving complaints by governments or individuals, of making inquiries and of taking decisions in regard to infringements which are found to exist, whilst the role of the Court of Justice consists in undertaking the legal review of the action taken by the Commission in these matters. In this regard, the rights of those concerned are safeguarded by the fact that if interim measures decided upon by the Commission adversely affect the legitimate interests of any party the person concerned may always obtain the revision of the decision made, by the appropriate judicial recourse, applying if necessary for emergency measures under Article 185 or Article 186 of the EEC Treaty. It follows from these considerations that the Commission possesses the powers needed to meet the request of the applicant if it thinks this request is justified in the circumstances. The applicant must therefore be referred back to the Commission so that it may, without prejudice to the rights and interests of the party concerned by the complaint, take a decision upon the request for interim measures upon the conditions set out above.

The same case illustrates the distinctive functions of the Court and of the Advocate General. The Advocate General delivers an Opinion in open court setting out the judgment that he would give if the matter were left to him alone. Such Opinions are apt to be highly persuasive and since they may deal with wider issues than those covered in the judgment, they may constitute a source of authority on issues that the Court has not addressed. The Opinion is, however, always subordinate to the judgment of the Court and in the *Camera Care* case Mr Advocate General Warner's Opinion was *not* followed by the Court.

Mr Advocate-General Warner

...I can dispose very shortly of the suggestion that the Commission may have an 'inherent' power to that effect. A body that is created by a legal instrument does not have 'inherent' powers. It has only the powers that are conferred upon it by that instrument or by necessary implication. It differs in that respect from, for instance, a natural person or an entity that exists independently of any instrument, such as a sovereign State.

So the question is whether the power in question is conferred on the Commission by necessary implication, either by the EEC Treaty or by legislation adopted thereunder, which means in effect Regulation No 17.

To imply such a power in the EEC Treaty would in my opinion be inconsistent with the terms of that Treaty. Article 87 clearly envisages that such a power can only be conferred on the Commission by an act of the Council. The transitional provisions in Articles 88 and 89 envisaged that, until the Council had adopted under Article 87 what that article called 'appropriate regulations and directives to give effect to the principles set out in Articles 85 and 86', the authorities in Member States should shoulder the main burden of giving effect to those principles. The Commission's powers were limited to proposing appropriate measures to those authorities and, in the ultimate resort, to recording an infringement of those principles in a reasoned decision and authorising Member States to take specified measures 'to remedy the situation'. I do not think one can divorce the first sentence of Article 89 from the rest of that Article in the manner that was suggested to us this morning. Nor do I think that one can interpret the general terms of Article 155 as overriding the specific provisions of Articles 87 to 89.

That seems to me to establish a clear distinction between what the Commission may do once it has made a finding of infringement and what it may do before it has reached that stage. Article 3 is inconsistent with the Commission having power, before it has issued a decision based on a finding of infringement, to go further than to address recommendations to the undertakings concerned. As we were reminded this morning, a decision under paragraph 1 of Article 3 can only be adopted after certain prescribed steps have been taken. In particular, a statement of objections must have been sent to the undertaking or undertakings concerned, they must have been heard in answer to it, and the Advisory Committee must have been consulted. No such formalities are required before a recommendation can be made under paragraph 3. The crux, however, in my opinion, is that, under Article 3, no decision binding on the undertaking or undertakings concerned can be adopted before there is a finding of infringement.

...

Other copious and detailed interim powers are conferred on the Commission by Articles 11 to 14 of the regulation, and they are backed up by the provisions about fines and penalties contained in Articles 15 and 16. None of those articles come anywhere near implying that the Commission has power to order interim measures of the kind here in question.

I conclude that, not only does Regulation No 17 not confer such a power on the Commission by necessary implication, but that, indeed, the necessary implication from the terms of that Regulation is that its authors had no intention of conferring such a power on the Commission.

Whether they were right or wrong is not the question. Arguments were addressed to us on behalf of the applicant and of the Commission, some of them attractive, to show that it was desirable that the Commission should have such a power. In my opinion those arguments should be addressed to the Council, not to this Court. This Court exists to say what the law is, not what it ought to be.

5. THE ECONOMIC AND SOCIAL COMMITTEE

The Parliament, Council, Commission and Court are the only institutions of the EEC, and their counterparts in the ECSC and Euratom are the only institutions of those Communities. The institutions, and they alone, are given 'powers' in the founding Treaties. The same Treaties, however, establish or authorise the establishment of various committees with consultative status. Among those are the Economic Study Committee set up by Article 16 of the ECSC Treaty, the Arbitration Committee and the Scientific and Technical Committee set up by Articles 18 and 134 of the Euratom Treaty and the Transport, Monetary, Competition and European Social Fund Committees set up under the EEC Treaty, by Articles 83, 105, 113 and 124 respectively. By far the most important of the Committees are the Economic and Social Committee (ECOSOC), which serves the EEC and Euratom, and its counterpart in the ECSC called the Consultative Committee.

Those two Committees contain representatives of employers (including those in the public as well as the private sector), employees (through trades unions) and others (particularly the self-employed). The Economic and Social Committee is divided into sections for the various activities regulated by the founding Treaties, and into sub-committees. It is these sections and sub-committees, rather than the Committee as a whole, that tend to play the more significant role in the devising of specific Community policies and in the drafting of Community legislation.

EEC Treaty

Article 193

An Economic and Social Committee is hereby established. It shall have advisory status.

The Committee shall consist of representatives of the various categories of economic and social activity, in particular, representatives of producers, farmers, carriers, workers, dealers, craftsmen, professional occupations and representatives of the general public.

Article 194

The number of members of the Committee shall be as follows:

Belgium	12
Denmark	9
Germany	24
Greece	12
Spain	21
France	24
Ireland	9
Italy	24
Luxembourg	5
Netherlands	12
Portugal	12
United Kingdom	24

The members of the Committee shall be appointed by the Council, acting unanimously, for four years. Their appointments shall be renewable.

The members of the Committee shall be appointed in their personal capacity and may not be bound by any mandatory instructions.

Article 195

1. For the appointment of the members of the Committee, each Member State shall provide the Council with a list containing twice as many candidates as there are seats allotted to its nationals.

The composition of the Committee shall take account of the need to ensure adequate representation of the various categories of economic and social activity.

2. The Council shall consult the Commission. It may obtain the opinion of European bodies which are representative of the various economic and social sectors to which the activities of the Community are of concern.

Article 196

The Committee shall elect its chairman and officers from among its members for a term of two years.

It shall adopt its rules of procedure and shall submit them to the Council for its approval, which must be unanimous.

The Council shall be convened by its chairman at the request of the Council or of the Commission.

Article 197

The Committee shall include specialised sections for the principal fields covered by this Treaty.

In particular, it shall contain an agricultural section and a transport section, which are the subject of special provisions in the Titles relating to agriculture and transport.

These specialised sections shall operate within the general terms of reference of the Committee. They may not be consulted independently of the Committee.

Sub-committees may also be established within the Committee to prepare, on specific questions or in specific fields, draft opinions to be submitted to the Committee for its consideration.

The rules of procedure shall lay down the methods of composition and the terms of reference of the specialised sections and of the sub-committees.

Article 198

The Committee must be consulted by the Council or by the Commission where this Treaty so provides. The Committee may be consulted by these institutions in all cases in which they consider it appropriate.

The Council or the Commission shall, if it considers it necessary, set the Committee, for the submission of its opinion, a time limit which may not be less than ten days from the date on which the chairman receives notification to this effect. Upon expiry of the time limit, the absence of an opinion shall not prevent further action.

The opinion of the Committee and that of the specialised section, together with a record of the proceedings, shall be forwarded to the Council and to the Commission.

6. THE STAFF OF THE COMMUNITIES

The Communities employ a staff of about fifteen thousand people, most of them being nationals of the Member States. They work at buildings of the Parliament in Luxembourg and Strasbourg, of the Council in Brussels, of the Commission in Brussels and Luxembourg, of the Court in Luxembourg and at the premises of the Economic and Social Committee in Brussels as well as in Euratom research centres and in various information and other offices in the Member States and beyond.

Their status and rights are governed by Staff Regulations made by Council Regulation No 31 of 18 December 1961, amended on numerous occasions. These regulations are lengthy and detailed. They contain, apart from general provisions, those dealing with officials' career structures, working conditions, emoluments, social security benefits and pensions as well as with discipline and resolution of disputes. In particular they provide in certain instances for proceedings before the Court of Justice of the European Communities for the annulment of decisions affecting staff. In this respect they are complemented by provisions in the founding Treaties, whereby the Court is invested with jurisdiction to entertain such appeals.

EEC Treaty

Article 179

The Court of Justice shall have jurisdiction in any dispute between the Community and its servants within the limits and under the conditions laid down in the Staff Regulations or the Conditions of Employment.

Council Regulation No 31 of 18 December 1961 laying down Staff Regulations (as amended)

JO 1962, 1385; OJ Sp Ed 1959-62, 135

Article 1

For the purposes of these Staff Regulations, 'official of the Communities' means any person who has been appointed, as provided in these Staff Regulations, to an established post on the staff of one of the institutions of the Communities by an instrument issued by the appointing authority of that institution.

Save as otherwise provided, the Economic and Social Committee shall, for the purposes of these Staff Regulations, be treated as one of the institutions of the Communities.

...

Article 9

1. There shall be set up:

(a) within each institution:

- a Staff Committee, which may be organised in sections for the different places of employment;
- one or more Joint Committees, as appropriate for the number of officials at the places of employment;
- one or more Disciplinary Boards, as appropriate for the number of officials at the places of employment;
- a Reports Committee, if required;

(b) for the Communities:

- an Invalidity Committee;

which shall perform the functions assigned to them by these Staff Regulations.

3. The Staff Committee shall represent the interests of the staff *vis-à-vis* their institution and maintain continuous contact between the institution and the staff. It shall contribute to the smooth running of the service by providing a channel for the expression of opinion by the staff...

4. In addition to the functions assigned to them by these Staff Regulations, the Joint Committee or Committees may be consulted by the appointing authority or by the Staff Committee on questions of a general nature which either of the latter thinks fit to submit.

Article 10

A Staff Regulations committee shall be set up consisting of representatives of the institutions of the Communities and an equal number of representatives of their Staff Committees. The procedure for appointing members of the Staff Regulations Committee shall be decided by agreement between the institutions.

In addition to the functions assigned to it by these Staff Regulations, the Committee may formulate suggestions for the revision of the Staff Regulations. The Committee shall meet at the request of its Chairman, an institution or the Staff Committee of an institution.

Minutes of the meetings of the Committee shall be communicated to the appropriate bodies.

Article 11

An official shall carry out his duties and conduct himself solely with the interests of the Communities in mind; he shall neither seek nor take instructions from any government, authority, organisation or person outside his institution.

An official shall not without the permission of the appointing authority accept from any government or from any other source outside the institution to which he belongs any honour, decoration, favour, gift or payment of any kind whatever, except for services rendered either before his appointment or during special leave for military or other national service and in respect of such service.

Article 12

An official shall abstain from any action and, in particular, any public expression of opinion which may reflect on his position. He may neither keep nor acquire, directly or indirectly, in undertakings which are subject to the authority of the institution to which he belongs or which have dealings with that institution, any interest of such kind of magnitude as might impair his independence in the performance of his duties...

...

Article 90(8)

[Words in brackets inserted by editors in substitution for obvious mistranslation.]

1. Any person to whom these Staff Regulations apply may submit to the appointing authority a request that it take a decision relating to him. The authority shall notify the person concerned of its reasoned decision within four months from the date on which the request was made. If at the end of that period no reply to the request has been received, this shall be deemed to constitute an implied decision rejecting it, against which a complaint may be lodged in accordance with the following paragraph.

2. Any person to whom these Staff Regulations apply may submit to the appointing authority a complaint against an act adversely affecting him, either where the said authority has taken a decision or where it has failed to adopt a measure prescribed by the Staff Regulations. The complaint must be lodged within three months. The period shall start to run:

- on the date of publication of the act if it is a measure of a general nature;
- on the date of notification of the decision to the person concerned, but in no case later than the date on which the latter received such notification, if the measure affects a specified person; if, however, an act affecting a specified person also [adversely affects] another person, the period shall start to run in respect of that other person on the date on which he receives notification thereof but in no case later than the date of publication;
- on the date of expiry of the period prescribed for reply where the complaint concerns an implied decision rejecting a request as provided in paragraph 1.

The authority shall notify the person concerned of its reasoned decision within four months from the date on which the complaint was lodged. If at the end of that period no reply to the complaint has been received, this shall be deemed to constitute an implied decision rejecting it, against which an appeal may be lodged under Article 91.

3. A request or complaint by an official shall be submitted through his immediate superior, except where it concerns that person, in which case it may be submitted direct to the authority next above.

Article 91(8)

[Words in brackets inserted by editors in substitution for obvious mistranslation.]

1. The Court of Justice of the European Communities shall have jurisdiction in any dispute between the Communities and any person to whom these Staff Regulations apply regarding the legality of an act [adversely affecting] such person ... In disputes of a financial character the Court of Justice shall have unlimited jurisdiction.

2. An appeal to the Court of Justice of the European Communities shall lie only if:

– the appointing authority has previously had a complaint submitted to it ... within the period prescribed ... and
– the complaint has been rejected by express decision or by implied decision.

3. Appeals under paragraph 2 shall be filed within three months. The period shall begin:

– on the date of notification of the decision taken in response to the complaint,
– on the date of expiry of the period described for the reply where the appeal is against an implied decision rejecting a complaint ... nevertheless, where a complaint is rejected by express decision after being rejected by implied decision but before the period for lodging an appeal has expired, the period for lodging the appeal shall start to run afresh.

4. By way of derogation from paragraph 2, the person concerned may, after submitting a complaint to the appointing authority ... immediately file an appeal with the Court of Justice, provided that such appeal is accompanied by an application either for a stay of execution of the contested act or for the adoption of interim measures. The proceedings in the principal action before the Court of Justice shall then be suspended until such time as an express or implied decision rejecting the complaint is taken.

5. Appeals under this article shall be investigated and heard as provided in the Rules of Procedure of the Court of Justice of the European Communities.

Staff Regulations modelled on those of the European Communities have been made for officials of the European Investment Bank. That Bank is not an institution of the Communities, but is established by the EEC Treaty and has the task of contributing to the balanced and stable development of the common market in the interest of the Community.

Case 110/75 John Mills v European Investment Bank
[1976] ECR 955

Mr Mills, a British subject and a Senior Lecturer in modern languages at the Polytechnic of the South Bank, entered the service of the European Investment Bank during his sabbatical leave in 1973. He was given an indefinite appointment at the Bank, as a translator, by a letter stating that the provisions of the Bank's Staff Regulations should form an integral part of the contract. In 1975 he was told that for reasons pertaining to the Bank's internal organisation his contract was to be terminated. He took the view that the decision to dismiss him was in the nature of a penalty, and was biased. He took the matter to the Bank's Conciliation Board, which failed to reach a settlement acceptable to both parties, and then decided to bring the case before the Court of Justice of the European Communities in pursuance of Article 41 of the Bank's Staff Regulations, which provides that 'Disputes, of any nature, between the Bank and individual members of staff, shall be brought before the Court of Justice of the European Communities'. He asked the Court to declare as void the decision to terminate his employment or to order the payment of compensation. The matter was first heard by a Chamber of Court (as is normal in staff cases), which referred it to the whole Court on the ground that it raised novel and important questions of jurisdiction.

Mr Advocate General Warner

Following that reference the full Court ordered that two points should be set down for argument as preliminary points, namely:

(1) Whether the Court had jurisdiction to entertain the application at all – in other words, whether Article 41 of the Staff Regulations of the Bank was valid; and

(2) Whether, if so, the Court had jurisdiction to declare void the notice terminating Mr Mills' contract.

Wrapped up in the latter point was the question whether the Court, if it found that that notice was unlawful, would have jurisdiction to order his reinstatement, or jurisdiction only to award him damages or compensation.

Those two points were argued before us on 1 April 1976 and I apprehend that it is on them, and them only, that I am now called upon to express my opinion. On the first point the parties were at one. They both submitted that the Court did have jurisdiction, though they both accepted that the point was not free from difficulty.

The difficulty is this.

Article 179 of the EEC Treaty provides:

> 'The Court of Justice shall have jurisdiction in any dispute between the Community and its servants within the limits and under the conditions laid down in the Staff Regulations or the Conditions of Employment.'

It has been suggested that the reference there to 'the Staff Regulations or the Conditions of Employment' is a reference exclusively to the 'Staff Regulations of Officials of the European Communities and the Conditions of Employment of other Servants of the Community' which were, under Article 212 of the Treaty (since replaced by Article 24 of the Merger Treaty) to be laid down by the Council. On this view, of course, the jurisdiction of the Court under Article 179 could not extend to disputes arising under the Staff Regulations of the Bank, for these were made by the Board of Directors of the Bank pursuant to Article 29 of the Rules of Procedure of the Bank, which were themselves made by the Board of Governors of the Bank under Article 9(3)(h) of the Protocol on the Statute of the Bank annexed to the Treaty.

In my opinion, however, that view is too narrow. It is to be observed that the rather precise reference in the authentic English text of Article 179 to 'the Staff Regulations or the Conditions of Employment' is not matched in the other authentic texts of the Treaty. For instance the French text states in general terms:

> *'La Cour de Justice est compétente pour statuer sur tout litige entre la Communauté et ses agents dans les limites et conditions determinées au statut ou résultant du régime applicable à ces derniers'.*

In Cases 43, 45 and 48/59 *von Lachmüller and Others* v *Commission* (Recueil 1960 (2) at 939, 952-953) it was held that those words were wide enough to cover disputes between the Commission and its staff arising before the adoption of the Staff Regulations and Conditions of Employment provided for by Article 212, when such staff were recruited under individual contracts pursuant to Article 246(3) of the Treaty.

The real difficulty in my opinion lies in the fact that Article 179 refers to disputes between 'the Community' and its servants. Article 210 of the Treaty provides that 'The Community shall have legal personality' and Article 4 that 'The tasks entrusted to the Community shall be carried out by' the Parliament, the Council, the Commission and the Court, the Council and the Commission being 'assisted by' the Economic and Social Committee. The Bank was on the other hand established by Article 129 which provides that 'it shall have legal personality'. The Bank is thus a separate legal person from 'the Community'. This suggests that references in the Treaty to 'the Community' should be construed as excluding the Bank...

The question, as I have indicated, is whether for the purposes of, at all events, the articles of the Treaty conferring jurisdiction on the Court (Article 164 *et seq.*), the references in it to 'the Community' were intended to include the Bank.

In approaching that question it is, I think, right to have in mind the following general consideration.

Article 3(j) of the Treaty provides that, for the purposes set out in Article 2, which are of course those of the Community, the activities of the Community shall include 'the establishment of a European Investment Bank to facilitate the economic expansion of the Community...', and Article 1 of the Protocol on the Statute of the Bank provides that the Bank 'shall perform its functions and carry out its activities in accordance with the provisions of this Treaty and of this Statute'. It is thus clear that the Bank is, if not a Community 'Institution' in the strict sense, at least an organ of the Community and that everything it does is in application of the Treaty. Its activities are therefore within the general field in which, by virtue of Article 164, the Court is to ensure that the law is observed.

Among the articles specifically conferring jurisdiction on the Court is one, Article 180 (which I have already mentioned), relating expressly to the Bank. This is to be found sandwiched between Articles 179 and 181, which, as we have seen, refer in general to 'the Community'. If the Bank was intended to be regarded for the purposes of those articles as being distinct from the Community, one would have expected Article 180 to be placed elsewhere, perhaps at or towards the end of the group of articles dealing with the Court's jurisdiction. Of even more significance, I think, is a consideration of the relationship between Article 181 and Article 29 of the Protocol on the Statute of the Bank. The latter, Your Lordships remember, expressly envisages that jurisdiction may be conferred on this Court in disputes between the Bank and, among others, its creditors or debtors. I can see no means by which such jurisdiction could be conferred on the Court other than an arbitration clause to which Article 181 applied. It must follow that, in the contemplation of the authors of the Treaty, the reference in Article 181 to 'the Community' included the Bank. If that is so, the same must be true of the reference to 'the Community' in Article 179.

I conclude that, on the true interpretation of the EEC Treaty taken alone, Article 179 applies to the servants of the Bank as much as to the servants of the 'Institutions'.

On the second question the Advocate General stated as his opinion that the Court had no jurisdiction to declare Mr Mills' dismissal void or to order (rather than recommend) his reinstatement. The Court agreed on the question of jurisdiction, but also held that the application for a declaration of nullity was admissible. The Court therefore remitted the case to the Chamber to determine whether the applicant was entitled to compensation.

FURTHER READING

Bieber, R., 'Legal Developments in the European Parliament' 6 YEL (1986) 357
Bieber, R et al., 'Implications of the Single European Act for the European Parliament' 23 CMLRev (1986) 767
Borgsmidt, K., 'The Advocate General at the European Court of Justice' 13 ELRev (1988) 106
Brown, L.N., 'Case 44/84, Hurd v Jones' 23 CMLRev (1986) 895
Campbell, A., 'The Single European Act and the Implications' 35 ICLQ (1986) 932
Edward, D., 'The Impact of the Single European Act on the Institutions' 24 CMLRev (1987) 9
Ehlermann, C-D., 'The Internal Market following the Single European Act' 24 CMLRev (1987) 361
Glaesner, H-J., 'Single European Act' 6 YEL (1986) 283
Pescatore, P., 'Some Critical Remarks on the Single European Act' 24 CMLRev (1987) 9
Plender, R., 'Interpretation of Community Acts by reference to the Intentions of the Authors' 2 YEL (1982) 57
Schepers, S., 'The Legal Force of the Preamble to the EEC Treaty' 6 ELRev (1981) 356
Usher, J., 'Presenting a Case before the European Court' 1 ELRev (1976) 109
Warner, J-P., 'Some Aspects of the European Court of Justice' 14 JSPTL (1976) 15
Weiler, J., 'The Community System: the Dual Character of Supranationalism' 1 YEL (1981) 276.

2

COMMUNITY LEGISLATION AND ITS EFFECTS

I THE FORMS OF LEGISLATION

The institutions of the European Communities have no general legislative powers. They may make laws only in those instances in which the power to do so is conferred on them by specific articles of the Treaties. The institutions' powers to make laws may take a variety of forms including the capacity to conclude treaties with third countries. The principal species of instruments by which the Council and Commission may legislate in pursuance of the EEC Treaty have, however, been set out in Article 189 of that document. First of these is the regulation, an instrument which (to paraphrase the Court's words in Case 6/68 *Zuckerfabrik Watenstedt* [1968] ECR 409) applies to situations which are objectively defined and has legal effect for individuals defined in a general and abstract way. The second is the Directive, which likewise applies to situations objectively defined but is binding only as to ends and not as to means. The third is the Decision, which applies not to situations but to the individuals to whom it is addressed and may be binding both as to ends and as to means.

EEC Treaty

Article 189

In order to carry out their task the Council and the Commission shall, in accordance with the provisions of this Treaty, make regulations, issue directives, take decisions, make recommendations or deliver opinions.

A regulation shall have general application. It shall be binding in its entirety and directly applicable in all Member States.

A directive shall be binding, as to the result to be achieved, upon each Member State to which it is addressed, but shall leave to the national authorities the choice of form and methods.

A decision shall be binding in its entirety upon those to whom it is addressed.

Recommendations and opinions shall have no binding force.

Article 190

Regulations, directives and decisions of the Council and of the Commission shall state the reasons on which they are based and shall refer to any proposals or opinions which were required to be obtained pursuant to this Treaty.

The Court has ruled that by imposing this obligation to state the reasons, Article 190 not only satisfies a formal requirement but aims at permitting the parties to defend their rights. To attain these objectives it is sufficient for the act to state explicitly the main factual and legal elements which support it: Case 24/62 *Germany* v *Commission* [1963] ECR 63.

Article 191

Regulations shall be published in the Official Journal of the Community. They shall enter into force on the date specified in them or, in the absence thereof, on the twentieth day following their publication.

Directives and decisions shall be notified to those to whom they are addressed and shall take effect upon such notification.

Euratom Treaty

[Articles 161-3 are worded identically to the EEC Treaty, Articles 189-191, above.]

The High Authority of the ECSC was also invested with legislative capacities and the ECSC Treaty specified that these might be exercised by certain forms of instruments including Decisions and Recommendations. Decisions, however, might be either 'general' or 'individual', so that there is a degree of correspondence between a regulation under the EEC and Euratom Treaties and a general decision under the ECSC Treaty; between a directive under the EEC and Euratom Treaties and a recommendation under the ECSC Treaty; and between a decision under the EEC and Euratom Treaties and an individual decision under the ECSC Treaty.

ECSC Treaty

Article 14

In order to carry out the tasks assigned to it the High Authority shall, in accordance with the provisions of this Treaty, take decisions, make recommendations or deliver opinions.

Decisions shall be binding in their entirety.

Recommendations shall be binding as to the aims to be pursued but shall leave the choice of the appropriate methods for achieving these aims to those to whom the recommendations are addressed.

Opinions shall have no binding force.

In cases where the High Authority is empowered to take a decision, it may confine itself to making a recommendation.

Article 15

Decisions, recommendations and opinions of the High Authority shall state the reasons on which they are based and shall refer to any opinions which were required to be obtained.

Where decisions and recommendations are individual in character, they shall become binding upon being notified to the party concerned.

In all other cases, they shall take effect by the mere fact of publication.

The High Authority shall determine the manner in which this article is to be implemented.

In determining the classification, and hence the application, of a particular instrument of European Community legislation, a court must if necessary have regard to its content rather than to its form alone. It should not treat as conclusive the classification accorded to the instrument by its author in the title.

Joined Cases 16 and 17/62 Confédération Nationale des Producteurs des fruits et légumes v Council
[1962] ECR 471, 8 Recueil (1962) 901; [1963] 2 CMLR 160

In April 1962 the EEC Council published a measure entitled 'Regulation on the Progressive Establishment of a Common Organisation of the Market in Fruit and Vegetables'. Article 9 of that instrument provided for the abolition, in accordance with a stated timetable, of quantitative restrictions on imports and measures having equivalent effect in trade between Member States in certain fruits and vegetables. An association of French fruit and vegetable producers applied to the Court of Justice of the European Communities for the annulment of the measure. In order to establish that they had sufficient standing to maintain the action, the applicants needed to satisfy the Court that the measure constituted a decision addressed to them, or a decision which although in the form of a regulation was of direct and individual concern to them.

The Court

Under the terms of the second paragraph of Article 173 of the EEC Treaty, any natural or legal person may institute proceedings against an act of the Commission or the Council only if that act constitutes either a decision addressed to that person or a decision which, although in the form of a regulation or a decision addressed to another person, is of direct and individual concern to the former. It follows that such a person is not entitled to make an application for annulment of regulations adopted by the Council or the Commission...

The Court is unable in particular to adopt the interpretation suggested by one of the applicants during the oral procedure, according to which the term 'decision', as used in the second paragraph of Article 173, could also cover regulations. Such a wide interpretation conflicts with the fact that Article 189 makes a clear distinction between the concept of a 'decision' and that of a 'regulation'. It is inconceivable that the term 'decision' would be used in Article 173 in a different sense from the technical sense as defined in Article 189. It follows from the foregoing considerations that the present applications should be dismissed as inadmissible if the measure in dispute constitutes a regulation.

In examining this question, the Court cannot restrict itself to considering the official title of the measure, but must first take into account its object and content.

Under the terms of Article 189 of the EEC Treaty, a regulation shall have general application and shall be directly applicable in all Member States, whereas a decision shall be binding only upon those to whom it is addressed. The criterion for the distinction must be sought in the general 'application' or otherwise of the measure in question.

The essential characteristics of a decision arise from the limitation of the persons to whom it is addressed, whereas a regulation, being essentially of a legislative nature, is applicable not to a limited number of persons, defined or identifiable, but to categories of persons viewed abstractly and in their entirety. Consequently, in order to determine in doubtful cases whether one is concerned with a decision or a regulation, it is necessary to ascertain whether the measure in question is of individual concern to specific individuals.

In these circumstances, if a measure entitled by its author a regulation contains provisions which are capable of being not only of direct but also of individual concern to certain natural or legal persons, it must be admitted, without prejudice to the question whether that measure considered in its entirety can be correctly called a regulation, that in any case those provisions do not have the character of a regulation and may therefore be impugned by those persons under the terms of the second paragraph of Article 173.

In this case the measure in dispute was entitled by its author a 'regulation'. However, the applicants maintain that the disputed provision is in fact 'a decision in the form of a regulation'. It is possible without doubt for a decision also to have a very wide field of application. However, a measure which is applicable to objectively determined situations and which involves immediate legal consequences in all Member States for categories of persons viewed in a general and abstract manner cannot be considered as constituting a decision, unless it can be proved that it is of individual concern to certain persons within the meaning of the second paragraph of Article 173.

In this particular case, the disputed provision involves immediate legal consequences in all Member States for categories of persons viewed in a general and abstract manner. In fact, Article 9 of the measure in dispute – the provision particularly at issue in the present dispute – abolishes, for certain products and subject to certain time limits, quantitative restrictions on imports and measures having equivalent effect. It involves in addition the requirement that Member States shall dispense with recourse to the provisions of Article 44 of the Treaty, in particular with regard to the right temporarily to suspend or reduce imports. Consequently, the said Article eliminates the restrictions on the freedom of traders to export or import within the Community.

It remains to be considered whether the disputed provision is of individual concern to the applicants.

Although this provision, by obliging Member States to put an end to or to dispense with various measures capable of favouring agricultural producers, affects in so doing their interests and the interests of the members of the applicant associations, it must be stated nevertheless that those members are concerned by the said provision in the same way as all other agricultural producers of the Community.

Moreover, one cannot accept the principle that an association, in its capacity as the representative of a category of businessmen, could be individually concerned by a measure affecting the general interests of that category.

Such a principle would result in the grouping, under the heading of a single legal person, of the interests properly attributed to the members of a category, who have been affected as individuals by genuine regulations, and would derogate from the system of the Treaty which allows application for annulment by private individuals only of decisions which have been addressed to them, or of acts which affect them in a similar manner.

In these circumstances, it cannot be admitted that the provision in dispute is of individual concern to the applicants. It follows that the defendant was correct in designating the provision in question as a regulation.

The preliminary objection of inadmissibility is therefore well founded and the applications must be declared inadmissible, without its being necessary to examine the question whether associations are entitled to act each time their members are enabled to do so.

The power of the Council and the Commission to legislate in any area is governed by specific articles of the Treaty conferring appropriate authority. Thus, Article 43 authorises the Council to make regulations, issue directives or take decisions for the purpose of implementing the Common Agricultural Policy (CAP) and specifies that after the end of the transitional period measures shall be taken by a qualified majority after consulting the Parliament and on a proposal from the Commission. Article 49 authorises the Council to issue directives or make regulations for the purpose of securing freedom of movement for workers and specifies that such measures shall be taken by a qualified majority, on a proposal from the Commission, in cooperation with the Parliament and after consulting the Economic and Social Committee (ECOSOC). Where provision is made for qualified majority, Article 148 applies (see above Chapter 1, p. 43).

Provision is made in two articles of the EEC Treaty for a more general power to adopt measures: a power not confined to specific Community programmes.

II THE TREATY BASIS

Any measure adopted by the Council or Commission must find its basis in an article (or two or more articles) of the Treaty authorising the adoption of an act to that effect. Thus, a measure designed to achieve one of the objectives of the Common Agricultural Policy, for example, must be based on Article 43. Two Treaty provisions, however, provide a more general basis for the adoption of Community acts: Articles 100 and 235.

EEC Treaty

Article 100

The Council shall, acting unanimously on a proposal from the Commission, issue directives for the approximation of such provisions laid down by law, regulation or administrative action in Member States as directly affect the establishment or functioning of the Common Market.

The Assembly and the Economic and Social Committee shall be consulted in the case of directives whose implementation would, in one or more Member States, involve the amendment of legislation.

Article 100A

1. By way of derogation from Article 100 and save where otherwise provided in this Treaty, the following provisions shall apply for the achievement of the objectives set out in Article 8A. The Council shall, acting by a qualified majority on a proposal from the Commission in cooperation with the European Parliament and after consulting the Economic and Social Committee, adopt the measures for the approximation of the provisions laid down by law, regulation or administrative action in Member States which have as their object the establishment and functioning of the internal market.

2. Paragraph 1 shall not apply to fiscal provisions, to those relating to the free movement of persons nor to those relating to the rights and interests of employed persons.

3. The Commission, in its proposals envisaged in paragraph 1 concerning health, safety, environmental protection and consumer protection, will take as a base a high level of protection.

4. If, after the adoption of a harmonisation measure by the Council acting by a qualified majority, a Member State deems it necessary to apply national provisions on grounds of major needs referred to in Article 36, or relating to protection of the environment or the working environment, it shall notify the Commission of these provisions.

The Commission shall confirm the provisions involved after having verified that they are not a means of arbitrary discrimination or a disguised restriction on trade between Member States.

By way of derogation from the procedure laid down in Articles 169 and 170, the Commission or any Member State may bring the matter directly before the Court of Justice if it considers that another Member State is making improper use of the powers provided for in this Article.

5. The harmonisation measures referred to above shall, in appropriate cases, include a safeguard clause authorising the Member States to take, for one or more of the non-economic reasons referred to in Article 36, provisional measures subject to a Community control procedure.

...

Article 235

If action by the Community should prove necessary to attain, in the course of the operation of the Common Market, one of the objectives of the Community and this Treaty has not provided the necessary powers, the Council shall, acting unanimously on a proposal from the Commission and after consulting the Assembly, take the appropriate measures.

Subject to Article 100A, Articles 100 and 235 require unanimity. Therefore, the Council has the incentive to use articles making provision for voting by simple or qualified majority, rather than Articles 100 or 235, where the subject-matter has a bearing on both provisions. It is of course possible to cite two or more articles of the Treaty, but if this is done it will be necessary to meet the procedural requirements of all of them.

Case 45/86 Commission v Council (Generalised Tariff Preferences)
26 March 1987

The Commission brought an action under Article 173 (see below, p. 97) for a declaration that two Council regulations dealing with generalised tariff preferences for products from third world countries were void.

The Court

The Commission raises two submissions in support of its action, which in its view merge into a single complaint: the absence of a precise legal basis, which is in itself contrary to Article 190 of the EEC Treaty, and in this case at the same time constitutes an infringement of the Treaty because it resulted in recourse being had to a procedure entailing a unanimous vote rather than the procedure applicable under Article 113 of the Treaty, which in the Commission's view is the only correct legal basis.

Article 190 of the Treaty provides that: 'Regulations, directives and decisions of the Council and of the Commission shall state the reasons on which they are based'. According to the case-law of the Court (in particular the judgment of 7 July 1981 in Case 158/80 *Rewe-Handelsgesellschaft Nord mbH and Another* v *Hauptzollamt Kiel* [1981] ECR 1805), in order to satisfy that requirement to state reasons, Community measures must include a statement of the facts and law which led the institution in question to adopt them, so as to make possible review by the Court and so that the Member State and the nationals concerned may have knowledge of the conditions under which the Community institutions have applied the Treaty.

It is therefore necessary to consider whether the contested regulations satisfy those requirements.

In that connection the Council contends that, although the indication of the legal basis is not precise, the recitals in the preambles to the regulations, taken as a whole, provide sufficient alternative information as to the aims pursued by the Council, that is to say both commercial aims and aims of development-aid policy.

However, those indications are not sufficient to identify the legal basis by virtue of which the Council acted. Although the recitals in the preambles to the regulations do refer to improving access for developing countries to the markets of the preference-giving countries, they merely state that adaptations to the Community system of generalised preferences have proved to be necessary in the light of experience in the first fifteen years. Moreover, according to information given to the Court by the Council itself, *the wording 'having regard to the Treaty' was adopted as a result of differences of opinion about the choice of the appropriate legal basis. Consequently, the wording chosen was designed precisely to leave the legal basis of the regulations in question vague.*

Admittedly, failure to refer to a precise provision of the Treaty need not necessarily constitute an infringement of essential procedural requirements when the legal basis for the measure may be determined from other parts of the measure. However, such explicit reference is indispensable where, in its absence, the parties concerned and the Court are left uncertain as to the precise legal basis.

In answer to a question put by the Court *the Council has stated that when it adopted the contested regulations it intended to base them on both Articles 113 and 235 of the EEC Treaty*. It has explained that it departed from the Commission's proposal to base the regulations on Article 113 alone because it was convinced that the contested regulations had not only commercial policy aims, but also major development policy aims. The implementation of development policy goes beyond the scope of Article 113 of the Treaty and necessitates recourse to Article 235.

It must be observed that *in the context of the organisation of the powers of the Community the choice of the legal basis for a measure may not depend simply on an institution's conviction as to the objective pursued but must be based on objective factors which are amenable to judicial review.*

In this case, the dispute as to the correct legal basis was not purely formal in scope since Articles 113 and 235 of the EEC Treaty lay down different rules governing the Council's decision-making process, and the choice of the legal basis was therefore liable to affect the determination of the content of the contested regulations.

It follows from the very wording of Article 235 that its use as the legal basis for a measure is justified only where no other provision of the Treaty gives the Community institutions the necessary power to adopt the measure in question.

It must therefore be considered whether in this case the Council was competent to adopt the contested regulations pursuant to Article 113 of the Treaty alone, as the Commission maintains.

On consideration, the Court decided that Article 113 would have been sufficient for the regulations and that the Council was not justified in taking as its basis Article 235. It concluded:

It is clear from the foregoing that the contested regulations do not satisfy the requirements laid down in Article 190 of the Treaty with regard to the statement of reasons and that, moreover, they were not adopted on the correct legal basis. Consequently, they must be declared void.

Case 68/86 United Kingdom v Council ('Hormones')
23 February 1988

The United Kingdom brought proceedings for the annulment of a Council directive prohibiting the use of certain hormones in livestock farming. The United Kingdom, along with Denmark, had voted against the measure. Among the submissions made to the Court by the United Kingdom under an Article 173 action was the argument that the directive had been adopted on an insufficient legal basis. It had been issued on the basis of Article 43, which permits the use of a qualified majority, whereas the United Kingdom and Denmark maintained that Article 100 was a necessary legal basis.

The Court

Legal Basis

The applicant, supported in all essential respects by the Danish Government, claims that the contested directive, which was adopted by a qualified majority on the basis of Article 43 of the Treaty, should have been based not only on that article, but also on Article 100, which requires unanimity on the part of the Council. It considers that it was necessary to base the directive at issue on those two articles since, in addition to having agricultural policy objectives, it was designed *inter alia* for the purpose of approximating the provisions laid down by law, regulation or administrative action in the Member States to safeguard the interests and health of consumers. In the applicant's view, that aim is not covered by Article 43 of the Treaty but comes under Article 100. Previous practice on the part of the Council bears out the need for that dual legal basis.

The Council, the defendant, and the Commission, intervening, do not deny that one aspect of the directive at issue deals with the harmonisation of national laws with a view to the protection of consumers and public health, but consider that that does not cause it to fall outside the sphere of the Common Agricultural Policy and that it is therefore covered by Article 43 of the Treaty.

It should be pointed out first of all that in this case the argument with regard to the correct legal basis is not a purely formal one, inasmuch as Articles 43 and 100 of the Treaty entail different rules regardingy the manner in which the Council may arrive at its decision. The choice of the legal basis could thus affect the determination of the content of the contested directive.

Consequently, in order to determine whether the submission based on the alleged insufficiency of the legal basis of the directive at issue is well-founded it is necessary to consider whether the Council had the power to adopt it on the basis of Article 43 alone.

By virtue of Article 38 of the Treaty, the provisions of Articles 30 to 46 apply to the products listed in Annex II to the Treaty.

Article 43, moreover, must be interpreted in the light of Article 39, which sets out the objectives of the Common Agricultural Policy, and Article 40, which governs its implementation, providing *inter alia* that in order to attain the objectives set out in Article 39 a common organisation of agricultural markets is to be established and that that organisation may include all measures required to attain those objectives (judgment of 21 February 1979 in Case 138/78 *Stölting* v *Hauptzollamt Hamburg-Jonas* [1979] ECR 713).

The agricultural policy objectives set out in Article 39 of the Treaty include in particular the increasing of productivity by promoting technical progress and by ensuring the rational development of agricultural production and the optimum utilisation of the factors of production. Moreover, Article 39 (2)(b) and (c) provides that in working out the Common Agricultural Policy account must be taken of the need to effect the appropriate adjustments by degrees and the fact that in the Member States agriculture constitutes a sector closely linked with the economy as a whole. It follows that agricultural policy objectives must be conceived in such a manner as to enable the Community institutions to carry out their duties in the light of developments in agriculture and in the economy as a whole.

Measures adopted on the basis of Article 43 of the Treaty with a view to achieving those objectives under a common organisation of the market as provided for in Article 40(2) may include rules governing conditions and methods of production, quality and marketing of agricultural products. The common organisations of the markets contain many rules in that regard.

Efforts to achieve objectives of the Common Agricultural Policy, in particular under common organisations of the markets, cannot disregard requirements relating to the public interest such as the protection of consumers or the protection of the health and life of humans and animals, requirements which the Community institutions must take into account in exercising their powers.

Finally, it must be observed that according to Article 42 of the Treaty the rules on competition are to apply to production of and trade in agricultural products only to the extent determined by the Council within the framework of provisions adopted pursuant to Article

43. Consequently, in adopting such provisions the Council must also take into consideration the requirements of competition policy.

It follows from the provisions discussed above, taken as a whole, that *Article 43 of the Treaty is the appropriate legal basis for any legislation concerning the production and marketing of agricultural products listed in Annex II to the Treaty which contributes to the achievement of one or more of the objectives of the Common Agricultural Policy set out in Article 39 of the Treaty. There is no need to have recourse to Article 100 of the Treaty where such legislation involves the harmonisation of provisions of national law in that field.*

As the Court has pointed out, in particular in its judgments of 29 November 1978 (Case 83/78 *Pigs Marketing Board* v *Redmond* [1978] ECR 2347) and 26 June 1979 (Case 177/78 *Pigs and Bacon Commission* v *McCarren* [1979] ECR 2161), Article 38(2) of the Treaty gives precedence to specific provisions in the agricultural field over general provisions relating to the establishment of the common market.

Consequently, *even where the legislation in question is directed both to objectives of agricultural policy and to other objectives which, in the absence of specific provisions, are pursued on the basis of Article 100 of the Treaty, that article, a general one under which directives may be adopted for the approximation of the laws of the Member States, cannot be relied on as a ground for restricting the field of application of Article 43 of the Treaty.*

It is on the basis of the foregoing considerations that it must be determined whether or not the contested directive falls within the scope of Article 43 of the Treaty as described above.

In that regard, it must first be observed that there are common organisations of the markets in the sectors of beef and veal (Regulation No 805/68 of the Council of 27 June 1968, Official Journal, English Special Edition 1968 (I), p. 187), pigmeat (Regulation No 2759/75 of the Council of 29 October 1975, Official Journal 1975 L 282, p. 1) and sheepmeat and goatmeat (Council Regulation No 1837/80 of 27 June 1980, Official Journal 1980 L 183, p. 1), and that Article 2 of each of those regulations provides for the adoption of Community measures designed to promote better organisation of production, processing and marketing, and to improve quality.

The directive at issue essentially contains, on the one hand, rules on the administration of certain substances having a hormonal action to farm animals whose meat is covered by the aforementioned common organisations of the markets and, on the other hand, rules concerning the requisite control measures. Those measures relate in particular to trade between Member States in live animals and meat and to imports of those products into the Community.

The aim of the directive, according to the recitals in its preamble, is to protect human health and consumer interests with a view to eliminating the distortion of conditions of competition and bringing about an increase in 'consumption of the production in question'.

In view of the content and objectives of the directive, it must be found that, in regulating conditions for the production and marketing of meat with a view to improving its quality, it comes into the category of measures provided for by the aforementioned common organisations of the markets in meat and thus contributes to the achievement of the objectives of the Common Agricultural Policy which are set out in Article 39 of the Treaty.

It follows from the foregoing that the directive at issue falls within the sphere of the Common Agricultural Policy and that the Council had the power to adopt it on the basis of Article 43 alone.

That finding cannot be affected by the fact, on which the applicant places some reliance, that the Council departed from its practice of basing measures in the field in question on Articles 43 and 100 of the Treaty.

On that point, it should be borne in mind that, as the Court held in its judgment of 26 March 1987 (in Case 45/86 *Commission* v *Council* [1988] 2 CMLR 131), in the context of the organisation of the powers of the Community the choice of the legal basis for a measure must be based on objective factors which are amenable to judicial review. A mere practice on the part of the Council cannot derogate from the rules laid down in the Treaty. Such a practice cannot therefore create a precedent binding on Community institutions with regard to the correct legal basis.

The applicant's first submission must therefore be rejected.

The Court however went on to consider an alleged infringement by the Council of its Rules of Procedure, and on this basis the Directive was declared void.

III DIRECT EFFECT

1 TREATY ARTICLES

Regulations are a 'directly applicable' source of rights and obligations in national courts, no less than national legislation (see Joined Cases 16 and 17/62 *Confédération Nationale*, above, p. 71). The European Court decided in an early case that Treaty articles, too, may be of direct effect.

Case 26/62 NV Algemene Transport-en Expeditie Onderneming van Gend en Loos v Nederlandse Administratie der Belastingen
[1963] ECR 1; [1963] CMLR 105

Van Gend en Loos engaged in the business of importing chemical products to the Netherlands. On 9 September 1960 they imported to that country from the Federal Republic of Germany a quantity of ureaformaldehyde. A Dutch law of 16 December 1959, passed in order to give effect to a Benelux agreement of 25 July 1958, imposed an *ad valorem* duty of eight per cent in the case of ureaformaldehyde. By Article 12 of the EEC Treaty, however, Member States had undertaken to refrain from introducing between themselves any new customs duties on imports, and from increasing those that they already applied in their trade with each other. That Treaty entered into force between the Netherlands and the Federal Republic of Germany on 1 January 1958, and Van Gend contended that on that date the duty exigible under Dutch law on the product in question was three per cent. Van Gend therefore objected to paying the additional five per cent. The matter came before the Tariefcommissie, Amsterdam, which asked the Court of Justice of the European Communities to rule on the question whether Article 12 of the EEC Treaty produces direct effects within the territory of a Member State such that nationals of the State can on the basis of that article lay claim to rights that national courts must protect; and if so, whether the application of an *ad valorem* duty of eight per cent to ureaformaldehyde in the circumstances of the case was prohibited by that article.

The Court

To ascertain whether the provisions of an international treaty extend so far in their effects it is necessary to consider the spirit, the general scheme and the wording of those provisions.

The objective of the EEC Treaty, which is to establish a Common Market, the functioning of which is of direct concern to interested parties in the Community, implies that this Treaty is more than an agreement which merely creates mutual obligations between the contracting states. This view is confirmed by the preamble to the Treaty which refers not only to governments but to peoples. It is also confirmed more specifically by the establishment of institutions endowed with sovereign rights, the exercise of which affects Member States and also their citizens. Furthermore, it must be noted that the nationals of the states brought together in the Community are called upon to cooperate in the functioning of this Community through the intermediary of the European Parliament and the Economic and Social Committee.

In addition the task assigned to the Court of Justice under Article 177, the object of which is to secure uniform interpretation of the Treaty by national courts and tribunals, confirms that the States have acknowledged that Community law has an authority which can be invoked by their nationals before those courts and tribunals.

The conclusion to be drawn from this is that *the Community constitutes a new legal order of international law for the benefit of which the States have limited their sovereign rights, albeit within limited fields, and the subjects of which comprise not only Member States but also their nationals. Independently of the legislation of Member States, Community law therefore not only imposes legislation on individuals but is also intended to confer upon them rights which become part of their legal heritage.* These rights arise not only where they are expressly granted by the Treaty, but also by reason of obligations which the Treaty imposes in a clearly defined way upon individuals as well as upon the Member States and upon the institutions of the Community.

With regard to the general scheme of the Treaty as it relates to customs duties and charges having equivalent effect it must be emphasised that Article 9, which bases the Community upon a customs union, includes as an essential provision the prohibition of these customs duties and charges. This provision is found at the beginning of the part of the Treaty which defines the 'Foundations of the Community'. It is applied and explained in Article 12.

The wording of Article 12 contains a clear and unconditional prohibition which is not a positive but a negative obligation. This obligation, moreover, is not qualified by any reservation on the part of States which would make its implementation conditional upon a positive legislative measure enacted under national law. The very nature of this prohibition makes it ideally adapted to produce direct effects in the legal relationship between Member States and their subjects.

The implementation of Article 12 does not require any legislative intervention on the part of the states. The fact that under this article it is the Member States who are made the subject of the negative obligation does not imply that their nationals cannot benefit from this obligation...

It follows from the foregoing considerations that, according to the spirit, the general scheme and the wording of the Treaty, Article 12 must be interpreted as producing direct effects and creating individual rights which national courts must protect.

On the second question the Court concluded that it was the function of the domestic court to enquire whether the dutiable product was in fact charged under the customs measures brought into force in the Netherlands with an import duty higher than that with which it was charged on 1 January 1958.

The Court did not decide in *Van Gend* that all Treaty articles would have direct effect. It would be a question of interpretation of the provisions. The test was set out in *Van Gend* – only if the Article was 1) clear 2) unconditional and 3) immediate would it be directly effective.

The judgment in *Van Gend* applied only to the EEC Treaty. The question whether treaties with third States could have direct effect was particularly controversial because there was no guarantee that the third State would recognise any such notion. The Court avoided dealing with this issue in Case 270/80 *Polydor* v *Harlequin Record Shops* [1982] ECR 329. In a later case, however, the Court ruled that within the Community, a provision in a treaty with a third State is capable of producing direct effects.

Case 104/81 Hauptzollamt Mainz v C. A. Kupferberg & Cie KG a. A.
[1982] ECR 3641; [1983] 1 CMLR 1

Kupferberg was charged a duty under German law on imports of Portuguese port wine. The Finanzgericht Rheinland-Pfalz (Finance Court) reduced this charge in accordance with Article 21 of an Agreement between the EEC and Portugal, which has similar provisions to Article 95 of the EEC Treaty (see below, Chapter 6 p. 200). When the tax authorities appealed to the Bundesfinanzhof a number of questions were referred to the Court, the first one relating to the issue of direct effect.

The Court

In the first place the Bundesfinanzhof wishes to know whether the German importer may rely on the said Article 21 before the German court in the proceedings which it has brought against the decision of the tax authorities.

In the observations which they have submitted to the Court, the Governments of the Kingdom of Denmark, the Federal Republic of Germany, the French Republic and the United Kingdom have laid the most stress on the question whether a provision which is part of one of the free-trade agreements made by the Community with the member countries of the European Free Trade Association is in principle capable of having direct effect in the Member States of the Community.

The Treaty establishing the Community has conferred upon the institutions the power not only of adopting measures applicable in the Community but also of making agreements with non-Member countries and international organisations in accordance with the provisions of the Treaty. According to Article 228(2) these agreements are binding on the institutions of the Community and on Member States. Consequently, it is incumbent upon the Community institutions, as well as upon the Member States, to ensure compliance with the obligations arising from such agreements.

The measures needed to implement the provisions of an agreement concluded by the Community are to be adopted, according to the state of Community law for the time being in the areas affected by the provisions of the agreements, either by the Community institutions or by the Member States. That is particularly true of agreements such as those concerning free trade where the obligations entered into extend to many areas of a very diverse nature.

In ensuring respect for commitments arising from an agreement concluded by the Community institutions the Member States fulfil an obligation not only in relation to the non-Member country concerned but also and above all in relation to the Community which has assumed responsibility for the due performance of the agreement. That is why the provisions of such an agreement, as the Court has already stated in its judgment of 30 April 1974 in Case 181/73 *Haegeman* [1974] ECR 449, form an integral part of the Community legal system.

It follows from the Community nature of such provisions that their effect in the Community may not be allowed to vary according to whether their application is in practice the responsibility of the Community institutions or of the Member States and, in the latter case, according to the effects in the internal legal order of each Member State which the law of that State assigns to international agreements concluded by it. Therefore it is for the Court, within the framework of its jurisdiction in interpreting the provisions of agreements, to ensure their uniform application throughout the Community.

The governments which have submitted observations to the Court do not deny the Community nature of the provisions of agreements concluded by the Community. They contend, however, that the generally recognised criteria for determining the effects of provisions of a purely Community origin may not be applied to provisions of a free-trade agreement concluded by the Community with a non-Member country.

In that respect the governments base their arguments in particular on the distribution of powers in regard to the external relations of the Community, the principle of reciprocity governing the application of free-trade agreements, the institutional framework established by such agreements in order to settle differences between the contracting parties and safeguard clauses allowing the parties to derogate from the agreements.

It is true that the effects within the Community of provisions of an agreement concluded by the Community with a non-Member country may not be determined without taking account of the international origin of the provisions in question. In conformity with the principles of public international law Community institutions which have power to negotiate and conclude an agreement with a non-Member country are free to agree with that country what effect the provisions of the agreement are to have in the internal legal order of the contracting parties. Only if that question has not been settled by the agreement does it fall for decision by the courts having jurisdiction in the matter, and in particular by the Court of Justice within the framework of its jurisdiction under the Treaty, in the same manner as any question of interpretation relating to the application of the agreement in the Community.

According to the general rules of international law there must be *bona fide* performance of every agreement. Although each contracting party is responsible for executing fully the commitments which it has undertaken it is nevertheless free to determine the legal means appropriate for attaining that end in its legal system unless the agreement, interpreted in the light of its subject-matter and purpose, itself specifies those means. Subject to that reservation the fact that the courts of one of the parties consider that certain of the stipulations in the agreement are of direct application whereas the courts of the other party do not recognise such direct application is not in itself such as to constitute a lack of reciprocity in the implementation of the agreement.

As the governments have emphasised, the free-trade agreements provide for joint committees responsible for the administration of the agreements and for their proper implementation. To that end they may make recommendations and, in the cases expressly provided for by the agreement in question, take decisions.

The mere fact that the contracting parties have established a special institutional framework for consultations and negotiations *inter se* in relation to the implementation of the agreement is not in itself sufficient to exclude all judicial application of that agreement. The fact that a court of one of the parties applies to a specific case before it a provision of the agreement involving an unconditional and precise obligation and therefore not requiring any prior intervention on the part of the joint committee does not adversely affect the powers that the agreement confers on that committee.

As regards the safeguard clauses which enable the parties to derogate from certain provisions of the agreement it should be observed that they apply only in specific circumstances and as a general rule after consideration within the joint committee in the presence of both parties. Apart from specific situations which may involve their application, the existence of such clauses, which, moreover, do not affect the provisions prohibiting tax discrimination, is not sufficient in itself to affect the direct applicability which may attach to certain stipulations in the agreement.

It follows from all the foregoing considerations that neither the nature nor the structure of the Agreement concluded with Portugal may prevent a trader from relying on the provisions of the said Agreement before a court in the Community.

Nevertheless the question whether such a stipulation is unconditional and sufficiently precise to have direct effect must be considered in the context of the Agreement of which it forms part. In order to reply to the question on the direct effect of the first paragraph of Article 21 of the Agreement between the Community and Portugal it is necessary to analyse the provision in the light of both the object and purpose of the Agreement and of its context.

The purpose of the Agreement is to create a system of free trade in which rules restricting commerce are eliminated in respect of virtually all trade in products originating in the territory of the parties, in particular by abolishing customs duties and charges having equivalent effect and eliminating quantitative restrictions and measures having equivalent effect.

Seen in context the first paragraph of Article 21 of the Agreement seeks to prevent the liberalisation of the trade in goods, through the abolition of customs duties and charges having equivalent effect and quantitative restrictions and measures having equivalent effect, from being rendered nugatory by fiscal practices of the Contracting Parties. That would be so if the product imported of one party were taxed more heavily than the similar domestic products which it encounters on the market of the other party.

It appears from the foregoing that the first paragraph of Article 21 of the Agreement imposes on the Contracting Parties an unconditional rule against discrimination in matters of taxation, which is dependent only on a finding that the products affected by a particular system of taxation are of like nature, and the limits of which are the direct consequence of the purpose of the Agreement. As such this provision may be applied by a court and thus produces direct effects throughout the Community.

The first part of the first question should therefore be answered to the effect that the first paragraph of Article 21 of the Agreement between the Community and Portugal is directly applicable and capable of conferring upon individual traders rights which the courts must protect.

Although the Court has tended to use the terms 'directly applicable' and 'directly effective' interchangeably (note particularly in *Van Gend*), the modern tendency is to distinguish between the two expressions. (See the wording of Article 189, above p. 69.)

Direct applicability connotes the quality of applying within the domestic legal system even in the absence of implementing legislation. Direct effect describes the quality of giving rise to the rights upon which an individual may rely in a domestic court. A Treaty provision or a provision in a directive can give rise to rights and therefore be called directly effective if it imposes a clear, immediate and unconditional obligation. In the case of the Treaty provision, the obligation may be imposed on an individual or on the State and in the case of the directive, the obligation is imposed on the State. Direct effects are created because it would frustrate the intentions of the authors of the provision to allow the Member State to rely, even in a domestic court, on its own failure to fulfil its obligations. But even in such an event, the Treaty provision may not and the provision in the directive will not give rise to rights and obligations between individuals. For this reason a provision in a directive is inherently dissimilar to a provision in a regulation.

2 DIRECTIVES

Also controversial for many years was the question whether directives may produce direct effect. It was argued by the United Kingdom that they could not, since they were addressed to the Member States. The European Court held otherwise.

Case 41/74 Yvonne van Duyn v Home Office
[1974] ECR 1337; [1975] 1 CMLR 1

Miss Van Duyn was a Dutch national and a Scientologist. On 9 May 1973 she arrived at Gatwick Airport in England, bearing a written offer of employment as a secretary at the Hubbard College of Scientology, East Grinstead. She was refused admission to the United Kingdom on the ground that the Home Secretary considers it undesirable to give anyone leave to enter the United Kingdom on the business of or in the employment of the Church of Scientology. Miss Van Duyn then sought a declaration from the Chancery Division of the High Court, claiming that she was entitled under European Community law to enter and remain in the United Kingdom for the purpose of employment. In particular she relied on Article 48 of the EEC Treaty and Council Directive No 64/221, Article 3. The High Court referred to the Court of Justice of the European Communities a number of questions concerning the interpretation of these provisions.

The Court

By the first question, the Court is asked to say whether Article 48 of the EEC Treaty is directly applicable so as to confer on individuals rights enforceable by them in the courts of a Member State.

It is provided, in Article 48(1) and (2), that freedom of movement for workers shall be secured by the end of the transitional period and that such freedom shall entail 'the abolition of any discrimination based on nationality between workers of Member States as regards employment, remuneration and other conditions of work and employment'.

These provisions impose on Member States a precise obligation which does not require the adoption of any further measure on the part either of the Community institutions or of the Member States and which leaves them, in relation to its implementation, no discretionary power.

Paragraph 3, which defines the rights implied by the principle of freedom of movement for workers, subjects them to limitations justified on grounds of public policy, public security or public health. The application of these limitations is, however, subject to judicial control, so that a Member State's right to invoke the limitations does not prevent the provisions of Article 48, which enshrine the principle of freedom of movement for workers, from conferring on individuals rights which are enforceable by them and which the national courts must protect.

The reply to the first question must therefore be in the affirmative...

The second question asks the Court to say whether Council Directive No 64/221 of 25 February 1964 on the coordination of special measures concerning the movement and residence of foreign nationals which are justified on grounds of public policy, public security or public health is directly applicable so as to confer on individuals rights enforceable by them in the courts of a Member State.

It emerges from the order making the reference that the only provision of the Directive which is relevant is that contained in Article 3(1) which provides that 'measures taken on grounds of public policy or public security shall be based exclusively on the personal conduct of the individual concerned'.

The United Kingdom observes that, since Article 189 of the Treaty distinguishes between the effects ascribed to regulations, directives and decisions, it must therefore be presumed that the Council, in issuing a directive rather than making a regulation, must have intended that the directive should have an effect other than that of a regulation and accordingly that the former should not be directly applicable.

If, however, by virtue of the provisions of Article 189 regulations are directly applicable and, consequently, may by their very nature have direct effects, it does not follow from this that other categories of acts mentioned in that article can never have similar effects. It would be incompatible with the binding effect attributed to a directive by Article 189 to exclude, in principle, the possibility that the obligation which it imposes may be invoked by those concerned. In particular, where the Community authorities have, by directive, imposed on Member States the obligation to pursue a particular course of conduct, the useful effect of such an act would be weakened if individuals were prevented from relying on it before their national courts and if the latter were prevented from taking it into consideration as an element of Community law. Article 177, which empowers national courts to refer to the Court questions concerning the validity and interpretation of all acts of the Community institutions, without distinction, implies furthermore that these acts may be invoked by individuals in the national courts. It is necessary to examine, in every case, whether the nature, general scheme and wording of the provision in question are capable of having direct effects on the relations between Member States and individuals.

By providing that measures taken on grounds of public policy shall be based exclusively on the personal conduct of the individual concerned, Article 3(1) of Directive No 64/221 is intended to limit the discretionary power which national laws generally confer on the authorities responsible for the entry and expulsion of foreign nationals. First, the provision lays down an obligation which is not subject to any exception or condition and which, by its very nature, does not require the intervention of any act on the part either of the institutions of the Community or of Member States. Secondly, because Member States are thereby obliged, in implementing a clause which derogates from one of the fundamental principles of the Treaty in favour of individuals, not to take account of factors extraneous to personal conduct, legal certainty for the persons concerned requires that they should be able to rely on this obligation even though it has been laid down in a legislative act which has no automatic direct effect in its entirety.

If the meaning and exact scope of the provision raises questions of interpretation, these questions can be resolved by the courts, taking into account also the procedure under Article 177 of the Treaty.

Accordingly, in reply to the second question, Article 3(1) of Council Directive No 64/221 of 25 February 1964 confers on individuals rights which are enforceable by them in the courts of a Member State and which the national courts must protect.

Case 148/78 Pubblico Ministero v Tullio Ratti

[1979] ECR 1629; [1980] 1 CMLR 96

Council directives were passed in 1973 and 1977 on the labelling and packaging of solvents and toxic substances respectively. Italy, which had more detailed requirements concerning the description of the contents on labels, had failed to implement the directives in national law. Criminal proceedings were brought in Italy against an undertaking whose labelling standards only reached the level required by Community law. The national court referred a number of questions to the European Court.

The Court

The national court, finding that 'there was a manifest contradiction between the Community rules and internal Italian law', wondered 'which of the two sets of rules should take precedence in the case before the court' and referred to the Court the first question, asking as follows:

> 'Does Council Directive No 73/173/EEC of 4 June 1973, in particular Article 8 thereof, constitute directly applicable legislation conferring upon individuals personal rights which the national courts must protect?'

This question raises the general problem of the legal nature of the provisions of a directive adopted under Article 189 of the Treaty.

In this regard the settled case-law of the Court, last reaffirmed by the judgment of 1 February 1977 in Case 51/76 *Nederlandse Ondernemingen* [1977] 1 ECR 113 at 126, lays down that, whilst under Article 189 regulations are directly applicable and, consequently, by their nature capable of producing direct effects, that does not mean that other categories of acts covered by that article can never produce similar effects.

It would be incompatible with the binding effect which Article 189 ascribes to directives to exclude on principle the possibility of the obligations imposed by them being relied on by persons concerned.

Particularly in cases in which the Community authorities have, by means of directive, placed Member States under a duty to adopt a certain course of action, the effectiveness of such an act would be weakened if persons were prevented from relying on it in legal proceedings and national courts prevented from taking it into consideration as an element of Community law.

Consequently *a Member State which has not adopted the implementing measures required by the directive in the prescribed periods may not rely, as against individuals, on its own failure to perform the obligations which the directive entails.*

It follows that a national court requested by a person who has complied with the provisions of a directive not to apply a national provision incompatible with the directive not incorporated into the internal legal order of a defaulting Member State, must uphold that request if the obligation in question is *unconditional* and *sufficiently precise*.

Therefore the answer to the first question must be that after the expiration of the period fixed for the implementation of a directive a Member State may not apply its internal law – even if it is provided with penal sanctions – which has not yet been adapted in compliance with the directive, to a person who has complied with the requirements of the directive.

In the second question the national court asks, essentially, whether, in incorporating the provisions of the directive on solvents into its internal legal order, the State to which it is addressed may prescribe 'obligations and limitations which are more precise and detailed than, or at all events different from, those set out in the directive', requiring in particular information not required by the directive to be affixed to the containers.

The combined effect of Articles 3 to 8 of Directive No 73/173 is that only solvents which 'comply with the provisions of this directive and the annex thereto' may be placed on the market and that Member States are not entitled to maintain, parallel with the rules laid down by the said directive for imports, different rules for the domestic market.

Thus it is a consequence of the system introduced by Directive No 73/173 that a Member State may not introduce into its national legislation conditions which are more restrictive than those laid down in the directive in question, or which are even more detailed or in any event different, as regards the classification, packaging and labelling of solvents, and that this prohibition on the imposition of restrictions not provided for applies both to the direct marketing of the products on the home market and to imported products.

The second question submitted by the national court must be answered in that way.

For some years thereafter, a dispute existed as to whether it was open to a litigant to rely on a directive not against a Member State (as in *Van Duyn*) but against another individual. This was known as 'horizontal' as opposed to 'vertical' direct effect.

Sir Gordon Slynn, the Advocate General in *Becker*, argued against horizontal direct effects.

Case 8/81 Ursula Becker v Finanzamt Münster-Innenstadt
[1982] 1 ECR 53; [1982] 1 CMLR 499

Council Directive No 77/388 provided rules for the harmonisation of turnover taxes in the Member States which were to be adopted by 1 January 1979. The Federal Republic of Germany failed to fulfil its obligations but Mrs Becker, a self-employed credit negotiator, calculated her tax returns for 1979 on the assumption that the new rules had been implemented. The Advocate General stated explicitly that there is a difference between direct applicability and direct effect of directives. In his view, directives produced direct effects against Member States.

Mr Advocate General Slynn:

...

Article 13B of Directive No 77/388 provides, so far as is relevant: 'Without prejudice to other Community provisions, Member States shall exempt the following under conditions which they shall lay down for the purpose of ensuring the correct and straightforward application of the exemptions and of preventing any possible evasion, avoidance or abuse:

...

(d) the following transactions:

(1) the granting and the negotiation of credit and the management of credit by the person granting it...'.

The question referred to the Court for a preliminary ruling by the Finanzgericht simply asks whether Article 13B(d)(1) is directly applicable in relation to transactions consisting of the negotiation of credit in Germany from 1 January 1979. Written and oral observations have been submitted on behalf of the French and German Governments and the Finanzamt, all to the effect that the question should be answered in the negative, and by the Commission, which is of the contrary opinion. Mrs Becker herself has not submitted observations.

Counsel for the German Government questioned whether the phrase 'directly applicable', used by the Finanzgericht in the order for reference, adequately expressed the principle laid down in a number of decisions of the Court that while, under Article 189 of the EEC Treaty regulations alone are said to be directly applicable, other acts, and in particular directives, may produce similar effects.

Previous decisions of the Court seem to me to make it plain that the right question is not whether a directive is 'directly applicable' in the strict sense i.e. in the sense in which that phrase is used in Article 189 of the EEC Treaty.

In Case 41/74 *van Duyn* v *Home Office* [1974] ECR 1337 (see above, p. 84) the Court made it clear that merely because 'by virtue of the provisions of Article 189 regulations are directly applicable and, consequently, may by their very nature have direct effects, it does not follow from this that other categories of acts mentioned in that article can never have similar effects ... *It is necessary to examine, in every case, whether the nature, general scheme and wording of the provision in question are capable of having direct effect on the relations between Member States and individuals*'. The Court's judgments in Case 51/76 *Nederlandse Ondernemingen* v *Inspecteur der Invoerrechten en Accijnzen* [1977] ECR 113, Case 148/78 *Pubblico Ministero* v *Ratti* [1979] ECR 1629 and Case 102/79 *Commission* v *Belgium* [1980] ECR 1473 establish that if a directive is addressed to a Member State, that State is under a duty to give effect to it even though the choice of form and methods by which the results of the directive are to be achieved is left to the Member State. *If the Member State fails to implement the directive, an individual may rely on its terms, if these are unconditional and sufficiently precise, as against the Member State. The latter cannot take advantage of its own failure to act in due time by contending that the directive is not yet in force.*

The question is thus not whether the directive is 'directly applicable' but whether its terms are such that the individual can rely upon it against the Member State who in breach of duty has failed to implement it.

...

Leaving aside these preliminary objections to Mrs Becker's claim, I turn to what seems to be the central question, namely, was the Federal Republic of Germany obliged to implement Article 13B(d)(1) and are the terms unconditional and sufficiently precise that an individual can rely on them even if the Member State has not implemented them?

It is said, first, that because of the opening words of Article 13B, there is no unconditional or sufficiently precise obligation to exempt the acts or transactions referred to. This is because there is reserved to the Member State the power to lay down conditions 'for the purpose of ensuring the correct and straightforward application of the exemptions and of preventing any possible evasion, avoidance or abuse'.

The Commission has submitted that the conditions to which exemption under Article 13B are subject are ancillary and do not affect the unconditional or imperative nature of the obligation imposed on the Member States. They only have discretion to ensure the correct application of the exemptions provided for, and the prevention of evasion, avoidance and abuse.

Article 189 of the EEC Treaty itself makes it plain that the choice of form and methods may be left to the national authorities. Such a discretion does not prevent a directive from being unconditional and sufficiently precise as to the result to be achieved. That a margin of discretion may be left to the national authorities, without the directive being put outside the category of those which can be relied upon, also appears from the Court's judgments in the *Nederlandse Ondernemingen* case (see above, p. 87) and in Case 131/79, *R.* v *Secretary of State for Home Affairs ex parte Santillo* [1980] ECR 1585 (see above, p. 321). If, on the other hand, it is left to the discretion of the Member State as to whether the provision is implemented at all, then the position is different.

In my opinion the Commission's contention here is clearly right. The conditions which may be laid down are limited to those which provide the means by which (a) the exemptions can be applied correctly and in a straightforward way so that justified exemptions are upheld, unjustified claims rejected; and (b) evasion, avoidance and abuse of the system of exemptions can be prevented. Where specific exempt transactions are defined, it is not open to the Member State to modify the description of the transaction. The fact that the Member State may by way of exclusion restrict the ambit of exemption B(b) in Article 13 does not take away the precision of the transactions exempted in B(d), nor does it do anything to render their application conditional. The power to lay down the conditions specified in the opening words of Article 13B does not in my opinion detract from the clear obligation to exempt 'the negotiation of credit'. The obligation to achieve that result is precise and unconditional.

...

Accordingly, it is my opinion that the question referred to the Court by the Finanzgericht should be answered to the effect that Article 13B(d)(1) may be relied on by private persons as against the Finanzamt in respect of their tax liability for the year 1979.

The arguments were finally laid to rest in the *Marshall* case.

Case 152/84 M. H. Marshall v Southampton and South-West Hampshire Area Health Authority (Teaching) [1986] ECR 723; [1986] 1 CMLR 688

Southampton AHA had a policy of compulsory retirement for women and men over the ages of 60 and 65 respectively, with extensions under exceptional circumstances.

Miss Marshall was a dietician employed by the AHA who was dismissed at the age of 62 on the ground that she was over the normal retirement age for women. Miss Marshall instituted proceedings against the AHA alleging sex discrimination contrary to Council Directive No 76/207 on equality of treatment of the sexes. The Court of Appeal referred two questions to the Court, the first asking whether the dismissal was contrary to the directive. This was answered in the affirmative by the Court, which then went on to consider whether the directive could be relied upon by an individual in the national courts.

The Court

...

The appellant and the Commission consider that that question must be answered in the affirmative. They contend in particular, with regard to Articles 2(1) and 5(1) of Directive No 76/207, that those provisions are sufficiently clear to enable national courts to apply them without legislative intervention by the Member States, at least so far as overt discrimination is concerned.

In support of that view, the appellant points out that directives are capable of conferring rights on individuals which may be relied upon directly before the courts of the Member States; national courts are obliged by virtue of the binding nature of a directive, in conjunction with Article 5 of the EEC Treaty, to give effect to the provisions of directives where possible, in particular when construing or applying relevant provisions of national law (judgment of 10 April 1984 in Case 14/83 *von Colson and Kamann* v *Land Nordrhein-Westfalen* [1984] ECR 1891). Where there is any inconsistency between national law and Community law which cannot be removed by means of such a construction, the appellant submits that a national court is obliged to declare that the provision of national law which is consistent with the directive is inapplicable.

The Commission is of the opinion that the provisions of Article 5(1) of Directive No 76/207 are sufficiently clear and unconditional to be relied upon before a national court.

They may therefore be set up against section 6(4) of the Sex Discrimination Act, which, according to the decisions of the Court of Appeal, has been extended to the question of compulsory retirement and has therefore become ineffective to prevent dismissals based upon the difference in retirement ages for men and for women.

The respondent and the United Kingdom propose, conversely, that the second question should be answered in the negative. They admit that a directive may, in certain specific circumstances, have direct effect as against a Member State in so far as the latter may not rely on its failure to perform its obligations under the directive. However, *they maintain that a directive can never impose obligations directly on individuals and that it can only have direct effect against a Member State* qua *public authority and not against a Member State* qua *employer*. As an employer a State is no different from a private employer. It would not therefore be proper to put persons employed by the State in a better position than those who are employed by a private employer.

With regard to the legal position of the respondent's employees the United Kingdom states that they are in the same position as the employees of a private employer. Although according to United Kingdom constitutional law the health authorities, created by the National Health Service Act 1977, as amended by the Health Services Act 1980 and other legislation, are Crown bodies and their employees are Crown servants, nevertheless the administration of the National Health Service by the health authorities is regarded as being separate from the Government's central administration and its employees are not regarded as civil servants.

Finally, both the respondent and the United Kingdom take the view that the provisions of Directive No 76/207 are neither unconditional nor sufficiently clear and precise to give rise to direct effect. The directive provides for a number of possible exemptions, the details of which are to be laid down by the Member States. Furthermore, the wording of Article 5 is quite imprecise and requires the adoption of measures for its implementation.

It is necessary to recall that, according to a long line of decisions of the Court (in particular its judgment of 19 January 1982 in Case 8/81 *Becker* v *Finanzamt Münster-Innenstadt* [1982] ECR 53), wherever the provisions of a directive appear, as far as their subject-matter is concerned, to be unconditional and sufficiently precise, those provisions may be relied upon by an individual against the State where that State fails to implement the directive in national law by the end of the period prescribed or where it fails to implement the directive correctly.

That view is based on the consideration that it would be incompatible with the binding nature which Article 189 confers on the directive to hold as a matter of principle that the obligation imposed thereby cannot be relied on by those concerned. From that the Court deduced that a Member State which has not adopted the implementing measures required by the directive within the prescribed period may not plead, as against individuals, its own failure to perform the obligations which the directive entails.

With regard to the argument that a directive may not be relied upon against an individual, it must be emphasised that according to Article 189 of the EEC Treaty the binding nature of a directive, which constitutes the basis for the possibility of relying on the directive before a national court, exists only in relation to 'each Member State to which it is addressed'. It follows that a directive may not of itself impose obligations on an individual and that a provision of a directive may not be relied upon as such against such a person. It must therefore be examined whether, in this case, the respondent must be regarded as having acted as an individual.

In that respect it must be pointed out that where a person involved in legal proceedings is able to rely on a directive as against the State he may do so regardless of the capacity in which the latter is acting, whether employer or public authority. In either case it is necessary to prevent the State from taking advantage of its own failure to comply with Community law.

It is for the national court to apply those considerations to the circumstances of each case; the Court of Appeal has, however, stated in the order for reference that the respondent, Southampton and South West Hampshire Area Health Authority (Teaching), is a public authority.

The argument submitted by the United Kingdom that the possibility of relying on provisions of the directive against the respondent *qua* organ of the State would give rise to an arbitrary and unfair distinction between the rights of State employees and those of private employees does not justify any other conclusion. Such a distinction may easily be avoided if the Member State concerned has correctly implemented the directive in national law.

Finally, with regard to the question whether the provision contained in Article 5(1) of Directive No 76/207, which implements the principle of equality of treatment set out in Article 2(1) of the directive, may be considered, as far as its contents are concerned, to be unconditional and sufficiently precise to be relied upon by an individual as against the State, it must be stated that the provision, taken by itself, prohibits any discrimination on grounds of sex with regard to working conditions, including the conditions governing dismissal, in a general manner and in unequivocal terms. The provision is therefore sufficiently precise to be relied on by an individual and to be applied by the national courts.

It is necessary to consider next whether the prohibition of discrimination laid down by the directive may be regarded as unconditional, in the light of the exceptions contained therein and of the fact that according to Article 5(2) thereof the Member States are to take the measures necessary to ensure the application of the principle of equality of treatment in the context of national law.

With regard, in the first place, to the reservation contained in Article 1(2) of Directive No 76/207 concerning the application of the principle of equality of treatment in matters of social security, it must be observed that, although the reservation limits the scope of the directive *ratione materiae*, it does not lay down any condition on the application of that principle in its field of operation and in particular in relation to Article 5 of the directive. Similarly, the exceptions to Directive No 76/207 provided for in Article 2 thereof are not relevant to this case.

It follows that Article 5 of Directive No 76/207 does not confer on the Member States the right to limit the application of the principle of equality of treatment in its field of operation or to subject it to conditions and that that provision is sufficiently precise and unconditional to be capable of being relied upon by an individual before a national court in order to avoid the application of any national provision which does not conform to Article 5(1).

Consequently, the answer to the second question must be that Article 5(1) of Council Directive No 76/207 of 9 February 1976, which prohibits any discrimination on grounds of sex with regard to working conditions, including the conditions governing dismissal, may be relied upon *as against a State authority acting in its capacity as employer*, in order to avoid the application of any national provision which does not conform to Article 5(1).

IV MEASURES OTHER THAN REGULATIONS, DIRECTIVES AND DECISIONS

The only legislative acts envisaged by the EEC Treaty are those in Article 189 (and in the case of the Euratom and ECSC Treaties in Articles 161 and 14 respectively). However, the Court may be called upon to have recourse to other measures, especially as a means of interpreting regulations and directives. In particular, it has applied the Commission's Explanatory Notes to the Common Customs Tariff (CCT) in construing Community regulations governing the Common External Tariff.

Case 149/73 Otto Witt KG v Hauptzollamt Hamburg-Ericus
[1973] ECR 1587

Between February and October 1970 Firma Witt imported frozen caribou meat into Germany from Greenland. Firma Witt maintained that these imports fell within CCT classification 02.04–B ('other meat and edible meat offals, fresh, chilled or frozen ... of game'). The German customs authorities, however, took the view that the imports fell within CCT classification 02.04–C–III ('other ... other'). In reaching this conclusion the German authorities relied on the Commission's Explanatory Notes to subheading 02.04–B which stated that 'reindeer are held to be domestic animals. Reindeer meat and offals do not therefore come under this subheading and are classified under subheading 02.04–C–III'. Firma Witt instituted proceedings before the Hamburg Finanzgericht, which asked the Court of Justice of the European Communities to rule 'what are the decisive criteria to be applied in interpreting the expression "game" in tariff heading 02.04–B?'.

In its submissions to the Court the Commission maintained that its Explanatory Notes, although not amounting to binding rules, constitute a commentary giving the authentic meaning attributed by the Community legislature to a given expression. As such, the Commission argued, they represent a basis and method for the interpretation of the tariff which are both essential and 'decisive'. To attempt to interpret the expression 'game' within the meaning of subheading 02.04–B, independently of the Explanatory Notes, in favour of a concept based on other contexts and definitions, would display a want of comprehension of these attributes of the Notes.

Firma Witt, after providing a learned zoological disquisition on the subspecies of *Rangifer tarandus*, replied that Explanatory Notes amount only to administrative guidelines intended for the federal administration of customs, and have no binding effect with regard to third parties or institutions.

The Court

The arguments put forward by the Commission to justify the classification of all reindeer meat under the same subheading in this way, leaving no possibility for a different treatment of the meat of wild reindeer as compared with that of domestic reindeer, consist in the absence as between the two products of objective characteristics and properties which would allow one to be distinguished from the other when submitted for customs clearance.

However, this similarity between the products is not such as to exclude treatment differentiated on the basis of other objective factors, of which evidence can be given when the products are submitted for customs clearance, for example by means of certificates of origin.

The Explanatory Notes to the Common Customs Tariff, although an important factor as regards interpretation in all cases where the provisions of the tariff provoke uncertainty, cannot amend those provisions, the meaning and scope of which are sufficiently clear.

The expression 'game' in its ordinary meaning designates those categories of animal living in the wild state which are hunted.

Although the customs authorities can legitimately require conclusive evidence that the animals whose meat is declared by the importer as being covered by subheading 02-04–B are game animals, the Explanatory Notes cannot, in contradiction to the text of the Common Customs Tariff, eliminate all differences of classification as between the meat of wild and domestic animals of the same species.

Accordingly, the answer to the questions referred is that the expression 'game' as it appears at subheading 02.04–B of the Common Customs Tariff 1970 is to be interpreted as applying to animals living in the wild state which are hunted.

There is a tendency on the part of the Ministers of the Member States to adopt acts other than regulations, directives and decisions, so as to avoid the possibility of such acts being characterised as Measures of the Council, especially where there is a desire to express political consensus short of legislation. An example of this is the Council Resolution on the adoption of a Community passport.

Resolution of the Representatives of the Governments of the Member States of the European Communities, Meeting within the Council of 23 June 1981

(OJ 1981 C 241/1)

THE REPRESENTATIVES OF THE GOVERNMENTS OF THE MEMBER STATES OF THE EUROPEAN COMMUNITIES, MEETING WITHIN THE COUNCIL,

recalling that the Heads of Governments meeting in Paris on 9 and 10 December 1974 requested that the possibility of creating a Passport Union and, in advance, the introduction of a uniform passport, be examined and that the European Council meeting in Rome on 3 and 4 December 1975, agreed on the basis of the report submitted to it to introduce a passport of uniform design,

anxious to promote any measures which might strengthen the feeling among nationals of the Member States that they belong to the same Community,

considering that the establishment of such a passport is likely to facilitate the movement of nationals of the Member States, *have drawn up* a passport of which the uniform format and scope are described in Annexes I and II respectively, which form an integral part of this resolution,

have resolved that the Member States will endeavour to issue the passport by 1 January 1985 at the latest.

Annex I

CHARACTERISTICS OF THE UNIFORM PASSPORT

A. Passport Format

The passport will be uniform. The format will be decided upon by a working party taking into account technical problems and in particular those posed by the possible insertion of a laminated card.

Should a laminated card be inserted, it should have the dimensions stated in the draft ICAO recommendation.

B. Passport Cover

(a) *Colour*: burgundy red.

(b) *Information on the cover*:

In the following order:

- the words 'European Community',
- name of the State issuing the passport,
- emblem of the State,
- the word 'Passport'.

The words 'European Community' and the name of the State will be printed in similar typeface.

(c) *Languages used on the cover*:

The above information will be given in the official language(s) of the State issuing the Passport.

(d) *Inside cover*:

Each State may give here whatever information it chooses. This optional information will be given in the official language(s) of the State issuing the passport.

C. Number of Pages in the Passport

The passport will normally contain 32 pages. However, a passport containing more pages may be issued to people who travel frequently.

The number of pages in the passport will appear at the bottom of the last page. This information will be given in the official languages of the Member States of the European Communities.

D. First Page

This page will contain the following items in the order given below:

- the words 'European Community',
- name of the State issuing the passport,
- the word 'Passport'.

The words 'European Community' and the name of the State will be printed in similar typeface.

This information will be given in the official languages of the European Communities.

The serial number of the passport will also be given on this page. The serial number may also be repeated on the other pages.

...

Annex II

SCOPE

A. The uniform passport will be available to nationals of the Member States of the European Communities.

B. Member States may decide to issue passports of this type to other persons.

C. Member States may in certain special cases issue passports in another form, e.g. diplomatic or service passports.

D. If necessary in particular cases, Member States may, without prejudice to the passport to be drawn up in accordance with this resolution, continue to issue the old type of passport.

FURTHER READING

Bebr, G., 'Directly Applicable Provisions of Community Law: the Development of a Community Concept' 19 ICLQ (1970) 257

Comment on the effect of the *Marshall* case 11 ELRev (1986) 117

Easson, A.J., 'EEC Directives for the Harmonisation of Laws' 1 YEL (1981) 1

Pescatore, P., 'The Doctrine of Direct Effect: an Infant Disease of Community Law' 8 ELRev (1983) 155

Shachor-Landau, C., 'International Legal Personality of the EEC and its Treaty making Power' 20 Israel Law Review (1985) 341

Winter, J., 'Direct Applicability and Direct Effect: Two Distinct and Different Concepts in Community Law' 9 CMLRev (1972) 425

Wyatt, D., 'New Legal Order, or Old?' 7 ELRev (1982) 147; 'The Direct Effect of Community Social Law – Not Forgetting Directives' 8 ELRev (1983) 241

3

ACTIONS AGAINST COMMUNITY INSTITUTIONS

The EEC Treaty envisages four principal methods by which the Court of Justice may control the legality or validity of acts of the Community institutions. They are the action for annulment; the action for failure to act; the plea of illegality; and the action for damages.

I THE ACTION FOR ANNULMENT

1. REVIEW

EEC Treaty

Article 173

The Court of Justice shall review the legality of acts of the Council and the Commission other than recommendations or opinions. It shall for this purpose have jurisdiction in actions brought by a Member State, the Council or the Commission on grounds of lack of competence, infringement of an essential procedural requirement, infringement of this Treaty or of any rule of law relating to its application, or misuse of powers.

Any natural or legal person may, under the same conditions, institute proceedings against a decision addressed to that person or against a decision which, although in the form of a regulation or a decision addressed to another person, is of direct and individual concern to the former.

The proceedings provided for in this article shall be instituted within two months of the publication of the measure, or of its notification to the plaintiff, or, in the absence thereof, of the day on which it came to the knowledge of the latter, as the case may be.

Article 174

If the action is well founded, the Court of Justice shall declare the act concerned to be void.

In the case of a regulation, however, the Court of Justice shall, if it considers this necessary, state which of the effects of the regulation which it has declared void shall be considered as definitive.

...

Article 176

The institution whose act has been declared void or whose failure to act has been declared contrary to this Treaty shall be required to take the necessary measures to comply with the judgment of the Court of Justice...

Articles 146, 147 and 149 of the Euratom Treaty are worded identically with Articles 173, 174 and 176 of the EEC Treaty. By contrast, Article 33 of the ECSC Treaty authorises the Court of Justice to review *decisions and recommendations* of the High Authority (now Commission) and Article 38 authorises review of the acts of the Assembly (now Parliament) and the Council.

ECSC Treaty

Article 33

The Court shall have jurisdiction in actions brought by a Member State or by the Council to have decisions or recommendations of the High Authority declared void on grounds of lack of competence, infringement of an essential procedural requirement, infringement of this Treaty or of any rule of law relating to its application, or misuse of powers. The Court may not, however, examine the evaluation of the situation, resulting from economic facts or circumstances, in the light of which the High Authority took its decisions or made its recommendations, save where the High Authority is alleged to have misused its powers or to have manifestly failed to observe the provisions of this Treaty or any rule of law relating to its application.

Undertakings or the associations referred to in Article 48 may, under the same conditions, institute proceedings against decisions or recommendations concerning them which are individual in character or against general decisions or recommendations which they consider to involve a misuse of powers affecting them.

The proceedings provided for in the first two paragraphs of this article shall be instituted within one month of the notification or publication, as the case may be, of the decision or recommendation.

Article 34

If the Court declares a decision or recommendation void, it shall refer the matter back to the High Authority. The High Authority shall take the necessary steps to comply with the judgment. If direct and special harm is suffered by an undertaking or group of undertakings by reason of a decision or recommendation held by the Court to involve a fault of such a nature as to render the Community liable, the High Authority shall, using the powers conferred upon it by this Treaty, take steps to ensure equitable redress for the harm resulting directly from the decision or recommendation declared void and, where necessary, pay appropriate damages.

If the High Authority fails to take within a reasonable time the necessary steps to comply with the judgment, proceedings for damages may be instituted before the Court.

...

Article 38

The Court may, on application by a Member State or the High Authority, declare an act of the Assembly or of the Council to be void.

Application shall be made within one month of the publication of the act of the Assembly or the notification of the act of the Council to the Member States or to the High Authority.

The only grounds for such application shall be lack of competence or infringement of an essential procedural requirement.

As we have seen, the 'acts' susceptible to review under Article 173 of the EEC Treaty are not confined to those listed in Article 189: Case 22/70 *Commission* v *Council* [1971] , (see above, p. 7). Measures of a purely preparatory character, on the other hand, are not susceptible of review. In order to be subject to the procedure envisaged by Article 173, the measure must produce binding legal effects of such a kind as to affect the applicant's interests by clearly altering his legal position.

Case 60/81 International Business Machines Corporation v Commission
[1981] ECR 2639; [1981] 3 CMLR 635

After receiving complaints from a competitor, the Commission conducted an investigation of IBM's marketing practices in order to determine whether these amounted to an abuse of a dominant position contrary to Article 86 of the EEC Treaty. By a letter dated 19 December 1980 the Commission informed IBM that it had initiated a procedure pursuant to Article 3 of Regulation No 17 of 6 February 1982, OJ Sp Ed 1959-62, 87, for the purpose of determining whether an infringement had occurred. The Commission sent with the letter a statement of objections of the kind envisaged by Article 19 of that Regulation. IBM lodged an application before the Court claiming that the Court should declare void the act or acts of the Commission by which a proceeding was initiated or a statement of objections notified to IBM. Further, it sought the annulment of the statement of objections itself. The Court dismissed the application.

The Court

...

According to Article 173 of the Treaty proceedings may be brought for a declaration that acts of the Council and the Commission other than recommendations or opinions are void. That remedy is available in order to ensure, as required by Article 164, that in the interpretation and application of the Treaty the law is observed, and it would be inconsistent with that objective to interpret restrictively the conditions under which the action is admissible by limiting its scope merely to the categories of measures referred to in Article 189.

In order to ascertain whether the measures in question are acts within the meaning of Article 173 it is necessary, therefore, to look at their substance. *According to the consistent case-law of the Court any measure the legal effects of which are binding on, and capable of affecting the interests of, the applicant by bringing about a distinct change in his legal position is an act or decision which may be the subject of an action under Article 173 for a declaration that it is void.* However, the form in which such acts or decisions are cast is, in principle, immaterial as regards the question whether they are open to challenge under that article.

In the case of acts or decisions adopted by a procedure involving several stages, in particular where they are the culmination of an internal procedure, it is clear from the case-law that in principle an act is open to review only if it is a measure definitively laying down the position of the Commission or the Council on the conclusion of that procedure, and not a provisional measure intended to pave the way for the final decision.

It would be otherwise only if acts or decisions adopted in the course of the preparatory proceedings not only bore all the legal characteristics referred to above but in addition were themselves the culmination of a special procedure distinct from that intended to permit the Commission or the Council to take a decision on the substance of the case.

Furthermore, it must be noted that whilst *measures of a purely preparatory character may not themselves be the subject of an application for a declaration that they are void,* any legal defects therein may be relied upon in an action directed against the definitive act for which they represent a preparatory step.

The effects and the legal character of the invitation of an administrative procedure pursuant to the provisions of Regulation No 17 and of the notification of objections as provided for in Article 2 of Regulation No 99/63 must be determined in the light of the purpose of such acts in the context of the Commission's administrative procedure in matters of competition, detailed rules for which have been laid down in the above-mentioned regulations.

The procedure was designed to enable the undertakings concerned to communicate their views and to provide the Commission with the fullest information possible before it adopted a decision affecting the interests of an undertaking. Its purpose is to create procedural guarantees for the benefit of the latter and, as may be seen in the eleventh recital in the preamble to Regulation No 17, to ensure that the undertakings have the right to be heard by the Commission.

That is why in accordance with Article 19(1) of Regulation No 17 and in order to guarantee observance of the rights of the defence, it is necessary to ensure that the undertaking concerned has the right to submit its observations on conclusion of the inquiry on all the objections which the Commission intends to raise against it in its decision and, therefore, to inform it of those objections in the document which is provided for in Article 2 of Regulation No 99/63. That is why, too, in order to remove any doubt as to the procedural position of the undertaking in question, initiation of the procedure under the abovementioned provisions is clearly marked by an act manifesting the intention to take a decision.

In support of its submission that the application is admissible IBM relies on a number of effects arising from the initiation of a procedure and from communication of the statement of objections.

Some of those effects amount to no more than the ordinary effects of any procedural step and, apart from the procedural aspect, do not affect the legal position of the undertaking concerned. That is so, in particular, of the interruption of the time-limit brought about both by the initiation of a procedure and by the communication of the statement of objections by virtue of Regulation (EEC) No 2988/74 of the Council of 26 November 1974 concerning limitation periods in proceedings and the enforcement of sanctions under the rules of the European Economic Community relating to transport and competition (Official

Journal 1974, L 319, p. 1). The same is true as regards the fact that the acts in question are necessary stages to be accomplished by the Commission pursuant to the provisions of Regulation No 17 before it is able to impose a fine or a periodic penalty payment on the undertaking concerned, and the fact that the acts oblige the undertaking concerned to put up a defence in administrative proceedings.

Other effects relied on by IBM do not adversely affect the interests of the undertaking concerned. One such is the fact that initiation of a procedure under Article 9(3) of Regulation No 17 puts an end to the jurisdiction of the authorities in the Member States – a result which did not in fact occur in this instance as there were no national proceedings, and which essentially results in protecting the undertaking concerned from parallel proceedings brought by the authorities of the Member States. Another such effect is the fact that communication of the statement of objections is recognised as crystallising the Commission's position, which means in effect that the Commission is prevented, pursuant to Article 4 of Regulation No 99/63, from relying in its decision, in the absence of a fresh statement of objections, on the existence of any objections other than those on which the undertaking has been given an opportunity to make known its views, though it does not prevent the Commission from withdrawing its objections and thereby altering its standpoint in favour of the undertaking.

A statement of objections does not compel the undertaking concerned to alter or reconsider its marketing practices and it does not have the effect of depriving it of the protection hitherto available to it against the application of a fine, as is the case when the Commission informs an undertaking, pursuant to Article 15(6) of Regulation No 17, of the results of the preliminary examination of an agreement which has been notified by the undertaking. Whilst a statement of objections may have the effect of showing the undertaking in question it is incurring a real risk of being fined by the Commission, that is merely a consequence of fact, and not a legal consequence which the statement of objections is intended to produce.

An application for a declaration that the initiation of a procedure and a statement of objections are void might make it necessary for the Court to arrive at a decision on questions on which the Commission has not yet had an opportunity to state its position and would as a result anticipate the arguments on the substance of the case, confusing different procedural stages both administrative and judicial. It would thus be incompatible with the system of the division of powers between the Commission and the Court and of the remedies laid down by the Treaty, as well as the requirements of the sound administration of justice and the proper course of the administrative procedure to be followed in the Commission.

It follows from the foregoing that *neither the initiation of a procedure nor a statement of objections may be considered, on the basis of their nature and the legal effects they produce, as being decisions within the meaning of Article 173 of the EEC Treaty which may be challenged in an action for a declaration that they are void.* In the context of the administrative procedure as laid down by Regulations No 17 and No 99/63, they are procedural measures adopted preparatory to the decision which represents their culmination.

2. RIGHT OF ACTION

All three of the founding Treaties put Member States and Community institutions in a different position from that of natural and legal persons as regards *locus standi*. The exercise by a Member State or Community institution of the right of action is not subject to any proof of legal interest. The Court had reason to emphasise this fact in a judgment rendered in 1979.

Case 166/78 Italy v **Council** [1979] ECR 2575; [1981] 3 CMLR 770

The Italian Government brought proceedings for the annulment of a Council regulation governing the premium payable to potato starch manufacturers. The Council argued that the action was inadmissible since the Italian representative had voted in favour of that regulation at the appropriate Council meeting.

The Court

The Council has invoked the plea that the application is inadmissible by reason of the affirmative unqualified vote cast by Italy when the regulations in question were adopted by the Council and also of the vote cast by the Italian representative on the Management Committee for Cereals when the implementing measures, which in the meantime have been brought into force by Commission Regulation (EEC) No 1809/78 of 28 July 1978 laying down rules for the payment of a premium to producers of potato starch, were considered (Official Journal L 205 of 29 July 1978, p. 69).

This plea of inadmissibility cannot be upheld. The first paragraph of Article 173 of the Treaty confers on every Member State the right to challenge, by an application for annulment, the legality of every Council regulation, without the exercise of this right being conditional upon the positions taken up by the representatives of the Member States of which the Council is composed when the regulation in question was adopted.

In the case of natural and legal persons, the situation under the ECSC Treaty is different from that under the other founding Treaties. Article 38 of the ECSC Treaty (concerning acts of the European Parliament and the Council) does not permit natural or legal persons to initiate proceedings at all; and Article 33 (concerning acts of the Commission) permits undertakings and associations to challenge individual decisions 'concerning them' and general decisions or recommendations which they consider to involve a misuse of powers affecting them. A decision affecting measures taken by a Member State in regard to its own undertakings may amount to a decision 'concerning' an association of undertakings in another Member State: Case 30/59 *De Gezamenlijke Steenkolenmijnen in Limburg* v *ECSC High Authority* [1961] ECR 1.

The EEC and Euratom Treaties draw a distinction between ordinary decisions, which may be challenged by natural and legal persons to whom they are addressed, and decisions in the form of regulations, which may be challenged by individuals who are directly and individually concerned thereby. For the purpose of determining whether a measure amounts to a decision, the Court will have regard to the substance rather than the form, and it will apply the following test: a regulation is a measure which applies to objectively determined situations and produces legal effects with regard to categories regarded generally and in the abstract: Case 101/76 *Koninklijke Scholten Honig* v *Council and Commission* [1977] ECR 797; [1980] 2 CMLR 669. The application of that test is illustrated in the *Nold* case (see below p. 115).

Joined Cases 41 to 44/70 NV International Fruit Company and Others v Commission [1971] ECR 411; [1975] 2 CMLR 515

The applicants sought the annulment of a decision adopted by the Commission pursuant to Regulation No 459/70 of 11 March 1970, JO 1970, L 57, whereby the Commission refused to grant them licences to import dessert apples from third countries, which was notified to them through the intermediary of the PGF in the Hague.

The Court

...

The defendant submits that no decision was addressed to the applicants, and that the refusal to grant them import licences emanates from the PGF and is in reality an administrative measure governed by national law.

It states that the only 'decisions' of the Commission concerning the grant of import licences were contained in Regulation No 565/70 and the subsequent amending regulations.

These 'decisions' were of general application and in the nature of regulations, and the defendant submits that they could not therefore be of individual concern to the applicants within the meaning of the second paragraph of Article 173.

By Regulation No 459/70, adopted on the basis of Regulations Nos 2513/69 and 2514/69 of the Council, protective measures were taken with the object of limiting the import of dessert apples from third countries into the Community in the period from 1 April 1970 to 30 June 1970.

This regulation provides for a system of import licences, which are granted to the extent to which the state of the Community market allows.

It follows that when the said regulation was adopted, the number of applications which could be affected by it was fixed.

No new application could be added.

To what extent, in percentage terms, the applications could be granted depended on the total quantity in respect of which applications had been submitted.

Accordingly, by providing that the system introduced by Article 1 of Regulation No 565/70 should be maintained for the relevant period, the Commission decided, even though it took account only of the quantities requested, on the subsequent fate of each application which had been lodged.

Consequently, Article 1 of Regulation No 983/70 is not a provision of general application within the meaning of the second paragraph of Article 189 of the Treaty, but must be regarded as a conglomeration of individual decisions taken by the Commission under the guise of a regulation pursuant to Article 2(2) of Regulation No 459/70, each of which decisions affects the legal position of each author of an application for a licence.

Thus, the decisions are of individual concern to the applicants.

Moreover, it is clear from the system introduced by Regulation No 459/70, and particularly from Article 2(2) thereof, that the decision on the grant of import licences is a matter for the Commission.

According to this provision, the Commission alone is competent to assess the economic situation in the light of which the grant of import licences should be granted.

Article 1(2) of Regulation No 459/70, by providing that 'the Member States shall, in accordance with the conditions laid down in Article 2, issue the licence to any interested party applying for it', makes it clear that the national authorities do not enjoy any discretion in the matter of the issue of licences and the conditions on which applications by the parties concerned should be granted.

The duty of such authorities is merely to collect the data necessary in order that the Commission may take its decision in accordance with Article 2(2) of that regulation, and subsequently adopt the national measures needed to give effect to that decision.

In these circumstances, as far as the interested parties are concerned, the issue of or refusal to issue the import licences must be bound up with this decision.

Under this system and in accordance with Article 2(1) of Regulation No 459/70, 'at the end of each week ... the Member States shall communicate to the Commission the quantities for which import licences have been requested during the preceding week, stating the months to which they relate'.

The following paragraph of the same article provides that the Commission, on the basis *inter alia* of these communications, 'shall assess the situation and decide on the issue of the licences'.

On the basis of the latter provision, the Commission subsequently stipulated in Article 1 of Regulation No 565/70 of 25 March 1970 that 'applications for import licences lodged up to 20 March 1970 shall be treated in accordance with the provisions of Article 1 of Regulation No 459/70, within the quantity limit shown in the application and up to 80% of a reference quantity'.

The criteria for fixing this reference quantity were stated in greater detail, and amended, by Article 2 of Regulation No 686/70 of 15 April 1970.

By various regulations published in the period between 2 April 1970 and 20 July 1970, the expiry date of 20 March 1970 specified in Article 1 of Regulation No 565/70 was repeatedly postponed.

By these postponements the said measures were periodically extended and made applicable to applications for import licences submitted within each period.

By virtue of Article 1 of Regulation No 983/70 of 28 May 1970, this system was applied in the period in which the applications for licences were submitted by the applicants.

Hence, the issue of admissibility in the present cases must be determined in the light of the last-mentioned regulation.

For this purpose, it is necessary to consider whether the provisions of that regulation – in so far as they make the system established by Article 1 of Regulation No 565/70 applicable – are of direct and individual concern to the applicants within the meaning of the second paragraph of Article 173 of the Treaty.

It is indisputable that Regulation No 983/70 was adopted with a view on the one hand to the state of the market and on the other to the quantities of dessert apples for which applications for import licences had been made in the week ending on 22 May 1970.

The measure whereby the Commission decides on the issues of the import licences thus directly affects the legal position of the parties concerned.

The applications thus fulfil the requirements of the second paragraph of Article 173 of the Treaty, and are therefore admissible.

3. DIRECT CONCERN

In the case of the EEC Treaty and the Euratom Treaty, a measure is subject to challenge at the suit of a natural or legal person. This may take place not only at the instance of the addressee but also at the instance of another person who is directly and individually concerned.

A person is said to be directly concerned if the effects of the decision on his or her interests do not depend on the discretion of another person. In Case 69/69 *Alcan Aluminium Raeren* v *Commission* [1970] 1 ECR 385, the Court held that the applicant was not directly concerned because the two Member States to whom the Commission had addressed a decision, refusing an import quota, retained full discretion as to the disposal of any quota that might have been addressed to them. Conversely, in the *Bock* case, the Court held that direct concern had been established because the addressee had already tied his own hands in advance of the decision.

Case 62/70 W. A. Bock KG v Commission [1971] ECR 897; [1972] CMLR 160

Bock sought the annulment of part of a decision addressed to the Federal Republic of Germany by the Commission, authorising the addressee to exclude from Community treatment certain products originating in China, which were in free circulation in the Benelux countries.

The Court

...

(1) The Commission first contends that the application is inadmissible because the contested provision is not of concern to the applicant. It maintains that the words 'currently and duly pending' exclude applications for import licences which the German authorities ought already to have granted before the entry into force of the contested decision, at the risk of infringing the prohibition of measures having an effect equivalent to quantitative restrictions. This is said to be the case with the plaintiff's application since the German authorities had permitted an excessively long period to elapse before replying to it.

The expression 'duly pending' must be understood as constituting an application of Article 10(1) of Regulation No 865/68/EEC of the Council of 28 June 1968 in conjunction with Article 2(3)(q) and 4(1) of the Commission's Directive of 22 December 1969; according to these provisions the Member States are obliged to grant applications for import licences for the products in question within a period which is not 'excessive', otherwise they contravene the prohibition of measures having an effect equivalent to quantitative restrictions.

In the present case it is sufficient to note that the Federal Government, which had justified its initiative by reference to an application submitted to it at the time, might have assumed that the provision at issue was precisely intended to cover applications which had already been submitted. On 15 September 1970, the date when the contested decision was taken, the defendant was aware that the authorisation was to extend, in accordance with the wishes of the Federal Government, to applications for licences which were already pending before the German authorities before 11 September 1970, the date on which the German Government applied to the defendant. Therefore if the defendant intended to exclude these applications from the protective measure it should have expressed this clearly, instead of using the words 'the present authorisation likewise covers', with which, by implication, it extended the scope of the first sentence of Article 1 of the decision.

Accordingly, since the second sentence of that article must be interpreted as applying to the applicant's case, the provision the annulment of which is sought is of concern to the applicant.

(2) The defendant contends that in any event an authorisation granted to the Federal Republic is not of direct concern to the applicant since the Federal Republic remained free to make use of it.

The appropriate German authorities had nevertheless already informed the applicant that they would reject its application as soon as the Commission had granted them the requisite authorisation. They had requested that authorisation with particular reference to the applications already before them at that time.

It follows therefore that the matter was of direct concern to the applicant.

...

In order to show that he is individually concerned by the contested measure, the applicant must show that the measure affects him by reason of certain attributes which are peculiar to him or by reason of circumstances differentiating him from all other persons and by virtue of which the applicant is distinguished individually, just as in the case of the person addressed: Case 25/62 *Plaumann* v *Commission* [1963] ECR 95; [1964] CMLR 29. The possibility of determining more or less precisely the number or even the identity of the persons to whom a measure applies by no means implies that it must be regarded as being of direct concern to them.

Case 123/77 Unione Nazionale Importatori e Commercianti Motoveicoli Esteri (UNICME) and Others v Council [1978] ECR 845

The applicants sought the annulment of Council Regulation No 1692/77 of 25 July 1977 concerning protective measures on the importation of motor-cycles originating in Japan (OJ 1977, L 188/11). The Council objected that the regulation was not of direct and individual concern to the applicants.

The Court

Regulation No 1692/77 establishes for a limited period a system covering the importation into Italy of motor-cycles specified therein and originating in Japan.

The system consists in introducing a requirement to produce an import authorisation issued by the Italian authorities, and for the year 1977 such authorisations were not to be issued for more than 18,000 items.

The system would only affect the interests of the importers in the event of the necessary authorisations being refused them.

Consequently Regulation No 1692/77 would only be of concern to the applicants if, pursuant to that measure, they were refused an import authorisation.

In that case they will be able to raise the matter before the national court having jurisdiction, if necessary raising before that court their questions concerning the validity of the regulation, which the court will, if it thinks fit, be able to deal with by means of the procedure under Article 177 of the Treaty.

In the present case the condition laid down in Article 173, to the effect that the contested measure must be of direct and individual concern to the applicants, is not fulfilled.

The applicants claim that, taken together, they represent all the importers affected by the import system introduced for motor-cycles originating in Japan.

They state that even before Regulation No 1692/77 was adopted it could have been established that they were the only persons concerned and that they were all concerned.

The possibility of determining more or less precisely the number or even the identity of the persons to whom a measure applies by no means implies that it must be regarded as being of individual concern to them.

In the present case the fact that all the applicants might possibly be refused an import authorisation pursuant to Regulation No 1692/77 does not provide a sufficient basis for regarding the regulation as being of individual concern to them in the same way as if a decision had been addressed to them.

On the contrary the regulation will not produce effects in individual cases until it is implemented by the Italian authorities.

Consequently, the second condition laid down by Article 173 likewise remains unfulfilled.

Since the conditions laid down by Article 173 have not been fulfilled the application must accordingly be dismissed as inadmissible.

On the other hand, the Court has held that a particular factual situation may differentiate the applicant from all other persons and distinguish him individually. This was the case when a wholesale importer of cereals in Germany sought the annulment of a Commission decision dated 3 October 1963 authorising Germany to maintain protective measures governing the importation of maize, millet and sorghum. The Court dismissed the Commission's argument that the application was inadmissible; for the only persons affected by the contested measure were importers who had applied for an import licence during 1 October 1963 and their number and identity was discoverable when the measure was made.

Joined Cases 106 and 107/63 Alfred Toepfer and Getreide-Import Gesellschaft v Commission [1965] ECR 405; [1966] CMLR 111

The Court

It is clear from the fact that on 1 October 1963 the Commission took a decision fixing new free-at-frontier prices for maize imported into the Federal Republic as from 2 October, that the danger which the protective measures retained by the Commission were to guard against no longer existed as from this latter date.

Therefore the only persons concerned by the said measures were importers who had applied for an import licence during the course of the day of 1 October 1963. The number and identity of these importers had already become fixed and ascertainable before 4 October, when the contested decision was made. The Commission was in a position to know that its decision affected the interests and the position of the said importers alone.

The factual situation thus created differentiates the said importers, including the applicants, from all other persons and distinguishes them individually just as in the case of the person addressed.

Therefore the objection of inadmissibility which has been raised is unfounded and the applications are admissible.

...

'Individual concern' was established in one case where a regulation named certain undertakings and applied specific measures to them, by stipulating the number of tons of isoglucose that six named manufacturers were allowed to produce.

Case 138/79 Roquette Frères SA v Council [1980] ECR 3333

The applicant sought the annulment of Council Regulation No 1293/79 of 25 June 1979 fixing a production quota for isoglucose (OJ 1979, L 162/10). The Council contended that the application was inadmissible since it was directed against a regulation and, in the Council's submission, the conditions set out in the second paragraph of Article 173 were not fulfilled.

The Court

Article 9(1), (2) and (3) of Regulation No 1111/77 as amended by Article 3 of Regulation No 1293/79 provides:

'1. A basic quota shall be allotted to each isoglucose- producing undertaking established in the Community, for the period referred to in Article 8(1).

Without prejudice to implementation of paragraph (3), the basic quota of each such undertaking shall be equal to twice its production as determined, under this regulation, during the period 1 November 1978 to 30 April 1979.

2. To each undertaking having a basic quota, there shall also be allotted a maximum quota equal to its basic quota multiplied by a coefficient. This coefficient shall be that fixed by virtue of the second paragraph of Article 25(2) of Regulation (EEC) No 3330/74 for the period 1 July 1979 to 30 June 1980.

3. The basic quota referred to in paragraph (1) shall, if necessary, be corrected so that the maximum quota determined in accordance with paragraph (2):

- does not exceed 85%,
- is not less than 65%

of the technical production capacity per annum of the undertaking in question.'

Article 9(4) provides that the basic quotas established pursuant to paragraphs (1) and (3) are fixed for each undertaking as set out in Annex II. That annex, which is an integral part of Article 9, provides that the applicant's basic quota is 15,887 tonnes.

It follows that Article 9(4) of Regulation No 1111/77 (as amended by Article 3 of Regulation No 1293/79), in conjunction with Annex II, itself applies the criteria laid down in Article 9(1) to (3) to each of the undertakings in question who are the addressees and thus directly and individually concerned. Regulation No 1293/79 therefore is a measure against which the undertakings concerned manufacturing isoglucose may bring proceedings for a declaration that is void pursuant to the second paragraph of Article 173 of the Treaty.

'Individual concern' was also established where the contested regulations had as their subject-matter the individual circumstances of three named exporters.

Joined Cases 239 and 257/82 Allied Corporation and Others v Commission [1984] ECR 1005; [1985] 3 CMLR 572

The applicants sought the annulment of two Commission regulations governing the imposition of anti-dumping duty on chemical fertiliser originating in the United States. These were adopted pursuant to Council Regulation No 3017/79 of 20 December 1979 on protection against dumped or subsidised imports (OJ 1979, L 339/1). The Commission questioned the admissibility of the application.

The Court

...

The questions of admissibility raised by the Commission must be resolved in the light of the system established by Regulation No 3017/79 and, more particularly, of the nature of the anti-dumping measures provided for by that regulation, regard being had to the provisions of the second paragraph of Article 173 of the EEC Treaty.

Article 13(1) of Regulation No 3017/79 provides that 'anti-dumping or countervailing duties, whether provisional or definitive, shall be imposed by regulation'. Although it is true that in the light of the criteria set out in the second paragraph of Article 173 such measures are in fact, as regards their nature and their scope, of a legislative character, inasmuch as they apply to all the traders concerned, taken as a whole, the provisions may nonetheless be of direct and individual concern to those producers and exporters who are charged with practising dumping. It is clear from Article 2 of Regulation No 3017/79 that anti-dumping duties may be imposed only on the basis of the findings resulting from investigations concerning the production prices and export prices of undertakings which have been individually identified.

It is thus clear that measures imposing anti-dumping duties are liable to be of direct and individual concern to those producers and exporters who are able to establish that they were identified in the measures adopted by the Commission or the Council or were concerned by the preliminary investigations.

As the Commission has rightly stated, to acknowledge that undertakings which fulfil those requirements have a right of action, in accordance with the principles laid down in the second paragraph of Article 173, does not give rise to a risk of duplication of means of redress since it is possible to bring an action in the national courts only following the collection of an anti-dumping duty which is normally paid by an importer residing within the Community. There is no risk of conflicting decisions in this area since, by virtue of the mechanism of the reference for a preliminary ruling under Article 177 of the EEC Treaty, it is for the Court of Justice alone to give a final decision on the validity of the contested regulations.

It follows that the applications lodged by Allied, Kaiser and Transcontinental are admissible. All three applicants gave an undertaking under Article 10 of Regulation No 3017/79, they were accordingly referred to individually in Article 2 of Regulation No 349/81 and, after withdrawing their undertakings, their individual circumstances formed the subject-matter of the two regulations contested in the applications.

Natural or legal persons who are entitled to request the Commission to find an infringement of Article 85 or 86 of the EEC Treaty are 'individually concerned' by a decision made by the Commission in response to their requests, although the decision is addressed to another person.

Case 75/84 Metro SB-Grossmarkte GmbH & Co v Commission
(No 2) [1986] ECR 3021; [1987] 1 CMLR 118

For some years 'Metro', a self-service wholesale trading organisation, challenged the distribution system of 'SABA', a German manufacturer of consumer electronics equipment. By a decision dated 15 December 1975, the Commission recognised that certain terms of SABA's standard contracts did not fall within the prohibition laid down in Article 85(1) of the EEC Treaty whereas other provisions were entitled to exemption. Metro applied to the Court for partial annulment of the decision. SABA argued that the application was inadmissible since Metro was not directly and individually concerned thereby. The objection was dismissed.

The Court

...

According to the second paragraph of Article 173 of the Treaty, any natural or legal person may institute proceedings against a decision addressed to that person or against a decision which, although in the form of a regulation or a decision addressed to another person, is of direct and individual concern to the former. Since the contested decision is not addressed to Metro, it is necessary to examine whether it is of direct and individual concern to Metro.

The Court has consistently held that persons other than those to whom a decision is addressed may claim to be concerned within the meaning of the second paragraph of Article 173 only if that decision affects them by reason of certain attributes which are peculiar to them, or by reason of circumstances in which they are differentiated from all other persons, and by virtue of these factors distinguishes them individually just as in the case of the person addressed (judgment of 28 January 1986 in Case 169/84 *COFAZ and Others* v *Commission* [1986] ECR 391).

In that regard it should be noted in the first place that Metro's applications for admission to the SABA system as a wholesaler have been refused.

It should be pointed out furthermore that Metro raised objections, in several letters of February 1983 and also later, following the publication of the Commission's Notice, pursuant to Article 19(3) of Regulation No 17, concerning its intention to grant SABA an exemption (Official Journal 1983, C 140, p. 3). The Commission recognised that Metro had a legitimate interest in submitting its observations, in accordance with Article 19(3) of Regulation No 17, and stated that the objections of Metro were precisely those which were rejected in Part IC of the contested decision. In spite of certain amendments to the original version of the SABA agreements, the decision maintains the special features of the distribution system which were criticised by Metro during the administrative procedure.

In those circumstances, the contested decision must be considered to be of direct and individual concern to Metro within the meaning of the second paragraph of Article 173. The application is therefore admissible.

4. GROUNDS FOR ANNULMENT

The grounds on which a measure may be annulled are set out exhaustively in Article 173 of the EEC Treaty, Article 146 of the Euratom Treaty and Articles 33 and 38 of the ECSC Treaty. There are four such grounds: lack of competence, infringement of an essential procedural requirement, infringement of the Treaty or of any rule of law relating to its application, and misuse of powers.

A. LACK OF COMPETENCE

'Lack of competence' means absence of the legal power to adopt the act in question. The plea was raised successfully in the *Meroni* case, where the Court annulled levies imposed on scrap iron by the High Authority on the basis of decisions taken by a subordinate body.

Case 9/56 Meroni and Co., Industrie Metallurgiche SpA v ECSC High Authority [1957-8] ECR 133

The Court

The applicant complains that the High Authority has, by its Decision No 14/55, delegated to the Brussels agencies powers which they are ill-qualified to exercise. Article 8 of the Treaty requires the High Authority

> '...to ensure that the objectives set out in this Treaty are attained in accordance with the provisions thereof'

and does not provide any power to delegate.

However, the possibility of entrusting to bodies established under private law, having a distinct legal personality and possessing powers of their own, the task of putting into effect certain 'financial arrangements common to several undertakings' as mentioned in subparagraph (a) of Article 53 cannot be excluded.

The financial arrangements made by the High Authority itself in application of subparagraph (b) of the same article must serve the same purposes as those authorised in application of subparagraph (a).

Therefore it must be possible for those arrangements to be similar in form and in particular to use the aid of bodies having a distinct legal personality.

Hence the power of the High Authority to authorise or itself to make the financial arrangements mentioned in Article 53 of the Treaty gives it the right to entrust certain powers to such bodies subject to conditions to be determined by it and subject to its supervision.

However, in the light of Article 53, such delegations of powers are only legitimate if the High Authority recognises them

> 'to be necessary for the performance of the tasks set out in Article 3 and compatible with this Treaty, and in particular with Article 65'.

Article 3 lays down no fewer than eight distinct, very general objectives, and it is not certain that they can all be simultaneously pursued in their entirety in all circumstances.

In pursuit of the objectives laid down in Article 3 of the Treaty, the High Authority must permanently reconcile any conflict which may be implied by these objectives when considered individually, and when such conflict arises must grant such priority to one or other of the objectives laid down in Article 3 as appears necessary having regard to the economic facts or circumstances in the light of which it adopts its decisions.

Reconciling the various objectives laid down in Article 3 implies a real discretion involving difficult choices, based on a consideration of the economic facts and circumstances in the light of which those choices are made.

The consequences resulting from a delegation of powers are very different depending on whether it involves clearly defined executive powers the exercise of which can, therefore, be subject to strict review in the light of objective criteria determined by the delegating authority, or whether it involves a discretionary power, implying a wide margin of discretion which may, according to the use which is made of it, make possible the execution of actual economic policy.

A delegation of the first kind cannot appreciably alter the consequences involved in the exercise of the powers concerned, whereas a delegation of the second kind, since it replaces the choices of the delegator by the choices of the delegate, brings about an actual transfer of responsibility.

In any event under Article 53 as regards the execution of the financial arrangements mentioned therein, it is only the delegation of those powers 'necessary for the performance of the tasks set out in Article 3' which may be authorised.

Such delegations of powers, however, can only relate to clearly defined executive powers, the use of which must be entirely subject to the supervision of the High Authority.

The objectives set out in Article 3 are binding not only on the High Authority, but on the 'institutions of the Community ... within the limits of their respective powers, in the common interest'.

From that provision there can be seen in the balance of powers which is characteristic of the institutional structure of the Community a fundamental guarantee granted by the Treaty in particular to the undertakings and associations of undertakings to which it applies.

To delegate a discretionary power, by entrusting it to bodies other than those which the Treaty has established to effect and supervise the exercise of such power each within the limits of its own authority, would render that guarantee ineffective.

In the light of the criteria set out above, it is appropriate to examine whether the delegation of powers granted by the High Authority to the Brussels agencies by virtue of Decision No 14/55 satisfies the requirements of the Treaty.

Article 5 of Decision No 14/55 provides that:

> 'The Joint Bureau may propose to the Fund:
>
> (a) the tonnages of scrap imported from third countries or scrap treated as such which may be entitled to equalisation;
>
> (b) the conditions to which the entitlement to equalisation subsidy is subject...;
>
> (c) the maximum import price;
>
> (d) the equalisation price, which may be fixed either for the date of order or for the date of delivery;

(e) the criteria for calculating economy in scrap due to an increased use of pig-iron;

(f) the amount of the bonus to be granted in regard to these economies'.

The Third General Report on the Activities of the Community published (p. 105) the general principles drawn up by the Council of Ministers and the High Authority 'on which the general policy in the matter of ferrous scrap is to be based'.

Those general principles state in the particular that

> 'the cost of ferrous scrap for the producer of steel – that is to say the sum of the purchase price and the equalisation levy – must not exceed a reasonable level in comparison with the level in fact borne by producers of steel in the principal competitor countries.
>
> In order to prevent cost prices from becoming too high in the Community as a whole, and in particular to prevent the net charge borne as a result of the functioning of the Fund in certain regions of the Community from being increased, the amount of the equalisation levy must not be increased without due cause. The effort made to encourage imports and a reasonable level of prices must not lead to an improvident increase in the consumption of ferrous scrap either in existing plant or by the creation of new plant.
>
> ...
>
> So far as is technically and economically possible, and to the extent to which other raw materials may be available, every effort should be made to reduce the consumption of ferrous scrap by an increased use of pig-iron'.

Several proposals which, under the above-mentioned Article 5, the competent office must submit to the Fund, in particular the fixing of the 'maximum import price', the 'equalisation price', the 'criteria for the calculation of economy in scrap' and the 'amount of the bonus to be granted for such economies' cannot be the result of mere accountancy procedures based on objective criteria laid down by the High Authority.

They imply a wide margin of discretion and are as such the outcome of the exercise of a discretionary power which tends to reconcile the many requirements of a complex and varied economic policy.

...

In those circumstances the delegation of powers granted to the Brussels agencies by Decision No 14/55 gives those agencies a degree of latitude which implies a wide margin of discretion and cannot be considered as compatible with the requirements of the Treaty.

The decision of 24 October 1956 is based on a general decision which is unlawful from the point of view of the Treaty and it must, for this reason also, be annulled.

B. INFRINGEMENT OF AN ESSENTIAL PROCEDURAL REQUIREMENT

Infringement of an essential procedural requirement was alleged in the *Roquette Frères* case of 1980. (For the facts see above, p. 108). The Court found that such an infringement had occurred where the opinion of the Parliament had not been obtained pursuant to Article 43 of the EEC Treaty.

Case 138/79 Roquette Frères SA v Council [1980] ECR 3333

The Court

The applicant and the Parliament in its intervention maintain that since Regulation No 1111/77 as amended was adopted by the Council without regard to the consultation procedure provided for in the second paragraph of Article 43 of the Treaty it must be treated as void for infringement of essential procedural requirements.

The consultation provided for in the third subparagraph of Article 43(2), as in other similar provisions of the Treaty, is the means which allows the Parliament to play an actual part in the legislative process of the Community. Such power represents an essential factor in the institutional balance intended by the Treaty. Although limited, it reflects at Community level the fundamental democratic principle that the peoples should take part in the exercise of power through the intermediary of a representative assembly. Due consultation of the Parliament in the cases provided for by the Treaty therefore constitutes an essential formality disregard of which means that the measure concerned is void.

In that respect it is pertinent to point out that observance of that requirement implies that the Parliament has expressed its opinion. It is impossible to take the view that the requirement is satisfied by the Council's simply asking for the opinion. The Council is, therefore, wrong to include in the references in the preamble to Regulation No 1293/79 a statement to the effect that the Parliament has been consulted.

The Council has not denied that consultation of the Parliament was in the nature of an essential procedural requirement. It maintains however that in the circumstances of the present case the Parliament, by its own conduct, made observance of that requirement impossible and that it is therefore not proper to rely on the infringement thereof.

Without prejudice to the questions of principle raised by that argument of the Council it suffices to observe that in the present case on 25 June 1979 when the Council adopted Regulation No 1293/79 amending Regulation No 1111/77 without the opinion of the Assembly, the Council had not exhausted all the possibilities of obtaining the preliminary opinion of the Parliament. In the first place the Council did not request the application of the emergency procedure provided for by the internal regulation of the Parliament although in other sectors and as regards other draft regulations it availed itself of that power at the same time. Further the Council could have made use of the possibility it had under Article 139 of the Treaty to ask for an extraordinary session of the Assembly especially as the Bureau of the Parliament on 1 March and 10 May 1979 drew its attention to that possibility.

It follows that in the absence of the opinion of the Parliament required by Article 43 of the Treaty, Regulation No 1293/79 amending Council Regulation No 1111/77 must be declared void without prejudice to the Council's power following the present judgment to take all appropriate measures pursuant to the first paragraph of Article 176 of the Treaty.

C. INFRINGEMENT OF THE TREATY OR OF A RULE OF LAW

The third ground for annulment embraces not only infringements of the Treaty but also infringements of rules of law relating to its application. It is on this basis that applicants are apt to base claims that Community measures have been adopted in breach of general principles of law, such as the principles of proportionality, legal certainty or equality, or in breach of principles governing respect for human rights.

Case 4/73 J. Nold, Kohlen- und Baustoffgrosshandlung v Commission
[1974] ECR 491; [1974] 2 CMLR 338

Nold, which carried on a wholesale coal and construction materials business, sought annulment of a Commission decision authorising new terms of business of the German coal undertaking, Ruhrkohle. One of its arguments was that the decision violated Nold's fundamental rights.

The Court

...

The applicant asserts finally that certain of its fundamental rights have been violated, in that the restrictions introduced by the new trading rules authorised by the Commission have the effect, by depriving it of direct supplies, of jeopardising both the profitability of the undertaking and the free development of its business activity, to the point of endangering its very existence.

In this way the decision is said to violate, in respect of the applicant, a right akin to a proprietary right, as well as its right to the free pursuit of business activity, as protected by the Grundgesetz of the Federal Republic of Germany and by the Constitutions of other Member States and various international treaties, including in particular the Convention for the Protection of Human Rights and Fundamental Freedoms of 4 November 1950 and the Protocol to that Convention of 20 March 1952.

As the Court has already stated, fundamental rights form an integral part of the general principles of law, the observance of which it ensures.

In safeguarding these rights, the Court is bound to draw inspiration from constitutional traditions common to the Member States, and it cannot therefore uphold measures which are incompatible with fundamental rights recognised and protected by the Constitutions of those States.

Similarly, international treaties for the protection of human rights on which the Member States have collaborated, or of which they are signatories, can supply guidelines which should be followed within the framework of Community law.

The submissions of the applicant must be examined in the light of these principles.

If rights of ownership are protected by the constitutional laws of all the Member States and if similar guarantees are given in respect of their right freely to choose and practice their trade or profession, the rights thereby guaranteed, far from constituting unfettered prerogatives, must be viewed in the light of the social function of the property and activities protected thereunder.

For this reason, rights of this nature are protected by law subject always to limitations laid down in accordance with the public interest.

Within the Community legal order it likewise seems legitimate that these rights should, if necessary, be subject to certain limits justified by the overall objectives pursued by the Community, on condition that the substance of these rights is left untouched.

As regards the guarantees accorded to a particular undertaking, they can in no respect be extended to protect mere commercial interests or opportunities, the uncertainties of which are part of the very essence of economic activity.

The disadvantages claimed by the applicant are in fact the result of economic change and not of the contested decision.

It was for the applicant, confronted by the economic changes brought about by the recession in coal production, to acknowledge the situation and itself carry out the necessary adaptations.

This submission must be dismissed for all the reasons outlined above.

D. MISUSE OF POWER

A misuse of power is the exercise of a power for a purpose other than that for which it was granted.

Case 105/75 Franco Giuffrida v Council [1976] ECR 1395

The applicant, a Council official, requested the annulment of a decision of the Council appointing one Emilio Martino to the post of principal administrator in the Directorate General for regional policy. He maintained that the decision was adopted following an internal competition organised for the purpose of appointing to the vacant post the candidate who was in fact successful. The Court annulled the decision.

The Court

The decision making the appointment in question was adopted following Internal Competition on the Basis of Qualifications No A/108, the notice of competition for which was published on 18 February 1975 in Communication No 11/75-I from the Secretary-General.

Under the terms of the first paragraph of Article 27 of the Staff Regulations, 'recruitment shall be directed to securing for the institution the services of officials of the highest standard of ability, efficiency and integrity...'.

In addition, Article 29 of the Staff Regulations lays down the necessary recruitment procedures – which, in paragraph 1(b), include the internal competition – so that vacant posts may be filled by officials chosen on the basis of objective criteria and only in the interests of the service.

In his note of 14 November 1974, in which he replied to the criticisms made by the Amalgamated European Public Service Union in its bulletin of 7 November 1974, the Secretary-General stated that:

> '– The question of the transfer of an official in Grade L/A4 to Grade A4 as a result of a competition arose out of a desire to mitigate an anomalous situation which has already lasted for some years and which came into existence as the result of excessive leniency on the part of the administration.
>
> – It will be impossible for such a situation to arise in future. Measures will be adopted to ensure that in the near future the tasks performed by each official are those of his category or service'.

The defendant has not contested the pertinence in this case of these statements and, during the written and oral procedure, has admitted that the 'situation which has already lasted for some years' to which the Secretary-General referred was that of Mr Martino who was classified in Grade L/A4 but who had for a considerable time been assigned to a post which was identical to the post in question.

In its rejoinder the defendant stated that as such a situation was anomalous 'it was appropriate... to remedy it' by means of the opportunity presented by Competition No A/108.

It is clear from the abovementioned note and from the foregoing statements that Internal Competition No A/108 was organised by the appointing authority for the sole purpose of remedying the anomalous administrative status of a specific official and of appointing that same official to the post declared vacant.

The pursuit of such a specific objective is contrary to the aims of any recruitment procedure, including the internal competition procedure, and thus constitutes a misuse of powers.

The existence of misuse of powers in this instance is moreover confirmed by the fact that one of the conditions for admission to the competition was that the successful candidate must have held the secretariat for meetings of Council working parties or committees on regional policy for at least four years.

It is not disputed that such a restrictive condition corresponds exactly to the duties performed by Emilio Martino in his previous post.

...

II THE ACTION FOR FAILURE TO ACT

EEC Treaty

Article 175

Should the Council or the Commission, in infringement of this Treaty, fail to act, the Member States and the other institutions of the Community may bring an action before the Court of Justice to have the infringement established.

The action shall be admissible only if the institution concerned has first been called upon to act. If, within two months of being so called upon, the institution concerned has not defined its position, the action may be brought within a further period of two months.

Any natural or legal person may, under the conditions laid down in the preceding paragraphs, complain to the Court of Justice that an institution of the Community has failed to address to that person any act other than a recommendation or an opinion.

Article 148 of the Euratom Treaty is in identical terms.

ECSC Treaty

Article 35

Wherever the High Authority is required by this Treaty, or by rules laid down for the implementation thereof, to take a decision or make a recommendation and fails to fulfil this obligation, it shall be for States, the Council, undertakings or associations, as the case may be, to raise the matter with the High Authority.

The same shall apply if the High Authority, where empowered by this Treaty, or by rules laid down for the implementation thereof, to take a decision or make a recommendation, abstains from doing so and such abstention constitutes a misuse of powers.

If at the end of two months the High Authority has not taken any decision or made any recommendation, proceedings may be instituted before the Court within one month against the implied decision of refusal which is to be inferred from the silence of the High Authority on the matter.

1. FAILURE TO DEFINE POSITION

In the case of the EEC and Euratom Treaties, the defendant institution will not have 'failed to act' if it has 'defined its position'. Thus, where an applicant has called on the Commission to initiate proceedings against a Member State and the Commission has decided not to initiate such proceedings, no action for annulment will lie against that decision.

Case 48/65 Alfons Lütticke GmbH and Others v Commission
[1966] ECR 19; [1966] CMLR 378

The Court

In a letter dated 15 March 1965, the applicants made an application to the Commission on the basis of Article 175 of the Treaty.

The applicants requested that the Commission take a decision ('Beschluß') to the effect that, as from 1 January 1962, the imposition by the Federal Republic of Germany of a turnover equalisation tax of 4% on the importation of powdered milk and other dried milk products is an infringement of Article 95 of the Treaty and that it should decide ('beschließen') to initiate against the Federal Republic the procedure laid down in Article 169 and inform the applicants of the decisions ('Beschlüsse') adopted.

After considering this request, the Commission informed the applicants in a letter dated 14 May 1965 that it did not share their opinion that the said turnover equalisation tax constituted an infringement of Article 95 of the Treaty.

...the applicants complain of failure to act under Article 175.

The defendant claims that the alternative application is ... inadmissible.

Under the terms of the second paragraph of Article 175, proceedings for failure to act may only be brought if at the end of a period of two months from being called upon to act the institution has not defined its position.

It is established that the Commission has defined its position and has notified this position to the applicants within the prescribed period.

The plea of inadmissibility is therefore well founded.

2. FAILURE TO ADOPT A MEASURE

Article 175 of the EEC Treaty, like Article 173, distinguishes between the Member States and institutions on the one hand and natural and legal persons on the other. The former are privileged applicants: they may initiate proceedings without proof of legal interest. The latter may challenge a failure to act only when the defendant was under a duty to adopt a measure in relation to the applicant.

Case 13/83 Parliament v Council
[1985] ECR 1513; [1986] 1 CMLR 138

The Parliament brought an action for a declaration that the Council had infringed the EEC Treaty by failing to introduce a common policy for transport and in particular by failing to reach a decision on sixteen specified proposals submitted by the Commission in relation to transport. The Council objected to the admissibility of the action on the ground, among others, that the Parliament lacked capacity. The Court rejected that objection to admissibility (for the appropriate extract, see Chapter 1, p. 35). The Council then raised the objection that the Parliament had failed to comply with the conditions laid down in Article 175 regarding the steps to be taken prior to bringing an action.

The Court

...

The Council considers that the conditions governing the procedure prior to an action which are laid down in Article 175 have not been complied with. In the first place the Council was not 'called upon to act', within the meaning of Article 175, by the letter from the President of the European Parliament of 21 September 1982, and in the second place the Council 'defined its position' with regard to that letter for the purposes of Article 175 by supplying the Parliament with a full report on its activities with regard to the common transport policy referred to in the aforementioned letter of 21 September 1982.

...

The Court is of the opinion that the conditions laid down by the second paragraph of Article 175 were satisfied in the present case. After expressly referring to that provision the Parliament clearly stated in the letter from its President that it was calling upon the Council to act pursuant to Article 175 and appended a list of actions which in its opinion ought to be undertaken by the Council to remedy its failure.

The Council's reply, on the other hand, was confined to setting out what action it had already taken in relation to transport without commenting 'on the legal aspects' of the correspondence initiated by the Parliament. *The reply neither denied nor confirmed the alleged failure to act nor gave any indication of the Council's views as to the measures which, according to the Parliament, remained to be taken. Such a reply cannot be regarded as a definition of position within the meaning of the second paragraph of Article 175.*

Moreover, the Court considers that in the present case the Council's observations in relation to its discretion in implementing the Common Transport Policy are not germane to the question whether the specific conditions in Article 175 were complied with. They relate to the more general issue of whether the absence of a Common Transport Policy can amount to a failure to act for the purposes of that provision, an issue which will be considered subsequently in this judgment.

It follows that the second objection of inadmissibility must also be rejected.

...

Case 246/81 Nicholas William Lord Bethell v Commission
[1982] ECR 2277; [1982] 3 CMLR 300

Lord Bethell, a Member of the European Parliament and Chairman of the Freedom of the Skies Campaign, wrote to the Commission calling upon it to take action under Article 89 of the EEC Treaty against agreements and concerted practices which, in his allegation, existed between airlines operating scheduled flights as regards passenger fares in Europe. The Director-General for Competition sent a reply, with which Lord Bethell was not satisfied. He therefore brought proceedings in the European Court, contending that in so far as the Commission's reply amounted to an 'act' it should be annulled under Article 173; and in so far as it amounted to a failure to act, it should be the subject of a declaration under Article 175. The Court dismissed the action as inadmissible.

The Court

In the words of the second paragraph of Article 173, any natural or legal person may, under the conditions laid down in that article, institute proceedings 'against a decision addressed to that person or against a decision which, although in the form of a regulation or a decision addressed to another person, is of direct and individual concern to the former'.

According to the third paragraph of Article 175, any natural or legal person may, under the conditions laid down in the article, complain to the Court that an institution of the Community 'has failed to address to that person any act other than a recommendation or an opinion'.

It appears from the provisions quoted that the applicant, for his application to be admissible, must be in a position to establish either that he is the addressee of a measure of the Commission having specific legal effects with regard to him, which is, as such, capable of being declared void, or that the Commission, having been duly called upon to act in pursuance of the second paragraph of Article 175, has failed to adopt in relation to him a measure which he was legally entitled to claim by virtue of the rules of Community law.

In reply to a question from the Court the applicant stated that the measure to which he believed himself to be entitled was 'a response, an adequate answer to his complaint saying either that the Commission was going to act upon it or saying that it was not and, if not, giving reasons'. Alternatively the applicant took the view that the letter addressed to him on 17 July 1981 by the Director-General for Competition was to be described as an act against which proceedings may be instituted under the second paragraph of Article 173.

The principal question to be resolved in this case is whether the Commission had, under the rules of Community law, the right and the duty to adopt in respect of the applicant a decision in the sense of the request made by the applicant to the Commission in his letter of 13 May 1981. It is apparent from the content of that letter and from the explanations given during the proceedings that the applicant is asking the Commission to undertake an investigation with regard to the airlines in the matter of the fixing of air fares with a view to a possible application to them of the provisions of the Treaty with regard to competition.

It is clear therefore that the applicant is asking the Commission not to take a decision in respect of him, but to open an inquiry with regard to third parties and to take decisions in respect of them. No doubt the applicant, in his double capacity as a user of the airlines and a leading member of an organisation of users of air passenger services, has an indirect interest, as other users may have, in such proceedings and their possible outcome, but he is nevertheless not in the precise legal position of the actual addressee of a decision which may be declared void under the second paragraph of Article 173 or in that of the potential addressee of a legal measure which the Commission has a duty to adopt with regard to him, as is the position under the third paragraph of Article 175.

It follows that the application is inadmissible from the point of view of both Article 175 and Article 173.

III THE PLEA OF ILLEGALITY

EEC Treaty

Article 184

Notwithstanding the expiry of the period laid down in the third paragraph of Article 173, any party may, in proceedings in which a regulation of the Council or of the Commission is in issue, plead the grounds specified in the first paragraph of Article 173, in order to invoke before the Court of Justice the inapplicability of that regulation.

Article 156 of the Euratom Treaty is in identical terms. In the case of the ECSC Treaty, Article 36 enables parties to plead the illegality of decisions or recommendations in the course of an appeal against a pecuniary sanction.

ECSC Treaty

Article 36

Before imposing a pecuniary sanction or ordering a periodic penalty payment as provided for in this Treaty, the High Authority must give the party concerned the opportunity to submit its comments.

The Court shall have unlimited jurisdiction in appeals against pecuniary sanctions and periodic penalty payments imposed under this Treaty.

In support of its appeal, a party may, under the same conditions as in the first paragraph of Article 33 of this Treaty, contest the legality of the decision or recommendation which that party is alleged not to have observed.

The plea of illegality does not constitute a separate cause of action. Its purpose is to enable a party to proceedings before the Court, which have already been initiated on some other jurisdictional basis, to plead that a regulation is inapplicable.

1. INAPPLICABILITY INVOKED BEFORE A NATIONAL COURT

Joined Cases 31 and 33/62 Milchwerke Heinz Wöhrmann & Sohn KG and Alfons Lütticke GmbH v Commission [1962] ECR 501; [1963] CMLR 152

The applicants initiated proceedings in the European Court for the purpose of challenging a decision by which the Commission had authorised Germany to impose countervailing duties on imports of powdered milk. Since the applicants were unable to invoke Article 173 (by reason of passage of time and apparently by reason of lack of legal interest) they relied on Article 184 of the EEC Treaty.

The Court

Before examining the question whether the contested measures are of their nature decisions or regulations, it is necessary to examine whether Article 184 empowers the Court to adjudicate upon the inapplicability of a regulation when this is invoked in proceedings – as in the present case – before a national court or tribunal.

Article 184 enables any party, notwithstanding the expiry of the period laid down in the third paragraph of Article 173, to invoke before the Court of Justice, for the purpose of making an application for annulment, the inapplicability of a regulation in proceedings in which it is at issue and to plead the grounds specified in the first paragraph of Article 173.

Because Article 184 does not specify before which court or tribunal the proceedings in which the regulation is at issue must be brought, the applicants conclude that the inapplicability of that regulation may in any event be invoked before the Court of Justice. This would mean that there would exist a method of recourse running concurrently with that available under Article 173.

This is however not the meaning of Article 184. *It is clear from the wording and the general scheme of this article that a declaration of the inapplicability of a regulation is only contemplated in proceedings brought before the Court of Justice itself under some other provision of the Treaty, and then only incidentally and with limited effect.*

More particularly, it is clear from the reference to the time limit laid down in Article 173 that Article 184 is applicable only in the context of proceedings brought before the Court of Justice and that it does not permit the said time limit to be avoided.

The sole object of Article 184 is thus to protect an interested party against the application of an illegal regulation, without thereby in any way calling in issue the regulation itself, which can no longer be challenged because of the expiry of the time limit laid down in Article 173.

It must be stressed that the Treaty clearly defines the respective jurisdictions of the Court of Justice and of national courts or tribunals. In fact, by virtue of both Article 177 and Article 20 of the Protocol on the Statute of the Court of Justice of the European Economic Community, the decision to suspend proceedings and to refer a case to this Court is one for the national court or tribunal.

If the parties to an action pending before a national court or tribunal were entitled to make a direct request to this Court for a preliminary ruling, they could compel the national court to suspend proceedings pending a decision of the Court of Justice. Neither the Treaty nor the Protocol, however, imposes such a limitation on the powers of the national court.

Although, therefore, Article 184 does not provide sufficient grounds to enable the Court of Justice to give a decision at the present stage, Article 177 does empower the Court to give a ruling if a national court or tribunal were to refer proceedings instituted before it to the Court.

In the light of all these considerations, the Court must declare that it has no jurisdiction to consider the present applications, both insofar as they seek the annulment of the contested measures and insofar as they seek to have them declared inapplicable. It is unnecessary therefore to decide upon the question of the Court's jurisdiction with regard to the exact nature of the measures of the Commission which are challenged by the applicants.

2. ACTS ANALOGOUS TO REGULATIONS IN THEIR EFFECTS

On the other hand, the field of application of Article 184 includes acts of the institutions which, although not in the form of regulations, nevertheless produce similar effects.

Case 92/78 Simmenthal SpA v Commission
[1979] ECR 777; [1980] 1 CMLR 25

Simmenthal, an Italian company engaged in trade in agricultural products, brought proceedings for the annulment of a decision fixing selling prices for frozen beef. In support of its application, it relied on Article 184 of the EEC Treaty for the purpose of pleading the illegality of certain regulations which constituted the legal basis of the contested decision. It also relied on that article for the purpose of pleading the illegality of certain 'notices of invitation to tender'. The Court ruled that it was open to Simmenthal to invoke Article 184 to that effect.

The Court

While the applicant formally challenges Commission Decision No 78/258 it has at the same time criticised, in reliance on Article 184 of the EEC Treaty, certain aspects of the 'linking' system in the form in which it has been implemented pursuant to the new Article 14 of Regulation No 805/68, by Regulations No 2900/77 and No 2901/77 and also by the notices of invitations to tender of 13 January 1978.

Article 184 reads: 'Notwithstanding the expiry of the period laid down in the third paragraph of Article 173, any party may, in proceedings in which a regulation of the Council or the Commission is in issue, plead the grounds specified in the first paragraph of Article 173, in order to invoke before the Court of Justice the inapplicability of that regulation'.

There is no doubt that this provision enables the applicant to challenge indirectly during the proceedings, with a view to obtaining the annulment of the contested decision, the validity of the measures laid down by regulation which form the legal basis of the latter.

On the other hand there are grounds for questioning whether Article 184 applies to the notices of invitations to tender of 13 January 1978 when according to its wording it only provides for the calling in question of 'regulations'.

These notices are general acts which determine in advance and objectively the rights and obligations of the traders who wish to participate in the invitations to tender which these notices make public.

As the Court in its judgment of 12 June 1958 in Case 15/57 *Compagnie des Hauts Fourneaux de Chasse* v *High Authority of the European Coal and Steel Community* [1957 and 1958] ECR 211, and in its judgment of 13 June 1956 in Case 9/56 *Meroni & Co., Industrie Metallurgidche SpA.* v *High Authority of the European Coal and Steel Community* [1957 and 1958] ECR 133, has already held in connection with Article 36 of the ECSC Treaty, Article 184 of the EEC Treaty gives expression to a general principle conferring upon any party to proceedings the right to challenge, for the purpose of obtaining the annulment of a decision of direct and individual concern to that party, the validity of previous acts of the institutions which form the legal basis of the decision which is being attacked, if that party was not entitled under Article 173 of the Treaty to bring a direct action challenging those acts by which it was thus affected without having been in a position to ask that they be declared void.

The field of application of the said article must therefore include acts of the institutions which, although they are not in the form of a regulation, nevertheless produce similar effects and on those grounds may not be challenged under Article 173 by natural or legal persons other than Community institutions and Member States.

This wide interpretation of Article 184 derives from the need to provide those persons who are precluded by the second paragraph of Article 173 from instituting proceedings directly in respect of general acts with the benefit of a judicial review of them at the time when they are affected by implementing decisions which are of direct and individual concern to them.

The notices of invitations to tender of 13 January 1978 in respect of which the applicant was unable to initiate proceedings are a case in point, seeing that only the decision taken in consequence of the tender which it had submitted in answer to a specific invitation to tender could be of direct and individual concern to it.

There are therefore good grounds for declaring that the applicant's challenge during the proceedings under Article 184, which relates not only to the above-mentioned regulations but also to the notices of invitations to tender of 13 January 1978, is admissible, though the latter are not in the strict sense measures laid down by regulation.

IV DAMAGES

The contractual liability of the Communities is governed by the law of the contract in question: and disputes to which the Community is a party are not for that reason alone excluded from national jurisdiction. It follows that proceedings to establish contractual liability may be initiated in national courts. The Protocol on Privileges and Immunities imposes limits on the enforcement of any judgment so obtained. In the case of non-contractual liability, jurisdiction is conferred on the Court of Justice of the European Communities.

EEC Treaty

Article 178

The Court of Justice shall have jurisdiction in disputes relating to the compensation for damage provided for in the second paragraph of Article 215.

...

Article 183

Save where jurisdiction is conferred on the Court by this Treaty, disputes to which the Community is a party shall not on that ground be excluded from the jurisdiction of the courts or tribunals of the Member States.

...

Article 215

The contractual liability of the Community shall be governed by the law applicable to the contract in question.

In the case of non-contractual liability, the Community shall, in accordance with the general principles common to the laws of the Member States, make good any damage caused by its institutions or by its servants in the performance of their duties.

Articles 151, 155 and 188 of the Euratom Treaty are worded identically. Article 40 of the ECSC Treaty limits non-contractual liability to cases where fault has occurred.

ECSC Treaty

Article 40

Without prejudice to the first paragraph of Article 34, the Court shall have jurisdiction to order pecuniary reparation from the Community, on application by the injured party, to make good any injury caused in carrying out this Treaty by a wrongful act or omission on the part of the Community in the performance of its functions.

The Court shall also have jurisdiction to order the Community to make good any injury caused by a personal wrong by a servant of the Community in the performance of his duties. The personal liability of its servants towards the Community shall be governed by the provisions laid down in their Staff Regulations or the Conditions of Employment applicable to them.

All other disputes between the Community and persons other than its servants to which the provisions of this Treaty or the rules laid down for the implementation thereof do not apply shall be brought before national courts or tribunals.

1. UNLAWFUL ACT OR OMISSION

The action for non-contractual liability (damages) is an autonomous form of action. It is not subject to the procedural rules, nor to the requirements as to *locus standi*, which are applicable in actions for annulment. The essential feature of the action is an unlawful act or omission attributable to the Community causing pecuniary loss to the applicant.

Case 175/84 Krohn Import-Export v Commission 26 February 1986

Krohn claimed compensation for damage suffered as a result of the refusal of the Bundesanstalt für Landwirtschaftliche Marketordnung, acting on instructions from the Commission, to grant it import licences for imports of manioc from Thailand. The instructions co-issued by the Commission (in November and December 1982) were given in pursuance of statutory power inferred by Regulation No 2029/82 of 22 July 1982, (OJ 1982, L 218/8). The Commission raised three objections to admissibility: (1) that the action for damages is not intended to enable the Court to examine the validity of decisions taken by national agencies; (2) that such an action is admissible only when the applicant has exhausted the procedure enabling him to seek the annulment of the national authority's decision in national courts; and (3) that an action for damages cannot be brought so as to nullify the legal effects of an individual decision which has become definitive.

The Court
First Argument against Inadmissibility

...

Where, as in this case, the decision adversely affecting the applicant was adopted by a national body acting in order to ensure the implementation of Community rules, it is necessary, in order to establish the jurisdiction of the Court, to determine whether the unlawful conduct alleged in support of the application for compensation is in fact the responsibility of a Community institution and cannot be attributed to the national body.

In support of its application for compensation, the applicant confines itself to pleading the illegality of the telex messages sent to the Bundesanstalt by the Commission on 23 November and 21 December 1982.

With regard to that point, it is clear from the very wording of Article 7(1) of Regulation No 2029/82 that its provisions do not merely confer upon the Commission the right to give an opinion on the decision to be adopted in the context of the cooperation between itself and the national bodies responsible for applying the Community rules, but actually empower it to insist that such national bodies refuse requests for import licences where the conditions laid down in the Cooperation Agreement have not been fulfilled.

Moreover, the information submitted by the parties and their arguments before the Court make it clear that the Commission's telex messages of 23 November and 21 December 1982 were intended as an effective exercise of the power conferred upon it by the provisions and that their effect was to instruct the Bundesanstalt to refuse the import licences at issue if no satisfactory reply was given to the requests for information made to Krohn.

It follows from the foregoing that *the unlawful conduct alleged by the applicant in order to establish its claim for compensation is to be attributed not to the Bundesanstalt, which was bound to comply with the Commission's instructions, but to the Commission itself.* The Court therefore has jurisdiction to entertain the action brought by Krohn, and the first argument against admissibility must be rejected.

Second Argument against Admissibility

...

According to an established body of decisions of the Court, the application for compensation provided for by Article 178 and the second paragraph of Article 215 of the Treaty was introduced as an autonomous form of action with a particular purpose to fulfil within the system of actions and subject to conditions on its use dictated by its specific nature.

Nonetheless, it is true that such actions must be examined in the light of the whole system of legal protection for the individual established by the Treaty and that *the admissibility of such an action may in certain cases be dependent on the exhaustion of all national rights of action available to obtain the annulment of a national authority's decision. In order for that to be the case, however, it is necessary that those national rights of action should provide an effective means of protection for the individual concerned and be capable of resulting in compensation for the damage alleged.*

That is not the case here. There is nothing to suggest that the annulment of the Bundesanstalt's decision and the issue, after a lapse of several years, of the import licences claimed in 1982 would compensate Krohn for the damage suffered by it at that time; such an annulment would therefore not remove the need for the applicant, if it is to obtain compensation, to bring an action before the Court under Article 178 and the second paragraph of Article 215 of the Treaty.

In those circumstances, the admissibility of this action cannot be made dependent on the exhaustion of the national rights of action available against the Bundesanstalt's decision, and the second argument against admissibility must also be rejected.

...

Third Argument against Admissibility

...

As the Court has pointed out above, the action provided for by Article 178 and the second paragraph of Article 215 of the Treaty was introduced as an autonomous form of action with a particular purpose to fulfil. It differs from an action for annulment in particular in that its purpose is not to set aside a specific measure but to repair the damage caused by an institution. It follows that *the existence of an individual decision which has become definitive cannot act as a bar to the admissibility of such an action.*

The decision cited by the Commission relates solely to the exceptional case where an application for compensation is brought for the payment of an amount precisely equal to the duty which the applicant was required to pay under an individual decision, so that the application seeks in fact the withdrawal of that individual decision. At all events, such considerations are foreign to this case.

It follows that the third argument against admissibility must also be rejected.

2. LIABILITY FOR ACTS OF SERVANTS OF THE COMMUNITIES

An act done by a servant of the Communities will be attributable to the Communities only if it is the necessary extension of tasks entrusted to the institutions. Thus, for example, the driving of a private car by a Community servant does not constitute the performance of his duties save in the exceptional cases in which this activity cannot be carried out other than under the authority of the Community. The parameters of this authority were outlined in the case of *Sayag* v *Leduc*.

Case 5/68 Sayag v Leduc [1968] ECR 395; [1969] CMLR 12

The Court

...

The immunity from legal proceedings conferred on officials and other agents of the Community thus only covers acts which, by their nature, represent a participation of the person entitled to the immunity in the performance of the tasks of the institution to which he belongs.

On the other hand it matters little whether it is a question of the actual exercise of 'normal duties or those prescribed under the Staff Regulations', only of an act performed on the occasion of the exercise of those duties if the position is that the act in question serves directly for the accomplishment of a Community task in the sense defined above.

Hence, driving a motor vehicle is not in the nature of an act performed in an official capacity save in the exceptional cases in which this activity cannot be carried out otherwise than under the authority of the Community and by its own servants.

3. LIABILITY FOR ACTS OF NATIONAL AUTHORITIES

Similarly, an action for repayment of sums paid to a national authority under Community law cannot be brought in the Court of Justice of the European Communities under Article 215; for in such proceedings the Commission is not the correct defendant. The plaintiff's proper course of action is to sue the national authority in the national courts.

Case 96/71 R. and V. Haegeman Sprl v Commission
[1972] ECR 1005; [1973] CMLR 365

Haegemann was a Belgian trading company engaged in the importation of wines from Greece, then outside the Community. It claimed to have suffered loss by reason of the levying of a countervailing charge on the import of wine from Greece to Belgium. The charge was levied by the Belgian authorities in pursuance of a provision in a Council regulation.

The Court

...

Disputes concerning the levying on individuals of the charges and levies referred to by this provision must be resolved, applying Community law, by the national authorities and following the practices laid down by the law of the Member States.

Issues, therefore, which are raised during a procedure as to the interpretation and validity of regulations establishing the Communities' own resources must be brought before the national courts which have at their disposal the procedure under Article 177 of the Treaty in order to ensure the uniform application of Community law.

...

The applicant maintains further that by reason of the defendant's behaviour it has suffered exceptional damage as a result of loss of profit, unforeseen financial outlay and losses on existing contracts.

The question of the possible liability of the Community is in the first place linked with that of the legality of the levying of the charge in question.

It has just been found that, in the context of the relationship between individuals and the taxation authority which has levied the charge in dispute, the latter question comes under the jurisdiction of the national courts.

Accordingly, at the present stage the claim for compensation for possible damage must be dismissed.

Case 99/74 Société des grands Moulins des Antilles v Commission [1975] ECR 1531

The applicants claimed damages allegedly occasioned by the implied refusal of the Commission to pay refunds due in respect of exports of cereals from the French Overseas Department to third countries.

The Court

The action for damages provided for in Articles 178 and 215 of the Treaty was included as an independent form of action, with a particular purpose to fulfil within the system of legal remedies, and subject to conditions on its use arising out of its specific nature.

The refusal by a Community institution to pay a debt which may be owed by a Member State under Community law is not a matter involving the non-contractual liability of the Community.

For an action involving non-contractual liability to lie it is necessary that an injury arising from an act or omission of the Community be alleged.

...

The provisions of Community law, especially Article 10 of Regulation No 1041/67 and Article 3 of Regulation No 1554/73, leave no doubt that payment or refusal of payment are measures appropriate to the national authorities.

It is thus for the national courts having jurisdiction in the matter to give a ruling on the legality of such measures, in pursuance of Community law, within the forms laid down by national law, following recourse, where necessary, to Article 177 of the Treaty.

Consequently, it is impossible to accept the applicant's attempt to disregard the precise wording of the implementing regulations, providing that the national authorities have the requisite powers, the more so since any rights which it may have against those authorities cannot depend upon a prior financial authorisation by the Community.

Since the applicant has failed to allege an injury arising from an act or omission of the Community capable of affecting it adversely, its application is inadmissible under Article 178 of the Treaty.

4. COMPETENCE TO AWARD DAMAGES

The fact that a remedy may be available before a national court is not sufficient to disseise the European Court of jurisdiction. For the purpose of determining whether the European Court is competent to make an award of damages, the test to be applied is as follows: is the action in fact directed against measures adopted by the Community institutions?

Case 126/76 Firma Gebrüder Dietz v Commission [1977] ECR 2431

The applicants, a German company trading with Italy, claimed damages to compensate them for losses suffered by reason of the application to Italy of a Commission regulation governing monetary compensatory amounts. They initiated proceedings in the German courts and in the European Court.

The Court

The applicant, which took the view that it was adversely affected by an implementing measure adopted by the national authorities, should have contested that measure before the national court since that course of action was, where appropriate, such as to prompt the German courts to submit to the Court of Justice under Article 177 of the Treaty the question of the validity of Regulation No 2887/71.

The applicant instituted proceedings in the Federal Republic of Germany but as it was uncertain whether the court would comply with its suggestion that the question should be referred to the Court of Justice for a preliminary ruling, it lodged the present application bearing in mind the period of limitation laid down in Article 43 of the Protocol on the Statute of the Court of Justice.

According to the applicant, the damage suffered does not result from measures adopted by the national authorities but from an omission on the part of the Commission within the context of the regulations issued in implementation of Article 6 of Regulation No 974/71.

The Court has only stated that it has no jurisdiction in cases in which the application was in fact directed against measures adopted by the national authorities for the purpose of applying provisions of Community law.

Even if the Court, within the context of proceedings for a preliminary ruling, considered that the rules applicable were such as to cause damage because of the absence of appropriate transitional measures, the national court would not be empowered to adopt those measures itself, with the result that a direct application to the Court on the basis of Article 215 of the Treaty would still be necessary.

The matter has been brought before the Court within the bounds of its jurisdiction and it is therefore under a duty to examine whether the alleged omission in the Community regulations issued in implementation of Article 6 of Regulation No 974/71 constitutes an infringement of the law such as to incur the liability of the Community.

The application is therefore admissible.

5. LIABILITY IN THE ABSENCE OF FAULT

It remains unsettled whether liability can be established under Article 215 in the absence of fault on the part of the Communities. The available indications suggest that fault is not an essential element in liability. Certainly the Court has been prepared to conclude that the Community incurred liability where it was at fault only to the extent of disclosing the identity of an informant, after he had left his employment, to the employer about whom he supplied information.

Case 145/83 Stanley George Adams v Commission
[1985] ECR 3539; [1986] 1 CMLR 506

In 1973 Stanley Adams sent a letter to the Commission describing a number of anti-competitive activities by his employer, Roche, in Basle. He stated in the letter that he was about to leave his employment with Roche and that thereafter he would be prepared to appear in any court to give sworn evidence on his statements. The Commission began an investigation into the activities of Roche and took a decision against the company. Roche asked the Commission to disclose the identity of their informant. The Commission refused to do so. Nevertheless the suspicion of Roche fell upon Mr Adams. On New Year's Eve 1974 Mr Adams was arrested in Switzerland and charged with economic espionage. He was held in solitary confinement and not permitted to communicate with his family. His wife was interrogated by the police and committed suicide. According to the police records, Mr Adams confessed that he was the Commission's informant. On February 1975 the Commission confirmed that he was their informant. In March 1975 Mr Adams was released on bail. He was subsequently sentenced to one year's imprisonment (suspended). He sued the Commission, claiming that the latter had incurred non-contractual liability by disclosing his identity to Roche.

The Court

...

As regards the existence of a duty of confidentiality it must be pointed out that Article 214 of the EEC Treaty lays down an obligation, in particular for the members and the servants of the institutions of the Community, 'not to disclose information of the kind covered by the obligation of professional secrecy, in particular information about undertakings, their business relations or their cost components'. Although that provision primarily refers to information gathered from undertakings, the expression 'in particular' shows that the principle in question is a general one which applies also to information supplied by natural persons, if that information is 'of the kind' that is confidential. That is particularly so in the case of information supplied on a purely voluntary basis but accompanied by a request for confidentiality in order to protect the informant's anonymity. An institution which accepts such information is bound to comply with such a condition.

As regards the case before the Court, it is quite clear from the applicant's letter of 25 February 1973 that he requested the Commission not to reveal his identity. It cannot therefore be denied that the Commission was bound by a duty of confidentiality towards the applicant in that respect. In fact the parties disagree not so much as to the existence of such a duty but as to whether the Commission was bound by a duty of confidentiality after the applicant had left his employment with Roche.

In that respect it must be pointed out that the applicant did not qualify his request by indicating a period upon the expiry of which the Commission would be released from its duty of confidentiality regarding the identity of its informant. No such indication can be inferred from the fact that the applicant was prepared to appear before any court after he had left Roche. The giving of evidence before a court implies that the witness has been duly summoned, that he is under a duty to answer the questions put to him, and is, in return, entitled to all the guarantees provided by a judicial procedure. The applicant's offer to confirm the accuracy of his information under such conditions cannot therefore be interpreted as a general statement releasing the Commission from its duty of confidentiality. Nor can any such intention be inferred from the applicant's subsequent conduct.

It must therefore be stated that the Commission was under a duty to keep the applicant's identity secret even after he had left his employer.

...

It must therefore be concluded that in principle the Community is bound to make good the damage resulting from the discovery of the applicant's identity by means of the documents handed over to Roche by the Commission. It must however be recognised that the extent of the Commission's liability is diminished by reason of the applicant's own negligence.

...

6. LIABILITY FOR LEGISLATIVE ACTS

Special problems arise when liability is attributed to the Community by reason of its legislative acts. The Court has held that where legislative action involving choices of economic policy is concerned, the Community does not incur non-contractual liability unless a sufficiently flagrant violation of a superior rule of law for the protection of the individual has occurred.

Case 5/71 Aktien-Zuckerfabrik Schöppenstedt v Council [1971] ECR 975

The applicant claimed that the Community incurred non-contractual liability by adopting Regulation No 769/68 of 18 June 1968, (OJ 1968, L 143/1) on sugar prices. In its submission, this regulation infringed Article 40(3) of the EEC Treaty according to which any common price policy should be based on common criteria and uniform methods of calculation.

The Court

In the present case the non-contractual liability of the Community presupposes at the very least the unlawful nature of the act alleged to be the cause of the damage. Where legislative action involving measures of economic policy is concerned, the Community does not incur non-contractual liability for damage suffered by individuals as a consequence of that action, by virtue of the provisions contained in Article 215, second paragraph, of the Treaty, unless a sufficiently flagrant violation of a superior rule of law for the protection of the individual has occurred. For that reason the Court, in the present case, must first consider whether such a violation has occurred.

...

The difference referred to does not constitute discrimination because it is the result of a new system of common organisation of the market in sugar which does not recognise a single fixed price but has a maximum and minimum price and lays down a framework of prices within which the level of actual prices depends on the development of the market. Thus it is not possible to challenge the justification of transitional rules which proceeded on the basis that where the previous prices were already within the framework set up they must be governed by market forces and which therefore required the payment of dues only in cases where the previous prices were still too low to come within the new framework of prices and authorised compensation only in cases where the previous prices were too high to come within the said framework.

In addition, having regard to the special features of the system established with effect from 1 July 1968, the Council by adopting Regulation No 769/68 satisfied the requirements of Article 37 of Regulation No 1009/67.

It is also necessary to dismiss the applicant's claim that Regulation No 769/68 infringed the provisions of Article 40 of the Treaty because the method of calculating the compensation and dues for the raw sugar stocks was derived from that adopted for white sugar, which could, according to the applicant, result in the unequal treatment of the producers of raw sugar. Although, relying on hypothetical cases, the applicant stated that the calculation methods selected did not necessarily lead to uniform results with regard to producers of raw sugar, it was not proved that this could have been the case on 1 July 1968.

The applicant's action founded upon the Council's liability does not therefore satisfy the first condition mentioned above and must be dismissed.

Case 238/78 Ireks-Arkady GmbH v Council and Commission [1979] ECR 2955

In Joined Cases 117/76 and 16/77 *Ruckdeschel* v *Hauptzollamt Hamburg* [1977] ECR 1753, the Court established that the abolition of refunds for quellmehl as from 1 August 1974, together with the retention of refunds for pre-gelatinised starch, was incompatible with the principle of equality. Ireks-Arkady, quellmehl producers, then brought an action for damages.

The Court

The finding that a legal situation resulting from the legislative measures of the Community is unlawful is not sufficient in itself to give rise to such liability. The Court has already expressed that view in its judgment of 25 May 1978 in Joined Cases 83/76 and others *Bayerische HNL Vermehrungsbetriebe GmbH and Co KG and Others* v *Council and Commission* [1978] ECR 1209. In this regard, the Court recalled its settled case-law, according to which the Community does not incur liability on account of a legislative measure which involves choices of economic policy unless a sufficiently serious breach of a superior rule of law for the protection of the individual has occurred. Taking into consideration the principles in the legal systems of the Member States governing the liability of public authorities for damage caused to individuals by legislative measures, the Court said that in the context of Community provisions in which one of the chief features was the exercise of a wide discretion essential for the implementation of the Common Agricultural Policy, the Community did not incur liability unless the institution concerned manifestly and gravely disregarded the limits on the exercise of its powers.

In the circumstances of this case, the Court is led to the conclusion that there was on the part of the Council such a grave and manifest disregard of the limits on the exercise of its discretionary powers in matters of the Common Agricultural Policy. In this regard the Court notes the following findings in particular.

In the first place it is necessary to take into consideration that the principle of equality, embodied in particular in the second subparagraph of Article 40(3) of the EEC Treaty, which prohibits any discrimination in the common organisation of the agricultural markets, occupies a particularly important place among the rules of Community law intended to protect the interests of the individual. Secondly, the disregard of that principle in this case affected a limited and clearly defined group of commercial operators. It seems, in fact, that the number of quellmehl producers in the Community is very limited. Further, the damage alleged by the applicants goes beyond the bounds of the economic risks inherent in the activities in the sector concerned. Finally, equality of treatment with the producers of maize starch, which had been observed from the beginning of the common organisation of the market in cereals, was ended by the Council in 1974 without sufficient justification.

For those reasons the Court arrives at the conclusion that the Community incurs liability for the abolition of the refunds for quellmehl under Regulation No 1125/74 of the Council.

FURTHER READING

Barav, A., 'The Exception of Illegality in Community Law' 11 CMLRev (1974) 366

Bradley, K. St. C., 'The European Court and the Legal Basis of Community Legislation', 13 ELRev (1988) 379

Dinnage, J., 'Locus Standi and Article 173 EEC', 4 ELRev (1979) 15

Durand, A., 'Restriction or Damages: National Court or European Court', 1 ELRev (1975-6) 431

Greaves, R.M., 'Locus Standi under Article 173 when seeking Annulment of a Regulation', 11 ELRev (1986) 119

Harding, C., 'The Choice of Court Problem in Cases of Non-Contractual Liability under EEC Law', 16 CMLRev (1979) 389

Harding, C., 'Decisions addressed to Member States and Article 173 of the Treaty of Rome', 25 ICLQ (1976) 15

March Hunnings, N., 'The *Stanley Adams* Affair or the Biter Bit', 24 CMLRev (1987) 65

Oliver, P., 'Enforcing Community Rights in the English Courts', 50 MLRev (1987) 881

Rasmussen, H., 'Between Self-Restraint and Activism: A Judicial Policy for the European Court', 13 ELRev (1988) 28

Toth, A., 'The Law as it stands in the Appeal for Failure to Act' [1975-2] LIEI 65

4

ACTIONS AGAINST MEMBER STATES

The founding Treaties make provision for actions against Member States on the initiative of the Commission and on that of other Member States. Moreover, without making explicit provision to that effect they create the possibility of actions in national courts against Member States for the purpose of enforcing obligations imposed by Community law.

I INFRINGEMENT PROCEEDINGS INITIATED BY THE COMMISSION

EEC Treaty

Article 169

If the Commission considers that a Member State has failed to fulfil an obligation under this Treaty, it shall deliver a reasoned opinion on the matter after giving the State concerned the opportunity to submit its observations.

If the State concerned does not comply with the opinion within the period laid down by the Commission the latter may bring the matter before the Court of Justice.

Article 141 of the Euratom Treaty is in identical terms.

ECSC Treaty

Article 88

If the High Authority considers that a State has failed to fulfil an obligation under this Treaty, it shall record this failure in a reasoned decision after giving the State concerned the opportunity to submit its comments. It shall set the State a time limit for the fulfilment of its obligation.

The State may institute proceedings before the Court within two months of notification of the decision; the Court shall have unlimited jurisdiction in such cases.

If the State has not fulfilled its obligation by the time limit set by the High Authority, or if it brings an action which is dismissed, the High Authority may, with the assent of the Council acting by a two-thirds majority:

(a) suspend the payment of any sums which it may be liable to pay to the State in question under this Treaty;

(b) take measures, or authorise the other Member States to take measures, by way of derogation from the provisions of Article 4, in order to correct the effects of the infringement of the obligation.

Proceedings may be instituted before the Court against decisions taken under subparagraphs (a) and (b) within two months of their notification; the Court shall have unlimited jurisdiction in such cases.

If these measures prove ineffective, the High Authority shall bring the matter before the Council.

As the language of Article 169 makes clear, it authorises the Commission to initiate proceedings only when it considers that there has been a failure *on the part of a Member State* to fulfil an obligation. The liability of the Member State may arise whatever may be the agency whose action or inaction is the cause of the failure to fulfil the obligation.

Case 77/69 Commission v Belgium

[1970] ECR 237; [1974] 1 CMLR 203

The Commission brought proceedings against Belgium alleging that the latter had failed to fulfil its obligations under Article 95 of the EEC Treaty by applying different methods of calculation of duty for home-grown and for imported wood.

The Court

The defendant does not dispute the existence of discrimination resulting from the provisions which form the subject-matter of the proceedings.

Following a series of steps taken by the Commission the first of which dates back to 1963, the Belgian Government has shown its willingness to take the necessary measures with a view to eliminating the discrimination complained of.

A draft law intended to make possible a revision of the disputed scheme was put before Parliament in 1967 and provisions were later adopted in order to revive this draft law which had lapsed owing to the dissolution of the Belgian Parliament in the meanwhile.

In these circumstances the Belgian Government considers that the delay in enacting the law amounts as far as it is concerned to a 'case of *force majeure*'.

The obligations arising from Article 95 of the Treaty devolve upon States as such and the liability of a Member State under Article 169 arises whatever the agency of the State whose action or inaction is the cause of the failure to fulfil its obligations, even in the case of a constitutionally independent institution.

The objection raised by the defendant cannot therefore be sustained.

Although each Member State is free to delegate powers to its domestic authorities as it thinks fit, it may not be released from the obligation to give effect to the provisions of a directive by means of national provisions. Mere administrative practices, which by their nature may be altered at the whim of the administration, do not amount to fulfilment of an obligation deriving from a directive.

Case 96/81 Commission v Netherlands [1982] ECR 1791

The Commission brought proceedings against the Netherlands for a declaration that the latter had failed to fulfil its obligations under the Treaty by omitting to implement a Council directive on the quality of bathing water. The Netherlands Government argued that there was no need to introduce legislation on the subject since regional and local authorities were directly bound by the directive and they implemented it in the practical management of water quality.

The Court

...

The Netherlands Government referred to the fact that the supervision of the quality of water is carried out in the Netherlands within a framework of a decentralised system. The regional and local authorities are directly bound by the provisions of the directive and they implement it in the practical management of water quality, under the control of the national authorities.

It is true that each Member State is free to delegate powers to its domestic authorities as it considers fit and to implement the directive by means of measures adopted by regional or local authorities. That does not however release it from the obligation to give effect to the provisions of the directive by means of national provisions of a binding nature. The directive in question, adopted *inter alia* pursuant to Article 100 of the EEC Treaty, is intended to approximate the applicable laws, regulations and administrative provisions in the Member States. Mere administrative practices, which by their nature may be altered at the whim of the administration, may not be considered as constituting the proper fulfilment of the obligation deriving from that directive.

None of the matters put forward by the Netherlands Government justifies the conclusion that provisions of a binding nature have actually been adopted either by the national authorities or by regional or local authorities in order to determine for all bathing areas or for each of them the values applicable to bathing water for all the parameters indicated in the annex to the directive and in order to ensure that the quality of bathing conforms with the values thus determined. In particular, the prospective multiennial programme to which the Netherlands Government referred in its correspondence with the Commission prior to the commencement of these proceedings, affirming that that programme adopted the rules contained in the directive, constituted, at that time, nothing more than a set of guidelines for those responsible for the supervision of water quality and had no legally binding force. That programme could not therefore be considered as sufficient for the purpose of implementation of the directive.

In its observations on the Commission's reply to the questions put by the Court before the oral procedure and also during the oral procedure, the Netherlands Government again referred to an amendment of the Wet Verontreiniging Oppervlaktewateren [Law relating to the Pollution of Surface Water], which entered into force on 1 January 1982, claiming that by virtue of that amendment the prospective multiennial programme would enable the directive to be fully implemented. At the hearing the Commission, whilst not departing from its views, declared that that amendment to the law would, if supplemented by certain administrative measures, make it possible for the directive to be implemented properly. In that regard it must be pointed out, without its being necessary to consider whether, merely by reason of that amendment, the failure to fulfil the obligation might have been wholly remedied, that the measures needed to ensure the full implementation of the directive were not adopted within the prescribed periods and in any case did not exist when this action was brought.

It follows from the foregoing that the Kingdom of the Netherlands did not adopt within the prescribed periods the provisions needed to ensure the full implementation of the directive in question and must be declared to have failed to fulfil its obligations under the Treaty.

Before initiating proceedings under Article 169 of the EEC Treaty the Commission must deliver a reasoned opinion. That opinion delimits the scope of the infraction proceedings. Therefore the two documents must be founded on the same grounds and submissions.

Case 31/69 Commission v Italy [1970] ECR 25; [1970] CMLR 175

By a letter dated 12 July 1968 the Commission gave the Italian Government an opportunity to submit observations on the former's allegation that the latter had failed to comply with a number of regulations governing refunds on exports of agricultural products to third countries. In November 1968 the Commission delivered a reasoned opinion finding that Italy had failed to fulfil its obligations under those regulations. The Commission then initiated proceedings against Italy in the Court. Among the regulations on which the Commission relied in the proceedings before the Court were two, dated 27 and 28 June 1968, which applied the system of refunds to milk and milk products and to beef and veal. These had not been mentioned expressly in the reasoned opinion.

The Court

...

The Italian Government further claims that the present proceedings can only concern its obligations relating to products made subject to an organisation of the markets during the year 1967 and not to obligations relating to products which were only made so from 1 July 1968.

Despite the general nature of its wording, the Commission's letter of 12 July 1968 requesting the Italian Government to submit its observations in accordance with Article 169 cannot relate to delays in payments for products which were not then subject to the system of uniform refunds or which had at most only been so for several days.

Even if the Member State concerned does not consider it necessary to avail itself of the opportunity to submit its observations, such an opportunity constitutes an essential guarantee required by the Treaty and amounts to an essential procedural requirement in proceedings relating to the finding of a failure on the part of a Member State.

Respect for this guarantee means that the alleged failure to fulfil an obligation under regulations issued during or after the month of June 1968 must be excluded from these proceedings.

The purpose of the pre-litigation procedure is to enable the Member State to justify its position or to comply with the Treaty. There is no obligation incumbent on the Commission to specify in the reasoned opinion a further period within which a Member State can amend its law or practice so as to comply with its existing obligation.

Case 85/85 Commission v Belgium 18 March 1986

The Commission brought proceedings against Belgium for a declaration that the latter had failed to fulfil its obligations under Article 12(b) of the Protocol on Privileges and Immunities of the European Communities, by failing to ensure that the bye-laws of certain municipalities exempted officials and servants of the European Communities from tax on certain secondary residences.

The Court

...

In its first objection, the Belgian Government contends that, by allowing altogether less than two months to elapse between the formal notification of the infringement (12 February 1985), the reasoned opinion (8 March 1985) and the submission of the application (3 April 1985), the Commission contravened the principle that every Member State is entitled to be allowed a reasonable period of time by the Commission. In its view, the Commission's conduct is contrary to both the spirit and the letter of Article 169 of the Treaty. The pre-litigation procedure provided for by Article 169 should not be a means of exerting pressure on national governments but a procedure designed to establish a dialogue between the parties and to enable the dispute to be resolved if possible. The Belgian Government maintains that it was impossible to comply with the reasoned opinion within such a short period, in view of the considerable autonomy that Belgian municipalities enjoy in this area.

The Commission maintains that the objection of inadmissibility is unfounded. In its view, the periods prescribed were reasonable and sufficient to enable Belgium to put into effect the measures needed to terminate the infringement. It contends that the Belgian Government is not being confronted with this problem for the first time since it is aware of the numerous representations that the Commission has been making for over a year. The municipal councils could have adopted appropriate decisions and the complaints lodged by the officials concerned against the notices of assessment demanding payment of the tax could have been adjudicated upon within the prescribed period. Moreover, such measures were envisaged in a letter of 25 January 1985 sent to the Commission by Belgium's Permanent Representative to the European Communities.

In that regard, it must be borne in mind that the purpose of the pre-litigation procedure provided for by Article 169 of the Treaty, which forms part of the general supervisory tasks entrusted to the Commission by the first indent of Article 155, is to give the Member State concerned an opportunity either to justify its position or, if it so wishes, to comply of its own accord with the requirements of the Treaty. If that attempt to reach a settlement proves unsuccessful, the Member State concerned is requested to comply with its obligations as set out in the reasoned opinion within the period prescribed therein.

With regard to the period prescribed by the letter giving formal notice of the infringement, the Belgian Government does not deny that it was aware of the Commission's point of view long before proceedings were brought against it for failing to fulfil its obligations. The first letter from the Commission's Director General for Personnel and Administration to Belgium's Permanent Representative to the Communities, calling for joint consideration of the problem and for suspension of the application of the contested tax bye-laws, is dated 24 May 1984. That letter was followed by further representations in the same year. In his letter of 25 January 1985, Belgium's Permanent Representative refers to the steps contemplated by the Belgian Government in relation to the municipalities concerned. Discussions with the Commission continued until the dispatch of the letter giving formal notice of the infringement. In those circumstances it must be held that the Belgian Government was in a position to submit its observations even within the limited period of 15 days prescribed in the letter giving formal notice of the infringement.

With regard to the period prescribed in the reasoned opinion, it is clear that the Belgian Government was aware of the Commission's point of view long before the pre-litigation procedure was initiated. It must also be pointed out that the Belgian Government did not challenge the Commission's point of view in the course of any of the numerous exchanges of views which preceded the initiation of the pre-litigation procedure. Furthermore, the Belgian Government does not even maintain that it subsequently set in motion appropriate procedures in order to comply with the Commission's wishes or at least to suspend the application of the contested bye-laws pending a definitive solution. In those specific circumstances, the Belgian Government's contention that the period prescribed in the reasoned opinion was too short is unjustified.

Moreover, even if a Member State puts an end to its failure to comply with its obligations, the Commission remains competent to begin proceedings for a declaration that the Member State did in fact fail to fulfil its obligations: Case 39/72 *Commission v Italy* [1973] ECR 101; [1973] CMLR 439. Equally, the Commission may if it so chooses discontinue any proceedings pending against the Member State, but such discontinuance does not imply that the State's conduct is lawful.

Joined Cases 15 and 16/76 France v Commission [1979] ECR 321

The French Government sought the annulment of a decision by the Commission refusing to charge to the European Agricultural Guidance and Guarantee Fund certain expenses incurred by that Government. The refusal had its origin in a dispute between the French Government and the Commission about calculation of aids for distillation of wine. In 1972 the Commission had initiated proceedings against France under Article 169 of the EEC Treaty for failure to fulfil its obligations on the matter, but in 1973 it discontinued those proceedings. The French Government argued that in refusing to charge to the EAGGF the expenses in dispute, the Commission had misused the procedure by reopening the matter, once it had discontinued the infraction proceedings.

The Court

...

That argument, however, cannot be upheld.

In fact, the two procedures are independent of each other as they serve different aims and are subject to different rules.

The procedure under Article 169 of the Treaty on the ground of failure to comply with Treaty obligations is for the purpose of obtaining a declaration that the conduct of a Member State infringes Community law and of terminating that conduct; the Commission remains at liberty, if the Member State has put an end to the alleged failure, to discontinue the proceedings but such discontinuance does not constitute recognition that the contested conduct is lawful.

As Community law now stands the procedure for the discharge of the accounts, on the other hand, serves to determine not only that the expenditure was actually and properly incurred but also that the financial burden of the Common Agricultural Policy is correctly apportioned between the Member States and the Community and in this respect the Commission has no discretionary power to derogate from the rules regulating the allocation of expenses.

The sum in question which, in the opinion of the French Government, should be charged to the EAGGF, represents, in respect of all the quantities of wine which have been distilled, that proportion of the aid granted which corresponds to the rates fixed by Community rules whilst the proportion corresponding to the additional national aid should be borne by France.

The Commission objects to such a calculation, arguing that the national measure had the effect of distorting the distillation operation by extending it, in France, to far greater quantities of wine than would have been distilled on the basis of the Community measure alone.

In applying Community rules the Member States cannot unilaterally adopt additional measures which are such as to compromise the equality of treatment of traders throughout the Community and thus to distort competitive conditions between the Member States.

As the French national measure in question is therefore incompatible with Community law it is impossible to ascertain to what extent the total effect of the combined national and Community measures is due to one or other component part.

It is, in particular, impossible to establish with certainty what quantities of wine would have been distilled in France if the national measure had not been adopted.

Consequently neither the method of calculation used by the French Government nor a method based on the distillation estimates relied on by the Commission when setting up the operation makes it possible to apportion the expenses chargeable to the Community and to the Member State respectively.

In those circumstances the Commission had no choice but to refuse to charge to the EAGGF the expenditure incurred by the French authorities.

The application for annulment lodged by the French Government must therefore be dismissed.

II EXPEDITED PROCEEDINGS

The EEC Treaty provides for three expedited forms of proceeding in actions against Member States. Article 225 establishes a procedure for expedited consideration, *in camera*, of a claim that a Member State is making improper use of its power to derogate from the provisions of the Treaty in the interests of national security. Article 100A(4) creates a new (and hitherto untried) procedure for testing the allegation that a Member State is making improper use of its power to apply national provisions in the face of a measure of harmonisation adopted by the Community by qualified majority. Article 93 establishes a well-tried procedure for expedited hearings in cases involving State aids.

EEC Treaty

Article 93

1. The Commission shall, in cooperation with Member States, keep under constant review all systems of aid existing in those States. It shall propose to the latter any appropriate measures required by the progressive development or by the functioning of the Common Market.

2. If, after giving notice to the parties concerned to submit their comments, the Commission finds that aid granted by a State or through State resources is not compatible with the Common Market having regard to Article 92, or that such aid is being misused, it shall decide that the State concerned shall abolish or alter such aid within a period of time to be determined by the Commission.

If the State concerned does not comply with this decision within the prescribed time, the Commission or any other interested State may, in derogation from the provisions of Articles 169 and 170, refer the matter to the Court of Justice direct.

...

Case 70/72 Commission v Germany [1973] ECR 813; [1973] CMLR 741

The Commission brought an action under Article 93(2) for a declaration that Germany had disregarded a decision requiring Germany to put an end to a system of investment grants for the mining regions of North Rhine-Westphalia. By the same action the Commission ordered Germany to recover from mining companies in North Rhine-Westphalia any grants paid to them after the date of the Commission's decision.

The Court

The Federal Republic of Germany disputes the admissibility of the action, which has been brought on the basis of the first subparagraph to Article 93(2), on the ground that the decision of the Commission of 17 February 1971, contrary to a formal requirement of the Treaty, does not fix a period of time for compliance, but requires the system of aid in dispute to be ended 'without delay'; and that according to the categorical requirements of Article 93(2) the determination of such a period of time is a necessary condition precedent to the reference of the matter to the Court in accordance with the special requirements of the provision in question.

In reality this plea is concerned not with the admissibility of the action but with the validity of the Decision of 17 February 1971. The plea of inadmissibility must therefore be rejected.

In the second place the defendant pleads in particular the inadmissibility of the second head of the action under which the defendant is to be ordered to require from the recipients the repayment, within certain time limits, of the grants awarded after the Decision of 17 February 1971. According to the defendant it follows from Article 171 of the Treaty that in the course of an action directed against a Member State, the Court of Justice must limit itself to finding a failure to fulfil an obligation, and has no power to order the Member State to take any specific steps, so that it is in fact the responsibility of the Member State alone to determine the necessary measures to comply with the judgment of the Court so as to eliminate the results of its failure to comply.

By the second subparagraph of Article 93(2) 'if the State ... does not comply with this decision within the prescribed time, the Commission ... may refer the matter to the Court of Justice direct'.

The head of submissions in question requests the Court to find that the defendant, by its failure to require the re-payment by the recipients of the aid wrongly received, has not fulfilled an obligation incumbent upon it by virtue of the Decision of 17 February 1971.

Such a request is admissible since *the Commission is competent, when it has found that aid is incompatible with the Common Market, to decide that the State concerned must abolish or alter it. To be of practical effect, this abolition or modification may include an obligation to require repayment of aid granted in breach of the Treaty, so that in the absence of measures for recovery, the Commission may bring the matter before the Court.* Moreover an application from the Commission, within the scope of the procedure under Articles 169 to 171, for a declaration that in omitting to take specific measures, a Member State has failed to fulfil an obligation under the Treaty, is equally admissible.

Since the aim of the Treaty is to achieve the practical elimination of infringements and the consequences thereof, past and future, it is a matter for the Community authorities whose task it is to ensure that the requirements of the Treaty are observed to determine the extent to which the obligation of the Member State concerned may be specified in the reasoned opinions or decisions delivered under Articles 169 and 93(2) respectively and in applications addressed to the Court.

This plea must therefore be rejected.

Case 173/73 Italy v Commission [1974] ECR 709; [1974] 2 CMLR 593

By a decision taken in 1973 the Commission required Italy to abolish the temporary and partial reduction of family allowances, for which provision had been made in an Italian law of 1971. That decision was made on the ground that the Italian law gave rise to a State aid contrary to Articles 92 and 93 of the EEC Treaty. Italy claimed that the decision did not fix a time for compliance and submitted that in the absence of this element, which was essential to the legality of the decision, the latter should be considered as void.

The Court

In order to ensure the progressive development and functioning of the Common Market in accordance with the provisions of Article 92, Article 93 provides for constant review of aids granted or planned by the Member States, an operation which assumes constant cooperation between these States and the Commission.

Article 93(2) envisages the case where during the course of such a review the Commission finds that aid granted by a Member State is not compatible with the provisions of Article 92, and provides for the situation to be resolved by decision of the Commission subject to appeal to the Court of Justice.

Because the article is based on the idea of cooperation, the Commission must, in such a case, allow the State concerned a period of time within which to comply with the decision taken.

However, in the situation envisaged by Article 93(3) where a proposed aid is considered incompatible with Article 92, the fixing of a time limit is unnecessary, as the aid in question cannot be put into effect.

The submissions amount to the assertion that a new aid granted by a Member State in contravention of paragraph (3) must be treated in the same way as aids granted legally and, consequently, should be subject only to the procedure prescribed by Article 93(2), including the compulsory fixing of a time limit.

This interpretation of Article 93 is however unacceptable because it would have the effect of depriving the provisions of Article 93(3) of their binding force and even that of encouraging their non-observance.

Moreover, *the spirit and general scheme of Article 93 imply that the Commission, when it establishes that an aid has been granted or altered in disregard of paragraph (3), must be able, in particular when it considers that this aid is not compatible with the Common Market having regard to Article 92, to decide that the State concerned must abolish or alter it, without being bound to fix a period of time for this purpose and with the possibility of referring the matter to the Court if the State in question does not comply with the required speed.*

In such a case, the means of recourse open to the Commission are not restricted to the more complicated procedure under Article 169.

Cases 31/77R and 53/77R Commission v United Kingdom and United Kingdom v Commission [1977] ECR 921; [1977] 2 CMLR 359

By a decision taken in February 1977 the Commission required the United Kingdom to terminate immediately a subsidy to pig producers, considered by the Commission to be a State aid contrary to Articles 92 and 93 of the EEC Treaty. The United Kingdom disputed the validity of the Commission's decision and maintained the subsidy in force. The Commission brought proceedings to enforce its decision and the United Kingdom brought proceedings to annul it.

The Court

In this interlocutory application the Commission is asking for the adoption of an interim measure, within the meaning of Article 186 of the Treaty, requiring the United Kingdom to cease infringing the said decision pending the decisions of the Court which will, in both cases, determine the questions of law at issue between the Commission and the United Kingdom.

Articles 92 and 93 lay down machinery for the review of the compatibility of State aids with the Common Market in such a way that any national measure instituting or altering any such aid shall be investigated by the Commission and that no such measure may be put into effect until the Commission has announced its decision.

It is therefore necessary to find, without pre-judging the question whether the decision of 17 February is or is not well founded, that by bringing the disputed aid measure into force from 31 January 1977 the United Kingdom has acted in contravention of this system, which is essential to protect the proper functioning of the Common Market.

Even if the Member State in question took the view that the aid measure was compatible with the Common Market and that the contrary decision of the Commission was vitiated by infringement of the rules of the Treaty, that fact could not entitle it to defy the clear provisions of Article 93 and to act as if that decision were non-existent in law.

Indeed, it is in order to prevent Member States from acting as judges in their own cause that the Treaty provides them, namely in Article 173 and the following articles, with the opportunity to refer to the Court any infringement of the law on the part of the institutions, so that a decision of the Commission remains 'binding in its entirety' upon the State to which it is addressed – as laid down by the fourth paragraph of Article 189 – unless the Court decides to the contrary.

Disregard of the provisions of the final sentence of Article 93, which is the means of safeguarding the machinery for review laid down by that article, interferes with the proper operation of that machinery to such an extent as to be capable by itself of giving rise to the application of Article 186.

The fact that the Commission originally tried to remedy the situation described above without recourse to the Court cannot affect the gravity of that interference and thus exclude the application of Article 186.

Nor can the fact that it may very shortly be possible to hear and adjudicate upon the substance of Cases 31/77 and 53/77 militate against the need to ensure that the dispute between the United Kingdom and the Commission with regard to the validity of the decision of 17 February shall be conducted with proper regard to the conditions and procedural requirements laid down by the Treaty.

Moreover the provisional measure sought will not necessarily have irreversible consequences as, if the decision of the Commission were to be annulled, the United Kingdom would still be in a position to provide the aid in dispute retroactively.

Having regard to the circumstances of the case, in particular of the failure to observe the provisions of the last sentence of Article 93, it is therefore necessary to order the United Kingdom of Great Britain and Northern Ireland to cease forthwith to apply the aid measure which it has been operating since 31 January 1977.

III INTERIM MEASURES

EEC Treaty

Article 186

The Court of Justice may in any cases before it prescribe any necessary interim measures.

Article 158 of the Euratom Treaty is in identical terms; and Article 39 of the ECSC Treaty contains a provision in substantially identical terms. Under Article 83 of the Court's Rules of Procedure an application for the adoption of interim measures may be made only by a party to a case before the Court. Article 85 of those Rules provides that the President may decide on the application himself or refer it to the Court.

Case 293/85R Commission v Belgium [1985] ECR 3521

The Commission initiated proceedings against Belgium under Article 169 of the EEC Treaty for a declaration that Belgium had failed to fulfil its obligations under Articles 5 and 7 of that Treaty by its policy of charging a supplementary enrolment fee known as a 'minerval' to students who were nationals of other Member States. On the same date the Commission sought an order pursuant to Article 186 of the EEC Treaty and Article 83 of the Rules of Procedure for an order requiring Belgium to ensure that pending judgment in the main action, students who were nationals of other Member States should have access to university education offered in Belgium on the same conditions as Belgian students. In support of this application the Commission relied on the recent judgment of the Court in Case 293/83 *Gravier* v *City of Liège* [1985] ECR 593 at 606.

The President

As a condition enabling interim measures such as those requested to be granted, Article 83(2) of the Rules of Procedure provides that applications for interim measures must state the circumstances giving rise to urgency and the factual and legal grounds establishing a *prima facie* case for the interim measures applied for.

...

In interim proceedings it is impossible for the Court, without prejudging the substance of the case, to determine whether vocational training within the meaning of the judgment in *Gravier* includes university studies. However, it may be that certain university studies, in particular those which lead to qualification for a particular profession, trade or employment or which provide the necessary training and skills for such a profession, trade or employment, constitute vocational training and therefore should not have conditions of access for students of other Member States different from those applicable to students of the host State. From the fact that Article 16(1) of the Law of 21 June 1985 requires students who are nationals of other Member States and who wish to follow university courses in Belgium to pay a supplementary enrolment fee, even if their studies seem to be closely linked with vocational training, it may therefore be inferred that the grounds relied upon by the applicant establish a *prima facie* case for the grant of the interim measure applied for.

The applicant in this case appears to have put forward factual and legal grounds which may be regarded as establishing a *prima facie* case for the grant of the interim measure applied for; however, the Court must also assess the urgency of such a measure and *whether it is necessary in order to avoid serious and irreparable damage.*

In that regard, the applicant submits that the academic year has already begun and students who are nationals of other Member States therefore urgently need to know whether they will be entitled to enrol, at least provisionally, or whether, on the contrary, depending on their financial resources, they will either have to pay the supplementary fee or abandon the studies which they proposed to undertake or have already begun. It seems obvious to the applicant that any such student whose enrolment or re-enrolment is refused because he is unable to pay the fee will suffer serious and irreparable damage. A student who has agreed to pay the fee would be in the same situation, in view of the amount which he will have to pay, which may be substantial. It is even more apparent that such a student will suffer irreparable damage if, though prepared to pay the fee, he is refused the right to enrol pursuant to Article 16(2) of the Law of 21 June 1985.

...

The information given to the Court by the Kingdom of Belgium at the hearing indicates that it is chiefly the students wishing to enrol in an independent university whose enrolment will be refused if they do not pay the fee in question. State universities are largely complying with the instructions communicated to them by the Minister in his letter of 2 September 1985.

Although the parties do not agree as to the precise number of students affected, it appears that at least some of them are being refused enrolment because they are unable or unwilling to pay the fee, although the academic year has already begun. The President of the Court therefore takes the view that it is a matter or urgency for those students to be able to enrol without having to pay the fee in order to prevent serious and irreparable damage to their interests.

However, *for the purposes of Article 186 of the EEC Treaty, it is necessary to balance all the interests concerned. Accordingly, the President of the Court considers that a balance will be achieved between the interests of the parties concerned if, on enrolment, students who are nationals of other Member States give a personal undertaking, in writing, to pay the fee if the main application is dismissed by the Court.*

On those grounds,

THE PRESIDENT,

by way of interim decision,

hereby orders as follows:

Pending the judgment on the main application, the Kingdom of Belgium is required:

(a) on notification of this order, immediately to adopt all the measures needed to ensure that students who are nationals of other Member States shall have access to vocational training offered by Belgian universities on the same conditions as Belgian students, provided that they give a personal undertaking, in writing, to pay the fee in question if the main application is dismissed by the Court. That personal undertaking in writing should take the form of an individual acknowledgment of liability to pay;

(b) to inform the Commission and the Court of Justice within one month at the latest of the measures which it has adopted in order to comply with paragraph 1(a) of the operative part of this order.

IV ACTIONS BETWEEN MEMBER STATES

EEC Treaty

Article 170

A Member State which considers that another Member State has failed to fulfil an obligation under this Treaty may bring the matter before the Court of Justice.

Before a Member State brings an action against another Member State for an alleged infringement of an obligation under this Treaty, it shall bring the matter before the Commission.

The Commission shall deliver a reasoned opinion after each of the States concerned has been given the opportunity to submit its own case and its observations on the other party's case both orally and in writing.

If the Commission has not delivered an opinion within three months of the date on which the matter was brought before it, the absence of such opinion shall not prevent the matter from being brought before the Court of Justice.

Article 142 of the Euratom Treaty is in identical terms. In the case of the ECSC Treaty, Article 89 provides that any dispute between Member States which cannot be settled by another procedure provided for in the Treaty may be submitted to the Court of Justice on application by one of the States parties to the dispute. Hitherto there has been no judgment on the basis of that article.

Until recently proceedings under Article 170 of the EEC Treaty were also rare; but an example is provided in Case 141/78.

Case 141/78 France v United Kingdom [1979] ECR 2923; [1980] 1 CMLR 6

In 1977 a French trawler, fishing within United Kingdom fishery limits, was boarded by British fishery protection officers. The master of the trawler was later convicted of using nets of a mesh smaller than the minimum authorised under an Order in Council made earlier that year.

The Court

The French Republic claims in particular that the disputed order, which was adopted in a matter reserved for the competence of the Community, was brought into force in disregard of the requirements set out in Annex VI to the resolution adopted by the Council at The Hague at its meetings on 30 October and 3 November 1976, under which, pending the implementation of the appropriate Community measures, Member States might, as an interim measure, adopt unilateral measures to ensure the protection of fishery resources on condition that they had first consulted the Commission and sought its approval. As these requirements were not observed by the Government of the United Kingdom the measure adopted is contrary to Community law. In the alternative the French Government also claims that the disputed order is, with regard to the measures adopted, excessive and thus does not constitute a reasonable measure of protection.

The French Government's position was supported by the Commission which intervened in the action. In the arguments presented to the Court the Commission stated that the Government of the United Kingdom had also failed to observe Article 3 of Council Regulation No 101/76 of 19 January 1976 laying down a common structural policy for the fishing industry, under which Member States are required to give prior notification of any alterations to fishery rules. Furthermore, the Commission emphasised particularly that Annex VI to The Hague Resolution is a specific expression of the duty of cooperation expressed in general terms by Article 5 of the EEC Treaty. Finally, the Commission claims that the British measures are excessive inasmuch as they involve certain specific conditions, in particular relative to the restrictions on by-catches, which are defined more strictly than in the proposals put forward by the Commission for determining common rules in the matter.

...

The Commission has rightly claimed that that resolution, in the particular field to which it applies, makes specific the duties of cooperation which the Member States assumed under Article 5 of the EEC Treaty when they acceded to the Community. Performance of these duties is particularly necessary in a situation in which it has appeared impossible, by reason of divergences of interest which it has not yet been possible to resolve, to establish a common policy and in a field such as that of the conservation of the biological resources of the sea in which worthwhile results can only be attained thanks to the cooperation of all the Member States.

It follows from the foregoing that the institution of measures of conservation by a Member State must first be notified to the other Member States and to the Commission and that such measures are in particular subject to the requirements laid down by Annex VI to The Hague resolution. In other words, a Member State proposing to bring such measures into force is required to seek the approval of the Commission, which must be consulted at all stages of the procedure.

It is common ground that these requirements have not been satisfied in this case. The Government of the United Kingdom, however, claims that it was not required to follow that procedure since it applies exclusively in the case of 'unilateral measures' of conservation of resources adopted by a Member State and that the measures which are the subject of the disputed order are not 'unilateral' measures, inasmuch as they were adopted in order to ensure, within the jurisdiction of the United Kingdom, the undertakings arising for the United Kingdom from the North-East Atlantic Fisheries Convention and the resolutions adopted thereunder.

Annex VI to The Hague Resolution, in the words of which 'the Member States will not take any unilateral measures in respect of the conservation of resources', except in certain circumstances and with due observance of the requirements set out above must be understood as referring to any measures of conservation emanating from the Member States and not from the Community authorities. The duty of consultation arising under that resolution thus also covers measures adopted by a Member State to comply with one of its international obligations in this matter. Such consultation was all the more necessary in this case since it is common ground, as has been emphasised by the French Government and the Commission and accepted by the Government of the United Kingdom itself, that the order in question, although carrying out certain recommendations of the North-East Atlantic Fisheries Convention, nevertheless in some respects goes beyond the requirements flowing from those recommendations.

It follows from the foregoing that, by not previously notifying the other Member States and the Commission of the measure adopted and seeking the approval of the Commission, the United Kingdom has failed to fulfil its obligations under Article 5 of the EEC Treaty, Annex VI to The Hague Resolution and Articles 2 and 3 of Regulation No 101/76.

V ACTIONS IN NATIONAL COURTS

The initiation of proceedings against Member States in national courts is in principle governed, as regards jurisdiction and procedure, by national law. This is so even though in substance the dispute may fall to be resolved in accordance with Community law. Community law requires that any right to which it gives rise at the national level should be enforceable in national courts by means of a remedy which is real and effective and is not tainted by discrimination. It seems, however, that Community law does not demand that damages should be available to compensate the victim of a breach by a Member State of an obligation arising under the founding Treaties, even when the article giving rise to the obligation produces direct effects.

Bourgoin SA and Others v Ministry of Agriculture, Fisheries and Food
[1985] 3 All ER 585; [1985] 3 WLR 1627; [1986] 1 CMLR 267

In August 1981 the Minister of Agriculture imposed restrictions on the importation of turkeys from certain countries, including most Member States of the EEC. In July 1982 the Court of Justice of the European Communities held that the Minister's action amounted to a breach of Article 30 of the EEC Treaty. It was not justified under Article 36 since the restrictions were apparently imposed for commercial and economic reasons rather than for reasons of animal health.

The plaintiffs, French turkey producers, claimed to have lost substantial sums of money by reason of the disruption of their trade. They brought an action in the High Court claiming damages on the ground, among others, that the defendant Minister had violated their directly-effective rights under Article 30 of the EEC Treaty. This, they said, gave rise to damages, even in the absence of evidence that the defendant was guilty of misfeasance. Mann J allowed that part of their claim but the Court of Appeal, by a majority, reversed the judge's decision. The principal judgment for the majority in the Court of Appeal was that of Parker LJ, who distinguished between public law rights enforceable by such remedies as declarations and judicial review, and private law rights enforceable by such remedies as damages.

Lord Justice Parker

...

Article 30 of the EEC Treaty falls to be read with Article 36 for, notwithstanding the unqualified terms of the earlier article, the latter article provides that the former shall not preclude prohibitions or restrictions –

> 'justified on grounds of public morality, public policy or public security; the protection of health and life of humans, animals or plants; the protection of national treasures possessing artistic, historic or archaeological value; or the protection of industrial and commercial property'.

The last sentence of Article 36 then provides:

> 'Such prohibitions or restrictions shall not, however, constitute a means of arbitrary discrimination or a disguised restriction on trade between Member States'.

...

Most, if not all, of the excepted matters are matters on which, when considering whether it can or should impose a prohibition or restriction, a Member State could be faced with conflicting evidence of fact and conflicting expert evidence. Even if it were not, there are many matters on which other experts might hold perfectly honest but different views. Moreover, when one is dealing with a matter such as public morality, one is of necessity operating in a field of moral judgment.

...

As to expert evidence, the problem which may face a Member State can be simply illustrated. The Member State may be advised by its experts that a particular drug has certain harmful side-effects which make prohibition on its import necessary for the protection of the life and health of humans. The exporting State or those desiring to import the drug may, however, produce evidence from equally highly qualified experts either (a) that the drug does not produce the harmful side-effects at all or (b) that, although it does, they only occur in certain types of individual and that a prohibition is therefore not necessary; a condition, for example, that every packet should carry a clear warning that it should not be prescribed for individuals of such types would be sufficient.

Suppose that in this situation a Member State imposes a complete ban but it is subsequently held, by either the European Court or a national court, after hearing a mass of conflicting evidence and perhaps stating that it has had great difficulty in reaching a decision, that the ban was not justified. Suppose also that the court reached its conclusion because, although it rejected the evidence that the drug caused no harmful side-effects, it accepted the evidence that such side-effects were limited and that import subject to conditions would have sufficed. In such a situation the Member State would have been in breach of Article 30; but is it the case that the exporting manufacturer and the importing distributor who have lost profits by reason of the ban, and perhaps others besides, could recover damages from the Member State? I pose the question generally although in this appeal we are of course concerned only with the question whether in such circumstances damages could be recovered from the government of this country in the courts of this country. Both in general and in particular, however, it would in my view be surprising if the answer was in the affirmative.

...

I must therefore examine the two English cases on which the plaintiffs found their claim.

In *Garden Cottage Foods Ltd* v *Milk Marketing Board* [1983] 2 All ER 770, [1984] AC 130 the plaintiffs alleged that the defendants had acted in breach of Article 86 and applied for an interlocutory injunction. I refused the injunction on the ground, principally, that if the plaintiffs succeeded they would be adequately compensated in damages (see [1982] 3 All ER 292, [1982] QB 1114). In the Court of Appeal doubts were expressed whether a remedy in damages was available and an injunction was granted (see [1982] 3 All ER 292, [1982] QB 1114). The defendants appealed to the House of Lords, which, Lord Wilberforce dissenting, allowed the appeal and discharged the injunction (see [1983] 2 All ER 770, [1984] AC 130).

In the course of his speech, with which Lord Keith, Lord Bridge and Lord Brandon concurred, Lord Diplock said ([1983] 2 All ER 770 at 775-776, [1984] AC 130 at 141):

> 'The rights which the article confers on citizens in the United Kingdom accordingly fall within Section 2(1) of the 1972 Act. They are without further enactment to be given legal effect in the United Kingdom and enforced accordingly. A breach of the duty imposed by Article 86 not to abuse a dominant position in the Common Market or in a substantial part of it can thus be categorised in English law as a breach of statutory duty that is imposed not only for the purpose of promoting the general economic prosperity of the Common Market but also for the benefit of private individuals to whom loss or damage is caused by a breach of that duty. If this categorisation be correct, and I can see none other that would be capable of giving rise to a civil cause of action in English private law on the part of a private individual who sustained loss or damage by reason of a breach of a directly applicable provision of the EEC Treaty, the nature of the cause of action cannot, in my view, be affected by the fact that the legislative provision by which the duty is imposed takes the negative form of a prohibition of particular kinds of conduct rather than the positive form of an obligation to do particular acts'.

As appears from the above passage, Lord Diplock was considering the case of a private individual asserting a civil course of action in English private law. There was nothing else to be considered. No question of public law arose. Article 86 imposed a negative obligation on undertakings and created a private right. Lord Diplock, dealing further with the matter, said ([1983] 2 All ER 770 at 777-778, [1984] AC 130 at 144):

> '...I, for my own part, find it difficult to see how it can ultimately be successfully argued, as the Board will seek to do, that a contravention of Article 86 which causes damage to an individual citizen does not give rise to a cause of action in English law of the nature of a cause of action for breach of statutory duty; but since it cannot be regarded as unarguable that is not a matter for final decision by your Lordships at the interlocutory stage that the instant case has reached. What, with great respect to those who think otherwise, I *do* regard as quite unarguable is the proposition, advanced by the Court of Appeal itself but disclaimed by both parties to the action, that, if such a contravention of Article 86 gives rise to any cause of action at all, it gives rise to a cause of action for which there is no remedy in damages to compensate for loss already caused by that contravention but only a remedy by way of injunction to prevent future loss being caused. A cause of action to which an unlawful act by the defendant causing pecuniary loss to the plaintiff gives rise, if it possessed those characteristics as respects the remedies available, would be one which, so far as my understanding goes, is unknown in English private law, at any rate since 1875 when the jurisdiction conferred on the Court of Chancery by Lord Cairns's Act, the Chancery Amendment Act 1858, passed to the High Court. I

> leave aside as irrelevant for present purposes injunctions granted in matrimonial causes or wardship proceedings which may have no connection with pecuniary loss. I likewise leave out of account injunctions obtainable as remedies in public law whether on application for judicial review or in an action brought by the Attorney General *ex officio* or *ex relatione* some private individual. It is private law, not public law, to which the company has had recourse. In its action it claims damages as well as an injunction. No reasons are to be found in any of the judgments of the Court of Appeal and none has been advanced at the hearing before your Lordships why in law, in logic or in justice, if contravention of Article 86 of the EEC Treaty is capable of giving rise to a cause of action in English private law at all, there is any need to invent a cause of action with characteristics that are wholly novel as respects the remedies that it attracts, in order to deal with breaches of articles of the EEC Treaty which have in the United Kingdom the same effect as statutes'.

That is clear authority that *a private law action for breach of Article 86 against an undertaking sounds in damages,* but it should be noted that Lord Diplock emphasises that the plaintiffs were resorting purely to private law, and that they could resort to nothing else.

It is, however, submitted that, as Lord Diplock categorised the action as one of breach of statutory duty creating rights in individuals, it follows that a breach of Article 30 by a Member State, which article also creates rights in individuals, also gives rise to an action for breach of statutory duty and that, this being so, it must by virtue of the decision give a remedy in damages.

I am unable to accept this. I can find nothing in Lord Diplock's speech to suggest that he had in mind for one moment that breach by a Member State of a negative obligation in relation to measures could be categorised as, or be of the nature of, a breach of statutory duty giving rise to a civil cause of action in private law. He expressly leaves out of account such matters. The reference to individual rights is in my judgment without significance. *An individual right may be a right in private law or in public law; Article 30 in my judgment creates individual rights both in public law and private law. A breach simpliciter of the article sounds only in public law.* A breach amounting to abuse of power sounds in private law. Neither can be categorised as, or be regarded as being of the nature of, a breach of statutory duty in any sense known to English law. Nothing in Lord Diplock's speech leads me to suppose that either he or those who agreed with him would have done so had they had to consider the matter.

The other case on which the plaintiffs principally rely, *An Bord Bainne Cooperative Ltd* v *Milk Marketing Board* [1984] 1 CMLR 519, concerned an alleged breach by the defendants of EEC regulations and of Article 86. The defendants contended that the matters complained of by the plaintiffs with regard to the regulations were public law decisions and that on the basis of *O'Reilly* v *Mackman* [1982] 3 All ER 1124, [1983] 2 AC 237 that head of claim should be struck out as an abuse of process and the plaintiffs left to their remedies by way of judicial review. Neill J accepted the argument that the decisions complained of were public law decisions but declined to strike out. The defendants appealed and the appeal was dismissed on the basis that the plaintiffs were undoubtedly asserting private law rights and if successful would be entitled to an injunction or damages, the court having no discretion to refuse a remedy (see [1984] 2 CMLR 584). The case does not in my judgment assist the plaintiffs.

Here the plaintiffs are, so far as this part of the case is concerned, asserting that the United Kingdom government are in breach of an obligation not to impose measures.

I regard this as wholly different from a claim under Article 86 and I do not consider that damages are available.

FURTHER READING

Bridge, J., 'Procedural Aspects of the Enforcement of European Community Law through the Legal Systems of the Member States', 9 ELRev (1984) 28

Cripps, Y., 'European Rights, Invalid Actions and Denial of Damages' [1986] CLJ 165

Durand, A., 'Restriction or Damages: National Court or the European Court' 1 ELRev (1975-6) 431

March Hunnings, N., 'Default Judgments in the EEC' [1985] Jo Bus L 303

Oliver, P., 'Enforcing Community Rights in the English Courts' 50 MLR (1987) 81

5

PRELIMINARY RULINGS

INTRODUCTION

One of the distinguishing features of European Community law is the capacity to give rise to rights and duties that must be protected, not by the Court of Justice of the European Communities, but by national courts. The European Court has, however, the duty to ensure the uniform interpretation and application of Community law in the courts of the several Member States. For this purpose the founding Treaties confer on some domestic courts the power, and impose on others the duty, of referring questions of Community law to the European Court for its rulings. Such rulings are designated as 'preliminary', for although the domestic courts must accept them as conclusive, they must apply them to the cases that gave rise to the questions in the form of judgments and must, if necessary, enforce them by the sanctions for which national law provides.

EEC Treaty

Article 177

The Court of Justice shall have jurisdiction to give preliminary rulings concerning:

(a) the interpretation of this Treaty;

(b) the validity and interpretation of acts of the institutions of the Community;

(c) the interpretation of the statutes of bodies established by an act of the Council, where those statutes so provide.

Where such a question is raised before any court or tribunal of a Member State that court or tribunal may, if it considers that a decision on the question is necessary to enable it to give judgment, request the Court of Justice to give a ruling thereon.

Where any such question is raised in a case pending before a court or tribunal of a Member State, against whose decisions there is no judicial remedy under national law, that court or tribunal shall bring the matter before the Court of Justice.

I THE 'QUESTION'

Article 177 provides for 'questions' to be referred to the European Court. It has long been accepted in the French Conseil d'Etat, which also has jurisdiction to answer questions from lower courts, that a point is not to be referred when the answer is so clear as to admit of no possible difficulty. The same court applied a similar technique when confronted with an application for reference under Article 177.

Re Société des Pétroles Shell-Berre and Others
[1964] CMLR 462

Shell and other oil companies claimed that a French decree governing the distribution arrangements for petroleum was incompatible with Article 37 of the EEC Treaty. In proceedings before the Conseil d'Etat, the companies sought the annulment of the French decree; and they asked the Conseil d'Etat to refer to the Court of Justice of the European Communities questions on the interpretation of Article 37.

The Conseil d'Etat

In accordance with Article 55 of the Constitution, the French courts are required to apply the Treaty instituting the European Economic Community. Although Article 177 of this Treaty stipulates that the Court of Justice of the EEC is 'competent to give preliminary rulings' especially on the 'interpretation' of that Treaty and lays down for this purpose a reference procedure from national courts to the Court of Justice, *it follows from the very terms of this article that a national court from the decisions of which there is no possibility of appeal under domestic law*, such as the Conseil d'Etat acting in its judicial capacity, *is only required to stay proceedings in a case pending before it and to seise the Court of Justice of the EEC if a 'question' relating to the interpretation of the Treaty is 'raised' in that case. That could only happen in a case in which there is a doubt as to the meaning or scope of one or several clauses of the Treaty applicable to the main action and if the issue of the action depends on the settlement of this difficulty.*

The plaintiff companies maintain that the provisions of the *arrêté* of 3 January 1959 relating to the creation and extension of distribution installations for petroleum products would or could involve restrictions on the import of the products coming from the States of the European Community, would introduce discrimination to the disadvantage of those companies distributing products originating in the Community and would, consequently, be incompatible with the provisions of the Treaty which forbid discrimination on grounds of nationality, aim at eliminating quantitative restrictions between the Member States, arrange for the freedom of provision of services and forbid State subsidies or measures which distort or threaten to distort competition. The plaintiff companies further maintain that even accepting that the system instituted by the Law of 30 March 1928 comes within the field of application of Article 37 of the Treaty, the ministerial *arrêté* of 3 January 1959 might contain provisions contrary to certain rules laid down by the said article.

Under subsection (1) of the afore mentioned Article 37,

> 'Member States shall gradually adjust any State trading monopolies so as to ensure that, when the transitional period expires, no discrimination exists between the nationals of Member States as regards the supply or marketing of goods.
>
> 'The provisions of this article shall apply to any organisation through which a Member State, *de jure* or *de facto*, either directly or indirectly controls, supervises or appreciably influences imports or exports as between Member States. These provisions shall likewise apply to monopolies delegated by the State to other legal entities.'

On the one hand, it follows clearly from this clause that its field of application includes systems such as that to which, by virtue of the provisions of the internal French legislation mentioned above, the undertakings holding special import authorisations for petroleum products are subject.

On the other hand, while the same clause has laid down that the national monopolies of a commercial nature and similar systems should be gradually adjusted so that when the transitional period expires no discrimination exists between the nationals of Member States, subsections (2) to (5) of Article 37 determine the rules which are imposed during the transitional period. Finally subsection (6) confers on the EEC Commission the power to make recommendations to the Member States as to the manner of effecting the adjustment of the national monopolies and similar systems and the timetable which should govern it. It also follows clearly from these latter clauses that they have the aim and effect of placing monopolies and similar systems, during the transitional period, under a special régime which departs from the rules of common law laid down by various other articles of the Treaty and the adaptation of which to the said rules should be realised gradually by the Member States, taking account of the recommendations of the EEC Commission.

Article 37(2) specifies that 'Member States shall abstain from introducing any new measure which is contrary to the principles laid down in subsection (1) of this article or which restricts the scope of the articles dealing with the abolition of customs duties and quantitative restrictions between Member States'. It is clear that this clause has the object of forbidding all new measures likely to create discrimination between nationals of the Member States or to increase existing discrimination. It does not follow from the *instruction* that the attacked *arrêté*, which relates only to the distribution of petroleum products and especially to the creation and installation of service stations by French companies benefiting from special import authorisations for petroleum products, has the effect of creating discrimination between nationals of the Member States of the EEC or of increasing the existing discrimination.

From the whole of the above, it follows that the plaintiff companies could not effectively use in support of their subsidiary claim analysed above the fact that the *arrêté* in dispute could conflict either with certain clauses of the EEC Treaty relating to the system under common law or with the clauses of Article 37 relating to national monopolies and similar systems. *In these circumstances, the settlement of the action is not subject to any question of interpretation of the Treaty. Therefore, the claim analysed above that the Conseil d'Etat should seise the Court of Justice of the European Economic Community cannot be accepted.*

The *Shell-Berre* case proved controversial. But it is at most an objectionable application of an unobjectionable principle. The European Court has since accepted that a national court need not refer points which present no interpretative difficulty.

Case 283/81 Srl CILFIT and Lanificio di Gavardo SpA v Ministry of Health
[1982] ECR 3415; [1983] 1 CMLR 472

Certain Italian wool importers and the Italian Ministry of Health were in dispute over the payment of a fixed health inspection levy on wool from outside the Community. The matter came before the Corte Suprema di Cassazione which referred the following question to the Court of Justice: 'Does the third paragraph of Article 177 of the EEC Treaty, which provides that where any question of the same kind as those listed in the first paragraph of that article is raised in a case pending before a national court or tribunal against whose decisions there is no judicial remedy under national law that court or tribunal must bring the matter before the Court of Justice, lay down an obligation so to submit the case which precludes the national court from determining whether the question raised is justified or does it, and if so within what time limits, make that obligation conditional on the prior finding of a reasonable interpretative doubt?'

The Court

In order to answer that question it is necessary to take account of the system established by Article 177 , which confers jurisdiction on the Court of Justice to give preliminary rulings on, inter alia, the interpretation of the Treaty and the measures adopted by the institutions of the Community.

The second paragraph of that article provides that any court or tribunal of a Member State *may*, if it considers that a decision on a question of interpretation is necessary to enable it to give judgment, request the Court of Justice to give a ruling thereon. The third paragraph of that article provides that, where a question of interpretation is raised in a case pending before a court or tribunal of a Member State against whose decisions there is no judicial remedy under national law, that court or tribunal *shall* bring the matter before the Court of Justice.

That obligation to refer a matter to the Court of Justice is based on cooperation, established with a view to ensuring the proper application and uniform interpretation of Community law in all the Member States, between national courts, in their capacity as courts responsible for the application of Community law, and the Court of Justice. More particularly, the third paragraph of Article 177 seeks to prevent the occurrence within the Community of divergences in judicial decisions on questions of Community law. The scope of that obligation must therefore be assessed, in view of those objectives, by reference to the powers of the national courts, on the one hand, and those of the Court of Justice, on the other, where such a question of interpretation is raised within the meaning of Article 177.

In this connection, it is necessary to define the meaning for the purposes of Community law of the expression 'where any such question is raised' in order to determine the circumstances in which a national court or tribunal against whose decisions there is no judicial remedy under national law is obliged to bring a matter before the Court of Justice.

In this regard, it must in the first place be pointed out that *Article 177 does not constitute a means of redress available to the parties to a case pending before a national court or tribunal. Therefore the mere fact that a party contends that the dispute gives rise to a question concerning the interpretation of Community law does not mean that the court or tribunal concerned is compelled to consider that a question has been raised within the meaning of Article 177.* On the other hand, a national court or tribunal may, in an appropriate case, refer a matter to the Court of Justice of its own motion.

Secondly, it follows from the relationship between the second and third paragraphs of Article 177 that the courts or tribunals referred to in the third paragraph have the same discretion as any other national court or tribunal to ascertain whether a decision on a question of Community law is necessary to enable them to give judgment. Accordingly, those courts or tribunals are not obliged to refer to the Court of Justice a question concerning the interpretation of Community law raised before them if that question is not relevant, that is to say, if the answer to that question, regardless of what it may be, can in no way affect the outcome of the case.

If, however, those courts or tribunals consider that recourse to Community law is necessary to enable them to decide a case, Article 177 imposes an obligation on them to refer to the Court of Justice any question of interpretation which may arise.

The question submitted by the Corte di Cassazione seeks to ascertain whether, in certain circumstances, the obligation laid down by the third paragraph of Article 177 might nonetheless be subject to certain restrictions.

It must be remembered in this connection that in its judgment of 27 March 1963 in Joined Cases 28 to 30/62 (*Da Costa* v *Nederlandse Belastingadministratie* [1963] ECR 31) the Court ruled that: 'Although the third paragraph of Article 177 unreservedly requires courts or tribunals of a Member State against whose decisions there is no judicial remedy under national law ... to refer to the Court every question of interpretation raised before them, the authority of an interpretation under Article 177 already given by the Court may deprive the obligation of its purpose and thus empty it of its substance. Such is the case especially when the question raised it materially identical with a question which has already been the subject of a preliminary ruling in a similar case.'

The same effect, as regards the limits set to the obligation laid down by the third paragraph of Article 177, may be produced where previous decisions of the Court have already dealt with the point of law in question, irrespective of the nature of the proceedings which led to those decisions, even though the questions at issue are not strictly identical.

However, it must not be forgotten that in all such circumstances national courts and tribunals, including those referred to in the third paragraph of Article 177, remain entirely at liberty to bring a matter before the Court of Justice if they consider it appropriate to do so.

Finally, the correct application of Community law may be so obvious as to leave no scope for any reasonable doubt as to the manner in which the question raised is to be resolved. Before it comes to the conclusion that such is the case, the national court or tribunal must be convinced that the matter is equally obvious to the courts of the other Member States and to the Court of Justice. Only if those conditions are satisfied may the national court or tribunal refrain from submitting the question to the Court of Justice and take upon itself the responsibility for resolving it.

However, the existence of such a possibility must be assessed on the basis of the characteristic features of Community law and the particular difficulties to which its interpretation gives rise.

To begin with, it must be borne in mind that Community legislation is drafted in several languages and that the different language versions are all equally authentic. An interpretation of a provision of Community law thus involves a comparison of the different language versions.

It must also be borne in mind, even where the different language versions are entirely in accord with one another, that Community law uses terminology which is peculiar to it. Furthermore, it must be emphasised that legal concepts do not necessarily have the same meaning in Community law and in the law of the various Member States.

Finally, every provision of Community law must be placed in its context and interpreted in the light of the provisions of Community law as a whole, regard being had to the objectives thereof and to its state of evolution at the date on which the provision in question is to be applied.

In the light of all those considerations, the answer to the question submitted by the Corte Suprema di Cassazione must be that the third paragraph of Article 177 of the EEC Treaty is to be interpreted as meaning that a court or tribunal against whose decisions there is no judicial remedy under national law is required, where a question of Community law is raised before it, to comply with its obligation to bring the matter before the Court of Justice, unless it has established that the question raised is irrelevant or that the Community provision in question has already been interpreted by the Court or that the correct application of Community law is so obvious as to leave no scope for any reasonable doubt. The existence of such a possibility must be assessed in the light of the specific characteristics of Community law, the particular difficulties to which its interpretation gives rise and the risk of divergences in judicial decisions within the Community.

Even a court from whose judgments there is no judicial remedy is entitled to refuse to refer a point on the ground that the answer is clear.

SA Magnavision NV v General Optical Council (No 2)

[1987] 2 CMLR 262

(For the facts of this case see below, p. 219).

Having reached a conclusion on the merits, the High Court was further called by counsel for the appellants to consider making a reference for a preliminary ruling to the European Court.

Watkins LJ

Now that judgments have been delivered, we are in this position. We were invited, at the conclusion of giving judgment, to certify points of law for consideration by the House of Lords. Having looked at the drafts of those points, we had no hesitation in coming to the conclusion that they did not call for certification by us. So we rejected the application therefor. There is no appeal against the refusal by this Court, in a criminal cause or matter, to certify a point of law for consideration by the House of Lords. There is, therefore, nothing a disappointed appellant, or respondent for that matter, can do if he applies for such a certificate and fails. It is, to put it in homely language, 'the end of the road' for him.

I am bound to say that when we announced that decision, I thought it was the end of the road for us. But my Lord and I were soon disabused of such a notion, for Mr Bellamy was once again on his feet, this time making what I regard as a most daring application. The purport of that was that although we had decided the appeal, and refused to certify points of law for the consideration of the House of Lords, we should, notwithstanding all that, refer the point which he had canvassed during argument in the course of the appeal to the European Court for the purpose of obtaining the opinion of that Court upon it.

As he said, and he was right so far as I know, that was the first time that an application of such a nature had been made, at the time when it was made.

...

His second argument is that by refusing to certify a point or points of law, we have turned ourselves into a final court, that is a court of final decision. In a sense, I agree with that. There is no appeal now from our decision to any other court in this country or elsewhere. Consequently, he submits that the prospect looms, if we do not make a reference to the European Court now, of the matter of which he complains being taken up either by the Commission of the European Community, or by a Member State of it. That may happen. But such a prospect cannot be permitted to sway this court away from considering the application now made to it otherwise than strictly in accordance with the law of this country. Likewise, when deciding whether to make a reference during the hearing of a case.

He says further that the European Court itself has, in recent times, made it clear that it expects courts of final decision in Member States to make a reference when a litigant has no other means of redress for a decision which has gone against him. In that connection, he made reference to a case which I shall call, for short, *CILFIT*. I do not propose to make any further reference to that case other than to observe, in agreement with the submission made by Mr Jacobs with regard to it, that if anything, it supports the proposition that when a court of final decision in a Member State has come to a decision as a consequence of being clear in its mind as to the construction to be put upon relevant legislation, then it is under no obligation at all to make a reference to the European Court.

Finally, I would look at the practical sense, if there is any, of making a reference to that Court at this stage and in the circumstances of this case. I examine therefore Article 177, the provisions of which commence with these words: 'The Court of Justice shall have jurisdiction to give preliminary rulings concerning...'. The matters of concern then follow. That means that the Court of Justice has referred to it and accepts for this purpose a reference so that it may give a ruling (called preliminary) to the court which has made the reference so that basing itself on that ruling it may make up its mind upon the issues arising in the case which stands adjourned before it. In other words, it is an indispensable aid to the domestic court leading it to its final conclusion. Reference now in this case to the European Court could, in no sense, be regarded as something which goes there for a preliminary ruling. The issues in the case have been resolved and final judgment given.

In subparagraph 3 of this article, it is provided: 'Where any such question is raised in a case pending before a court or tribunal of a Member State, against whose decisions there is no judicial remedy under national law, that court or tribunal shall bring the matter before the Court of Justice'. Putting aside as I think we should all such considerations as *acte clair* and so on, this subparagraph must be put in context. The real context in which it must be placed is in contemplation of a court or tribunal requiring from the European Court a preliminary ruling. That is what Article 177 is all about. We require no such ruling and I cannot regard ourselves as having to bring in all the circumstances the law which was in issue but is no longer before the European Court. The submission to that effect I reject without hesitation.

II 'COURT OR TRIBUNAL' 'OF A MEMBER STATE'

1. 'COURT OR TRIBUNAL'

Under Article 177 only a court or tribunal may refer questions to the European Court. The French and German versions of Article 177 use only one word for "court or tribunal", *juridiction* and *Gericht* respectively. The meaning is not confined to the central judicial arms of the state but extends also to other tribunals which are authorised to give binding decisions of a judicial nature. On the other hand, the expression is not broad enough to embrace a body which has before it a request for a declaration relating to a dispute which it is under no legal obligation to resolve.

Case 138/80 Jules Borker [1980] 2 ECR 1975; [1980] 3 CMLR 638

The Bar Council of the Cour de Paris referred a question to the Court relating to the direct effect of Directive No 77/249 on the effective exercise by lawyers of the freedom to provide services (see below, Chapter 8, p. 351). The Court responded as follows:

The Court

...

Under Article 177 of the EEC Treaty the Court of Justice has jurisdiction to give preliminary rulings concerning the interpretation of the Treaty and of acts of the institutions of the Community. The second paragraph of the article adds that: 'Where such a question is raised before any court or tribunal of a Member State, that court or tribunal may, if it considers that a decision on the question is necessary to enable it to give judgment, request the Court of Justice to give a ruling thereon'.

It is apparent from that provision that the Court can only be requested to give a preliminary ruling under Article 177 by a court or tribunal which is called upon to give judgment in proceedings intended to lead to a decision of a judicial nature. That is not the position in this case since the Conseil de l'Ordre does not have before it a case which it is under a legal duty to try but a request for a declaration relating to a dispute between a member of the Bar and the courts or tribunals of another Member State.

It is therefore clear that the Court has no jurisdiction to give a ruling in connection with the decision sent to it by the Conseil de l'Ordre des Avocats à la Cour de Paris.

Circumstances may arise in which a professional body amounts to a 'court or tribunal' within the meaning of Article 177. This will be the case where the professional body is established, in conjunction with public authorities of the state, as an appellate authority with the power to affect the exercise of rights granted by Community law.

Case 246/80 C. Broekmeulen v Huisarts Registratie Commissie
[1981] ECR 2311; [1982] 1 CMLR 91

(For the facts of this case see below, Chapter 8, p. 341).

Before answering the question submitted by the Appeals Committee for General Medicine, the Court considered the standing of this body in the light of Article 177.

The Court

...

The Appeals Committee is a body set up by the Society and it is appropriate therefore to deal first with the question whether it ought to be considered as a 'court or tribunal' of a Member State within the meaning of Article 177 of the Treaty.

According to the internal rules of the Society, the Appeals Committee, appointed for a period of five years, is composed of three members appointed by the Netherlands medical faculties, three members appointed by the Board of the Society and three members, including the chairman (preferably a high-ranking judge), who are appointed by the ministers responsible for higher education and health respectively. It may therefore be seen that the composition of the Appeals Committee entails a significant degree of involvement on the part of the Netherlands public authorities.

Pursuant to those rules, the Appeals Committee determines disputes on the adversarial principle, that is to say having heard the Registration Committee and the doctor concerned, as well as his adviser or lawyer, if necessary.

The Netherlands Government stated that, in its opinion, the Appeals Committee cannot be considered a court or tribunal under Netherlands law. However, it pointed out that that fact is not decisive for the interpretation of Article 177 of the Treaty and suggested that the question whether a body such as the Appeals Committee is entitled to refer a case to the Court under that provision should be determined in the light of the function performed by that body within the system of remedies available to those who consider that their rights under Community law have been infringed.

In this regard, the order for reference mentions a Royal Decree of 1966, the decree concerning benefits ('Verstreckingenbesluit'), adopted under the Sickness Fund Law; for the purposes of that decree the term 'general practitioner' refers exclusively to a doctor enrolled on the register of general practitioners maintained by the Society. The practice of a doctor who is not enrolled on the register would thus not be recognised by the sickness insurance schemes. Under those circumstances a doctor who is not enrolled on the register is unable to treat, as a general practitioner, patients covered by the social security system. In fact, private practice is likewise made impossible by the fact that private insurers also define the term 'general practitioner' in their policies in the same way as the provisions of the decree concerning benefits.

A study of the Netherlands legislation and of the statutes and internal rules of the Society shows that a doctor who intends to establish himself in the Netherlands may not in fact practise either as a specialist, or as an expert in social medicine, or as a general practitioner, without being recognised and registered by the organs of the Society. In the same way it may be seen that the system thus established is the result of close cooperation between doctors who are members of the Society, the medical faculties and the departments of State responsible for higher education and health.

It is thus clear that both in the sector covered by the social security system and in the field of private medicine the Netherlands system of public health operates on the basis of the status accorded to doctors by the Society and that registration as a general practitioner is essential to every doctor wishing to establish himself in the Netherlands as a general practitioner.

Therefore a general practitioner who avails himself of the right of establishment and the freedom to provide services conferred upon him by Community law is faced with the necessity of applying to the Registration Committee established by the Society, and, in the event of his application's being refused, must appeal to the Appeals Committee. The Netherlands Government expressed the opinion that a doctor who is not a member of the Society would have the right to appeal against such a refusal to the ordinary courts, but stated that the point had never been decided by the Netherlands courts. Indeed all doctors, whether members of the Society or not, whose application to be registered as a general practitioner is refused, appeal to the Appeals Committee, whose decisions to the knowledge of the Netherlands Government have never been challenged in the ordinary courts.

In order to deal with the question of applicability in the present case of Article 177 of the Treaty, it should be noted that it is incumbent upon Member States to take the necessary steps to ensure that within their own territory the provisions adopted by the Community institutions are implemented in their entirety. If, under the legal system of a Member State, the task of implementing such provisions is assigned to a professional body acting under a degree of governmental supervision, and if that body, in conjunction with the public authorities concerned, creates appeal procedures which may affect the exercise of rights granted by Community law, it is imperative, in order to ensure the proper functioning of Community law, that the Court should have an opportunity of ruling on issues of interpretation and validity arising out of such proceedings.

As a result of all the foregoing considerations and in the absence, in practice, of any right of appeal to the ordinary courts, the Appeals Committee, which operates with the consent of the public authorities and with their cooperation, and which, after an adversarial procedure, delivers decisions which are in fact recognised as final, must, in a matter involving the application of Community law, be considered as a court or tribunal of a Member State within the meaning of Article 177 of the Treaty. Therefore, the Court has jurisdiction to reply to the question asked.

2. 'OF A MEMBER STATE'

The preceding two cases were concerned principally with the expression 'court or tribunal'; but in order to refer a question to the European Court under Article 177 a body must be a 'court or tribunal of a Member State'. Where the parties to a dispute agree to submit their differences to arbitration and to be bound by the arbitrator's decision, the arbitrator is by no means necessarily a court or tribunal of a Member State. He may well be independent of the State, even though his decision is binding and even though the person chosen as arbitrator may be in fact a national judge.

Case 102/81 Nordsee Deutsche Hochseefischerei GmbH v Reederei Mond Hochseefischerei Nordstern AG & Co KG and Another
[1982] ECR 1095

In the course of proceedings relating to ship building contracts, the arbitrator referred to the European Court several questions. By the first of these he asked whether the Court was competent to dispose under Article 177 of questions referred by such an arbitrator.

The Court

Since the arbitration tribunal which referred the matter to the Court for a preliminary ruling was established pursuant to a contract between private individuals the question arises whether it may be considered as a court or tribunal of one of the Member States within the meaning of Article 177 of the Treaty.

The first question put by the arbitrator concerns that problem. It is worded as follows:

'Is a German arbitration court, which must decide not according to equity but according to law, and whose decision has the same effects as regards the parties as a definitive judgment of a court of law (Article 1040 of the Zivilprozeßordnung [rules of civil procedure]) authorised to make a reference to the Court of Justice of the European Communities for a preliminary ruling pursuant to the second paragraph of Article 177 of the EEC Treaty?'

It must be noted that, as the question indicates, the jurisdiction of the Court to rule on questions referred to it depends on the nature of the arbitration in question.

It is true, as the arbitrator noted in his question, that there are certain similarities between the activities of the arbitration tribunal in question and those of an ordinary court or tribunal inasmuch as the arbitration is provided for within the framework of the law, the arbitrator must decide according to law and his award has, as between the parties, the force of *res judicata*, and may be enforceable if leave to issue execution is obtained. However, those characteristics are not sufficient to give the arbitrator the status of a 'court or tribunal of a Member State' within the meaning of Article 177 of the Treaty.

The first important point to note is that when the contract was entered into in 1973 the parties were free to leave their disputes to be resolved by the ordinary courts or to opt for arbitration by inserting a clause to that effect in the contract. From the facts of the case it appears that the parties were under no obligation, whether in law or in fact, to refer their disputes to arbitration.

The second point to be noted is that the German public authorities are not involved in the decision to opt for arbitration nor are they called upon to intervene automatically in the proceedings before the arbitrator. The Federal Republic of Germany, as a Member State of the Community responsible for the performance of obligations arising from Community law within its territory pursuant to Article 5 and Articles 169 to 171 of the Treaty, has not entrusted or left to private individuals the duty of ensuring that such obligations are complied with in the sphere in question in this case.

It follows from these considerations that the link between the arbitration procedure in this instance and the organisation of legal remedies through the courts in the Member State in question is not sufficiently close for the arbitrator to be considered as a 'court or tribunal of a Member State' within the meaning of Article 177.

As the court has confirmed in its judgment of 6 October 1981 (Case 246/80 *Broekmeulen* [1981] ECR 2311), Community law must be observed in its entirety throughout the territory of all the Member States; parties to a contract are not, therefore, free to create exceptions to it. In that context attention must be drawn to the fact that if questions of Community law are raised in an arbitration resorted to by agreement the ordinary courts may be called upon to examine them either in the context of their collaboration with arbitration tribunals, in particular to order to assist them in certain procedural matters or to interpret the law applicable, or in the course of a review of an arbitration award – which may be more or less extensive depending on the circumstances – and which they may be required to effect in case of an appeal or objection, in proceedings for leave to issue execution or by any other method of recourse available under the relevant national legislation.

It is for those national courts and tribunals to ascertain whether it is necessary for them to make a reference to the Court under Article 177 of the Treaty in order to obtain the interpretation or assessment of the validity of provisions of Community law which they may need to apply when exercising such auxiliary or supervisory functions.

It follows that in this instance the Court has no jurisdiction to give a ruling.

III EXERCISE OF DISCRETION

If a question is to be referred from a national court to the Court of Justice, the national judge must consider that a *decision* on the question is necessary to enable him to give judgment. In an early case Lord Denning stated that the *reference* itself must be considered as necessary.

H. P. Bulmer Ltd and Another v J. Bollinger SA and Others

[1974] 2 All ER 1226; [1974] 2 CMLR 91

Lord Denning MR

For many years now some producers of cider in England have been marketing some of their drinks as 'champagne cider' and 'champagne perry'. When it started the French producers of champagne took no steps to stop it. It went on for a long time. But in 1970 the French producers brought an action against an English firm, claiming an injunction. They sought to stop the use of the name champagne in these drinks. To counter this, two of the biggest producers of cider in England on 8 October 1970 brought an action against the French producers. They claimed declarations that they were entitled to use the expression 'champagne cider' and 'champagne perry'. They said that they had used those expressions for 70 or 80 years in England; that many millions of bottles had been marketed under those descriptions; and that the government of the United Kingdom had recognised it in the various regulations. They said further that the French producers had acquiesced in the use and were estopped from complaining. In answer the French producers of champagne claimed that the use of the word 'champagne' in connection with any beverage other than champagne was likely to lead to the belief that such beverage was or resembled champagne, or was a substitute for it, or was in some way connected with champagne. They claimed an injunction to stop the English producers from using the word 'champagne' in connection with any beverages not being a wine produced in the Champagne district of France.

After England joined the Common Market
Thus far it was a straightforward action for passing-off. It was to be determined by well-known principles of English law. But on 1 January 1973 England joined the Common Market. On 26 March 1973 the French producers amended their pleading so as to add these claims:

> '9A. Following the adhesion of the United Kingdom to the European Economic Community the use of the word "champagne" in connection with any beverage other than champagne will contravene European Community Law'.

They relied on EEC Regulation No 816/70, Article 30, and EEC Regulation No 817/70, Articles 12 and 13. By a further amendment they counterclaimed for:

> 'A declaration that the use by the [English producers] of the expression "Champagne Cider" and "Champagne Perry" in relation to beverages other than wine produced in the Champagne District of France is contrary to European Community Law'.

Reference to Luxembourg
Now the French producers ask that two points of European Community law should be referred to the European Court at Luxembourg. Shortened, they are:

(a) 'Whether ... the use of the word "champagne" in connection with any beverage other than champagne is a contravention of ... the provisions of European Community law'.

(b) 'Whether ... a national court of a Member State should ... refer to the Court of Justice [of the European Community] such a question as has been raised herein...'

The judge at first instance refused to refer either question at this stage. He said that he would try the whole case out before he came to a decision on it. The French producers appeal to this court.

...

To answer these questions, we must consider several points of fundamental importance. To make the discussion easier to understand, I will speak only of the interpretation of 'the Treaty', but this must be regarded as including the regulations and directions under it. I will make reference to the English courts because I am specially concerned with them; but this must be regarded as including the national courts of any Member State.

The Impact of the Treaty on English Law
The first and fundamental point is that the Treaty concerns only those matters which have a European element, that is to say, matters which affect people or property in the nine countries of the Common Market besides ourselves. The Treaty does not touch any of the matters which concern solely the mainland of England and the people in it. These are still governed by English law. They are not affected by the Treaty. But when we come to matters with a European element, the Treaty is like an incoming tide. It flows into estuaries and up the rivers. It cannot be held back. Parliament has decreed that the Treaty is henceforward to be part of our law. It is equal in force to any statute...

The Discretion to refer or not to refer
Short of the House of Lords, no other English court is bound to refer a question to the European Court at Luxembourg. Not even a question on the *interpretation* of the Treaty. Article 177(2) uses the permissive word 'may' in contrast to 'shall' in Article 177(3). In England the trial judge has complete *discretion*. If a question arises on the interpretation of

the Treaty, an English judge can decide it for himself. He need not refer it to the Court at Luxembourg unless he wishes. He can say: 'It will be too costly', or 'It will take too long to get an answer', or 'I am well able to decide it myself'. If he does decide it himself, the European Court cannot interfere. None of the parties can go off to the European Court and complain. The European Court would not listen to any party who went moaning to them. The European Court take the view that the trial judge has a complete discretion to refer or not to refer (see *Firma Rheinmühlen Düsseldorf* v *German Intervention Agency for Cereals and Feeding-stuffs*) with which they cannot interfere (see *Milchwerke Heinz Wöhrmann & Sohn KG* and *Alfons Lütticke GmbH* v *Commission*, above p. 122). If a party wishes to challenge the decision of the trial judge in England – to refer or not to refer – he must appeal to the Court of Appeal in England. (If the judge makes an order referring the question to Luxembourg, the party can appeal *without leave*: see RSC Order 114. If the judge refuses to make an order, he needs leave, because it is an interlocutory order: see the Supreme Court of Judicature (Consolidation) Act 1925, Section 31.) The judges of the Court of Appeal, in their turn, have complete discretion. They can interpret the Treaty themselves if they think fit. If the Court of Appeal do interpret it themselves, the European Court will not rebuke them for doing so. If a party wishes to challenge the decision of the Court of Appeal – to refer or not to refer – he must get leave to go to the House of Lords and go there. It is only in that august place that there is no discretion. If the point of interpretation is one which is 'necessary' to give a ruling, the House *must* refer it to the European Court at Luxembourg. The reason behind this imperative is this. The cases which get to the House of Lords are substantial cases of the first importance. If a point of interpretation arises there, it is assumed to be worthy of reference to the European Court at Luxembourg. Whereas the points in the lower courts may not be worth troubling the European Court about. See the judgment of the German Court of Appeal at Frankfurt in *Re Export of Oat Flakes*.

The Condition Precedent to a Reference: it must be 'Necessary'

Whenever any English court thinks it would be helpful to get the view of the European Court – on the interpretation of the Treaty – there is a *condition precedent* to be fulfilled. It is a condition which applies to the House of Lords as well as to the lower courts. It is contained in the same paragraph of Article 177(2) of the Treaty and applies in Article 177(3) as well. It is this. An English court can only refer the matter to the European Court '*if it considers* that a decision on the question is necessary to enable it to give judgment'. Note the words 'if *it* considers'. That is, 'if the *English court* considers'. On this point again the opinion of the English courts is final, just as it is on the matter of discretion. An English judge can say either: 'I consider it necessary', or 'I do not consider it necessary'. His discretion in that respect is final. Let me take the two in order.

(i) If the English judge considers it *necessary* to refer the matter, no one can gainsay it save the Court of Appeal. The European Court will accept his opinion. It will not go into the grounds on which he based it. The European Court so held in *van Gend en Loos* (see p. 79 above) and *Albatros* v *Sopéco* (Case 20/64 [1965] ECR 29). It will accept the question as he formulates it: *Fratelli Grassi* v *Amministrazione delle Finanze* (Case 5/72 [1972] ECR 443). It will not alter it or send it back. Even if it is a faulty question, it will do the best it can with it: see *Deutsche Grammophon Gesellschaft mbH* v *Metro-SB-Grossmärkte GmbH & Co KG* (below p. 261). The European Court treated it as a matter between the English courts and themselves – to be dealt with in a spirit of cooperation – in which the parties have no place save that they are invited to be heard. It was so held in *Hessische Knappschaft* v *Maison Singer et Fils*.

(ii) If the English judge considers it *not necessary* to refer a question of interpretation to the European Court – but instead decides it himself – that is the end of the matter. It is no good a party going off to the European Court. They would not listen to him. They are conscious that the Treaty gives the final word in this respect to the English courts. From all I have read of their cases, they are very careful not to exceed their jurisdiction. They never do anything to trespass on any ground which is properly the province of the national courts.

The better view, and the one more faithful to the text of the article, is that it is the *decision* on the question that must be considered as necessary. If a question necessarily arises, a court other than one from whose judgment no remedy is available has the discretion whether or not to refer. A useful guide to the exercise of discretion was given in *Bulmer* v *Bollinger*.

The Guidelines

Seeing that these matters of 'necessary' and 'discretion' are the concern of the English courts, it will fall to the English judges to rule on them. Likewise the national courts of other Member States have to rule on them. They are matters on which guidance is needed. It may not be out of place, therefore, to draw attention to the way in which other national courts have dealt with them.

(1) *Guidelines as to whether a decision is necessary*

(i) *The point must be conclusive.* The English court has to consider whether 'a decision of the question is *necessary* to enable it to give *judgment*'. That means judgment in the very case which is before the court. The judge must have got to the stage when he says to himself: 'This clause of the Treaty is capable of two or more meanings. If it means *this*, I give judgment for the plaintiff. If it means *that*, I give judgment for the defendant'. In short, the point must be such that, whichever way the point is decided, it is conclusive of the case. Nothing more remains but to give judgment. The Hamburg court stressed the necessity in *Re Adjustment of Tax on Petrol*. In *van Duyn* v *Home Office* Pennycuick V-C said: 'It would be quite impossible to give judgment without such a decision'.

(ii) *Previous ruling.* In some cases, however, it may be found that the same point – or substantially the same point – has already been decided by the European Court in a previous case. In that event it is not necessary for the English court to decide it. It will follow the previous decision without troubling the European Court. But, as I have said, the European Court is *not* bound by its previous decisions. So if the English court thinks that a previous decision of the European court may have been wrong – or if there are new factors which ought to be brought to the notice of the European Court – the English court may consider it *necessary* to re-submit the point to the European Court. In that event, the European Court will consider the point again. It was so held by the European Court itself in the *Da Costa* case, in Holland in *Vereniging van Fabrikanten en Importeurs van Verbruiksartikelen (FIVA)* v *Mertens*, and in Germany in *Re Import of Powdered Milk*.

(iii) *Acte clair.* In other cases the English court may consider the point is reasonably clear and free from doubt. In that event there is no need to interpret the Treaty but only to apply it, and that is the task of the English court. It was so submitted by the Advocate General to the European Court in the *Da Costa* case. It has been so held by the highest courts in France: by the Conseil d'Etat in *Re Société des Pétroles Shell-Berre* (see above p.

156), by the Cour de Cassation in *State* v *Cornet,* and *Lapeyre* v *Administration de Douanes*; also by a superior court in Germany in *Re French Widow's Pension Settlement*.

(iv) *Decide the facts first.* It is to be noticed, too, that the word is 'necessary'. This is much stronger than 'desirable' or 'convenient'. There are some cases where the point, if decided one way, would shorten the trial greatly. But, if decided the other way, it would mean that the trial would have to go its full length. In such a case it might be 'convenient' or 'desirable' to take it as a preliminary point because it might save much time and expense. But it would not be 'necessary' at that stage. When the facts were investigated, it might turn out to have been quite unnecessary. The case would be determined on another ground altogether. As a rule you cannot tell whether it is necessary to decide a point until all the facts are ascertained. So in general it is best to decide the facts first.

Lord Denning then laid down guidelines to be followed by national courts, both in deciding whether to refer questions to the European Court and in interpreting European Community legislation.

I come now to the two specific questions sought to be referred. The first question raised is:

> 'Whether ... the use of the word 'champagne' in connection with any beverage other than champagne is a contravention of the provisions of European Community law'.

I do not think it is *necessary* at this stage to decide that question. Take the claim in passing-off. If the French growers succeeded in this claim for passing-off in English law – for an injunction and damages – it would not be necessary to decide the point under the regulations. So the facts must be found before it can be said that a reference is 'necessary'.

Next take the claim of the French growers for a declaration that the use of the expression 'Champagne Cider' and 'Champagne Perry' was contrary to European Community law. Counsel for the French producers said that it would be necessary on this issue to decide the point on the regulations. I do not agree. It is always a matter for the discretion of the judge whether to grant a declaration or not. He could very properly say in the present case: whatever the true interpretation of the regulations, it is not a case in which I would make any declaration on the point. Taking that view, it would not be necessary to decide the point.

Even if it could be said to be necessary to decide the point, I think that an English court (short of the House of Lords) should not, as a matter of discretion, refer it to the European Court. It should decide the point itself. It would take much time and money to get a ruling from the European Court. Meanwhile the whole action would be held up. It is, no doubt, an important point, but not a difficult one to decide. I think it would be better to deal with it as part of the whole case, both by the trial judge and by the Court of Appeal. If it should then go to the House of Lords, it will by that time have become clear whether it is a 'necessary' point or not. If it is, then the House of Lords will refer it.

The second point is: 'Whether a national court should ... refer to the Court of Justice such a question as has been raised herein'. The object of this question is to get a ruling from the European Court as to the circumstances in which a national court should refer a question of interpretation to the European Court. I am quite clear that it is unnecessary to ask this question. The answer is clear. It is not the province of the European Court to give any guidance or advice to the national court when it should, or should not, refer a question. That is a matter for the national court itself. It is no concern of the European Court.

In my opinion Whitford J was right in refusing to refer either of the questions. I would dismiss the appeal.

In a separate judgment, with which Stamp LJ concurred, Stephenson LJ explained that a reference should be made under Article 177 of the EEC Treaty only if a decision on the question was necessary, and not merely convenient or expedient. He refrained from laying down guidelines for the judge of first instance, except by observing that it is often difficult to isolate an issue for preliminary decision before ascertaining all the facts. Lord Denning's judgment in this case has been subjected to criticism, notably by F. Jacobs at 90 LQR (1974) 486.

In the *Samex* case, Bingham J gave an interpretation more in line with the contemporary view governing the exercise of discretion:

Customs and Excise Commissioners v ApS Samex
[1983] 1 All ER 1042

Bingham J

In this case the plaintiffs, the Commissioners of Customs and Excise, seek an order for condemnation of 199 bales of acrylic yarn under para 6 of Schedule 3 to the Customs and Excise Management Act 1979. The defendant, ApS Samex, a Danish company, resists that order. It contends that it has a defence to the Commissioners' action under Community law, in particular, under EEC Council Regulation No 3059/78 and under general principles of Community law. It accordingly seeks a reference to the Court of Justice of the European Communities at Luxembourg in order that those questions may be determined.

...

I turn to consider whether in all the circumstances it is proper for the questions which counsel for the defendant has raised to be referred to the Court of Justice under Article 177 of the Treaty. Article 177 reads:

> 'The Court of Justice shall have jurisdiction to give preliminary rulings concerning: (a) the interpretation of this Treaty; (b) the validity and interpretation of acts of the institutions of the Community; (c) the interpretation of the statutes of bodies established by an act of the Council, where those statutes so provide.
>
> Where such a question is raised before any court or tribunal of a Member State, that court or tribunal may, if it considers that a decision on the question is necessary to enable it to give judgment, request the Court of Justice to give a ruling thereon.
>
> Where any such question is raised in a case pending before a court or tribunal of a Member State, against whose decisions there is no judicial remedy under national law, that court or tribunal shall bring the matter before the Court of Justice'.

From the language of the article it is, I think, clear that, so far as the court of first instance is concerned, there are two questions to be answered: first, whether a decision on the question of Community law is necessary to enable it to give judgment, and, if it is so necessary, whether the court should in the exercise of its discretion order that a reference be made.

The guidelines as to the proper approach on both those questions were given by the Court of Appeal in *H. P. Bulmer Ltd* v *J. Bollinger SA* [1974] 2 All ER 1226 at 1234ff, [1974] Ch 401 at 422ff. Lord Denning MR draws attention to four points relevant to the question whether a decision is necessary. The first of those is that the point must be conclusive. On the facts of this case, as I understand it, the answer to be given by the Court of Justice will be conclusive in this sense, that if the answers are adverse to the defendant that will admittedly be the end of its case. If the answers are given favourably to the defendant, then depending on what those answers are and which of them are favourable, there may be some short issues or a short issue to be tried, but there is, I think, no doubt that the answer which the Court of Justice will give will be substantially, if not quite totally, determinative of this litigation.

The second point raised with reference to the necessity of a decision is previous ruling. Lord Denning MR says ([1974] 2 All ER 1226 at 1235, [1974] Ch 401 at 422):

> 'In some cases, however, it may be found that the same point – or substantially the same point – has already been decided by the European Court in a previous case. In that event it is not necessary for the English court to decide it. It can follow the previous decision without troubling the European Court'.

That, no doubt true in some cases, does not, I think, apply in this case, since it is not suggested that there is any previous ruling either on this regulation or on any analogous regulation which yields a clear answer to the present litigation.

Third, Lord Denning MR lists *acte clair* and says ([1974] 2 All ER 1226 at 1235, [1974] Ch 401 at 423):

> 'In other cases the English court may consider the point is reasonably clear and free from doubt. In that event there is no need to interpret the Treaty but only to apply it, and that is the task of the English court'.

It certainly is of course the task of the English court to apply it, but it must apply the Treaty properly interpreted. As I have indicated, I myself feel that the first three questions raised should certainly, if it rested with me, be answered in favour of the Commissioners, but I do not regard the matter as so free from doubt as to render those points *acte clair*, and I certainly do not regard the fourth point on the principle of proportionality as either reasonably clear or reasonably free from doubt.

Point four: Lord Denning MR says, 'Decide the facts first'. That, with respect, is an injunction of obvious merit. The present case is one in which the essential facts are agreed and on the very minor areas of disagreement or non-agreement the facts can without doubt be settled in a form which will enable the relevant question to be answered.

I therefore turn to the guidelines which Lord Denning MR has indicated governing the exercise of discretion. He mentions, first, the time to get a ruling, second, the undesirability of overloading the Court of Justice, third, the need to formulate the question clearly, fourth, the difficulty and importance of the point. Under that head he says ([1974] 2 All ER 1226 at 1236, [1974] Ch 401 at 424):

> '*Difficulty and importance.* Unless the point is really difficult and important, it would seem better for the English judge to decide it himself. For in so doing, much delay and expense will be saved. So far the English judges have not shirked their responsibilities. They have decided several points of interpretation on the Treaty to the satisfaction, I hope, of the parties'.

He refers, fifth, to expense, and, sixth, to the wishes of the parties. Under that head he says ([1974] 2 All ER 1226 at 1236, [1974] Ch 401 at 425):

> 'If both parties want the point to be referred to the European Court, the English court should have regard to their wishes, but it should not give them undue weight. The English court should hesitate before making a reference against the wishes of one of the parties, seeing the expense and delay which it involves'.

Lord Denning MR then goes on to discuss the principles of interpretation and draws attention to the different approach which is required in interpreting Community legislation as compared with our own domestic legislation.

In endeavouring to follow and respect these guidelines I find myself in some difficulty, because it was submitted by counsel on behalf of the defendant that the issues raised by his client should be resolved by the Court of Justice as the court best fitted to do so, and I find this a consideration which does give me some pause for thought. *Sitting as a judge in a national court, asked to decide questions of Community law, I am very conscious of the advantages enjoyed by the Court of Justice.* It has a panoramic view of the Community and its institutions, a detailed knowledge of the Treaties and of much subordinate legislation made under them, and an intimate familiarity with the functioning of the Community market which no national judge denied the collective experience of the Court of Justice could hope to achieve. Where questions of administrative intention and practice arise the Court of Justice can receive submissions from the Community institutions, as also where relations between the Community and non-Member States are in issue. Where the interests of Member States are affected they can intervene to make their views known. That is a material consideration in this case since there is some slight evidence that the practice of different Member States is divergent. Where comparison falls to be made between Community texts in different languages, all texts being equally authentic, the multinational Court of Justice is equipped to carry out the task in a way which no national judge, whatever his linguistic skills, could rival. The interpretation of Community instruments involves very often not the process familiar to common lawyers of laboriously extracting the meaning from words used but the more creative process of supplying flesh to a spare and loosely constructed skeleton. The choice between alternative submissions may turn not on purely legal considerations, but on a broader view of what the orderly development of the Community requires. These are matters which the Court of Justice is very much better placed to assess and determine than a national court.

It does not follow from this that a reference should be made by a national court of first instance wherever a litigant raises a serious point of Community law and seeks a reference, or wherever he indicates an intention to appeal, even if he announces an intention to appeal, if necessary, to the highest court which is effectively bound to refer the question to the Court of Justice. For example, as *H. P. Bulmer Ltd* v *J. Bollinger SA* points out, it can rarely be necessary to make a reference until the relevant facts have been found, and unless the points raised are substantially determinative of the action. Or the question raised may admit of one one possible answer, or it may be covered by Community authority precisely in point, although even here some slight caution is necessary since the Court of Justice is not strictly bound by its own decisions. These considerations relate to whether a decision is necessary. Other considerations may affect the exercise of discretion. Sometimes no doubt it may appear that the question is raised mischievously, not in the bona fide hope of success but in order to obstruct or delay an almost inevitable adverse judgment, denying the other party his remedy meanwhile. In my judgment none of these contra-indications obtains here. While I think the defendant unlikely to succeed, I do not regard its arguments as hopeless and they are of potential importance. I have been referred to no authority precisely in point and, so far as I know, Regulation No 3059/78 has never been considered by the Court of Justice. The defendant is at present denied the possession or use of the yarn but is paying and will continue to pay for its storage, at least unless some other arrangement is made for disposal of the goods. It has already given security for the Commissioners' costs under para 10(2) of Sch 3 to the Customs and Excise Management Act 1979, and has expressed willingness to increase that security. If a reference produces a ruling unfavourable to it, it will almost certainly be ordered to pay the costs incurred by the Commissioners as a result of it. It has nothing to hope from delay, save the hope of success. The reference to the Court of Justice would be unlikely to take longer than appeals have normally taken to reach the Court of Appeal, at least until recently, and unlikely to cost much more. If, at the Court of Appeal stage, a reference were held to be necessary, the delay and expense would be roughly doubled. I discount the indication of counsel for the defendant that if denied a reference in this court his client would probably, according to his present instructions, appeal to the Court of Appeal and seek a reference there, but in all the circumstances this does appear to me to be an appropriate case in which questions of potentially great importance in the operation of the Community's system for regulating imports to Member States should be reviewed.

I shall accordingly order a reference under Article 177 of the EEC Treaty. The precise form of that reference is something that I think will have to be the subject of discussion hereafter.

IV THE DUTY TO REFER

It will be noted that in *Bulmer* v *Bollinger* [1974] 2 All ER 1226; [1974] 2 CMLR 97 Lord Denning said that 'short of the House of Lords, no other English court is bound to refer a question to the European Court at Luxembourg' (see above, p. 167). He was there referring to the final paragraph of Article 177 which requires the court to refer when there is no judicial remedy under national law against its decision. An obligation may well arise for a court other than the highest national court to refer a question under Article 177. Even an inferior court is under the obligation to refer when, in the particular case, there is no judicial remedy under national law against its decision. In Case 6/64 *Costa* v *Enel* [1964] ECR 585; [1964] CMLR 425 (see above p. 4) the Italian giudice conciliatore correctly considered that he was under an obligation to refer the questions even though he occupied an inferior rank within the Italian judiciary; for the case before him was a small claim and in such a case there was in Italian law no judicial remedy against his decision.

The European Court has now established that a national court has no jurisdiction to declare that measures taken by Community institutions are invalid. Accordingly, even a national judge against whose decision there *is* a judicial remedy will have no option other than to refer to the European Court a question on the invalidity of Community legislation if he considers that a decision on that question is necessary to enable him to give judgment, and if the point is not so clear that he can simply declare the legislation to be *valid*.

Case 314/85 Firma Foto-Frost v Hauptzollamt Lübeck-Ost
22 October 1987

The Court
In its first question the Finanzgericht asks whether it itself is competent to declare invalid a Commission decision such as the decision of 6 May 1983. It casts doubt on the validity of that decision on the ground that all the requirements laid down by Article 5(2) of Regulation No 1697/79 for taking no action for the post-clearance recovery of duty seem to be fulfilled in this case. However, it considers that in view of the division of jurisdiction between the Court of Justice and the national courts set out in Article 177 of the EEC Treaty only the Court of Justice is competent to declare invalid acts of the Community institutions.

Article 177 confers on the Court jurisdiction to give preliminary rulings on the interpretation of the Treaty and of acts of the Community institutions and on the validity of such acts. The second paragraph of that article provides that national courts may refer such questions to the Court and the third paragraph of that article puts them under an obligation to do so where there is no judicial remedy under national law against their decisions.

In enabling national courts against whose decisions there is a judicial remedy under national law to refer to the Court for a preliminary ruling questions on interpretation or validity, Article 177 did not settle the question whether those courts themselves may declare that acts of Community institutions are invalid.

Those courts may consider the validity of a Community act and, if they consider that the grounds put forward before them by the parties in support of invalidity are unfounded, they may reject them, concluding that the measure is completely valid. By taking that action they are not calling the existence of the Community measure into question.

On the other hand, those courts do not have the power to declare acts of the Community institutions invalid. As the Court emphasised in the judgment of 13 May 1981 (Case 66/80 *International Chemical Corporation* v *Amministrazione delle Finanze* [1981] ECR 1191), the main purpose of the powers accorded to the Court by Article 177 is to ensure that Community law is applied uniformly by national courts. That requirement of uniformity is particularly imperative when the validity of a Community act is in question. *Divergences between courts in the Member States as to the validity of Community acts would be liable to place in jeopardy the very unity of the Community legal order and detract from the fundamental requirement of legal certainty.*

The same conclusion is dictated by consideration of the necessary coherence of the system of judicial protection established by the Treaty. In that regard it must be observed that requests for preliminary rulings, like actions for annulment, constitute means for reviewing the legality of acts of the Community institutions. As the Court pointed out in its judgment of 23 April 1986 (Case 294/83 *Parti écologiste 'Les Verts'* v *Parliament* [1986] ECR 1339), 'in Articles 173 and 184, on the one hand, and in Article 177, on the other, the Treaty established a complete system of legal remedies and procedures designed to permit the Court of Justice to review the legality of measures adopted by the institutions'.

Since Article 173 gives the Court exclusive jurisdiction to declare void an act of a Community institution, the coherence of the system requires that where the validity of a Community act is challenged before a national court the power to declare the act invalid must also be reserved to the Court of Justice.

It must also be emphasised that the Court of Justice is in the best position to decide on the validity of Community acts. Under Article 20 of the Protocol on the Statute of the Court of Justice of the EEC, Community institutions whose acts are challenged are entitled to participate in the proceedings in order to defend the validity of the acts in question. Furthermore, under the second paragraph of Article 21 of that Protocol the Court may require the Member States and institutions which are not participating in the proceedings to supply all information which it considers necessary for the purpose of the case before it.

It should be added that the rule that national courts may not themselves declare Community acts invalid may have to be qualified in certain circumstances in the case of proceedings relating to an application for interim measures; however, that case is not referred to in the national court's question.

The answer to the first question must therefore be that national courts have no jurisdiction themselves to declare that acts of Community institutions are invalid.

V LEGAL AID

When it answers questions referred to it by a national court or tribunal, the European Court does not make an award of costs in favour of either of the parties. This is so even when it is plain from the answer that the national judge can only give judgment in favour of one party rather than another. The Court explains its practice by observing that the proceedings before the European Court are to be regarded as a stage of the proceedings before the national court; and it is for the national court to make any award of costs that may be appropriate. The national rules of procedure may well provide that the successful party may be awarded costs in respect of the entire proceedings including those before the European Court.

By parity of reasoning, the Divisional Court has held that a legal aid order, made to cover proceedings before a Magistrates' Court, automatically covers proceedings before the European Court if the magistrates have referred questions to it under Article 177.

Regina v Marlborough Street Stipendiary Magistrate ex parte Bouchereau
[1977] 1 WLR 414; [1977] 3 All ER 365; [1977] 1 CMLR 269

Bouchereau, a French national working in England, appeared before the Marlborough Street Magistrate charged with the possession of dangerous drugs. The Magistrate had it in mind to recommend Bouchereau's deportation. It was argued on Bouchereau's behalf that such a recommendation would be inconsistent with Article 48 of the EEC Treaty (see below, Chapter 7). Accordingly the Magistrate decided to refer to the European Court questions on the meaning of Article 48. The Magistrate was asked to certify that the legal aid certificate, granted for the appearance in the Magistrates' Court, extended to the proceedings in Luxembourg. He refused so to certify; and Bouchereau's counsel sought judicial review of that refusal.

Lord Widgery CJ

The vital question as I see it is whether legal aid to go to Luxembourg, if one may so put it, is legal aid given for the purposes of the proceedings at Marlborough Street because it is only if the legal aid is granted for the purposes of proceedings at Marlborough Street that it comes within section 28(2) [of the Criminal Justice Act 1967, on the provisions of legal aid in proceedings before a Magistrate's Court]. The language is not particularly helpful in itself and the question is in my judgment a somewhat open one, save of course that it would be a very strange thing if Parliament had made comprehensive provisions for legal aid in criminal proceedings by this Act and its predecessor and had in any sense deliberately excluded proceedings which take place on a reference either at the time now in question or other references concerning other persons.

However, looking at the authorities under the guidance of counsel, there seem to me to be two which do point quite clearly in which way the decision in this court should go. Mr Newman has been very active in giving us every possible assistance in the form of authority, but, as I have indicated, I do not get very much out of most of the cases which have been cited to us. There are however two which I feel provide a solution to the problem.

The first is *van Duyn* v *Home Office* [1975] Ch. 358. I cite it for it is a reference to the European Court under Article 177 of the Treaty and, in particular, because it shows the attitude of the European Court towards costs. One finds in the judgment, at p. 379:

> 'The costs incurred by the United Kingdom and by the Commission of the European Communities, which have submitted observations to the court, are not recoverable, and as these proceedings are, in so far as the parties to the main action are concerned, a step in the action pending before the national court, costs are a matter for that court'.

A flood of light, I think, is thrown on this problem by those few lines because it makes perfectly clear that the attitude of the European Court is that costs are matters for the domestic tribunals. The European Court answers the problem and the parties go home and their national courts deal with questions of costs which have arisen during the course of proceedings, and that is because the reference to the European Court is just a step in the proceedings. It could not be more than that. It could not be simpler.

One gets the same sort of guidance from Case 62/72 *Bollmann* v *Hauptzollamt Hamburg-Waltershof* [1973] ECR 269. I do not find it necessary to go in any way into the matters for decision in that case, but merely to look again at what happened about costs. On p. 271 one finds this phrase contained in the judgment at the issues of fact and law stage. These are the words that impress me:

> 'Where the Court of Justice has ruled that the decision as to costs in an application for a preliminary ruling is a matter for the national court, should (a) the procedure for the recovery of costs, and (b) the recoverability of expenses necessarily incurred by the parties for the purposes of the proceedings, in particular the remuneration of lawyers, be determined by reference to Community law (Articles 73 and 74 of the Rules of Procedure of the Court of Justice), or by reference to the rules laid down by national law in the matter?'

That question having been posed at an early stage in the judgment which is the practice of the European Court, we find the answers on pp. 275 and 276. It is said, at p. 275:

> 'Proceedings instituted under Article 177 are non-contentious and are in the nature of a step in the action pending before a national court, as the parties to the main action are merely invited to state their case within the legal limits laid down by the national court'.

It is said, at p. 276:

> 'The costs incurred by the Government of the Federal Republic of Germany and the Commission of the European Communities, which have submitted observations to the Court, are not recoverable, and as these proceedings are, in so far as the parties to the main action are concerned, in the nature of a step in the action pending before the national court, the decision on costs is a matter for that court'.

Not only does that seem to me to make the position clear, but it also provides a perfectly sensible and workmanlike scheme. I have been troubled earlier on in the argument lest we were being invited to say that English costs would have to be taxed in Luxembourg or vice versa. But when one realises that the excursion to Luxembourg is merely a step in the proceedings, and when it is realised that all questions of costs are still dealt with domestically and nationally, it seems to me that any doubts about the efficiency of this procedure disappear and I am pleased to find it possible to say that this is a case in which legal aid can, and indeed should, be extended for the purpose under review.

VI THE RESPECTIVE FUNCTIONS OF THE NATIONAL AND EUROPEAN COURTS

The European Court has on several occasions stated that Article 177 presupposes distinct and separate functions for the national and European courts. In principle, it is the exclusive function of the national court to determine issues of fact and to determine whether a reference shall be made. The European Court's function is in principle confined to that of determining authoritatively and conclusively the answer to the question put by the national court.

Case 35/76 Simmenthal SpA v Ministero delle Finanze
[1976] ECR 1871; [1977] 2 CMLR 1

Simmenthal imported to Italy from France a consignment of beef and veal for human consumption. The meat was subjected to public health inspection on crossing the frontier and the appropriate Italian administration passed on to Simmenthal the cost of the inspection. Maintaining that the charges were equivalent in effect to customs duties on trade between Member States, Simmenthal demanded their recovery. It instituted proceedings before the Pretura of Susa; and the Pretura referred to the European Court questions about the interpretation of the pertinent articles in the EEC Treaty.

The Court

The plaintiff in the main action takes the view that the fees have been charged unlawfully, on the one hand because the organisation of compulsory and systematic veterinary and public health inspections – which are concerned in the present case – since the implementation of the veterinary and public health directives of 26 June 1964 has been a measure having an effect equivalent to a quantitative restriction prohibited by the Treaty, which is the reason why the imposition of fees on this occasion was unlawful and, on the other hand because, in any event, the charging of fees for such inspections is an infringement of Articles 9 and 13 of the Treaty which prohibit the imposition of any charges having an effect equivalent to a customs duty on imports. Since these directives standardise national provisions relating to the veterinary and public health inspection of certain meat, bovine animals and swine and lay down that measures ensuring that this supervision is carried out must be taken by the exporting Member State, they have made systematic inspections at the frontiers of the said products unnecessary and, consequently, unjustifiable under Article 36 of the Treaty.

The Government of the Italian Republic has denied that the veterinary and public health inspections of the products referred to in the directives which it organised were carried out systematically and produces documents in support of its view that this is not the case. Consequently it has expressed doubts as to the relevance of the questions referred.

Article 177 of the EEC Treaty is based on a distinct separation of functions between national courts and tribunals on the one hand and the Court of Justice on the other hand and it does not give the Court jurisdiction to take cognisance *of the facts of the case, or to criticise the reasons for the reference.*

The Court is entitled to pronounce on the interpretation of the Treaty and of acts of the institutions but cannot apply them to the case in question since such application falls within the jurisdiction of the national court.

In the event the European Court ruled that it was immaterial whether the veterinary and health inspections were carried out systematically or not. In either case, such inspections constituted in the Court's view measures having an effect equivalent to quantitative restrictions within the meaning of Article 30 of the EEC Treaty; and charges for such inspections were prohibited unless they related to a general system of internal dues applied systematically in accordance with the same criteria to domestic and imported products alike.

From the fact that the European Court's function, in cases brought under Article 177, is one of interpretation, it may also be inferred that the national court alone must determine whether a question is to be referred. It is not open to the European Court to refuse to consider a question validly posed by a national court, even on the ground that the question has already been answered in some other case.

Joined Cases 28, 29 and 30/62 Da Costa en Schaake NV, Jacob Meijer NV and Hoechst-Holland NV v Nederlandse Belastingadministratie

[1963] ECR 31; [1963] CMLR 224

In Spring 1960 the three plaintiffs, all Dutch companies, imported to the Netherlands goods from the Federal Republic of Germany. In all three cases the defendant classified the imports for customs purposes in accordance with the Brussels Protocol of 25 July 1968, concluded between the Member States of the Benelux Economic Union and approved by the Dutch Law of 16 December 1959. On the basis of this classification, the defendant in all three cases subjected the imports to a rate of duty higher than that which was applied on 1 January 1958. All the plaintiffs maintained that the imposition of such a duty was invalid since it contravened Article 12 of the EEC Treaty, which prohibits any increase in the customs duties levied by Member States in their trade with each other, beyond the rate applicable at the beginning of 1958. The respondent replied in the first two cases that Article 12 of the EEC Treaty does not have direct effects for the nationals of the signatory states, and in the third case it made a similar (but not identical) reply. The cases were heard by the Tariefcommissie, a Dutch tribunal from which there is no right of appeal. The Tariefcommissie suspended the proceedings in accordance with Article 177 of the EEC Treaty and in each case referred to the Court of Justice of the European Communities the questions:

(1) Whether Article 12 of the EEC Treaty produces direct effect within the territory of a Member State;

(2) If so, whether there had been an unlawful increase in customs duty.

These questions were materially identical with those that had been the subject of a preliminary ruling in Case 26/62 *van Gend en Loos* v *Nederlandse Administratie der Belastingen* [1963] (see above p. 79).

The Court

The regularity of the procedure followed by the Tariefcommissie in requesting the Court for a preliminary ruling under Article 177 of the EEC Treaty has not been disputed and there is no ground for the Court to raise the matter of its own motion.

The Commission, appearing by virtue of the provisions of Article 20 of the Statute of the Court of Justice of the EEC, urges that the request should be dismissed for lack of substance, since the questions on which an interpretation is requested from the Court in the present cases have already been decided by the judgment of 5 February 1963 in Case 26/62, which covered identical questions raised in a similar case.

This contention is not justified. A distinction should be made between the obligation imposed by the third paragraph of Article 177 upon national courts or tribunals of last instance and the power granted by the second paragraph of Article 177 to every national court or tribunal to refer to the Court of the Communities a question on the interpretation of the Treaty. Although the third paragraph of Article 177 unreservedly requires courts or tribunals of a Member State against whose decisions there is no judicial remedy under national law – like the Tariefcommissie – to refer to the Court every question of interpreta-

/tion raised before them, the authority of an interpretation under Article 177 already given by the Court may deprive the obligation of its purpose and thus empty it of its substance. Such is the case especially when the question raised is materially identical with a question which has already been the subject of a preliminary ruling in a similar case.

When it gives an interpretation of the Treaty in a specific action pending before a national court, the Court limits itself to deducing the meaning of the Community rules from the wording and spirit of the Treaty, it being left to the national court to apply in the particular case the rules which are thus interpreted. Such an attitude conforms with the function assigned to the Court by Article 177 of ensuring unity of interpretation of Community law within the six Member States. If Article 177 had not such a scope, the procedural requirements of Article 20 of the Statute of the Court of Justice, which provides for the participation in the hearing of the Member States and the Community institutions, and of the third paragraph of Article 165 of the Treaty, which requires the Court to sit in plenary session, would not be justified. This aspect of the activity of the Court within the framework of Article 177 is confirmed by the absence of parties, in the proper sense of the word, which is characteristic of this procedure.

It is no less true that Article 177 always allows a national court, if it considers it desirable, to refer questions of interpretation to the Court again. This follows from Article 20 of the Statute of the Court of Justice, under which the procedure laid down for the settlement of preliminary questions is automatically set in motion as soon as such a question is referred by a national court.

The Court must, therefore, give a judgment on the present application.

The interpretation of Article 12 of the EEC Treaty, which is here requested, was given in the Court's judgment of 5 February 1963 in Case 26/62. This ruled that:

'1. Article 12 of the Treaty establishing the European Economic Community produces direct effects and creates individual rights which national courts must protect.

2. In order to ascertain whether customs duties or charges having equivalent effect have been increased contrary to the prohibition contained in Article 12 of the Treaty, regard must be had to the duties and charges actually applied by the Member State in question at the date of the entry into force of the Treaty. Such an increase can arise both from a re-arrangement of the tariff resulting in the classification of the product under a more highly taxed heading and from an increase in the rate of customs duty applied'.

The questions of interpretation posed in this case are identical with those settled as above and no new factor has been presented to the Court.

In these circumstances the Tariefcommissie must be referred to the previous judgment.

Case 117/77 Bestuur van het Algemeen Ziekenfonds, Drenthe-Platteland v G. Pierik [1978] ECR 825; [1978] 3 CMLR 343

The Court

The Centrale Raad van Beroep by a letter from its President of 28 September 1977 which reached the Court on 30 September 1977 has submitted to the Court of Justice pursuant to Article 177 of the EEC Treaty questions on the interpretation of certain provisions of Regulation (EEC) No 1408/71 of the Council of 14 June 1971 on the application of social security schemes to employed persons and their families moving within the Community (Official Journal, English Special Edition, 1971 (II), p. 416).

These questions were submitted within the framework of a dispute concerning the refusal of the competent Netherlands social security institution to refund to a worker residing in the Netherlands and entitled to invalidity benefit in pursuance of Netherlands legislation the costs incurred in a course of hydrotherapy in the Federal Republic of Germany.

The above-mentioned social security institution based its refusal on the Wet op Arbeidsongeschiktheidsverzekering (law on insurance against incapacity for work) in accordance with which measures intended to maintain, re-establish or improve capacity for work shall be accorded to a person entitled to invalidity benefits only in so far as they are not included amongst the benefits in kind governed by certain provisions of Netherlands social security legislation.

The Commission in its observations expressed doubts regarding the relevance and utility in the present case of the questions submitted since it considered that Article 22 of Regulation No 1408/71 does not relate to the matter before the national court.

It suggested that the Court of Justice should make a statement to this effect in its decision.

Article 177 of the Treaty, which is based on a clear separation of functions between national courts and the Court of Justice, does not permit the latter to pass judgment on the relevance of the questions submitted.

Accordingly the question whether the provisions or concepts of Community law whose interpretation is requested are in fact applicable to the case in question lies outside the jurisdiction of the Court of Justice and falls within the jurisdiction of the national court.

Nevertheless, circumstances may arise in which it is necessary for the European Court to do rather more than answer the question as it has been framed by the national court. In order to assist the national court, the European Court may need to enquire into the facts, as they appear from the record, for the purpose of 'defining the legal context' of the European Court's ruling.

Case 244/78 Union Laitière Normande, a group of agricultural cooperatives v French Dairy Farmers Limited
[1979] ECR 2663; [1980] 1 CMLR 314

In the context of an action between a group of French agricultural cooperatives and its English subsidiary, concerning the performance of a contract to supply standardised whole milk from France to England, the Tribunal de Commerce of Paris referred five questions to the European Court. The questions related to various aspects of the packaging and licensing regulations concerning milk, but the European Court did not consider them in the order in which they had been submitted.

The Court

Before proceeding to examine the questions which have been referred to the Court for a preliminary ruling, it should be noted that, whilst Article 177 of the Treaty does not permit the Court to evaluate the grounds for making the reference, the need to afford a helpful

interpretation of Community law makes it essential to define the legal context in which the interpretation requested should be placed.

Although the national court did not give its reasons for asking the Court to interpret the Community law, it appears from the file on the case that it considers an interpretation necessary for its decision on the consequences which are to follow from the non-performance of the disputed contract to ascertain whether the English legislation which prevents the marketing of the products in question within the United Kingdom was or was not, at the date on which those products were imported, justified under Community law.

It also appears from the file on the case that, whereas certain provisions in that legislation, such as Regulation 4 in Part II of the British Statutory Instrument No 1033 of 16 June 1977, read together with the provisions in Schedule 2, Part IV require, for obtaining a dealer's licence for whole milk bearing the special designation 'UHT', that the product, immediately after having been treated by the UHT method, be packaged on 'registered premises', other provisions in the same legislation, especially those in the Weights and Measures Act 1963, provide in paragraph 3, Part V of Schedule 4 that for the marketing of any 'pre-packaged' milk, whether imported or not, the product must be made available for distribution in containers of a capacity of one third of a pint, half a pint, or a multiple of half a pint.

It is accepted that in this case the milk in question was imported into the United Kingdom and made available for distribution in that Member State in containers with a capacity of one litre. Since this milk was 'pre-packed' in a way which did not comply with the requirements laid down by the British Weights and Measures Act 1963, the first difficulty in marketing the goods in England was presented by the provisions in that act, so that in fact the question of the compatibility with Community law of the British legislation concerning the marketing of UHT whole milk in the United Kingdom must, in the case of the imports concerned in this dispute, be considered first with reference to that act.

That being so, the fourth question should be answered first and the others examined only if it appears that the British national legislation concerning the packaging of pre-packed milk could have applied in this case to the marketing in England of the product under discussion.

...

The Court answered that question in a way that made it unnecessary to answer the other questions, so it declined to answer them.

In its controversial judgments in the two *Foglia* v *Novello* cases the European Court refused to give a ruling on questions referred by the national judge, even though the questions indisputably involved the interpretation of articles of the EEC Treaty and the national judge declared that he considered it necessary to obtain answers to the questions in order to give judgment. There were several factors in those two cases leading the European Court to decline jurisdiction:

1) the parties were agreed as to the outcome and there appeared to be no genuine dispute before the national court,
2) the litigation was artificial in the sense that the parties appeared to have concluded a contract with the object of creating a factual situation to support a reference to the European Court,

3) by proceedings before an Italian court the parties called in question the validity of French law.

Case 104/79 Pasquale Foglia v Mariella Novello
[1980] ECR 745; [1981] 1 CMLR 45

The Court

By an order of 6 June 1979 which was received at the Court on 29 June 1979 the Pretura di Bra referred to the Court pursuant to Article 177 of the EEC Treaty five questions on the interpretation of Articles 92, 95 and 177 of the Treaty.

The proceedings before the Pretura di Bra concern the costs incurred by the plaintiff Mr Foglia, a wine dealer having his place of business at Santa Vittoria d'Alba in the province of Cuneo, Piedmont, Italy, in the dispatch to Menton, France of some cases of Italian liqueur wines which he sold to the defendant, Mrs Novello.

The file on the case shows that the contract of sale between Foglia and Novello stipulated that Novello should not be liable for any duties which were claimed by the Italian or French authorities contrary to the provisions on the free movement of goods between the two countries or which were at least not due. Foglia adopted a similar clause in his contract with the Danzas undertaking to which he entrusted the transport of the cases of liqueur wine to Menton; that clause provided that Foglia should not be liable for such unlawful charges or charges which were not due.

The order making the reference finds that the subject-matter of the dispute is restricted exclusively to the sum paid as a consumption tax when the liqueur wines were imported into French territory. The file and the oral argument before the Court of Justice have established that that tax was paid by Danzas to the French authorities, without protest or complaint; that the bill for transport which Danzas submitted to Foglia and which was settled included the amount of that tax and that Mrs Novello refused to reimburse the latter amount to Foglia in reliance on the clause on unlawful charges or charges which were not due expressly included in the contract of sale.

In the view of the Pretura the defences advanced by Novello entail calling into question the validity of French legislation concerning the consumption tax on liqueur wines in relation to Article 95 of the EEC Treaty.

The attitude of Foglia in the course of the proceedings before the Pretura may be described as neutral. Foglia has in fact maintained that he could not in any case be liable for the amount corresponding to the French consumption tax since, if it was lawfully charged, it should have been borne by Novello whilst Danzas would be liable if it were unlawful.

This point of view prompted Foglia to request the national court to increase the scope of the proceedings and to summon Danzas as a third party having an interest in the action. The court nevertheless considered that before it could give a ruling on that request it was necessary to settle the problem whether the imposition of the consumption tax paid by Danzas was in accordance with the provisions of the EEC Treaty or not.

The parties to the main action submitted a certain number of documents to the Pretura which enabled it to investigate the French legislation concerning the taxation of liqueur wines and other comparable products. The court concluded from its investigation that such legislation created a 'serious discrimination' against Italian liqueur wines and natural wines having a high degree of alcoholic strength by means of special arrangements made for French liqueur wines termed 'natural sweet wines' and preferential tax treatment accorded certain French natural wines with a high degree of alcoholic strength and bearing a designation of origin. On the basis of that conclusion the court formulated the questions which it has submitted to the Court of Justice.

In their written observations submitted to the Court of Justice the two parties to the main action have provided an essentially identical description of the tax discrimination which is a feature of the French legislation concerning the taxation of liqueur wines; the two parties consider that that legislation is incompatible with Community law. In the course of the oral procedure before the Court Foglia stated that he was participating in the procedure before the Court in view of the interest of his undertaking as such and as an undertaking belonging to a certain category of Italian traders in the outcome of the legal issues involved in the dispute.

It thus appears that the parties to the main action are concerned to obtain a ruling that the French tax system is invalid for liqueur wines by the expedient of proceedings before an Italian court between two private individuals who are in agreement as to the result to be attained and who have inserted a clause in their contract in order to induce the Italian court to give a ruling on the point. The artificial nature of this expedient is underlined by the fact that Danzas did not exercise its rights under French law to institute proceedings over the consumption tax although it undoubtedly had an interest in doing so in view of the clause in the contract by which it was also bound and moreover of the fact that Foglia paid without protest that undertaking's bill which included a sum paid in respect of that tax.

The duty of the Court of Justice under Article 177 of the EEC Treaty is to supply all courts in the Community with the information on the interpretation of Community law which is necessary to enable them to settle genuine disputes which are brought before them. A situation in which the Court was obliged by the expedient of arrangement like those described above to give rulings would jeopardise the whole system of legal remedies available to private individuals to enable them to protect themselves against tax provisions which are contrary to the Treaty.

This means that the questions asked by the national court, having regard to the circumstances of this case, do not fall within the framework of the duties of the Court of Justice under Article 177 of the Treaty.

The Court of Justice accordingly has no jurisdiction to give a ruling on the questions asked by the national court.

On receiving the European Court's reply, the national judge referred further questions. In short, he asked whether the judgment in *Foglia* v *Novello* (No 1) was consistent with the principle whereby the national judge alone must determine the facts. Further, he asked what a national judge must do when confronted with a question on the interpretation of the EEC Treaty to which the European Court was not prepared to reply. The Advocate General, Sir Gordon Slynn, was prepared at this stage to answer the questions put by the national judge. In his view, *Foglia* v *Novello* (No 1) was to be explained on the ground that the European Court could not establish on the basis of the file transmitted from the national judge that the national judge had *considered* whether it was necessary to refer the questions. The Advocate General concluded that the file submitted in connection with *Foglia* v *Novello* (No 2) established that the national judge had by that stage considered the necessity of the reference. Nevertheless, the Court adhered to the view that the questions were still inadmissible.

Case 244/80 Pasquale Foglia v Mariella Novello (No 2)
[1981] ECR 3045; [1982] 1 CMLR 585

The Court
In his first question the Pretore requested clarification of the limits of the power of appraisal reserved by the Treaty to the national court on the one hand and the Court of Justice on the other with regard to the wording of references for a preliminary ruling and of the appraisal of the circumstances of fact and of law in the main action, in particular where the national court is requested to give a declaratory judgment.

...

With regard to the first question it should be recalled, as the Court has had occasion to emphasise in very varied contexts, that Article 177 is based on cooperation which entails a division of duties between the national courts and the Court of Justice in the interest of the proper application and uniform interpretation of Community law throughout all the Member States.

With this in view it is for the national court – by reason of the fact that it is seised of the substance of the dispute and that it must bear the responsibility for the decision to be taken – to assess, having regard to the facts of the case, the need to obtain a preliminary ruling to enable it to give judgment.

In exercising that power of appraisal the national court, in collaboration with the Court of Justice, fulfils a duty entrusted to them both of ensuring that in the interpretation and application of the Treaty the law is observed. Accordingly the problems which may be entailed in the exercise of its power of appraisal by the national court and the relations which it maintains within the framework of Article 177 with the Court of Justice are governed exclusively by the provisions of Community law.

In order that the Court of Justice may perform its task in accordance with the Treaty it is essential for national courts to explain, when the reasons do not emerge beyond any doubt from the file, why they consider that a reply to their questions is necessary to enable them to give judgment.

It must in fact be emphasised that the duty assigned to the Court by Article 177 is not that of delivering advisory opinions on general or hypothetical questions but of assisting in the administration of justice in the Member States. It accordingly does not have jurisdiction to reply to questions of interpretation which are submitted to it within the framework of procedural devices arranged by the parties in order to induce the Court to give its views on certain problems of Community law which do not correspond to an objective requirement inherent in the resolution of a dispute. A declaration by the Court that it has no jurisdiction in such circumstances does not in any way trespass upon the prerogatives of the national court but makes it possible to prevent the application of the procedure under Article 177 for purposes other than those appropriate for it.

Furthermore, it should be pointed out that, whilst the Court of Justice must be able to place as much reliance as possible upon the assessment by the national court of the extent to which the questions submitted are essential, it must be in a position to make any assessment inherent in the performance of its own duties in particular in order to check, as all courts must, whether it has jurisdiction. Thus the Court, taking into account the repercussions of its decisions in this matter, must have regard, in exercising the jurisdiction conferred upon it by Article 177, not only to the interests of the parties to the proceedings but also to those of the Community and of the Member States. Accordingly it cannot, without disregarding the duties assigned to it, remain indifferent to the assessments made by the courts of the Member States in the exceptional cases in which such assessments may affect the proper working of the procedure laid down by Article 177.

Whilst the spirit of cooperation which must govern the performance of the duties assigned by Article 177 to the national courts on the one hand and the Court of Justice on the other requires the latter to have regard to the national court's proper responsibilities, it implies at the same time that the national court, in the use which it makes of the facilities provided by Article 177, should have regard to the proper function of the Court of Justice in this field.

The reply to the first question must accordingly be that whilst, according to the intended role of Article 177, an assessment of the need to obtain an answer to the questions of interpretation raised, regard being had to the circumstances of fact and of law involved in the main action, is a matter for the national court it is nevertheless for the Court of Justice, in order to confirm its own jurisdiction, to examine, where necessary, the conditions in which the case has been referred to it by the national court.

...

The third question concerns circumstances in which, in proceedings between individuals before a court of a Member State, a dispute arises as to the compatibility with Community law of the legislation of a Member State other than that of the State in which the court is situated. The Pretore has submitted in this connection the question whether in such a case the Member State whose legislation is at issue may be joined in the proceedings instituted before the court in question.

The reply on this point must be that in the absence of provisions of Community law in the matter, the possibility of taking proceedings before a national court against a Member State other than that in which the court is situated depends both on the laws of the latter and on the principles of international law.

...

In the fifth question the Pretore, Bra, repeats in abbreviated form the first question submitted in his first order concerning the interpretation of Article 95 of the Treaty. In its above-mentioned judgment of 11 March 1980 the Court of Justice found that the parties took the same view as to the lawfulness of the French legislation at issue and in reality sought to obtain by the device of a special clause inserted in their contract a ruling by an Italian court that the French legislation was unlawful although French law provided appropriate remedies. The Court of Justice concluded that to reply to the questions submitted in such circumstances would be to exceed the duty entrusted to it by Article 177 of the Treaty, which is to supply all courts in the Community with the information on the interpretation of Community law which is necessary to enable them to settle genuine disputes which are brought before them. It accordingly declared that it had no jurisdiction to give a ruling on the questions raised.

In his second order making a reference to the Court the Pretore has specially emphasised that the defendant had requested him to deliver a declaratory judgment. In this connection it must be pointed out that the conditions in which the Court of Justice performs its duties in this field are independent of the nature and objective of proceedings brought before the national courts. Article 177 refers to the 'judgment' to be given by the national court without laying down special rules in terms of the nature of such judgments.

...

The circumstance referred to by the national court in its second order for reference does not appear to constitute a new fact which would justify the Court of Justice in making a fresh appraisal of its jurisdiction. It is therefore for the Pretore, within the framework of the collaboration between a national court and the Court of Justice to ascertain in the light of the foregoing considerations whether there is any need to obtain an answer from the Court of Justice to the fifth question and, if so, to indicate to the Court any new factor which might justify it in taking a different view of its jurisdiction...

It seems clear that the judgments in *Foglia* v *Novello* cannot be explained on the ground that the parties before the national court sought in effect to challenge the legislation of one Member State before the court of another Member State. The European Court has accepted a reference for preliminary rulings from a German court concerned about the validity of Belgian legislation.

Case 261/81 Walter Rau Lebensmittelwerke v De Smedt PvbA
[1982] ECR 3961; [1983] 2 CMLR 496

Belgian legislation stipulated that margarine may only be retailed in cube-shaped blocks. In the course of proceedings in the Landgericht Hamburg between a German seller and Belgian buyer relating to a contract for margarine in cone-shaped plastic tubs, the question of the compatibility of the Belgian legislation with Article 30 of the EEC Treaty was raised. The Landgericht therefore referred a question on the interpretation of Article 30.

The Court

The Belgian Government points out that the importation of margarine into Belgium by the defendant in the main action is already the subject of criminal proceedings in Belgium and that the Court should therefore inquire whether a dispute which gave rise to the request for a preliminary ruling is a genuine dispute. In this regard the Belgian Government recalls the judgment of the Court of 16 December 1981 in Case 244/80 *Foglia* [1981] ECR 3045.

In this instance there is nothing in the file on the case which provides grounds for doubting that the dispute is genuine. Therefore there is no reason for concluding that the Court has no jurisdiction.

The explanation of the two *Foglia* v *Novello* cases appears to be that the Court has no jurisdiction to answer questions which are put to it as a result of collusion between the parties before the national court, who are agreed as to the outcome of the case. It is not possible to be entirely certain of this explanation for there was little disagreement between the parties in *Union Laitière* (above). Nevertheless, this explanation appears to be offered in a passage of the European Court's ruling in *Vinal* v *Orbat*.

Case 46/80 Vinal SpA v Orbat SpA
[1981] ECR 77; [1981] 3 CMLR 524

In January 1980 Vinal, an Italian importer of alcohol, concluded a contract with Orbat relating to a supply of denatured synthetic alcohol from France. Orbat did not dispute that it was bound to pay the agreed price for the goods but challenged the imposition of a revenue charge on the ground that it was inconsistent with Article 95 of the EEC Treaty. In those circumstances, the national judge referred questions on the interpretation of Article 95.

The Court

The Italian Government has put in issue the admissibility of the request for a preliminary ruling submitted by the Pretura, Casteggio. It raises the question whether the action brought before the national court is not really a fictitious dispute and whether the procedure under Article 177 has not been employed in this case to impeach the Italian State in the absence of any actual dispute giving rise to questions of Community law as between the parties. In these circumstances the Italian Government asks whether the situation should not be compared to that which formed the subject-matter of the judgment of the Court of 11 March 1980 in Case 104/79 *Foglia* v *Novello* [1980] ECR 745 in which the Court held that it had no jurisdiction to give a ruling on the questions put by the national court.

In view of that contention, which the Italian Government set out in its written observations, the Court requested the parties to supply it with additional information.

Having studied the replies given to those questions the Court considers that in this case it is possible to set aside the doubts expressed by the Italian Government and to broach the substance of the case.

FURTHER READING

Barav, A., 'Preliminary Censorship..?' 5 ELR (1980) 443

Bebr, G., 'Arbitration Tribunals and Article 177 of the EEC Treaty' 22 (1985) CMLRev 489

Gray, C., 'Advisory Opinions and the European Court of Justice' 8 ELRev (1983) 2

Harding, C., 'The Impact of Article 177 of the EEC Treaty on the Review of Community Action' 1 YEL (1981) 93

O' Keefe, D., 'Appeals against an Order to Refer under Article 177' 9 (1984) ELR 87

Rasmussen, H., 'The European Court's *Acte Clair* Strategy in *CILFIT*' 9 (1984) ELR 242

Schermers, H., 'The Law as it Stands on Preliminary Rulings' [1974] I LIEI 93

Wyatt, D., 'Following up *Foglia*: Why the Court is Right to Stick to its Guns' 6 ELR (1981) 447

6

FREE MOVEMENT OF GOODS

INTRODUCTION

Within the scheme established by the EEC Treaty, the free movement of goods results from a number of interlinked but conceptually separate provisions. The principle, however, underlies other sections of the Treaty, such as those relating to competition (Chapters 9-11 below). It presents both external and internal characteristics.

Externally, the Common Market within which free movement occurs is surrounded by a Common Customs Tariff: within this market, imported goods upon which the common duties or charges (if any) have been paid are in principle to be treated on the same footing as domestic products.

Internally, free movement is ensured by three main sets of provisions, relating to customs duties and charges having equivalent effect, domestic taxation, and quantitative restrictions and measures having equivalent effect. Member States are required to eliminate customs duties and quantitative restrictions and charges or measures having equivalent effect within a set timetable, and to refrain from introducing new charges or restrictions in trade between Member States. They must also ensure that internal taxation on products imported from other Member States does not exceed that on domestic products.

The prohibition on measures having equivalent effect to quantitative restrictions has a particularly wide scope. Not only measures invoked on the initiative of Member States but also legally enforced restrictions invoked by private individuals or enterprises fall within its terms. This is of considerable importance in relation to the exercise of industrial property rights.

I THE CUSTOMS UNION – EXTERNAL ASPECTS

EEC Treaty

Article 8A

The Community shall adopt measures with the aim of progressively establishing the internal market over a period expiring on 31 December 1992, in accordance with the provisions of this Article and of Articles 8B, 8C, 28, 57(2), 59, 70(1), 84, 99, 100A and 100B and without prejudice to the other provisions of this Treaty.

The internal market shall comprise an area without internal frontiers in which the free movement of goods, persons, services and capital is ensured in accordance with the provisions of this Treaty.

...

Article 9

1. The Community shall be based upon a customs union which shall cover all trade in goods and which shall involve the prohibition between Member States of customs duties on imports and exports and of all charges having equivalent effect, and the adoption of a Common Customs Tariff in their relations with third countries.

2. The provisions of Chapter 1, Section 1, and of Chapter 2 of this Title shall apply to products originating in Member States and to products coming from third countries which are in free circulation in Member States.

Article 10

1. Products coming from a third country shall be considered to be in free circulation in a Member State if the import formalities have been complied with and any customs duties or charges having equivalent effect which are payable have been levied in that Member State, and if they have not benefited from a total or partial drawback of such duties or charges.

...

Article 18

The Member States declare their readiness to contribute to the development of international trade and the lowering of barriers to trade by entering into agreement designed, on a basis of reciprocity and mutual advantage, to reduce customs duties below the general level of which they could avail themselves as a result of the establishment of a customs union between them.

Article 19

1. Subject to the conditions and within the limits provided for hereinafter, duties in the Common Customs Tariff shall be at the level of the arithmetical average of the duties applied in the four customs territories comprised in the Community.

...

Article 23

...

3. The Common Customs Tariff shall be applied in its entirety by the end of the transitional period at the latest.

Article 24

Member States shall remain free to change their duties more rapidly than is provided for in Article 23 in order to bring them into line with the Common Customs Tariff.

By a Council Decision of 26 July 1966 (JO 1966, p. 2971/66) the original Member States agreed to apply the Common Customs Tariff as from 1 July 1968, eighteen months before the end of the transitional period, for all products other than those falling within the scope of the common agricultural policy. (In fact certain Regulations establishing common organisations of agricultural markets provided for the relevant nomenclature to be included in the common tariff). The Common Customs Tariff was enacted by Regulation No 950/68 of the Council of 28 June 1968 (OJ Special Edition 1968, p. 275). Consolidated versions of the tariff are published regularly, the 1988 version being contained in Council Regulation (EEC) No 2658/87 of 7 September 1987 (OJ 1987, L 256).

Hence the Act of Accession contained provisions enabling new Member States to adapt to an already existing tariff.

Act of Accession

Article 39

1. For the purpose of the progressive introduction of the Common Customs Tariff and the the ECSC unified tariff, the new Member States shall amend their tariffs applicable to third countries as follows:

(a) in the case of tariff headings in respect of which the basic duties do not differ by more than 15% in either direction from the duties in the Common Customs Tariff or the ECSC unified tariff, these latter duties shall be applied from 1 January 1974;

(b) in other cases, each new Member State shall, from the same date, apply a duty reducing by 40% the difference between the basic duty and the duty in the Common Customs Tariff or the ECSC unified tariff.

This difference shall be further reduced by 20% on 1 January 1975 and by 20% on 1 January 1976.

The new Member States shall apply in full the Common Customs Tariff and the ECSC unified tariff from 1 July 1977.

2. From 1 January 1974, if any duties in the Common Customs Tariff are altered or suspended, the new Member States shall simultaneously amend or suspend their tariffs in the proportion resulting from the implementation of paragraph 1.

3. The new Member States shall apply the Common Customs Tariff from 1 January 1974 in respect of the products listed in Annex III to this Act.

4. The new Member States shall apply the Common Customs Tariff nomenclature from the date of accession. Denmark and the United Kingdom are, however, authorised to defer their application of the nomenclature until 1 January 1974.

The new Member States may include within this nomenclature existing national subdivisions which are indispensable in order that the progressive alignment of their customs duties with those in the Common Customs Tariff be carried out under the conditions laid down in this Act.

5. With a view to facilitating the progressive introduction of the Common Customs Tariff by the new Member States, the Commission shall determine, if necessary, the provisions whereby new Member States alter their customs duties.

...

Article 41

In order to bring their tariffs into line with the Common Customs Tariff and the ECSC unified tariff, the new Member States shall remain free to alter their customs duties more rapidly than is provided for in Article 39(1) and (3). They shall inform other Member States and the Commission thereof.

The relevant Treaty provisions (and the Common Customs Tariff itself) deal in terms only with customs duties as such and not with measures having equivalent effect. Hence the Court has had to consider the degree to which the existence of the Common Tariff prevents Member States imposing such measures.

Joined Cases 37 and 38/73 Sociaal Fonds voor de Diamantarbeiders v NV Indiamex and Association de fait de Belder
[1973] ECR 1609; [1976] 2 CMLR 222

Under Belgian law, importers of rough diamonds were liable to pay a contribution, calculated on the basis of the value of the diamonds imported, to the Social Fund for diamond workers. In an action before the Arbeidsrechtbank of Antwerp, which referred the matter for a preliminary ruling, Indiamex, a firm importing rough diamonds from third countries, claimed that after the coming into force of the Common Customs Tariff, the levying of the contribution was incompatible with Community law as being a measure having equivalent effect to a customs duty on imports from third countries.

The Court

The essential purpose of the questions referred is to have it made known whether, and to what extent, the Member States may introduce or maintain, after 1 July 1968, charges having an effect equivalent to customs duties, levied on goods imported directly from third countries, and under what conditions they may be required to eliminate them.

The application of such charges in this case is dependent upon the trade arrangements with third countries, instituted at Article 3(b) of the Treaty, and especially upon the principles governing the customs union, such as those set out at Article 9.

The customs union, which is one of the foundations of the Community, involves, on the one hand, the elimination of customs duties between the Member States and of all charges having equivalent effect.

The elimination of such charges is designed to promote the free movement of goods within the Community.

It must therefore be sufficiently comprehensive to include the abolition of all pecuniary, administrative or other obstacles, for the purpose of achieving a unified market between the Member States.

On the other hand, the customs union involves the establishment of a single customs tariff for the whole Community, as envisaged at Articles 18 to 29 of the Treaty.

This common tariff is intended to achieve an equalisation of customs charges levied at the frontiers of the Community on products imported from third countries, in order to avoid any deflection of trade in relations with those countries and any distortion of free internal circulation or of competitive conditions.

Although, unlike the first Section of the Chapter of the Treaty relating to the customs union (Articles 12 to 17), Section 2 of the same Chapter (Articles 18 to 29) makes no mention of 'charges having an effect equivalent to customs duties', this omission does not mean that such charges may be maintained, still less introduced.

In answering the question as to the application of such charges in trade with third countries, account must be taken both of the requirements resulting from the establishment of the Common Customs Tariff, and of those resulting from a common commercial policy, within the meaning of Articles 110 to 116 of the Treaty, which, according to the abovementioned Article 3(b), regulates trade arrangements with third countries.

The Common Customs Tariff was introduced, for the Community as originally constituted, by Regulation No. 950/68 of the Council, which came into force on 1 July 1968.

Although that Regulation does not expressly allow for the elimination or equalisation of charges other than customs duties as such, it is nevertheless clear from its objective that under it Member States are prohibited from amending, by means of charges supplementing such duties, the level of protection as defined by the Common Customs Tariff.

Even if they are not protective in character the existence of such charges may be irreconcilable with the requirements of a common commercial policy.

According to Article 113(1) of the Treaty, the common commercial policy shall be based on uniform principles, particularly in regard to changes in tariff rates, the conclusion of tariff and trade agreements, the achievement of uniformity in measures of liberalisation, export policy and measures to protect trade.

The definition of these uniform principles involves, as does the common tariff itself, the elimination of national disparities, whether in the field of taxation or of commerce, affecting trade with third countries.

It is for the Commission or the Council to evaluate these requirements in each case both as regards the establishment of the Common Customs Tariff and the adoption of the commercial policy.

It follows therefore that subsequent to the introduction of the Common Customs Tariff all Member States are prohibited from introducing, on a unilateral basis, any new charges or from raising the level of those already in force.

As regards charges already in existence, prior evaluation by the Community authorities is necessary in order to establish their incompatibility with the Treaty and the obligation to eliminate them.

It follows that such charges may only be considered to be incompatible with Community law pursuant to provisions adopted by the Community.

Therefore a prohibition upon charges of that nature is the result in particular of provisions, which are not in issue here, adopted in the context of the common agricultural policy, of trade agreements concluded by the Community and of association arrangements existing between the Community and certain states.

Accordingly, the questions referred should be answered to the effect that the Member States may not, subsequent to the establishment of the Common Customs Tariff, introduce, in a unilateral manner, new charges on goods imported directly from third countries or raise the level of those in existence at that time.

As regards charges already in existence, the introduction of the common commercial policy must involve the elimination of all national disparities, whether in the field of taxation or of commerce, which regulate trade with third countries.

Since the adoption of this common commercial policy falls within the exclusive jurisdiction of the Community, the equalisation of charges other than customs duties as such for all the Member States or their elimination is dependent upon an intervention by the Community.

Accordingly, the reduction or elimination of existing charges on goods imported directly from third countries is a matter for the institutions of the Community.

II THE CUSTOMS UNION – INTERNAL ASPECTS

1. CUSTOMS DUTIES AND CHARGES HAVING EQUIVALENT EFFECT

EEC Treaty

Article 12

Member States shall refrain from introducing between themselves any new customs duties on imports or exports or any charges having equivalent effect, and from increasing those which they already apply in their trade with each other.

...

Article 16

...

Member States shall abolish between themselves customs duties on exports and charges having equivalent effect by the end of the first stage at the latest.

Act of Accession

Article 32

1. Customs duties on imports between the Community as originally constituted and the new Member States and between the new Member States themselves shall be progressively abolished in accordance with the following timetable:
   - on 1 April 1973, each duty shall be reduced to 80% of the basic duty;
   - the four other reductions of 20% each shall be made on:

1 January 1974,
1 January 1975,
1 January 1976,
1 July 1977.

...

Article 33

In no case shall customs duties higher than those applied to third countries enjoying most-favoured-nation treatment be applied within the Community.

In the event of the Common Customs Tariff duties being amended or suspended or the new Member States applying Article 41, the Council, acting by a qualified majority on a proposal from the Commission, may take the necessary measures for the maintenance of Community preference.

Article 34

Any new Member State may suspend in whole or in part the levying of duties on products imported from other Member States. It shall inform the other Member States and the Commission thereof.

Article 35

Any charge having equivalent effect to a customs duty on imports, introduced after 1 January 1972 in trade between the Community as originally constituted and the new Member States or between the new Member States themselves, shall be abolished on 1 January 1973.

Any charge having equivalent effect to a customs duty on imports the rate of which on 31 December 1972 is higher than that actually applied on 1 January 1972 shall be reduced to the latter rate on 1 January 1973.

Article 36

1. Charges having equivalent effect to customs duties on imports shall be progressively abolished between the Community as originally constituted and the new Member States and between the new Member States themselves in accordance with the following timetable:

- by 1 January 1974 at the latest, each charge shall be reduced to 60% of the rate applied on 1 January 1972:
- the three other reductions of 20% each shall be made on:
  1 January 1975,
  1 January 1976,
  1 July 1977.

...

Article 37

Customs duties on exports and charges having equivalent effect shall be abolished between the Community as originally constituted and the new Member States and between the new Member States themselves by 1 January 1974 at the latest.

It was held in Case 26/62 *van Gend en Loos* [1963] (see above, p 79) that Article 12 of the EEC Treaty produced direct effects from its entry into force. (For the facts and judgment see Chapter 1, above.) In fact the original Member States, in the Council Decision of 26 July 1966 (JO 1966, p. 2971/66) by which they agreed to apply the Common Customs Tariff from 1 July 1968, also agreed to eliminate customs duties between themselves from that date. The European Court considered the effects of this 'Acceleration Decision', and of a Commission Directive issued under Article 13(2), requiring the abolition by 1 July 1968 of a particular Italian duty, in Case 33/70 *SACE* v *Italian Ministry of Finance* [1970] ECR 1213. It held that the material part of the directive produced direct effects from 1 July 1968. In general, however, measures having equivalent effect to customs duties as such, were only required to be abolished as from the end of the transitional period.

The essential feature in the Community concept of a charge having equivalent effect to a customs duty is that it is levied by reason of the fact that a frontier has been crossed (see Joined Cases 2 and 3/69 *Sociaal Fonds voor de Diamantarbeiders* v *SA Ch. Brachfeld and Sons and Chougol Diamond Co* [1969] ECR 211 at 244; [1969] CMLR 335).

In the *'Statistical Levy'* case (Case 24/68 *Commission* v *Italy* [1969] ECR 193; [1971] CMLR 611), the Court gave a clear definition of charges within Article 12 on being confronted with a 10 lira charge imposed by the Italian Government on all imported goods for the purpose of a statistical survey:

> 'Any pecuniary charge, however small and whatever its designation and mode of application, which is imposed unilaterally on domestic or foreign goods by reason of the fact that they cross a frontier, and which is not a customs duty in the strict sense, constitutes a charge having equivalent effect within the meaning of Articles 9, 12, 13 and 16 of the Treaty, even if it is not imposed for the benefit of the State, is not discriminatory or protective in effect and if the product on which the charge is imposed is not in competition with any domestic product.'

The claim that a charge is actually a payment for administrative services has usually been met with scepticism by the Court, which has held that the service must be of direct benefit to the goods or traders (see Cases 52 and 55/65 *Germany* v *Commission* [1966] ECR 159; [1967] CMLR 22 and Case 39/73 *Rewe-Zentralfinanz* v *Landwirtschaftskammer Westfalen-Lippe* [1973] ECR 1039; [1977] 1 CMLR 630).

Case 132/82 Commission v Belgium
[1983] ECR 1649; [1983] 3 CMLR 600

Goods in Community transit could undergo customs clearance either at the border or in special warehouses situated in the interior of the country. At issue was whether storage charges could be levied if the latter method was chosen.

The Court

It is appropriate to recall, in the first place, that according to the established case-law of the Court, any pecuniary charge, however small and whatever its designation and mode of application, which is imposed unilaterally on the goods by reason of the fact that they cross a frontier and which is not a customs duty in the strict sense, constitutes a charge having equivalent effect within the meaning of Articles 9, 12, 13 and 16 of the Treaty, even if it is not levied by the State. *The position is different only if the charge in question is the consideration for a service actually rendered to the importer and is of an amount commensurate with that service, when the charge concerned, as in this case, is payable exclusively on imported products.*

The prohibition of charges having an effect equivalent to customs duties, laid down in provisions of the Treaty, is justified on the ground that pecuniary charges imposed by reason or on the occasion of the crossing of the frontier represent an obstacle to the free movement of goods.

It is in the light of those principles that the question whether the disputed storage charges may be classified as charges having an effect equivalent to customs duties must be assessed. It should therefore be noted, in the first place, that the placing of imported goods in temporary storage in the special stores of public warehouses clearly represents a service rendered to traders. A decision to deposit the goods there can indeed be taken only at the request of the trader concerned and then ensures their storage without payment of duties, until the trader has decided how they are to be dealt with.

...

However, it appears ... that the storage charges are payable equally when the goods are presented at the public warehouse solely for the completion of customs formalities, even though they have been exempted from storage and the importer has not requested that they be put in temporary storage.

Admittedly the Belgian Government claims that even in that case a service is rendered to the importer. It is always open to the latter to avoid payment of the disputed charges by choosing to have his goods cleared through customs at the frontier, where such a procedure is free. Moreover, by using a public warehouse, the importer is enabled to have the goods declared through customs near the places for which his products are bound and he is therefore relieved of the necessity of himself either having at his own disposal premises suitable for their clearance or having recourse to private premises, the use of which is more expensive that that of the public warehouses. It is therefore legitimate, in the Belgian Government's view, to impose a charge commensurate with that service.

That argument cannot however be accepted. Whilst it is true that the use of a public warehouse in the interior of the country offers certain advantages to importers it seems clear first of all that such advantages are linked solely with the completion of customs formalities which, whatever the place, is always compulsory. It should moreover be noted that such advantages result from the scheme of Community transit, ... in order to increase the fluidity of the movement of goods and to facilitate transport within the Community.

There can therefore be no question of levying any charges for customs clearance facilities accorded in the interests of the Common Market.

It follows from the foregoing, that *when payment of storage charges is demanded solely in connection with the completion of customs formalities, it cannot be regarded as the consideration for a service actually rendered to the importer*.

Consequently, it must be declared that, by levying storage charges on goods which originate in a Member State or are in free circulation, and which are imported into Belgium, and presented merely for the completion of customs formalities at a special store, the Kingdom of Belgium has failed to fulfil its obligations under Articles 9 and 12 of the Treaty.

It is, however, clear that charges imposed in relation to health controls required by Community law are not regarded as having equivalent effect to customs duties. (See Case 46/76 *Bauhuis* v *Netherlands* [1977] ECR 5.) The same is true with regard to charges for health controls required under an international convention, intended to facilitate the free movement of goods, to which all the Member States are parties. (See Case 89/76 *Commission* v *Netherlands* [1977] ECR 1355; [1978] 3 CMLR 630.)

2. DOMESTIC TAXATION

EEC Treaty

Article 95

No Member State shall impose, directly or indirectly, on the products of other Member States any internal taxation of any kind in excess of that imposed directly or indirectly on similar domestic products.

Furthermore, no Member State shall impose on the products of other Member States any internal taxation of such a nature as to afford indirect protection to other products.

Member States shall, not later than at the beginning of the second stage, repeal or amend any provisions existing when this Treaty enters into force which conflict with the preceding rules.

As was mentioned at the beginning of this chapter, the provisions of the EEC Treaty relating to the free movement of goods are interlinked but conceptually separate. Hence a charge may not at the same time be treated as having equivalent effect to a customs duty and as falling within a system of internal taxation. In a number of cases the Court has held that a charge apparently within a system of internal taxation but producing the effects of a customs duty is to be treated as a charge having equivalent effect to a customs duty.

All three paragraphs of Article 95 have been held to produce direct effects, as will appear from the extracts from the following two cases. These also illustrate the problem of distinguishing internal taxation from measures having equivalent effect to customs duties and that of distinguishing internal taxation from measures having equivalent effect to quantitative restrictions. Both cases arose from the levying of 'turnover equalisation tax' *(Umsatzausgleichsteuer)* on the import of goods into Germany.

Case 57/65 Alfons Lütticke GmbH v Hauptzollamt Saarlouis [1966] ECR 205; [1971] CMLR 674

Lütticke asked the German authorities to give customs clearance for the import of a consignment of milk powder originating in Luxembourg. Clearance was given subject to payment of turnover equalisation tax. Lütticke appealed to the Finanzgericht against assessments to tax. The Finanzgericht referred questions to the European Court.

The Court

In its first question, the Finanzgericht des Saarlandes requests the court to rule whether the first paragraph of Article 95 of the Treaty produces direct effects and creates individual rights of which national courts must take account. If a negative answer is given to this question, the Finanzgericht asks whether, as from 1 January 1962, the third paragraph of the same article, together with the first paragraph, produces the effects and creates the rights mentioned above.

It is necessary to consider the two questions together and first of all to clarify the relationship between the said paragraphs of Article 95.

The first paragraph of Article 95 sets forth, as a general and permanent rule of Community law, that Member States shall not impose on the products of other Member States any internal taxation in excess of that imposed on similar domestic products. Such a system, often adopted by the Treaty to ensure the equal treatment of nationals within the Community under national legal systems, constitutes in fiscal matters the indispensable foundation of the Common Market. In order to facilitate the adaptation of national legal systems to this rule, the third paragraph of Article 95 allows Member States a period of grace lasting until the beginning of the second stage of the transitional period, that is to say, until 1 January 1962, to repeal or amend any 'provisions existing when this Treaty enters into force which conflict with the preceding rules'. *Article 95 thus contains a general rule provided with a simple suspensory clause with regard to provisions existing when it entered into force. From this it must be concluded that on the expiry of the said period the general rule emerges unconditionally into full force.*

The questions raised by the Finanzgericht must be considered in the light of the foregoing conclusions.

The first paragraph of Article 95 contains a prohibition against discrimination, constituting a clear and unconditional obligation. With the exception of the third paragraph this obligation is not qualified by any condition, or subject, in its implementation or effects, to the taking of any measure either by the institutions of the Community or by the Member States. This prohibition is therefore complete, legally perfect and consequently capable of producing direct effects on the legal relationships between the Member States and persons within their jurisdiction. The fact that this article describes the Member States as being subject to the obligation of non-discrimination does not imply that individuals cannot benefit from it.

With regard to the third paragraph of Article 95, it indeed imposes an obligation on the Member States to 'repeal' or 'amend' any provisions which conflict with the rules set out in the preceding paragraphs. The said obligation however leaves no discretion to the Member States with regard to the date by which these operations must have been carried out, that is to say, before 1 January 1962. After this date it is sufficient for the national court to find, should the case arise, that the measures implementing the contested national rules of law were adopted after 1 January 1962 in order to be able to apply the first paragraph directly in any event. Thus the provisions of the third paragraph prevent the application of the general rule only with regard to implementing measures adopted before 1 January 1962, and founded upon provisions existing when the Treaty entered into force.

In the oral and written observations which have been submitted in the course of the proceedings, three governments have relied on Article 97 in order to support a different interpretation of Article 95.

In empowering Member States which levy a turnover tax calculated on a cumulative multi-stage tax system to establish average rates for products or groups of products, the said article thus constitutes a special rule for adapting Article 95 and this rule is, by its nature, incapable of creating direct effects on the relationships between the Member States and persons subject to their jurisdiction. This situation is peculiar to Article 97, and can in no circumstances influence the interpretation of Article 95.

It follows from the foregoing that, *notwithstanding the exception in the third paragraph for provisions existing when the Treaty entered into force until 1 January 1962, the prohibition contained in Article 95 produces direct effects and creates individual rights of which national courts must take account.*

In its third question, the Finanzgericht requests the Court to rule whether 'the first and third paragraphs of Article 95 of the EEC Treaty in conjunction with Articles 12 and 13 thereof have direct effect creating individual rights of which the national courts must take account'.

Since this question was only raised in the event of the Court's answering the first two questions in the negative, it is unnecessary to give a reply to it. It should however be made clear that *Articles 12 and 13 on the one hand and Article 95 on the other cannot be applied jointly to one and the same case.* Charges having an effect equivalent to customs duties on the one hand and internal taxation on the other hand are governed by different systems. In this respect it should be noted that a charge intended to offset the effect of internal taxation thereby takes on the internal character of the taxation whose effect it is intended to offset.

Case 27/67 Firma Fink-Frucht GmbH v Hauptzollamt München-Landsbergerstrasse [1968] ECR 223; [1968] CMLR 228

Fink-Frucht imported to Germany from Italy a consignment of sweet peppers on which the German authorities charged turnover equalisation tax. Fink-Frucht appealed to the Finanzgericht, contending that the imposition of the tax entailed a breach of Article 95. The Finanzgericht referred questions to the European Court.

The Court

The court making the reference asks whether the first paragraph of Article 95 prohibits a Member State from imposing turnover equalisation tax on products imported from another Member State where there are no similar or comparable domestic products, and whether the equalisation tax in such cases amounts to a measure having equivalent effect to quantitative restrictions within the meaning of Article 30.

The first and second paragraphs of Article 95 prohibit Member States from imposing on imports from other Member States any internal taxation in excess of that imposed on similar domestic products, or of such a nature as to afford indirect protection to other domestic products. *Article 95 is intended to remove certain restrictions on the free movement of goods. But to conclude that it prohibits the imposition of any internal taxation on imported goods which do not compete with domestic products would appear to give it a scope exceeding its purpose.* Internal taxes, and turnover tax in particular, are essentially fiscal in purpose. There is therefore no reason why certain imported products should be given privileged treatment, because they do not compete with any domestic products capable of being protected. Where such a tax is imposed at the import stage, even on the products which do not compete with domestic products, its purpose is to put every kind of product, whatever its origin, in a comparable fiscal situation in the territory of the state imposing the tax. *It must therefore be concluded that Article 95 does not prohibit Member States from imposing internal taxation on imported products when there is no similar domestic product, or any other domestic products capable of being protected.*

Nor does internal taxation imposed under the conditions set out above come within the prohibition on quantitative restrictions and measures having equivalent effect, within the meaning of Article 30 of the Treaty. Such restrictions, which are intended to limit the quantities imported, are in fact different both in their purpose and in the way in which they operate from measures of a fiscal nature. Furthermore, since Articles 30 *et seq.*, on the one hand, and Article 95, on the other, lay down different periods of time and different procedures for the elimination of the restrictions to which they refer, *it would be difficult to concede that one and the same tax could be both a measure having an effect equivalent to a quantitative restriction and internal taxation.*

In its third question the court making the reference asks the Court of Justice to rule whether 'the second paragraph of Article 95 has direct effects and creates individual rights which national courts must protect'.

This provision contains a straightforward prohibition against protection which is the necessary complement to the prohibition set out in the first paragraph of the article. The obligation which results from that prohibition is unconditional, and no action is required on the part of the institutions of the Community or the Member States for its implementation or its entry into force. The prohibition is therefore self-sufficient and legally complete, and is thus capable of having direct effects on the legal relationships between Member States and those subject to their jurisdiction. Although this provision involves the evaluation of economic factors, this does not exclude the right and duty of national courts to ensure that the rules of the Treaty are observed whenever they can ascertain, in the light of the interpretation given below in answer to Questions 2, 4 and 5, that the conditions necessary for the application of the article are fulfilled. The answer to this question, therefore, must be that *the provision in question is capable of producing direct effects and creating individual rights which national courts must protect.*

The object of Questions 2, 4 and 5 is, in substance, to establish the conditions under which an imported product, as compared with a domestic product, comes within one or other of the situations referred to in the first two paragraphs of Article 95, and also to have the conditions under which the second paragraph applies and its effects defined.

Under the terms of Article 95 no Member State shall impose, directly or indirectly, on the products of other Member States internal taxation of any kind in excess of that imposed directly or indirectly on 'similar domestic products'. Similarity between products within the meaning of the first paragraph of Article 95 exists when the products in question are normally to be considered as coming within the same fiscal, customs or statistical classification, as the case may be.

In addition to the prohibition imposed in the first paragraph of Article 95, the second paragraph of the same article forbids the imposition on imported products of any form of taxation 'of such nature as to afford indirect protection to other products'. Such protection would occur in particular if internal taxation were to impose a heavier burden on an imported product than on a domestic product with which the imported product is, by reason of one or more economic uses to which it may be put, in competition, even though the condition of similarity for the purposes of the first paragraph of Article 95 is not fulfilled. Even if there is no direct competition of any sort with a domestic product, such protection would still exist if it were established that the imported product bore a specific fiscal charge because of its state of manufacture or distribution or because of any other economic circumstances in such a way as to protect certain activities distinct from those used in the manufacture of the imported product. In the interests of legal certainty, however, it is necessary for the various economic relationships covered by the second paragraph of Article 95 not to be merely fortuitous, but lasting and characteristic.

The effects of a tax on the economic relationships referred to in the second paragraph of Article 95 must be assessed in the light of the objectives of Article 95, which are to ensure normal conditions of competition and to remove all restrictions of a fiscal nature capable of hindering the free movement of goods within the Common Market. *Whereas the first paragraph of Article 95 only prohibits taxation in so far as it exceeds a clearly defined level, the prohibition laid down in the second paragraph is based on the protective effect of the taxation in question to the exclusion of any exact standard of reference.* A tax must therefore be considered as incompatible with the Treaty if it is capable of having the effect referred to above. In fact the Treaty does not prevent national courts from deciding, where necessary, the level below which the tax in question would cease to have the protective effects prohibited by the Treaty and from drawing all appropriate conclusions therefrom.

The point that the absence of a domestic equivalent to the taxed product does not necessarily make the taxation discriminatory was reiterated by the Court in its judgment in Case 78/76 *Steinike und Weinlig* v *Germany* [1977] ECR 595 (but compare Case 112/84 *Humblot* [1986] 2 CMLR 338).

Article 95 prohibits both discriminatory taxation of similar products (paragraph 1) and also that which gives indirect protection to other products (paragraph 2). The relevant criterion here is that products must be in actual or potential competition and this has been particularly widely construed in the area of alcoholic beverages.

Case 170/78 Commission v United Kingdom ('Wine and Beer')

[1983] ECR 2265; [1983] 3 CMLR 512

The Commission's claim was that tax on wines (an almost exclusively imported product) was protection of the UK beer market, since wine was a potential competitor to beer and such differentiation caused artificial separation of the market.

The Court

In its judgment of 27 February 1980, the Court emphasised that the second paragraph of Article 95 applied to the treatment for tax purposes of products which, without fulfilling the criterion of similarity laid down in the first paragraph of that article, were nevertheless in competition, either partially or potentially, with certain products of the importing country. It added that, in order to determine the existence of a competitive relationship within the meaning of the second paragraph of Article 95, it was necessary to consider not only the present state of the market but also possible developments regarding the free movement of goods within the Community and the further potential for the substitution of products for one another which might be revealed by intensification of trade, so as fully to develop the complementary features of the economies of the Member States in accordance with the objectives laid down by Article 2 of the Treaty.

As regards the question of competition between wine and beer, the Court considered that, to a certain extent at least, the two beverages in question were capable of meeting identical needs, so that it had to be acknowledged that there was a degree of substitution for one another. It pointed out that, for the purpose of measuring the possible degree of substitution, attention should not be confined to consumer habits in a Member State or in a given region. Those habits, which were essentially variable in time and space, could not be considered to be immutable; the tax policy of a Member State must not therefore crystallise given consumer habits so as to consolidate an advantage acquired by national industries concerned to respond to them.

The Court nonetheless recognised that, in view of the substantial differences between wine and beer, it was difficult to compare the manufacturing processes and the natural properties of those beverages, as the Government of the United Kingdom had rightly observed. For that reason, the Court requested the parties to provide additional information with a view to dispelling the doubts which existed concerning the nature of the competitive relationship between the two products.

The Government of the United Kingdom did not give any opinion on that question in its subsequent statements. The Commission expressed the view that the difference in the conditions of production, to which the Court had attached some importance, was not significant from the point of view of the price structures of the two products, particularly in relation to the competitive relationship between beer and wines of popular quality.

The Italian Government contended in that connection that it was inappropriate to compare beer with wines of average strength or, *a fortiori*, with wines of greater alcoholic strength. In its opinion, it was the lightest wines with an alcoholic strength in the region of 9°, that is to say the most popular and cheapest wines, which were genuinely in competition with beer. It therefore took the view that those wines should be chosen for purposes of comparison where it was a question of measuring the incidence of taxation on the basis of either alcoholic strength of the price of the products.

The Court considers that observation by the Italian Government to be pertinent. In view of the substantial differences in the quality and, therefore, in the price of wines, the decisive competitive relationship between beer, a popular and widely consumed beverage, and wine must be established by reference to those wines which are the most accessible to the public at large, that is to say, generally speaking, the lightest and cheapest varieties. Accordingly, that is the appropriate basis for making fiscal comparisons by reference to the alcoholic strength or to the price of the two beverages in question.

The essential aim of Article 95 is that imported products should be taxed at the same rate, on the same basis, and by the same methods as domestic products – or indeed at a lower rate if the possibility of higher taxation cannot otherwise be avoided (see Case 127/75 *Bobie* v *Hauptzollamt Aachen-Nord* [1976] 2 ECR 1079 at 1088)

The use to which the tax is put may also be a relevant consideration.

Case 77/72 Carmine Capolongo v Azienda Agricola Maya
[1973] ECR 611; [1974] 1 CMLR 230

Capolongo imported to Italy from Germany a large quantity of eggs. The invoice charged Capolongo not only for the price of the eggs and their containers but also for a tax levied in Italy on cardboard products including containers. A similar tax was levied on cardboard containers made in Italy. The proceeds of the tax were devoted to the promotion of the Italian paper and cardboard industry.

The Court

Article 13(2), therefore, comprises a clear and precise prohibition, as from the end of the transitional period at the latest and for all charges having an effect equivalent to customs duties, on the collecting of the said charges, which prohibition has no reservation allowing States to subject its implementation to a positive measure of domestic law or to an intervention by the institutions of the Community.

This prohibition lends itself, by its very nature, to producing direct effects in the legal relations between Member States and their subjects.

It is aimed at any tax demanded at the time or or by reason of importation and which, being imposed specifically on an imported product to the exclusion of the similar domestic product, results in the same restrictive consequences on the free movement of goods as a customs duty by altering the cost price of that product.

Even pecuniary charges intended to finance the activities of an agency governed by public law can constitute taxes having equivalent effect within the meaning of Article 13(2) of the Treaty.

On the other hand, financial charges within a general system of internal taxation applying systematically to domestic and imported products according to the same criteria are not to be considered as charges having equivalent effect.

In the interpretation of the concept 'charge having an effect equivalent to a customs duty on imports', the destination of the financial charges levied must be taken into account.

In effect, when such a financial charge or duty is intended exclusively to support activities which specifically profit taxed domestic products, it can follow that the general duty levied according to the same criteria on the imported product and the domestic product nevertheless constitutes for the former a net supplementary tax burden, whilst for the latter it constitutes in reality a set-off against benefits or aids previously received.

Consequently a duty within the general system of internal taxation, applying systematically to domestic and imported products according to the same criteria, can nevertheless constitute a charge having an effect equivalent to customs duty on imports, when such contribution is intended exclusively to support activities which specifically benefit the taxed domestic product.

In its decision in Case 77/76 *Cucchi* v *Avez* [1977] ECR 987, the Court further refined the view expressed in the last paragraph of the above extract, stating that such a duty can constitute a charge having an effect equivalent to a customs duty on imports 'only if it has the sole purpose of financing activities for the specific advantage of the taxed domestic product; if the taxed product and the domestic product benefiting from it are the same; and if the charges imposed on the domestic product are made good in full' (at p. 1006).

Case 94/74 Industria Gomma Articoli Vari (IGAV) v Ente Nazionale per la Cellulosa e per la Carta (ENCC)
[1975] ECR 699; [1976] 2 CMLR 37

IGAV brought an action before the Pretore of Abbiategrasso claiming repayment of levies paid to ENCC on the import of paper products into Italy. IGAV argued *inter alia* that since the levy was used to finance activities encouraging Italian domestic cellulose and paper production, its effect was that of a customs duty.

The Court

The first question asks for an interpretation of the concept in Article 13(2) of 'charges having an effect equivalent to customs duties' in relation to dues such as the duty levied by the ENCC at the marketing stage of imported paper, cardboard and pulp, taking into account both the manner of collecting these dues and the purpose to which the revenue derived therefrom is applied.

In order to interpret this concept the following three factors must be remembered in connection with the duty in dispute:

(a) the duty is levied by an autonomous institution governed by public law, devoid of any commercial character,
(b) it is applied without distinction to domestic products and to products from other Member States,
(c) the proceeds are allocated to certain development and research activities of interest to the cellulose and paper industry, the major part however being reserved for the payment of subsidies to newsprint, which is itself exempt from the duty.

As was ruled in the judgment of 19 June 1973 (Case 77/72 *Capolongo* v *Maya* [1973] ECR 611) to which the national court refers, the prohibition contained in Article 13(2) is aimed at any tax demanded at the time of or by reason of importation and which, being imposed specifically on an imported product to the exclusion of a similar domestic product, results in the same restrictive consequences on the free movement of goods as a customs duty by altering the cost price of that product. The fact that a duty is levied by an independent institution governed by public law rather than levied by the State itself and is used by that institution for purposes intended by the relevant legislation involves no difference with regard to the possible definition of that fiscal charge as a charge having an effect equivalent to customs duties, since the prohibition under Article 13(2) attaches solely to the effect of such charges and not to the manner in which they are imposed.

On the other hand, the fact that a charge applied without distinction to domestic products as well as to products from other Member States gives rise to the question whether the taxation at issue falls within the prohibition of Article 13(2) or the rule against discrimination in matters of internal taxation laid down by Article 95.

One and the same scheme of taxation cannot, under the system of the Treaty, belong simultaneously to both the categories mentioned, having regard to the fact that the charges referred to in Article 13(2) must be purely and simply abolished whilst, for the purpose of applying internal taxation, Article 95 provides solely for the elimination of any form of discrimination, direct or indirect, in the treatment of the domestic products of the Member States and of products originating in other Member States.

Financial charges within a general system of internal taxation applying systematically to domestic and imported products according to the same criteria are not to be considered as charges having equivalent effect.

The situation would be different, however, if such a duty, which is limited to particular products, had the sole purpose of financing activities for the specific advantage of the taxed domestic products, so as to make good, wholly or in part, the fiscal charge imposed upon them. Such a fiscal device would in fact only appear to be a system of internal taxation and accordingly could by reason of its protective character be termed a charge having an effect equivalent to customs duties, so as to bring Article 13(2) into operation. Such a definition would nevertheless imply a clearly established likeness between, on the one hand, the collection of a fiscal duty levied without distinction on the products in question, whether domestic or imported and, on the other hand, the advantage which enures only for the benefit of the domestic products by reason of the proceeds of that same duty.

Accordingly the answer to the first question must be that a duty falling within a general system of internal taxation applying systematically to domestic and imported products according to the same criteria can nevertheless constitute a charge having an effect equivalent to a customs duty on imports when such duty is intended exclusively to support activities which specifically benefit the taxed domestic product.

The same formula was repeated by the Court in its judgment in Case 78/76 *Steinike und Weinlig* v *Germany* [1977] ECR 595, which refers expressly to the above passage.

Case 73/79 Commission v Italy [1980] ECR 1533; [1982] 1 CMLR 1

A surcharge was imposed on all white sugar used in Italy (imported and domestic produce), the revenue from which was received by the 'Sugar Equalisation Fund' for the purpose of subsidising the national sugar industry.

The Court

The first paragraph of Article 95 of the Treaty prohibits Member States from imposing, directly or indirectly, on the products of other Member States any internal taxation of any kind in excess of that imposed directly or indirectly on similar domestic products.

The Italian Government claims first of all that the surcharge constitutes an identical burden on sugar produced in Italy and imported sugar and that the discrimination of which the Commission complains resides in the amount of the aid granted for domestic sugar. That aid is authorised under Article 38 of Regulation No 3330/74; its objective is to compensate for the economic difference in the sugar sector between Italy and the other Member States in order to ensure the integration of the Italian sugar industry into the Community system. Accordingly the aid in question must constitute a clear and constant difference in favour of Italian sugar.

In connection with this last point it should be recalled that the Court has already declared, in its judgment of 25 May 1977 (Case 105/76 *Interzuccheri* [1977] ECR 1029), that authorisation under Article 38 of Regulation (EEC) No 3330/74 to grant the aids provided for therein cannot be taken to mean that any method of financing such aids, whatever its character or conditions, is compatible with Community law and that in the financing of the aid granted, the national authorities remain in particular subject to the obligations arising under the Treaty.

The surcharge is indeed a charge imposed on domestic products and imported products on the basis of identical criteria. However, *in an interpretation of the concept 'internal taxation' for the purposes of Article 95 it may be necessary to take into account the purpose to which the revenue from the charge is put.* In fact, if the revenue from such a charge is intended to finance activities for the special advantage of the taxed domestic products it may follow that the charge imposed on the basis of the same criteria nevertheless constitutes discriminatory taxation in so far as the fiscal burden on domestic products is neutralised by the advantages which the charge is used to finance whilst the charge on the imported products constitutes a net burden.

It follows that *internal taxation is of such a nature as indirectly to impose a heavier burden on products from other Member States than on domestic products if it is used exclusively or principally to finance aids for the sole benefit of domestic products.*

The Italian Government objects that such an attitude would lead in this case to adopting a formalistic view of Article 95. It claims that in fact it would be permissible for the Italian Republic to maintain the surcharge as it is at present applied if the revenue from that charge were paid to the Italian treasury and thence into the general budget of the State; the Government could then provide from that budget the funds intended for financing the aids authorised by Article 38 of Regulation No 3330/74. In that case, too, the imported product would be no better off than at present since the surcharge would continue to be imposed on it without benefiting aids granted for the domestic product.

It must be observed that the situation envisaged by the Italian Government is not comparable to that which forms the subject-matter of this action. These proceedings concern the surcharge, in its capacity as taxation which, although imposing an equal charge on domestic sugar and imported sugar, is allotted to the financing of aids for the benefit of domestic sugar. If the surcharge were not in the nature of taxation allotted to the financing of aids for the domestic product the conditions for the application of Article 95 would not be present. In that case however the grant of the adaptation aids would no longer be the automatic result of equalisation arrangements burdening only the sugar-production and importation sectors but would have its origin in legislative or governmental decisions in which the different trade interests in question were brought into equilibrium.

Finally the Italian Government emphasises that the surcharge is imposed on sugar released for consumption and that the charge which it represents forms an integral part of the selling price of the sugar. It follows, in its view, that the charge in question is ultimately borne by the consumer of the product and that the producers and importers of the sugar are acting on behalf of the consumer when they pay the amount of the charge.

However, as the Commission pertinently remarks, the fact that the financial burdens arising from the imposition of a charge are passed on to the consumers does not alter the legal nature of the charge in question. Furthermore the Italian Government has not contested the fact that the surcharge is imposed on producers and importers of sugar. The fact, alleged by the Italian Government, that the selling prices of sugar in Italy at the various stages of marketing include the amount of the surcharge is irrelevant in classifying it in relation to Article 95 of the Treaty.

It follows from the foregoing that the arguments advanced by the Italian Government cannot be upheld.

Consequently the surcharge must be considered as a charge which, although levied at the same rate on sugar produced in Italy and sugar from other Member States, does not constitute a uniform imposition on those products since it constitutes an unequal burden on the domestic products which benefit from its imposition and on the imported products which are liable to the charge but do not derive the benefit.

3. QUANTITATIVE RESTRICTIONS AND MEASURES HAVING EQUIVALENT EFFECT

A) THE RULE IN ARTICLE 30

EEC Treaty

Article 30

Quantitative restrictions on imports and all measures having equivalent effect shall, without prejudice to the following provisions, be prohibited between Member States.

...

Article 34

1. Quantitative restrictions on exports, and all measures having equivalent effect, shall be prohibited between Member States.

The quantitative restrictions prohibited by Article 30 had largely been eliminated by the Member States before the EEC Treaty came into force and were all abolished by the end of the first four year period, but the meaning of 'measures having equivalent effect' has caused great problems. The last directive issued by the Commission during the transitional period contains an interesting catalogue.

Commission Directive No 70/50 of 22 December 1969, based on the Provisions of Article 33(7), on the Abolition of Measures which have an Effect Equivalent to Quantitative Restrictions on Imports and are not covered by Other Provisions adopted in Pursuance of the EEC Treaty

(OJ Special Edition 1970, p. 17)

Article 1

The purpose of this directive is to abolish the measures referred to in Articles 2 and 3, which were operative at the date of entry into force of the EEC Treaty.

Article 2

1. This directive covers measures, other than those applicable equally to domestic or imported products, which hinder imports which could otherwise take place, including measures which make importation more difficult or costly than the disposal of domestic production.

2. In particular, it covers measures which make imports or the disposal, at any marketing stage, of imported products subject to a condition – other than a formality – which is

required in respect of imported products only, or a condition differing from that required for domestic products and more difficult to satisfy. Equally, it covers, in particular, measures which favour domestic products or grant them a preference, other than an aid, to which conditions may or may not be attached.

3. The measures referred to must be taken to include those measures which:

(a) lay down, for imported products only, minimum or maximum prices below or above which imports are prohibited, reduced or made subject to conditions liable to hinder importation;

(b) lay down less favourable prices for imported products than for domestic products;

(c) fix profit margins or any other price components for imported products only or fix these differently for domestic products and for imported products, to the detriment of the latter;

(d) preclude any increase in the price of the imported product corresponding to the supplementary costs and charges inherent in importation;

(e) fix the prices of products solely on the basis of the cost price or the quality of domestic products at such a level as to create a hindrance to importation;

(f) lower the value of an imported product, in particular by causing a reduction in its intrinsic value, or increase its costs;

(g) make access of imported products to the domestic market conditional upon having an agent or representative in the territory of the importing Member State;

(h) lay down conditions of payment in respect of imported products only, or subject imported products to conditions which are different from those laid down for domestic products and more difficult to satisfy;

(i) require, for imports only, the giving of guarantees or making of payments on account;

(j) subject imported products only to conditions, in respect in particular of shape, size, weight, composition, presentation, identification or putting up, or subject imported products to conditions which are different from those for domestic products and more difficult to satisfy;

(k) hinder the purchase by individuals of imported products only, or encourage, require or give preference to the purchase of domestic products only;

(l) totally or partially preclude the use of national facilities or equipment in respect of imported products only, or totally or partially confine the use of such facilities or equipment to domestic products only;

(m) prohibit or limit publicity in respect of imported products only, or totally or partially confine publicity to domestic products only;

(n) prohibit, limit or require stocking in respect of imported products only; totally or partially confine the use of stocking facilities to domestic products only, or make the stocking of imported products subject to conditions which are different from those required for domestic products and more difficult to satisfy;

(o) make importation subject to the granting of reciprocity by one or more Member States;

(p) prescribe that imported products are to conform, totally or partially, to rules other than those of the importing country;

(q) specify time limits for imported products which are insufficient or excessive in relation to the normal course of the various transactions to which these time limits apply;
(r) subject imported products to controls, other than those inherent in the customs clearance procedure, to which domestic products are not subject or which are stricter in respect of imported products than they are in respect of domestic products, without this being necessary in order to ensure equivalent protection;
(s) confine names which are not indicative of origin or source to domestic products only;

Article 3

This directive also covers measures governing the marketing of products which deal, in particular, with shape, size, weight, composition, presentation, identification or putting up and which are equally applicable to domestic and imported products, where the restrictive effect of such measures on the free movement of goods exceeds the effects intrinsic to trade rules.

This is the case, in particular, where:

– the restrictive effects on the free movement of goods are out of proportion to their purpose;
– the same objective can be attained by other means which are less of a hindrance to trade.

Article 4

1. Member States shall take all necessary steps in respect of products which must be allowed to enjoy free movement pursuant to Articles 9 and 10 of the Treaty to abolish measures having an effect equivalent to quantitative restrictions on imports and covered by this directive.

2. Member States shall inform the Commission of measures taken pursuant to this directive.

Article 5

1. This directive does not apply to measures:
(a) which fall under Article 37(1) of the EEC Treaty;
(b) which are referred to in Article 44 of the EEC Treaty or form an integral part of a national organisation of an agricultural market not yet replaced by a common organisation.

2. This directive shall apply without prejudice to the application, in particular, of Articles 36 and 223 of the EEC Treaty.

...

The prohibition extends not only to quantitative restrictions properly so called, but also to measures producing equivalent effects. A measure applied indiscriminately to domestic and imported products may produce effects equivalent to a quantitative restriction.

Case 8/74 Procureur du Roi v Benoît and Gustave Dassonville
[1974] ECR 837; [1974] 2 CMLR 436

The Court

By the first question it is asked whether a national provision prohibiting the import of goods bearing a designation of origin where such goods are not accompanied by an official document issued by the Government of the exporting country certifying their right to such designation constitutes a measure having an effect equivalent to a quantitative restriction within the meaning of Article 30 of the Treaty.

This question was raised within the context of criminal proceedings instituted in Belgium against traders who duly acquired a consignment of Scotch whisky in free circulation in France and imported it into Belgium without being in possession of a certificate of origin from the British customs authorities, thereby infringing Belgian rules.

It emerges from the file and from the oral proceedings that a trader, wishing to import into Belgium Scotch whisky which is already in free circulation in France, can obtain such a certificate only with great difficulty, unlike the importer who imports directly from the producer country.

All trading rules enacted by Member States which are capable of hindering directly or indirectly, actually or potentially, intra-Community trade are to be considered as measures having an effect equivalent to quantitative restrictions.

In the absence of a Community system guaranteeing for consumers the authenticity of a product's designation of origin, if a Member State takes measures to prevent unfair practices in this connection, it is however subject to the condition that these measures should be reasonable and that the means of proof required should not act as a hindrance to trade between Member States and should, in consequence, be accessible to all Community nationals.

Even without having to examine whether or not such measures are covered by Article 36, they must not, in any case, by virtue of the principle expressed in the second sentence of that article, constitute a means of arbitrary discrimination or a disguised restriction on trade between Member States.

That may be the case with formalities, required by a Member State for the purpose of proving the origin of a product, which only direct importers are really in a position to satisfy without facing serious difficulties.

Consequently, the requirement by a Member State of a certificate of authenticity which is less easily obtainable by importers of an authentic product which has been put into free circulation in a regular manner in another Member State than by importers of the same product coming directly from the country of origin constitutes a measure having an effect equivalent to a quantitative restriction as prohibited by the Treaty.

The Court occupied itself with the issue again in 1978, in an important judgment which has since been the subject of conflicting interpretations.

Case 120/78 Rewe-Zentral AG v Bundesmonopolverwaltung für Branntwein ('Cassis de Dijon') [1979] ECR 649; [1979] 3 CMLR 494

A German prohibition on the marketing of liqueurs with an alcoholic strength of less than 25% made it impossible for the plaintiff to import a consignment of

Cassis de Dijon, a French liqueur with a strength of between 15-20%, into the Federal Republic.

The Court

The plaintiff takes the view that the fixing by the German rules of a minimum alcohol content leads to the result that well-known spirits products from other Member States of the Community cannot be sold in the Federal Republic of Germany and that the said provision therefore constitutes a restriction on the free movement of goods between Member States which exceeds the bounds of the trade rules reserved to the latter.

In its view it is a measure having an effect equivalent to a quantitative restriction on imports contrary to Article 30 of the EEC Treaty.

In the absence of common rules relating to the production and marketing of alcohol – a proposal for a regulation submitted to the Council by the Commission on 7 December 1976 (Official Journal, C 309, p. 2) not yet having received the Council's approval – it is for the Member States to regulate all matters relating to the production and marketing of alcohol and alcoholic beverages on their own territory.

Obstacles to movement within the Community resulting from disparities between the national laws relating to the marketing of the products in question must be accepted in so far as those provisions may be recognised as being necessary in order to satisfy mandatory requirements relating in particular to the effectiveness of fiscal supervision, the protection of public health, the fairness of commercial transactions and the defence of the consumer.

After laying down these four exceptions, the Court continued to dispense with the German Government's claim that an exception was justified in this case.

The Government of the Federal Republic of Germany, intervening in the proceedings, put forward various arguments which, in its view, justify the application of provisions relating to the minimum alcohol content of alcoholic beverages, adducing considerations relating on the one hand to the protection of public health and on the other to the protection of the consumer against unfair commercial practices.

As regards the protection of public health the German Government states that the purpose of the fixing of minimum alcohol contents by national legislation is to avoid the proliferation of alcoholic beverages on the national market, in particular alcoholic beverages with a low alcoholic content, since, in its view, such products may more easily induce a tolerance towards alcohol than more highly alcoholic beverages.

Such considerations are not decisive since the consumer can obtain on the market an extremely wide range of weakly or moderately alcoholic products and furthermore a large proportion of alcoholic beverages with a high alcohol content freely sold on the German market is generally consumed in a diluted form.

The German Government also claims that the fixing of a lower limit for the alcohol content of certain liqueurs is designed to protect the consumer against unfair practices on the part of producers and distributors of alcoholic beverages.

This argument is based on the consideration that the lowering of the alcohol content secures a competitive advantage in relation to beverages with a higher alcohol content, since alcohol constitutes by far the most expensive constituent of beverages by reason of the high rate of tax to which it is subject.

Furthermore, according to the German Government, to allow alcoholic products into free circulation wherever, as regards their alcohol content, they comply with the rules laid down in the country of production would have the effect of imposing as a common standard within the Community the lowest alcohol content permitted in any of the Member States, and even of rendering any requirements in this field inoperative since a lower limit of this nature is foreign to the rules of several Member States.

As the Commission rightly observed, the fixing of limits in relation to the alcohol content of beverages may lead to the standardisation of products placed on the market and of their designations, in the interests of a greater transparency of commercial transactions and offers for sale to the public.

However, this line of argument cannot be taken so far as to regard the mandatory fixing of minimum alcohol contents as being an essential guarantee of the fairness of commercial transactions, since it is a simple matter to ensure that suitable information is conveyed to the purchaser by requiring the display of an indication of origin and of the alcohol content on the packaging of products.

It is clear from the foregoing that the requirements relating to the minimum alcohol content of alcoholic beverages do not serve a purpose which is in the general interest and such as to take precedence over the requirements of the free movement of goods, which constitutes one of the fundamental rules of the Community.

In practice, the principal effect of requirements of this nature is to promote alcoholic beverages having a high alcohol content by excluding from the national market products of other Member States which do not answer that description.

It therefore appears that the unilateral requirement imposed by the rules of a Member States of a minimum alcohol content for the purposes of the sale of alcoholic beverages constitutes an obstacle to trade which is incompatible with the provisions of Article 30 of the Treaty.

There is therefore no valid reason why, provided that they have been lawfully produced and marketed in one of the Member States, alcoholic beverages should not be introduced into any other Member State; the sale of such products may not be subject to a legal prohibition on the marketing of beverages with an alcohol content lower than the limit set by the national rules.

Consequently ... the concept of 'measures having an effect equivalent to quantitative restrictions on imports' contained in Article 30 of the Treaty is to be understood to mean that the fixing of a minimum alcohol content for alcoholic beverages intended for human consumption by the legislation of a Member State also falls within the prohibition laid down in that provision where the importation of alcoholic beverages lawfully produced and marketed in another Member State is concerned.

The *'Cassis de Dijon'* judgment seems to be an attempt on the part of the Court to limit the effect of the *Dassonville* rule. It is clear that the exceptions laid down in *'Cassis de Dijon'* can apply only to measures which are formally or materially non-discriminatory and the effect seems to be that such measures which are justified by the exceptions are thus taken out of Article 30 altogether rather than subject to Article 36 (see below p. 223).

Case 286/81 Criminal Proceedings against Oosthoek's Uitgeversmaatschappij BV
[1982] ECR 4575; [1983] 3 CMLR 428

A Belgian manufacturer of encyclopaedias offered a free dictionary as a purchase incentive and was prosecuted for breach of Netherlands legislation which restricted the freedom to offer or give free gifts within the framework of a commercial activity. The manufacturer argued in its defence that the Netherlands prohibition was incompatible with Community law.

The Court

In its question, the national court seeks in substance to ascertain whether Articles 30 and 34 of the EEC Treaty preclude the application by a Member State to products from, or intended for, another Member State of national legislation which prohibits the offering or giving, for sales promotion purposes, of free gifts in the form of books to purchasers of an encyclopaedia and requires, for the application of an exception to that prohibition, the existence of a relationship between the consumption or use of the free gift and the product sold.

In their observations, the Netherlands, German and Danish Governments express the view, *in limine,* that national legislation such as that at issue has no particular impact on intra-Community trade and does not fall within the scope of Articles 30 and 34 of the EEC Treaty.

In that regard, it must be stated that the application of the Netherlands legislation to the sale in the Netherlands of encyclopaedias produced in that country is in no way linked to the importation of goods and does not fall within the scope of Articles 30 and 34 of the EEC Treaty. However, the sale in the Netherlands of encyclopaedias produced in Belgium and the sale in other Member States of encyclopaedias produced in the Netherlands are transactions forming part of intra-Community trade. In view of the question raised by the national court, it is therefore necessary to determine whether provisions of the type contained in the Netherlands legislation are compatible with both Article 30 and Article 34 of the EEC Treaty.

Oosthoek maintains that the Netherlands legislation obliges it to adopt different sales promotion schemes in the various Member States which constitute a single market, involves it in additional costs and further difficulties and thus hinders the importation and exportation of the encyclopaedias in question. The requirement of related consumption or use is not justified by the need either to protect consumers or to safeguard competition.

The Commission considers that although the possibility that such a measure may indirectly hinder the importation of encyclopaedias cannot be ruled out, it is not contrary to Article 30 since it applies to all products without distinction and is justified by the objectives of consumer protection and organisation of the economy.

In order to answer the question raised by the national court, it is necessary to consider the question relating to exportation separately from that relating to importation.

As regards exportation, Article 34 is concerned with national measures the aim or effect of which is specifically to restrict the flow of exports and thus establish a difference in treatment between the domestic trade of a Member State and its export trade, in such a way as to confer a particular advantage on domestic production or on the domestic market of the State in question. That is evidently not the position in the case of legislation such as that at issue as regards the sale in other Member States of the Community of encyclopaedias produced in the Netherlands. That legislation merely imposes certain restrictions on marketing conditions within the Netherlands without affecting the sale of goods intended for exportation.

As regards the restrictions on imports referred to in Article 30 of the EEC Treaty, it must be remembered that the Court has repeatedly held, since its judgment of 20 February 1979 in Case 120/78 *Rewe* [1979] ECR 649, that in the absence of common rules relating to marketing, obstacles to movement within the Community resulting from disparities between national rules must be accepted in so far as those rules, being applicable to domestic products and imported products without distinction, are justifiable as being necessary in order to satisfy mandatory requirements relating, *inter alia,* to consumer protection and fair trading.

Legislation which restricts or prohibits certain forms of advertising and certain means of sales promotion may, although it does not directly affect imports, be such as to restrict their volume because it affects marketing opportunities for the imported products. The possibility cannot be ruled out that to compel a producer either to adopt advertising or sales promotion schemes which differ from one Member State to another or to discontinue a scheme which he considers to be particularly effective may constitute an obstacle to imports even if the legislation in question applies to domestic products and imported products without distinction.

It is therefore necessary to consider whether a prohibition of a free gift scheme, such as that contained in the Netherlands legislation, may be justified by requirements relating to consumer protection and fair trading.

In that regard, it is clear from the evidence before the Court that the Wet Beperking Cadeaustelsel 1977 pursues a twofold objective which is, in the first place, to prevent the disruption of normal competition by undertakings which offer products as free gifts or at very low prices with a view to promoting the sale of their own range of goods and, secondly, to protect consumers by the attainment of greater market transparency.

It is undeniable that the offering of free gifts as a means of sales promotion may mislead consumers as to the real prices of certain products and distort the conditions on which genuine competition is based. Legislation which restricts or even prohibits such commercial practices for that reason is therefore capable of contributing to consumer protection and fair trading.

The question raised by the national court with regard to legislation of that kind concerns, in particular, the criterion of relation consumption or use the purpose of which, in the present case, is to define the scope of one of the exceptions relaxing the rule which in principle prohibits the offering of free gifts.

Even though no such criterion has been incorporated in the laws of other Member States, and in particular that of Belgium, it does not appear to be unrelated to the above-mentioned objectives of the Netherlands legislation or, in particular, to the desire to achieve market transparency to the extent considered necessary for the protection of consumers and to ensure fair trading. Accordingly, the incorporation of such a criterion in national legislation in order to define the scope of an exception to a rule which prohibits the offering of free gifts does not exceed what is necessary for the attainment of the objectives in question.

The answer to the question raised must therefore be that Articles 30 and 34 of the EEC Treaty do not preclude the application by a Member State to products from, or intended for, another Member State of national legislation which prohibits the offering or giving, for sales promotion purposes, of free gifts in the form of books to purchasers of an encyclopaedia and requires, for the application of an exception to that prohibition, the existence of a relationship between the consumption or the use of the free gift and the product constituting the basis for the offering of the gift.

The Court thus gave the concept of measures with equivalent effect a very broad meaning, but used the *'Cassis de Dijon'* rule to take the measure back out of Article 30. Compare this approach with that in the next two cases. (For further comments on the distinction between the application of Article 30 and that of Article 34 see Case 15/79 *Groenveld* [1979] ECR 3409; [1981] 1 CMLR 207 and Case 155/80 *Oebel* [1981] ECR 1993; [1983] 1 CMLR 390.)

Case 75/81 Joseph Henri Thomas Blesgen v State of Belgium
[1982] 1 ECR 1211; [1983] 1 CMLR 431

A restaurateur who stocked imported spirits was prosecuted for alleged breach of a prohibition on the sale of spirits in certain public places. The Belgian Cour de Cassation asked the European Court whether the law in question fell within the ambit of Article 30.

The Court

Both before the Cour de Cassation and in his observations to the Court of Justice the accused maintained that even if they applied without distinction to domestic and imported products the rules laid down by Articles 1 and 2 of the Law of 29 August 1919 constituted measures having an effect equivalent to quantitative restrictions on the importation of spirits contrary to Article 30 of the EEC Treaty.

In the view of the Belgian Government the law in question does not fall under the prohibition of Article 30 of the EEC Treaty because it has no restrictive effect upon intra-Community trade in the absence of any discrimination between imported and domestic products. The objective of the Law of 29 August 1919 is a general one and forms part of the campaign against alcoholism. The Belgian Government points out that the ban on keeping and consuming certain spirits in places open to the public is intended to combat alcoholism and its spread and in particular to protect youth against its harmful effects both from a personal and social point of view. It therefore constitutes a legitimate choice of social policy in accordance with the objectives of general interest pursued by the Treaty. The absence of Community rules in the matter justifies national action in so far as it is considered necessary to satisfy imperative requirements which in any event have precedence over the requirements of free movements of goods.

Article 30 of the EEC Treaty provides that quantitative restrictions on imports and all measures having equivalent effect shall be prohibited between Member States. It follows that any national measure likely to hinder, directly or indirectly, actually or potentially, intra-Community trade is to be regarded as a measure having an effect equivalent to quantitative restrictions. As the Court pointed out in its judgment of 10 July 1980 in Case 152/78 *Commission* v *France* [1980] ECR 2299, even though a law on the marketing of products does not directly concern imports, it may, according to the circumstances, affect prospects for importing products from other Member States and thus fall under the prohibition in Article 30 of the Treaty.

Moreover according to Article 3 of Commission Directive No 70/50 of 22 December 1969 (Official Journal, English Special Edition 1970, I p. 17) on the abolition of measures which have an effect equivalent to quantitative restrictions on imports and are not covered by other provisions adopted in pursuance of the EEC Treaty, the prohibition in Article 30 of the Treaty also covers national measures governing the marketing of products even though equally applicable to domestic and imported products, where the restrictive effect of such measures on the free movement of goods exceeds the effects intrinsic to trade rules.

That is not however the case with a legislative provision concerning only the sale of strong spirits for consumption on the premises in all places open to the public and not concerning other forms of marketing the same drinks. It is to be observed in addition that the restrictions placed on the sale of the spirits in question make no distinction whatsoever based on their nature or origin. Such a legislative measure has therefore in fact no connection with the importation of the products and for that reason is not of such a nature as to impede trade between Member States.

The same considerations also apply to the prohibition of keeping the drinks in question in premises appurtenant to the establishment open to the public. In so far as that provision is ancillary to the prohibition of consumption on the premises its effect cannot be to restrict the importation of products originating in other Member States.

The first question must therefore be answered to the effect that *the concept in Article 30 of the EEC Treaty of measures having an effect equivalent to quantitative restrictions on imports is to be understood as meaning that the prohibition laid down by that provision does not cover a national measure applicable without distinction to domestic and imported products which prohibits the consumption, sale or offering even without charge of spirituous beverages of a certain alcoholic strength for consumption on the premises in all places open to the public* as well as the stocking of such drinks on premises to which consumers are admitted or in other parts of the establishment or in the dwelling appurtenant thereto, in so far as the latter prohibition is complementary to the prohibition of consumption on the premises.

SA Magnavision NV v General Optical Council (No 1)
[1987] 1 CMLR 887

MacPherson J

SA Magnavision NV is a Belgian company which markets reading glasses in England and Wales. These glasses are sold through a chain of concessions which operate in shops. In the present case the shop holding the concession was David Morgan Stores, which is a department store in Cardiff. The customer can roughly test his own need for magnifying glasses by means of a simple test-card. According to the scale or size of writing that the customer can read he can then buy glasses which will correct his deficiency in sight without prescription and without the supervision of an optician.

Section 21 of the Opticians Act 1958 provides as follows:

(1) Subject to the following provisions of this Section, a person shall not sell any optical appliance unless the sale is effected by or under the supervision of a registered medical practitioner or registered optician...

By Section 30 'optical appliance' means an appliance designed to correct, remedy or relieve a defect of sight.

Certain sales are excluded from the ambit of Section 21(1), but sales of the spectacles with which we are concerned are not within the excluded categories, and the law says in effect that such spectacles may not be sold otherwise than under the supervision of a doctor or an optician on the premises or after the production of a prescription given by an optician.

On 15 July 1985 an information was laid in Cardiff alleging breaches of Section 21 (1). Magistrates heard the case on 19 and 20 December 1985 and on 15 January 1986.

After a lengthy hearing the Magistrates found the case proved and the appellants were fined £250.

The appellants now appeal by way of case stated, and the question to be resolved is:

> 'Whether we [the Magistrates] were correct in law in interpreting Article 30 of the Treaty of Rome so as to determine that the same would not apply on the facts as we found?'

In this connection it is important to set out that which the Magistrates found to be established. Paragraph 6 of the case stated reads as follows:

> 'We were of the opinion that all the respondent's contentions were correct. We were of the opinion that presbyopia constitutes a defect of sight within the meaning of the Act and that the Act does not contravene Article 30 of the Treaty of Rome in that the Act regulates sales and not importation and does not place at any disadvantage those seeking to sell imported glasses'.

Among the respondent's contentions which were thus accepted by the Magistrates were the following:

'(c) The operation of the Opticians Act 1958 is indiscriminate in its application as between glasses sold by domestic suppliers imported from other Member States of the European Economic Community.

'(d) The Opticians Act is a statute concerned with public health and designed *inter alia* to aid the detection and treatment of eye abnormalities which would otherwise go undetected and as such fell within the provisions of Article 36 of the Treaty of Rome'.

That sub-paragraph (c) is on analysis ineptly worded, but its meaning is in my judgment apparent.

In my judgment those contentions and the Magistrates' acceptance of them were fully justified and, for reasons which follow, the Magistrates were in my judgment correct in law and right to convict in this case.

Articles 30 and 36 of the Treaty read as follows:

[See above, p. 210 and below, p. 223.]

In essence the appellants' argument is simple. They say that the practical result of the operation of Section 21(1) of the 1958 Act is to hinder them selling their product in this country, since opticians cannot and do not prescribe Magnavision glasses, and since sale under the supervision of an optician would involve hiring and paying an optician in each shop where a concession is held, which would be uneconomic.

And they argue that while Section 21(1) is indistinctly applicable to domestic and imported products alike and regulates sales and not importation as such, yet the Section 21(1) prohibition is caught by Article 30. This is illustrated by a number of European Court cases, say the appellants, and is contrary to the basic test set out in the case of *Procureur du Roi* v *Dassonville* (see above, p. 213). That ... case undoubtedly confirms that *prima facie* all trading rules enacted by Member States which are capable of hindering directly or indirectly, actually or potentially, intra-Community trade are to be considered as measures having an effect equivalent to quantitative restrictions. Such measures must not constitute a means of arbitrary discrimination or a disguised restriction on trade between Member States.

...

It should be noted however that *Dassonville* was of course a case dealing with trading rules between States as such which involved discrimination against imported products.

As Mr Jacobs says (for the respondents), *Dassonville* stresses the fact that trade was made more difficult for the importer than for the domestic producer.

Similarly in the now classic case of *Rewe-Zentral AG v Bundesmonopolverwaltung für Branntwein* (more conveniently known by its shorthand names as *Rewe* or *'Cassis de Dijon'*) the appellants argue that the European Court held that a unilateral requirement imposed by the rules of a Member State of a minimum alcohol content for the purposes of the sale of alcoholic beverages constituted an obstacle to trade which was incompatible with Article 30.

The case further established that 'obstacles to movement within the Community resulting from disparities between the national laws relating to the marketing of the products in question must be accepted in so far as those provisions may be recognised as being necessary in order to satisfy marketing requirements relating in particular to the effectiveness of fiscal supervision, the protection of public health, the fairness of commercial transactions and the defence of the consumer'.

It is true that the *'Cassis De Dijon'* case shows that national measures can infringe Article 30 even though they apply to both imported and domestic products, subject to justification by reference to the mandatory requirement under examination. That is further established by other cases referred to by the appellants (see *Eyssen* and *Cinethèque*).

But *'Cassis De Dijon'* involved effectively a direct ban upon the sale of the low alcohol beverage and thus upon its import to Germany. So that the measures were plainly discriminatory and protectionist in their effect.

And similarly other cases cited involved in practice the prohibition upon sale of the proposed imports.

Other cases concerning the presentation of goods, such as their packaging or labelling, may similarly be caught by Article 30; since such measures impose an additional barrier upon imported goods and have some particular restrictive effect (see *Walter Rau* (above, p. 188) concerning the packaging of margarine).

But the cases show that before Article 30 will bite there must be proved to exist some particular restrictive effect upon imports. If this were not so then any sales restriction (such as a requirement that guns can only be sold by licensed dealers, or that alcohol may only be sold by the holders of Justices' licences) *could similarly involve breach of Article 30...*

It is thus a prerequisite to reliance upon Article 30 that the measures under attack must have some real connection with the importation of the product... If there is no true connection between the restriction and the importation of the product then Article 30 has no effect. This is perhaps best of all illustrated by the case of *Blesgen* (see above p. 218), where it was held expressly that the law in question did not fall within Article 30 because the legislative measure had in fact no connection with the importation of the products and for that reason was not of such a nature as to impede trade between Member States.

Mr Bellamy plainly has difficulty with this case (*Blesgen*) and while he seeks to distinguish it, I am, for my part, convinced that it is in point and strongly favours the respondents' arguments.

In parenthesis I add that the case of *Oosthoek* (the encyclopaedia sales case (above, p. 216)), upon which the applicants rely, appears to be out of line with the other cases cited to us. This may be because in any event the Court was to hold that the relevant legislation was justified in consumer protection terms (see *Rewe*). It is not in my judgment helpful further to analyse that case in all the circumstances.

I am convinced upon consideration of these and all the cases to which we were referred that in the present case the respondents' arguments prevail.

Before Article 30 could catch the 1958 Act restrictions it would have to be established that the measures did truly affect the Belgian imports adversely. It is not enough simply to prove that sales are affected, since otherwise all such measures could be caught.

That adverse effect may be either some discrimination in favour of the domestic product or against the import. Member States may not regulate trade in such a way that imports are adversely affected, but regulation is within the competence of Member States if it does not impede imports.

In the present case it is in my judgment clear that the 1958 Act measure was not in the outlawed category. Certainly there is in my judgment no evidence that it was in that category, and the Magistrates were entitled to conclude that Article 30 did not bite at all in this case.

For good measure the Magistrates seem to me also to have been fully justified in their conclusion as to Article 36.

In this context Mr Bellamy relies strongly upon the question in accordance with the rules laid down in *R.* v *Goldstein.*

For further good measure it is in my judgment open to the prosecution to say (as they do) that the measure is plainly justifiable also in *Rewe* or '*Cassis De Dijon*' terms. It is a mandatory requirement . But it is plainly a requirement imposed 'for the protection of public health ... and the defence of the consumer'. It is perfectly true that the Magistrates do not deal expressly with this aspect of the case. But they rule that Article 30 does not bite, and that Article 36 does. And in my judgment it can be inferred from the case that the '*Cassis De Dijon*' argument also prevailed.

I confess however that my heart is not in these latter conclusions as to the justification since I am convinced that this is not an Article 30 case at all. But (as in *Oosthoek*) the respondents can in my judgment argue the matter by reference to justification in case it should be held elsewhere that Article 30 has been breached.

I would uphold the Magistrates' decision, and would certainly conclude that they were entitled to find as they did; and my conclusion is so clear that (as I have already said) I would not order a reference to the European Court of preliminary ruling upon this case.

Finally I add that I am comforted in this conclusion since *it seems plain to me that the spirit of Article 30 of the Treaty is concerned to prohibit discriminatory and protectionist measures*. And in the absence of harmonisation of the laws of Member States, each Member can pursue its own measures provided they are not in their aim or effect discriminatory or protectionist. In my judgment Section 21(1) of the 1958 Act is neither of those things.

Appeal dismissed.

B) THE EXCEPTIONS TO THE RULE IN ARTICLE 30

Two provisions in the EEC Treaty set out express derogations from the basic rules relating to the free movement of goods. Article 36 sets out a series of exceptions to the prohibition on quantitative restrictions and measures having equivalent effect, the most important of which in practice have been those relating to industrial property and public health. Article 115 provides the basis of an exception to the principle of free movement of goods as such to prevent what might generically be termed 'deflection of trade'. What Articles 36 and 115 have in common is that, as exceptions, they have been construed very strictly.

EEC Treaty

Article 36

The provisions of Articles 30 to 34 shall not preclude prohibitions or restrictions on imports, exports or goods in transit justified on grounds of public morality, public policy or public security; the protection of health and life of humans, animals or plants; the protection of national treasures possessing artistic, historic or archaeological value; or the protection of industrial and commercial property. Such prohibitions or restrictions shall not, however, constitute a means of arbitrary discrimination or a disguised restriction on trade between Member States.

Article 115

In order to ensure that the execution of measures of commercial policy taken in accordance with this Treaty by any Member State is not obstructed by deflection of trade, or where differences between such measures lead to economic difficulties in one or more of the Member States, the Commission shall recommend the methods for the requisite cooperation between Member States. Failing this, the Commission shall authorise Member States to take the necessary protective measures, the conditions and details of which it shall determine.

In case of urgency during the transitional period, Member States may themselves take the necessary measures and shall notify them to the other Member States and to the Commission, which may decide that the States concerned shall amend or abolish such measures.

In the selection of such measures, priority shall be given to those which cause the least disturbance to the functioning of the common market and which take into account the need to expedite, as far as possible, the introduction of the Common Customs Tariff.

Act of Accession

Article 135

1. If, before 31 December 1977, difficulties arise which are serious and liable to persist in any sector of the economy or which could bring about serious deterioration in the economic situation of a given area, a new Member State may apply for authorisation to take protective measures in order to rectify the situation and adjust the sector concerned to the economy of the Common Market.

2. On application by the State concerned, the Commission shall by emergency procedure determine without delay the protective measures which it considers necessary, specifying the circumstances and the manner in which they are to be put into effect.

3. The measures authorised under paragraph 2 may involve derogations from the rules of the EEC Treaty and of this Act to such an extent and for such periods as are strictly necessary in order to attain the objective referred to in paragraph 1. Priority shall be given to such measures as will least disturb the functioning of the Common Market.

4. In the same circumstances and according to the same procedure, any original Member State may apply for authorisation to take protective measures in regard to one or more new Member States.

i) Public Morality

It appeared from early cases that Member States were to be allowed a margin of discretion in the field of public morality (see Case 34/79 *Regina* v *Maurice Donald Henn and John Frederick Ernest Darby* [1979] ECR 3795; [1980] 1 CMLR 246), but the Court subsequently made it clear that Article 36 is to be restrictively construed.

Case 121/85 Conegate Limited v H. M. Customs and Excise
11 March 1986

The defendant company was engaged in the importation from the Federal Republic of Germany of inflatable dolls of an erotic nature. The United Kingdom's customs authorities took the view that the dolls were 'indecent or obscene' and accordingly subject to a prohibition on importation under the Customs Consolidation Act 1876. No United Kingdom legislation prohibited the *manufacture* of such items.

The Court

The Court would observe that the ... question raises, in the first place, the general problem of whether a prohibition on the importation of certain goods may be justified on grounds of public morality where the legislation of the Member State concerned contains no prohibition on the manufacture or marketing of the same products within the national territory.

So far as that problem is concerned, it must be borne in mind that according to Article 36 of the EEC Treaty the provisions relating to the free movement of goods within the Community do not preclude prohibitions on imports justified 'on grounds of public morality'. As the Court held in its judgment of 14 December 1979, cited above, in principle it is for each Member State to determine in accordance with its own scale of values and in the form selected by it the requirements of public morality in its territory.

However, although Community law leaves the Member States free to make their own assessments of the indecent or obscene character of certain articles, it must be pointed out that the fact that goods cause offence cannot be regarded as sufficiently serious to justify restrictions on the free movement of goods where the Member State concerned does not adopt, with respect to the same goods manufactured or marketed within its territory, penal measures or other serious and effective measures intended to prevent the distribution of such goods in its territory.

It follows that a Member State may not rely on grounds of public morality in order to prohibit the importation of goods from other Member States when its legislation contains no prohibition on the manufacture or marketing of the same goods on its territory.

ii) Public Policy

Although the exceptions listed in Article 36 are to be construed restrictively, the term 'public policy' (or, in the French, *ordre public*) is not to be construed as narrowly as 'public order'.

Case 7/78 Regina v Ernest George Thompson and Others
[1978] ECR 2247; [1979] 1 CMLR 47

The defendants traded in coins, some of which were old British silver coins that were no longer legal tender. They were convicted in England of being knowingly concerned in the fraudulent evasion of the prohibition on importation of gold coins into the United Kingdom. On appeal they argued that the provisions of English law prohibiting the imports infringed Article 30 to 34 of the Treaty. The Court of appeal referred questions to the European Court. The Court, having held that such coins were goods rather than capital since they were not a normal means of payment, went on to consider whether a prohibition on their import was justified on grounds of public policy.

The Court
The appellants ... submitted that the restrictions on exports and imports contained in British legislation cannot be justified on grounds of public policy on the basis of Article 36 of the Treaty.

On the other hand the British Government has maintained that ... even if the coins in question were to be regarded as goods falling within the scope of Article 30 *et seq.* of the Treaty the restrictions on imports and exports would be authorised under Article 36 of the Treaty, since they could be justified on grounds of public policy.

As far as concerns the restrictions on exports, the ban on exports from the United Kingdom of silver coins minted before 1947 was enacted in order:

(i) to ensure that there is no shortage of current coins for use of the public;
(ii) to ensure that any profit resulting from any increase in the value of metal content of the coin accrues to the Member State rather than to an individual and
(iii) to prevent the destruction of these United Kingdom coins – which if it occurred within its jurisdiction would be a criminal offence – from occurring outside its jurisdiction...

It is for the Member States to mint their own coinage and to protect it from destruction.

The Court's file shows that in the United Kingdom the melting down or destruction of national coins in prohibited, even if they are no longer legal tender.

A ban on destroying such coins with a view to preventing their being melted down or destroyed in another Member State is justified on grounds of public policy within the meaning of Article 36 of the Treaty, because it stems from the need to protect the right to mint coinage which is traditionally regarded as involving the fundamental interests of the State.

iii) Public Health

Article 36 attempts to strike a balance between the interests involved in the creation of a single market (see below, p. 260) and the protection of health. What appears to be of particular relevance is whether, if the measure is discriminatory, it can be shown to be reasonable, in which case it is justified. The word 'justified' has been held to mean 'necessary' (see Case 153/78 *Commission* v *Germany* [1979] ECR 2555; [1980] 1 CMLR 198) and the Court has repeatedly concerned itself with the principle of proportionality.

Case 104/75 Adriaan De Peijper, Managing Director of Centrafarm BV
[1976] ECR 613; [1976] 2 CMLR 271

Under Dutch health legislation, before drugs could be put on the market, certain information had to be communicated to the relevant authorities which could in fact only be supplied by the manufacturer or with his consent. De Peijper, the managing director of Centrafarm, marketed drugs bought in the United Kingdom which were very similar if not identical to those marketed by the same manufacturer in the Netherlands. He was unable to supply the necessary information, and was prosecuted before the Kantongerecht of Rotterdam, which referred two questions for a preliminary ruling.

The Court

First Question

The Court is asked to rule whether national authorities faced with such a situation adopt a measure equivalent to a quantitative restriction and prohibited by the Treaty when they make the authorisation to place a product on the market, for which a parallel importer has applied, conditional upon the production of documents identical with those which the manufacturer or his duly appointed importer has already lodged with them.

1. National measures of the kind in question have an effect equivalent to a quantitative restriction and are prohibited under Article 30 of the Treaty if they are likely to constitute an obstacle, directly or indirectly, actually or potentially, to imports between Member States.

Rules or practices which result in imports being channelled in such a way that only certain traders can effect these imports, whereas others are prevented from doing so, constitute such an obstacle to imports.

2A. However, according to Article 36, 'the provisions of Articles 30 to 34 shall not preclude prohibitions or restrictions on imports ... justified on grounds of ... the protection of health and the life of humans' which do not 'constitute a means of arbitrary discrimination or a disguised restriction on trade between Member States'.

Health and the life of humans rank first among the property or interests protected by Article 36 and it is for the Member States, within the limits imposed by the Treaty, to decide what degree of protection they intend to assure and in particular how strict the checks to be carried out are to be.

Nevertheless it emerges from Article 36 that national rules or practices which do restrict imports of pharmaceutical products or are capable of doing so are only compatible with the Treaty to the extent to which they are necessary for the effective protection of health and life of humans.

National rules or practices do not fall within the exception specified in Article 36 if the health and life of humans can be as effectively protected by measures which do not restrict intra-Community trade so much.

In particular Article 36 cannot be relied on to justify rules or practices which, even though they are beneficial, contain restrictions which are explained primarily by a concern to lighten the administration's burden or reduce public expenditure, unless, in the absence of the said rules or practices, this burden or expenditure clearly would exceed the limits of what can reasonably be required.

The situation described by the national court must be examined in the light of these considerations.

B. For this purpose a distinction must be drawn between, on the one hand, the documents relating to a medicinal preparation in general, in this case the 'file' prescribed by the Netherlands legislation, and, on the other hand, those relating to a specific batch of this medicinal preparation imported by a particular trader, in this case the 'records' which have to be kept under the said legislation.

(a) With regard to the documents relating to the medicinal preparation in general, if the public health authorities of the importing Member State already have in their possession, as a result of importation on a previous occasion, all the pharmaceutical particulars relating to the medicinal preparation in question and considered to be absolutely necessary for the purpose of checking that the medicinal preparation is effective and not harmful, it is clearly unnecessary, in order to protect the health and life of humans, for the said authorities to require a second trader who has imported a medicinal preparation, which is in every respect the same, to produce the above-mentioned particulars to them again.

Therefore national rules or practices which lay down such a requirement are not justified on grounds of the protection of health and life of humans within the meaning of Article 36 of the Treaty.

(b) With regard to the documents relating to a specific batch of a medicinal preparation imported at a time when the public health authorities of the Member State of importation already have in their possession a file relating to this medicinal preparation, these authorities have a legitimate interest in being able at any time to carry out a thorough check to make certain that the said batch complies with the particulars on the file.

Nevertheless, having regard to the nature of the market for the pharmaceutical product in question, it is necessary to ask whether this objective cannot be equally well achieved if the national administrations, instead of waiting passively for the desired evidence to be produced to them – and in a form calculated to give the manufacturer of the product and his duly appointed representatives an advantage – were to admit, where appropriate, similar evidence and, in particular, to adopt a more active policy which could enable every trader to obtain the necessary evidence.

This question is all the more important because parallel importers are very often in a position to offer the goods at a price lower than the one applied by the duly appointed importer for the same product, a fact which, where medicinal preparations are concerned, should, where appropriate, encourage the public health authorities not to place parallel imports at a disadvantage, since the effective protection of health and life of humans also demands that medicinal preparations should be sold at reasonable prices.

National authorities possess legislative and administrative methods capable of compelling the manufacturer or his duly appointed representative to supply particulars making it possible to ascertain that the medicinal preparation which is in fact the subject of parallel importation is identical with the medicinal preparation in respect of which they are already informed.

Moreover, simple cooperation between the authorities of the Member States would enable them to obtain on a reciprocal basis the documents necessary for checking certain largely standardised and widely distributed products.

Taking into account all these possible ways of obtaining information the national public health authorities must consider whether the effective protection of health and life of humans justifies a presumption of the non-conformity of an imported batch with the description of the medicinal preparation, or whether on the contrary it would not be sufficient to lay down a presumption of conformity with the result that, in appropriate cases, it would be for the administration to rebut this presumption.

Finally, even if it were absolutely necessary to require the parallel importer to prove this conformity, there would in any case be no justification under Article 36 for compelling him to do so with the help of documents to which he does not have access, when the administration, or as the case may be, the court, finds that the evidence can be produced by other means.

The British, Danish and Netherlands Governments are of the opinion that measures such as those which are the subject-matter of the main proceedings are necessary in order to comply with the requirements of Council Directives Nos 65/65/EEC, 75/318/EEC and 75/319/EEC (OJ, English Special Edition 1965, p. 20; OJL 147 of 9/6/1975, p. 1 and p. 13) concerning the approximation of national provisions relating to proprietary medicinal products.

However the sole aim of these directives is to harmonise national provisions in this field; they do not and cannot aim at extending the very considerable powers left to Member States in the field of public health by Article 36.

Given a factual situation such as that described in the first question the answer must therefore be that *rules or practices which make it possible for a manufacturer and his duly appointed representatives simply by refusing to produce the 'file' or the 'records' to enjoy a monopoly of the importation and marketing of the product in question must be regarded as being unnecessarily restrictive and cannot therefore come within the exceptions specified in Article 36 of the Treaty, unless it is clearly proved that any other rules or practices would obviously be beyond the means which can reasonably be expected of an administration operating in a normal manner.*

Second Question

By the second question the Court is asked to say whether in principle the answer which must be given to the first question also applies to the case where (a) the process of manufacture and the qualitative and quantitative composition of the medicinal preparation imported by the parallel importer coming from another Member State are different from those of the medicinal preparation bearing the same name and in respect of which the authorities of the Member State into which it has been imported already have these data but (b) 'the differences between the one and the other product are of such minor importance that it is likely that the manufacturer is applying or introducing ... these differences with the conscious and exclusive intention of using these differences ... in order to prevent or impede the possibility of the parallel importation of the proprietary medicinal product'.

The answer must be in the affirmative.

The competent administration of the importing Member State is clearly entitled to require the manufacturer or his duly appointed importer, when the person concerned applies for an authorisation to market the medicinal preparation and lodges the relevant documentation, (a) to state whether the manufacturer or, as the case may be, the group of manufacturers to which he belongs, manufactures under the same name for different Member States several variants of the medicinal preparation and (b) if his answer is in the affirmative, to produce similar documentation for the other variants too, specifying what are differences between all these variants.

It is only if the documents produced in this way show that there are differences which have a therapeutic effect that there would be any justification for treating the variants as different medicinal preparations, for the purposes of authorising them to be placed on the market and as regards producing the relevant documents, it being understood that the answer to the first question remains valid as regards each of the authorisation procedures which have become necessary.

Case 174/82 Officier van Justitie v Sandoz BV
[1983] ECR 2445; [1984] 3 CMLR 43

Sandoz sold, amongst other things, muesli bars which had been lawfully produced in Germany, to which vitamins A and D had been added. They were prosecuted for alleged breach of a Netherlands law prohibiting the marketing without authorisation of food to which vitamins have been added. The matter came before the Economische Politierechter, which took the view that the decision depended on whether the Netherlands legislation was compatible with Articles 30 *et seq.* of the EEC Treaty. It therefore referred questions to the European Court.

The Court

First Question

In the first question the national court seeks in essence to know whether, and if so in what circumstances, the provisions of the Treaty on free movement of goods preclude national rules prohibiting without prior administrative authorisation the marketing of food to which vitamins have been added and which are lawfully marketed in another Member State.

Article 30 of the Treaty prohibits in trade between Member States quantitative restrictions on imports and all measures having equivalent effect. According to established case-law of the Court all commercial rules of the Member States likely to impede directly or indirectly, actually or potentially, intra-Community trade are to be regarded as measures having an effect equivalent to quantitative restrictions. Nevertheless, according to Article 36 of the Treaty the provision in Article 30 does not preclude prohibitions or restrictions on imports justified on grounds *inter alia* of the protection of human health provided that such prohibitions or restrictions do not constitute a means of arbitrary discrimination or a disguised restriction on trade between Member States.

It is apparent that national rules of the kind referred to by the national court prohibiting without prior administrative authorisation the marketing of food to which vitamins have been added are likely to impede trade between Member States and must therefore be regarded as a measure having an effect equivalent to quantitative restrictions within the meaning of Article 30 of the Treaty. The answer to the question therefore depends on the applicability of Article 36 to such rules.

In that respect and in the opinion of Sandoz and the Commission, it is only in the event of excessive consumption, which is excluded however in the case of products of the kind in question, that vitamins and in particular vitamins soluble in fat, such as vitamins A and D, may have harmful effects. A general prohibition on the marketing of food to which vitamins of any kind have been added is therefore not justified within the meaning of Article 36 of the Treaty on grounds of the protection of health and is in any event excessive within the meaning of the last sentence of that article.

On the other hand the Netherlands and Danish Governments contend that such rules are necessary owing to the very nature of the substances added since the absorption of any vitamins in high doses or for a prolonged period may entail risks to health or at least undesirable side-effects such as malnutrition. In view on the one hand of scientific uncertainties and on the other of the fact that the harmfulness of vitamins depends on the quantity absorbed with the whole nutrition of a person it is not possible to say with certainty whether any food to which vitamins have been added is harmful or not.

It appears from the file that vitamins are not in themselves harmful substances but on the contrary are recognised by modern science as necessary for the human organism. Nevertheless excessive consumption of them over a prolonged period may have harmful effects, the extent of which varies according to the type of vitamin: there is generally a greater risk with vitamins soluble in fat than with those soluble in water. According to the observations submitted to the Court, however, scientific research does not appear to be sufficiently advanced to be able to determine with certainty the critical quantities and the precise effects.

It is not disputed by the parties who have submitted observations that the concentration of vitamins contained in the foodstuffs of the kind in issue is far from attaining the critical threshold of harmfulness so that even excessive consumption thereof cannot in itself involve a risk to public health. Nevertheless such a risk cannot be excluded in so far as the consumer absorbs with other foods further quantities of vitamins which it is impossible to monitor or foresee.

...

As the Court found in its judgment of 17 December 1981 in Case 272/80 *Frans-Nederlandse Maatschappij voor Biologische Producten BV* [1981] ECR 3277, in so far as there are uncertainties at the present state of scientific research it is for the Member States, in the absence of harmonisation, to decide what degree of protection of the health and life of humans they intend to assure, having regard however for the requirements of the free movement of goods within the Community.

Those principles also apply to substances such as vitamins which are not as a general rule harmful in themselves but may have special harmful effects solely if taken to excess as part of the general nutrition, the composition of which is unforeseeable and cannot be monitored. In view of the uncertainties inherent in the scientific assessment, national rules prohibiting, without prior authorisation, the marketing of foodstuffs to which vitamins have been added are justified on principle within the meaning of Article 36 of the Treaty on grounds of the protection of human health.

Nevertheless the principle of proportionality which underlies the last sentence of Article 36 of the Treaty requires that the power of the Member States to prohibit imports of the products in question from other Member States should be restricted to what is necessary to attain the legitimate aim of protecting health. Accordingly, national rules providing for such a prohibition are justified only if authorisations to market are granted when they are compatible with the need to protect health.

Such an assessment is, however, difficult to make in relation to additives such as vitamins, the abovementioned characteristics of which exclude the possibility of foreseeing or monitoring the quantities consumed as part of the general nutrition, and the degree of harmfulness of which cannot be determined with sufficient certainty. Nevertheless, although in view of the present stage of harmonisation of national laws at the Community level a wide discretion must be left to the Member States, they must, in order to observe the principle of proportionality, authorise marketing when the addition of vitamins to foodstuffs meets a real need, especially a technical or nutritional one.

The first question must therefore be answered to the effect that Community law permits national rules prohibiting without prior authorisation the marketing of foodstuffs lawfully marketed in another Member State to which vitamins have been added, provided that the marketing is authorised when the addition of vitamins meets a real need, especially a technical or nutritional one.

Second Question

In the second question the national court asks in essence whether Community law precludes national rules such as those referred to by the national court where the authorisation to market is subject to proof by the importer that the product in question is not harmful to health.

Inasmuch as the question arises as to where the onus of proof lies when there is a request for authorisation, in view of the answer to the first question, it must be remembered that Article 36 of the Treaty creates an exception, which must be strictly interpreted, to the rule of free movement of goods within the Community which is one of the fundamental principles of the common market. It is therefore for the national authorities who rely on that provision in order to adopt a measure restricting intra-Community trade to check in each instance that the measure contemplated satisfies the criteria of that provision.

Accordingly, although the national authorities may, in so far as they do not have it themselves, ask the importer to produce the information in his possession relating to the composition of the product and the technical or nutritional reasons for adding vitamins, they must themselves assess, in the light of all the relevant information, whether authorisation must be granted pursuant to Community law.

The second question must therefore be answered to the effect that Community law does not permit national rules which subject authorisation to market to proof by the importer that the product in question is not harmful to health, without prejudice to the right of the national authorities to ask the importer to submit all the information in his possession needed to assess the facts...

Another case concerning additives – this time to animal fodder – raised the issue of a Member State's freedom to implement national legislation with more restrictive effect than existing Community directives dealing with the same subject matter.

Case 28/84 Commission v Germany
[1985] ECR 3097

German legislation on additives to feedingstuffs for calves prohibited importation into the country of products which were legally produced in other Member States.

The Court

The Commission contends, in essence, that the three directives constitute a complete and exhaustive set of rules covering the whole field of production and marketing of compound feedingstuffs, including questions of public health which may be raised by the use of certain ingredients. According to Article 13 of the additives directive (Council Directive No 70/524/EEC of 23 November 1970 concerning Additives in Feedingstuffs (Official Journal, English Special Edition 1970 (III), p. 840)), Article 7 of the undesirable substances directive (Directive No 74/63/EEC of 17 December 1973 on the Fixing of Maximum Permitted Levels for Undesirable Substances and Products in Feedingstuffs (Official Journal 1974, L 38, p. 31)), and Article 9 of the compound feedingstuffs directive (Council Directive No 79/373/EEC of 2 April 1979 on the Marketing of Compound Feedingstuffs (Official Journal 1979, L 86, p. 30)), products which conform to the standards laid down by the Commission ought to be able to circulate freely subject only to the emergency measures provided for by Article 7 of the additives directive and Article 5 of the undesirable substances directive. A Member State is therefore unable, save in the exceptional circumstances laid down by those directives, to adopt unilaterally measures concerning the composition of feedingstuffs that have the effect of creating obstacles to the marketing of feedingstuffs in other Member States. In the Commission's view the compound feedingstuffs directive clearly shows that the Community legislature did not intend to prescribe to manufacturers of feedingstuffs what had to be contained in their products but did intend, in principle, to enable products whatever their composition to be marketed freely in the Community.

...

In its defence the Federal Republic of Germany explains the reason for the adoption of the measure to which the Commission objects. Its purpose is to prohibit certain undesirable practices in the feeding of calves. One such practice is the use of feedingstuffs which are deficient in iron to induce artificial anaemia in calves so as to produce a white meat which is particularly highly regarded by consumers; the other practice is the administering of excessive quantities of salt so as to make the calves artificially thirsty which causes them to absorb excessive quantities of liquid feedingstuffs in order to increase their slaughter liveweight.

From a legal point of view the German Government's arguments may be summarised as follows:

(a) According to the principle of proportionality, or, in the form relevant to this case, the principle of minimum intervention, when interpreting measures of secondary Community law which encroach upon the sovereignty of the Member States, preference should be given to the interpretation which keeps the intervention to a minimum.

(b) In addition to additives and undesirable substances, the use or presence of which is the specific subject of Directives Nos 70/542 and 74/64, it is necessary to take account, for the purpose of applying those directives, of the rules relating to 'constituent elements', that is to say the substances which essentially determine the quality of feedingstuffs. Since the question of the composition of feedingstuffs is not regulated by the directive in question, that is to say the compound feedingstuffs directive, that question continues to lie within the remit of the Member States. It is for that reason that the rules of which the Commission complains are justified...

(c) The contested measure is justified for the protection of animal health, which falls within the powers reserved to the Member States by Article 36. That power is reaffirmed in Article 3 of the compound feedingstuffs directive according to which the Member States must ensure that compound feedingstuffs are wholesome and do not represent a danger to health.

(d) Finally, the Commission misinterpreted Article 15 of the compound feedingstuffs directive which requires it, on the basis of experience acquired, to forward to the Council within a certain period proposals for amendments to the directive such as to achieve free movement of compound feedingstuffs and to eliminate certain disparities concerning in particular the use of ingredients. Since the Commission has not taken appropriate steps, the German Government is authorised to adopt at national level such measures as it considers necessary.

Substance

Before examining the arguments put forward by the Federal Republic of Germany it is necessary to make certain preliminary observations regarding the general background to the aforementioned directives and their relationship with Article 30 of the EEC Treaty.

First, it should be noted that the three directives are based on Articles 43 and 100 of the EEC Treaty. In other words they form part of the framework of the common agricultural policy and at the same time that of the harmonisation of legislation capable of directly affecting the functioning of the common market. In view of that dual legal basis the purpose of the directives is to contribute specifically in the area in question to achieving the free movement of goods which is one of the fundamental elements of the common market.

Although the directives came into force over a period of time from 1970 to 1979 they form a coherent system, as is clear from the first two recitals in their respective preambles. According to those recitals the common objective of the directives is to increase agricultural productivity by promoting the quality of animal production by means of the use of 'appropriate good-quality feedingstuffs'. Within that framework the specific purpose of the additives directive and the undesirable substances directive is to define those aspects which require particular supervision on account, in particular, of their effect on animal or human health (see the fifth to eleventh recitals in the preamble to the additives directive and the third and eighth recitals in the preamble to the undesirable substances directive). Each of those directives provides for a Community procedure for laying down special rules, whether in the form of maximum or minimum contents or in the form of prohibitions, which are contained in the annexes to those directives (see Article 6 of the additives directive, as amended by Council Directive No 73/103/EEC of 28 July 1973, Official Journal 1973, L 124, p. 17, and Article 6 of the undesirable substances directive).

In addition, the additives directive and the undesirable substances directive both provide for the provisional adoption of emergency measures by the Member States in the event of danger to animal or human health (Article 7 of the additives directive and Article 5 of the undesirable substances directive). Any Member State which adopts such measures must inform the other Member States and the Commission without delay. Such notification sets in motion a procedure under which appropriate measures may be adopted at Community level.

It therefore appears that, in relation to all constituents capable of giving rise to problems or dangers from the point of view of proper animal nutrition or from the point of view of animal or human health, the two directives have set up a comprehensive system which enables account to be taken of the need to amend the directives periodically and of urgent problems which may arise in practice.

The compound feedingstuffs directive relates, as is clear from its title, to the marketing of compound feedingstuffs. In that connection it lays down a number of rules concerning packaging of feedstuffs and the information relating to their composition contained on their labelling or in the accompanying documents.

According to Article 3 of the compound feedingstuffs directive:

'Member States shall prescribe that compound feedingstuffs may be marketed only if they are wholesome, unadulterated and of merchantable quality. They shall also prescribe that compound feedingstuffs may not represent a danger to animal or human health and may not be presented or marketed in a manner liable to mislead'.

...

Article 14 of the directive reserves to the Member States the right, *inter alia*, 'to recommend types of compound feedingstuffs which meet certain analytical characteristics'.

Finally, Article 15 of the directive requires the Commission, on the basis of experience acquired, to forward to the Council, not later than three years following notification of the directive, 'proposals for amendments to the directive such as to achieve free movement of compound feedingstuffs and to eliminate certain disparities concerning the use of ingredients and labelling in particular'.

Each of the directives contains a provision according to which compound feedingstuffs which conform to the directive in question may not be subjected to any marketing restrictions other than those provided for in the directive itself (Article 13 of the additives directive, Article 7 of the undesirable substances directive and Article 9 of the compound feedingstuffs directive). *They therefore constitute a coherent system covering the manufacture and marketing of compound feedingstuffs, including the question of additives and undesirable substances.*

The defence put forward by the Federal Republic of Germany must therefore be examined in the light of those considerations.

(a) With regard to the argument based on the 'principle of minimum intervention' it should be stated that that method of interpretation overlooks the fact that the directives in question form part of the common agricultural policy and are intended to facilitate the free movement of feedingstuffs within the common market. *They must therefore be interpreted in the light of their objectives, which are to improve livestock production throughout the Community according to common rules and at the same time to eliminate the obstacles arising from differences in the relevant national legislation.*

(b) The distinction between 'constituent elements', on the one hand, and 'additives' and 'undesirable substances', on the other, also overlooks the coherent scheme of the three directives. In principle, compound feedingstuffs should be able to circulate freely within the Community if they satisfy the requirements of the compound feedingstuffs directive and if they also comply with the rules laid down by the additives directive and the undesirable substances directive. The German Government was wrong to try to confine the argument to the compound feedingstuffs directive by refusing to deal with the matters which are the subject of the contested provisions of the Futtermittelverordnung by means of the procedures provided for by the additives directive and the undesirable substances directive, even though the two substances in question, iron and sodium, fall within the scope of one or the other of those two directives. According to those directives the Member States may adopt unilateral measures only by following the emergency procedure. The German Government has never asserted that the contested provisions of the Futtermittelverordnung were a matter of urgency.

...

(c) With regard to the Federal Republic of Germany's reliance on Article 36 of the EEC Treaty, which authorises the Member States to maintain restrictions on imports justified on the ground of the protection health and life of humans and animals, it follows from the scheme of the additives directive and the undesirable substances directive that questions of public health relating to the use of substances covered by the directives are regulated exhaustively by those directives. In that respect, therefore, a Member State may no longer rely on the exception contained in Article 36 as is clear from the Court's established case-law (see primarily the judgment of 5 October 1977, Case 5/77 *Tedeschi* v *Denkavit* [1977] ECR 1555, paragraph 35 of the decision). Only the procedures provided for by the additives directive and the undesirable substances directive could have been used to resolve any public health problems to which the contested measure is alleged to be addressed.

The argument based on Article 3 of the compound feedingstuffs directive cannot be accepted either, since that provision can have neither the purpose nor the effect of derogating from the exhaustive nature of the additives directive and the undesirable substances directive.

(d) With regard to the charge that the Commission failed to fulfil its obligations under Article 15 of the compound feedingstuffs directive, it suffices to observe that that provision, which is of a general nature, does not in any way oblige the Commission to take up on its own account, in the form of proposals, the provisions adopted unilaterally by the Federal Republic of Germany. The Commission has a discretion with regard to the steps it takes toward amending the directive; with regard to the contested measures, the discussion within the Working Party on feedingstuffs legislation shows that the other Member States were not in favour of extending the measures adopted unilaterally by the Federal Republic of Germany to the whole of the Community. Accordingly, the Commission cannot be criticised for failing to take such an initiative on its own authority pursuant to Article 15 of the compound feedingstuffs directive.

It appears from all the foregoing that the measure adopted by the German authorities derogates from the division of powers laid down by the directives pursuant to the EEC Treaty since a measure of that type could have been adopted only for the whole of the Community in accordance with the procedures provided for by the additives directive and the undesirable substances directive. The unilateral adoption of those measures by the Federal Republic of Germany also constitutes an infringement of the principle of the free movement of goods set out in Article 30 of the EEC Treaty and confirmed by the relevant provisions of the three directives.

Case 178/84 Commission v Germany ('German Beer')
[1988] 1 CMLR 780

Production and sale of beer in the Federal Republic of Germany was covered by rules contained in the Biersteuergesetz, the provisions of particular interest concerning the Reinheitsgebot, a prohibition on additives to beer. The Commission argued that the German Government had failed to fulfil its obligations under the Treaty on two counts: first, a prohibition on the designation 'Bier' for beers not complying with the requirements of Paragraph 9 of the statute; and secondly, the absolute prohibition on the importation of any beers containing additives.

The Court

The Prohibition on the marketing under the designation 'Bier' of Beers not complying with the Requirements of Paragraph 9 of the Biersteuergesetz.

It must be noted in the first place that the provision on the manufacture of beer set out in Paragraph 9 of the Biersteuergesetz cannot in itself constitute a measure having an equivalent effect to a quantitative restriction on imports contrary to Article 30 of the EEC Treaty, since it applies only to breweries in the Federal Republic of Germany. Paragraph 9 of the Biersteuergesetz is at issue in this case only in so far as Paragraph 10 of that law, which covers both products imported from other Member States and products manufactured in Germany, refers thereto in order to determine the beverages which may be marketed under the designation 'Bier'.

As far as those rules on designation are concerned, the Commission concedes that as long as harmonisation has not been achieved at Community level the Member States have the power in principle to lay down rules governing the manufacture, the composition and the marketing of beverages. It stresses, however, that rules which, like Paragraph 10 of the Biersteuergesetz, prohibit the use of a generic designation for the marketing of products manufactured partly from raw materials such as rice and maize, other than those whose use is prescribed in the national territory, are contrary to Community law. In any event, such rules go beyond what is necessary in order to protect the German consumer, since that could be done simply by means of labelling or notices. Those rules therefore constitute an impediment to trade contrary to Article 30 of the EEC Treaty.

The German Government has first sought to justify its rules on public health grounds. It maintains that the use of raw materials other than those permitted by Paragraph 9 of the Biersteuergesetz would inevitably entail the use of additives. However, at the hearing the German Government conceded that Paragraph 10 of the Biersteuergesetz, which is merely a rule on designation, was exclusively intended to protect consumers. In its view, consumers associate the designation 'Bier' with a beverage manufactured from only the raw materials listed in Paragraph 9 of the Biersteuergesetz. Consequently, it is necessary to prevent them from being misled as to the nature of the product by being led to believe that a beverage called 'Bier' complies with the Reinheitsgebot when that is not the case. The German Government maintains that its rules are not protectionist in aim. It stresses in that regard that the raw materials whose use is specified in Paragraph 9 (1) and (2) of the Biersteuergesetz are not necessarily of national origin. Any trader marketing products satisfying the prescribed rules is free to use the designation 'Bier' and those rules can readily be complied with outside the Federal Republic of Germany.

According to a consistent line of decisions of the Court (above all, the judgment of 11 July 1974 in Case 8/74 *Procureur du Roi* v *Dassonville* [1974] ECR 837) the prohibition of measures having an effect equivalent to quantitative restrictions under Article 30 of the EEC Treaty covers 'all trading rules enacted by Member States which are capable of hindering, directly or indirectly, actually or potentially, intra-Community trade'.

The Court has also consistently held (in particular in the judgment of 20 February 1979 in Case 120/78 *Rewe-Zentral AG* v *Bundesmonopolverwaltung* [1979] ECR 649, and the judgment of 10 November 1982 in Case 261/81 *Walter Rau Lebensmittelwerke* v *De Smedt* [1982] ECR 3961, see above p.188) that 'in the absence of common rules relating to the marketing of the products concerned, obstacles to free movement within the Community resulting from disparities between the national laws must be accepted in so far as such rules, applicable to domestic and to imported products without distinction, may be recognised as being necessary in order to satisfy mandatory requirements relating *inter alia* to consumer protection. It is also necessary for such rules to be proportionate to the aim in view. If a Member State has a choice between various measures to attain the same objective it should choose the means which least restricts the free movement of goods'.

It is not contested that the application of Paragraph 10 of the Biersteuergesetz to beers from other Member States in whose manufacture raw materials other than malted barley have been lawfully used, in particular rice and maize, is liable to constitute an obstacle to their importation into the Federal Republic of Germany.

Accordingly, it must be established whether the application of that provision may be justified by imperative requirements relating to consumer protection.

The German Government's argument that Paragraph 10 of the Biersteuergesetz is essential in order to protect German consumers because, in their minds, the designation 'Bier' is inseparably linked to the beverage manufactured solely from the ingredients laid down in Paragraph 9 of the Biersteuergesetz must be rejected.

First, consumers' conceptions which vary from one Member State to the other are also likely to evolve in the course of time within a Member State. The establishment of the Common Market is, it should be added, one of the factors that may play a major contributory role in that development. Whereas rules protecting consumers against misleading practices enable such a development to be taken into account, legislation of the kind contained in Paragraph 10 of the Biersteuergesetz prevents it from taking place. As the Court has already held in another context (judgment of 27 February 1980 in Case 170/78 *Commission* v *United Kingdom* [1980] ECR 417), the legislation of a Member State must not 'crystallise given consumer habits so as to consolidate an advantage acquired by national industries concerned to comply with them'.

Secondly, in the other Member States of the Community the designations corresponding to the German designation 'Bier' are generic designations for a fermented beverage manufactured from malted barley, whether malted barley on its own or with the addition of rice or maize. The same approach is taken in Community law as can be seen from Heading No 22.03 of the Common Customs Tariff. The German legislature itself utilises the designation 'Bier' in that way in Paragraph 9 (7) and (8) of the Biersteuergesetz in order to refer to beverages not complying with the manufacturing rules laid down in Paragraph 9 (1) and (2).

The German designation 'Bier' and its equivalents in the languages of the other Member States of the Community may therefore not be restricted to beers manufactured in accordance with the rules in force in the Federal Republic of Germany.

It is admittedly legitimate to seek to enable consumers who attribute specific qualities to beers manufactured from particular raw materials to make their choice in the light of that consideration. However, as the Court has already emphasised (judgment of 9 December 1981 in Case 193/80 *Commission* v *Italy* [1981] ECR 3019), that possibility may be ensured by means which do not prevent the importation of products which have been lawfully manufactured and marketed in other Member States and, in particular, 'by the compulsory affixing of suitable labels giving the nature of the product sold'. By indicating the raw materials utilised in the manufacture of beer 'such a course would enable the consumer to make his choice in full knowledge of the facts and would guarantee transparency in trading and in offers to the public'. It must be added that such a system of mandatory consumer information must not entail negative assessments for beers not complying with the requirements of Paragraph 9 of the Biersteuergesetz.

Contrary to the German Government's view, such a system of consumer information may operate perfectly well even in the case of a product which, like beer, is not necessarily supplied to consumers in bottles or in cans capable of bearing the appropriate details. That is borne out, once again, by the German legislation itself. Paragraph 26(1) and (2) of the aforementioned regulation implementing the Biersteuergesetz provides for a system of consumer information in respect of certain beers, even where those beers are sold on draught, when the requisite information must appear on the casks or the beer taps.

It follows from the foregoing that by applying the rules on designation in Paragraph 10 of the Biersteuergesetz to beers imported from other Member States which were manufactured and marketed lawfully in those States the Federal Republic of Germany has failed to fulfil its obligations under Article 30 of the EEC Treaty.

The Absolute Ban on the marketing of Beers containing Additives

...

It is not contested that the prohibition on the marketing of beers containing additives constitutes a barrier to the importation from other Member States of beers containing additives authorised in those States, and is to that extent covered by Article 30 of the EEC Treaty. However, it must be ascertained whether it is possible to justify that prohibition under Article 36 of the Treaty on grounds of the protection of human health.

The Court has consistently held (in particular in the judgment of 14 July 1983 in Case 174/82 *Criminal Proceedings against Sandoz BV* [1983] ECR 2445) that 'in so far as there are uncertainties at the present state of scientific research it is for the Member States, in the absence of harmonisation, to decide what degree of protection of the health and life of humans they intend to assure, having regard however to the requirements of the free movement of goods within the Community'.

As may also be seen from the decisions of the Court (and especially the judgment of 14 July 1983 in the *Sandoz* case, cited above, the judgment of 10 December 1985 in Case 247/84 *Motte* [1985] ECR 3887, and the judgment of 6 May 1986 in Case 304/84 *Ministère Public* v *Muller and Others* [1986] ECR 1511), in such circumstances Community law does not preclude the adoption by the Member States of legislation whereby the use of additives is subjected to prior authorisation granted by a measure of general application for specific additives, in respect of all products, for certain products only or for certain uses. Such legislation meets a genuine need of health policy, namely that of restricting the uncontrolled consumption of food additives.

However, *the application to imported products of prohibitions on marketing products containing additives which are authorised in the Member State of production but prohibited in the Member State of importation is permissible only in so far as it complies with the requirements of Article 36 of the Treaty as it has been interpreted by the Court.*

It must be borne in mind, in the first place, that in its judgments in the *Sandoz, Motte* and *Muller* cases, cited above, the Court inferred from the principle of proportionality underlying the last sentence of Article 36 of the Treaty that prohibitions on the marketing of products containing additives authorised in the Member State of production but prohibited in the Member State of importation must be *restricted to what is actually necessary to secure the protection of public health. The Court also concluded that the use of a specific additive which is authorised in another Member State must be authorised* in the case of a product imported from that Member State *where, in view, on the one hand, of the eating habits prevailing in the importing Member State, of the findings of international scientific research,* and in particular of the work of the Community's Scientific Committee for Food, the Codex Alimentarius Committee of the Food and Agriculture Organisation of the United Nations (FAO) and the World Health Organisation, *and, on the other hand, of the eating habits prevailing in the importing Member State the additive in question does not present a risk to public health and meets a real need, especially a technical one.*

Secondly, it should be remembered that, as the Court held in its judgment of 6 May 1986 in the *Muller* case, cited above, by virtue of the principle of proportionality, traders must also be able to apply, under a procedure which is easily accessible to them and can be concluded within a reasonable time, for the use of specific additives to be authorised by a measure of general application.

It should be pointed out that it must be open to traders to challenge before the courts an unjustified failure to grant authorisation. Without prejudice to the right of the competent national authorities of the importing Member State to ask traders to produce the information in their possession which may be useful for the purpose of assessing the facts, it is for those authorities to demonstrate, as the Court held in its judgment of 6 May 1986 in the *Muller* case, cited above, that the prohibition is justified on grounds relating to the protection of the health of its population.

It must be observed that the German rules on additives applicable to beer result in the exclusion of all the additives authorised in the other Member States and not the exclusion of just some of them for which there is concrete justification by reason of the risks which they involve in view of the eating habits of the German population; moreover those rules do not lay down any procedure whereby traders can obtain authorisation for the use of a specific additive in the manufacture of beer by means of a measure of general application.

...

Consequently, in so far as the German rules on additives in beer entail a general ban on additives, their application to beers imported from other Member States is contrary to the requirements of Community law as laid down in the case-law of the Court, since that prohibition is contrary to the principle of proportionality and is therefore not covered by the exception provided for in Article 36 of the EEC Treaty.

In view of the foregoing considerations it must be held that by prohibiting the marketing of beers lawfully manufactured and marketed in another Member State if they do not comply with Paragraphs 9 and 10 of the Biersteuergesetz, the Federal Republic of Germany has failed to fulfil its obligations under Article 30 of the EEC Treaty...

(iv) Industrial Property

Case 15/74 Centrafarm BV and Adriaan de Peijper v Sterling Drug Inc. [1974] ECR 1147; [1974] 2 CMLR 480

An American company, Sterling Drug, held British and Dutch patents relating to the mode of preparation of a medicament marketed under the trade name 'Negram'. In Great Britain this trade mark was owned by a subsidiary of Sterling Drug, and in the Netherlands it was owned by a subsidiary of that subsidiary. Centrafarm, a Dutch independent company, bought 'Negram' on the open market in Britain and Germany, and imported it into the Netherlands. Sterling Drug and its subsidiaries invoked their respective patent and trade mark rights before the Dutch courts to prevent the parallel imports. The cases came before the Hoge Raad, which referred a series of questions for a preliminary ruling.

The Court

As a result of the provisions in the Treaty relating to the free movement of goods and in particular of Article 30, quantitative restrictions on imports and all measures having equivalent effect are prohibited between Member States.

By Article 36 these provisions shall nevertheless not include provisions or restrictions justified on grounds of the protection of industrial or commercial property.

Nevertheless, it is clear from this same article, in particular its second sentence, as well as from the context, that whilst the Treaty does not affect the existence of rights recognised by the legislation of a Member State in matters of industrial and commercial property, yet the exercise of these rights may nevertheless, depending on the circumstances, be affected by the prohibitions in the Treaty.

Inasmuch as it provides an exception to one of the fundamental principles of the Common Market, Article 36 in fact only admits of derogations from the free movement of goods where such derogations are justified for the purpose of safeguarding rights which constitute the specific matter of this property.

In relation to patents, the specific subject matter of the industrial property is the guarantee that the patentee, to reward the creative effort of the inventor, has the exclusive right to use an invention with a view to manufacturing industrial products and putting them into circulation for the first time, either directly or by the grant of licences to third parties, as well as the right to oppose infringements.

An obstacle to the free movement of goods may arise out of the existence, within a national legislation concerning industrial and commercial property, of provisions laying down that a patentee's right is not exhausted when the product protected by the patent is marketed in another Member State, with the result that the patentee can prevent importation of the product into his own Member State when it has been marketed in another State.

Whereas an obstacle to the free movement of goods of this kind may be justified on the ground of protection of industrial property where such protection is invoked against a product coming from a Member State where it is not patentable and has been manufactured by third parties without the consent of the patentee and in cases where there exist patents, the original proprietors of which are legally and economically independent, a derogation from the principle of the free movement of goods is not, however, justified where the product has been put onto the market in a legal manner, by the patentee himself or with his consent, in the Member State from which it has been imported, in particular in the case of a proprietor of parallel patents.

In fact, if a patentee could prevent the import of protected products marketed by him or with his consent in another Member State, he would be able to partition off national markets and thereby restrict trade between Member States, in a situation where no such restriction was necessary to guarantee the essence of the exclusive rights flowing from the parallel patents.

The plaintiff in the main action claims, in this connection, that by reason of divergences between national legislations and practice, truly identical or parallel patents can hardly be said to exist.

It should be noted here that, in spite of the divergences which remain in the absence of any unification of national rules concerning industrial property, the identity of the protected invention is clearly the essential element of the concept of parallel patents which it is for the courts to assess.

The question referred should therefore be answered to be effect that the exercise, by a patentee, of the right which he enjoys under the legislation of a Member State to prohibit the sale, in that State, of a product protected by the patent which has been marketed in another Member State by the patentee or with his consent is incompatible with the rules of the EEC Treaty concerning the free movement of goods within the Common Market.

Case 16/74 Centrafarm BV and Adriaan de Peijper v Winthrop BV [1974] ECR 1183; [1974] 2 CMLR 480 at 508

The Court

In relation to trade marks, the specific subject-matter of the industrial property is the guarantee that the owner of the trade mark has the exclusive right to use that trade mark, for the purpose of putting products protected by the trade mark into circulation for the first time, and is therefore intended to protect him against competitors wishing to take advantage of the status and reputation of the trade mark by selling products illegally bearing that trade mark.

An obstacle to the free movement of goods may arise out of the existence, within a national legislation concerning industrial and commercial property, of provisions laying down that a trade mark owner's right is not exhausted when the product protected by the trade mark is marketed in another Member State, with the result that the trade mark owner can prevent importation of the product into his own Member State when it has been marketed in another Member State.

Such an obstacle is not justified when the product has been put onto the market in a legal manner in the Member State from which it has been imported, by the trade mark owner himself or with his consent, so that there can be no question of abuse or infringement of the trade mark.

In fact, if a trade mark owner could prevent the import of protected products marketed by him or with his consent in another Member State, he would be able to partition off national markets and thereby restrict trade between Member States, in a situation where no such restriction was necessary to guarantee the essence of the exclusive right flowing from the trade mark.

The question referred should therefore be answered to the effect that the exercise, by the owner of a trade mark, of the right which he enjoys under the legislation of a Member State to prohibit the sale, in that State, of a product which has been marketed under the trade mark in another Member State by the trade mark owner or with his consent is incompatible with the rules of the EEC Treaty concerning the free movement of goods within the Common Market.

Although these decisions caused a certain amount of controversy at the time, their result has been provisionally accepted by the Member States in the Community Patent Convention, which has not yet entered into force.

Convention for the European Patent for the Common Market
(OJ 1976, No L 17, p. 1)

Article 81

Exhaustion of the Rights conferred by a National Patent

1. The rights conferred by a national patent in a Contracting State shall not extend to acts concerning a product covered by that patent which are done within the territory of that Contracting State after that product has been put on the market in any Contracting State by the proprietor of the patent or with his express consent, unless there are grounds which, under Community law, would justify the extension to such acts of the rights conferred by the patent.

2. Paragraph 1 shall also apply with regard to a product put on the market by the proprietor of a national patent, granted for the same invention in another Contracting State, who has economic connections with the proprietor of the patent referred to in Paragraph 1. For the purpose of this paragraph, two persons shall be deemed to have economic connections where one of them is in a position to exert a decisive influence on the other, directly or indirectly, with regard to the exploitation of a patent, or where a third party is in a position to exercise such an influence on both persons.

3. The preceding paragraphs shall not apply in the case of a product put on the market under a compulsory licence.

Just as a patentee or trade mark holder may not exercise his rights to prevent the sale in a Member State of goods marketed in another Member State by him or with his consent, so also it would appear that his successors in title cannot claim greater rights. The owner of an industrial property right cannot evade the restrictions on the exercise of his right by splitting it and granting its benefits to different assignees in different countries. Further down the line of succession, particularly if certain of the transactions involved were not voluntary, it becomes rather artificial to speak of marketing in one Member State with the consent of the holder of the right in another Member State. The view of the Court is that the holder of a trade mark in one Member State may not prevent the importation of goods lawfully produced in another Member State bearing a trade mark having the same origin. It might be suggested that this is because at the level of the original owner it would be a case of preventing the importation of goods marketed by him or with his consent.

Case 192/73 Van Zuylen Frères v HAG AG
[1974] ECR 731; [1974] 2 CMLR 127

Hag AG was the original owner of the 'Hag' decaffeinated coffee trade mark in, *inter alia,* both Germany and Belgium-Luxembourg. In 1935 it assigned its Belgium-Luxembourg marks to a wholly-owned subsidiary. After the Second World War the shares in the subsidiary were placed under sequestration and sold as enemy property, and the Belgium-Luxembourg trade marks were eventually acquired by Van Zuylen. In 1972 Hag AG began to deliver coffee under the 'Hag' trade mark to Luxembourg retailers. Van Zuylen commenced proceedings to prevent these deliveries before the Tribunal d'Arrondissement of Luxembourg, which referred two questions for a preliminary ruling.

The Court

First Question

The first question asks whether the Community rules on competition or those relating to the free movement of goods prohibit the holder of a trade mark enjoying legal protection in a Member State from opposing the importation of products that legally bear 'the same trade mark' in another Member State, where at the outset the two marks belonged to the same holder.

The file shows that the original holder, carrying on business in Germany, had assigned his trade mark as regards Belgium to a subsidiary established and controlled by him, but which became independent as a result of an act by a public authority.

As it is expressed in the question, there exists between the two present holders 'no legal, financial, technical or economic link'.

Article 85 not being in these circumstances applicable, the question must be examined by reference only to the rules relating to the free movement of goods.

As a result of the provisions in the Treaty relating to the free movement of goods and in particular of Article 30, quantitative restrictions on imports and all measures having equivalent effect are prohibited between Member States.

By Article 36 these provisions shall nevertheless not preclude prohibitions or restrictions on imports justified on grounds of the protection of industrial or commercial property.

Nevertheless, it is shown by this very article, in particular its second sentence, as well as by the context, that whilst the Treaty does not affect the existence of rights recognised by the legislation of a Member State in matters of industrial and commercial property, yet the exercise of these rights may nevertheless, depending on the circumstances, be affected by the prohibitions in the Treaty.

Inasmuch as it provides an exception to one of the fundamental principles of the Common Market, Article 36 in fact only admits derogations from the free movement of goods to the extent that such derogations are justified for the purpose of safeguarding rights that constitute the specific subject-matter of this property.

Thus the application of the legislation relating to the protection of trade marks at any rate protects the legitimate holder of the trade mark against infringement on the part of persons who lack any legal title.

The exercise of a trade mark right tends to contribute to the partitioning off of the markets and thus to affect the free movement of goods between Member States, all the more so since – unlike other rights of industrial and commercial property – it is not subject to limitations in point of time.

Accordingly, one cannot allow the holder of a trade mark to rely upon the exclusiveness of a trade mark right – which may be the consequence of the territorial limitation of national legislations – with a view to prohibiting the marketing in a Member State of goods legally produced in another Member State under an identical trade mark having the same origin.

Such a prohibition, which would legitimise the isolation of national markets, would collide with one of the essential objects of the Treaty, which is to unite national markets in a single market.

Whilst in such a market the indication of origin of a product covered by a trade mark is useful, information to consumers on this point may be ensured by means other than such as would affect the free movement of goods.

Accordingly, to prohibit the marketing in a Member State of a product legally bearing a trade mark in another Member State, for the sole reason that an identical trade mark having the same origin exists in the first State, is incompatible with the provisions for free movement of goods within the Common Market.

Second Question

The second question asks whether the same would be the case if the marketing of the product covered by trade mark were effected not by the holder of the trade mark in the other Member State but by a third party, who has duly acquired the product in that State.

If the holder of a trade mark in one Member State may himself market the product covered by the trade mark in another Member State, then this also applies to a third party who has duly acquired this product in the first State.

Where, on the other hand, the holder of industrial property rights seeks to prevent the importation of goods produced independently either under different industrial property rights or indeed in a State where no such protection is available, then the balance of the equation between the single market and the industrial property rights changes. Although the effect may be that of a quantitative restriction, the industrial property owner is permitted to prevent the importation; otherwise the 'specific subject-matter' of his right would not be protected. This was mentioned by the Court in the *Centrafarm* patent judgment at pp. 1162-3. It arose on the facts in Case 24/67 *Parke, Davis* v *Centrafarm* [1968] ECR 55, which involved the use by Parke, Davis of their Dutch patent to prevent the importation into the Netherlands of 'chloramphenicol' manufactured in Italy, where patents could not be granted for medicaments.

A synthesis of this case law is to be found in the judgment given in the *Terrapin* case, a reference for a preliminary ruling from the Bundesgerichtshof in an action relating to the alleged potential confusion arising from the use of the names 'Terrapin' and 'Terranova' by separate and independent undertakings.

Case 119/75 Terrapin (Overseas) Ltd v Terranova Industrie CA Kapferer & Co [1976] ECR 1039

The Court

As a result of the provisions in the Treaty relating to the free movement of goods and in particular of Article 30, quantitative restrictions on imports and all measures having equivalent effect are prohibited between Member States. By Article 36 these provisions nevertheless do not preclude prohibitions or restrictions on imports justified on grounds of the protection of industrial or commercial property. However, it is clear from that same article, in particular the second sentence, as well as from the context, that whilst the Treaty does not affect the existence of rights recognised by the legislation of a Member State in matters of industrial and commercial property, yet the exercise of those rights may nevertheless, depending on the circumstances, be restricted by the prohibitions in the Treaty. Inasmuch as it provides an exception to one of the fundamental principles of the Common Market, Article 36 in fact admits exceptions to the free movement of goods only to the extent to which such exceptions are justified for the purpose of safeguarding rights which constitute the specific subject-matter of that property.

It follows from the above that the proprietor of an industrial or commercial property right protected by the law of a Member State cannot rely on that law to prevent the importation of a product which has lawfully been marketed in another Member State by the proprietor himself or with his consent. It is the same when the right relied on is the result of the subdivision, either by voluntary act or as a result of public constraint, of a trade-mark right which originally belonged to one and the same proprietor. In these cases the basic function of the trade mark to guarantee to consumers that the product has the same origin is already undermined by the subdivision of the original right. Even where the rights in question belong to different proprietors the protection given to industrial and commercial property by national law may not be relied on when the exercise of those rights is the purpose, the means or the result of an agreement prohibited by the Treaty. In all these cases the effect of invoking the territorial nature of national laws protecting industrial and commercial property is to legitimise the insulation of national markets without this partitioning within the Common Market being justified by the protection of a legitimate interest on the part of the proprietor of the trade mark or business name.

On the other hand in the present state of Community law *an industrial or commercial property right legally acquired in a Member State may legally be used to prevent under the first sentence of Article 36 of the Treaty the import of products marketed under a name giving rise to confusion where the rights in question have been acquired by different and independent proprietors under different national laws.* If in such a case the principle of the free movement of goods were to prevail over the protection given by the respective national laws, the specific objective of industrial and commercial property rights would be undermined. In the particular situation the requirements of the free movement of goods and the safeguarding of industrial and commercial property rights must be so reconciled that protection is ensured for the legitimate use of the rights conferred by national laws, coming within the prohibitions on imports 'justified' within the meaning of Article 36 of the Treaty, but denied on the other hand in respect of any improper exercise of the same rights of such a nature as to maintain or effect artificial partitions within the Common Market.

It is appropriate therefore to reply to the question referred to the Court that it is compatible with the provisions of the EEC Treaty relating to the free movement of goods for an undertaking established in a Member State, by virtue of a right to a trade mark and a right to a commercial name which are protected by the legislation of that State, to prevent the importation of products of an undertaking established in another Member State and bearing by virtue of the legislation of that State a name giving rise to confusion with the trade mark and commercial name of the first undertaking, provided that there are no agreements restricting competition and no legal or economic ties between the undertakings and that their respective rights have arisen independently of one another.

Case 3/78 Centrafarm BV v American Home Products Corporation
[1978] ECR 1823; [1979] 1 CMLR 326

Centrafarm played a more active role in the resale of the medication here than in the previous case. A tranquiliser marketed in the UK under the name Serenid was known in Benelux as Seresta, and Centrafarm repackaged the tablets bought in the UK, labelling them with the trade mark owned by the Belgian arm of the American Home Products Corporation before placing them on the market in the Benelux countries.

The Court

The purpose of the first question is to establish whether, in the given circumstances, the rules of the Treaty, in particular Article 36, prevent the proprietor of a trade mark from exercising the right conferred upon him under the national law.

As a result of the provisions of the Treaty relating to the free movement of goods, and in particular Article 30, quantitative restrictions on imports and all measures having equivalent effect are prohibited between Member States.

Under Article 36 those provisions nevertheless do not preclude prohibitions or restrictions on imports justified on grounds of the protection of industrial and commercial property.

However, it is clear from that same article, in particular its second sentence, as well as from the context, that whilst the Treaty does not affect the existence of rights recognised by the laws of a Member State in matters of industrial and commercial property, the exercise of those rights may nevertheless, depending on the circumstances, be restricted by the prohibitions contained in the Treaty.

Inasmuch as it creates an exception to one of the fundamental principles of the Common Market, Article 36 in fact admits of exceptions to the rules on the free movement of goods only to the extent to which such exceptions are justified for the purpose of safeguarding the rights which constitute the specific subject-matter of that property.

In relation to trade marks, the specific subject-matter is in particular the guarantee to the proprietor of the trade mark that he has the exclusive right to use that trade mark for the purpose of putting a product into circulation for the first time and therefore his protection against competitors wishing to take advantage of the status and reputation of the mark by selling products illegally bearing that trade mark.

In order to establish in exceptional circumstances the precise scope of that exclusive right granted to the proprietor of the mark, regard must be had to the essential function of the trade mark, which is to guarantee the identity of the origin of the trade-marked product to the consumer or ultimate user.

This guarantee of origin means that only the proprietor may confer an identity upon the product by affixing the mark.

The guarantee of origin would in fact be jeopardised if it were permissible for a third party to affix the mark to the product, even to an original product.

It is thus in accordance with the essential function of the mark that national legislation, even where the manufacturer or distributor is the proprietor of two different marks for the same product, prevents an unauthorised third party from usurping the right to affix one or other mark to any part whatsoever of the production or to change the marks affixed by the proprietor to different parts of the production.

The guarantee of the origin of the product requires that the exclusive right of the proprietor should be protected in the same manner where the different parts of the production, bearing different marks, come from two different Member States.

The right granted to the proprietor to prohibit any unauthorised affixing of his mark to his product accordingly comes within the specific subject-matter of the trade mark.

The proprietor of a trade mark which is protected in one Member State is accordingly justified pursuant to the first sentence of Article 36 in preventing a product from being marketed by a third party in that Member State under the mark in question even if previously that product has been lawfully marketed in another Member State under another mark held in the latter State by the same proprietor.

Nevertheless it is still necessary to consider whether the exercise of that right may constitute a 'disguised restriction on trade between Member States' within the meaning of the second sentence of Article 36.

In this connection it should be observed that it may be lawful for the manufacturer of a product to use in different Member States different marks for the same product.

Nevertheless it is possible for such a practice to be followed by the proprietor of the marks as part of a system of marketing intended to partition the markets artificially.

In such a case the prohibition by the proprietor of the unauthorised affixing of the mark by a third party constitutes a disguised restriction on intra-Community trade for the purposes of the above-mentioned provision.

It is for the national court to settle in each particular case whether the proprietor has followed the practice of using different marks for the same product for the purpose of partitioning the markets.

See Case 1/81 *Pfizer* v *Eurim-Pharm* [1981] ECR 2913; [1982] 1 CMLR 406 for an example of a situation where an importer repackaged marked products in a way that avoided compromising the guarantee of origin.

Joined Cases 55 and 57/80 Musik-Vertrieb membran GmbH and K-tel International v GEMA [1981] ECR 147; [1981] 2 CMLR 44

The Court made it clear that copyright was subject to the same limitations as patents and trade marks when it came to consider the attempt by the German copyright management society, GEMA, to recover the difference between UK and German royalties on recordings being imported into the Federal Republic of Germany. The Court dealt specifically with three points.

The Court

...the question submitted by the national court is, in effect, whether Articles 30 and 36 of the Treaty must be interpreted as precluding the application of national legislation under which a copyright management society, empowered to exercise the copyrights of composers of musical works reproduced on gramophone records or other sound recording in another Member State, is permitted to invoke those rights where such sound recordings are distributed on the national market after having been put into circulation in the Member State of manufacture by or with the consent of the owners of those copyrights, in order to claim payment of a fee equal to the royalties ordinarily paid for marketing on the national market less the lower royalties paid in the Member State of manufacture for marketing in that Member State alone.

It should first be emphasised that sound recordings, even if incorporating protected musical works, are products to which the system of free movement of goods provided for by the Treaty applies. It follows that national legislation whose application results in obstructing trade in sound recordings between Member States must be regarded as a measure having an effect equivalent to a quantitative restriction within the meaning of Article 30 of the Treaty. That is the case where such legislation permits a copyright management society to object to the distribution of sound recordings originating in another Member State on the basis of the exclusive exploitation right which it exercises in the name of the copyright owner.

However, Article 36 of the Treaty provides that the provisions of Articles 30 to 34 shall not preclude prohibitions or restrictions on imports justified on grounds of the protection of industrial and commercial property. The latter expression includes the protection conferred by copyright, especially when exploited commercially in the form of licences capable of affecting distribution in the various Member States of goods incorporating the protected literary or artistic work.

It is apparent from the well-established case-law of the Court and most recently from the judgment of 22 June 1976 in Case 119/75 *Terrapin* v *Terranova* [1976] ECR 1039 (above p. 244) that the proprietor of an industrial or commercial property right protected by the law of a Member State cannot rely on that law to prevent the importation of a product which has been lawfully marketed in another Member State by the proprietor himself or with his consent.

In the proceedings before the Court the French Government has argued that that case-law cannot be applied to copyright, which comprises *inter alia* the right of an author to claim authorship of the work and to object to any distortion, mutilation or other alteration thereof, or any other action in relation to the said work which would be prejudicial to his honour or reputation. It is contended that, in thus conferring extended protection, copyright is not comparable to other industrial and commercial property rights such as patents or trade marks.

It is true that copyright comprises moral rights of the kind indicated by the French Government. However, it also comprises other rights, notably the right to exploit commercially the marketing of the protected work, particularly in the form of licences granted in return for payment of royalties. *It is this economic aspect of copyright which is the subject of the question submitted by the national court and, in this regard, in the application of Article 36 of the Treaty there is no reason to make a distinction between copyright and other industrial and commercial property rights.*

While the commercial exploitation of copyright is a source of remuneration for the owner it also constitutes a form of control on marketing exercisable by the owner, the copyright management societies acting in his name and the grantees of licences. From this point of view commercial exploitation of copyright raises the same issues as that of any other industrial or commercial property right.

The argument put to the Court by the Belgian and Italian Governments that in the absence of harmonisation in this sector the principle of the territoriality of copyright laws always prevails over the principle of freedom of movement of goods within the Common Market cannot be accepted. Indeed, the essential purpose of the Treaty, which is to unite national markets into a single market, could not be attained if, under the various legal systems of the Member States, nationals of those Member States were able to partition the market and bring about arbitrary discrimination or disguised restrictions on trade between Member States.

It follows from the foregoing considerations that neither the copyright owner or his licensee, nor a copyright management society acting in the owner's or licensee's name, may rely on the exclusive exploitation right conferred by copyright to prevent or restrict the importation of sound recordings which have been lawfully marketed in another Member State by the owner himself or with his consent.

GEMA has argued that such an interpretation of Articles 30 and 36 of the Treaty is not sufficient to resolve the problem facing the national court since GEMA's application to the German courts is not for the prohibition or restriction of the marketing of the gramophone records and tape cassettes in question on German territory but for equality in the royalties paid for any distribution of those sound recordings on the German market. The owner of a copyright in a recorded musical work has a legitimate interest in receiving and retaining the benefit of his intellectual or artistic effort regardless of the degree to which his work is distributed and consequently it is maintained that he should not lose the right to claim royalties equal to those paid in the country in which the recorded work is marketed.

It should first be observed that the question put by the national court is concerned with the legal consequences of infringement of copyright. GEMA seeks damages for that infringement pursuant to the applicable national legislation and it is immaterial whether the quantum of damages which it seeks is calculated according to the difference between the rate of royalty payable on distribution in the national market and the rate of royalty paid in the country of manufacture or in any other manner. On any view its claims are in fact founded on the copyright owner's exclusive right of exploitation, which enables him to prohibit or restrict the free movement of the products incorporating the protected musical work.

It should be observed next that no provision of national legislation may permit an undertaking which is responsible for the management of copyrights and has a monopoly on the territory of a Member State by virtue of that management to charge a levy on products imported from another Member State where they were put into circulation by or with the consent of the copyright owner and thereby cause the Common Market to be partitioned. Such a practice would amount to allowing a private undertaking to impose a charge on the importation of sound recordings which are already in free circulation in the Common Market on account of their crossing a frontier; it would therefore have the effect of entrenching the isolation of national markets which the Treaty seeks to abolish.

It follows from those considerations that this argument must be rejected as being incompatible with the operation of the Common Market and with the aims of the Treaty.

GEMA and the Belgian Government have represented to the Court that, in any event, a system of free movement of sound recordings may not be permitted as regards sound recordings manufactured in the United Kingdom because the provisions of Section 8 of the United Kingdom Copyright Act 1956 have the effect of instituting a statutory licence in return for payment of a royalty at a reduced rate and the extension of such a statutory licence to other countries is contrary to the provisions of the Berne Convention for the Protection of Literary and Artistic Works.

Section 8 of the Copyright Act provides in effect that the copyright of a composer of a musical work is not infringed by the manufacture of a sound recording of that work if the work has already been reproduced in the United Kingdom on a sound recording for the purpose of retail sale by the author himself or with his consent and if, in addition, the manufacturer notifies the copyright owner of his intention to make a recording of the work for the purpose of sale and pays him a royalty of 6.25% of the retail selling price of the sound recording.

It appears from the papers before the Court that the practical result of that system is that the royalty for any manufacture of a sound recording is established at 6.25% of the retail selling price since no prospective licensee is willing to agree to a higher rate. As the rate of 6.25% is thus the rate which is in fact agreed for contractual licences, the United Kingdom legislation has the effect of putting a ceiling on the remuneration of the copyright holder.

Where, therefore, a copyright management society exercising an exclusive right of exploitation in the name of an owner claims the difference between the rate of 6.25% already paid and that charged on its domestic market, it is in fact seeking to neutralise the price differences arising from the conditions existing in the United Kingdom and thereby eliminate the economic advantage accruing to the importers of the sound recordings from the establishment of the Common Market.

As the Court held in another context in its judgment of 31 October 1974 in Case 15/74 *Centrafarm BV and Adriaan de Peijper* v *Sterling Drug Inc.* [1974] ECR 1147, the existence of a disparity between national laws which is capable of distorting competition between Member States cannot justify a Member State's giving legal protection to practices of a private body which are incompatible with the rules concerning free movement of goods.

It should further be observed that in a Common Market distinguished by free movement of goods and freedom to provide services an author, acting directly or through his publisher, is free to choose the place, in any of the Member States, in which to put his work into circulation. He may make that choice according to his best interests, which involve not only the level of remuneration provided in the Member State in question but other factors such as, for example, the opportunities for distributing his work and the marketing facilities which are further enhanced by virtue of the free movement of goods within the Community. In those circumstances, a copyright management society may not be permitted to claim, on the importation of sound recordings into another Member State, payment of additional fees based on the difference in the rates of remuneration existing in the various Member States.

It follows from the foregoing considerations that the disparities which continue to exist in the absence of any harmonisation of national rules on the commercial exploitation of copyrights may not be used to impede the free movement of goods in the Common Market.

The answer to the question put by the Bundesgerichtshof should therefore be that Articles 30 and 36 of the Treaty must be interpreted as precluding the application of national legislation under which a copyright management society empowered to exercise the copyrights of composers of musical work reproduced on gramophone records or other sound recordings in another Member State is permitted to invoke those rights where those sound recordings are distributed on the national market after having been put into circulation in that other Member State by or with the consent of the owners of those copyrights, in order to claim payment of a fee equal to the royalties ordinarily paid for marketing on the national market less the lower royalties paid in the Member State of manufacture.

Case 144/81 Keurkoop BV v Nancy Kean Gifts BV
[1982] ECR 2853; [1983] 2 CMLR 47

Nancy Kean Gifts registered the design of a handbag imported by them into the Netherlands and then brought proceedings against Keurkoop who were importing handbags of the same design.

The Court

First Question

The first question is essentially concerned with the question whether the provisions of Article 36 of the Treaty allow the application of a national law which, like the Uniform Benelux Law on Designs, gives an exclusive right to the first person to file a design, without persons other than the author or those claiming under him being entitled, in order to challenge such exclusive right or defend an action for an injunction brought by the holder of the right, to contend that the person filing the design is not the author of it, the person who commissioned the design from him or his employee.

By way of a preliminary observation it should be stated that, as the Court has already held as regards patent rights, trade marks and copyright, the protection of designs comes under the protection of industrial and commercial property within the meaning of Article 36 inasmuch as its aim is to define exclusive rights which are characteristic of that property.

According to Article 1 of the Uniform Benelux Law protection is afforded by that law only to the novel feature of a product serving a utility purpose, that is to say, according to Article 4, a product which in fact has not been commonly known in the industrial or commercial circles concerned in the Benelux territory during the 50 years prior to the filing of the design. According to Article 3 the exclusive right to a design is acquired by the first person to file it without it being necessary to inquire whether that person is also the author of the design or a person entitled under him. The reason for the rule is to be found in the function of the right to the design in economic life and in a concern for simplicity and efficacy. Finally, by virtue of the detailed rules laid down in Article 5 of the law the author of the design may, during a period of five years, claim the right to its registration and may at any time claim to have the registration annulled.

Those features, which are neither exhaustive nor limitative, nevertheless allow it to be said that legislation having characteristics of the kind of those which have just been described constitutes legislation for the protection of industrial and commercial property for the purposes of Article 36 of the Treaty.

Although it is true that, by virtue of Article 15 of the Uniform Benelux Law on Designs, any person or body concerned, including the Public Prosecutor's Department, may claim that the rights attached to the registration are null and void by contesting, in particular, the novelty of the product in the territory concerned, they may not, on the other hand, allege that the person filing the design is not the author, the person commissioning him or his employer. In view of this restriction the national court wonders whether the Uniform Law comes within the scope of Article 36 of the Treaty.

On that issue the Court can only state that in the present state of Community law and in the absence of Community standardisation or of a harmonisation of laws the determination of the conditions and procedures under which protection of designs is granted is a matter for national rules and, in this instance, for the common legislation established under the regional union between Belgium, Luxembourg and the Netherlands referred to in Article 233 of the Treaty.

Consequently the rules on the free movement of goods do not constitute an obstacle to the adoption of provisions of the kind contained in the Uniform Benelux Law on Designs, as described by the national court.

The answer to the first question must therefore be that national legislation having the characteristics of the Uniform Benelux Law on Designs falls within the scope of the provisions of Article 36 of the Treaty on the protection of industrial and commercial property. In the present state of its development Community law does not prevent the adoption of national provisions of the kind contained in the Uniform Benelux Law, as described by the national court.

Second Question

The second question is essentially concerned with the question whether, in view of the provisions of the Treaty, the owner of an exclusive right to a design protected by the legislation of a Member State may rely on that legislation in order to oppose the importation of products, whose appearance is identical to the design which has been filed, from one of the Member States of the Community where their marketing does not infringe any right of the owner to the exclusive right in the country of importation.

First of all it must be observed that in principle the protection of industrial and commercial property established by Article 36 would be rendered meaningless if a person other than the owner of the right to the design in a Member State could be allowed to market in that State a product which is identical in appearance to the protected design. That observation loses none of its force in the particular case, cited by the national court, where a person who wishes to market a product in a Member State has obtained supplies for that purpose in another Member State where the marketing of the product does not infringe the rights of the person who filed the design and who is the owner of the exclusive right thereto in the first State.

It must however be borne in mind that as far as the provisions on the free movement of goods are concerned prohibitions and restrictions on imports must, by virtue of Article 36, be justified *inter alia* on grounds of the protection of industrial and commercial property and must not in particular constitute disguised restrictions on trade between Member States.

Article 36 is thus intended to emphasise that the reconciliation between the requirements of the free movement of goods and the respect to which industrial and commercial property rights are entitled must be achieved in such a way that protection is ensured for the legitimate exercise, in the form of prohibitions on imports which are 'justified' within the meaning of that article, of the rights conferred by national legislation, but is refused, on the other hand, in respect of any improper exercise of the same rights which is of such a nature as to maintain or establish artificial partitions within the Common Market. The exercise of industrial and commercial property rights conferred by national legislation must consequently be restricted as far as is necessary for that reconciliation.

The Court has consistently held that the proprietor of an industrial or commercial property right protected by the legislation of a Member State may not rely on that legislation in order to oppose the importation of a product which has lawfully been marketed in another Member State by, or with the consent of, the proprietor of the right himself or a person legally or economically dependent on him.

Furthermore, the proprietor of an exclusive right may not rely on his right if the prohibition on importation or marketing of which he wishes to avail himself could be connected with an agreement or practice in restraint of competition within the Community contrary to the provisions of the Treaty, in particular to those of Article 85.

Although a right to a design, as a legal entity, does not as such fall within the class of agreements or concerted practices envisaged by Article 85(1), the exercise of that right may be subject to the prohibitions contained in the Treaty when it is the purpose, the means or the result of an agreement, decision or concerted practice.

It is therefore for the national court to ascertain in each case whether the exercise of the exclusive right in question leads to one of the situations which fall under the prohibitions contained in Article 85 and which may, in the context of the exercise of exclusive rights to designs, take very different forms, such as, for example, the situation where persons simultaneously or successively file the same design in various Member States in order to divide up the markets within the Community among themselves.

It follows from the foregoing that the answer to be given to the second question is that the proprietor of a right to a design acquired under the legislation of a Member State may oppose the importation of products from another Member State which are identical in appearance to the design which has been filed, provided that the products in question have not been put into circulation in the other Member State by, or with the consent of, the proprietor of the right or a person legally or economically dependent on him, that as between the natural or legal persons in question there is no kind of agreement or concerted practice in restraint of competition, and finally that the respective rights of the proprietors of the right to the design in the various Member States were created independently of one another.

(v) Deflection of Trade

The archetypal situation envisaged in Article 115 is that in which a Member State, which imposes quotas on the importation of certain goods from a non-Member State, seeks to prevent their importation via a second Member State which imposes less restrictive quotas or no quotas at all. In so far as a Member State is permitted, under Article 115, the benefit of a derogation from the rules relating to free movement of goods, it must, since the end of the transitional period, obtain the Commission's authorisation.

It might be noted that the Member States' policies with regard to imports of such products have in fact been coordinated by Council Regulation (EEC) No 1927/75 establishing the system of trade with third countries in the market in products processed from fruit and vegetables. The usual way in which Member States inform themselves as to likely deflection of trade is by requiring an importer to declare the origin of his goods, but the requirement of an import licence is regarded as having effect equivalent to a quantitative restriction. Even so, the Court has held that a Member State may require a declaration as to origin provided that no disproportionate sanction is involved and that the importer is required to state only information which he could reasonably know. The Court has gone so far as to say, in fact, that after the end of the transitional period, the national measures of commercial policy which are to be protected should themselves be approved by the Community.

Case 41/76 Suzanne Criel (née Donckerwolke) and Henri Schou v Procureur de la République au Tribunal de Grande Instance, Lille, and Director General of Customs [1976] ECR 1921; [1977] 2 CMLR 535

The appellants, Belgian traders, imported into France cloth and sacking, which had been in free circulation in Belgium. On a French customs form, they stated the origin of the goods to be the Belgium-Luxembourg Economic Union, but it eventually transpired that the goods came from the Lebanon and Syria. The Tribunal Correctionnel of Lille sentenced the appellants to suspended prison sentences, a fine equal to the value of the goods in lieu of confiscation, and a supplementary fine equal to twice the value of the goods. On appeal, the Cour d'Appel of Douai referred two questions for a preliminary ruling.

The Court

The questions referred concern the rules applicable to products originating in third countries not yet subject to common provisions of commercial policy and which, after being put into free circulation in one Member State, are re-exported to another Member State.

They concern more particularly the compatibility with the Treaty of monitoring measures introduced unilaterally by the importing Member State before obtaining a derogation, pursuant to the second sentence of the first paragraph of Article 115, from the rules of free circulation within the Community.

The monitoring measures in question consist of the importer's obligation to declare the actual origin of the imported goods and the issue of an import licence.

The answer to these questions must be derived from the provisions of the Treaty concerning the customs union and from the closely related provisions concerning the common commercial policy.

According to Article 9 of the Treaty the Community shall be based upon a customs union which shall cover all trade in goods between Member States.

According to Article 9(2) the provisions adopted for the liberalisation of intra-Community trade apply in identical fashion to products originating in Member States and to products coming from third countries which are in 'free circulation' in the Community.

Products in free circulation are to be understood as meaning those products which, coming from third countries, were duly imported into any one of the Member States in accordance with the requirements laid down by Article 10.

It appears from Article 9 that, as regards free circulation of goods within the Community, products entitled to 'free circulation' are definitely and wholly assimilated to products originating in Member States.

The result of this assimilation is that the provisions of Article 30 concerning the elimination of quantitative restrictions and all measures having equivalent effect are applicable without distinction to products originating in the Community and to those which were put into free circulation in any one of the Member States, irrespective of the actual origin of these products.

Measures having an effect equivalent to quantitative restrictions prohibited by the Treaty include all trading rules enacted by Member States which are capable of hindering, directly or indirectly, actually or potentially, intra-Community trade.

This provision precludes the application to intra-Community trade of a national provision which requires, even purely as a formality, import licences or any other similar procedure.

In addition Article 9(2) excludes any administrative procedure intended to establish between products different rules with regard to movement depending on whether they originate in the Community or, having originated in third countries, were put into free circulation in one of the Member States, since both types of product are included without distinction in the same system of free circulation.

Consequently the movement certificate DD1 established by the Decision of Commission of 5 December 1960 (Official Journal 1961, p. 29) and intended to cover the movement of goods which comply with the conditions required for the application of the Treaty provisions concerning the elimination of customs duties and quantitative restrictions and any measures having equivalent effect between the Member States contains no indication concerning the origin of the products.

In the system of Community law this authorisation must, of itself and without the addition of any measure of national law, guarantee to the person holding it the benefit of free circulation for the goods which it is intended to cover.

However it results from the system of the Treaty that the application of the principles referred to above is conditional upon the establishment of a common commercial policy.

The assimilation to products originating with the Member States of goods in 'free circulation' may only take full effect if these goods are subject to the same conditions of importation with regard both to customs and to commercial considerations, irrespective of the State in which they were put in free circulation.

Under Article 113 of the Treaty this unification should have been achieved by the expiry of the transitional period and supplanted by the establishment of a common commercial policy based on uniform principles.

The fact that at the expiry of the transitional period the Community commercial policy was not fully achieved is one of a number of circumstances calculated to maintain in being between the Member States differences in commercial policy capable of bringing about deflections of trade or of causing economic difficulties in certain Member States.

Because they constitute not only an exception to the provisions of Articles 9 and 30 of the Treaty which are fundamental to the operation of the Common Market, but also an obstacle to the implementation of the common commercial policy provided for by Article 113, the derogations allowed under Article 115 must be strictly interpreted and applied.

It is in the light of this interpretation that the compatibility of the 'monitoring measures' described above with the rules concerning the free circulation of goods within the Community should be considered.

First of all it should be stressed with regard to the scope of such provisions, that *under Article 115 limitations may only be placed on the free movement within the Community of goods enjoying the right to free circulation by virtue of measures of commercial policy adopted by the importing Member State in accordance with the Treaty.*

As full responsibility in the matter of commercial policy was transferred to the Community by means of Article 113(1), measures of commercial policy of a national character are only permissible after the end of the transitional period by virtue of specific authorisation by the Community.

Within the context thus defined the Member States are not prevented from requiring from an importer a declaration concerning the actual origin of the goods in question even in the case of goods put into free circulation in another Member State and covered by a Community movement certificate.

In these circumstances it may be admitted that knowledge of that origin is necessary both for the Member State concerned, so that it may determine the scope of commercial policy measures which it is authorised to adopt pursuant to the Treaty, and for the Commission, for the purpose of exercising the right of supervision and decision conferred on it by Article 115.

Nevertheless *the Member States may not require from the importer more in this respect than an indication of the origin of the products in so far as he knows it or may reasonably be expected to know it.*

In addition the fact that the importer did not comply with the obligation to declare the real origin of goods cannot give rise to the application of penalties which are disproportionate taking account of the purely administrative nature of the contravention.

In this respect the seizure of the goods or any pecuniary penalty fixed according to the value of the goods would certainly be incompatible with the provisions of the Treaty as being equivalent to an obstacle to the free movement of goods.

In general terms, any administrative or penal measure which goes beyond what is strictly necessary for the purposes of enabling the importing Member State to obtain reasonably complete and accurate information on the movement of goods falling within specific measures of commercial policy must be regarded as a measure having an effect equivalent to a quantitative restriction prohibited by the Treaty.

A fortiori the requirement of an import licence for the introduction into a Member State of goods put into free circulation in another Member State is incompatible with the provisions of the Treaty in so far as the goods are not the subject of a derogation properly authorised by the Commission by virtue of the second sentence of the first paragraph of Article 115.

Consequently *the refusal to issue an import permit, as an interim measure with a view to a possible application of Article 115, constitutes a restriction which is incompatible with Article 30 of the Treaty.*

The reply to be given to the first question is, therefore, that the requirement by the importing Member State of the indication of the country of origin on the customs declaration document for products in free circulation whose Community status is attested by the Community movement certificate does not in itself constitute a measure equivalent to a quantitative restriction if the goods in question are covered by measures of commercial policy adopted by that State in conformity with the Treaty.

Such a requirement would, however, fall under the prohibition contained in Article 30 of the Treaty if the importer were required to declare, with regard to origin, something other than what he knows or may reasonably be expected to know, or if the omission or inaccuracy of that declaration were to attract penalties disproportionate to the nature of a contravention of a purely administrative character.

The reply to be given to the second question is, therefore, that national rules making the importation of products coming from and in free circulation in a Member State and originating in a third country subject to the issue of a licence for the purposes of a possible future application of Article 115 of the Treaty in any event constitute a quantitative restriction prohibited by Article 30 of the Treaty.

4. NATIONAL MONOPOLIES

EEC Treaty

Article 37

1. Member States shall progressively adjust any State monopolies of a commercial character so as to ensure that when the transitional period has ended no discrimination regarding the conditions under which goods are procured and marketed exists between nationals of Member States.

The provisions of this Article shall apply to any body through which a Member State, in law or in fact, either directly or indirectly supervises, determines or appreciably influences imports or exports between Member States. These provisions shall likewise apply to monopolies delegated by the State to others.

2. Member States shall refrain from introducing any new measure which is contrary to the principles laid down in paragraph 1 or which restricts the scope of the Articles dealing with the abolition of customs duties and quantitative restrictions between Member States.

3. The timetable for the measures referred to in paragraph 1 shall be harmonised with the abolition of quantitative restrictions on the same products provided for in Articles 30 to 34.

If a product is subject to a State monopoly of a commercial character in only one or some Member States, the Commission may authorise the other Member States to apply protective measures until the adjustment provided for in paragraph 1 has been effected; the Commission shall determine the conditions and details of such measures.

4. If a State monopoly of a commercial character has rules which are designed to make it easier to dispose of agricultural products or obtain for them the best return, steps should be taken in applying the rules contained in this article to ensure equivalent safeguards for the employment and standard of living of the producers concerned, account being taken of the adjustments that will be possible and the specialisation that will be needed with the passage of time.

5. The obligations on Member States shall be binding only in so far as they are compatible with existing international agreements.

6. With effect from the first stage the Commission shall make recommendations as to the manner in which and the timetable according to which the adjustment provided for in this article shall be carried out.

Act of Accession

Article 44

1. The new Member States shall progressively adjust State monopolies of a commercial character within the meaning of Article 37(1) of the EEC Treaty so as to ensure that by 31 December 1977 no discrimination regarding the conditions under which goods are procured and marketed exists between nationals of Member States.

The original Member States shall have equivalent obligations in relation to the new Member States.

2 From the beginning of 1973 the Commission shall make recommendations as to the manner in which and the timetable according to which the adjustment provided for in this article must be carried out, it being understood that the manner and timetable must be the same for the new Member States and the original Member States.

It is significant that Article 37, requiring the adjustment of State monopolies, is contained in the chapter of the Treaty relating to the elimination of quantitative restrictions and refers expressly to the abolition of customs duties and quantitative restrictions. The European Court has held, in Case 155/73 *Sacchi* [1974] ECR 409 at 428 (see p. 444 below), that this article does not apply to a monopoly in the supply of services. More importantly, however, the position of Article 37 has led to its being interpreted as one intended to promote the free movement of goods. Indeed, the aspects of national monopolies that the Court has had to consider under Article 37 have often involved also the application of the more general provisions relating to the free movement of goods. Article 37(2) has been held to produce direct effects since the entry into force of the EEC Treaty (see Case 6/64 *Costa* v *ENEL* [1964] ECR 585 at 597-598, Chapter 1, above, p. 4), and Article 37(1) has been held to produce such effects since the end of the transitional period.

Case 59/75 Pubblico Ministero v Flavia Manghera and Others
[1976] ECR 91; [1976] 1 CMLR 557

The Italian tobacco monopoly had, *inter alia*, an exclusive right to import manufactured tobacco. The defendants had imported tobacco, some of it manufactured in other Member States, into Italy without passing through the State monopoly (and indeed without paying the relevant duties). In criminal proceedings before the Tribunale of Como, the defendants raised the question of the legality of the monopoly's exclusive right to import cigarettes.

The Court

The national court is concerned with the application of the Italian criminal law to facts described as constituting an infringement of the legal provisions granting an exclusive right of import to the State monopoly in manufactured tobacco.

The First Question

The first question asks whether Article 37(1) of the Treaty is to be interpreted as meaning that, with effect from 31 December 1969 (the date when the transitional period expired), the trade monopoly should have been reorganised in such a way as to eliminate even the possibility of any discrimination being practised against Community exporters, with the consequential extinction, with effect from 1 January 1970, of the exclusive right to import from other Member States.

Under Article 37(1) Member States must progressively adjust any State monopolies of a commercial character so as to ensure that when the transitional period has ended no discrimination regarding the conditions under which goods are procured and marketed exists between the nationals of Member States.

Without requiring the abolition of the said monopolies, this provision prescribes in mandatory terms that they must be adjusted in such a way as to ensure that when the transitional period has ended such discrimination shall cease to exist.

For the purposes of interpreting Article 37 as regards the nature and scope of the adjustment prescribed it must be considered in its context in relation to the other paragraphs of the same article and in its place in the general scheme of the Treaty.

This article comes under the title of the free movement of goods and in particular under Chapter II on the abolition of quantitative restrictions between Member States.

It applies to any body through which a Member State either directly or indirectly supervises, determines or appreciably influences imports or exports between Member States.

Article 37(3), moreover, provides that the time table for adjustment provided for in paragraph (1) must be harmonised with the abolition of quantitative restrictions on the same products provided for in Articles 30 to 34.

It follows from these provisions and their structure that the obligation laid down in paragraph (1) aims at ensuring compliance with the fundamental rule of the free movement of goods throughout the Common Market, in particular by the abolition of quantitative restrictions and measures having equivalent effect in trade between Member States.

This objective would not be attained if, in a Member State where a commercial monopoly exists, the free movement of goods from other Member States similar to those with which the national monopoly is concerned were not ensured.

The Council's Resolution of 21 April 1970 on national monopolies of a commercial character in manufactured tobacco itself refers to the obligation to abolish exclusive rights to import and market manufactured tobacco.

The exclusive right to import manufactured products of the monopoly in question thus constitutes, in respect of Community exporters, discrimination prohibited by Article 37(1).

The answer to the first question should therefore be that Article 37(1) of the EEC Treaty must be interpreted as meaning that as from 31 December 1969 every national monopoly of a commercial character must be adjusted so as to eliminate the exclusive right to import from other Member States.

The Second Question

The second question asks whether Article 37(1) of the Treaty is directly applicable and whether it has created individual rights which the national judicial bodies must protect.

The fact that at the end of the transitional period no discrimination regarding the conditions under which goods are procured and marketed must exist between nationals of Member States constitutes an obligation with a very precise objective subject to a clause postponing its operation.

Upon the expiry of the transitional period this obligation is no longer subject to any condition nor contingent, in its execution or in its effects, upon the introduction of any measure, either by the Community or by the Member States, and by its nature is capable of being relied on by nationals of Member States before national courts.

....

The fourth question asks whether the Council Resolution of 21 April 1970 can vary the effect of the provisions of Article 37(1) of the Treaty and, if the answer is in the affirmative, whether it is, so far as the Member States are concerned, binding in such a way as immediately to remove all restrictions on the importation of products covered by the monopoly without any need for further Community legislation, thus extinguishing the exclusive rights of the tobacco monopoly.

Under the terms of the said resolution 'the French and Italian Governments undertake to take all necessary measures for the abolition of discrimination arising out of national monopolies of a commercial nature. The abolition of exclusive rights relating to importation and wholesale marketing must be achieved by 1 January 1976 at the latest'.

The said resolution, which basically expresses the political will of the Council and the French and Italian Governments to put an end to a state of affairs contravening Article 37(1), cannot engender effects which can be used against individuals.

In particular the time-scale referred to in the resolution cannot prevail over that contained in the Treaty.

The fourth question must therefore be answered in the negative.

In Case 20/64 *Albatros* v *Sopéco* [1965] 1 ECR 29, the Court found it unnecessary to decide whether the requirements of Article 37 and the general provisions relating to the abolition of quantitative restrictions are mutually exclusive. However, Article 95 on internal taxation and Article 37 are not treated as being mutually exclusive. Nor are they treated as being necessarily coextensive (see Case 45/75 *Rewe-Zentrale des Lebensmittel-Grosshandels GmbH* v *Hauptzollamt Landau/Pfalz* [1976] ECR 181; [1976] 2 CMLR 1).

5. THE SINGLE MARKET

The objective pursued by the rules of the free movement of goods is the establishment of a single, common market between Member States. This objective also underlies the other trading rules in the EEC Treaty, for example the rules on competition, as the Court pointed out even in Cases 56 and 58/64 *Consten and Grundig* v *Commission* [1966] ECR 299 at 341 (see Chapter 9 below, p. 404).

In June 1985 the Commission published a white paper in response to a request made to it by the Heads of State and Government of all the Member States. This white paper sets out an ambitious programme of legislative activity to be accomplished by the Commission and Council by 1992 for the purpose of removing physical, technical and fiscal barriers to trade between Member States. It puts forward more than 300 legislative proposals, some very limited or technical in character (including those designed to establish common safety standards or manufacturing standards for specified goods) and others of a more far-reaching nature, addressing entire sectors of economic activity (like the UCITS Directive of 20 December 1985 (OJ L375/3) governing the liberalisation of the unit trusts industry). The white paper envisages that the legislative programme will be accomplished gradually, in the period between 1985 and 1992, not all at a stroke. Initial progress was slow and while it must be expected that the programme will quicken towards the end of the timetable, it remains to be seen whether the Community institutions will accomplish the task that they have set themselves.

The concept of a single market has already exercised a considerable influence on the judges of the European Court and this is particularly the case in actions involving industrial property rights. For in deciding how far the exercise of industrial property rights benefits from the exemption in Article 36, the Court has used the single market as the Community interest to weigh against that of the holders of industrial property rights.

Case 78/70 Deutsche Grammophon Gesellschaft mbH v Metro-SB-Grossmärkte GmbH & Co KG [1971] ECR 487; [1971] CMLR 631

The Court

In the first question the Court is asked to rule whether it is contrary to the second paragraph of Article 5 or Article 85(1) of the EEC Treaty to interpret Articles 97 and 85 of the German Law of 9 September 1965 on Copyright and Related Rights to mean that a German undertaking manufacturing sound recordings may rely on its exclusive right of distribution to prohibit the marketing in the Federal Republic of Germany of sound recordings which it has itself supplied to the French subsidiary which, although independent at law, is wholly subordinate to it commercially.

...

If, however, the exercise of the right does not exhibit those elements of contract or concerted practice referred to in Article 85(1) it is necessary, in order to answer the question referred, further to consider whether the exercise of the right in question is compatible with other provisions of the Treaty, in particular those relating to the free movement of goods.

The principles to be considered in the present case are those concerned with the attainment of a single market between the Member States, which are placed both in Part Two of the Treaty devoted to the foundations of the Community, under the free movement of goods, and in Article 3(f) of the Treaty which prescribes the institution of a system ensuring that competition in the Common Market is not distorted.

Moreover, where certain prohibitions or restrictions on trade between Member States are conceded in Article 36, the Treaty makes express reference to them, providing that such derogations shall not constitute 'a means of arbitrary discrimination or a disguised restriction on trade between Member States'.

It is thus in the light of those provisions, especially of Articles 36, 85 and 86, that an appraisal should be made as to how far the exercise of a national right related to copyright may impede the marketing of products from another Member State.

Amongst the prohibitions or restrictions on the free movement of goods which it concedes, Article 36 refers to industrial and commercial property. On the assumption that those provisions may be relevant to a right related to copyright, it is nevertheless clear from that article that, *although the Treaty does not affect the existence of rights recognised by the legislation of a Member State with regard to industrial and commercial property, the exercise of such rights may nevertheless fall within the prohibitions laid down by the Treaty*. Although it permits prohibitions or restrictions on the free movement of products which are justified for the purpose of protecting industrial and commercial property, Article 36 only admits derogations from that freedom to the extent to which they are justified for the purpose of safeguarding rights which constitute the specific subject-matter of such property.

If a right related to copyright is relied upon to prevent the marketing in a Member State of products distributed by the holder of the right or with his consent on the territory of another Member State on the sole ground that such distribution did not take place on the national territory, such a prohibition, which would legitimise the isolation of national markets, would be repugnant to the essential purpose of the Treaty, which is to unite national markets into a single market.

That purpose could not be attained if, under the various legal systems of the Member States, nationals of those States were able to partition the market and bring about arbitrary discrimination or disguised restrictions on trade between Member States.

Consequently, it would be in conflict with the provisions prescribing the free movement of products within the Common Market for a manufacturer of sound recordings to exercise the exclusive right to distribute the protected articles, conferred upon him by the legislation of a Member State, in such a way as to prohibit the sale in that State of products placed on the market by him or with his consent in another Member State solely because such distribution did not occur within the territory of the first Member State.

The 'specific subject-matter' of a patent was defined by the Court in Case 15/74 *Centrafarm* v *Sterling Drug* [1974] ECR 1147 at 1162 (p. 239 above), and that of a trade mark in Case 16/74 *Centrafarm* v *Winthrop* [1974] ECR 1183 at 1194 (p. 241 above).

However, the single market in this context is only an objective with regard to trade between Member States. For this reason the use of industrial property rights at the borders of the Community, to prevent imports from a non-Member State, does not contravene the principle. This is the case even if it does have an effect equivalent to a quantitative restriction, provided it does not lead to partitioning of the internal Common Market.

Case 51/75 EMI Records Limited v CBS United Kingdom Limited [1976] ECR 811; [1976] 2 CMLR 235

The trademark 'Columbia' originally belonged to an American company which, in 1917, transferred to its English subsidiary its interests in various countries including the states which later made up the European Community. At the same time the American company transferred to its English subsidiary a number of trademarks, including the Columbia mark, in respect of those states; but it retained the trademark in the United States and other third countries. After 1922 the trademark was acquired by various American and English undertakings. Among those American undertakings was CBS Inc, of which CBS UK was an English subsidiary. Among the English undertakings which acquired the trademark was EMI Records. EMI sought to rely on its trademark in order to prevent the importation and marketing in England of records and tapes bearing the Columbia mark which originated in the United States or had been manufactured in the Community by a subsidiary of the proprietor of the American trademark.

The Court

Within the framework of the provisions of the Treaty relating to the free movement of goods and in accordance with Article 3(a), Articles 30 *et seq.* on the elimination of quantitative restrictions and of measures having equivalent effect expressly provide that such restrictions and measures shall be prohibited 'between Member States'.

Article 36, in particular, after stipulating that Articles 30 to 34 shall not preclude restrictions on imports, exports or goods in transit justified *inter alia* on grounds of the protection of industrial and commercial property, states that such restrictions shall in no instance constitute a means of arbitrary discrimination or disguised restriction on trade 'between Member States'.

Consequently *the exercise of a trade-mark right in order to prevent the marketing of products coming from a third country under an identical mark, even if this constitutes a measure having an effect equivalent to a quantitative restriction, does not affect the free movement of goods between Member States and thus does not come under the prohibitions set out in Articles 30* et seq. *of the Treaty.*

In such circumstances the exercise of a trade-mark right does not in fact jeopardise the unity of the Common Market which Articles 30 *et seq.* are intended to ensure.

Furthermore if the same proprietor holds the trade-mark right in respect of the same product in all the Member States there are no grounds for examining whether those marks have a common origin with an identical mark recognised in a third country, since that question is relevant only in relation to considering whether within the Community there are opportunities for partitioning the market.

It is impossible to avoid these conclusions by relying on Articles 9 and 10 of the Treaty.

According to Article 10(1) of the Treaty, products coming from a third country shall be considered to be in free circulation in a Member State if the import formalities have been complied with and any customs duties or charges having equivalent effect which are payable have been levied in the importing Member State.

According to Article 9(2) of the Treaty, the provisions of Chapter 1, Section 1 and of Chapter 2 of Title I of Part Two shall apply to products coming from third countries which are in free circulation in Member States.

Since those provisions only refer to the effects of compliance with customs formalities and paying customs duties and charges having equivalent effect, they cannot be interpreted as meaning that it would be sufficient for products bearing a mark applied in a third country and imported into the Community to comply with the customs formalities in the first Member State where they were imported in order to be able then to be marketed in the Common Market as a whole in contravention of the rules relating to the protection of the mark.

Furthermore the provisions of the Treaty on commercial policy do not, in Articles 110 *et seq.*, lay down any obligation on the part of the Member States to extend to trade with third countries the binding principles governing the free movement of goods between Member States and in particular the prohibition of measures having an effect equivalent to quantitative restrictions.

The arrangements concluded by the Community in certain international agreements such as the ACP-EEC Convention of Lomé of 28 February 1975 or the agreements with

Sweden and Switzerland of 22 July 1972 form part of such a policy and do not constitute the performance of a duty incumbent on the Member States under the Treaty.

The binding effect of commitments undertaken by the Community with regard to certain countries cannot be extended to others.

Furthermore with regard to the provisions of Regulation No 1439/74 of 4 June 1974 (OJ, L 1974, L 159, p.1) introducing common rules for imports these provisions relate only to quantitative restrictions to the exclusion of measures having equivalent effect.

It follows that neither the rules of the Treaty on the free movement of goods nor those on the putting into free circulation of products coming from third countries nor, finally, the principles governing the common commercial policy, prohibit the proprietor of a mark in all the Member States of the Community from exercising his right in order to prevent the importation of similar products bearing the same mark and coming from a third country.

Nor may the provisions of the Treaty on the free movement of goods be invoked for the purpose of prohibiting the proprietor of the mark in the territories of the Member States from exercising his right in order to prevent another proprietor of the same mark in a third country from manufacturing and marketing his products within the Community, either himself or through his subsidiaries established in the Community.

In fact the protection of industrial and commercial property established by Article 36 would be rendered meaningless if an undertaking other than the proprietor of a mark in the Member States could be allowed there to manufacture and market products bearing the same mark since such conduct would amount to an actual infringement of the protected mark.

The steps taken by the proprietor of a mark to prevent a person other than the proprietor of that mark in the Member States from manufacturing and distributing their products bearing the same mark cannot be classified as a means of arbitrary discrimination or as a disguised restriction on trade between Member States within the meaning of Article 36.

6. CAPITAL MOVEMENTS

The provisions of the EEC Treaty governing movement of capital are contained in the title dealing also with persons and services; but they have a bearing on the free movement of goods insofar as limitations on capital movements may affect movement of goods.

EEC Treaty

Article 67

1. During the transitional period and to the extent necessary to ensure the proper functioning of the Common Market, Member States shall progressively abolish between themselves all restrictions on the movement of capital belonging to persons resident in Member States and any discrimination based on the nationality or on the place of residence of the parties or on the place where such capital is invested...

Article 68

1. Member States shall, as regards the matters dealt with in this chapter, be as liberal as possible in granting such exchange authorisations as are still necessary after the entry into force of this Treaty.

2. Where a Member State applies to the movements of capital liberalised in accordance with the provisions of this chapter the domestic rules governing the capital market and the credit system, it shall do so in a non-discriminatory manner...

Article 69

The Council shall, on a proposal from the Commission, which for this purpose shall consult the Monetary Committee provided for in Article 105, issue the necessary directives for the progressive implementation of the provisions of Article 67, acting unanimously during the first two stages and by a qualified majority thereafter.

Article 70

1. The Commission shall propose to the Council measures for the progressive coordination of the exchange policies of Member States in respect of the movement of capital between those States and third countries. For this purpose the Council shall issue directives, acting by a qualified majority. It shall endeavour to attain the highest possible degree of liberalisation. Unanimity shall be required for measures which constitute a step back as regards the liberalisation of capital movements.

2. Where the measures taken in accordance with paragraph 1 do not permit the elimination of differences between the exchange rules of Member States and where such differences could lead persons resident in one of the Member States to use the freer transfer facilities within the Community which are provided for in Article 67 in order to evade the rules of one of the Member States concerning the movement of capital to or from third countries, that State may, after consulting the other Member States and the Commission, take appropriate measures to overcome these difficulties.

Should the Council find that these measures are restricting the free movement of capital within the Community to a greater extent than is required for the purpose of overcoming the difficulties, it may, acting by a qualified majority on a proposal from the Commission, decide that the State concerned shall amend or abolish these measures.

Article 71

Member States shall endeavour to avoid introducing within the Community any new exchange restrictions on the movement of capital and current payments connected with such movements, and shall endeavour not to make existing rules more restrictive.

They declare their readiness to go beyond the degree of liberalisation of capital movements provided for in the preceding articles in so far as their economic situation, in particular the situation of their balance of payments, so permits.

The Commission may, after consulting the Monetary Committee, make recommendations to Member States on this subject.

Article 106

1. Each Member State undertakes to authorise, in the currency of the Member State in which the creditor or the beneficiary resides, any payments connected with the movement of goods, services or capital, and any transfers of capital and earnings, to the extent that the movement of goods, services, capital and persons between Member States has been liberalised pursuant to this Treaty.

The Member States declare their readiness to undertake the liberalisation of payments beyond the extent provided in the preceding subparagraph, in so far as their economic situation in general and the state of their balance of payments in particular so permit.

2. In so far as movement of goods, services and capital are limited only by restrictions on payments connected therewith, these restrictions shall be progressively abolished by applying, *mutatis mutandis,* the provisions of the chapters relating to the abolition of quantitative restrictions, to the liberalisation of services and to the free movement of capital.

3. Member States undertake not to introduce between themselves any new restrictions on transfers connected with the invisible transactions listed in Annex III to this Treaty...

Case 203/80 Criminal Proceedings against Guerrino Casati
[1981] ECR 2595; [1982] 1 CMLR 365

Casati was an Italian businessman living in Germany who was charged with the attempted illegal exportation from Italy of 24,000 DM. The sum had been brought into the country for the purpose of purchasing equipment for commercial purposes and was being re-exported, Casati having been unable to obtain the goods required.

The Court

The First Question

The first question concerns the effects of Article 67 and, more particularly, Article 67(1), after the expiry of the transitional period. That article heads the chapter on capital which belongs to Title II, 'Free movement of persons, services and capital', incorporated in Part Two of the EEC Treaty, entitled 'Foundations of the Community'. The general scheme of those provisions is in keeping with the list, set out in Article 3 of the EEC Treaty, of the methods provided for the attainment of the Community's objectives. Those methods include, according to Article 3(c), 'the abolition, as between Member States, of obstacles to freedom of movement for persons, services and capital'. Thus the free movement of capital constitutes, alongside that of persons and services, one of the fundamental freedoms of the Community. Furthermore, freedom to move certain types of capital is, in practice, a pre-condition for the effective exercise of other freedoms guaranteed by the Treaty, in particular the right of establishment.

However, capital movements are also closely connected with the economic and monetary policy of the Member States. *At present, it cannot be denied that complete freedom of movement of capital may undermine the economic policy of one of the Member States or create an imbalance in its balance of payments, thereby impairing the proper functioning of the Common Market.*

For those reasons, Article 67(1) differs from the provisions on the free movements of goods, persons and services in the sense that there is an obligation to liberalise capital movements only 'to the extent necessary to ensure the proper functioning of the Common Market'. The scope of that restriction, which remained in force after the expiry of the transitional period, varies in time and depends on an assessment of the requirements of the Common Market and on an appraisal of both the advantages and the risks which liberalisation might entail for the latter, having regard to the stage it has reached and, in particular, to the level of integration attained in matters in respect of which capital movements are particularly significant.

Such an assessment is, first and foremost, a matter for the Council, in accordance with the procedure provided for by Article 69. The Council has adopted two directives under that article, the first on 11 May 1960 (Official Journal, English Special Edition 1959-1962, p. 49) and the second, which adds to and amends the first, on 18 December 1962 (Official Journal, English Special Edition 1963-1964, p. 5). All the movements of capital are divided into four lists (A, B, C, & D) annexed to the directives. In the case of the movements covered by Lists A and B, unconditional liberalisation is prescribed by the directives. However, in the case of movements covered by List C, the directives authorise the Member States to maintain or to reimpose the exchange restrictions in existence on the date of the entry into force of the fist directive if the freedom of movement of capital is capable of forming an obstacle to the achievement of the economic policy objectives of the State concerned. Finally, in the case of the movements referred to in List D, the directives do not require the Member States to adopt any liberalising measures. List D covers, *inter alia,* the physical importation and exportation of financial assets, including bank notes.

The conclusion must be drawn that the obligation contained in Article 67(1) to abolish restrictions on movements of capital cannot be defined, in relation to a specific category of such movements, in isolation from the Council's assessment under Article 69 of the need to liberalise that category in order to ensure the proper functioning of the Common Market. The Council has so far taken the view that it is unnecessary to liberalise the exportation of bank notes, the operation with which the accused in the main proceedings is charged, and there is no reason to suppose that, by adopting that position, it has overstepped the limits of it discretionary power.

The answer to the first question should therefore be that Article 67(1) must be interpreted as meaning that restrictions on the exportation of bank notes may not be regarded as abolished as from the expiry of the transitional period, irrespective of the provisions of Article 69...

The Third Question

In its third question, the national court asks essentially whether a principle of Community law or any provision of the Treaty guarantees the right of non-residents to re-export currency previously imported and not used.

To begin with it is necessary to observe that, as the replies given to the first two questions show, the extent to which capital movements are liberalised and exchange restrictions gradually abolished does not depend on a general principle but is governed by the provisions of Article 67 and 69 of the EEC Treaty and by those of the aforesaid directives of 11 May 1960 and 18 December 1962 adopted to give effect to those articles. However, it is necessary to consider whether, in matters where, according to those provisions, there is so far no obligation to liberalise movements of capital – for example, transfers of currency – individuals may derive rights, which the Member States are bound to respect, either from the standstill provisions contained in Article 71 of the EEC Treaty or from Article 106 of the EEC Treaty, both of which are referred to by the national court, though in another context, in its sixth and eighth questions.

According to the first paragraph of Article 71, the Member States must endeavour to avoid introducing within the Community any new exchange restrictions on the movement of capital and must endeavour not to make existing rules more restrictive.

By using the term 'shall endeavour', the wording of that provision departs noticeably from the more imperative forms of wording employed in other similar provisions concerning restrictions on the free movement of goods, persons and services. It is apparent from that wording that, in any event, the first paragraph of Article 71 does not impose on the Member States an unconditional obligation capable of being relied upon by individuals.

Capital movements account for only a part of the transactions involving transfers of currency. With good reason, therefore, the national court draws attention to Article 106 which is designed to ensure that the necessary transfers of currency be made both for the liberalisation of capital movements and for the free movement of goods, services and persons and which, moreover, does not contain the same restrictions as those expressly provided for by the provisions already considered.

More specifically, in its sixth question, the national court refers to the standstill obligation contained in the first sub paragraph of Article 106(3). According to that provision, the Member States undertake not to introduce between themselves any new restrictions on transfers connected with the so-called 'invisible' transactions listed in Annex III to the Treaty.

In that regard, it is necessary to recall that the defendant in the main proceedings has stated that he intended to re-export a sum of money previously imported with a view to making purchases of a commercial nature, not an amount corresponding to a transaction actually listed in Annex III.

The answer to the questions relating to Article 106(3)) should therefore be that the latter provision is inapplicable to the re-exportation of a sum of money previously imported with a view to making purchases of a commercial nature if such purchases have not in fact been effected.

The order referring the matter to the Court contains no express reference to the first two paragraphs of Article 106. In view of the alleged purpose of the importation of the sum of money in question, those two paragraphs are significant in relation to the third question. According to those provisions, the Member States undertake to authorise on the expiry of the transitional period, any payments connected with, *inter alia,* the movement of goods. *The first two paragraphs of Article 106 are thus designed to ensure the free movement of goods in practice by authorising all the transfers of currency necessary to achieve that aim. However, those provisions do not require the Member States to authorise the importation and exportation of bank notes for the performance of commercial transactions, if such transfers are not necessary for the free movement of goods.* In connection with commercial transactions, that method of transfer which, moreover, is not in conformity with standard practice cannot be regarded as necessary to ensure such free movement.

In the light of the foregoing considerations, the answer to the third question should be that the right of non-residents to re-export bank notes which were previously imported with a view to performing commercial transactions but have not been used is not guaranteed by any principle of Community law or by any provisions of Community law relating to capital movements or by the rules of Article 106 concerning payments connected with the movement of goods...

Although the movement of bank notes is still subject to restrictions, those restrictions will not be justified if their effect is to hinder the free movement of goods and services.

Joined Cases 286/82 and 26/83 Graziana Luisi and Giuseppe Carbone v Ministero del Tesoro [1984] ECR 377; [1985] 3 CMLR 52

The Ministero del Tesoro imposed on Mrs Luisi and Mr Carbone fines for exporting foreign currency in amounts greater than those permitted by Italian law. Both challenged the validity of the fines on the ground that the Italian restriction on export of currency constituted an impediment to their freedom to travel throughout the Community. Mrs Luisi maintained that she had exported the currency in question for the purposes of her visits to France and Germany as a tourist and for the purpose of meeting costs of medical treatment in Germany. Mr Carbone maintained that he had used the currency for the purposes of his stay in Germany for three months as a tourist.

The Court

...

It is apparent from the wording of the questions submitted for a preliminary ruling and from the statement of reasons contained in the two orders for reference that the problems of interpretation of Community law arising in these cases are:

(a) whether tourism and travel for the purposes of business, education and medical treatment fall within the scope of services, or of invisible transactions within the meaning of Article 106(3) of the Treaty, or of both those categories at once;

(b) whether the transfer of foreign currency for those four purposes must be regarded as a current payment or as a movement of capital, in particular when bank notes are transferred physically...

(a) 'Services' and 'Invisible Transactions'

According to Article 60 of the Treaty, services are deemed to be 'services' within the meaning of the Treaty where they are normally provided for remuneration, in so far as they are not governed by the provisions relating to freedom of movement for goods, capital and persons. Within the context of Title III of Part Two of the Treaty ('Free movement of persons, services and capital'), the free movement of persons includes the movement of workers within the Community and freedom of establishment within the territory of the Member States.

By virtue of Article 59 of the Treaty, restrictions on freedom to provide such services are to be abolished in respect of nationals of Member States who are established in a Member State other than that of the person for whom the service is intended. In order to enable services to be provided, the persons providing the service may go to the Member State where the person for whom it is provided is established or else the latter may go to the State in which the person providing the service is established. Whilst the former case is expressly mentioned in the third paragraph of Article 60, which permits the person providing the service to pursue his activity temporarily in the Member State where the service is provided, the latter case is the necessary corollary thereof, which fulfils the objective of liberalising all gainful activity not covered by the free movement of goods, persons and capital.

For the implementation of those provisions, Title II of the General Programme for the Abolition of Restrictions on Freedom to Provide Services (Official Journal, English Special Edition, Second Series IX, p. 3), which was drawn up by the Council pursuant to Article 63 of the Treaty on 18 December 1961, envisages *inter alia* the repeal of provisions laid down by law, regulation or administrative action which in any Member State govern, for economic purposes, the entry, exit and residence of nationals of Member States, where such provisions are not justified on grounds of public policy, public security or public health and are liable to hinder the provision of services by such persons.

According to Article 1 thereof, Council Directive No 64/221/EEC of 25 February 1964 on the coordination of special measures concerning the movement and residence of foreign nationals which are justified on grounds of public policy, public security or public health (Official Journal, English Special Edition 1963-1964, p. 117) applies *inter alia* to any national of a Member State who travels to another Member State 'as a recipient of services'. Council Directive No 73/148/EEC of 21 May 1973 on the abolition of restrictions on movement and residence within the Community for nationals of Member States with regard to establishment and the provision of services (Official Journal 1973, L 172, p. 14) grants both the provider and the recipient of a service a right of residence co terminous with the period during which the service is provided.

By basing the General Programme for the Abolition of Restrictions on the Freedom to provide Services partly on Article 106 of the Treaty, its authors showed that they were aware of the effect of the liberalisation of services on the liberalisation of payments. In fact, the first paragraph of that article provides that any payments connected with the movement of goods or services are to be liberalised to the extent to which the movement of goods and services has been liberalised between Member States.

Among the restrictions on the freedom to provide services which must be abolished, the General Programme mentions, in Section C of Title III, impediments to payments for services, particularly where, according to section D of Title III and in conformity with Article 106(2), the provision of such services is limited only by restrictions in respect of the payments therefor. By virtue of section B of Title V of the General Programme, those restrictions were to be abolished before the end of the first stage of the transitional period, subject to a proviso permitting limits on 'foreign currency allowances for tourists' to be retained during that period. Those provisions were implemented by Council Directive No 63/340/EEC of 31 May 1963 on the abolition of all prohibitions on or obstacles to payments for services where the only restrictions on exchange of services are those governing such payments (Official Journal, English Special Edition 1963-1964, p. 31). Article 3 of that directive also refers to foreign exchange allowances for tourists.

However, both the General Programme and the aforesaid directive reserve the right for Member States to verify the nature and genuineness of transfers of funds and of payments and to take all necessary measures in order to prevent contravention of their laws and regulations, 'in particular as regards the issue of foreign currency to tourists'.

It follows that the freedom to provide services includes the freedom, for the recipients of services, to go to another Member State in order to receive a service there, without being obstructed by restrictions even in relation to payments, *and that tourists, persons receiving medical treatment and persons travelling for the purpose of education or business are to be regarded as recipients of services.*

Article 106(3) provides for the progressive abolition of restrictions on transfers connected with 'invisible transactions' listed in Annex III to the Treaty. As the national court correctly stated, that list includes, *inter alia,* business travel, tourism, private travel for the purpose of education and private travel on health grounds.

However, since that paragraph is merely subordinate to paragraphs (1) and (2) of Article 106, as is apparent from the second subparagraph thereof, it cannot be applied to the four types of transaction in question.

(b) 'Current Payments' and 'Movements of Capital'

The national court has pointed out that the physical transfer of bank notes is included in List D in the annexes to the two directives which the Council adopted pursuant to Article 69 of the Treaty in relation to the movement of capital (Official Journal, English Special Edition 1959-1962, p. 49, and 1963-1964, p. 5). List D enumerates the movements of capital for which the directives do not require the Member States to adopt any liberalising measure. The question therefore arises whether the reference in the list to the physical transfer of bank notes implies that such a transfer itself constitutes a movement of capital.

The Treaty does not specify what is to be understood by the movements of capital. However, in the annexes to the two above-mentioned directives a list is given of the various movement of capital, together with a nomenclature. Although the physical transfer of financial assets, in particular bank notes, is included in that list, that does not mean that any such transfer must in all circumstances be regarded as a movement of capital.

The general scheme of the Treaty shows, and a comparison between Articles 67 and 106 confirms, that current payments are transfers of foreign exchange which constitute the consideration within the context of an underlying transaction, whilst movements of capital are financial operations essentially concerned with the investment of the funds in question rather than remuneration for a service. For that reason movements of capital may themselves give rise to current payments, as is implied by Articles 67(2) and 106(1).

The physical transfer of bank notes may not therefore be classified as a movement of capital where the transfer in question corresponds to an obligation to pay arising from a transaction involving the movement of goods or services.

Consequently, payments in connection with tourism or travel for the purposes of business, education or medical treatment cannot be classified as movements of capital, even where they are effected by means of the physical transfer of bank notes.

...

FURTHER READING

Baden-Fuller, C., 'Economic Issues relating to Property Rights in Trade Marks' 6 ELR (1981) 162

Barents, R., 'Recent Case Law on the Prohibition of Fiscal Discrimination under Article 95' 23 (1986) CMLRev 641

Brouwer, O., 'Free Movement of Foodstuffs and Quality Requirements: has the Commission got it wrong?' 25 (1988) CMLRev 237

Ehlermann, C. D., 'The Internal Market following the Single European Act' 24 (1987) CMLRev 361

Harris, B., 'Appellations of Origin and other Geographical Indications used in Trade' [1979] EIPR 205

Oliver, P., 'A Review of the Case Law of the European Court of Justice on Articles 30-36 in 1985' 23 CMLRev (1986) 325

Perrott, D., 'Pricing Policy and Community Rules on Competition and Free Movement of Goods' 1 Ybk EL (1981) 207

Petersen, M., 'Capital Movements and Payments under the EEC Treaty after Casati' 7 ELR (1982) 167

Quinn, M. and MacGowan, N., 'Could Article 30 impose Obligations on Individuals?' 12 ELR (1987) 163

Usher, J., 'The Consequences of the Notion of a Single Market' [1977] II LIEI 39

Van Ballegooijen, D., 'Free Movement of Capital in the European Economic Community' [1976] II LIEI 1

Woolridge, F. and Plender, R., 'Charges having an Effect Equivalent to Customs Duties' 3 ELR (1978) 101

7

FREE MOVEMENT OF WORKERS

I THE PROGRAMME

The States parties to the ECSC Treaty took only a small and hesitant step towards the creation of a free market in labour for the coal and steel industries.

ECSC Treaty

Article 69

1. Member States undertake to remove any restriction based on nationality upon the employment in the coal and steel industries of workers who are nationals of Member States and have recognised qualifications in a coalmining or steelmaking occupation, subject to the limitations imposed by the basic requirements of health and public policy.

2. For the purpose of applying this provision, Member States shall draw up common definitions of skilled trades and qualifications therefor, shall determine by common accord the limitations provided for in paragraph 1, and shall endeavour to work out arrangements on a Community-wide basis for bringing offers of employment into touch with applications for employment.

3. In addition, with regard to workers not covered by paragraph 2, they shall, should growth of coal or steel production be hampered by a shortage of suitable labour, adjust their immigration rules to the extent needed to remedy this state of affairs; in particular, they shall facilitate the re-employment of workers from the coal and steel industries of other Member States.

4. They shall prohibit any discrimination in remuneration and working conditions between nationals and immigrant workers, without prejudice to special measures concerning frontier workers; in particular, they shall endeavour to settle among themselves any matters remaining to be dealt with in order to ensure that social security arrangements do not inhibit labour mobility...

This article shall not affect the international obligations of Member States.

They took a step only slightly larger in the Euratom Treaty. Article 96 of that Treaty makes provision similar, *mutatis mutandis,* to that of Article 69 of the

ECSC Treaty; and Article 97 proscribes the application of restrictions based on nationality to persons in a Member State desiring to participate in the construction of nuclear installations in the Community. In the case of the EEC Treaty, however, the contracting parties felt able to make a more confident stride. For the purpose of promoting the homogeneous development of economic activities within their several territories, in accordance with Article 2 of the EEC Treaty, the Member States agreed in Article 3(c) that the Community's activities should include the abolition of obstacles to the free movement of persons. To that end they set out a number of principles designed to secure freedom of movement for workers by the end of 1969.

EEC Treaty

Article 48

1. Freedom of movement for workers shall be secured within the Community by the end of the transitional period at the latest.

2. Such freedom of movement shall entail the abolition of any discrimination based on nationality between workers of the Member States as regards employment, remuneration and other conditions of work and employment.

3. It shall entail the right, subject to limitations justified on grounds of public policy, public security or public health:

(a) to accept offers of employment actually made;
(b) to move freely within the territory of Member States for this purpose;
(c) to stay in a Member State for the purpose of employment in accordance with the provisions governing the employment of nationals of that State laid down by law, regulation or administrative action;
(d) to remain in the territory of a Member State after having been employed in that State, subject to conditions which shall be embodied in implementing regulations to be drawn up by the Commission.

4. The provisions of this article shall not apply to employment in the public service.

Article 49

As soon as this Treaty enters into force, the Council shall, acting on a proposal from the Commission and after consulting the Economic and Social Committee, issue directives or make regulations setting out the measures required to bring about, by progressive stages, freedom of movement for workers, as defined in Article 48, in particular:

(a) by ensuring close cooperation between national employment services;
(b) by systematically and progressively abolishing those administrative procedures and practices and those qualifying periods in respect of eligibility for available employment, whether resulting from national legislation or from agreements previously concluded between Member States, the maintenance of which would form an obstacle to liberalisation of the movement of workers;
(c) by systematically and progressively abolishing all such qualifying periods and other restrictions, provided for either under national legislation or under agreements previously concluded between Member States, as imposed on

workers of other Member States conditions regarding the free choice of employment other than those imposed on workers of the State concerned;

(d) by setting up appropriate machinery to bring offers of employment into touch with applications for employment and to facilitate the achievement of a balance between supply and demand in the employment market in such a way as to avoid serious threats to the standard of living and level of employment in the various regions and industries.

Article 50

Member States shall, within the framework of a joint programme, encourage the exchange of young workers.

Acting in pursuance of Article 49 the Council set out to achieve the objects defined in the antecedent article in three stages. The first stage was initiated by Regulation No 15 of 15 August 1961 (JO, p. 1073/61), which established the principle that every national of a Member State is free to take employment in the territory of another Member State provided that no suitable employee is available among the work force of the other State. The same regulation stipulated that provision should be made to facilitate the admission of migrant workers' families to the Member States in which those workers are employed. It set out to abolish discrimination on grounds of nationality between workers of the several Member States in the case of recruitment of personnel already resident in the country of proposed employment. The second stage of the Council's programme was initiated by Regulation No 38 of 25 March 1964 which reduced the preferences enjoyed by members of the work force of the State of employment, while permitting Member States to restore the priority of the domestic labour market in certain well-defined situations. The third stage was initiated by Council Regulation No 1612 of 15 October 1968 (JO, p. 295/12), which remains in force, although amended in 1976.

Council Regulation No 1612/68 of 15 October 1968 on freedom of movement for workers within the Community JO 1968 L 257/2; OJ Sp Ed 1968-69 475

[Amended by Council Regulation No 312/76 of 9 February 1976, OJ 1976 L 39/3]

THE COUNCIL OF THE EUROPEAN COMMUNITIES,

...

Whereas freedom of movement constitutes a fundamental right of workers and their families; whereas mobility of labour within the Community must be one of the means by which the worker is guaranteed the possibility of improving his living and working conditions and promoting his social advancement, while helping to satisfy the requirements of the economies of the Member States; whereas the right of all workers in the Member States to pursue the activity of their choice within the Community should be affirmed,

Whereas such right must be enjoyed without discrimination by permanent, seasonal and frontier workers and by those who pursue their activities for the purpose of providing services...

HAS ADOPTED THIS REGULATION:

PART I

EMPLOYMENT AND WORKERS' FAMILIES

Article 1

1. Any national of a Member State shall, irrespective of his place of residence, have the right to take up an activity as an employed person, and to pursue such activity within the territory of another Member State in accordance with the provisions laid down by law, regulation or administrative action governing the employment of nationals of that State.

2. He shall, in particular, have the right to take up available employment in the territory of another Member State with the same priority as nationals of that State.

Article 2

Any national of a Member State and any employer pursuing an activity in the territory of a Member State may exchange their applications for any offers of employment, and may conclude and perform contracts of employment in accordance with the provisions in force laid down by law, regulation or administrative action, without any discrimination resulting therefrom.

Article 3

1. Under this regulation, provisions laid down by law, regulation or administrative action or administrative practices of a Member State shall not apply:

– where they limit application for and offers of employment or the right of foreign nationals to take up and pursue employment, or subject these to conditions not applicable in respect of their own nationals; or

– where, though applicable irrespective of nationality, their exclusive or principal aim or effect is to keep nationals of other Member States away from the employment offered.

This provision shall not apply to conditions relating to linguistic knowledge required by reason of the nature of the post to be filled...

Article 4

1. Provisions laid down by law, regulation or administrative action of the Member States which restrict by number or percentage the employment of foreign nationals in any undertaking, branch of activity or region, or at a national level, shall not apply to nationals of the other Member States...

Article 5

A national of a Member State who seeks employment in the territory of another Member State shall receive the same assistance there as that afforded by the employment offices in that State to their own nationals seeking employment.

Article 6

1. The engagement and recruitment of a national of one Member State for a post in another Member State shall not depend on medical, vocational or other criteria which are discriminatory on grounds of nationality by comparison with those applied to nationals of the other Member State who wish to pursue the same activity...

Article 7

1. A worker who is a national of a Member State may not, in the territory of another Member State, be treated differently from national workers by reason of his nationality in respect of any conditions of employment and work, in particular as regards remuneration, dismissal and, should he become unemployed, reinstatement or re-employment.
2. He shall enjoy the same social and tax advantages as national workers.
3. He shall also, by virtue of the same right and under the same conditions as national workers, have access to training in vocational schools and retraining centres.
4. Any clause of a collective or individual agreement or of any other collective regulation concerning eligibility for employment, employment, remuneration and other conditions of work or dismissal shall be null and void in so far as it lays down or authorises discriminatory conditions in respect of workers who are nationals of the other Member States.

Article 8

1. A worker who is a national of a Member State and who is employed in the territory of another Member State shall enjoy equality of treatment as regards membership of trade unions and the exercise of rights attaching thereto, including the right to vote and to be eligible for the administration or management posts of a trade union; he may be excluded from taking part in the management of bodies governed by public law and from holding an office governed by public law. Furthermore, he shall have the right of eligibility for workers' representative bodies in the undertaking. The provisions of this article shall not affect laws or regulations in certain Member States which grant more extensive rights to workers coming from the other Member States.

Article 9

1. A worker who is a national of a Member State and who is employed in the territory of another Member State shall enjoy all the rights and benefits accorded to national workers in matters of housing, including ownership of the housing he needs.
2. Such worker may, with the same right as nationals, put his name down on the housing lists in the region in which he is employed, where such lists exist; he shall enjoy the resultant benefits and priorities.

If his family has remained in the country whence he came, they shall be considered for this purpose as residing in the said region, where national workers benefit from a similar presumption...

Article 10

1. The following shall, irrespective of their nationality, have the right to install themselves with a worker who is a national of one Member State and who is employed in the territory of another Member State:
   (a) his spouse and their descendants who are under the age of 21 years or are dependants;

(b) dependent relatives in the ascending line of the worker and his spouse.

2. Member States shall facilitate the admission of any member of the family not coming within the provisions of paragraph 1 if dependent on the worker referred to above or living under his roof in the country whence he comes.

3. For the purposes of paragraphs 1 and 2, the worker must have available for his family housing considered as normal for national workers in the region where he is employed; this provision, however, must not give rise to discrimination between national workers and workers from the other Member States.

Article 11

Where a national of a Member State is pursuing an activity as an employed or self-employed person in the territory of another Member State, his spouse and those of the children who are under the age of 21 years or dependent on him shall have the right to take up any activity as an employed person throughout the territory of that same State even if they are not nationals of any Member State...

PART II

CLEARANCE OF VACANCIES
AND APPLICATIONS FOR EMPLOYMENT

Article 15

1. At least once a month the specialist service of each Member State shall send to the specialist services of the other Member States and to the European Coordination Office a return showing by occupation and by region:

(a) vacancies unfilled or unlikely to be filled by manpower from the national labour market;

(b) applicants for employment who have declared themselves actually ready and able to accept employment in another country.

The specialist service of each Member States shall forward such information to the appropriate employment services and agencies.

2. The returns referred to in paragraph 1 shall be circulated according to a uniform system to be established by the European Coordination Office in collaboration with the Technical Committee, within eighteen months following the entry into force of this regulation.

Article 16

1. Any vacancy communicated to the employment services of a Member State which cannot be filled from the national labour market and which, on the basis of the returns referred to in Article 15, can be cleared within the Community, shall be notified to the competent employment services of the Member State which has indicated that it has manpower available in the same occupation...

Article 19

1. Twice a year, on the basis of a report from the Commission drawn up from information supplied by the Member States, the latter and the Commission shall together analyse:

- the results of Community arrangements for vacancy clearance;
- the number of placings of nationals of non-Member States;
- the foreseeable developments in the state of the labour market and, as far as possible, the movements of manpower within the Community.

2. The Member States shall examine with the Commission all the possibilities of giving priority to nationals of Member States when filling employment vacancies in order to achieve a balance between vacancies and applications for employment within the Community. They shall adopt all measures necessary for this purpose.

Article 20

1. When a Member State undergoes or foresees disturbances on its labour market which could seriously threaten the standard of living or level of employment in a given region or occupation, that State shall inform the Commission and the other Member States thereof and shall supply them with all relevant particulars.

2. The Member States and the Commission shall take all suitable measures to inform Community workers so that they shall not apply for employment in that region or occupation.

3. Without prejudice to the application of the Treaty and of the Protocols annexed thereto, the Member State referred to in paragraph 1 may request the Commission to state that, in order to restore to normal the situation in that region or occupation, the operation of the clearance machinery provided for in Articles 15, 16 and 17 should be partially or totally suspended.

The Commission shall decide on the suspension as such and on the duration thereof not later than two weeks after receiving such request. Any Member State may, within a strict time limit of two weeks, request the Council to annul or amend any such decision. The Council shall act on any such request within two weeks.

4. Where such suspension does take place, the employment services of the other Member States which have indicated that they have workers available shall not take any action to fill vacancies notified directly to them by employers in the Member States referred to in paragraph 1.

Article 21

The European Office for Coordinating the Clearance of Vacancies and Applications for Employment, established within the Commission (called in this regulation the 'European Coordination Office') shall have the general task of promoting vacancy clearance at Community level. It shall be responsible in particular for all the technical duties in this field which, under the provisions of this regulation, are assigned to the Commission, and especially for assisting the national employment services.

It shall summarise the information referred to in Articles 14 and 15 and the data arising out of the studies and research carried out pursuant to Article 13, so as to bring to light any useful facts about foreseeable developments on the Community labour market; such facts shall be communicated to the specialist services of the Member States and to the Advisory and Technical Committees...

PART III
COMMITTEES FOR ENSURING CLOSE COOPERATION BETWEEN THE MEMBER STATES IN MATTERS CONCERNING THE FREEDOM OF MOVEMENT OF WORKERS AND THEIR EMPLOYMENT

Article 24

The Advisory Committee shall be responsible for assisting the Commission in the examination of any questions arising from the application of the Treaty and measures taken in pursuance thereof, in matters concerning the freedom of movement of workers and their employment...

Article 26

1. The Advisory Committee shall be composed of six members for each Member State, two of whom shall represent the Government, two the trade unions and two the employers' associations.

2. For each of the categories referred to in paragraph 1, one alternate member shall be appointed by each Member State...

Article 32

The Technical Committee shall be responsible for assisting the Commission to prepare, promote and follow up all technical work and measures for giving effect to this regulation and any supplementary measures...

Article 34

1. The Technical Committee shall be composed of representatives of the Governments of the Member States. Each Government shall appoint as member of the Technical Committee one of the members who represent it on the Advisory Committee.

2. Each Government shall appoint an alternate from among its other representatives – members or alternates – on the Advisory Committee...

PART IV
TRANSITIONAL AND FINAL PROVISIONS

Article 42

1. This regulation shall not affect the provisions of the Treaty establishing the European Coal and Steel Community which relate to workers with recognised qualifications in coalmining or steelmaking, nor those of the Treaty establishing the European Atomic Energy Community which deal with eligibility for skilled employment in the field of nuclear energy, nor any measures taken in pursuance of those Treaties.

Nevertheless, this regulation shall apply to categories of workers referred to in the first subparagraph and to members of their families in so far as their legal position is not governed by the above-mentioned Treaties or measures.

2. This regulation shall not affect measures taken in accordance with Article 51 of the Treaty.

3. This regulation shall not affect the obligations of Member States arising out of:

- special relations or future agreements with certain non-European countries or territories, based on institutional ties existing at the time of the entry into force of this regulation: or
- agreements in existence at the time of entry into force of this regulation with certain non-European countries or territories, based on institutional ties between them.

Workers from such countries or territories who, in accordance with this provision, are pursuing activities as employed persons in the territory of one of the Member States may not invoke the benefit of the provision of this regulation in the territory of the other Member States.

This regulation shall be binding in its entirety and directly applicable in all Member States.

On the day on which it made Regulation No 1612/68 the Council issued Directive No 68/360 which provides for the issuance of Community 'residence permits' to workers of Member States. These are valid for a minimum of five years and are to be renewed automatically on production of evidence of identity and of documentary proof that employment will remain available to the worker in the State in question.

Council Directive No 68/360 of 15 October 1968 on the Abolition of Restrictions on Movement and Residence within the Community for Workers of Member States and their families

JO 1968 L 257/13; OJ Sp Ed 1968-69, 485.

THE COUNCIL OF THE EUROPEAN COMMUNITIES,

...

Whereas Council Regulation (EEC) No 1612/68 fixed the provisions governing freedom of movement for workers within the Community; whereas, consequently, measures should be adopted for the abolition of restrictions which still exist concerning movement and residence within the Community, which conform to the rights and privileges accorded by the said regulation to nationals of any Member State who move in order to pursue activities as employed persons and to members of their families;

Whereas the rules applicable to residence should, as far as possible, bring the position of workers from other Member States and members of their families into line with that of nationals;

...

HAS ADOPTED THIS DIRECTIVE:

Article 1

Member States shall, acting as provided in this directive, abolish restrictions on the movement and residence of nationals of the said States and of members of their families to whom Regulation (EEC) No 1612/68 applies.

Article 2

1. Member States shall grant the nationals referred to in Article 1 the right to leave their territory in order to take up activities as employed persons and to pursue such activities in the territory of another Member State. Such right shall be exercised simply on production of a valid identity card or passport. Members of the family shall enjoy the same right as the national on whom they are dependent.

2. Member States shall, acting in accordance with their laws, issue to such nationals, or renew, an identity card or passport which shall state in particular the holder's nationality.

3. The passport must be valid at least for all Member States and for countries through which the holder must pass when travelling between Member States. Where a passport is the only document on which the holder may lawfully leave the country, its period of validity shall be not less than five years.

4. Member States may not demand from the nationals referred to in Article 1 any exit visa or any equivalent document.

Article 3

1. Member States shall allow the persons referred to in Article 1 to enter their territory simply on production of a valid identity card or passport.

2. No entry visa or equivalent document may be demanded save from members of the family who are not nationals of a Member State. Member States shall accord to such persons every facility for obtaining any necessary visas.

Article 4

1. Member States shall grant the right of residence in their territory to the persons referred to in Article 1 who are able to produce the documents listed in paragraph 3.

2. As proof of the right of residence, a document entitled 'Residence Permit for a National of a Member State of the EEC' shall be issued. This document must include a statement that it has been issued pursuant to Regulation (EEC) No 1612/68 and to the measures taken by the Member States for the implementation of the present directive. The text of such statement is given in the Annex to this directive.

3. For the issue of a Residence Permit for a National of a Member State of the EEC, Member States may require only the production of the following documents;

– by the worker:
  (a) the document with which he entered their territory;
  (b) a confirmation of engagement from the employer or a certificate of employment;
– by the members of the worker's family:
  (c) the document with which they entered the territory;
  (d) a document issued by the competent authority of the State of origin or the State whence they came, proving their relationship;
  (e) in the cases referred to in Article 10(1) and (2) of Regulation (EEC) No 1612/68, a document issued by the competent authority of the State of origin or the State whence they came, testifying that they are dependent on the worker or that they live under his roof in such country.

4. A member of the family who is not a national of a Member State shall be issued with a residence document which shall have the same validity as that issued to the worker on whom he is dependent.

Article 5

Completion of the formalities for obtaining a residence permit shall not hinder the immediate beginning of employment under a contract concluded by the applicants.

Article 6

1. The residence permit:
   (a) must be valid throughout the territory of the Member State which issued it;
   (b) must be valid for at least five years from the date of issue and be automatically renewable.

2. Breaks in residence not exceeding six consecutive months and absence on military service shall not affect the validity of a residence permit.

3. Where a worker is employed for a period exceeding three months but not exceeding a year in the service of an employer in the host State or in the employ of a person providing services, the host Member State shall issue him a temporary residence permit, the validity of which may be limited to the expected period of the employment.

Subject to the provisions of Article 8(1)(c), a temporary residence permit shall be issued also to a seasonal worker employed for a period of more than three months. The period of employment must be shown in the documents referred to in paragraph 4(3)(b).

Article 7

1. A valid residence permit may not be withdrawn from a worker solely on the grounds that he is no longer in employment, either because he is temporarily incapable of work as a result of illness or accident, or because he is involuntarily unemployed, this being duly confirmed by the competent employment office.

2. When the residence permit is renewed for the first time, the period of residence may be restricted, but not to less than twelve months, where the worker has been involuntarily unemployed in the Member State for more than twelve consecutive months.

Article 8

1. Member States shall, without issuing a residence permit, recognise the right of residence in their territory of:
   (a) a worker pursuing an activity as an employed person, where the activity is not expected to last for more than three months. The document with which the person concerned entered the territory and a statement by the employer on the expected duration of the employment shall be sufficient to cover his stay; a statement by the employer shall not, however, be required in the case of workers coming within the provisions of the Council Directive of 25 February 1964 on the attainment of freedom of establishment and freedom to provide services in respect of the activities of intermediaries in commerce, industry and small craft industries;
   (b) a worker who, while having his residence in the territory of a Member State to which he returns, as a rule, each day or at least once a week, is employed in the territory of another Member State. The competent authority of the State where he is employed may issue such worker with a special permit valid for five years and automatically renewable;
   (c) a seasonal worker who holds a contract of employment stamped by the competent authority of the Member State on whose territory he has come to pursue his activities.

2. In all cases referred to in paragraph 1, the competent authorities of the host Member State may require the worker to report his presence in the territory.

Article 9

1. The residence documents granted to nationals of a Member State of the EEC referred to in this directive shall be issued and renewed free of charge or on payment of an amount not exceeding the dues and taxes charged for the issue of identity cards to nationals.

2. The visa referred to in Article 3(2) and the stamp referred to in Article 8(1)(c) shall be free of charge.

3. Member States shall take the necessary steps to simplify as much as possible the formalities and procedure for obtaining the documents mentioned in paragraph 1.

Article 10

Member States shall not derogate from the provisions of this directive save on grounds of public policy, public security or public health.

Article 11

1. This directive shall not affect the provisions of the Treaty establishing the European Coal and Steel Community which relate to workers with recognised skills in coalmining and steelmaking, or the provisions of the Treaty establishing the European Atomic Energy Community which deal with the right to take up skilled employment in the field of nuclear energy, or any measures taken in implementation of those Treaties.

2. Nevertheless, this directive shall apply to the categories of workers referred to in paragraph 1, and to members of their families, in so far as their legal position is not governed by the above-mentioned Treaties or measures.

...

ANNEX

Text of the statement referred to in Article 4(2):

'This permit is issued pursuant to Regulation (EEC) No 1612/68 of the Council of the European Communities of 15 October 1968 and to the measures taken in implementation of the Council Directive of 15 October 1968.

'In accordance with the provisions of the above-mentioned regulation, the holder of this permit has the right to take up and pursue an activity as an employed person in ....* territory under the same conditions as ....* workers'.

* Belgian, German, French, Italian, Luxembourg, Netherlands, according to the country issuing the permit.

More recently the Commission has made a regulation designed to implement Article 48(3)(d) of the EEC Treaty.

Commission Regulation No 1251/70 of 29 June 1970
JO 1970 L 142/24; OJ Sp Ed 1970 402

Article 2

1. The following shall have the right to remain permanently in the territory of a Member State:

(a) a worker who, at the time of termination of his activity, has reached the age laid down by the law of that Member State for entitlement to an old-age pension and who has been employed in that State for at least the last twelve months and has resided there continuously for more than three years;

(b) a worker who, having resided continuously in the territory of that State for more than two years, ceases to work there as an employed person as a result of permanent incapacity to work. If such incapacity is the result of an accident at work or an occupational disease entitling him to a pension for which an institution of that State is entirely or partially responsible, no condition shall be imposed as to length of residence;

(c) a worker who, after three years' continuous employment and residence in the territory of that State, works as an employed person in the territory of another Member State, while retaining his residence in the territory of the first State, to which he returns, as a rule, each day or at least once a week.

Periods of employment completed in this way in the territory of the other Member State shall, for the purposes of entitlement to the rights referred to in subparagraphs (a) and (b), be considered as having been completed in the territory of the State of residence...

II TERRITORIAL APPLICATION

Article 48 of the EEC Treaty and Article 1 of Council Regulation No 1612/68 stipulate that the free movement of labour, and its associated rights, are to be secured or enjoyed within 'the Community' or 'the territory of Member States'. For guidance as to the meaning of these expressions, we must look elsewhere.

EEC Treaty

[Amended by Act of Accession, Article 26 and Adaptation Decision, Article 15.]

Article 227

1. This Treaty shall apply to the Kingdom of Belgium, the Kingdom of Denmark, the Federal Republic of Germany, the French Republic, Ireland, the Italian Republic, the Grand Duchy of Luxembourg, the Kingdom of the Netherlands and the United Kingdom of Great Britain and Northern Ireland.

2. With regard to Algeria and the French overseas departments, the general and particular provisions of this Treaty relating to:

- the free movement of goods;
- agriculture, save for Article 40(4);
- the liberalisation of services;

– the rules on competition;
– the protective measures provided for in Articles 108, 109 and 226;
– the institutions,

shall apply as soon as this Treaty enters into force.

The conditions under which the other provisions of this Treaty are to apply shall be determined, within two years of the entry into force of this Treaty, by decisions of the Council, acting unanimously on a proposal from the Commission...

4. The provisions of this Treaty shall apply to the European territories for whose external relations a Member State is responsible.

5. Notwithstanding the preceding paragraphs:

(a) This Treaty shall not apply to the Faroe Islands. The Government of the Kingdom of Denmark may, however, give notice, by a declaration deposited by 31 December 1975 at the latest with the Government of the Italian Republic, which shall transmit a certified copy thereof to each of the Governments of the other Member States, that this Treaty shall apply to those Islands. In that event, this Treaty shall apply to those Islands from the first day of the second month following the deposit of the declaration.

(b) This Treaty shall not apply to the Sovereign Base Areas of the United Kingdom of Great Britain and Northern Ireland in Cyprus.

(c) This Treaty shall apply to the Channel Islands and the Isle of Man only to the extent necessary to ensure the implementation of the arrangements for those Islands set out in the Treaty concerning the accession of new Member States to the European Economic Community and to the European Atomic Energy Community signed on 22 January 1972.

In accordance with Article 227(2), the Council on 15 October 1968 made a decision extending to the French Overseas Territories Articles 48 and 49 of the EEC Treaty as well as the measures taken in their application (Decision No 68/359, JO L 257, p. 1). French Guyana, Guadeloupe, Martinique and Réunion are thus included in the area within which the free movement of labour is to be secured.

Algeria is not included in that area. Even so, for the purpose of determining the social security rights of migrant workers who have spent parts of their lives in Algeria it remains important that, despite the advent of independence in 1962, Algeria was not until 30 June 1965 eliminated from the definition of French territory annexed to Council Regulation No 3 on the social security of migrants (JO 1958, p. 561). Thus, in 1976 the European Court considered the case of a Belgian national, then resident in France, who had been resident in Algeria from 1957 to 1961. It ruled that the principle of the equal treatment of workers, laid down by Articles 48 to 51 of the EEC Treaty, implied that provisions of French law could not be applied to the Belgian worker so as to deprive him of a benefit awarded to French workers, namely the inclusion of insurance periods completed in Algeria in the calculation of old-age pension: Case 112/75 *Sécurité Sociale Nancy* v *Hirardin* [1976] ECR 553.

On ratifying the EEC Treaty the Government of the Federal Republic of Germany declared that it applied equally to the *Land* Berlin.

The Dutch Antilles, although constitutionally part of the Kingdom of the Netherlands, are excluded from the area within which free movement of labour is secured, by an annexure to the EEC Treaty (Protocol on the Application of the Treaty establishing the EEC to Non-European Parts of the Kingdom of the Netherlands). Although the Member States have expressed willingness to include them within the area of free movement of labour, the Netherlands Antilles have preferred to remain outside it.

III PERSONAL APPLICATION

Articles 48 and 49 of the EEC Treaty identify as the beneficiaries of the programme 'workers' or 'workers of the Member States'.

To determine whether a person is a 'worker' it is appropriate to apply a uniform criterion of European Community law. It is not appropriate to apply the law of employment or contract in the particular Member State in which the individual is engaged: Case 75/63 *Hoekstra (née Unger)* v *Bestuur der Bedrijfs-vereniging voor Detailhandel en Ambachten* [1964] ECR 177. According to the European Court, the determining characteristic of a 'worker' is that he or she performs services of some economic value for and under the direction of another person, in return for which he or she receives remuneration.

Case 66/85 Deborah Lawrie-Blum v Land Baden-Württemberg
[1986] ECR 2121; [1987] 3 CMLR 389

Deborah Lawrie-Blum was a British national. After passing at the University of Freiburg the first examination for the profession of teacher at a Gymnasium, she was refused admission to the period of probationary service leading to the second examination, which qualifies successful candidates for appointment as teachers. The refusal was based on a law of the *Land* which required possession of German nationality for admission to probationary service. Mrs Lawrie-Blum contended that in refusing on grounds of nationality to admit her to probationary service, the authorities of the *Land* had infringed her rights under Article 48(2) of the EEC Treaty. The *Land* contended, *inter alia,* that a probationary teacher is not a 'worker' within the meaning of Article 48.

The Court

Mrs Lawrie-Blum considers that any paid activity must be regarded as an economic activity and that the sphere in which it is exercised must necessarily be of an economic nature. A restrictive interpretation of Article 48(1) would reduce freedom of movement to a mere instrument of economic integration, would be contrary to its broader objective of creating an area in which Community citizens enjoy freedom of movement and would deprive the exception in Article 48(4) of any meaning of its own. The term 'worker' covers any person performing for remuneration work the nature of which is not determined by himself for and under the control of another, regardless of the legal nature of the employment relationship.

The *Land* Baden-Württemberg espouses the considerations put forward by the Bundesverwaltungsgericht in its order for reference to the effect that, since a trainee teacher's activity falls under education policy, it is not an economic activity within the meaning of Article 2 of the Treaty. The term 'worker' within the meaning of Article 48 of the Treaty and Regulation No 1612/68 covers only persons whose relationship to their employer is governed by a contract subject to private law and not persons whose employment relationship is subject to public law. The period of preparatory service should be regarded as the last stage of the professional training of future teachers.

The United Kingdom considers that a distinction between students and workers must be made on the basis of objective criteria and that the term 'worker' in Article 48 must be given a Community definition. Objectively defined, a 'worker' is a person who is obliged to provide services to another in return for monetary reward and who is subject to the direction or control of the other person as regards the way in which the work is done. In the present case, account must be taken of the fact that a trainee teacher is required, at least towards the end of the period of preparatory service, to conduct lessons and therefore provides an economically valuable service for which he receives remuneration which is based on the starting salary of a duly appointed teacher.

The Commission takes the view that the criterion for the application of Article 48 is the existence of an employment relationship, regardless of the legal nature of that relationship and its purpose. The fact that the period of preparatory service is a compulsory stage in the preparation for the practice of a profession and that it is spent in the public service is irrelevant if the objective criteria for defining the term 'worker', namely the existence of a relationship of subordination *vis-à-vis* the employer, irrespective of the nature of that relationship, the actual provision of services and the payment of remuneration, are satisfied.

Since freedom of movement for workers constitutes one of the fundamental principles of the Community, the term 'worker' in Article 48 may not be interpreted differently according to the law of each Member State but has a Community meaning. Since it defines the scope of that fundamental freedom, the Community concept of a 'worker' must be interpreted broadly...

That concept must be defined in accordance with objective criteria which distinguish the employment relationship by reference to the rights and duties of the persons concerned. *The essential feature of an employment relationship, however, is that for a certain period of time a person performs services for and under the direction of another person in return for which he receives remuneration.*

In the present case, it is clear that during the entire period of preparatory service the trainee teacher is under the direction and supervision of the school to which he is assigned. It is the school that determines the services to be performed by him and his working hours and it is the school's instructions that he must carry out and its rules that he must observe. During a substantial part of the preparatory service he is required to give lessons to the school's pupils and thus provides a service of some economic value to the school. The amounts which he receives may be regarded as remuneration for the services provided and for the duties involved in completing the period of preparatory service. Consequently, the three criteria for the existence of an employment relationship are fulfilled in this case.

The fact that teachers' preparatory service, like apprenticeships in other occupations, may be regarded as practical preparation directly related to the actual pursuit of the occupation in point is not a bar to the application of Article 48(1) if the service is performed under the conditions of an activity as an employed person.

Nor may it be objected that services performed in education do not fall within the scope of the EEC Treaty because they are not of an economic nature. All that is required for the application of Article 48 is that the activity should be in the nature of work performed for remuneration, irrespective of the sphere in which it is carried out (see the judgment of 12 December 1974 in Case 36/74 *Walrave* v *Union Cycliste Internationale* [1974] ECR 1405). Nor may the economic nature of those activities be denied on the ground that they are performed by persons whose status is governed by public law since, as the Court pointed out in its judgment of 12 February 1974 in Case 152/73 (*Sotgiu* v *Deutsche Bundespost* [1974] ECR 153), the nature of the legal relationship between employee and employer, whether involving public law status or a private law contract, is immaterial as regards the application of Article 48.

The fact that trainee teachers give lessons for only a few hours a week and are paid remuneration below the starting salary of a qualified teacher does not prevent them from being regarded as workers. In its judgment in *Levin* [see below, p. 290], the Court held that the expressions 'worker' and 'activity as an employed person' must be understood as including persons who, because they are not employed full time, receive lower pay than that for full-time employment, provided that the activities performed are effective and genuine. The latter requirement is not called into question in this case.

Consequently, the reply to the first part of the question must be that a trainee teacher who, under the direction and supervision of the school authorities, is undergoing a period of service in preparation for the teaching profession during which he provides services by giving lessons and receives remuneration must be regarded as a worker within the meaning of Article 48(1) of the EEC Treaty, irrespective of the legal nature of the employment relationship.

A person who is employed as a worker for only part of his or her time benefits from Articles 48–50 of the EEC Treaty provided that he or she pursues an activity as an employed person which is effective and genuine. It is immaterial that the employment yields an income lower than that considered as the minimum for subsistence; and despite the implication to the contrary in the final three words of Article 48(3)(b) of the EEC Treaty, the motives which may have prompted the worker to seek employment in another Member State are of no account.

Case 53/81 D.M. Levin v Staatssecretaris van Justitie

[1982] ECR 1035; [1982] 2 CMLR 454

[typographical error corrected by editor]

The Court

...

The appellant in the main proceedings, Mrs Levin, of British nationality and the wife of a national of a non-Member country, applied for a permit to reside in the Netherlands. The permit was refused, on the basis of Netherlands legislation, on the ground, amongst others, that Mrs Levin was not engaged in a gainful occupation in the Netherlands and therefore could not be described as a 'favoured EEC citizen' within the meaning of that legislation.

...

Under Article 48 of the Treaty freedom of movement for workers is to be secured within the Community. That freedom is to entail the abolition of any discrimination based on nationality between workers of the Member States as regards employment, remuneration and other conditions of work and is to include the right, subject to limitations justified on grounds of public policy, public security or public health, to accept offers of employment actually made, to move freely within the territory of Member States for this purpose, to stay in a Member State for the purpose of employment and to remain there after the termination of that employment.

That provision was implemented *inter alia* by Regulation (EEC) No 1612/68 of the Council of 15 October 1968 on freedom of movement for workers within the Community ... and Council Directive No 68/360/EEC of the same date on the abolition of restrictions on movement and residence within the Community for workers of the Member States and their families ... Under Article 1 of Regulation (EEC) No 1612/68 any national of a Member State is, irrespective of his place of residence, to have the right to take up activity as an employed person, and to pursue such activity, within the territory of another Member State, in accordance with the provisions laid down by law, regulation or administrative action governing the employment of nationals of that State.

Although the rights deriving from the principle of freedom of movement for workers and more particularly the right to enter and stay in the territory of a Member State are thus linked to the status of a worker or of a person pursuing an activity as an employed person or desirous of so doing, the terms 'worker' and 'activity as an employed person' are not expressly defined in any of the provisions on the subject. It is appropriate, therefore, in order to determine their meaning, to have recourse to the generally recognised principles of interpretation, beginning with the ordinary meaning to be attributed to those terms in their context and in the light of the objectives of the Treaty.

The Netherlands and Danish Governments have maintained that the provisions of Article 48 may only be relied upon by persons who receive a wage at least commensurate with the means of subsistence considered as necessary by the legislation of the Member State in which they work, or who work at least for the number of hours considered as usual in respect of full-time employment in the sector in question. In the absence of any provisions to that effect in Community legislation, it is suggested that it is necessary to have recourse to national criteria for the purpose of defining both the minimum wage and the minimum number of hours.

That argument cannot, however, be accepted. As the Court has already stated in its judgment of 19 March 1964 in Case 75/63 *Hoekstra (née Unger)* [1964] ECR 177 the terms 'worker' and 'activity as an employed person' may not be defined by reference to the national laws of the Member States but have a Community meaning. If that were not the case, the Community rules on freedom of movement for workers would be frustrated, as the meaning of those terms could be fixed and modified unilaterally, without any control by the Community institutions, by national laws which would thus be able to exclude at will certain categories of persons from the benefit of the Treaty.

Such would, in particular, be the case if the enjoyment of the rights conferred by the principle of freedom of movement for workers could be made subject to the criterion of what the legislation of the host State declares to be a minimum wage, so that the field of application *ratione personae* of the Community rules on this subject might vary from one Member State to another. The meaning and the scope of the terms 'worker' and 'activity as an employed person' should thus be clarified in the light of the principles of the legal order of the Community.

In this respect it must be stressed that these concepts define the field of application of one of the fundamental freedoms guaranteed by the Treaty and, as such, may not be interpreted restrictively.

In conformity with this view the recitals in the preamble to Regulation (EEC) No 1612/68 contain a general affirmation to the right of all workers in the Member States to pursue the activity of their choice within the Community, irrespective of whether they are permanent, seasonal or frontier workers or workers who pursue their activities for the purpose of providing services. Furthermore, although Article 4 of Directive No 68/360/EEC grants the right of residence to workers upon the mere production of the document on the basis of which they entered the territory and of a confirmation of engagement from the employer or a certificate of employment, it does not subject this right to any condition relating to the kind of employment or to the amount of income derived from it.

An interpretation which reflects the full scope of these concepts is also in conformity with the objectives of the Treaty which include, according to Articles 2 and 3, the abolition, as between Member States, of obstacles to freedom of movement for persons, with the purpose *inter alia* of promoting throughout the Community a harmonious development of economic activities and a raising of the standard of living. Since part-time employment, although it may provide an income lower than what is considered to be the minimum required for subsistence, constitutes for a large number of persons an effective means of improving their living conditions, the effectiveness of Community law would be impaired and the achievement of the objectives of the Treaty would be jeopardised if the enjoyment of rights conferred by the principle of freedom of movement for workers were reserved solely to persons engaged in full-time employment and earning, as a result, a wage at least equivalent to the guaranteed minimum wage in the sector under consideration.

It follows that the concepts of 'worker' and 'activity as an employed person' must be interpreted as meaning that the rules relating to freedom of movement for workers also concern persons who pursue or wish to pursue an activity as an employed person on a part-time basis only and who, by virtue of that fact, obtain or would obtain only remuneration lower than the minimum guaranteed remuneration in the sector under consideration. In this regard no distinction may be made between those who wish to make do with their income from such an activity and those who supplement that income with other income, whether the latter is derived from property or from the employment of a member of their family who accompanies them.

It should however be stated that whilst part-time employment is not excluded from the field of application of the rules of freedom of movement for workers, those rules cover only the pursuit of effective and genuine activities, to the exclusion of activities on such a small scale as to be regarded as purely marginal and ancillary. It follows both from the statement of the principle of freedom of movement for workers and from the place occupied by the rules relating to that principle in the system of the Treaty as a whole that those rules guarantee only the free movement of persons who pursue or are desirous of pursuing an economic activity.

The Court took its reasoning one step further in the *Kempf* case, where it added that a person who pursues a part-time activity may qualify as a 'worker' even if he supplements his income by recourse to public assistance.

Case 139/85 R.H. Kempf v Staatssecretaris van Justitie

[1986] ECR 1741; [1987] 1 CMLR 764

The Court

The plaintiff in the main action, Mr R. H. Kempf, a German national, entered the Netherlands on 1 September 1981 and worked there as a part-time music teacher giving 12 lessons a week from 26 October 1981 to 14 July 1982; at the end of that period the gross wages he was receiving for that work amounted to HFL 984 per month. In the same period he applied for and received supplementary benefit under the Wet Werkloosheids-voorziening [Law on Unemployment Benefit]. Benefits under that law, which come out of public funds, are payable to persons having the status of workers.

Mr Kempf subsequently became unable to work as a result of sickness and obtained social security benefits under the Ziektewet [Law on Sickness Insurance]. He also received supplementary benefits under both the above-mentioned Law on Unemployment Benefit and the Algemene Bijstandswet [Law on Social Assistance]. The last-mentioned law provides for general social assistance to the needy which is wholly financed out of public funds.

On 30 November 1981 Mr Kempf applied for a residence permit in the Netherlands in order to 'pursue an activity as an employed person' in that country. It was refused by a decision of the local chief of police dated 17 August 1982. The plaintiff then made an application for review to the Staatssecretaris van Justitie, which was rejected by a decision of 9 December 1982 on the ground, *inter alia,* that he did not qualify as a favoured EEC citizen within the meaning of the Netherlands legislation on immigration matters because he had had recourse to public funds in the Netherlands and was therefore manifestly unable to meet his needs out of the income received from his employment.

By an application dated 10 January 1983 Mr Kempf appealed against the decision of the Staatssecretaris van Justitie before the Judicial Division of the Raad van Staat. That is the background to the action before the Raad van Staat, which stayed the proceedings and referred the following question to this Court for a preliminary ruling:

'Where a national of a Member State pursues within the territory of another Member State an activity which may in itself be regarded as effective and genuine work within the meaning of the Court's judgment in Levin v Staatssecretaris *van Justitie, does the fact that*

he claims financial assistance payable out of the public funds of the latter Member State in order to supplement the income he receives from that activity exclude him from the provisions of Community law relating to freedom of movement for workers?'

...

The Court has consistently held that freedom of movement for workers forms one of the foundations of the Community. The provisions laying down that fundamental freedom and, more particularly, the terms 'worker' and 'activity as an employed person' defining the sphere of application of those freedoms must be given a broad interpretation in that regard, whereas exceptions to and derogations from the principle of freedom of movement for workers must be interpreted strictly.

It follows that the rules on this topic must be interpreted as meaning that a person in effective and genuine part-time employment cannot be excluded from their sphere of application merely because the remuneration he derives from it is below the level of the minimum means of subsistence and he seeks to supplement it by other lawful means of subsistence. In that regard it is irrelevant whether those supplementary means of subsistence are derived from property or from the employment of a member of his family, as was the case in Levin, *or whether, as in this instance, they are obtained from financial assistance drawn from the public funds of the Member State in which he resides, provided that the effective and genuine nature of his work is established.*

...

It will be noted that in Case 53/81 *Levin* v *Staatssecretaris van Justitie* the Court stated that the term 'worker' must be interpreted to embrace 'persons who pursue *or wish to pursue* an activity as an employed person' (emphasis added). The Court used similar language in Case 48/75 *Jean Noel Royer* [1976] ECR 497 at 512 ('to look for or pursue an occupation'). The language is consistent with the Opinion of Mr Advocate General Trabucchi in Case 118/75 *Watson and Belmann* [1976] ECR 1185 at 1204, where he stated that

> 'by placing a wide interpretation upon Article 48, notwithstanding the term of subparagraphs (a) and (b) of paragraph (3) ... it is, in my opinion, possible to recognise workers who have not previously received an offer of employment in another Member State as having the right to move freely'.

The point is not yet firmly decided, but indications are strong that a person may qualify as a 'worker' when he is unemployed but is actively in search of work.

The expression used in Article 48(2) of the EEC Treaty is not simply 'workers' but 'workers of the Member States'. It is plain from Article 1 of Council Regulation No 1612/68 that this expression must be taken to mean 'workers who are nationals of a Member State'. Indeed, the European Court has treated with the greatest of reserve the suggestion that the Commission is competent to regulate the admission or treatment of nationals of third States, even if acting in the exercise of the power under Article 118 to deal with social affairs: Joined Cases 281/86, 283/86, 284/86 and 287/86 *Germany and Netherlands* v *Commission*,

Parliament Intervening 9 July 1987. To determine whether a worker is a national of a Member State one must apply the law of that State. For the purposes of the free movement of workers, certain Member States have attributed a special meaning to the term 'national'.

Declaration by the Government of the Federal Republic of Germany on the Definition of the Expression 'German National'

At the time of signature of the Treaty establishing the European Economic Community and the Treaty establishing the European Atomic Energy Community, the Government of the Federal Republic of Germany makes the following declaration:

'All Germans as defined in the Basic Law for the Federal Republic of Germany shall be considered nationals of the Federal Republic of Germany'.

German Basic Law

Article 116 (DEFINITION OF 'GERMAN')

[Editor's Translation]

(1) Unless otherwise provided by law, a German within the meaning of this Basic Law is a person who possesses German citizenship or who has been admitted to the territory of the German Reich within the frontiers of 31 December 1937 as a refugee or expellee of German stock (Volkszugehoerigkeit) or as the spouse or descendant of such person...

Note from the Government of the United Kingdom of Great Britain and Northern Ireland to the Government of the Italian Republic concerning a Declaration by the Government of the United Kingdom of Great Britain and Northern Ireland replacing the Declaration on the Definition of the Term 'Nationals' made at the Time of Signature of the Treaty of Accession of 22 January 1972 by the United Kingdom of Great Britain and Northern Ireland to the European Communities

Her Majesty's Ambassador at Rome to the Minister for Foreign Affairs of Italy

British Embassy

Rome

December 31, 1982

Sir,

On instructions from Her Majesty's Principal Secretary of State for Foreign and Commonwealth Affairs, I have the honour to refer to the Treaty between the Member States of the European Communities and the Kingdom of Denmark, Ireland, the Kingdom of Norway and the United Kingdom of Great Britain and Northern Ireland concerning the accession of the latter State to the European Economic Community and to the European Atomic Energy Community, done at Brussels on January 22, 1972.

When the United Kingdom joined the European Communities in 1973 there was annexed to the Treaty of Accession a formal Declaration by the United Kingdom defining the term 'national' in relation to the United Kingdom for the purposes of the Treaties and Community legislation. A precise definition was necessary to identify in terms of United Kingdom legislation those persons who by virtue of their close connection with the United Kingdom itself or with Gibraltar would be entitled to the rights conferred by the Treaties, particularly in regard to free movement and the right of establishment.

Last year the United Kingdom Parliament revised British nationality law in terms of the British Nationality Act 1981. The entry into force of this Act on January 1, 1983 will mean that the United Kingdom Declaration no longer corresponds exactly with United Kingdom legislation. I am to inform you therefore that that Declaration is no longer valid and to communicate the following Declaration on behalf of the Government of the United Kingdom of Great Britain and Northern Ireland to replace it:

> 'In view of the entry into force of the British Nationality Act 1981, the Government of the United Kingdom of Great Britain and Northern Ireland makes the following Declaration, which will replace, as from January 1, 1983, that made at the time of signature of the Treaty of Accession by the United Kingdom to the European Communities:
>
> 'As to the United Kingdom of Great Britain and Northern Ireland the terms "nationals", "nationals of Member States" or "nationals of Member States and overseas countries and territories" wherever used in the Treaty establishing the European Economic Community, the Treaty establishing the European Atomic Energy Community or the Treaty establishing the European Coal and Steel Community, or in any of the Community acts deriving from those Treaties, are to be understood to refer to:
>
> (a)British citizens;
>
> (b) Persons who are British subjects by virtue of Part IV of the British Nationality Act 1981 and who have the right of abode in the United Kingdom and are therefore exempt from United Kingdom immigration control;
>
> (c) British Dependent Territories citizens who acquire their citizenship from a connection with Gibraltar.

'The reference in Article 6 of the third Protocol to the Act of Accession of January 22, 1972, on the Channel Islands and the Isle of Man to "any citizen of the United Kingdom and Colonies" is to be understood as referring to "any British citizen'.

The term 'national' has also been qualified, in relation to both the United Kingdom and Denmark, by Protocols to the Treaty of Accession.

Protocol No 3, on the Channel Islands and the Isle of Man

Article 2

The rights enjoyed by Channel Islanders or Manxmen in the United Kingdom shall not be affected by the Act of Accession. However, such persons shall not benefit from Community provisions relating to the free movement of persons and services.

...

Article 6

In this Protocol, Channel Islander or Manxman shall mean any citizen of the United Kingdom and Colonies who holds that citizenship by virtue of the fact that he, a parent or grandparent was born, adopted, naturalised or registered in the Island in question; but such a person shall not for this purpose be regarded as a Channel Islander or Manxman if he, a parent or a grandparent was born, adopted, naturalised or registered in the United Kingdom. Nor shall he be so regarded if he has at any time been ordinarily resident in the United Kingdom for five years.

The administrative arrangements necessary to identify these persons will be notified to the Commission.

Protocol No 2, on the Faroe Islands

Article 4

Danish nationals resident in the Faroe Islands will be considered to be nationals of a Member State within the meaning of the original Treaties only from the date on which those original Treaties become applicable to those Islands.

Additionally, certain association agreements between the EEC and third countries envisage extending freedom of movement to those countries' territories and nationals. The most advanced of these is the 'Ankara Agreement' of association between the EEC and Turkey, which provides in Article 12 that the parties will be guided by Articles 48–50 of the EEC Treaty for the purpose of progressively assuring free movement of workers between them. Article 36 of an Additional Protocol annexed to that Agreement provides that this freedom of movement shall be secured by progressive stages between 1976 and 1986. The first stage has been initiated by Decision No 2/76 of 20 December 1976. It seems clear, however, that these provisions do not produce direct effects: see Case 12/86 *Denirel* v *Stadt Schwabisch Gmund* 30 September 1987.

Decision of the Association Council No 2/76

Article 2

(a) After three years of legal employment in a Member State of the Community, a Turkish worker shall be entitled, subject to the priority to be given to workers of Member States of the Community, to respond to an offer of employment, made under normal conditions and registered with the employment services of that State, for the same occupation, branch of activity and region.

(b) After five years of legal employment in a Member State of the Community, a Turkish worker shall enjoy free access in that country to any paid employment of his choice.

(c) Annual holidays and short absences for reasons of sickness, maternity or an accident at work shall be treated as periods of legal employment. Periods of involuntary unemployment duly certified by the relevant authorities and long absences on account of sickness shall not be treated as periods of legal employment, but shall not affect rights acquired as the result of the preceding period of employment.

IV DIRECT EFFECTS

The Court of Justice of the European Communities has held that, irrespective of Regulation No 1612/68, nationals of Member States are entitled to equality of treatment with nationals of any other Member State in which they may find themselves, in consequence and within the limits of Article 48(2) of the EEC Treaty.

Case 167/73 Commission v France
[1974] ECR 359; [1974] 2 CMLR 216

By Article 3 of the French Code du Travail Maritime, such proportion of the crew of a ship as was laid down by an order of the Minister of the Merchant Fleet had to be of French nationality.

The Commission brought proceedings against France under Article 169 of the EEC Treaty contending that in so far as it applied to nationals of other Member States the French Code was incompatible with Article 48 of the EEC Treaty and Article 4 of Regulation No 1612/68. The French Government declared its intention to amend the Code in order to confer on mariners from other Member States formal equality with French nationals. It argued, however, that the maintenance of the Code entailed no breach of the Treaty since in practice the Government had exempted nationals of other Member States from the disparity for which the Code provided, and since the rules of the EEC Treaty regarding freedom of movement for workers did not (in the French Government's submission) apply to sea transport so long as the Council had not so decided under Article 84(2) of the EEC Treaty.

The Court

It appears from the argument before the Court and from the position adopted during the parliamentary proceedings that the present state of affairs is that freedom of movement for workers in the sector in question continues to be considered by the French authorities not as a matter of right but as dependent on their unilateral will.

It follows that although the objective legal position is clear, namely, that Article 48 and Regulation No 1612/68 are directly applicable in the territory of the French Republic, nevertheless the maintenance in these circumstances of the wording of the Code du Travail Maritime gives rise to an ambiguous state of affairs by maintaining, as regards those subject to the law who are concerned, a state of uncertainty as to the possibilities available to them of relying on Community law.

This uncertainty can only be reinforced by the internal and verbal character of the purely administrative directions to waive the application of the national law.

The free movement of persons, and in particular workers, constitutes, as appears both from Article 3(c) of the Treaty and from the place of Articles 48 to 51 in Part Two of the Treaty, one of the foundations of the Community.

According to Article 48(2) it entails the abolition of any discrimination based on nationality, whatever be its nature or extent, between workers of the Member States as regards employment, remuneration and other conditions of work and employment.

The absolute nature of this prohibition, moreover, has the effect of not only allowing in each State equal access to employment to the nationals of other Member States, but also, in accordance with the aim of Article 177 of the Treaty, of guaranteeing to the States' own nationals that they shall not suffer the unfavourable consequences which could result from the offer or acceptance by nationals of other Member States of conditions of employment or remuneration less advantageous than those obtaining under national law since such acceptance is prohibited.

It thus follows from the general character of the prohibition on discrimination in Article 48 and the objective pursued by the abolition of discrimination that discrimination is prohibited even if it constitutes only an obstacle of secondary importance as regards the equality of access to employment and other conditions of work and employment.

The uncertainty created by the maintenance unamended of the wording of Article 3 of the Code du Travail Maritime constitutes such an obstacle.

It follows that in maintaining unamended, in these circumstances, the provisions of Article 3(2) of the Code du Travail Maritime as regards the nationals of other Member States, the French Republic has failed to fulfil its obligations under Article 48 of the Treaty and Article 4 of Regulation No 1612/68 of the Council of 15 October 1968.

In Case 41/74 *van Duyn* v *Home Office* the European Court expressly articulated its conclusion that Article 48 of the EEC Treaty is directly applicable so as to confer upon individuals rights enforceable by them in a Member State. The appropriate extract is set out at p. 84.

Since the right of a worker of one Member State to enter and reside in another, for the purpose of employment, is conferred directly by Article 48 of the EEC Treaty, the exercise of that right cannot be subject to the issuance of a residence permit.

Case 48/75 The State v Jean Noël Royer

[1976] ECR 497; [1976] 2 CMLR 619

Jean Royer was a French national whose police file in his country of origin showed that he had been convicted of procuring and had been prosecuted (but not, apparently, convicted) for various armed robberies. His wife, also a French national, was employed as manageress of a *café dancing* near Liège (Belgium). M. Royer had joined his wife there but failed to comply with the administrative formalities of entry on the population register. He was convicted of illegal residence in Belgium, left the country but returned shortly thereafter, again failing to comply with the administrative formalities. He was served with a ministerial decree of expulsion on the ground that his conduct showed his presence to be a danger to public policy. He contested the decree before the Tribunal de Première Instance of Liège, arguing that he was entitled to enter and remain in France as a worker, alternatively as the spouse of a worker, alternatively as a self-employed person. By a judgment confirmed by the Cour d'Appel of Liège, the Tribunal asked the Court of Justice of the European Communities to give preliminary rulings on several questions. Among these were the questions whether the right of a worker or spouse to enter and reside in a Member State other than his own arises directly from the Treaty or by means of the issuance of a residence permit; and whether the failure by a national of a Member State to comply with the legal formalities for the control of aliens may justify a decision ordering expulsion.

The Court

Article 48 provides that freedom of movement for workers shall be secured within the Community.

Paragraph (3) of that article provides that it shall entail the right to enter the territory of Member States, to move freely there, to stay there for the purpose of employment and to remain there after the end of this employment...

Article 1 of Regulation No 1612/68 provides that any national of a Member State shall, irrespective of his place of residence, have 'the right to take up activity as an employed person and to pursue such activity within the territory of another Member State' and Article 10 of the same regulation extends the 'right to install themselves' to the members of the family of such a national.

Article 4 of Directive No 68/360 provides that 'Member States shall grant the right of residence in their territory' to the persons referred to and further states that as 'proof' of this right an individual residence permit shall be issued...

These provisions show that *the legislative authorities of the Community were aware that, while not creating new rights in favour of persons protected by Community law, the regulation and directives concerned determined the scope and detailed rules for the exercise of rights conferred directly by the Treaty.*

It is therefore evident that the exception concerning the safeguard of public policy, public security and public health contained in Articles 48(3) and 56(1) of the Treaty must be regarded not as a condition precedent to the acquisition of the right of entry and residence but as providing the possibility, in individual cases where there is sufficient justification, of imposing restrictions on the exercise of a right derived directly from the Treaty...

It must therefore be concluded that this right is acquired independently of the issue of a residence permit by the competent authority of a Member State.

The grant of this permit is therefore to be regarded not as a measure giving rise to rights but as a measure by a Member State serving to prove the individual position of a national of another Member State with regard to provisions of Community law...

The logical consequence of the foregoing is that the mere failure by a national of a Member State to complete the legal formalities concerning access, movement and residence of aliens does not justify a decision ordering expulsion.

Since it is a question of the exercise of a right acquired under the Treaty itself, such conduct cannot be regarded as constituting in itself a breach of public policy or public security.

Consequently any decision ordering expulsion made by the authorities of a Member State against a national of another Member State covered by the Treaty would, if it were based solely on that person's failure to comply with the legal formalities concerning the control of aliens or on the lack of a residence permit, be contrary to the provisions of the Treaty...

By the same token, the Court has ruled that the right of Community workers to enter the territory of a Member State may not be made subject to the issuance of a written clearance, in the form of a grant of 'leave to enter' the State, issued by the authorities of that State.

Case 157/79 Regina v Stanislaus Pieck
[1980] ECR 2171; [1980] 3 CMLR 220

Criminal proceedings were brought in the Pontypridd Magistrates' Court against a Dutch national, living and working in Wales. The charge was that having only limited leave to enter the United Kingdom, he had remained beyond the expiry of his leave. The Magistrates referred to the European Court a series of questions designed to determine whether a Member State may require a worker of another Member State to obtain a written 'leave' to enter.

The Court

The Court has already stated on several occasions that the right of nationals of a Member State to enter the territory of another Member State and reside there for the purposes intended by the Treaty is a right conferred directly by the Treaty or, as the case may be, by the provisions adopted for its implementation.

The aim of Directive No 68/360, as the recitals in the preamble thereto show, is to adopt measures for the abolition of restrictions which still exist concerning movement and residence within the Community, which conform to the rights and privileges accorded to nationals of Member States by Regulation No 1612/68 of the Council of 15 October 1968 in freedom of movement for workers within the Community. To this end the directive lays down the conditions on which nationals of Member States may exercise their right to leave their State of origin to take up activities as employed persons in the territory of another Member State and their right to enter the territory of that State and reside there.

In this connection Article 3(1) of the directive provides that Member States shall allow the persons to whom Regulation No 1612/68 applies to enter their territory on production of a valid identity card or passport. Article 3(2) contains the further provision that no entry visa or equivalent requirement may be demanded from these workers.

In the course of the procedure before the Court the British Government maintained that the phrase 'entry visa' means exclusively a documentary clearance issued before the traveller arrives at the frontier in the form of an endorsement on his passport or of a separate document. On the contrary an endorsement stamped on a passport at the time of arrival giving leave to enter the territory may not be regarded as an entry visa or equivalent document.

This argument cannot be upheld. For the purpose of applying the directive, the object of which is to abolish restrictions on movement and residence for Community workers within the Community, the time at which clearance to enter the territory of a Member State has been given and indicated on a passport or by another document is immaterial. *Furthermore the right of Community workers to enter the territory of a Member State which Community law confers may not be made subject to the issue of a clearance to this effect by the authorities of that Member State.*

...

V DISCRIMINATION

The prohibition of discrimination on grounds of nationality, contained in Article 48(2) of the EEC Treaty, was the subject of the European Court's preliminary ruling in Case 15/69 *Württembergische Milchverwertung-Südmilch-AG* v *Salvatore Ugliola* [1969] ECR 363. In that case an Italian national, obliged to interrupt his employment in Germany to perform his national service in Italy, established his entitlement to the same protection against loss of employment prospects and benefits as was conferred by German law upon German nationals performing national service in the German forces.

The Court addressed its attention to Article 48(2) again in 1976.

Case 118/75 Lynne Watson and Alessandro Belmann
[1976] ECR 1185; [1976] 2 CMLR 552

Miss Watson, a national of the United Kingdom, spent several months in Italy where she was provided with accommodation by Mr Belmann, an Italian national. She was charged with failing to report to the police authorities within three days of her arrival in Italy, in accordance with an obligation imposed by Italian legislation upon all foreign nationals with the exception of certain categories of employed workers from other Member States. He was charged with failing to inform the authorities within twenty-four hours of the identity of Miss Watson, in accordance with an obligation imposed by Italian legislation on 'any person who provides board and lodging...to a foreign national'.

They were brought before the Pretura di Milano, who asked the European Court to rule whether national laws such as those invoked against Miss Watson and Mr Belmann were contrary to the provisions of Articles 7 and 48–66 of the EEC Treaty on the ground that they constituted discrimination based on nationality and a restriction on the freedom of movement of persons within the Community.

The Court

...

By creating the principle of freedom of movement for persons and by conferring on any person falling within its ambit the right of access to the territory of the Member States, for the purposes intended by the Treaty, Community law has not excluded the power of

Member States to adopt measures enabling the national authorities to have an exact knowledge of population movements affecting their territory.

Under the terms of Article 8(2) of Directive No 68/360 and Article 4(2) of Directive No 73/148, the competent authorities in Member States may require nationals of other Member States to report their presence to the authorities of the State concerned.

Such an obligation could not in itself be regarded as an infringement of the rules concerning freedom of movement for persons.

However, such an infringement might result from the legal formalities in question if the control procedures to which they refer were such as to restrict the freedom of movement required by the Treaty or to limit the right conferred by the Treaty on nationals of the Member States to enter and reside in the territory of any other Member State for the purposes intended by Community law.

In particular as regards the period within which the arrival of foreign nationals must be reported, the provisions of the Treaty are only infringed if the period fixed is unreasonable.

Among the penalties attaching to a failure to comply with the prescribed declaration and registration formalities, deportation, in relation to persons protected by Community law, is certainly incompatible with the provisions of the Treaty since, as the Court has already confirmed in other cases, such a measure negates the very right conferred and guaranteed by the Treaty.

As regards other penalties, such as fines and detention, whilst the national authorities are entitled to impose penalties in respect of a failure to comply with the terms of provisions requiring foreign nationals to notify their presence which are comparable to those attaching to infringements of provisions of equal importance by nationals, they are not justified in imposing a penalty so disproportionate to the gravity of the infringement that it becomes an obstacle to the free movement of persons.

In so far as national rules concerning the control of foreign nationals do not involve restrictions on freedom of movement for persons and on the right, conferred by the Treaty on persons protected by Community law, to enter and reside in the territory of the Member States, the application of such legislation, where it is based upon objective factors, cannot constitute 'discrimination on grounds of nationality', prohibited under Article 7 of the Treaty.

Provisions which require residents of the host State to inform the public authorities of the identity of foreign nationals for whom they provide accommodation, and which are for the most part connected with the internal order of the State, can only be called into question from the point of view of Community law if they place an indirect restriction on freedom of movement for persons.

In the same year, however, the European Court noted that limitations on the right of a professional football player to take part in football matches in a Member State other than that of which he is a national can indeed 'involve restrictions on freedom of movement' contrary to Article 48 of the EEC Treaty. Relying on a precedent set when the Court was interpreting the provisions relating to the rights of establishment of self-employed persons, the Court deduced that a national court must protect an individual against such restrictions on his freedom of movement, even when they are imposed not by the State but by a sporting federation competent to control football in a Member State.

Case 13/76 Gaetano Donà v Mario Mantero
[1976] ECR 1333; [1976] 2 CMLR 578

Sig. Mantero, former chairman of the Rovigo Football Club, asked Sig. Donà to undertake enquiries in football circles abroad in order to discover players willing to play in the Rovigo team. Sig. Donà therefore arranged for the publication of an advertisement in a Belgian newspaper, but Sig. Mantero refused to consider the offers resulting from the advertisement or to reimburse Sig. Donà for his expenses. Sig. Donà brought proceedings against Sig. Mantero for the recovery of his expenses.

The case was heard by a Giudice Conciliatore before whom Sig. Mantero contended that Sig. Donà had acted prematurely, since the Rules of the Italian Football Federation effectively prohibited the recruitment of foreign players for Italian teams. Sig. Donà contended that those Rules were invalid to the extent that they purported to restrict the employment in Italy of footballers being nationals of other Member States. The Giudice Conciliatore referred to the European Court for preliminary ruling four questions concerning the compatibility of the Rules of the Italian Football Federation with Article 48 of the EEC Treaty.

The Court

Having regard to the objectives of the Community, the practice of sport is subject to Community law only in so far as it constitutes an economic activity within the meaning of Article 2 of the Treaty.

This applies to the activities of professional or semi-professional football players, which are in the nature of gainful employment or remunerated service.

Where such players are nationals of a Member State they benefit in all the other Member States from the provisions of Community law concerning freedom of movement of persons and of provision of services.

However, those provisions do not prevent the adoption of rules or of a practice excluding foreign players from participation in certain matches for reasons which are not of an economic nature, which relate to the particular nature and context of such matches and are thus of sporting interest only, such as, for example, matches between national teams from different countries.

This restriction on the scope of the provisions in question must however remain limited to its proper objective.

Having regard to the above, it is for the national court to determine the nature of the activity submitted to its judgment.

As the Court has already ruled in its judgment of 12 December 1974 in Case 36/74 *Walrave* v *Union Cycliste Internationale* [1974] ECR 1405, the prohibition on discrimination based on nationality does not only apply to the action of public authorities but extends likewise to rules of any other nature aimed at collectively regulating gainful employment and services.

It follows that the provisions of Articles 7, 48 and 59 of the Treaty, which are mandatory in nature, must be taken into account by the national court in judging the validity or the effects of a provision inserted in the rules of a sporting organisation.

The answer to the questions referred to the Court must therefore be that *rules or a national practice, even adopted by a sporting organisation, which limit the right to take part in football matches as professional or semi-professional players solely to the nationals of the State in question, are incompatible with Article 7 and, as the case may be, with Articles 48 to 51 or 59 to 66 of the Treaty unless such rules or practice exclude foreign players from participation in certain matches for reasons which are not of an economic nature, which relate to the particular nature and context of such matches and are thus of sporting interest only.*

The prohibition of discrimination on grounds of nationality appears not only in Articles 7 and 48(2) of the EEC Treaty but also in Article 7 of Council Regulation No 1612/68 (see above, p. 277). In that context, the prohibition of discrimination is declared to apply not only in respect of conditions of employment and work but also in respect of 'social and tax advantages'. The term 'social ... advantage' encompasses not only the benefits accorded by virtue of a right but also those granted on a discretionary basis. More particularly it encompasses interest-free loans granted on childbirth by a credit institution incorporated under public law.

Case 65/81 Francesco and Letizia Reina v Landeskreditbank Baden-Württemberg [1982] ECR 33; [1982] 1 CMLR 744

The Court

...

The Landeskreditbank grants loans, upon application, on the basis of guidelines laid down by the competent authority of the *Land* of Baden-Württemberg, *inter alia* on the birth of a child. The childbirth loans, which are free of interest as a result of subsidies allocated by the *Land*, are granted for a term of seven years up to an amount of DM 8,000, which may be increased to DM 12,000 in exceptional cases. They may be granted to married couples only where at least one of the spouses is a German national and the family income does not exceed a specified amount. According to the information provided by the national court, this system of childbirth loans was introduced with a view to stimulating the birth rate of the German population and in order to reduce the number of voluntary abortions.

In the present case, the plaintiffs in the main action, Mr and Mrs Reina, applied for the grant of a loan on the birth of twins. The Landeskreditbank Baden-Württemberg rejected their application on the ground that under the above-mentioned guidelines, a loan may be granted only if at least one spouse is a German national. The plaintiffs then brought an action before the Verwaltungsgericht Stuttgart challenging the conformity of that requirement with Community law.

Since it took the view that it required a ruling of the Court of Justice to enable it to give judgment, the Verwaltungsgericht Stuttgart referred the following question ... to the Court of Justice for a preliminary ruling.

'Must Article 7(2) of Regulation (EEC) No 1612/68 of the Council of 15 October 1968 on freedom of movement for workers within the Community ... be construed as meaning that it puts other nationals of the EEC on an equal footing with German nationals if, pursuant to internal administrative guidelines and without there being any legal entitlement thereto, a credit institution incorporated under public law grants upon application in the event of the birth of a child interest-free loans to married couples whose income does not exceed a certain amount for the purpose of averting, alleviating or removing financial difficulties...?'

...

The Landeskreditbank contends in the first place that Article 7(2) may not be applied to the loans in question in view of the absence of any connection between the grant of the loan and the recipient's status as a worker and on the ground that the refusal to grant the loan in no way hinders the mobility of workers within the Community.

It should be recalled that Regulation No 1612/68, adopted *inter alia* pursuant to Article 49 of the EEC Treaty with a view to achieving freedom of movement for workers, provides, in Article 7(1), that a worker who is a national of a Member State may not, in the territory of another Member State, be treated differently from national workers by reason of his nationality in respect of any conditions of employment and work. Paragraph (2) of the same article adds that such a worker is to enjoy the same social and tax advantages as national workers.

As the Court has repeatedly held, most recently in its judgment of 31 May 1979 in Case 207/78 *Even* [1979] ECR 2019, it follows from those provisions and from the objective pursued that the advantages which that regulation extends to workers who are nationals of other Member States are all those which, whether or not linked to a contract of employment, are generally granted to national workers primarily because of their objective status as workers or by virtue of the mere fact of their residence on the national territory and the extension of which to workers who are nationals of other Member States therefore seems suitable to facilitate their mobility within the Community.

Consequently, *childbirth loans such as those referred to by the national court satisfy in principle the criteria enabling them to be classified as social advantages to be granted to workers of all the Member States without any discrimination whatever on grounds of nationality in particular in view of their aim which is to alleviate, in the case of families with a low income, the financial burden resulting from the birth of a child.*

...

The Landeskreditbank contends in addition that the loans in question constitute voluntary benefits within the limits of the budgetary resources allocated for that purpose, with the result that no entitlement to those benefits is created. Similarly, it is proper to take into account the fact that many foreign workers return to their countries of origin before the expiry of the period prescribed for the repayment of a loan, so that the repayment is put in jeopardy.

However, it must be observed in that connection that *the concept of 'social advantage' referred to in Article 7(2) of the regulation encompasses not only the benefits accorded by virtue of a right but also those granted on a discretionary basis.* In the latter case, the principle of equal treatment requires the benefits to be made available to nationals of other Member States on the same conditions as those which apply to a State's own nationals and on the basis of the same guidelines as those which govern the grant of the loans to the latter...

VI PUBLIC SERVICE

By Article 48(4) of the EEC Treaty, the provisions of that article do not apply to employment in the 'public service'. The several Member States differ in their characterisation of the public service for purposes of domestic law. In Case 152/73 *Sotgiu* v *Bundespost,* Mr Advocate General Mayras offered a definition of the expression 'public service' for the purposes of the EEC Treaty.

Case 152/73 Giovanni Maria Sotgiu v Deutsche Bundespost
[1974] ECR 153 at 169—172

Mr Advocate General Mayras

...

Every State certainly has the power to define the field of action of its administration, to assume responsibility either directly or through the intermediary of decentralised organisations under public law for activities which elsewhere are left to private initiative. In doing this it asserts its own concept of State intervention in national life. But it cannot rest with the State as a member of the Community to limit by this means the actual extent of freedom of movement for workers.

I therefore share the opinion of the Commission, according to which the concept of employment in the public service must be given an independent definition, unaffected by variable national criteria which depend upon the conception which each State has of its tasks and upon the structure of the bodies responsible for carrying them out.

It is for this Court to provide such a definition if possible.

As the wording itself gives little help, we must first look for the *ratio* in the intentions of the authors of the Treaty. There is no doubt that they meant by the exception in paragraph (4) to allow States to reserve for their own nationals such of the public appointments as put those who hold them in a position to participate directly in the exercise of official authority, or to put it in more general terms, to avail themselves of the prerogatives of public authority with regard to individuals. It is in this sense that it can be said that *the expression 'the public service' implies a power exercised directly by the State. Mere participation in a public service would not be sufficient to exclude a given employment from the field of application of Article 48* (Mégret, *Le Droit de la Communauté Européene,* Vol. 3, p. 6). This restrictive interpretation is also adopted by the majority of commentators on the Treaty.

...

As for the nature of the legal relationship between the employee and the employing administration, it seems to me that this can in no way supply the basis for a decisive criterion for the application of Community law.

In States like the Federal Republic of Germany and France there is an independent administrative law which is characterised in particular by the power of the administration to take enforceable decisions and to avail itself of prerogatives of public authority. The distinction between on the one hand officials subject to legislative provisions whose position as regards the administration is governed by statutes and regulations and on the other hand employees of public service of an industrial or commercial nature whose relationship with their employer is subject to contracts of employment under private law is of significance inasmuch as the legal nature of the employment relationship determines the type of court with jurisdiction to take cognisance of law suits concerning them and moreover involves important consequences in substantive law.

On the other hand this distinction seems to me to have little genuine relevance to Article 48 of the Treaty of Rome. In fact although it is possible to assume that the exception provided for by paragraph (4) of this article should in principle apply to officials [*fonctionnaires*] because they are normally entrusted with tasks which involve more or less directly the national interest, it does happen that employees recruited on the basis of a contract under private law [*agents recrutés sous contrat de droit privé*] find themselves entrusted with duties closely related to the actual exercise of official authority. Thus it has been stated that the Federal German delegate to the Coal Industry is a contractual employee [*agent contractuel*] under private law, even though he exercises powers of decision which plainly derive from State authority.

Are we to say, conversely, that a maintenance employee or a driver who occupies an established post as an official in a central administration is carrying out duties which involve the interests of the State or the prerogatives of public authority by virtue of the mere fact that he is governed by a legislative provision?

It is clear then that for the interpretation of Article 48(4) the concept of employment in the public service cannot be defined in terms of the legal status of the holder of the post.

A Community interpretation which would allow a uniform application of the exception provided for by this provision requires us therefore to have resort to factual criteria based upon the duties which the post held within the administration entails and the activities actually performed by the holder of this post.

The exception will only be applicable if this person possesses a power of discretion with regard to individuals or if his activity involves national interests – in particular those which are concerned with the internal or external security of the State.

Consequently however it is for the national court to apply these criteria to the actual cases which come before it. Moreover, in the present case we do not know what is the exact nature of the duties carried out by the plaintiff in the main action.

...

In the event, the Court found it possible to dispose of the case without deciding the question of the meaning of 'public service'. In a later case, the Court was confronted with an unavoidable question on the meaning of that phrase. Its judgment shows the influence of Mr Mayras' Opinion.

Case 149/79 Commission v Belgium
[1980] ECR 3881 and [1982] ECR 1845;
[1981] 2 CMLR 413 and [1982] 3 CMLR 539

The Court

By application lodged at the Court Registry on 28 September 1979 the Commission brought an action under Article 169 of the EEC Treaty for a declaration that by requiring or permitting to be required the possession of Belgian nationality as a condition of recruitment to posts not covered by Article 48(4) of the Treaty, the Kingdom of Belgium has failed to fulfil its obligations under Article 48 of the Treaty and Regulation (EEC) No 1612/68 on freedom of movement for workers within the Community...

In its reasoned opinion and application to the Court the Commission referred generally to 'various vacancies' advertised by the Société Nationale des Chemins de Fer Belges [Belgian National Railway Company] and the Société Nationale des Chemins de Fer Vicinaux [National Local Railway Company] concerning posts for unskilled workers, and to vacancies advertised 'during recent years' by the City of Brussels and the Commune of

Auderghem, and the Commission gave only a brief indication of the posts involved. Through information requested by the Court during the written and oral procedures and produced by the Government of the Kingdom of Belgium and after the Commission had specified the posts during the oral procedure without challenge from the Belgian Government, it became possible to establish an exact list of the posts in issue.

From that information and that list it emerges that the vacancies referred to concern posts for trainee locomotive drivers, loaders, plate-layers, shunters and signallers with the national railways and unskilled workers with the local railways as well as posts for hospital nurses, children's nurses, night-watchmen, plumbers, carpenters, electricians, garden hands, architects, and supervisors with the City of Brussels and the Commune of Auderghem. Nevertheless the information obtained during the inquiry has not enabled the Court to gain a precise idea of the nature of the duties involved in the posts for which it has been possible to draw up a precise list.

...

Article 48(4) of the Treaty provides that 'the provisions of this article shall not apply to employment in the public service'.

That provision removes from the ambit of Article 48(1) to (3) a series of posts which involve direct or indirect participation in the exercise of powers conferred by public law and duties designed to safeguard the general interests of the State or of other public authorities. Such posts in fact presume on the part of those occupying them the existence of a special relationship of allegiance to the State and reciprocity of rights and duties which form the foundation of the bond of nationality.

The scope of the derogation made by Article 48(4) to the principles of freedom of movement and equality of treatment laid down in the first three paragraphs of the article should therefore be determined on the basis of the aim pursued by the article. However, determining the sphere of application of Article 48(4) raises special difficulties since in the various Member States authorities acting under powers conferred by public law have assumed responsibilities of an economic and social nature or are involved in activities which are not identifiable with the functions which are typical of the public service yet which by their nature still come under the sphere of application of the Treaty. In these circumstances the effect of extending the exception contained in Article 48(4) to posts which, whilst coming under the State or other organisations governed by public law, still do not involve any association with tasks belonging to the public service properly so called, would be to remove a considerable number of posts from the ambit of the principles set out in the Treaty and to create inequalities between Member States according to the different ways in which the State and certain sectors of economic life are organised.

Consequently it is appropriate to examine whether the posts covered by the action may be associated with the concept of public service within the meaning of Article 48(4), which requires uniform interpretation and application throughout the Community. It must be acknowledged that the application of the distinguishing criteria indicated above gives rise to problems of appraisal and demarcation in specific cases. *It follows from the foregoing that such a classification depends on whether or not the posts in question are typical of the specific activities of the public service in so far as the exercise of powers conferred by public law and responsibility for safeguarding the general interests of the State are vested in it.*

Where, in the case of posts which, although offered by public authorities, are not within the sphere to which Article 48(4) applies, a worker from another Member State is, like a national worker, required to satisfy all other conditions of recruitment, in particular concerning the competence and vocational training required, the provisions of the first three paragraphs of Article 48 and Regulation No 1612/68 do not allow him to be debarred from those posts simply on the grounds of his nationality.

Since the Court had insufficient information about the nature of the posts in question, it ordered the parties to re-examine the issue between them in the light of the judgment. The parties were unable to agree upon the application to certain posts of the Court's criterion. Accordingly, the Court itself applied its own criterion to the posts in issue.

The Court

It follows from that judgment, in particular from paragraphs 12 and 19, that employment within the meaning of Article 48(4) of the Treaty must be connected with the specific activities of the public service in so far as it is entrusted with the exercise of powers conferred by public law and with responsibility for safeguarding the general interests of the State, to which the specific interests of local authorities such as municipalities must be assimilated.

The Commission has rightly acknowledged that, regard being had to the duties and responsibilities attached to some of the posts at issue described in the aforesaid reports, they may have characteristics which bring them within the scope of the exception contained in Article 48(4) of the Treaty in the light of the criteria established in the judgment of the Court of 17 December 1980. The posts are those described as head technical office supervisor, principal supervisor, works supervisor, stock controller and night-watchman with the municipality of Brussels and architect with the municipalities of Brussels and Auderghem. Those matters may therefore be regarded as being no longer at issue.

However, as far as the other posts dealt with in the two reports in question are concerned, it does not appear form the nature of the duties and responsibilities which they involve that they constitute 'employment in the public service' within the meaning of Article 48(4) of the Treaty.

The arguments put forward by the Kingdom of Belgium with regard to certain posts with the Société Nationale des Chemins de Fer Belges ... and the Société Nationale des Chemins de Fer Vicinaux ... according to which the question of the admission of foreign staff must be considered above all in terms of the possibility that a situation may arise in which the security of the State is jeopardised cannot be accepted in the context of Article 48(4) of the Treaty. Such a line of argument is based on an hypothesis which has no connection with the legal context of that provision.

For those reasons it must be declared that by making Belgian nationality or allowing it to be made a condition of entry for the posts referred to in the reports lodged by the parties on 29 and 30 October 1981, other than those of head technical office supervisor, principal supervisor, works supervisor, stock controller and night-watchman with the municipality of Brussels and that of architect with the municipalities of Brussels and Auderghem, the Kingdom of Belgium has failed to fulfil its obligations under the EEC Treaty.

VII PUBLIC POLICY, SECURITY AND HEALTH

In identifying the rights entailed by freedom of movement for workers, Article 48(3) of the EEC Treaty stipulates that such rights are to be enjoyed 'subject to limitations justified on grounds of public policy, public security or public health'. That phrase is amplified by a Council Directive of 1964.

Council Directive No 64/221 of 25 February 1964 on the Coordination of Special Measures concerning the Movement and Residence of Foreign Nationals which are justified on Grounds of Public Policy, Public Security or Public Health

JO 1964 850; OJ Sp Ed 1963-4 117

Article 2

1. This directive relates to all measures concerning entry into their territory, issue or renewal of residence permits, or expulsion from their territory, taken by Member States on grounds of public policy, public security or public health.
2. Such grounds shall not be invoked to service economic ends.

Article 3

1. Measures taken on grounds of public policy or of public security shall be based exclusively on the personal conduct of the individual concerned.
2. Previous criminal convictions shall not in themselves constitute grounds for the taking of such measures.
3. Expiry of the identity card or passport used by the person concerned to enter the host country and to obtain a residence permit shall not justify expulsion from the territory.
4. The State which issued the identity card or passport shall allow the holder of such document to re-enter its territory without any formality even if the document is no longer valid or the nationality of the holder is in dispute.

Article 4

1. The only diseases or disabilities justifying refusal of entry into a territory or refusal to issue a first residence permit shall be those listed in the Annex to this directive.
2. Diseases or disabilities occurring after a first residence permit has been issued shall not justify refusal to renew the residence permit or expulsion from the territory.
3. Member States shall not introduce new provisions or practices which are more restrictive than those in force at the date of notification of this directive.

...

Article 6

The person concerned shall be informed of the grounds of public policy, public security, or public health upon which the decision taken in his case is based, unless this is contrary to the interests of the security of the State involved.

Article 7

The person concerned shall be officially notified of any decision to refuse the issue or renewal of a residence permit or to expel him from the territory. The period allowed for leaving the territory shall be stated in this notification. Save in cases of urgency, this period shall be not less than 15 days if the person concerned has not yet been granted a residence permit and not less than one month in all other cases.

Article 8

The person concerned shall have the same legal remedies in respect of any decision concerning entry, or refusing the issue or renewal of a residence permit, or ordering expulsion from the territory, as are available to nationals of the State concerned in respect of acts of the administration.

Article 9

1. Where there is no right of appeal to a court of law, or where such appeal may be only in respect of the legal validity of the decision, or where the appeal cannot have suspensory effect, a decision refusing renewal of a residence permit or ordering the expulsion of the holder of a residence permit from the territory shall not be taken by the administrative authority, save in cases of urgency, until an opinion has been obtained from a competent authority of the host country before which the person concerned enjoys such rights of defence and of assistance or representation as the domestic law of that country provides for.

This authority shall not be the same as that empowered to take the decision refusing renewal of the residence permit or ordering expulsion.

2. Any decision refusing the issue of a first residence permit or ordering expulsion of the person concerned before the issue of the permit shall, where that person so requests, be referred for consideration to the authority whose prior opinion is required under paragraph (1). The person concerned shall then be entitled to submit his defence in person, except where this would be contrary to the interests of national security.

Article 10

1. Member States shall within six months of notification of this directive put into force the measures necessary to comply with its provisions and shall forthwith inform the Commission thereof.

2. Member States shall ensure that the texts of the main provisions of national law which they adopt in the field governed by this directive are communicated to the Commission.

Article 11

This directive is addressed to the Member States.

Done at Brussels, February 25 1964.

Annex

A. *Diseases which might endanger Public Health:*

1. Diseases subject to quarantine listed in International Health Regulation No 2 of the World Health Organisation of May 25, 1951;

2. Tuberculosis of the respiratory system in an active state or showing a tendency to develop;
3. Syphilis;
4. Other infectious disease or contagious parasitic diseases if they are subject of provisions for the protection of nationals of the host country.

B. *Diseases and Disabilities which might threaten Public Policy or Public Security:*
1. Drug addiction;
2. Profound mental disturbance; manifest conditions of psychotic disturbance with agitation, delirium, hallucinations or confusion.

This directive has been the subject of more than a little litigation. In *Van Duyn* v *Home Office* the Court of Justice of the European Communities ruled *inter alia* that Article 3(1) of the directive was directly aplicable, but found that present association with a body or organisation reflecting participation in its activities as well as identification with its aims and designs might be considered as 'personal conduct' within the meaning of that article.

Case 41/74 Yvonne van Duyn v Home Office
[1974] ECR 1337; [1975] 1 CMLR 1

The Government of the United Kingdom took the view that Scientology is a 'pseudo-philosophical cult' which is 'socially harmful'. Accordingly, the Government's policy was that foreign nationals would not be admitted to the Kingdom to study at the Church of Scientology nor would work permits or employment vouchers be issued for foreign nationals for work at a Scientology establishment.

Miss Van Duyn, a Dutch national, was offered employment as a secretary at the Church of Scientology's premises in Sussex. On her arrival at Gatwick Airport, she was refused leave to enter the Kingdom, on the ground that 'the Secretary of State considers it undesirable to give anyone leave to enter the United Kingdom on the business of or in the employment of that organisation'.

Miss Van Duyn sought a declaration in the High Court that she was entitled to enter the United Kingdom as a 'worker' within the meaning of Article 48 of the EEC Treaty. She relied on Article 3(1) of the directive, contending that the refusal to grant leave was not based exclusively on her personal conduct.

The Court

...

By the third question the Court is asked to rule whether Article 48 of the Treaty and Article 3 of Directive No 64/221 must be interpreted as meaning that

> 'a Member State, in the performance of its duty to base a measure taken on grounds of public policy exclusively on the personal conduct of the individual concerned is entitled to take into account as matters of personal conduct:

(a) the fact that the individual is or has been associated with some body or organisation the activities of which the Member State considers contrary to the public good but which are not unlawful in that State;
(b) the fact that the individual intends to take employment in the Member State with such a body or organisation it being the case that no restrictions are placed upon nationals of the Member State who wish to take similar employment with such a body or organisation'.

It is necessary, first, to consider whether association with a body or an organisation can in itself constitute personal conduct within the meaning of Article 3 of Directive No 64/221. Although a person's past association cannot in general justify a decision refusing him the right to move freely within the Community, it is nevertheless the case that present association, which reflects participation in the activities of the body or of the organisation as well as identification with its aims and its designs, may be considered a voluntary act of the person concerned and, consequently, as part of his personal conduct within the meaning of the provision cited.

This third question further raises the problem of what importance must be attributed to the fact that the activities of the organisation in question, which are considered by the Member State as contrary to the public good, are not however prohibited by national law. It should be emphasised that the concept of public policy in the context of the Community and where, in particular, it is used as a justification for derogating from the fundamental principle of freedom of movement for workers, must be interpreted strictly, so that its scope cannot be determined unilaterally by each Member State without being subject to control by the institutions of the Community. Nevertheless, the particular circumstances justifying recourse to the concept of public policy may vary from one country to another and from one period to another, and it is therefore necessary in this matter to allow the competent national authorities an area of discretion within the limits imposed by the Treaty.

It follows from the above that where the competent authorities of a Member State have clearly defined their standpoint as regards the activities of a particular organisation and where, considering it to be socially harmful, they have taken administrative measures to counteract these activities, the Member State cannot be required, before it can rely on the concept of public policy, to make such activities unlawful, if recourse to such a measure is not thought appropriate in the circumstances.

The question raises finally the problem of whether a Member State is entitled, on grounds of public policy, to prevent a national of another Member State from taking gainful employment within its territory with a body or organisation, it being the case that no similar restriction is placed upon its own nationals.

In this connection, the Treaty, while enshrining the principle of freedom of movement for workers without any discrimination on grounds of nationality, admits, in Article 48(3), limitations justified on grounds of public policy, public security or public health to the rights deriving from this principle. Under the terms of the provision cited above, the right to accept offers of employment actually made, the right to move freely within the territory of Member States for this purpose, and the right to stay in a Member State for the purpose of employment are, among others, all subject to such limitations. Consequently, the effect of such limitations, when they apply, is that leave to enter the territory of a Member State and the right to reside there may be refused to a national of another Member State.

Furthermore, it is a principle of international law, which the EEC Treaty cannot be assumed to disregard in the relations between Member States, that a State is precluded from refusing its own nationals the right of entry or residence.

It follows that a Member State, for reasons of public policy, can, where it deems necessary, refuse a national of another Member State the benefit of the principle of freedom of movement for workers in a case where such a national proposes to take up a particular offer of employment even though the Member State does not place a similar restriction upon its own nationals.

Accordingly, the reply to the third question must be that Article 48 of the EEC Treaty and Article 3(1) of Directive No 64/221 are to be interpreted as meaning that a Member State, in imposing restrictions justified on grounds of public policy, is entitled to take into account, as a matter of personal conduct of the individual concerned, the fact that the individual is associated with some body or organisation the activities of which the Member State considers socially harmful but which are not unlawful in that State, despite the fact that no restriction is placed upon nationals of the said Member State who wish to take similar employment with these same bodies or organisations.

In *Bonsignore* the question before the European Court was whether Article 3 of Directive No 64/221 prohibited the expulsion of an EEC national from a Member State for reasons of a general preventive nature.

Case 67/74 Carmelo Angelo Bonsignore v Oberstadtdirektor der Stadt Köln
[1975] ECR 297; [1975] CMLR 472

The Court

...

By order of 30 July 1974 received at the Court Registry on 14 September 1974, the Verwaltungsgericht Köln referred to the Court, under Article 177 of the EEC Treaty, two questions concerning the interpretation of Article 3(1) and (2) of Council Directive No 64/221/EEC of 25 February 1964 on the coordination of special measures concerning the movement and residence of foreign nationals which are justified on grounds of public policy, public security or public health.

These questions arose within the context of an appeal brought by an Italian national residing in the Federal Republic of Germany against a decision to deport him taken by the Ausländerbehörde [Aliens Authority] following his conviction for an offence against the Firearms Law and for causing death by negligence.

The order containing the reference shows that the plaintiff in the main action, who was unlawfully in possession of a firearm, accidentally caused the death of his brother by his careless handling of the firearm concerned.

For this reason the relevant criminal court sentenced him to a fine for an offence against the firearms legislation.

The court also found him guilty of causing death by negligence but imposed no punishment on this count, considering that no purpose would be served thereby in view of the circumstances, notably the mental suffering caused to the individual concerned as a result of the consequences of his carelessness.

Following the criminal conviction the Ausländerbehörde ordered the individual concerned to be deported in accordance with the Ausländergesetz [Aliens Law] of 28 April

1965 ... in conjunction with the Gesetz über Einreise und Aufenthalt von Staatsangehörigen der Mitgliedstaaten der Europäischen Wirtschaftsgemeinschaft [Law on the Entry and Residence of Nationals of Member States of the European Community] of 22 July 1969 ... which was adopted in order to implement Directive No 64/221 in the Federal Republic of Germany.

The Verwaltungsgericht, which heard the appeal against this decision, considered that by reason of the particular circumstances of the case the deportation could not be justified on grounds of a 'special preventive nature' based either on the facts which had given rise to the criminal conviction or on the present and foreseeable conduct of the plaintiff in the main action.

The Verwaltungsgericht considered that the only possible justification for the measure adopted would be the reasons of a 'general preventive nature', which were emphasised both by the Ausländerbehörde and by the representative of the public interest and were based on the deterrent effect which the deportation of an alien found in illegal possession of a firearm would have in immigrant circles having regard to the resurgence of violence in the large urban centres.

As it is required to apply legislative provisions adopted for the implementation of a Community directive – in particular Article 12 of the Law of 22 July 1969 – the Verwaltungsgericht takes the view that it is necessary to request the Court to give an interpretation of the relevant provisions of that directive, in order to ensure that national law is applied in accordance with the requirements of Community law.

In these circumstances the Verwaltungsgericht has referred to the Court the following two questions:

'1. Is Article 3(1) and (2) of Directive No 64/221/EEC of the Council of 25 February 1964 on the coordination of special measures concerning the movement and residence of foreign nationals which are justified on grounds of public policy, public security or public health, to be interpreted as excluding the deportation of a national of a Member State of the European Economic Community by the State authority of another Member State for the purpose of deterring other foreign nationals from committing such criminal offences as those with which the person deported was charged or similar offences or other infringements of public security or public policy, that is, for reasons of a general preventive nature?

2. Does the said provision mean that the deportation of a national of a Member State of the EEC is possible only when there are clear indications that the EEC national, who has been convicted of an offence, will commit further offences or will in some other way disregard public security or public policy of a Member State of the EEC, that is, for reasons of a special preventive nature?'

According to Article 3(1) and (2) of Directive No 64/221, 'measures taken on grounds of public policy or of public security shall be based exclusively on the personal conduct of the individual concerned' and 'previous criminal convictions shall not in themselves constitute grounds for the taking of such measures'.

These provisions must be interpreted in the light of the objectives of the directive which seeks in particular to coordinate the measures justified on grounds of public policy and for the maintenance of public security envisaged by Articles 48 and 56 of the Treaty, in order to reconcile the application of these measures with the basic principle of the free movement of persons within the Community and the elimination of all discrimination, in the application of the Treaty, between the nationals of the State in question and those of the other Member States.

With this in view, Article 3 of the directive provides that measures adopted on grounds of public policy and for the maintenance of public security against the nationals of Member States of the Community cannot be justified on grounds extraneous to the individual case, as is shown in particular by the requirement set out in paragraph (1) that 'only' the 'personal conduct' of those affected by the measures is to be regarded as determinative.

As departures from the rules concerning the free movement of persons constitute exceptions which must be strictly construed, the concept of 'personal conduct' expresses the requirement that a deportation order may only be made for breaches of the peace and public security which might be committed by the individual affected.

The reply to the questions referred should therefore be that *Article 3(1) and (2) of Directive No 64/221 prevents the deportation of a national of a Member State if such deportation is ordered for the purpose of deterring other aliens, that is, if it is based, in the words of the national court, on reasons of a 'general preventive nature'*.

In 1975, the European Court was faced with two questions about limitations on the free movement of workers justified on grounds of public policy. The first was whether individual decisions taken by national authorities, and not only the legislation authorising them to take such decisions, must be justified. The second question concerned the meaning of 'justified' and in particular whether a Member State may be justified in imposing on a worker from another Member State a restriction on his freedom of movement within the former State's territory, in circumstances in which it could not impose a similar restriction on one of its own nationals.

Case 36/75 Roland Rutili v Minister of the Interior

[1975] ECR 1219; [1976] 1 CMLR 140

The plaintiff was an Italian national resident in France. During 1967 and 1968 he took an active part in political and trade union activities. As a result the French authorities took the view that his presence in certain *départements* was 'likely to disturb public policy'. In 1968 he was subject first to a deportation order and later to an order directing him to reside in a particular *département*. In 1970 he was forbidden to reside in four *départements*, including the one in which he was habitually resident and in which his family continued to live. In proceedings before the Tribunal administratif, the plaintiff contested the measure taken against him in 1970. The Tribunal referred two questions to the Court of Justice of the European Communities for a preliminary ruling.

The Court

The First Question

The first question asks whether the expression 'subject to limitations justified on grounds of public policy' in Article 48 of the Treaty concerns only the legislative decisions which each Member State has decided to take in order to limit within its territory the freedom of movement and residence for nationals of other Member States or whether it also concerns individual decisions taken in application of such legislative provisions...

Inasmuch as the object of the provisions of the Treaty and of secondary legislation is to regulate the situation of individuals and to ensure their protection, it is also for the national courts to examine whether individual decisions are compatible with the relevant provisions of Community law.

This applies not only to the rules prohibiting discrimination and those concerning freedom of movement enshrined in Articles 7 and 48 of the Treaty and in Regulation No 1612/68, but also to the provisions of Directive No 64/221, which are intended both to define the scope of the reservation concerning public policy and to ensure certain minimal procedural safeguards for persons who are the subject of measures restricting their freedom of movement or their right of residence.

This conclusion is based in equal measure on due respect for the rights of the nationals of Member States, which are directly conferred by the Treaty and by Regulation No 1612/68, and the express provision in Article 3 of Directive No 64/221 which requires that measures taken on grounds of public policy or of public security 'shall be based exclusively on the personal conduct of the individual concerned'.

It is all the more necessary to adopt this view of the matter inasmuch as national legislation concerned with the protection of public policy and security usually reserves to the national authorities discretionary powers which might well escape all judicial review if the courts were unable to extend their consideration to individual decisions taken pursuant to the reservation contained in Article 48(3) of the Treaty.

The reply to the question referred to the Court must therefore be that the expression 'subject to limitations justified on grounds of public policy' in Article 48 concerns not only the legislative provisions which each Member State has adopted to limit within its territory freedom of movement and residence for nationals of other Member States but concerns also individual decisions taken in application of such legislative provisions...

The Second Question

The second question asks what is the precise meaning to be attributed to the word 'justified' in the phrase 'subject to limitations justified on grounds of public policy' in Article 48(3) of the Treaty...

In this context, regard must be had both to the rules of substantive law and to the formal or procedural rules subject to which Member States exercise the powers reserved under Article 48(3) in respect of public policy and public security.

Justification of Measures adopted on Grounds of Public Policy from the Point of View of Substantive Law

By virtue of the reservation contained in Article 48(3), Member States continue to be, in principle, free to determine the requirements of public policy in the light of their national needs.

Nevertheless, *the concept of public policy must, in the Community context and where, in particular, it is used as a justification for derogating from the fundamental principles of equality of treatment and freedom of movement for workers, be interpreted strictly,* so that its scope cannot be determined unilaterally by each Member State without being subject to control by the institutions of the Community...

In this connection Article 3 of Directive No 64/221 imposes on Member States the duty to base their decision on the individual circumstances of any person under the protection of Community law and not on general considerations.

Moreover, Article 2 of the same directive provides that grounds of public policy shall not be put to improper use by being 'invoked to service economic ends'.

Nor, under Article 8 of Regulation No 1612/68, which ensures equality of treatment as regards membership of trade unions and the exercise of rights attaching thereto, may the reservation relating to public policy be invoked on grounds arising from the exercise of those rights.

Taken as a whole, *these limitations placed on the powers of Member States in respect of control of aliens are a specific manifestation of the more general principle, enshrined in Articles 8, 9, 10 and 11 of the Convention for the Protection of Human Rights and Fundamental Freedoms, signed in Rome on 4 November 1950 and ratified by all the Member States, and in Article 2 of Protocol No 4 of the same Convention, signed in Strasbourg on 16 September 1963, which provide, in identical terms, that no restrictions in the interests of national security or public safety shall be placed on the rights secured by the above-quoted articles other than such as are necessary for the protection of those interests 'in a democratic society'.*

Measures adopted on Grounds of Public Policy: Justification from the Procedural Point of View

According to the third recital of the preamble to Directive No 64/221, one of the aims which it pursues is that 'in each Member State, nationals of other Member States should have adequate legal remedies available to them in respect of the decisions of the administration' in respect of measures based on the protection of public policy.

Under Article 8 of the same directive, the person concerned shall, in respect of any decision affecting him, have 'the same legal remedies ... as are available to nationals of the State concerned in respect of acts of the administration'.

In default of this, the person concerned must, under Article 9, at the very least be able to exercise his right of defence before a competent authority which must not be the same as that which adopted the measure restricting his freedom.

Furthermore, Article 6 of the directive provides that the person concerned shall be informed of the grounds upon which the decision taken in his case is based, unless this is contrary to the interests of the security of the State.

It is clear from these provisions that any person enjoying the protection of the provisions quoted must be entitled to a double safeguard comprising notification to him of the grounds on which any restrictive measure has been adopted in his case and the availability of a right of appeal.

The Justification for, in particular, a Prohibition on Residence in Part of the National Territory

The questions put by the Tribunal administratif were raised in connection with a measure prohibiting residence in a limited part of the national territory.

Right of entry into the territory of Member States and the right to stay there and to move freely within it is defined in the Treaty by reference to the whole territory of these States and not by reference to its internal subdivisions.

The reservation contained in Article 48(3) concerning the protection of public policy has the same scope as the rights the exercise of which may, under that paragraph, be subject to limitations.

It follows that prohibitions on residence under the reservation inserted to this effect in Article 48(3) may be imposed only in respect of the whole of the national territory.

On the other hand, in the case of partial prohibitions on residence, limited to certain areas of the territory, persons covered by Community law must, under Article 7 of the Treaty and within the field of application of that provision, be treated on a footing of equality with the nationals of the Member State concerned.

It follows that *a Member State cannot, in the case of a national of another Member State covered by the provisions of the Treaty, impose prohibitions on residence which are territorially limited except in circumstances where such prohibitions may be imposed on its own nationals.*

The answers to the second question must, therefore, be that an appraisal as to whether measures designed to safeguard public policy are justified must have regard to all rules of Community law the object of which is, on the one hand, to limit the discretionary power of Member States in this respect and, on the other, to ensure that the rights of persons subject thereunder to restrictive measures are protected.

The *Rutili* case stands for the proposition that a State which has no power to restrict the residence of its own nationals, in particular circumstances, may not exercise a power to restrict the movement of nationals of other Member States in like circumstances. It is not concerned with the question whether a State may prohibit in the case of nationals of other Member States an activity which is lawful when conducted by its own nationals. It might appear from Case 41/74 *van Duyn* v *Home Office* (see above, p. 312) that a Member State may prohibit such activities. In that case the Court sanctioned as a ground for restricting the admission of national of other Member States the fact that they were members of an organisation to which nationals of the United Kingdom were free to belong. It is now established, however, that a Member State may not impose restrictions on the admission of nationals of other Member States on the ground that they have engaged in particular conduct unless the State adopts, with respect to the same conduct on the part of its own nationals, repressive measures or other genuine and effective measures intended to combat such conduct.

Joined Cases 115 and 116/81 Adoui and Cornuaille v Belgian State
[1982] ECR 1665; [1982] 3 CMLR 631

The Court

By orders of 8 May 1981, received at the Court Registry on 12 May 1981, the President of the Tribunal de Première Instance, Liège, in interlocutory proceedings, referred to the Court for a preliminary ruling under Article 177 of the EEC Treaty a number of questions on the interpretation of Articles 7, 48(3), 56(1) and 66 of the Treaty and of Directive No 64/221/EEC of the Council of 25 February 1964 on the coordination of special measures concerning the movement and residence of foreign nationals which are justified on grounds of public policy, public security or public health...

The questions were raised in actions brought against the Belgian State by the plaintiffs in the main proceedings, who are of French nationality, in connection with the refusal by the administrative authority to issue a permit enabling them to reside in Belgian territory, on the ground that their conduct was considered to be contrary to public policy by virtue of the fact that they were waitresses in a bar which was suspect from the point of view of morals.

The Belgian Law of 21 August 1948 terminating official regulation of prostitution prohibits soliciting, incitement to debauchery, exploitation of prostitution, the keeping of a disorderly house or brothel and living on immoral earnings. It provides that supplementary regulations may be adopted by municipal councils, provided that their purpose is to uphold public morality or to ensure the keeping of the public peace. The police regulation of the City of Liège of 25 March 1957 and subsequent orders provide that persons engaged in prostitution may not display themselves to passers-by, that the doors and windows of the premises where they pursue their activity are to be closed and covered so that it is impossible to see inside and that those persons may not stand in the street near such premises.

... Prostitution as such is not prohibited by Belgian legislation, although the Law does prohibit certain incidental activities which are particularly harmful from the social point of view, such as the exploitation of prostitution by third parties and various forms of incitement to debauchery.

The reservations contained in Articles 48 and 56 of the EEC Treaty permit Member States to adopt, with respect to the nationals of other Member States and on the grounds specified in those provisions, in particular grounds justified by the requirements of public policy, measures which they cannot apply to their own nationals, inasmuch as they have no authority to expel the latter from the national territory or to deny them access thereto. Although that difference of treatment, which bears upon the nature of the measures available, must therefore be allowed, it must nevertheless be stressed that, in a Member State, the authority empowered to adopt such measures must not base the exercise of its powers on assessments of certain conduct which would have the effect of applying an arbitrary distinction to the detriment of nationals of other Member States.

It should be noted in that regard that reliance by a national authority upon the concept of public policy presupposes, as the Court held in its judgment of 27 October 1977 in Case 30/77 *R.* v *Pierre Bouchereau* [1977] ECR 1999, the existence of 'a genuine and sufficiently serious threat affecting one of the fundamental interests of society'. *Although Community law does not impose upon the Member States a uniform scale of values as regards the assessment of conduct which may be considered as contrary to public policy, it should nevertheless be stated that conduct may not be considered as being of a sufficiently serious nature to justify restrictions on the admission to or residence within the territory of a Member State of a national of another Member State in a case where the former Member State does not adopt, with respect to the same conduct on the part of its own nationals, repressive measures or other genuine and effective measures intended to combat such conduct.*

...Therefore ... a Member State may not, by virtue of the reservation relating to public policy contained in Articles 48 and 56 of the Treaty, expel a national of another Member State from its territory or refuse him access to its territory by reason of conduct which, when attributable to the former State's own nationals, does not give rise to repressive measures or other genuine and effective measures intended to combat such conduct.

Article 9 of Council Directive No 64/221 provides that where there is no right of appeal to a court of law, a decision ordering expulsion shall not be taken until an opinion has been obtained from a competent authority. That opinion must be sufficiently proximate in time to the decision ordering expulsion to provide an assurance that there are no new factors to be taken into consideration. Moreover, Article 9 produces direct effects.

Case 131/79 Regina v Secretary of State for Home Affairs, ex parte Mario Santillo [1980] ECR 1585; [1980] 2 CMLR 308

The Court

...

It may be seen from the order making the reference and the documents in the file that on 13 December 1973 the applicant was convicted before the Central Criminal Court of buggery and rape committed on 18 December 1972 on a prostitute and of indecent assault and assault occasioning actual bodily harm on 14 April 1973 on another prostitute. On 21 January 1974 he was sentenced to a total of eight years' imprisonment for these four offences. When giving judgment the Central Criminal Court made a recommendation for deportation under the Immigration Act.

On 10 October 1974 the Court of Appeal (Criminal Division) refused the applicant leave to appeal against the prison sentence and the recommendation for deportation. On 28 September 1978 the Secretary of State made a deportation order against him to take effect when his prison sentence was completed. Having completed his prison sentence on 3 April 1979 after remission of one third for good behaviour, the applicant was due to be released but remained in detention under the Immigration Act. On 10 April 1979 the applicant applied to the High Court to set aside the deportation order on the ground that, having been made more than four years after the recommendation for deportation by the Central Criminal Court, it infringed his individual rights for failure to comply with the provisions of Article 9(1) of Directive No 64/221.

Article 48 of the Treaty ensures freedom of movement for workers within the Community. This comprises the right of nationals of Member States, subject to restrictions justified on grounds of public policy, public security or public health, to move freely in the territory of Member States and to stay in a Member State to take up a post there in accordance with the laws, regulations and administrative provisions governing the employment of national workers.

According to the third recital in the preamble to Directive No 64/221, one of the aims which it pursues is that 'in each Member State, nationals of other Member States should have adequate legal remedies available to them in respect of the decisions of the administration' in the sphere of public policy, public security and public health.

Under Article 8 of the same directive the person concerned must, in respect of any decision affecting him, have 'the same legal remedies ... as are available to nationals of the State concerned in respect of acts of the administration'; in default of this, the person concerned must, under Article 9, at least be able to exercise his rights of defence before a competent authority which must not be the same as that empowered to take the decision ordering expulsion.

...

Article 9(1) of the directive is one of a number of provisions designed to ensure that the rights of nationals of a Member State regarding the freedom of movement and residence in the territory of other Member States are observed. Articles 3 and 4 of the directive restrict the grounds for deportation or for refusing a worker leave to enter a Member State. Article

6 provides that the person concerned shall be informed of the grounds of public policy, public security or public health upon which the decision taken in his case is based, unless this is contrary to the interests of the security of the State involved. Article 7 provides *inter alia* that the person concerned shall be notified of any decision to refuse the issue or renewal of a residence permit to expel him from the territory. Article 8 gives the person concerned access to the same legal remedies as are available to nationals in respect of acts of the administration.

The provisions of Article 9 are complementary to those of Article 8. Their object is to ensure a minimum procedural safeguard for persons affected by one of the measures referred to in the three cases set out in paragraph (1) of that article. Where the right of appeal relates only to the legal validity of a decision, the purpose of the intervention of the 'competent authority' referred to in Article 9(1) is to enable an exhaustive examination of all the facts and circumstances including the expediency of the proposed measure to be carried out before the decision is finally taken. Furthermore the person concerned must be able to exercise before that authority such rights of defence and of assistance or representation as the domestic law of that country provides for.

These provisions, taken together, are sufficiently well-defined and specific to enable them to be relied upon by any person concerned and capable, as such, of being applied by any court...

The requirement contained in Article 9(1) that any decision ordering expulsion must be preceded by the opinion of a 'competent authority' and that the person concerned must be able to enjoy such rights of defence and of assistance or representation as the domestic law of that country provides for, can only constitute a real safeguard if all the factors to be taken into consideration by the administration are put before the competent authority, if the opinion of the competent authority is sufficiently proximate in time to the decision ordering expulsion to ensure that there are no new factors to be taken into consideration, and if both the administration and the person concerned are in a position to take cognisance of the reasons which led the 'competent authority' to give its opinion – save where grounds touching the security of the State referred to in Article 6 of the directive make this undesirable.

FURTHER READING

Barav, A. and Thomson, S., 'Deportation of EEC Nationals from the United Kingdom in the Light of the Bouchereau Case' [1977-2] LIEI 1

Boehning, W., *The Migration of Workers in the United Kingdom and the European Community*, 1972

Durand, A., 'European Citizenship' 4 ELRev (1979) 3

Evans, A, 'Entry Formalities in the European Community' 6 ELRev (1981) 3

Hardoll, J., 'Article 48(4) EEC and Non-National Access to Public Employment' 13 ELRev (1988) 223

Hartley, T., *EEC Immigration Law*, 1978

Hartley, T., 'Are British Immigration Rules Contrary to Community Law?' 6 ELRev (1981) 280

Jacobs, F., 'The Free Movement of Persons within the EEC' 30 CLP (1977) 123

Lewis, C., 'Freedom of Movement and Community Law' 75 Law Soc Gaz (1978) 818
Pickup, D., 'Reverse Discrimination and Freedom of Movement for Workers' 23 CMLRev (1986) 135
Plender, R., 'Deportation and EEC Law' [1976] Crim L Rev 676
Plender, R., '*La libre circulation des personnes*' 104 Gazette du palais (1984) 2
Plender, R., 'Freedom of Movement in the EEC' 80 Law Soc Gaz (1983) 37 and 90
Sundberg-Weitman, B., *Discrimination on Grounds of Nationality*, 1977
Usher, J., 'Establishment, Services and Lawyers' [1979] SLT 65
van de Woude, M. and Mead, P., 'Free Movement of the Tourist in Community Law' 25 CMLRev (1988) 117
Wooldridge, F., 'Free Movement of EEC Nationals: the Limitation based on Public Policy and Public Security' 2 ELRev (1977) 190

8

ESTABLISHMENT AND SERVICES

I RELATIONSHIP TO FREE MOVEMENT OF WORKERS

Freedom of establishment and the freedom to supply services are closely linked to the free movement of workers. The same economic activity may fall within any one of these titles, depending upon the legal status of the person performing it. The example might be taken of a UK national who is a restorer of antique furniture. If he wishes to take up salaried employment with antique dealers in Luxembourg, it will be a question of free movement of workers; if, being self-employed, he wishes to move his business to Luxembourg or indeed to set up a branch there, it will be a question of freedom of establishment; if, finally, he wishes, while keeping his place of business within the United Kingdom, to fly to Luxembourg from time to time so as to restore specific items, it will be a question of freedom to supply services.

Hence it is hardly surprising that the Court of Justice has found itself confronted with cases referred for a preliminary ruling where the legal status of the person wishing to perform the particular economic activity has not been clear. In so far as all three freedoms involve common problems, the Court has given answers equally applicable to any of the situations. The most basic common problem is that of discrimination on the basis of nationality. Thus, the judgment in Case 13/76 *Donà* v *Mantero* [1976] ECR 1333 at 1339–41, involving attempts to recruit foreign players for an Italian football team, is expressed to relate both to free movement of workers and to freedom to supply services. Council Directive No 64/221/EEC of 25 February 1964 on the coordination of special measures concerning the movement and residence of foreign nationals which are justified on grounds of public policy, public security or public health states in its Article 1(1) that:

The provisions of this directive shall apply to any national of a Member State who resides in or travels to another Member State of the Community, either *in order to pursue an activity as an employed or self-employed person, or as a recipient of services.*

Likewise, Council Directive No 68/360/EEC of 15 October 1968 on the abolition of restrictions on movement and residence within the Community for workers of Member States and their families is parallelled by Council Directive No 73/148/EEC of 21 May 1973 on the abolition of restrictions on movement and residence within the Community for nationals of Member States with regard to establishment and the provision of services (OJ 1973, L 172, p. 14). Council Regulation No 1251/70 of 29 June 1970 on the right of workers to remain in the territory of a Member State after having been employed in that State is parallelled by Council Directive No 75/34/EEC of 17 December 1974 (OJ 1975, L 14, p. 10) concerning the right of nationals of a Member State to remain in the territory of another Member State after having pursued therein an activity in a self-employed capacity.

Hence the judgment of the Court in the *Royer* case is expressed to be equally applicable in all three situations.

Case 48/75 The State v Jean Noël Royer [1976] ECR 497; [1976] 2 CMLR 619

The Court

The facts submitted by the national court and the choice of the provisions of Community law of which it seeks interpretation allows of different hypotheses according to whether the accused falls within the provisions of Community law by virtue of an occupation which he carried out himself or by virtue of a post which he had himself found or again as the husband of a person subject to the provisions of Community law because of her occupation so that the accused's position may be regulated by either:

(a) the chapter of the Treaty concerning workers and, more especially, Article 48 which was implemented by Regulation (EEC) No 1612/68 of the Council of 15 October 1968 on freedom of movement for workers within the Community (OJ, English Sp Ed 1968 (II), p. 475) and Council Directive No 68/360/EEC or

(b) the chapters concerning the right of establishment and freedom to provide services, in particular Articles 52, 53, 56, 62 and 66 implemented by Council Directive No 73/148 of 21 May 1973 concerning the removal of restrictions on the movement and residence of nationals of the Member States within the Community for establishment and provision of services (OJ, L 172, p. 14).

Nevertheless comparison of these different provisions shows that they are based on the same principles both in so far as they concern the entry into and residence in the territory of Member States of persons covered by Community law and the prohibition of all discrimination between them on grounds of nationality.

In particular Article 10 of Regulation (EEC) No 1612/68, Article 1 of Directive No 68/360 and Article 1 of Directive No 73/148 extend in identical terms the application of Community law relating to entry into and residence in the territory of the Member States to the spouse of any person covered by these provisions.

Further, Article 1 of Directive No 64/221 states that the directive shall apply to any national of a Member State who resides in or travels to another Member State of the Community either in order to pursue an activity as an employed or self-employed person, or as a recipient of services, and his or her spouse and members of their family.

It is apparent from the foregoing that substantially identical provisions of Community law apply in a case such as the one at issue if there exists either with regard to the party concerned or his spouse a connection with Community law under any of the above-mentioned provisions.

The questions referred by the Tribunal de Première Instance will be answered in the light of these considerations and without prejudice to the national court's right to determine the situation before it with respect to provisions of Community law.

The present chapter is concerned with those matters which, if not specific to the freedom of establishment and the freedom to supply services, are of particular importance in the exercise of those freedoms.

II FREEDOM OF ESTABLISHMENT

1. TREATY PROVISIONS

EEC Treaty

Article 52

Within the framework of the provisions set out below, *restrictions on the freedom of establishment* of nationals of a Member State in the territory of another Member State *shall be abolished by progressive stages in the course of the transitional period.* Such progressive abolition shall also apply to restrictions on the setting up of agencies, branches or subsidiaries by nationals of any Member State established in the territory of any Member State.

Freedom of establishment shall include the right to take up and pursue activities as self-employed persons and to set up and manage undertakings, in particular companies or firms within the meaning of the second paragraph of Article 58, *under the conditions laid down for its own nationals by the law of the country* where such establishment is effected, subject to the provisions of the chapter relating to capital.

Article 53

Member States shall not introduce any new restrictions on the right of establishment in their territories of nationals of other Member States, save as otherwise provided in this Treaty.

Article 54

1. Before the end of the first stage, *the Council shall,* acting unanimously on a proposal from the Commission and after consulting the Economic and Social Committee and the Assembly, *draw up a general programme* for the abolition of existing restrictions

on freedom of establishment within the Community. The Commission shall submit its proposal to the Council during the first two years of the first stage.

The programme shall set out the general conditions under which freedom of establishment is to be attained in the case of each type of activity and in particular the stages by which it is to be attained.

2 *In order to implement this general programme* or, in the absence of such programme, in order to achieve a stage in attaining freedom of establishment as regards a particular activity, *the Council shall,* on a proposal from the Commission and after consulting the Economic and Social Committee and the Assembly, *issue directives,* acting unanimously until the end of the first stage and by a qualified majority thereafter.

...

Article 55

The provisions of *this chapter shall not apply,* so far as any given Member State is concerned, *to activities* which in that State are *connected,* even occasionally, *with the exercise of official authority.*

The Council may, acting by a qualified majority on a proposal from the Commission, rule that the provisions of this chapter shall not apply to certain activities.

Article 56

1. The provisions of this chapter and measures taken in pursuance thereof shall not prejudice the applicability of provisions laid down by law, regulation or administrative action providing for special treatment for foreign nationals on grounds of public policy, public security or public health.

2 Before the end of the transitional period, the Council shall, acting unanimously on a proposal from the Commission and after consulting the Assembly, issue directives for the coordination of the aforementioned provisions laid down by law, regulation or administrative action. After the end of the second stage, however, the Council shall, acting by a qualified majority on a proposal from the Commission, issue directives for the coordination of such provisions as, in each Member State, are a matter for regulation or administrative action.

Article 57

1. In order to make it easier for persons to take up and pursue activities as self-employed persons, the Council shall, on a proposal from the Commission and after consulting the Assembly, acting unanimously during the first stage and by a qualified majority thereafter, issue directives for the mutual recognition of diplomas, certificates and other evidence of formal qualifications.

2 For the same purpose, *the Council shall, before the end of the transitional period,* acting on a proposal from the Commission and after consulting the Assembly, *issue directives* for the coordination of the provisions laid down by law, regulation or administrative action in Member States concerning the taking up and pursuit of activities as self-employed persons...

3. In the case of the medical and allied and pharmaceutical professions, the progressive abolition of restrictions shall be dependent upon coordination of the conditions for their exercise in the various Member States.

2. THE GENERAL PROGRAMME

The 'General Programme' referred to in Article 54(1) was published in January 1962 (JO 36/62, OJ Sp Ed, Second Series, No 9, p. 7), and contains an illustrative list of restrictions on freedom of establishment which should be abolished.

General Programme for the Abolition of Restrictions on Freedom of Establishment OJ Sp Ed 2nd Series IX, p. 7

The Council of the European Economic Community,

Having regard to the provisions of the Treaty, and in particular Articles 54 and 132(5) thereof;

...

Title I

Beneficiaries

Subject to any decisions taken by the Council under the second subparagraph of Article 227(2) of the Treaty and without prejudice to subsequent provisions laying down association arrangements between the European Economic Community and the overseas countries and territories having attained independence after the entry into force of the Treaty, the persons entitled to benefit from the abolition of restrictions on freedom of establishment as set out in this General Programme are:

- nationals of Member States or of the overseas countries and territories, and
- companies and firms formed under the law of a Member State or of an overseas country or territory and having either the seat prescribed by their statutes, or their centre of administration, or their main establishment situated within the Community or in an overseas country or territory,

who wish to establish themselves in order to pursue activities as self-employed persons in a Member State; and

- nationals of Member States or of the overseas countries and territories who are established in a Member State or in an overseas country or territory, and
- companies and firms as above, provided that, where only the seat prescribed by their statutes is situated within the Community or in an overseas country or territory, their activity shows a real and continuous link with the economy of a Member State or of an overseas country or territory; such link shall not be one of nationality, whether of the members of the company or firm, or of the persons holding managerial or supervisory posts therein, or of the holders of the capital,

who wish to set up agencies, branches or subsidiaries in a Member State.

...

Title III

A. ...

Such restrictive provisions and practices are in particular those which, in respect of foreign nationals only:

(a) prohibit the taking up or pursuit of an activity as a self-employed person;
(b) make the taking up or pursuit of an activity as a self-employed person subject to an authorisation or to the issue of a document such as a foreign trader's permit;
(c) impose additional conditions in respect of the granting of any authorisation required for the taking up or pursuit of an activity as a self-employed person;
(d) make the taking up or pursuit of an activity as a self-employed person subject to a period of prior residence or training in the host country;
(e) make the taking up or pursuit of an activity as a self-employed person more costly through taxation or other financial burdens, such as a requirement that the person concerned shall lodge a deposit or provide security in the host country;
(f) limit or hinder, by making more costly or more difficult access to sources of supply or to distribution outlets;
(g) prohibit or hinder access to any vocational training which is necessary or useful for the pursuit of an activity as a self-employed person;
(h) prohibit foreign nationals from becoming members of companies or firms, or restrict their rights as members, in particular as regards the functions which they may perform within the company or firm;
(i) deny or restrict the right to participate in social security schemes, in particular sickness, accident, invalidity or old age insurance schemes, or the right to receive family allowances;
(j) grant less favourable treatment in the event of nationalisation, expropriation or requisition.

The like shall apply to provisions and practices which, in respect of foreign nationals only, exclude, limit or impose conditions on the power to exercise rights normally attaching to an activity as a self-employed person, and in particular the power:

(a) to enter into contracts, in particular contracts for work, business or agricultural tenancies, and contracts of employment, and to enjoy all rights arising under such contracts;
(b) to submit tenders for or to act directly as a party or as a subcontractor in contracts with the State or with any other legal person governed by public law;
(c) to obtain licences or authorisations issued by the State or by any other legal person governed by public law;
(d) to acquire, use or dispose of movable or immovable property or rights therein;
(e) to acquire, use or dispose of intellectual property and all rights deriving therefrom;
(f) to borrow, and in particular to have access to the various forms of credit;
(g) to receive aids granted by the State, whether direct or indirect;
(h) to be a party to legal or administrative proceedings;
(i) to join professional or trade organisations;

where the professional or trade activities of the person concerned necessarily involve the exercise of such power.

Furthermore, included among the abovementioned provisions and practices are those which limit or impair the freedom of personnel belonging to the main establishment in one Member State to take up managerial or supervisory posts in agencies, branches or subsidiaries in another Member State.

B. Any requirements imposed, pursuant to any provision laid down by law, regulation or administrative action or in consequence of any administrative practice, in respect of the taking up or pursuit of an activity as a self-employed person, where, although applicable irrespective of nationality, their effect is exclusively or principally to hinder the taking up or pursuit of such activity by foreign nationals.

...

Title V

Mutual Recognition of Diplomas and Other Evidence of Formal Qualifications – Coordination

...

Pending such mutual recognition of diplomas, or such coordination, and in order to facilitate the taking up and pursuit of activities as self-employed persons and to avoid distortions, a transitional system may be applied; such system may where appropriate include provision for the production of a certificate establishing that the activity in question was actually and lawfully carried on in the country of origin.

3. THE POSITION OF THOSE WITH PROFESSIONAL QUALIFICATIONS

Although quite a number of directives under Article 54 had been issued by the end of the transitional period, they were limited in scope and did not concern the 'professions'. The general structure of these directives is to define a particular economic activity, often by reference to the ISIC* nomenclature, and to require the elimination of restrictions preventing nationals of other Member States from taking part in such activities. In the case of the professions, there is the further problem of the mutual recognition of professional qualifications, which Article 57 was intended to overcome. By the end of the transitional period, the Commission had put forward a number of proposed directives, but they had not been adopted by the Council.

A. THE LEGAL PROFESSION

The common underlying feature of the directives and proposed directives was that all of them linked the elimination of discrimination on the grounds of nationality to the liberalisation of a defined activity. In 1974, however, the Court was faced

---

* International Standard Industrial Classification of all Economic Activities (Statistical Office of the United Nations, Statistical Papers, Series M, no 4, rev. 1, New York, 1958).

with a case involving a Dutch national wishing to be called to the Bar in Belgium who had obtained the necessary qualifications, and whose application was refused solely on the grounds of nationality. The Court held that, although no directive on freedom of establishment for lawyers had been issued, the prohibition of discrimination on the grounds of nationality as such produced direct effects, and was not inextricably interlinked with the liberalisation of a defined activity and the recognition of foreign qualifications.

Case 2/74 Jean Reyners v Belgian State
[1974] ECR 631; [1974] 2 CMLR 305

The plaintiff, a Dutch national resident in Belgium, wished to be admitted to the profession of avocat in Belgium. He had the necessary academic qualification, a Belgian diploma of docteur en droit, but under the Belgian legislation only Belgians could be admitted as practitioners. The plaintiff challenged one provision of the Belgian legislation before the Conseil d'Etat on the grounds that it infringed the EEC Treaty. The Conseil d'Etat referred a number of questions for a preliminary ruling.

The Court

The Conseil d'Etat inquires whether Article 52 of the EEC Treaty is, since the end of the transitional period, a 'directly applicable provision' despite the absence of directives as prescribed by Articles 54(2) and 57(1) of the Treaty.

...

Article 7 of the Treaty, which forms part of the 'principles' of the Community, provides that within the scope of application of the Treaty and without prejudice to any special provisions contained therein, 'any discrimination on grounds of nationality shall be prohibited'.

Article 52 provides for the implementation of this general provision in the special sphere of the right of establishment.

The words 'within the framework of the provisions set out below' refer to the chapter relating to the right of establishment taken as a whole and require, in consequence, to be interpreted in this general context.

After having stated that 'restrictions on the freedom of establishment of nationals of a Member State in the territory of another Member State shall be abolished by progressive stages in the course of the transitional period', Article 52 expresses the guiding principle in the matter by providing that freedom of establishment shall include the right to take up and pursue activities as self-employed persons 'under the conditions laid down for its own nationals by the law of the country where such establishment is effected'.

For the purpose of achieving this objective by progressive stages during the transitional period Article 54 provides for the drawing up by the Council of a 'general programme' and, for the implementation of this programme, directives intended to attain freedom of establishment in respect of the various activities in question.

Besides these liberalising measures, Article 57 provides for directives intended to ensure mutual recognition of diplomas, certificates and other evidence of formal qualifications and in a general way for the coordination of laws with regard to establishment and the pursuit of activities as self-employed persons.

It appears from the above that in the system of the chapter on the right of establishment the 'general programme' and the directives provided for by the Treaty are intended to accomplish two functions, the first being to eliminate obstacles in the way of attaining freedom of establishment during the transitional period, the second being to introduce into the law of Member States a set of provisions intended to facilitate the effective exercise of this freedom for the purpose of assisting economic and social interpenetration within the Community in the sphere of activities as self-employed persons.

This second objective is the one referred to, first, by certain provisions of Article 54(3), relating in particular to cooperation between the competent authorities in the Member States and adjustment of administrative procedures and practices, and, secondly, by the set of provisions in Article 57.

The effect of the provisions of Article 52 must be decided within the framework of this system.

The rule on equal treatment with nationals is one of the fundamental legal provisions of the Community.

As a reference to a set of legislative provisions effectively applied by the country of establishment to its own nationals, this rule is, by its essence, capable of being directly invoked by nationals of all the other Member States.

In laying down that freedom of establishment shall be attained at the end of the transitional period, Article 52 thus imposes an obligation to attain a precise result, the fulfilment of which had to be made easier by, but not made dependent on, the implementation of a programme of progressive measures.

The fact that this progression has not been adhered to leaves the obligation itself intact beyond the end of the period provided for its fulfilment.

This interpretation is in accordance with Article 8(7) of the Treaty, according to which the expiry of the transitional period shall constitute the latest date by which all the rules laid down must enter into force and all the measures required for establishing the Common Market must be implemented.

It is not possible to invoke against such an effect the fact that the Council has failed to issue the directives provided for by Articles 54 and 57 or the fact that certain of the directives actually issued have not fully attained the objective of non-discrimination required by Article 52.

After the expiry of the transitional period the directives provided for by the chapter on the right of establishment have become superfluous with regard to implementing the rule on nationality, since this is henceforth sanctioned by the Treaty itself with direct effect.

These directives have however not lost all interest since they preserve an important scope in the field of measures intended to make easier the effective exercise of the right of freedom of establishment.

It is right therefore to reply to the question raised that, since the end of the transitional period, Article 52 of the Treaty is a directly applicable provision despite the absence in a particular sphere of the directives prescribed by Articles 54(2) and 57(1) of the Treaty.

The Court also dealt in its judgment with the question of the exercise of official authority mentioned in Article 55 of the EEC Treaty, a question which had given rise to much debate with regard to freedom of establishment for lawyers.

The Court

The Conseil d'Etat has also requested a definition of what is meant in the first paragraph of Article 55 by 'activities which in that State are connected, even occasionally, with the exercise of official authority'.

...

Under the terms of the first paragraph of Article 55 the provisions of the Chapter on the right of establishment shall not apply 'so far as any given Member State is concerned, to activities which in that State are connected, even occasionally, with the exercise of official authority'.

Having regard to the fundamental character of freedom of establishment and the rule on equal treatment with nationals in the system of the Treaty, the exceptions allowed by the first paragraph of Article 55 cannot be given a scope which would exceed the objective for which this exemption clause was inserted.

The first paragraph of Article 55 must enable Member States to exclude non-nationals from taking up functions involving the exercise of official authority which are connected with one of the activities of self-employed persons provided for in Article 52.

This need is fully satisfied when the exclusion of nationals is limited to those activities which, taken on their own, constitute a direct and specific connection with the exercise of official authority.

An extension of the exception allowed by Article 55 to a whole profession would be possible only in cases where such activities were linked with that profession in such a way that freedom of establishment would result in imposing on the Member State concerned the obligation to allow the exercise, even occasionally, by non-nationals of functions appertaining to official authority.

This extension is on the other hand not possible when, within the framework of an independent profession, the activities connected with the exercise of official authority are separable from the professional activity in question taken as a whole.

In the absence of any directive issued under Article 57 for the purpose of harmonising the national provisions relating, in particular, to professions such as that of avocat, the practice of such professions remains governed by the laws of the various Member States.

The possible application of the restrictions on freedom of establishment provided for by the first paragraph of Article 55 must therefore be considered separately in connection with each Member State having regard to the national provisions applicable to the organisation and the practice of this profession.

This consideration must however take into account the Community character of the limits imposed by Article 55 on the exceptions permitted to the principle of freedom of establishment in order to avoid the effectiveness of the Treaty being defeated by unilateral provisions of Member States.

Professional activities involving contacts, even regular and organic, with the courts, including even compulsory cooperation in their functioning, do not constitute, as such, connection with the exercise of official authority.

The most typical activities of the profession of avocat, in particular, such as consultation and legal assistance and also representation and the defence of parties in court, even when the intervention or assistance of the avocat is compulsory or is a legal monopoly, cannot be considered as connected with the exercise of official authority.

The exercise of these activities leaves the discretion of judicial authority and the free exercise of judicial power intact.

It is therefore right to reply to the question raised that the exception to freedom of establishment provided for by the first paragraph of Article 55 must be restricted to those of the activities referred to in Article 52 which in themselves involve a direct and specific connection with the exercise of official authority.

In any case it is not possible to give this description, in the context of a profession such as that of avocat, to activities such as consultation and legal assistance or the representation and defence of parties in court, even if the performance of these activities is compulsory or there is a legal monopoly in respect of it.

B. ARCHITECTS

The decision in *Reyners* was followed in Case 11/77 *Patrick* v *Ministre des Affaires Culturelles* [1977] ECR 1199. In this case, a British architect wished to practise in France. Although he did not have a French qualification, his British qualification was expressly recognised under French legislation, and his application was refused solely on the grounds of nationality. The Court held that in the case of a national of a new Member State, Article 52 produced direct effects as from 1 January 1973, and that therefore, provided he had the necessary qualifications, such a person was entitled to practise as an architect in another Member State. Less clear is the situation where a person wishing to exercise an activity in another Member State has a qualification which is recognised only to a limited extent in the host country.

Case 71/76 Jean Thieffry v Conseil de l'Ordre des Avocats à la Cour de Paris [1977] ECR 765; [1977] 2 CMLR 373

The Court

By order of 13 July 1976, lodged at the Court Registry on 19 July 1976, the Cour d'Appel, Paris, put to the Court under Article 177 of the EEC Treaty a question concerning the interpretation of Article 57 of the Treaty, which relates to the mutual recognition of evidence of professional qualifications for the purpose of access to activities as self-employed persons, with regard in particular to admission to exercise the profession of advocate.

The case before the Cour d'Appel concerns the admission to the Ordre des Avocats auprès de la Cour de Paris [the Paris Bar] of a Belgian advocate, who is the holder of a Belgian diploma of Doctor of Laws which has been recognised by a French university as equivalent to the French licenciate's degree in law, and who subsequently obtained the Certificat d'Aptitude à la Profession d'Avocat'[Qualifying Certificate for the Profession of Advocate], having sat and passed that examination, in accordance with French legislation.

The appellant in the main action applied for admission to the Paris Bar, but by an order of 9 March 1976 the Conseil de l'Ordre [Bar Council] rejected his application on the ground that the person concerned 'offers no French diploma evidencing a licentiate's degree or a doctor's degree'.

...

With a view to making it easier for persons to take up and pursue activities as self-employed persons, Article 57 assigns to the Council the duty of issuing directives concerning, first, the mutual recognition of diplomas, and secondly, the coordination of the provisions laid down by law or administrative action in Member States concerning the taking up and pursuit of activities as self-employed persons.

That article is therefore directed towards reconciling freedom of establishment with the application of national professional rules justified by the general good, in particular rules relating to organisation, qualifications, professional ethics, supervision and liability, provided that such application is effected without discrimination.

In the General Programme for the abolition of restrictions on freedom of establishment, adopted on 18 December 1961 pursuant to Article 54 of the Treaty, the Council proposed to eliminate not only overt discrimination, but also any form of disguised discrimination, by designating in Title III (B) as restrictions which are to be eliminated 'any requirements imposed, pursuant to any provision laid down by law, regulation or administrative action or in consequence of any administrative practice, in respect of the taking up or pursuit of an activity as a self-employed person where, although applicable irrespective of nationality, their effect is exclusively or principally to hinder the taking up or pursuit of such activity by foreign nationals' (OJ, Sp Ed, Second Series, no 9, p. 8).

In the context of the abolition of restrictions on freedom of establishment, that programme provides useful guidance for the implementation of the relevant provisions of the Treaty.

It follows from the provisions cited taken as a whole that freedom of establishment, subject to observance of professional rules justified by the general good, is one of the objectives of the Treaty.

In so far as Community law makes no special provision, these objectives may be attained by measures enacted by the Member States, which under Article 5 of the Treaty are bound to take 'all appropriate measures, whether general or particular, to ensure fulfilment of the obligations arising out of this Treaty or resulting from action taken by the institutions of the Community', and to abstain 'from any measure which could jeopardise the attainment of the objectives of this Treaty'.

Consequently, *if the freedom of establishment provided for by Article 52 can be ensured in a Member State either under the provisions of the laws and regulations in force, or by virtue of the practices of the public service or of professional bodies, a person subject to Community law cannot be denied the practical benefit of that freedom solely by virtue of the fact that, for a particular profession, the directives provided for by Article 57 of the Treaty have not yet been adopted.*

Since the practical enjoyment of freedom of establishment can thus in certain circumstances depend upon national practice or legislation, it is incumbent upon the competent public authorities – including legally recognised professional bodies – to ensure that such practice or legislation are applied in accordance with the objective defined by the provisions of the Treaty relating to freedom of establishment.

In particular, *there is an unjustified restriction on that freedom where, in a Member State, admission to a particular profession is refused to a person covered by the Treaty who holds a diploma which has been recognised as an equivalent qualification by the competent authority of the country of establishment and who furthermore has fulfilled the specific conditions regarding professional training in force in that country,* solely by reason of the fact that the person concerned does not possess the national diploma corresponding to the diploma which he holds and which has been recognised as an equivalent qualification.

The national court specifically referred to the effect of a recognition of equivalence 'by the university authority of the country of establishment', and in the course of the proceedings the question has been raised whether a distinction should be drawn, as regards the equivalence of diplomas, between university recognition, granted with a view to permitting the pursuit of certain studies, and a recognition having 'civil effect', granted with a view to permitting the pursuit of a professional activity.

It emerges from the information supplied in this connection by the Commission and the Governments which took part in the proceedings that the distinction between the academic effect and the civil effect of the recognition of foreign diplomas is acknowledged, in various forms, in the legislation and practice of several Member States.

Since this distinction falls within the ambit of the national law of the different States, it is for the national authorities to assess the consequences thereof, taking account, however, of the objectives of Community law.

In this connection it is important that, in each Member State, the recognition of evidence of a professional qualification for the purposes of establishment may be accepted to the full extent compatible with the observance of the professional requirements mentioned above.

Consequently, *it is for the competent national authorities, taking account of the requirements of Community law set out above, to make such assessments of the facts as will enable them to judge whether a recognition granted by a university authority can, in addition to its academic effect, constitute valid evidence of a professional qualification.*

The fact that a national legislation provides for recognition of equivalence only for university purposes does not of itself justify the refusal to recognise such equivalence as evidence of a professional qualification.

This is particularly so when a diploma recognised for university purposes is supplemented by a professional qualifying certificate obtained according to the legislation of the country of establishment.

In these circumstances, the answer to the question referred to the Court should be that when a national of one Member State desirous of exercising a professional activity such as the profession of advocate in another Member State has obtained a diploma in his country of origin which has been recognised as an equivalent qualification by the competent authority under the legislation of the country of establishment and which has thus enabled him to sit and pass the special qualifying examination for the profession in question, the act of demanding the national diploma prescribed by the legislation of the country of establishment constitutes, even in the absence of the directives provided for in Article 57, a restriction incompatible with the freedom of establishment guaranteed by Article 52 of the Treaty.

C. THE MEDICAL PROFESSION

Following the decision in *Reyners,* the importance of directives (other than those of general scope) in the matter of freedom of establishment has been as a method of facilitating the mutual recognition of professional qualifications. This is particularly the case with regard to the two directives made, together with certain correlative decisions and recommendations, on 16 June 1975, and taking effect from 20 December 1976, on freedom of establishment for doctors. Two main problems are dealt with by the directives. Council Directive No 75/362 concerning the mutual recognition of diplomas, certificates and other evidence of formal qualifications in medicine, including measures to facilitate the effective exercise of the right of establishment and freedom to provide services (OJ 1975, L 167, p. 1) is, as its title implies, concerned basically with the mutual recognition of qualifications, and the following extracts are taken solely from that part of the directive. Council Directive No 75/363/EEC concerning the coordination of provisions laid down by law, regulation or administrative action in respect of activities of doctors (*ibid.*, p. 14) performs the important correlative function of ensuring that these qualifications conform to certain minimum standards.

Both directives are expressed to apply to *employed* as well as self-employed doctors (Directive No 75/362 Article 24, Directive No 75/363 Article 6).

Council Directive No 75/362/EEC

Article 1

This directive shall apply to the activities of doctors.

Article 2

Each Member State shall recognise the diplomas, certificates and other evidence of formal qualifications awarded to nationals of Member States by the other Member States in accordance with Article 1 of Directive No 75/363/EEC and which are listed in Article 3, by giving such qualifications, as far as the right to take up and pursue the self-employed activities of a doctor is concerned, the same effect in its territory as those which the Member State itself awards.

[Article 3 lists the relevant diplomas etc.]

Article 4

Each Member State shall recognise the diplomas, certificates and other evidence of formal qualifications in specialised medicine awarded to nationals of Member States by the other Member States in accordance with Articles 2, 3, 4 and 8 of Directive No 75/363/EEC and which are listed in Article 5, by giving such qualifications the same effect in its territory as those which the Member State itself awards.

Article 5

1. The diplomas, certificates and other evidence of formal qualifications referred to in Article 4 shall be those which, having been awarded by the competent authorities or bodies listed in paragraph 2, correspond, for the purpose of the specialised training concerned, to the qualifications recognised in the various Member States and listed in paragraph 3.

[Paragraphs 2 and 3 contain the relevant lists.]

Article 6

Each Member State with provisions on this matter laid down by law, regulation or administrative action shall recognise the diplomas, certificates and other evidence of formal qualifications in specialised medicine awarded to nationals of Member States by other Member States in accordance with Articles 2, 3, 5 and 8 of Directive No 75/363/EEC and which are listed in Article 7, by giving such qualifications the same effect in its territory as those which the Member State itself awards.

...

Article 8

1. Nationals of Member States wishing to acquire one of the diplomas, certificates or other evidence of formal qualifications of specialist doctors not referred to in Articles 4 and 6, or which, although referred to in Article 6, are not awarded in the Member State of origin or the Member State from which the foreign national comes, may be required by a host Member State to fulfil the conditions of training laid down in respect of the specialty by its own law, regulation or administrative action.

2. The host Member State shall, however, take into account, in whole or in part, the training periods completed by the nationals referred to in paragraph 1 and attested by the award of a diploma, certificate or other evidence of formal training by the competent authorities of the Member State of origin or the Member State from which the foreign national comes provided such training periods correspond to those required in the host Member State for the specialised training in question.

3. The competent authorities or bodies of the host Member State, having verified the content and duration of the specialist training of the person concerned on the basis of the diplomas, certificates and other evidence of formal qualifications submitted, shall inform him of the period of additional training required and of the fields to be covered by it.

Council Directive No 75/363/EEC

Article 1

1. The Member States shall require persons wishing to take up and pursue a medical profession to hold a diploma, certificate or other evidence of formal qualifications in medicine referred to in Article 3 of Directive No 75/362/EEC which guarantees that during his complete training period the person concerned has acquired:

(a) adequate knowledge of the sciences on which medicine is based and a good understanding of the scientific methods including the principles of measuring biological functions, the evaluation of scientifically established facts and the analysis of data;

(b) sufficient understanding of the structure, functions and behaviour of healthy and sick persons, as well as relations between the state of health and the physical and social surroundings of the human being;

(c) adequate knowledge of clinical disciplines and practices, providing him with a coherent picture of mental and physical diseases, of medicine from the points of view of prophylaxis, diagnosis and therapy and of human reproduction;

(d) suitable clinical experience in hospitals under appropriate supervision.

2. A complete period of medical training of this kind shall comprise at least a six-year course or 5,500 hours of theoretical and practical instruction given in a university or under the supervision of a university.

3. In order to be accepted for this training, the candidate must have a diploma or a certificate which entitles him to be admitted to the universities of a Member State for the course of study concerned .

4. In the case of persons who started their training before 1 January 1972, the training referred to in paragraph 2 may include six months' full-time practical training at university level under the supervision of the competent authorities.

5. Nothing in this directive shall prejudice any facility which may be granted in accordance with their own rules by Member States in respect of their own territory to authorise holders of diplomas, certificates or other evidence of formal qualifications which have not been obtained in a Member State to take up and pursue the activities of a doctor.

Article 2

1. Member States shall ensure that the training leading to a diploma, certificate or other evidence of formal qualifications in specialised medicine meets the following requirements at least:

(a) it shall entail the successful completion of six years' study within the framework of the training course referred to in Article 1;

(b) it shall comprise theoretical and practical instruction;

(c) it shall be a full-time course supervised by the competent authorities or bodies;

(d) it shall be in a university centre, in a teaching hospital or, where appropriate in a health establishment approved for this purpose by the competent authorities or bodies;

(e) it shall involve the personal participation of the doctor training to be a specialist in the activity and in the responsibilities of the establishments concerned.

2. Member States shall make the award of a diploma, certificate or other evidence of formal qualifications in specialised medicine subject to the possession of one of the diplomas, certificates or other evidence of formal qualifications in medicine referred to in Article 1.

3. Within the time limit laid down in Article 7, Member States shall designate the authorities or bodies competent to issue the diplomas, certificates or other evidence of formal qualifications referred to in paragraph 1.

Article 3

1. Without prejudice to the principle of full-time training as set out in Article 2(1)(c), and until such time as the Council makes a decision in accordance with paragraph 3, Member States may permit part-time specialist training, under conditions approved by the competent national authorities, when training on a full-time basis would not be practicable for well-founded reasons.

2. The total period of specialised training may not be shortened by virtue of paragraph 1. The standard of the training may not be impaired, either by its part-time nature or by the practice of private, remunerated professional activity.

3. Four years at the latest after notification of this directive and in the light of a review of the situation, acting on a proposal from the Commission, and bearing in mind that the possibility of part-time training should continue to exist in certain circumstances to

be examined separately for each specialty, the Council shall decide whether the provisions of paragraphs 1 and 2 should be retained or amended.

[Articles 4 and 5 deal with the minimum length of certain specialised training courses.]

The distinction between mutual recognition and minimum standards was applied also in facilitating freedom of establishment for nurses (Council Directives Nos 77/452/EEC and 77/453/EEC of 27 June 1977: OJ 1977, L 176, pp. 1 and 8).

The Court has interpreted Directive No 75/362 in the sense that it agrees that it gives rise to rights on the part of individuals against the Member States of which they are nationals.

Case 246/80 Broekmeulen v Huisarts Registratie Commissie
[1981] ECR 2311; [1982] 1 CMLR 91

The Court

By an order dated 21 October 1980 which was received at the Court on 11 November 1980 the Commissie van Beroep Huisartsgeneeskunde [Appeals Committee for General Medicine, hereinafter referred to as 'the Appeals Committee'], which sits in The Hague, referred to the Court for a preliminary ruling under Article 177 of the EEC Treaty a question as to the interpretation of Council Directive No 75/362/EEC of 16 June 1975 concerning the mutual recognition of diplomas, certificates and other evidence of formal qualifications in medicine, including measures to facilitate the effective exercise of the right of establishment and freedom to provide services, and Council Directive No 75/363/EEC of 16 June 1975 concerning the coordination of provisions laid down by law, regulation or administrative action in respect of activities of doctors...

The question was raised in the context of an appeal lodged by a doctor of Netherlands nationality, Dr Broekmeulen, who, having obtained a diploma of doctor of medicine, surgery and obstetrics at the Catholic University of Louvain, Belgium, was authorised by the Netherlands Secretary of State for Health and the Environment to practice medicine in the Netherlands; however, the Huisarts Registratie Commissie [General Practitioners' Registration Committee, hereinafter referred to as the 'Registration Committee'] refused to register him as a huisarts' [general practitioner].

...

The Registration Committee took the view that the orders of the Council for General Medicine expressly provided that nationals of other Member States, who hold a diploma of doctor of medicine awarded by one of the other Member States and recognised by virtue of Directives Nos 75/362/EEC and 75/363/EEC and who have been authorised to practise medicine in the Netherlands, must at their request be enrolled on the register of general practitioners, but that that exception did not apply to Dr Broekmeulen on account of his Netherlands nationality.

That decision was challenged before the Appeals Committee, which stayed the proceedings in order to refer the following question to the Court for a preliminary ruling: 'Does it follow from Directives Nos 75/362/EEC and 75/363/EEC (Official Journal L 167 of 30 June 1975) that a Netherlands national who has obtained in Belgium the *Wettelijk*

Diploma van Doctor in de Genees-, Heel- en Verloskunde [Diploma of Doctor of Medicine, Surgery and Obstetrics] and who is consequently entitled to practise in Belgium as a general practitioner has the right, on becoming established in the Netherlands, to be enrolled on the register of recognised general practitioners of the Royal Netherlands Society for the Promotion of Medicine without first having undergone training in the Netherlands as a general practitioner?' The Appeals Committee stated that by virtue of mandatory provisions of Netherlands law enrolment on the said register is possible only after that training has been undergone and that a doctor may practise in the Netherlands as a general practitioner only after enrolment on the said register.

...

In the question referred to the Court the Appeals Committee seeks in the first place to ascertain whether a Netherlands national holding a Belgian diploma listed under Article 3 of Directive No 75/362/EEC and recognised in every Member State by virtue of Article 2 of that directive may avail himself of those provisions if he intends to establish himself in the Netherlands.

Under Article 2 of the directive each Member State is to recognise the diplomas listed in Article 3 'awarded to nationals of Member States by the other Member States'. It follows from that wording that the provision may be invoked in one Member State by the nationals of all Member States who have obtained, in another Member State, a diploma listed under Article 3.

Such an interpretation accords, moreover, with the requirements flowing from the free movement of persons, the right of establishment and the freedom to provide services guaranteed by Articles 3(c), 48, 52 and 59 of the Treaty. *Those freedoms, which are fundamental to the system set up by the Community, would not be fully realised if Member States were able to deny the benefit of provisions of Community law to those of their nationals who have availed themselves of the freedom of movement and the right of establishment and who have attained, by those means, the professional qualifications mentioned in the directive in a Member State other than the State whose nationality they hold.*

The second problem envisaged by the question asked is whether a Member State may make the practice of general medicine, by the holder of a diploma awarded in another Member State and recognised by virtue of the provisions of Directive No 75/362/EEC, subject to the completion of a period of additional training, a requirement which that Member State also imposes on holders of diplomas of medicine awarded within its own territory.

The Registration Committee, the defendant in the main proceedings, argued that Directive No 75/362/EEC does not contain any rules concerning the recognition of the professional training for general practice undergone subsequent to the university examination in medicine. Recent thinking had shown that general medicine was a specific discipline akin to the specialised disciplines in regard to which Article 8 of the directive conceded to Member States the right to require, even of holders of diplomas awarded in other Member States, an additional period of training. Moreover, the right of establishment of doctors must not be allowed to undermine the efforts of Member States to establish the best possible system of health care.

That line of reasoning, however, runs counter to the general structure of Directive No 75/362/EEC, which is based on the distinction between the recognition of diplomas of medicine (Articles 2 and 3) and recognition of diplomas of specialised medicine (Articles 4 to 8). Article 2 of the directive requires Member States to recognise as equivalent the diplomas listed in Article 3, as far as the right to take up and pursue the self-employed activities of a doctor is concerned. It is only in so far as the training of specialists is concerned that Articles 4 to 8 of the directive permit the Member State in which the doctor wishes to practise to lay down additional requirements. Such an interpretation is, moreover, reinforced by the preamble to the directive, which states that 'the aim of this directive is the recognition of diplomas ... whereby activities in the field of medicine can be taken up and pursued, and the recognition of diplomas ... in respect of specialists'.

It is not disputed – and is in any case clear from the wording of Articles 5 and 7 of the directive – that general practice, as understood by the Netherlands legislation, is not recognised as a branch of specialised medicine by the directive. Therefore, in a situation such as that existing in the Netherlands, where the practice of medicine is made subject to the recognition of the doctor as a general practitioner, the right to practise of a holder of a diploma awarded in another Member State flows directly from recognition of the diploma under Article 2 of the directive and does not depend upon any additional qualification obtained in the State in which the doctor wishes to practise.

It should be noted, moreover, that doctors who are nationals of another Member State and who have obtained a diploma recognised by virtue of Directive No 75/362/EEC in a Member State other than the Netherlands are admitted to the profession of general practitioner in the Netherlands without having undergone an additional period of training. It is clear from the considerations set forth above that entry to the profession of general practitioner by a doctor of Netherlands nationality who has obtained a similar diploma may not be made subject to other requirements.

Finally, it should be observed that Article 21 of Directive No 75/362/EEC expressly permits Member States to require completion of a preparatory training period during a transitional period of five years. Thus at the end of that period the Member State is no longer entitled to impose such a requirement or to require any other additional training of doctors who establish themselves within the territory of that Member State as general practitioners and who are holders of diplomas obtained in other Member State and recognised by virtue of the directive.

Therefore the reply to the question asked by the Appeals Committee must be that Directive No 75/362/EEC is to be interpreted as meaning that a national of a Member State who has obtained a diploma listed under Article 3 of the directive in another Member State and who, by that token, may practise general medicine in that other Member State is entitled to establish himself as a general practitioner in the Member State of which he is a national, even if that Member State makes entry to that profession by holders of diplomas of medicine obtained within its own borders subject to additional training requirements...

III FREEDOM TO SUPPLY SERVICES

1. TREATY PROVISIONS

EEC Treaty

Article 59

Within the framework of the provisions set out below, *restrictions on freedom to provide services* within the Community *shall be progressively abolished during the transitional period in respect of nationals of Member States who are established in a State of the Community other than that of the person for whom the services are intended.*

The Council may, acting unanimously on a proposal from the Commission, extend the provisions of this Chapter to nationals of a third country who provide services and who are established within the Community.

Article 60

Services shall be considered to be 'services' within the meaning of this Treaty where they are normally provided for remuneration, *in so far as they are not governed by the provisions relating to freedom of movement for goods, capital and persons.*

'Services' shall in particular include:

(a) activities of an industrial character;
(b) activities of a commercial character;
(c) activities of craftsmen;
(d) activities of the professions.

Without prejudice to the provisions of the chapter relating to the right of establishment, the person providing a service may, in order to do so, temporarily pursue his activity in the State where the service is provided, under the same conditions as are imposed by that State on its own nationals.

Article 61

1. Freedom to provide services in the field of transport shall be governed by the provisions of the Title relating to transport.

2. The liberalisation of banking and insurance services connected with movements of capital shall be effected in step with the progressive liberalisation of movement of capital.

Article 62

Save as otherwise provided in this Treaty, Member States shall not introduce any new restrictions on the freedom to provide services which have in fact been attained at the date of the entry into force of this Treaty.

Article 63

1. Before the end of the first stage, the Council shall, acting unanimously on a proposal from the Commission and after consulting the Economic and Social Committee and the Assembly, draw up a general programme for the abolition of existing restrictions on freedom to provide services within the Community. The Commission shall submit its proposal to the Council during the first two years of the first stage.

The programme shall set out the general conditions under which and the stages by which each type of service is to be liberalised.

2. In order to implement this general programme or, in the absence of such programme, in order to achieve a stage in the liberalisation of a specific service, the Council shall, on a proposal from the Commission and after consulting the Economic and Social Committee and the Assembly, issue directives acting unanimously until the end of the first stage and by a qualified majority thereafter.

...

Article 66

The provisions of Articles 55 to 58 shall apply to the matters covered by this chapter.

Under Article 60 of the EEC Treaty, the supply of 'services' is treated as a residual concept comprising activities not covered by other provisions. Under Article 59 these services are supplied by a person established (and hence very probably resident) in another Member State. This has meant that cases concerned specifically with the supply of services have often involved discrimination on the grounds of residence rather than on the grounds of nationality as such. Indeed, in the two leading cases from which excerpts are given later in this section, the person wishing to supply the service was himself a national of the State in question.

2. THE GENERAL PROGRAMME

Hence, although the General Programme again gives interesting illustrations of the types of restriction which should be eliminated, it was pointed out by Advocate General Warner in his Opinion in Case 36/74 *Walrave* v *Union Cycliste Internationale* [1974] ECR 1405 at 1425 that it does not deal with this problem, concerning itself only with restrictions imposed by a Member State on nationals of other Member States.

General Programme for the Abolition of Restrictions on Freedom to Provide Services JO 32/62; OJ Sp Ed 2nd Series No IX p. 3

The Council of the European Economic Community,

Having regard to the provisions of the Treaty, and in particular Articles 63, 106 and 227(2) thereof;

...

Title I

Beneficiaries

The persons entitled to benefit from the abolition of restrictions on freedom to provide services as set out in this General Programme are:

- nationals of Member States who are established within the Community;
- companies or firms formed under the law of a Member State and having the seat prescribed by their statutes, or their centre of administration, or their main establishment situated within the Community, provided that where only that seat is situated within the Community their activity shows a real and continuous link with the economy of a Member State; such link shall not be one of nationality, whether of the members of the company or firm, or of the persons holding managerial or supervisory posts therein, or of the holders of the capital;

subject to the condition that the service is carried out either personally by the person contracting to provide it or by one of his agencies or branches established in the Community.

...

Title III

A. Any measures which, pursuant to any provision laid down by law, regulation or administrative action in a Member State, or as a result of the application of such a provision, or of administrative practices, prohibits or hinders the person providing services in his pursuit of an activity as a self-employed person by treating him differently from nationals of the State concerned.

Such restrictive provisions and practices are in particular those which, in respect of foreign nationals only:

[The list is identical to subparagraphs (a) to (h) of the first list in the extract from the General Programme for the abolition of restrictions on freedom of establishment (see above p. 329) with the substitution of the words 'the provision of services' for the words 'the taking up or pursuit of an activity as a self-employed person'.]

The like shall apply to provisions and practices which, in respect of foreign nationals only, exclude, limit or impose conditions on the power to exercise rights normally attaching to the provision of services and in particular the power:

...[The list is identical to subparagraphs (a) to (h) of the second list in the extract from the General Programme for the Abolition of Restrictions on Freedom of Establishment (see above p. 329).]

B. Any prohibition of, or hindrance to, the movement of the item to be supplied in the course of the service or of the materials comprising such item or of the tools, machinery, equipment and other means to be employed in the provision of the service.

C. Any prohibition of, or impediment to, the transfer of the funds needed to perform the service.

D. Any prohibition of, or hindrance to, payments for services, where the provision of such services between the Member States is limited only by restrictions in respect of the payments therefor.

However, in respect of the provisions referred to in paragraphs C and D, Member States shall retain the right to verify the nature and genuineness of transfer of funds and of payments and to take all necessary measures in order to prevent contravention of their laws and regulations, in particular as regards the issue of foreign currency to tourists.

B. Transfer of Funds. Payment

...

...Limits on foreign currency allowances for tourists may be maintained in force during the transitional period, but they are to be progressively raised from the end of the first stage.

Title VI

Mutual Recognition of Diplomas and Other Evidence of Formal Qualifications – Coordination

...

Pending such mutual recognition of diplomas, or such coordination, and in order to facilitate the provision of services and to avoid distortions, a transitional system may be applied; such system may where appropriate include provision for the production of a certificate establishing that the activity in question was actually and lawfully carried on in the country of origin.

3. THE QUESTION OF RESIDENCE

With regard to the issue of directives on the provision of services before the end of the transitional period, the same situation existed as in the matter of freedom of establishment. Indeed, most of the directives on freedom of establishment which were issued also dealt with the provision of services in the context of the activity with which they were concerned. Again in 1974 (and again in a case connected, at least peripherally, with the legal profession) the Court held that the abolition of discrimination based on nationality *or residence* is separate from the issue of directives to facilitate the provision of services.

Case 33/74 Johannes Henricus Maria van Binsbergen v Bestuur van de Bedrijfsvereniging voor de Metaalnijverheid

[1974] ECR 1299; [1975] 1 CMLR 298

In an appeal to the Centrale Raad van Beroep [the Netherlands Appeal Court in social matters], Van Binsbergen was represented by Kortmann, an unqualified legal adviser, representation by a qualified advocaat not being obligatory before that court. During the course of the proceedings, Kortmann changed his habitual residence from the Netherlands to Belgium, and was informed that he could no longer represent Van Binsbergen since under Dutch legislation a legal representative must be established in the Netherlands. Kortmann invoked Article 59 of the EEC Treaty, and questions relating to the interpretation of it and Article 60 were referred for a preliminary ruling.

The Court

The Court ... is asked whether the first paragraph of Article 59 and the third paragraph of Article 60 of the EEC Treaty are directly applicable and create individual rights which national courts must protect.

This question must be resolved with reference to the whole of the chapter relating to services, taking account, moreover, of the provisions relating to the right of establishment to which reference is made in Article 66.

With a view to the progressive abolition during the transitional period of the restrictions referred to in Article 59, Article 63 has provided for the drawing up of a General Programme – laid down by Council Decision of 18 December 1961 (1962, p. 32) – to be implemented by a series of directives.

Within the scheme of the chapter relating to the provision of services, these directives are intended to accomplish different functions, the first being to abolish, during the transitional period, restrictions on freedom to provide services, the second being to introduce into the law of Member States a set of provisions intended to facilitate the effective exercise of this freedom, in particular by the mutual recognition of professional qualifications and the coordination of laws with regard to the pursuit of activities as self-employed persons.

These directives also have the task of resolving the specific problems resulting from the fact that where the person providing the service is not established, on a habitual basis, in the State where the service is performed he may not be fully subject to the professional rules of conduct in force in that State.

As regards the phased implementation of the chapter relating to services, Article 59, interpreted in the light of the general provisions of Article 8(7) of the Treaty, expresses the intention to abolish restrictions on freedom to provide services by the end of the transitional period, the latest date for the entry into force of all the rules laid down by the Treaty.

The provisions of Article 59, the application of which was to be prepared by directives issued during the transitional period, therefore became unconditional on the expiry of that period.

The provisions of that article abolish all discrimination against the person providing the service by reason of his nationality or the fact that he is established in a Member State other than that in which the service is to be provided.

Therefore, as regards at least the specific requirement of nationality or of residence, Articles 59 and 60 impose a well-defined obligation, the fulfilment of which by the Member States cannot be delayed or jeopardised by the absence of provisions which were to be adopted in pursuance of powers conferred under Articles 63 and 66.

Accordingly, the reply should be that the first paragraph of Article 59 and the third paragraph of Article 60 have direct effect and may therefore be relied on before national courts, at least in so far as they seek to abolish any discrimination against a person for providing a service by reason of his nationality or of the fact that he resides in a Member State other than that in which the service is to be provided.

Earlier in its judgment, the Court considered the scope of the freedom to supply services, and, given that the case itself involved representation in legal proceedings, indicated what limitations on that freedom might be justified.

The Court

The Court is requested to interpret Articles 59 and 60 in relation to a provision of national law whereby only persons established in the territory of the State concerned are entitled to act as legal representatives before certain courts or tribunals.

Article 59, the first paragraph of which is the only provision in question in this connection, provides that: 'Within the framework of the provisions set out below, restrictions on freedom to provide services within the Community shall be progressively abolished during the transitional period in respect of nationals of Member States who are established in a State of the Community other than that of the person for whom the services are intended'.

Having defined the concept 'services' within the meaning of the Treaty in its first and second paragraphs, Article 60 lays down in the third paragraph that, without prejudice to the provisions of the chapter relating to the right of establishment, the person providing a service may, in order to provide that service, temporarily pursue his activity in the State where the service is provided, under the same conditions as are imposed by that State on its own nationals.

The question put by the national court therefore seeks to determine whether the requirement that legal representatives be permanently established within the territory of the State where the service is to be provided can be reconciled with the prohibition, under Articles 59 and 60, on all restrictions on freedom to provide services within the Community.

The restrictions to be abolished pursuant to Articles 59 and 60 include all requirements imposed on the person providing the service by reason in particular of his nationality or of the fact that he does not habitually reside in the State where the service is provided, which do not apply to persons established within the national territory or which may prevent or otherwise obstruct the activities of the person providing the service.

In particular, *a requirement that the person providing the service must be habitually resident within the territory of the State where the service is to be provided may, according to the circumstances, have the result of depriving Article 59 of all useful effect,* in view of the fact that the precise object of that article is to abolish restrictions on freedom to provide services imposed on persons who are not established in the State where the service is to be provided.

However, taking into account the particular nature of the services to be provided, *specific requirements imposed on the person providing the service cannot be considered incompatible with the Treaty where they have as their purpose the application of professional rules justified by the general good* – in particular rules relating to organisation, qualifications, professional ethics, supervision and liability – which are binding upon any person established in the State in which the service is provided, where the person providing the service would escape from the ambit of those rules by being established in another Member State.

Likewise, a Member State cannot be denied the right to take measures to prevent the exercise by a person providing services whose activity is entirely or principally directed towards its territory of the freedom guaranteed by Article 59 for the purpose of avoiding the professional rules of conduct which would be applicable to him if he were established within that State; such a situation may be subject to judicial control under the provisions of the chapter relating to the right of establishment and not of that on the provision of services.

In accordance with these principles, *the requirement that persons whose functions are to assist the administration of justice must be permanently established for professional purposes within the jurisdiction of certain courts or tribunals cannot be considered incompatible with the provisions of Articles 59 and 60, where such requirement is objectively justified* by the need to ensure observance of professional rules of conduct connected, in particular, with the administration of justice and with respect for professional ethics.

That cannot, however, *be the case when the provision of certain services in a Member State is not subject to any sort of qualification* or professional regulation and when the requirement of habitual residence is fixed by reference to the territory of the State in question.

In relation to a professional activity the exercise of which is similarly unrestricted within the territory of a particular Member State, the requirement of residence within that State constitutes a restriction which is incompatible with Articles 59 and 60 of the Treaty if the administration of justice can satisfactorily be ensured by measures which are less restrictive, such as the choosing of an address for service.

It must therefore be stated in reply to the question put to the Court that the first paragraph of Article 59 and the third paragraph of Article 60 of the EEC Treaty must be interpreted as meaning that the national law of a Member State cannot, by imposing a requirement as to habitual residence within that State, deny persons established in another Member State the right to provide services, where the provision of services is not subject to any special condition under the national law applicable.

In a second case involving the provision of services by a Dutch national resident in Belgium, the Court went a little further in elucidating the safeguards a Member State may require of those providing services within its territory, emphasising that a requirement of residence as such should be regarded as a last resort.

Case 39/75 Robert Gerardus Coenen and Others v Sociaal-Economische Raad [1975] ECR 1547; [1976] 1 CMLR 30

The Court

This question has been raised within the context of an action concerning the application to a Netherlands national who resides in Belgium and has an office in the Netherlands, where he acts as an insurance intermediary, of the provisions of Article 5(1)(f) of the Wet Assurantiebemiddeling which provides that a natural person who intends to act as an intermediary within the meaning of this law shall be bound to reside in the Netherlands.

The grounds of the order making the reference state that the above-mentioned provision must be understood to mean that in order to carry on the business of an insurance intermediary in the Netherlands a natural person must both reside in that country and have an office there.

...

Although, in the light of the special nature of certain services, it cannot be denied that a Member State is entitled to adopt measures which are intended to prevent the freedom guaranteed by Article 59 being used by a person whose activities are entirely or chiefly directed towards his territory in order to avoid the professional rules which would apply to him if he resided in that State, *the requirement of residence in the territory of the State where the service is provided can only be allowed as an exception where the Member State is unable to apply other, less restrictive, measures* to ensure respect for these rules.

In particular, where a person providing services who is residing abroad has, in the national territory in which the service is provided, a place of business for the purposes of providing it, then, if such place of business is *bona fide*, the Member State in question normally has effective means at its disposal for carrying out the necessary supervision of the activities of that person and to ensure that the service is provided in accordance with the rules issued under its national legislation.

In that case, the additional requirement that a person providing services in the territory of a State must also have a permanent private residence in that State is a restriction on the freedom to provide services which is incompatible with the provisions of the Treaty.

On these grounds it must be concluded that the provisions of the EEC Treaty, in particular Articles 59, 60 and 65, must be interpreted as meaning that national legislation may not, by means of a requirement of residence in the territory, make it impossible for persons residing in another Member State to provide services when less restrictive measures enable the professional rules to which provision of the service is subject in that territory to be complied with.

In this context, the existence might be noted of Council Directive No 77/92/EEC of 13 December 1976 on measures to facilitate the effective exercise of freedom of establishment and freedom to provide services in respect of the activities of insurance agents and brokers (OJ 1977, L 26, p. 14), which is concerned largely with the question of professional qualifications.

The problem of preserving necessary safeguards whilst eliminating residence requirements is faced squarely in Council Directive No 77/249/EEC of 22 March 1977, intended 'to facilitate the effective exercise by lawyers of freedom to provide services'.

Council Directive No 77/249 of 22 March 1977 OJ 1977 L 78/17

Article 1

1. This directive shall apply, within the limits and under the conditions laid down herein, to the activities of lawyers pursued by way of provision of services.

Notwithstanding anything contained in this directive, Member States may reserve to prescribed categories of lawyers the preparation of formal documents for obtaining title to administer estates of deceased persons, and the drafting of formal documents creating or transferring interests in land.

2. 'Lawyer' means any person entitled to pursue his professional activities under one of the following designations:

Belgium:	Avocat - Advocaat
Denmark:	Advokat
Germany:	Rechtsanwalt
France:	Avocat
Ireland:	Barrister Solicitor
Italy:	Avvocato
Luxembourg:	Avocat-avoué
Netherlands:	Advocaat
United Kingdom:	Advocate Barrister Solicitor

Article 2

Each Member State shall recognise as a lawyer for the purpose of pursuing the activities specified in Article 1(1) any person listed in paragraph 2 of that article.

Article 3

A person referred to in Article 1 shall adopt the professional title used in the Member State from which he comes, expressed in the language or one of the languages of that State, with an indication of the professional organisation by which he is authorised to practise or the court of law before which he is entitled to practise pursuant to the laws of that State.

Article 4

1. Activities relating to the representation of a client in legal proceedings or before public authorities shall be pursued in each host Member State under the conditions laid down for lawyers established in that State, *with the exception of any conditions requiring residence,* or registration with a professional organisation, in that State.

2. *A lawyer pursuing these activities shall observe the rules of professional conduct of the host Member State,* without prejudice to his obligations in the Member State from which he comes.

3. When these activities are pursued in the United Kingdom, 'rules of professional conduct of the host Member State' means the rules of professional conduct applicable to solicitors, where such activities are not reserved for barristers and advocates. Otherwise the rules of professional conduct applicable to the latter shall apply. However, barristers from Ireland shall always be subject to the rules of professional conduct applicable in the United Kingdom to barristers and advocates.

When these activities are pursued in Ireland 'rules of professional conduct of the host Member State' means, in so far as they govern the oral presentation of a case in court, the rules of professional conduct applicable to barristers. In all other cases the rules of professional conduct applicable to solicitors shall apply. However, barristers and advocates from the United Kingdom shall always be subject to the rules of professional conduct applicable in Ireland to barristers.

4. A lawyer pursuing activities other than those referred to in paragraph 1 shall remain subject to the conditions and rules of professional conduct of the Member State from which he comes without prejudice to respect for the rules, whatever their source, which govern the profession in the host Member State, especially those concerning the incompatibility of the exercise of the activities of a lawyer with the exercise of other activities in that State, professional secrecy, relations with other lawyers, the prohibition on the same lawyer acting for parties with mutually conflicting interests, and publicity. The latter rules are applicable only if they are capable of being observed by a lawyer who is not established in the host Member State and to the extent to which their observance is objectively justified to ensure, in that State, the proper exercise of a lawyer's activities, the standing of the profession and respect for the rules concerning incompatibility.

Article 5

For the pursuit of activities relating to the representation of a client in legal proceedings, *a Member State may require lawyers* to whom Article 1 applies:

- to be introduced, in accordance with local rules or customs, to the presiding judge and, where appropriate, to the President of the relevant Bar in the host Member State;

– *to work in conjunction with a lawyer who practises before the judicial authority in question* and who would, where necessary, be answerable to that authority, or with an 'avoué' or 'procuratore' practising before it.

Article 6

Any Member State may exclude lawyers who are in the salaried employment of a public or private undertaking from pursuing activities relating to the representation of that undertaking in legal proceedings in so far as lawyers established in that State are not permitted to pursue those activities.

Article 7

1. The competent authority of the host Member State may request the person providing the services to establish his qualifications as a lawyer.

2. In the event of non-compliance with the obligations referred to in Article 4 and in force in the host Member State, the competent authority of the latter shall determine in accordance with its own rules and procedures the consequences of such non-compliance, and to this end may obtain any appropriate professional information concerning the person providing services. It shall notify the competent authority of the Member State from which the person comes of any decision taken. Such exchanges shall not affect the confidential nature of the information supplied.

Article 8

1. Member States shall bring into force the measures necessary to comply with this directive within two years of its notification and shall forthwith inform the Commission thereof.

2. Member States shall communicate to the Commission the texts of the main provisions of national law which they adopt in the field covered by this directive.

Article 9

This directive is addressed to the Member States.

4. SUPERVISORY POWERS OF MEMBER STATES

Freedom to supply services presents a unique difficulty in cases in which Member States make the pursuit of an economic activity subject to requirements that the operator should maintain a place of business within the jurisdiction, so as to be amenable to the exercise of local supervisory powers. If Member States were entirely free to apply such requirements to nationals of other Member States, based in other Member States, the freedom to supply services would be reduced to a freedom of establishment. In a pair of cases involving fee-charging employment agencies, the European Court ruled that Member States are not entirely free to impose such requirements on such nationals.

Joined Cases 110 and 111/78 Ministère Public and Others v Willy van Waesemael and Others [1979] ECR 35

The Court

By two judgments both delivered on 21 March 1978 and received at the Court of Justice on 8 May 1978, the Tribunal de Première Instance de Tournai referred under Article 177 of the EEC Treaty several questions on the interpretation of Council Directive No 67/43/EEC of 12 January 1967 and of certain provisions of the EEC Treaty relating to freedom to provide services.

These questions were raised in the context of two cases of criminal proceedings each against a person established in Belgium and a French employment agent for entertainers established in France, who are charged with having infringed the provisions of Articles 6 and 20 of the Belgian Arrêté Royal of 28 November 1975 relating to the operation of fee-charging employment agencies for entertainers.

It provides that 'the operation of a fee-charging employment agency for entertainers shall be subject to the grant of a licence by the Minister responsible for employment', and that 'foreign employment agencies for entertainers may not, in the absence of a reciprocal convention between Belgium and their country, place anyone in employment in Belgium except through a fee-charging employment agency holding a licence'.

In each of the two cases the first accused is charged with having, for the purpose of engaging entertainers, resorted to a fee-charging employment agency situated in France the operator of which does not hold a licence in Belgium, and the second accused is charged with having placed persons in employment in that State without acting through an agency holding a licence in Belgium.

The accused pleaded that the aforementioned provisions of national law were incompatible with the Treaty in that they restricted the freedom to provide services referred to in Articles 52, 55, 59 and 60.

...

The first paragraph of Article 59 of the Treaty provides that '...restrictions on freedom to provide services within the Community shall be progressively abolished during the transitional period in respect of nationals of Member States...' of the Community.

In laying down that freedom to provide services shall be attained by the end of the transitional period, that provision, interpreted in the light of Article 8(7) of the Treaty, imposes an obligation to attain a precise result, the fulfilment of which had to be made easier by, but not made dependent on, the implementation of a programme of progressive measures.

It follows that the essential requirements of Article 59 of the Treaty, which was to be implemented progressively during the transitional period by means of the directives referred to in Article 63, became directly and unconditionally applicable on the expiry of that period.

Those essential requirements, which lay down the freedom to provide services, abolish all discrimination against the person providing the service by reason of his nationality or the fact that he is established in a Member State other than that in which the service is to be provided.

Taking into account the particular nature of certain services to be provided, such as the placing of entertainers in employment, specific requirements imposed on persons providing services cannot be considered incompatible with the Treaty where they have as their purpose the application of professional rules, justified by the general good or by the need to ensure the protection of the entertainer, which are binding upon any person established in the said State, in so far as the person providing the service is not subject to similar requirements in the Member State in which he is established.

However, *when the pursuit of the employment agency activity at issue is made subject in the State in which the service is provided to the issue of a licence and to supervision by the competent authorities, that State may not, without failing to fulfil the essential requirements of Article 59 of the Treaty, impose on the persons providing the service who are established in another Member State any obligation either to satisfy such requirements or to act through the holder of a licence, except where such requirement is objectively justified by the need to ensure observance of the professional rules of conduct and to ensure the said protection.*

Such a requirement is not objectively justified when the service is provided by an employment agency which comes under the public administration of a Member State or when the person providing the service is established in another Member State and in that State holds a licence issued under conditions comparable to those required by the State in which the service is provided and his activities are subject in the first State to proper supervision covering all employment agency activity whatever may be the Member State in which the service is provided.

...

Case 279/80 Alfred John Webb [1981] ECR 3305

The Court

By a judgment of 9 December 1980 which was received at the Court on 30 December 1980 the Hoge Raad der Nederlanden [Supreme Court of the Netherlands] referred to the Court for a preliminary ruling under Article 177 of the EEC Treaty three questions concerning the interpretation of Articles 59 and 60 of the Treaty in connection with the Netherlands legislation governing the provision of manpower.

The questions arose in the course of criminal proceedings for offences against Article 1 of the Koninklijk Besluit [Royal Decree] of 10 September 1970 (Staatsblad 410). That article prohibits the provision of manpower without authorisation from the Minister for Social Affairs.

The above-mentioned Royal Decree was adopted pursuant to the opening words of Article 2(1) and subparagraph (a) thereof of the Wet op het ter Beschikkingstellen van Arbeidskrachten [Law on the Provision of Manpower] of 31 July 1965 (Staatsblad 379), as amended by the Law of 30 June 1967 (Staatsblad 377). That article provides that the provision of manpower without authorisation may be prohibited by means of a Royal Decree if required in the interests of good relations on the labour market or of the labour force affected. Article 6(1) of the Law provides, however, that the authorisation may be refused only when there is reasonable cause to fear that the provision of manpower by the applicant might harm good relations on the labour market or if the interests of the labour force in question are inadequately safeguarded.

Article 1(1)(b) of the above-mentioned Law defines the activity in question as the provision of manpower for another person for hire or reward and otherwise than in pursuance of a contract of employment with that other person, for the performance of work usually carried on in his undertaking.

The accused in the main action, Alfred John Webb, who is the manager of a company incorporated under English law and established in the United Kingdom, holds a licence under United Kingdom law for the provision of manpower. The company provides technical staff for the Netherlands in particular. The staff are recruited by the company and made available, temporarily and for consideration, to undertakings located in the Netherlands, no contract of employment being entered into as between such staff and the undertakings. In the case at issue it was established by the court considering the facts that in February 1978 the company had on three occasions, not being in possession of a licence issued by the Netherlands Minister for Social Affairs, supplied workers for undertakings in the Netherlands, for consideration and otherwise than in pursuance of a contract of employment concluded with the latter, for the performance of work usually carried on in those undertakings.

...

The first paragraph of Article 59 of the Treaty requires restrictions on freedom to provide services within the Community to be progressively abolished during the transitional period in respect of nationals of Member States of the Community. As stated by the Court in its judgment of 18 January 1979 (Joined Cases 110 and 111/78 *van Waesemael* [1979] ECR 35, above p.354) that provision, interpreted in the light of Article 8(7) of the Treaty, imposes an obligation to obtain a precise result, the fulfilment of which had to be made easier by, but not made dependent on, the implementation of a programme of progressive measures. It follows that the essential requirements of Article 59 of the Treaty became directly and unconditionally applicable on the expiry of that period.

...

The principal aim of the third paragraph in Article 60 is to enable the provider of the service to pursue his activities in the Member State where the service is given without suffering discrimination in favour of the nationals of that State. However, it does not mean that all national legislation applicable to nationals of that State and usually applied to the permanent activities of undertakings established therein may be similarly applied in its entirety to the temporary activities of undertakings which are established in other Member States.

In the above-mentioned judgment of 18 January 1979 the Court held that, regard being had to the particular nature of certain services, specific requirements imposed on the provider of the services cannot be considered incompatible with the Treaty where they have as their purpose the application of rules governing such activities. However, the freedom to provide services is one of the fundamental principles of the Treaty and may be restricted only by provisions which are justified by the general good and which are imposed on all persons or undertakings operating in the said State in so far as that interest is not safeguarded by the provisions to which the provider of the service is subject in the Member State of his establishment.

It must be noted in this respect that the provision of manpower is a particularly sensitive matter from the occupational and social point of view. Owing to the special nature of the employment relationships inherent in that kind of activity, pursuit of such a business directly affects both relations on the labour market and the lawful interests of the workforce concerned. That is evident, moreover, in the legislation of some of the Member States in this matter, which is designed first to eliminate possible abuse and secondly to restrict the scope of such activities or even prohibit them altogether.

It follows in particular that it is permissible for Member States, and amounts for them to a legitimate choice of policy pursued in the public interest, to subject the provision of manpower within their orders to a system of licensing in order to be able to refuse licences where there is reason to fear that such activities may harm good relations on the labour market or that the interests of the workforce affected are not adequately safeguarded. In view of the differences there may be in conditions on the labour market between one Member State and another, on the one hand, and the diversity of the criteria which may be applied with regard to the pursuit of activities of that nature on the other hand, the Member State in which the services are to be supplied has unquestionably the right to require possession of a licence issued on the same conditions as the in the case of its own nationals.

Such a measure would be excessive in relation to the aim pursued, however, if the requirements to which the issue of a licence is subject coincided with the proofs and guarantees required in the State of establishment. In order to maintain the principle of freedom to provide services the first requirement is that in considering applications for licences and in granting them the Member State in which the service is to be provided may not make any distinction based on the nationality of the provider of the services or the place of his establishment; the second requirement is that it must take into account the evidence and guarantees already furnished by the provider of the services for the pursuit of his activities in the Member State of his establishment.

...

More recently the European Court applied the same reasoning to the insurance sector. It held that the Federal Republic of Germany failed to fulfil its obligations under Articles 59 and 60 of the EEC Treaty by providing that where insurance undertakings wish to provide services in Germany in relation to direct insurance business, other than transport insurance, through intermediaries, they must be established in a German territory.

Case 205/84 Commission v Germany [1987] 2 CMLR 69

The Court

By an application lodged at the Court Registry on 14 August 1984 the Commission of the European Communities brought an action before the Court under Article 169 EEC for a declaration that,

(a) by applying the Versicherungsaufsichtsgesetz [Insurance Supervision Act] as amended by the Vierzehntes Änderungsgesetz zum Versicherungsaufsichtsgesetz [Fourteenth Act amending the Versicherungsaufsichtsgesetz] of 29 March 1983 which provides that where insurance undertakings in the Community wish to provide services in the Federal Republic of Germany in relation to direct insurance business, other than transport insurance, through salesmen, representatives, agents or other intermediaries, such persons must be established and authorised in the Federal Republic of Germany and which provides that insurance brokers established in the Federal Republic of Germany may not arrange contracts of insurance for persons resident in the Federal Republic of Germany with insurers established in another Member State, the Federal Republic has failed to fulfil its obligations under Articles 59 and 60 of the EEC Treaty;

(b) by bringing into force and applying the Vierzehntes Änderungsgesetz zum Versicherungsaufsichtsgesetz, which was intended to transpose into national law Council Directive No 78/473 of 30 May 1978 on the coordination of laws, regulations and administrative provisions relating to Community co-insurance, the Federal Republic of Germany has failed to fulfil its obligations under Articles 59 and 60 of the EEC Treaty and under the aforementioned directive in so far as that Act provides in relation to the Community co-insurance operations that the leading insurer (in the case of risks situated in the Federal Republic of Germany) must be established in that State and authorised there to cover the risks insured also as sole insurer;

(c) by the fixing through the Bundesaufsichtsamt für das Versicherungswesen [Federal Insurance Supervision Office], in the context of the transposition into national law of the aforementioned directive, excessively high threshholds in respect of the risks arising in connection with free insurance, civil liability aircraft insurance and general civil liability insurance, which may be the subject of Community co-insurance, so that as a result co-insurance as a service is excluded in the Federal Republic of Germany for risks below those threshholds, the Federal Republic of Germany has failed to fulfil its obligations under Articles 1(2) and 8 of the said directive and under Articles 59 and 60 of the EEC Treaty.

...

According to Article 59(1) EEC, the abolition of restrictions on the freedom to provide services within the Community concerns all services provided by nationals to Member States who are established in a State of the Community other than that of the person for whom the services are intended. Article 60(1) provides that services are to be considered to be 'services' within the meaning of the Treaty where they are normally provided for remuneration, in so far as they are not governed by the provisions relating to freedom of movement for goods, capital and persons.

Those articles require the abolition of all restrictions on the free movement of the provision of services, as thus defined, subject nevertheless to the provisions of Article 61 and those of Articles 55 and 56 to which Article 66 refers.

...

If the requirement of an authorisation constitutes a restriction on the freedom to provide services, the requirement of a permanent establishment is the very negation of that freedom. It has the result of depriving Article 59 of the Treaty of all effectiveness, a provision whose very purpose is to abolish restrictions on the freedom to provide services of persons who are not established in the State in which the service is to be provided (see in particular *Van Binsbergen* (see above p. 347), and also Case 39/75 *Coenen* v *Sociaal-Economische Raad* [1975] ECR 1547, and Case 76/81 *Transporoute v Minister of Public Works* [1982] ECR 417). If such a requirement is to be accepted, it must be shown that it constitutes a condition which is indispensable for attaining the objective pursued.

In that respect, the German Government points out in particular that the requirement of an establishment in the State in which the service is provided makes it possible for the supervisory authority of that State to carry out verifications *in situ* and to monitor continuously the activities carried on by the authorised insurer and that, without that requirement, the authority would be unable to perform its task.

The Court has already stressed in its decisions, most recently in Case 29/82 *van Luipen* [1983] ECR 151, that *considerations of an administrative nature cannot justify derogation by a Member State from the rules of Community law. That principle applies with even greater force where the derogation in question amounts to preventing the exercise of one of the fundamental freedoms guaranteed by the Treaty.* In this instance it is therefore not sufficient that the presence on the undertaking's premises of all the documents needed for supervision by the authorities of the State in which the service is provided may make it easier for those authorities to perform their task. It must also be shown that those authorities cannot, even under an authorisation procedure, carry out their supervisory tasks effectively unless the undertaking has in the aforesaid State a permanent establishment at which all the necessary documents are kept.

That has not been shown to be the case. As has been stated above, Community law on insurance does not, as it stands at present, prohibit the State in which the service is provided from requiring that the assets representing the technical reserves covering business conducted on its territory be localised in that State. In that case the presence of such assets may be verified *in situ*, even if the undertaking does not have any permanent establishment in the State. As regards the other conditions for the conduct of business which are subject to supervision, it appears to the Court that such supervision may be effected on the basis of copies of balance sheets, accounts and commercial documents, including the conditions of insurance and schemes of operation, sent from the State of establishment and duly certified by the authorities of that Member State. It is possible under an authorisation procedure to subject the undertaking to such conditions of supervision by means of a provision in the certificate of authorisation and to ensure compliance with those conditions, if necessary by withdrawing that certificate.

It has therefore not been established that the considerations acknowledged above concerning the protection of policy-holders and insured persons make the establishment of the insurer in the territory of the State in which the service is provided an indispensable requirement.

As regards the Commission's first head of claim, it must therefore be concluded that the Federal Republic of Germany has failed to fulfil its obligations under Articles 59 and 60 of the Treaty by providing in the Versicherungsaufsichtsgesetz that where insurance undertakings in the Community wish to provide services in relation to direct insurance business, other than transport insurance, through salesmen, representatives, agents or other intermediaries, they must have an establishment in its territory; however, that failure does not extend to compulsory insurance and insurance for which the insurer either maintains a permanent presence equivalent to an agency or a branch or directs his business entirely or principally towards the territory of the Federal Republic of Germany.

...

IV COMPANIES

1. TREATY PROVISIONS

The chapters of the EEC Treaty relating to freedom of establishment and freedom to supply services contain special provisions relating to companies.

EEC Treaty

Article 58

Companies or firms formed in accordance with the law of a Member State and having their registered office, central administration or principal place of business within the Community shall, for the purposes of this chapter, be treated in the same way as natural persons who are nationals of Member States.

'Companies or firms' means companies or firms constituted under civil or commercial law, including cooperative societies, and other legal persons governed by public or private law, save for those which are non-profit-making.

Article 66

[Applies Article 58 to the provision of services.]

Article 54

[For paragraphs 1 and 2 see p. 327, above.]

3. The Council and the Commission shall carry out the duties devolving upon them under the preceding provisions, in particular:

...

(g) by coordinating to the necessary extent the safeguards which, for the protection of the interests of members and others, are required by Member States of companies or firms within the meaning of the second paragraph of Article 58 with a view to making such safeguards equivalent throughout the Community;

...

The basic idea underlying Articles 58 and 66 is that companies should be treated in the same way as natural persons for the purposes of establishment and provision of services in another Member State. This, however, is more easily stated than done, largely because, although human beings have a generally recognisable format, companies are creatures of the legislation under which they were incorporated, and may not be so easily recognised in another Member State.

The use of the phrase 'companies or firms' in the authentic English text preempts the debate as to how far legal personality is necessary in order to take advantage of the provisions, since English partnerships (unlike Scottish ones) do not have legal personality. In any event, certain German, Italian and Dutch partnerships do not have legal personality but are comprised in the single words *Gesellschaften, società* and *vennootschappen* used in the German, Italian and Dutch texts.

The real problem, in terms of legal theory at least, arises, as a result of different national rules of private international law, when a company wishes to avail itself of the freedom of establishment.

Under English law, a company is governed by the law of its domicile, i.e. it is governed by the law of the place where it was incorporated, and this domicile cannot be changed (see *Gasque* v *IRC* [1940] 2 KB 80, 84). Hence, if a company incorporated in Belgium decided to establish itself in England, it would still be treated as a Belgian company, and no particular problem would arise. However, in Belgium, for example, commercial companies are governed by the law of their principal establishment (Law of 18 May 1873, Articles 196–7), and an English company which established itself there would become subject to Belgian law (see the decision of the Belgian Cour de Cassation of 12 November 1965, *Pasicrisie Belge* 1966, I, p. 336). Given the substantial differences between English and Belgian company law, this could cause considerable problems. Further, in French law, it would appear that if the company's *siège réel* differs from the place where it was incorporated, it will be regarded as a nullity;* hence an English company wishing to establish itself in France would have to re-form under French law.

Admittedly this problem could only arise in the rare case where a company wished to move all or the bulk of its activities to another Member State; the action of setting up a subsidiary or branch or of providing services will not cause a change in the status of the company in the eyes of the host country, whether it applies a test based on incorporation or one based on the real activities of the company. Even in this case, however, problems may be caused by the different extent and legal effects of recognition under the laws of the different Member States, as well as by, for example, the existence of special rules relating to foreign shareholders, or requirements that branches of foreign companies comply with certain domestic rules.

The EEC Treaty in fact provides for the problem of recognition to be resolved by separate Conventions between the Member States.

EEC Treaty

Article 220

Member States shall, so far as is necessary, enter into negotiations with each other with a view to securing for the benefit of their nationals:

...

– *the mutual recognition of companies or firms* within the meaning of the second paragraph of Article 58, *the retention of legal personality in the event of transfer of their seat from one country to another,* and the possibility of mergers between companies or firms governed by the laws of different countries;

2. HARMONISATION AND COORDINATION

A Convention on the Mutual Recognition of Companies and Bodies Corporate was signed by the original Member States on 29 February 1968, and under Article 3(2) of the Act of Accession the new Member States undertook to accede, *inter alia,* to this Convention. It has not yet, however, been ratified by all the signatory States, and has not therefore entered into force. In principle it provides that companies formed under the law of one contracting State shall be recognised in another as having the capacity accorded to them by the law under which they were formed, subject however to a limited number of possible derogations. There is also an express declaration that certain named partnerships which do not have legal personality fall within its scope.

---

* See, e.g., J-G Renauld, '*La Reconnaissance mutuelle des Sociétés dans le Marché commun*' (Rev Pract des Soc Civ et Com (1968) 207, at 211).

Given a satisfactory solution to the question of recognition, the problem remains that those dealing with foreign companies taking advantage of their freedom of establishment and their freedom to provide services may, as a result of divergences between national systems of company legislation, find themselves faced with entities whose capacities and mode of conduct differ from those of the companies with which they are familiar. Hence the programme of harmonisation provided for in Article 54(3)(g) is intended to protect both members and others, interests which in fact do not always coincide, particularly if the 'others' are creditors.

A series of directives has been issued under this article. The first, Council Directive No 68/151/EEC of 9 March 1968 (JO 1968, L 65, p. 8; OJ Sp Ed, 1968, p. 41), appears largely to protect outsiders dealing with companies. It falls into three parts intended to ensure: (i) that publicity is given to essential information; (ii) that effect is given to a company's contracts made before its incorporation, which are beyond its powers, or where questions of the powers of its officers arise; and (iii) that the causes and effects of nullity shall be limited. Nullity is a concept effectively unknown to English company law (see *Peel's* case (1867) 2 Ch App 674). The directive defines by name the companies to which it applies: in the United Kingdom (as amended by Article 29 and Annex I (III) H of the Act of Accession) these are 'companies incorporated with limited liability'.

First Council Directive No 68/151 on Coordination of Safeguards ... required ... of Companies OJ Sp Ed 1968 p. 41 (as amended)

Article 1

The coordination measures prescribed by this directive shall apply to the laws, regulations and administrative provisions of the Member States relating to the following types of company:

– *In Germany:*
die Aktiengesellschaft, die Kommanditgesellschaft auf Aktien, die Gesellschaft mit beschränkter Haftung;

– *In Belgium:*

de naamloze vennootschap,	la société anonyme,
de commanditaire vennootschap op aandelen,	la société en commandite par actions,
de personenvennootschap met beperkte aansprakelijkheid;	la société de personnes à responsabilité limitée;

– *In France:*
la société anonyme, la société en commandite par actions, la société à responsabilité limitée;

– *In Italy:*
società per azioni, società in accomandita per azioni, società a responsabilità limitata;

– *In Luxembourg:*
la société anonyme, la société en commandite par actions, la société à responsabilité limitée;
– *In the Netherlands:*
de naamloze vennootschap, de commanditaire vennootschap op aandelen;
[– *In the United Kingdom:*
companies incorporated with limited liability;
– *In Ireland:*
companies incorporated with limited liability;
– *In Denmark:*
aktieselskab; komandit-aktieselskot;
[...]
[– *In Greece:*
ανωνυμη εταιρια, εταιρια, περιωρισμενης ευθυνης, ετερορρυθμη χατα μετοχες εταιρια.];
[– *In Spain:*
la sociedad anónima, la sociedad comanditaria por acciones, la sociedad de responsabilidad limitada;
[– *In Portugal:*
a sociedade anónima de responsabilidade limitada, a sociedade em comandita por acçoes, a sociedade por quotas de responsabilidade limitada.]

Section I

Disclosure

Article 2

1. Member States shall take the measures required to ensure compulsory disclosure by companies of at least the following documents and particulars:

(a) The instrument of constitution, and the statutes if they are contained in a separate instrument;

(b) Any amendments to the instruments mentioned in (a), including any extension of the duration of the company;

(c) After every amendment of the instrument of constitution or of the statutes, the complete text of the instrument or statutes as amended to date;

(d) The appointment, termination of office and particulars of the persons who either as a body constituted pursuant to law or as members of any such body:

(i) are authorised to represent the company in dealings with third parties and in legal proceedings;

(ii) take part in the administration, supervision or control of the company.

It must appear from the disclosure whether the persons authorised to represent the company may do so alone or must act jointly;

(e) At least once a year, the amount of the capital subscribed, where the instrument of constitution or the statutes mention an authorised capital, unless any increase in the capital subscribed necessitates an amendment of the statutes;

(f) The balance sheet and the profit and loss account for each financial year. The document containing the balance sheet must give details of the persons who are required by law to certify it. However, in respect of the Gesellschaft mit beschränkter Haftung, société de personnes à responsabilité limitée, personenvennootschap met beperkte aansprakelijkheid, société à responsabilité limitée, εταιρια περιωρισμενης ευθυνης, società a responsabilità limitata and sociedade em comandita por acçoes under German, Belgian, French, Greek, Italian, Luxembourg or Portuguese law referred to in Article 1, the besloten naamloze vennootschap under Netherlands law, the private company under the law of Ireland and the private company under the law of Northern Ireland, the compulsory application of this provision shall be postponed until the date of implementation of a directive concerning coordination of the contents of balance sheets and of profit and loss accounts and concerning exemption of such of those companies whose balance sheet total is less than that specified in the directive from the obligation to make disclosure in full or in part of the said documents. The Council will adopt such a directive within two years following adoption of the present directive].

(g) Any transfer of the seat of the company;

(h) The winding up of the company;

(i) Any declaration of nullity of the company by the courts;

(j) The appointment of liquidators, particulars concerning them, and their respective powers, unless such powers are expressly and exclusively derived from law or from the statutes of the company;

(k) The termination of the liquidation and, in Member States where the striking off the register entails legal consequences, the fact of any such striking off.

2. For purposes of paragraph 1(f), companies which fulfil the following conditions shall be considered as besloten naamloze vennootschappen:

(a) They cannot issue bearer shares;

(b) No bearer certificate of registered shares within the meaning of Article 42(c) of the Netherlands Commercial Code can be issued by any person whatsoever;

(c) Their shares cannot be quoted on a stock exchange;

(d) Their statutes contain a clause requiring approval by the company before the transfer of shares to third parties, except in the case of transfer in the event of death and, if the statutes so provide, in the case of transfer to a spouse, forebears or issue; transfers shall not be in blank, but otherwise each transfer shall be in writing under hand, signed by the transferor and transferee or by notarial act;

(e) Their statutes specify that the company is a besloten naamloze vennootschap; the name of the company includes the words 'Besloten Naamloze Vennootschap' or the initials 'BNV'.

Article 3

1. In each Member State a file shall be opened in a central register, commercial register or companies register, for each of the companies registered therein.

2. All documents and particulars which must be disclosed in pursuance of Article 2 shall be kept in the file or entered in the register; the subject matter of the entries must in every case appear in the file.

3. A copy of the whole or any part of the documents or particulars referred to in Article 2 must be obtainable by application in writing at a price not exceeding the administrative cost thereof.

Copies supplied shall be certified as 'true copies', unless the applicant dispenses with such certification.

4. Disclosure of the documents and particulars referred to in paragraph 2 shall be effected by publication in the national gazette appointed for that purpose by the Member State, either of the full or partial text, or by means of a reference to the document which has been deposited in the file or entered in the register.

5. The documents and particulars may be relied on by the company as against third parties only after they have been published in accordance with paragraph 4, unless the company proves that the third parties had knowledge thereof. However, with regard to transactions taking place before the sixteenth day following the publication, the documents and particulars shall not be relied on as against third parties who prove that it was impossible for them to have had knowledge thereof.

6. Member States shall take the necessary measures to avoid any discrepancy between what is disclosed by publication in the press and what appears in the register or file.

However, in cases of discrepancy, the text published in the press may not be relied on as against third parties; the latter may nevertheless rely thereon, unless the company proves that they had knowledge of the texts deposited in the file or entered in the register.

7. Third parties may, moreover, always rely on any documents and particulars in respect of which the disclosure formalities have not yet been completed, save where non-disclosure causes them not to have effect.

Article 4

Member States shall prescribe that letters and order forms shall state the following particulars:

– the register in which the file mentioned in Article 3 is kept, together with the number of the company in that register;
– the legal form of the company, the location of its seat and, where appropriate, the fact that the company is being wound up.

Where in these documents mention is made of the capital of the company, the reference shall be to the capital subscribed and paid up.

Article 5

Each Member State shall determine by which persons the disclosure formalities are to be carried out.

Article 6

Member States shall provide for appropriate penalties in case of:

– failure to disclose the balance sheet and profit and loss account as required by Article 2(1) (f);
– omission from commercial documents of the compulsory particulars provided for in Article 4.

Section II

Validity of Obligations entered into by a Company

Article 7

If, before a company being formed has acquired legal personality, action has been carried out in its name and the company does not assume the obligations arising from such action, the persons who acted shall, without limit, be jointly and severally liable therefor, unless otherwise agreed.

Article 8

Completion of the formalities of disclosure of the particulars concerning the persons who, as an organ of the company, are authorised to represent it shall constitute a bar to any irregularity in their appointment being relied upon as against third parties unless the company proves that such third parties had knowledge thereof.

Article 9

1. Acts done by the organs of the company shall be binding upon it even if those acts are not within the objects of the company, unless such acts exceed the powers that the law confers or allows to be conferred on those organs.

However, Member States may provide that the company shall not be bound where such acts are outside the objects of the company, if it proves that the third party knew that the act was outside those objects or could not in view of the circumstances have been unaware of it; disclosure of the statutes shall not of itself be sufficient proof thereof.

2. The limits on the powers of the organs of the company, arising under the statutes or from a decision of the competent organs, may never be relied on as against third parties, even if they have been disclosed.

3. If the national law provides that authority to represent a company may, in derogation from the legal rules governing the subject, be conferred by the statutes on a single person or on several persons acting jointly, that law may provide that such a provision in the statutes may be relied on as against third parties on condition that it relates to the general power of representation; the question whether such a provision in the statutes can be relied on as against third parties shall be governed by Article 3.

Section III

Nullity of the Company

Article 10

In all Member States whose laws do not provide for preventive control, administrative or judicial, at the time of formation of a company, the instrument of constitution, the company statutes and any amendments to those documents shall be drawn up and certified in due legal form.

Article 11

The laws of the Member States may not provide for the nullity of companies otherwise than in accordance with the following provisions:

1. Nullity must be ordered by decision of a court of law;
2. Nullity may be ordered only on the following grounds:
   (a) that no instrument of constitution was executed or that the rules of preventive control or the requisite legal formalities were not complied with;
   (b) that the objects of the company are unlawful or contrary to public policy;
   (c) that the instrument of constitution or the statutes do not state the name of the company, the amount of the individual subscriptions of capital, the total amount of the capital subscribed or the objects of the company;

(d) failure to comply with the provisions of the national law concerning the minimum amount of capital to be paid up;

(e) the incapacity of all the founder members;

(f) that, contrary to the national law governing the company, the number of founder members is less than two.

Apart from the foregoing grounds of nullity, a company shall not be subject to any cause of non-existence, nullity absolute, nullity relative or declaration of nullity.

Article 12

1. The question whether a decision of nullity pronounced by a court of law may be relied on as against third parties shall be governed by Article 3. Where the national law entitles a third party to challenge the decision, he may do so only within six months of public notice of the decision of the court being given.

2. Nullity shall entail the winding up of the company, as may dissolution.

3. Nullity shall not of itself affect the validity of any commitments entered into by or with the company, without prejudice to the consequences of the company's being wound up.

4. The laws of each Member State may make provision for the consequences of nullity as between members of the company.

5. Holders of shares in the capital shall remain obliged to pay up the capital agreed to be subscribed by them but which has not been paid up, to the extent that commitments entered into with creditors so require.

Section IV

General Provisions

Article 13

Member States shall put into force, within eighteen months following notification of this directive, all amendments to their laws, regulations or administrative provisions required in order to comply with provisions of this directive and shall forthwith inform the Commission thereof.

The obligation of disclosure provided for in Article 2(1)(f)shall not enter into force until thirty months after notification of this directive in respect of naamloze vennootschappen under Netherlands law other than those referred to in the present Article 42(c) of the Netherlands Commercial Code.

Member States may provide that initial disclosure of the full text of the statutes as amended since the formation of the company shall not be required until the statutes are next amended or until 31 December 1970, whichever shall be the earlier.

Member States shall ensure that they communicate to the Commission the text of the main provisions of national law which they adopt in the field covered by this directive.

Article 14

This directive is addressed to the Member States.

The first decision of the Court on this directive illustrates clearly its view of the function of directives issued under Article 54(3)(g).

Case 32/74 Friedrich Haaga GmbH [1974] ECR 1201; [1975] 1 CMLR 32

The Court

...

It appears from the order for reference that this question was referred as the result of an objection raised in non-contentious proceedings against an order issued by the Registrar of Companies, requiring the private limited liability company concerned to indicate the directors' power of representation and, in particular, to specify that, in the event of any one director being appointed, he is authorised to represent the company alone. The company opposed this requirement on the ground that the entry demanded was superfluous, since from the wording of the entries on the register it was already clear that if only one director was appointed, he alone represented the company, according to the legislation in force in the Federal Republic of Germany.

...

Article 2(1) of the Directive of 9 March 1968 lays down that:

> 'Member States shall take the measures required to ensure compulsory disclosure by companies of at least the following documents and particulars:
>
> ...
>
> (d) the appointment, termination of office and particulars of the persons who either as a body constituted pursuant to law or as members of any such body:
>
> – are authorised to represent the company in dealings with third parties and in legal proceedings;
>
> – take part in the administration, supervision or control of the company'.

The second sentence of Article 2(1)(d), the interpretation of which is sought, adds that 'it must appear from the disclosure whether the persons authorised to represent the company may do so alone or must act jointly'.

According to the rules of legal construction, the expression 'persons who are authorised to represent the company' must be understood as being a generic expression, so that the grammatical plural may indicate, without distinction, the case of a single person and that of several persons authorised to represent the company. This provision therefore implies that, in the event of a single person being authorised to represent the company, the power of representation of that person is required to be made known expressly.

This interpretation is in conformity with the objective of the directive, which is to guarantee legal certainty in dealings between companies and third parties in view of the intensification of trade between Member States following the creation of the Common Market. In view of this fact, *it is important that any person wishing to establish and develop trading relations with companies situated in other Member States should be able easily to obtain essential information relating to the constitution of trading companies and to the powers of persons authorised to represent them.* In the interest of legal transactions between nationals of different Member States, it is therefore important that all the relevant information should be expressly stated in official registers or records, even if certain information follows automatically from national legislation or may appear self-evident. In fact, *third parties cannot be expected to have a full knowledge of the legislations or current commercial practices of other Member States.* It therefore appears necessary to require, insofar as the power of representation of directors of a limited liability company is concerned, that an entry should appear on the Companies Register conveying this information to third parties, even if it seems possible to deduce this information, in the absence of any entry on the Register, by logical reasoning or reference to national law.

The answer to the question referred should therefore be that Article 2(1)(d), second sentence, of the First Council Directive of 9 March 1968 on coordination of company law must be interpreted as meaning that where the body authorised to represent a company may consist of one or of several members, disclosure must be made not only of the provisions as to representation applicable in the event of the appointment of several directors, but also, in the event of the appointment of a single director, of the fact that the latter represents the company alone, even if his authority to do so clearly flows from national law.

The second section of the directive, and its enactment into United Kingdom law in Section 9(1) and (2) of the European Communities Act 1972, throws an interesting light on the use of directives as a method of harmonisation.

Article 9

1. Acts done by the organs of the company shall be binding upon it even if those acts are not within the objects of the company, unless such acts exceed the powers that the law confers or allows to be conferred on those organs.

However, Member States may provide that the company shall not be bound where such acts are outside the objects of the company, if it proves that the third party knew that the act was outside those objects or could not in view of the circumstances have been unaware of it; disclosure of the statutes shall not of itself be sufficient proof thereof.

2. The limits on the powers of the organs of the company, arising under the statutes or from a decision of the competent organs, may never be relied on as against third parties, even if they have been disclosed.

3. If the national law provides that authority to represent a company may, in derogation from the legal rules governing the subject, be conferred by the statutes on a single person or on several persons acting jointly, that law may provide that such a provision in the statutes may be relied on as against third parties on condition that it relates to the general power of representation; the question whether such a provision in the statutes can be relied on as against third parties shall be governed by Article 3.

European Communities Act 1972

Section 9

(1) In favour of a person dealing with a company in good faith, any transaction decided on by the directors shall be deemed to be one which it is within the capacity of the company to enter into, and the power of the directors to bind the company shall be deemed to be free of any limitation under the memorandum or articles of association; and a party to a transaction so decided on shall not be bound to enquire as to the capacity of the company to enter into it or as to any such limitation on the powers of the directors, and shall be presumed to have acted in good faith unless the contrary is proved.

(2) Where a contract purports to be made by a company, or by a person as agent for a company, at a time when the company has not been formed, then subject to any agreement to the contrary the contract shall have effect as a contract entered into by the person purporting act for the company or as agent for it, and he shall be personally liable on the contract accordingly.

Although the requirement of good faith on the part of a person dealing with a company in Section 9(1) of the Act may roughly correspond to the exception in Article 9(1) of the directive to the effect that the company will not be bound if it proves actual knowledge on the part of the third party, this requirement of good faith does not appear to correspond to anything in Article 9(2) of the directive. More generally it may be doubted whether the directors are the only 'organs' of an English or Scottish company, since, to take a single example, companies are required to have a secretary, who is recognised as having capacity to bind the company with regard to certain types of act (see the Companies Act 1948, Sections 176-7, *Panorama* v *Fidelis* [1971] 3 All ER 16, and more generally L. Gower: *Principles of Modern Company Law*, London, 1969, 17–21). Finally it might be noted that Section 9(2) of the Act does not take up the hint in Article 7 of the directive that companies may assume obligations arising under pre-incorporation contracts.

The second directive, Council Directive No 77/91/EEC of 13 December 1976, applies in the United Kingdom only to public companies limited by shares and public companies limited by guarantee and having a share capital (Article 1). It again requires that certain basic information, including the type of the company, should appear in the memorandum and articles of association, or their equivalents in other legal systems (Article 2). Its basic function, however, is to lay down minimum capital requirements for public companies, and to ensure that they actually receive and, in principle, retain this capital.

Bearing in mind the problems caused in calculating uniform prices under the common agricultural policy, it is interesting to see that this minimum capital is expressed in a unit of account based on the daily values of a 'basket' of Community currencies.

Second Council Directive No 77/91 of 13 December 1976 on coordination of safeguards ... required ... of companies (as amended) OJ 1977 L 26/1

Article 1

1. The coordination measures prescribed by this directive shall apply to the provisions laid down by law, regulation or administrative action in Member States relating to the following types of company:

– *In Belgium:*
  la société anonyme/de naamloze vennootschap;
– *In Denmark:*
  aktieselskabet;
– *In France:*
  la société anonyme;
– *In Germany:*
  die Aktiengesellschaft;

– *In Ireland:*
the public company limited by shares,
the public company limited by guarantee and having a share capital;
– *In Italy:*
la società per azioni;
– *In Luxembourg:*
la société anonyme;
– *In the Netherlands;*
de naamloze vennootschap;
– *In the United Kingdom:*
the public company limited by shares,
the public company limited by guarantee and having a share capital;
[– *In Greece:*
η ανωνυμη εταιρια;]
[– *In Spain:*
la sociedad anónima;
– *In Portugal:*
a sociedade anónima de responsabilidade limitada.]

The name for any company of the above types shall comprise or be accompanied by a description which is distinct from the description required of other types of companies.

2. The Member States may decide not to apply this directive to investment companies with variable capital and to cooperatives incorporated as one of the types of company listed in paragraph 1. In so far as the laws of the Member States make use of this option, they shall require such companies to include the words 'investment company with variable capital' or 'cooperative' in all documents indicated in Article 4 of Directive 68/151.

The expression 'investment company with variable capital', within the meaning of this directive, means only those companies:

– the exclusive object of which is to invest their funds in various stocks and shares, land or other assets with the sole aim of spreading investment risks and giving their shareholders the benefit of the results of the management of their assets,
– which offer their own shares for subscription by the public, and
– the statutes of which provide that, within the limits of a minimum and maximum capital, they may at any time issue, redeem or resell their shares.

Article 2

The statutes or the instrument of incorporation of the company shall always give at least the following information:

(a) the type and name of the company;
(b) the objects of the company;
(c) – when the company has no authorised capital, the amount of the subscribed capital,
– when the company has an authorised capital, the amount thereof and also the amount of the capital subscribed at the time the company is incorporated or is authorised to commence business, and at the time of any change in the authorised capital, without prejudice to Article 2(1)(e) of Directive No 68/151;

(d) in so far as they are not legally determined, the rules governing the number of and the procedure for appointing members of the bodies responsible for representing the company with regard to third parties, administration, management, supervision or control of the company and the allocation of powers among those bodies;

(e) the duration of the company, except where this is indefinite.

Article 3

The following information at least must appear in either the statutes or the instrument of incorporation or a separate document published in accordance with the procedure laid down in the laws of each Member State in accordance with Article 3 of Directive No 68/151:

(a) the registered office;

(b) the nominal value of the shares subscribed and, at least once a year, the number thereof;

(c) the number of shares subscribed without stating the nominal value, where such shares may be issued under national law;

(d) the special conditions if any limiting the transfer of shares;

(e) where there are several classes of shares, the information under (b), (c), and (d) for each class and the rights attaching to the shares of each class;

(f) whether the shares are registered or bearer, where national law provides for both types, and any provisions relating to the conversion of such shares unless the procedure is laid down by law;

(g) the amount of the subscribed capital paid up at the time the company is incorporated or is authorised to commence business;

(h) the nominal value of the shares or, where there is no nominal value, the number of shares issued for a consideration other than in cash, together with the nature of the consideration and the name of the person providing this consideration;

(i) the identity of the natural or legal persons or companies or firms by whom or in whose name the statutes or the instrument of incorporation, or where the company was not formed at the same time, the drafts of these documents, have been signed;

(j) the total amount, or at least an estimate, of all the costs payable by the company or chargeable to it by reason of its formation and, where appropriate, before the company is authorised to commence business;

(k) any special advantage granted, at the time the company is formed or up to the time it receives authorisation to commence business, to anyone who has taken part in the formation of the company or in transactions leading to the grant of such authorisation.

Article 4

1. Where the laws of a Member State prescribe that a company may not commence business without authorisation, they shall also make provision for responsibility for liabilities incurred by or on behalf of the company during the period before such authorisation is granted or refused.

2 Paragraph 1 shall not apply to liabilities under contracts concluded by the company conditionally upon its being granted authorisation to commence business.

Article 5

1. Where the laws of a Member State require a company to be formed by more than one member, the fact that all the shares are held by one person or that the number of members has fallen below the legal minimum after incorporation of the company shall not lead to the automatic dissolution of the company.

2. If in the cases referred to in paragraph 1, the laws of a Member State permit the company to be wound up by order of the court, the judge having jurisdiction must be able to give the company sufficient time to regularise its position.

3. Where such a winding up order is made the company shall enter into liquidation.

Article 6

1. The laws of the Member States shall require that, in order that a company may be incorporated or obtain authorisation to commence business, a minimum capital shall be subscribed the amount of which shall be not less than 25,000 European units of account.

The European unit of account shall be that defined by Commission Decision No 3289/75/ECSC.* The equivalent in national currency shall be calculated initially at the rate applicable on the date of adoption of this directive.

2. If the equivalent of the European unit of account in national currency is altered so that the value of the minimum capital in national currency remains less than 22,500 European units of account for a period of one year, the Commission shall inform the Member State concerned that it must amend its legislation to comply with paragraph 1 within 12 months following the expiry of that period. However, the Member State may provide that the amended legislation shall not apply to companies already in existence until 18 months after its entry into force.

3. Every five years the Council, acting on a proposal from the Commission, shall examine and, if need be, revise the amounts expressed in this article in European units of account in the light of economic and monetary trends in the Community and of the tendency towards allowing only large and medium-sized undertakings to opt for the types of company listed in Article 1.

Article 7

The subscribed capital may be formed only of assets capable of economic assessment. However, an undertaking to perform work or supply services may not form part of these assets.

Article 8

1. Shares may not be issued at a price lower than their nominal value, or, where there is no nominal value, their accountable par.

2. However, Member States may allow those who undertake to place shares in the exercise of their profession to pay less than the total price of the shares for which they subscribe in the course of this transaction.

---

* OJ L 327, 19.12.1975, p. 4.

Article 9

1. Shares issued for a consideration must be paid up at the time the company is incorporated or is authorised to commence business at not less than 25% of their nominal value or, in the absence of a nominal value, their accountable par.

2 However, where shares are issued for a consideration other than in cash at the time the company is incorporated or is authorised to commence business, the consideration must be transferred in full within five years of that time.

Article 10

1. A report on any consideration other than in cash shall be drawn up before the company is incorporated or is authorised to commence business, by one or more independent experts appointed or approved by an administrative or judicial authority. Such experts may be natural persons as well as legal persons and companies or firms under the laws of each Member State.

2 The expert's report shall contain at least a description of each of the assets comprising the consideration as well as of the methods of valuation used and shall state whether the values arrived at by the application of these methods correspond at least to the number and nominal value or, where there is no nominal value, to the accountable par and, where appropriate, to the premium on the shares to be issued for them.

3. The expert's report shall be published in the manner laid down by the laws of each Member State, in accordance with Article 3 of Directive No 68/151/EEC.

4. Member States may decide not to apply this article where 90% of the nominal value, or where there is no nominal value, of the accountable par of all the shares is issued to one or more companies for a consideration other than in cash, and where the following requirements are met:

(a) with regard to the company in receipt of such consideration, the persons referred to in Article 3(i) have agreed to dispense with the expert's report;

(b) such agreement has been published as provided for in paragraph 3;

(c) the companies furnishing such consideration have reserves which may not be distributed under the law or the statutes and which are at least equal to the nominal value or, where there is no nominal value, the accountable par of the shares issued for consideration other than in cash;

(d) the companies furnishing such consideration guarantee, up to an amount equal to that indicated in subparagraph (c), the debts of the recipient company arising between the time the shares are issued for a consideration other than in cash and one year after the publication of that company's annual accounts for the financial year during which such consideration was furnished. Any transfer of these shares is prohibited within this period;

(e) the guarantee referred to in (d) has been published as provided for in paragraph 3;

(f) the companies furnishing such consideration shall place a sum equal to that indicated in (c) into a reserve which may not be distributed until three years after publication of the annual accounts of the recipient company for the financial year during which such consideration was furnished or, if necessary, until such later date as all claims relating to the guarantee referred to in (d) which are submitted during this period have been settled.

Article 11

1. If, before the expiry of a time limit laid down by national law of at least two years from the time the company is incorporated or is authorised to commence business, the company acquires any asset belonging to a person or company or firm referred to in Article 3(i) for a consideration of not less than one-tenth of the subscribed capital, the acquisition shall be examined and details of it published in the manner provided for in Article 10 and it shall be submitted for the approval of the general meeting.

Member States may also require these provisions to be applied when the assets belong to a shareholder or to any other person.

2. Paragraph 1 shall not apply to acquisitions effected in the normal course of the company's business, to acquisitions effected at the instance or under the supervision of an administrative or judicial authority, or to stock exchange acquisitions.

Article 12

Subject to the provisions relating to the reduction of subscribed capital, the shareholders may not be released from the obligation to pay up their contributions.

Article 13

Pending coordination of national laws at a subsequent date, Member States shall adopt the measures necessary to require provision of at least the same safeguards as are laid down in Articles 2 to 12 in the event of the conversion of another type of company into a public limited liability company.

Article 14

Articles 2 to 13 shall not prejudice the provisions of Member States on competence and procedure relating to the modification of the statutes or of the instrument of incorporation.

Article 15

1.(a) Except for cases of reductions of subscribed capital, no distribution to shareholders may be made when on the closing date of the last financial year the net assets as set out in the company's annual accounts are, or following such a distribution would become, lower than the amount of the subscribed capital plus those reserves which may not be distributed under the law or the statutes.

(b) Where the uncalled part of the subscribed capital is not included in the assets shown in the balance sheet, this amount shall be deducted from the amount of subscribed capital referred to in subparagraph (a).

(c) The amount of a distribution to shareholders may not exceed the amount of the profits at the end of the last financial year plus any profits brought forward and sums drawn from reserves available for this purpose, less any losses brought forward and sums placed to reserve in accordance with the law or the statutes.

(d) The expression 'distribution' used in subparagraphs (a) and (c) includes in particular the payment of dividends and of interest relating to shares.

2. When the laws of a Member State allow the payment of interim dividends, the following conditions at least shall apply:

(a) interim accounts shall be drawn up showing that the funds available for distribution are sufficient;

(b) the amount to be distributed may not exceed the total profits made since the end of the last financial year for which the annual accounts have been drawn up, plus any profits brought forward and sums drawn from reserves available for this purpose, less losses brought forward and sums to be placed to reserve pursuant to the requirements of the law or the statutes.

3. Paragraphs 1 and 2 shall not affect the provisions of the Member States as regards increases in subscribed capital by capitalisation of reserves.

4. The laws of a Member State may provide for derogations from paragraph 1(a) in the case of investment companies with fixed capital.

The expression 'investment company with fixed capital', within the meaning of this paragraph, means only those companies:

- the exclusive object of which is to invest their funds in various stocks and shares, land or other assets with the sole aim of spreading investment risks and giving their shareholders the benefit of the results of the management of their assets, and
- which offer their own shares for subscription by the public.

In so far as the laws of Member States make use of this option they shall:

(a) require such companies to include the expression 'investment company' in all documents indicated in Article 4 of Directive No 68/151/EEC;

(b) not permit any such company whose net assets fall below the amount specified in paragraph 1(a) to make a distribution to shareholders when on the closing date of the last financial year the company's total assets as set out in the annual accounts are, or following such distribution would become, less than one-and-a-half times the amount of the company's total liabilities to creditors as set out in the annual accounts;

(c) require any such company which makes a distribution when its net assets fall below the amount specified in paragraph 1(a) to include in its annual accounts a note to that effect.

Article 16

Any distribution made contrary to Article 15 must be returned by shareholders who have received it if the company proves that these shareholders knew of the irregularity of the distributions made to them, or could not in view of the circumstances have been unaware of it.

Article 17

1. In the case of a serious loss of the subscribed capital, a general meeting of shareholders must be called within the period laid down by the laws of the Member States, to consider whether the company should be wound up or any other measures taken.

2. The amount of a loss deemed to be serious within the meaning of paragraph 1 may not be set by the laws of Member States at a figure higher than half the subscribed capital.

Article 18

1. The shares of a company may not be subscribed for by the company itself.

2. If the shares of a company have been subscribed for by a person acting in his own name, but on behalf of the company, the subscriber shall be deemed to have subscribed for them for his own account.

3. The persons or companies or firms referred to in Article 3(i) or, in cases of an increase in subscribed capital, the members of the administrative or management body shall be liable to pay for shares subscribed in contravention of this article.

However, the laws of a Member State may provide that any such person may be released from his obligation if he proves that no fault is attributable to him personally.

Article 19

1. Where the laws of a Member State permit a company to acquire its own shares, either itself or through a person acting in his own name but on the company's behalf, they shall make such acquisitions subject to at least the following conditions:

(a) authorisation shall be given by the general meeting, which shall determine the terms and conditions of such acquisitions, and in particular the maximum number of shares to be acquired, the duration of the period for which the authorisation is given and which may not exceed 18 months, and, in the case of acquisition for value, the maximum and minimum consideration. Members of the administrative or management body shall be required to satisfy themselves that at the time when each authorised acquisition is effected the conditions referred to in subparagraphs (b), (c) and (d) are respected.

(b) the nominal value or, in the absence thereof, the accountable par of the acquired shares, including shares previously acquired by the company and held by it, and shares acquired by a person acting in his own name but on the company's behalf, may not exceed 10% of the subscribed capital;

(c) the acquisitions may not have the effect of reducing the net assets below the amount mentioned in Article 15(1)(a);

(d) only fully paid-up shares may be included in the transaction.

2. The laws of a Member State may provide for derogations from the first sentence of paragraph 1(a) where the acquisition of a company's own shares is necessary to prevent serious and imminent harm to the company. In such a case, the next general meeting must be informed by the administrative or management body of the reasons for and nature of the acquisitions effected, of the number and nominal value or, in the absence of a nominal value, the accountable par of the shares acquired, of the proportion of the subscribed capital which they represent, and of the consideration for these shares.

3. Member States may decide not to apply the first sentence of paragraph (1)(a) to shares acquired by either the company itself or by a person acting in his own name but on the company's behalf, for distribution to that company's employees or to the employees of an associate company. Such shares must be distributed within 12 months of their acquisition.

Article 20

1. Member States may decide not to apply Article 19 to:

(a) shares acquired in carrying out a decision to reduce capital, or in the circumstances referred to in Article 39;

(b) shares acquired as a result of a universal transfer of assets;

(c) fully paid-up shares acquired free of charge or by banks and other financial institutions as purchasing commission;

(d) shares acquired by virtue of a legal obligation or resulting from a court ruling for the protection of minority shareholders in the event, particularly, of a merger, a change in the company's object or form, transfer abroad of the registered office, or the introduction of restrictions on the transfer of shares;

(e) shares acquired from a shareholder in the event of failure to pay them up;

(f) shares acquired in order to indemnify minority shareholders in associated companies;

(g) fully paid-up shares acquired under a sale enforced by a court order for the payment of a debt owed to the company by the owner of the shares;

(h) fully paid-up shares issued by an investment company with fixed capital, as defined in the second subparagraph of Article 15(4), and acquired at the investor's request by that company or by an associate company. Article 15(4)(a) shall apply. These acquisitions may not have the effect of reducing the net assets below the amount of the subscribed capital plus any reserves the distribution of which is forbidden by law.

2. Shares acquired in the cases listed in paragraph 1(b) to (g) above must, however, be disposed of within not more than three years of their acquisition unless the nominal value or, in the absence of a nominal value, the accountable par of the shares acquired, including shares which the company may have acquired through a person acting in his own name but on the company's behalf, does not exceed 10% of the subscribed capital.

3. If the shares are not disposed of within the period laid down in paragraph 2, they must be cancelled. The laws of a Member State may make this cancellation subject to a corresponding reduction in the subscribed capital. Such a reduction must be prescribed where the acquisition of shares to be cancelled results in the net assets having fallen below the amount specified in Article 15(1)(a).

Article 21

Shares acquired in contravention of Articles 19 and 20 shall be disposed of within one year of their acquisition. Should they not be disposed of within that period, Article 20(3) shall apply.

Article 22

1. Where the laws of a Member State permit a company to acquire its own shares, either itself or through a person acting in his own name but on the company's behalf, they shall make the holding of these shares at all times subject to at least the following conditions:

(a) among the rights attaching to the shares, the right to vote attaching to the company's own shares shall in any event be suspended;

(b) if the shares are included among the assets shown in the balance sheet, a reserve of the same amount, unavailable for distribution, shall be included among the liabilities.

2. Where the laws of a Member State permit a company to acquire its own shares, either itself or through a person acting in his own name but on the company's behalf, they shall require the annual report to state at least:

(a) the reasons for acquisitions made during the financial year;

(b) the number and nominal value or, in the absence of a nominal value, the accountable par of the shares acquired and disposed of during the financial year and the proportion of the subscribed capital which they represent;

(c) in the case of acquisition or disposal for a value, the consideration for the shares;

(d) the number and nominal value or, in the absence of a nominal value, the accountable par of all the shares acquired and held by the company and the proportion of the subscribed capital which they represent.

Article 23

1. A company may not advance funds, nor make loans, nor provide security, with a view to the acquisition of its shares by a third party.

2. Paragraph 1 shall not apply to transactions concluded by banks and other financial institutions in the normal course of business, nor to transactions effected with a view to the acquisition of shares by or for the company's employees or the employees of an associate company. However, these transactions may not have the effect of reducing the net assets below the amount specified in Article 15(1)(a).

3. Paragraph 1 shall not apply to transactions effected with a view to acquisition of shares as described in Article 20(1)(h).

Article 24

1. The acceptance of the company's own shares as security, either by the company itself or through a person acting in his own name but on the company's behalf, shall be treated as an acquisition for the purposes of Articles 19, 20(1), 22 and 23.

2. The Member States may decide not to apply paragraph 1 to transactions concluded by banks and other financial institutions in the normal course of business.

Article 25

1. Any increase in capital must be decided upon by the general meeting. Both this decision and the increase in the subscribed capital shall be published in the manner laid down by the laws of each Member State, in accordance with Article 3 of Directive No 68/151/EEC.

2. Nevertheless, the statutes or instrument of incorporation or the general meeting, the decision of which must be published in accordance with the rules referred to in paragraph 1, may authorise an increase in the subscribed capital up to a maximum amount which they shall fix with due regard for any maximum amount provided for by law. Where appropriate, the increase in the subscribed capital shall be decided on within the limits of the amount fixed, by the company body empowered to do so. The power of such body in this respect shall be for a maximum period of five years and may be renewed one or more times by the general meeting, each time for a period not exceeding five years.

3. Where there are several classes of shares, the decision by the general meeting concerning the increase in capital referred to in paragraph 1, or the authorisation to increase the capital referred to in paragraph 2, shall be subject to a separate vote at least for each class of shareholder whose rights are affected by the transaction.

4. This article shall apply to the issue of all securities which are convertible into shares or which carry the right to subscribe for shares, but not to the conversion of such securities, nor to the exercise of the right to subscribe.

Article 26

Shares issued for a consideration, in the course of an increase in subscribed capital, must be paid up to at least 25% of their nominal value or, in the absence of a nominal value, of their accountable par. Where provision is made for an issue premium, it must be paid in full.

Article 27

1. Where shares are issued for consideration other than in cash in the course of an increase in the subscribed capital the consideration must be transferred in full within a period of five years from the decision to increase the subscribed capital.

2 The consideration referred to in paragraph 1 shall be the subject of a report drawn up before the increase in capital is made by one or more experts who are independent of the company and appointed or approved by an administrative or judicial authority. Such experts may be natural persons as well as legal persons and companies and firms under the laws of each Member State.

Article 10(2) and (3) shall apply.

3. Member States may decide not to apply paragraph 2 in the event of an increase in subscribed capital made in order to give effect to a merger or a public offer for the purchase or exchange of shares and to pay the shareholders of the company which is being absorbed or which is the object of the public offer for the purchase or exchange of shares.

4. Member States may decide not to apply paragraph 2 if all the shares issued in the course of an increase in subscribed capital are issued for a consideration other than in cash to one or more companies, on condition that all the shareholders in the company which receive the consideration have agreed not to have an experts' report drawn up and that the requirements of Article 4(b) to (f) are met.

Article 28

Where an increase in capital is not fully subscribed, the capital will be increased by the amount of the subscriptions received only if the conditions of the issue so provide.

Article 29

1. Whenever the capital is increased by consideration in cash, the shares must be offered on a pre-emptive basis to shareholders in proportion to the capital represented by their shares.

2. The laws of a Member State:

(a) need not apply paragraph 1 above to shares which carry a limited right to participate in distributions within the meaning of Article 15 and/or in the company's assets in the event of liquidation; or

(b) may permit, where the subscribed capital of a company having several classes of shares carrying different rights with regard to voting, or participation in distributions within the meaning of Article 15 or in assets in the event of liquidation, is increased by issuing new shares in only one of these classes, the right of pre-emption of shareholders of the other classes to be exercised only after the exercise of this right by the shareholders of the class in which the new shares are being issued.

3. Any offer of subscription on a pre-emptive basis and the period within which this right must be exercised shall be published in the national gazette appointed in accordance with Directive No 68/151/EEC. However, the laws of a Member State need not provide for such publication where all a company's shares are registered. In such case, all the company's shareholders must be informed in writing. The right of pre-emption must be exercised within a period which shall not be less than 14 days from the date of publication of the offer or from the date of dispatch of the letters to the shareholders.

4. The right of pre-emption may not be restricted or withdrawn by the statutes or instrument of incorporation. This may, however, be done by decision of the general meeting. The administrative or management body shall be required to present to such a meeting a written report indicating the reasons for restriction or withdrawal of the right of pre-emption, and justifying the proposed issue price. The general meeting shall act in accordance with the rules of a quorum and a majority laid down in Article 40. Its decision

shall be published in the manner laid down by the laws of each Member State, in accordance with Article 3 of Directive No 68/151/EEC.

5. The laws of a Member State may provide that the statutes, the instrument of incorporation or the general meeting, acting in accordance with the rules for a quorum, a majority and publication set out in paragraph 4, may give the power to restrict or withdraw the right of pre-emption to the company body which is empowered to decide on an increase in subscribed capital within the limits of the authorised capital. This power may not be granted for a longer period than the power for which provision is made in Article 25(2).

6. Paragraphs 1 to 5 shall apply to the issue of all securities which are convertible into shares or which carry the right to subscribe for shares, but not to the conversion of such securities, nor to the exercise of the right to subscribe.

7. The right of pre-emption is not excluded for the purposes of paragraphs 4 and 5 where, in accordance with the decision to increase the subscribed capital, shares are issued to banks or other financial institutions with a view to their being offered to shareholders of the company in accordance with paragraphs 1 and 3.

Article 30

Any reduction in the subscribed capital, except under a court order, must be subject at least to a decision of the general meeting acting in accordance with the rules for a quorum and a majority laid down in Article 40 without prejudice to Articles 36 and 37. Such decision shall be published in the manner laid down by the laws of each Member State in accordance with Article 3 of Directive No 68/151/EEC.

The notice convening the meeting must specify at least the purpose of the reduction and the way in which it is to be carried out.

Article 31

Where there a several classes of shares, the decision by the general meeting concerning a reduction in the subscribed capital shall be subject to a separate vote, at least for each class of shareholders whose rights are affected by the transaction.

Article 32

1. In the event of a reduction in the subscribed capital, at least the creditors whose claims antedate the publication of the decision to make the reduction shall be entitled at least to have the right to obtain security for claims which have not fallen due by the date of that publication. The laws of a Member State shall lay down the conditions for the exercise of this right. They may not set aside such right unless the creditor has adequate safeguards, or unless the latter are not necessary in view of the assets of the company.

2. The laws of the Member States shall also stipulate at least that the reduction shall be void or that no payment may be made for the benefit of the shareholders, until the creditors have obtained satisfaction or a court has decided that their application should not be acceded to.

3. This article shall apply where the reduction in the subscribed capital is brought about by the total or partial waiving of the payment of the balance of the shareholders' contributions.

Article 33

1. Member States need not apply Article 32 to a reduction in the subscribed capital whose purpose is to offset losses incurred or to include sums of money in a reserve

provided that, following this operation, the amount of such reserve is not more than 10% of the reduced subscribed capital. Except in the event of a reduction in the subscribed capital, this reserve may not be distributed to shareholders; it may be used only for offsetting losses incurred or for increasing the subscribed capital by the capitalisation of such reserve, in so far as the Member States permit such an operation.

2. In the cases referred to in paragraph 1 the laws of the Member States must at least provide for the measures necessary to ensure that the amounts deriving from the reduction of subscribed capital may not be used for making payments or distributions to shareholders or discharging shareholders from the obligation to make their contributions.

Article 34

The subscribed capital may not be reduced to an amount less than the minimum capital laid down in accordance with Article 6. However, Member States may permit such a reduction if they also provide that the decision to reduce the subscribed capital may take effect only when the subscribed capital is increased to an amount at least equal to the prescribed minimum.

Article 35

Where the laws of a Member State authorise total or partial redemption of the subscribed capital without reduction of the latter, they shall at least require that the following conditions are observed:

(a) where the statutes or instrument of incorporation provide for redemption, the latter shall be decided on by the general meeting voting at least under the usual conditions of quorum and majority. Where the statutes or instrument of incorporation do not provide for redemption, the latter shall be decided upon by the general meeting acting at least under the conditions of quorum and majority laid down in Article 40. The decision must be published in the manner prescribed by the laws of each Member State, in accordance with Article 3 of Directive No 68/151/EEC;

(b) only sums which are available for distribution within the meaning of Article 15(1) may be used for redemption purposes;

(c) shareholders whose shares are redeemed shall retain their rights in the company, with the exception of their rights to the repayment of their investment and participation in the distribution of an initial dividend on unredeemed shares.

Article 36

1. Where the laws of a Member State may allow companies to reduce their subscribed capital by compulsory withdrawal of shares, they shall require that at least the following conditions are observed:

(a) compulsory withdrawal must be prescribed or authorised by the statutes or instrument of incorporation before subscription of the shares which are to be withdrawn are subscribed for;

(b) where the compulsory withdrawal is merely authorised by the statutes or instrument of incorporation, it shall be decided upon by the general meeting unless it has been unanimously approved by the shareholders concerned;

(c) the company body deciding on the compulsory withdrawal shall fix the terms and manner thereof, where they have not already been fixed by the statutes or instrument of incorporation;

(d) Article 32 shall apply except in the case of fully paid-up shares which are made available to the company free of charge or are withdrawn using sums available for distribution in accordance with Article 15(1); in these cases, an amount equal to the nominal value or, in the absence thereof, to the accountable par of all the withdrawn shares must be included in a reserve. Except in the event of a reduction in the subscribed capital this reserve may not be distributed to shareholders. It can be used only for offsetting losses incurred or for increasing the subscribed capital by the capitalization of such reserve, in so far as Member States permit such an operation;

(e) the decision on compulsory withdrawal shall be published in the manner laid down by the laws of each Member State in accordance with Article 3 of Directive No 68/151/EEC.

2. Articles 30(1), 31, 33 and 40 shall not apply to the cases to which paragraph 1 refers.

Article 37

1. In the case of a reduction in the subscribed capital by the withdrawal of shares acquired by the company itself or by a person acting in his own name but on behalf of the company, the withdrawal must always be decided on by the general meeting.

2. Article 32 shall apply unless the shares are fully paid up and are acquired free of charge or using sums available for distribution in accordance with Article 15(1); in these cases an amount equal to the nominal value or, in the absence thereof, to the accountable par of all the shares withdrawn must be included in a reserve. Except in the event of a reduction in the subscribed capital, this reserve may not be distributed to shareholders. It may be used only for offsetting losses incurred or for increasing the subscribed capital by the capitalisation of such reserve, in so far as the Member States permit such an operation.

3. Articles 31, 33 and 40 shall not apply to the cases to which paragraph 1 refers.

Article 38

In the cases covered by Articles 35, 36(1)(b) and 37(1), when there are several classes of shares, the decision by the general meeting concerning redemption of the subscribed capital or its reduction by withdrawal of shares shall be subject to a separate vote, at least for each class of shareholders whose rights are affected by the transaction.

Article 39

Where the laws of a Member State authorise companies to issue redeemable shares, they shall require that the following conditions, at least, are complied with for the redemption of such shares:

(a) redemption must be authorised by the company's statutes or instrument of incorporation before the redeemable shares are subscribed for;

(b) the shares must be fully paid up;

(c) the terms and manner of redemption must be laid down in the company's statutes or instrument of incorporation;

(d) redemption can be only effected by using sums available for distribution in accordance with Article 15(1) or the proceeds of a new issue made with a view to effecting such redemption;

(e) an amount equal to the nominal value or, in the absence thereof, to the accountable par of all the redeemed shares must be included in a reserve which cannot be distributed to the shareholders, except in the event of a reduction in the subscribed capital; it may be used only for the purpose of increasing the subscribed capital by the capitalisation of reserves;

(f) subparagraph (e) shall not apply to redemption using the proceeds of a new issue made with a view to effecting such redemption;

(g) where provision is made for the payment of a premium to shareholders in consequence of a redemption, the premium may be paid only from sums available for distribution in accordance with Article 15(1), or from a reserve other than that referred to in (e) which may not be distributed to shareholders except in the event of a reduction in the subscribed capital; this reserve may be used only for the purposes of increasing the subscribed capital for the capitalisation of reserves or for covering the costs referred to in Article 3(j) or the cost of issuing shares or debentures or for the payment of a premium to holders of redeemable shares or debentures;

(h) notification of redemption shall be published in the manner laid down by the laws of each Member State in accordance with Article 3 of Directive No 68/151/EEC.

Article 40

1. The laws of the Member States shall provide that the decisions referred to in Articles 29(4) and (5), 30, 31, 35 and 38 must be taken at least by a majority of not less than two-thirds of the votes attaching to the securities or the subscribed capital represented.

2. The laws of the Member States may, however, lay down that a simple majority of the votes specified in paragraph 1 is sufficient when at least half the subscribed capital is represented.

Article 41

1. Member States may derogate from Article 9(1), Article 19(1)(a) first sentence and (b), and from Articles 25, 26 and 29 to the extent that such derogations are necessary for the adoption or application of provisions designed to encourage the participation of employees, or other groups of persons defined by national law, in the capital of undertakings.

2. Member States may decide not to apply Article 19(1)(a) first sentence, and Articles 30, 31, 36, 37, 38 and 39, to companies incorporated under a special law which issue both capital shares and workers' shares, the latter being issued to the company's employees as a body, who are represented at general meetings of shareholders by delegates having the right to vote.

Article 42

For the purposes of the implementation of this directive, the laws of the Member States shall ensure equal treatment to all shareholders who are in the same position.

Article 43

1. Member States shall bring into force the laws, regulations and administrative provisions needed in order to comply with this directive within two years of its notification. They shall forthwith inform the Commission thereof.

2. Member States may decide not to apply Article 3(g), (i), (j) and (k) to companies already in existence at the date of entry into force of the provisions referred to in paragraph 1.

They may provide that the other provisions of this directive shall not apply to such companies until 18 months after that date.

However, this time limit may be three years in the case of Articles 6 and 9 and five years in the case of unregistered companies in the United Kingdom and Ireland.

All Member States shall ensure that they communicate to the Commission the text of the main provisions of national law which they adopt in the field covered by this directive.

Article 44

This directive is addressed to the Member States.

In addition the Council has issued the following directives (among others) dealing with companies:

- Third Council Directive of 9 October 1978, based on Article 54(3)(g) of the Treaty, concerning mergers: OJ 1978, L, 295/36;
- Fourth Council Directive of 25 July 1978, based on Article 54(3)(g) of the Treaty, on annual accounts: OJ 1978, L, 222/11;
- Sixth Council Directive of 17 December 1982, based on Article 54(3)(g) of the Treaty, concerning the division of companies: OJ 1982, L, 378/47;
- Seventh Council Directive of 13 June 1983, based on Article 54(3)(g) of the Treaty, on consolidated accounts: OJ 1983, L, 193/1;
- Eighth Council Directive of 10 April 1984, based on Article 54(3)(g) of the Treaty, on the approval of persons responsible for carrying out audits: OJ 1984, L, 126/20.

V DEROGATIONS

In general the provisions of law governing derogations from freedom of establishment and freedom to supply services follow those governing derogations from the free movement of persons. Council Directive No 64/221 of 25 February 1964 applies to all these titles (see above p. 310).

In one respect, however, freedom to supply services calls for a separate consideration. The Court has held that those provisions do not preclude an assignee of the performing right in a cinematographic film in a Member State from relying on his right to prohibit the exhibition of that film in that State without his authority, by means of cable diffusion, if the film so exhibited is picked up and transmitted after being broadcast in another Member State by a third party with the consent of the original owner of the right.

Case 62/79 SA Coditel and Others v SA Ciné Vog Films and Others
[1980] ECR 881

The Court

By a judgment of 30 March 1979, which was received at the Court on 17 April 1979, the Cour d'Appel, Brussels, referred two questions to the Court under Article 177 of the EEC Treaty for a preliminary ruling on the interpretation of Article 59 and other provisions of the Treaty on freedom to provide services.

Those questions were raised during an action brought by a Belgian cinematographic film distribution company, Ciné Vog Films S.A., the respondent before the Cour d'Appel, for infringement of copyright. The action is against a French company, Les Films la Boétie, and three Belgian cable television diffusion companies, which are hereafter referred to collectively as the Coditel companies. Compensation is sought for the damage allegedly caused to Ciné Vog by the reception in Belgium of a broadcast by German television of the film 'Le Boucher' for which Ciné Vog obtained exclusive distribution rights in Belgium from Les Films la Boétie.

It is apparent from the file that the Coditel companies provide, with the authority of the Belgian administration, a cable television diffusion service covering part of Belgium. Television sets belonging to subscribers to the service are linked by cable to a central aerial having special technical features which enable Belgian broadcasts to be picked up as well as certain foreign broadcasts which the subscriber cannot always receive with a private aerial, and which furthermore improve the quality of the pictures and sound received by the subscribers.

The court before which the claim was made, the Tribunal de Première Instance, Brussels, declared that it was unfounded as against Les Films le Boétie, but it ordered the Coditel companies to pay damages to Ciné Vog. The Coditel companies appealed against that judgment. That appeal was declared inadmissible by the Cour d'Appel to the extent to which it was brought against the company Les Films la Boétie, which is not now therefore a party to the dispute.

The facts of the case bearing upon the outcome of the dispute were summarised by the Cour d'Appel as follows. By an agreement of 8 July 1969 Les Films la Boétie, acting as an owner of all the proprietary rights in the film 'Le Boucher', gave Ciné Vog the 'exclusive right' to distribute the film in Belgium for seven years. The film was shown in cinemas in Belgium starting on 15 May 1970. However, on 5 January 1971 German television's first channel broadcast a German version of the film and this broadcast could be picked up in Belgium. Ciné Vog considered that the broadcast had jeopardised the commercial future of the film in Belgium. It relied upon this ground of complaint both against Les Films la Boétie, for not having observed the exclusivity of the rights which it had transferred to it, and against the Coditel companies for having relayed the relevant broadcast over their cable diffusion networks.

The Cour d'Appel first of all examined the activities of the cable television diffusion companies from the point of view of copyright infringement. It considered that those companies had made a 'communication to the public' of the film within the meaning of the provisions applying in this field and that, as regards copyright law and subject to the effect thereon of Community law, they therefore needed the authorisation of Ciné Vog to relay the film over their networks. The effect of this reasoning by the Cour d'Appel is that the authorisation given by the copyright owner to German television to broadcast the film did not include authority to relay the film over cable diffusion networks outside Germany, or at least those existing in Belgium.

The Cour d'Appel then went on to examine in the light of Community law the argument of the Coditel companies that any prohibition on the transmission of films, the copyright in which has been assigned by the producer to a distribution company covering the whole of Belgium, is contrary to the provisions of the EEC Treaty, in particular to Article 85 and Articles 59 and 60. After rejecting the argument based on Article 85, the Cour d'Appel wondered if the action undertaken against the cable television diffusion companies by Ciné Vog infringed Article 59 'in so far as it limits the possibility for a transmitting station established in a country which borders on Belgium, and which is the country of the persons for whom a service is intended, freely to provide that service'.

In the opinion of the appellant companies, Article 59 must be understood to mean that it prohibits restrictions on freedom to provide services and not merely restrictions on the freedom of activity of those providing services, and that it covers all cases where the provision of a service involves or has involved at an earlier stage or will involve at a later stage the crossing of intra-Community frontiers.

Believing that that submission bears upon the interpretation of the Treaty, the Cour d'Appel referred to the Court of Justice the following two questions:

'1. Are the restrictions prohibited by Article 59 of the Treaty establishing the European Economic Community only those which prejudice the provision of services between nationals established in different Member States, or do they also comprise restrictions on the provision of services between nationals established in the same Member State which however concern services the substance of which originates in another Member State?

2. If the first limb of the preceding question is answered in the affirmative, is it in accordance with the provisions of the Treaty on freedom to provide services for the assignee of the performing right in a cinematographic film in one Member State to rely upon his right in order to prevent the defendant from showing that film in that State by means of cable television where the film thus shown is picked up by the defendant in the said Member State after having been broadcast by a third party in another Member State with the consent of the original owner of the right?'

According to its wording the second question is asked in case the answer to the first limb of the question should be in the affirmative; but the Cour d'Appel evidently had in mind an answer stating that in principle Article 59 *et seq.* of the Treaty apply to the provision of the services concerned because only in that case can the second question have any meaning.

The Court of Justice will first of all examine the second question. If the answer to this question is in the negative because the practice it describes is not contrary to the provisions of the Treaty on freedom to provide services – on the assumption that those provisions are applicable – the national court will have all the information necessary for it to be able to resolve the legal problem before it in conformity with Community law.

The second question raises the problem of whether Articles 59 and 60 of the Treaty prohibit an assignment, limited to the territory of a Member State, of the copyright in a film, in view of the fact that a series of such assignments might result in the partitioning of the Common Market as regards the undertaking of economic activity in the film industry.

A cinematographic film belongs to the category of literary and artistic works made available to the public by performances which may be infinitely repeated. In this respect the problems involved in the observance of copyright in relation to the requirements of the Treaty are not the same as those which arise in connection with literary and artistic works the placing of which at the disposal of the public is inseparable from the circulation of the material form of the works, as in the case of books or records.

In these circumstances *the owner of the copyright in a film and his assigns have a legitimate interest in calculating the fees due in respect of the authorisation to exhibit the film on the basis of the actual or probable number of performances and in authorising a television broadcast of the film only after it has been exhibited in cinemas for a certain period of time.* It appears from the file on the present case that the contract made between Les Films la Boétie and Ciné Vog stipulated that the exclusive right which was assigned included the right to exhibit the film 'Le Boucher' publicly in Belgium by way of projection in cinemas and on television but that the right to have the film diffused by Belgian television could not be exercised until 40 months after the first showing of the film in Belgium.

These facts are important in two regards. On the one hand, they highlight the fact that the right of a copyright owner and his assigns to require fees for any showing of a film is part of the essential function of copyright in this type of literary and artistic work. On the other hand, they demonstrate that the exploitation of copyright in films and the fees attaching thereto cannot be regulated without regard being had to the possibility of television broadcasts of those films. The question whether an assignment of copyright limited to the territory of a Member State is capable of constituting a restriction on freedom to provide services must be examined in this context.

Whilst Article 59 of the Treaty prohibits restrictions upon freedom to provide services, it does not thereby encompass limits upon the exercise of certain economic activities which have their origin in the application of national legislation for the protection of intellectual property, save where such application constitutes a means of arbitrary discrimination or a disguised restriction on trade between Member States. Such would be the case if that application enabled parties to an assignment of copyright to create artificial barriers to trade between Member States.

The effect of this is that, whilst copyright entails the right to demand fees for any showing or performance, the rules of the Treaty cannot in principle constitute an obstacle to the geographical limits which the parties to a contract of assignment have agreed upon in order to protect the author and his assigns in this regard. The mere fact that those geographical limits may coincide with national frontiers does not point to a different solution in a situation where television is organised in the Member States largely on the basis of legal broadcasting monopolies, which indicates that a limitation other than the geographical field of application of an assignment is often impracticable.

The exclusive assignee of the performing right in a film for the whole of a Member State may therefore rely upon his right against cable television diffusion companies which have transmitted that film on their diffusion network having received it from a television broadcasting station established in another Member State, without thereby infringing Community law.

...

For the sequel to this case, see Case 262/81 *Coditel and Others v Ciné Vog Films and Others* [1982] ECR 3381.

FURTHER READING

Boutard Labarde, M.-C., 'Activité de l'Assurance' 114 JDI (1987) 436
Chappatte, P., 'Freedom to Provide Insurance Services in the EEC' 9 ELRev (1984) 3
Edward, D., 'The Convention between the Member States of the EEC on the Mutual Recognition of Companies and Legal Persons' 6 CMLRev (1968) 104
Edward, D., 'Establishment and Services: An Analysis of the Insurance Cases' 12 ELRev (1987) 231
Gormley, L., 'Public Works Contracts and Freedom to Supply Services' 133 NLJ (1983) 533
Hodgin, R., 'Case-Law: Court of Justice' 24 CMLRev (1987) 273
Hurst, J., 'Harmonisation of Company Law in the EEC' LIEI (1974–I) 63
Kuyper, P., 'Case-Law: Court of Justice' 23 CMLRev (1986) 661
Maestripieri, C., 'Freedom of Establishment and Freedom to Supply Services' 10 CMLRev (1973) 150
Morse, G., 'Mutual Recognition of Companies in England and the EEC' JBL (1972) 195
Oliver, P., 'Directive 71/305: Criteria for Selecting Public Works Contractors' 7 ELRev (1982) 233
Prentice, D., 'Section 9 of the European Communities Act' 89 LQR (1973) 518
Sanders, P. , 'Structure and Progress of the European Company' *Harmonisation of European Company Law*, ed. C. Schmitthof, London, 1973, 1983
Schmitthof, C., 'The Success of the Harmonisation of European Company Law' 2 ELR (1976) 100

9

CONCERTED BEHAVIOUR

INTRODUCTION

Among the activities of the Community listed in Article 3 of the EEC Treaty is the institution of a system designed to ensure that competition in the Common Market should not be distorted. Such a system is necessary for the reason, among others, that in its absence the differences between national rules governing competition, and the behaviour of undertakings trading in the Community, could create obstacles to trade between Member States no less substantial than those arising from customs duties, quantitative restrictions and equivalent charges and measures. In other words, no useful purpose would be served by the prohibition of restrictions imposed by States on the free movement of goods and services, if private traders remained free to impose their own restrictions. There is also a long-term objective: the undertakings and industries which are efficient at providing what consumers want should grow at the expense of the less efficient. The latter should not be able to protect themselves by anti-competitive agreements or practices.

EEC Treaty

Article 85

1. The following shall be prohibited as incompatible with the Common Market: all agreements between undertakings, decisions by associations of undertakings and concerted practices which may affect trade between Member States and which have as their object or effect the prevention, restriction or distortion of competition within the Common Market, and in particular those which:

(a) directly or indirectly fix purchase or selling prices or any other trading conditions;

(b) limit or control production, markets, technical development, or investment;

(c) share markets or sources of supply;

(d) apply dissimilar conditions to equivalent transactions with other trading parties, thereby placing them at a competitive disadvantage;

(e) make the conclusion of contracts subject to acceptance by the other parties of supplementary obligations which, by their nature or according to commercial use, have no connection with the subject of such contracts.

2. Any agreements or decisions prohibited pursuant to this article shall be automatically void.

3. The provisions of paragraph 1 may, however, be declared inapplicable in the case of:

- any agreement or category of agreements between undertakings;
- any decision or category of decisions by associations of undertakings;
- any concerted practice or category of concerted practices;

which contributes to improving the production or distribution of goods or to promoting technical or economic progress, while allowing consumers a fair share of the resulting benefit, and which does not:

(a) impose on the undertakings concerned restrictions which are not indispensable to the attainment of these objectives;

(b) afford such undertakings the possibility of eliminating competition in respect of a substantial part of the products in question.

I AGREEMENTS, DECISIONS OR CONCERTED PRACTICES

The essence of an 'agreement' within Article 85 is that one party voluntarily undertakes to limit its freedom with regard to another. It is not necessary that there should be a contract binding in law: Decision No 74/634 *Franco-Japanese Ballbearings Agreement* OJ 1974 L 343/19; [1975] 1 CMLR D8. The expression 'decisions by associations of undertakings' includes a recommendation which, without having binding force, has an appreciable influence on competition in the market in question.

Joined Cases 96–102, 104, 105, 108 and 110/82 NV IAZ International Belgium and Others v Commission ('ANSEAU-NAVEWA')

[1983] ECR 3369; [1984] 3 CMLR 276

Two Belgian Royal Decrees, made in 1965 and 1966, provided that washing machines and dishwashers might be connected with the water supply only if they satisfied relevant Belgian standards. For the purpose of monitoring the conformity of washing machines and dishwashers with those Belgian standards, the manufacturers and sole importers of electrical appliances affiliated to certain trade organisations concluded an agreement with the national association of water suppliers (the 'ANSEAU–NAVEWA' agreement). Under that agreement, all appliances placed in commercial distribution were to bear a label, to be issued by a designated trade organisation (CEG). The Commission made a decision that certain provisions of the agreement infringed Article 85(1) of the EEC Treaty. In the Commission's view the provisions in question excluded 'the possibility for importers other than sole importers to obtain a conformity check for the washing machines and dishwashers which they import into Belgium under conditions which are not discriminatory by comparison with those which apply to manufacturers and sole importers'.

The Court

...

ANSEAU (Case 108/82) and Miele (Case 110/82) contend ... that the agreement does not exhibit the characteristics constituting an infringement of Article 85(1) of the Treaty.

In the first place, ANSEAU observes that there can be no question of an 'agreement between undertakings' within the meaning of the above-mentioned provision. ANSEAU is an association of undertakings which does not itself carry on any economic activity. Article 85(1) of the Treaty is therefore applicable to it only in so far as its member undertakings are legally bound by the agreement. In fact they are not since, under both the agreement and the statutes of ANSEAU, the latter is empowered only to make recommendations.

As the Court has already held, in its judgments of 15 May 1975 in Case 71/74 *Frubo* [1975] ECR 563 and of 29 October 1980 in Joined Cases 209 to 215 and 218/78 *van Landewyck* (see below, p. 396), Article 85(1) of the Treaty also applies to associations of undertakings in so far as their own activities or those of the undertakings affiliated to them are calculated to produce the results which it aims to suppress. It is clear particularly from the latter judgment that a recommendation, even if it has no binding effect, cannot escape Article 85(1) where compliance with the recommendation by the undertakings to which it is addressed has an appreciable influence on competition in the market in question.

In the light of that case-law, it must be emphasised, as the Commission has pertinently stated, that the recommendations made by ANSEAU under the agreement, to the effect that its member undertakings were to take account of the terms and of the purpose of the agreement and were to inform consumers thereof, in fact produced a situation in which the water-supply undertakings in the built-up areas of Brussels, Antwerp and Ghent carried out checks on consumers' premises to determine whether machines connected to the water-supply system were provided with a conformity label. Those recommendations therefore determined the conduct of a large number of ANSEAU's members and consequently exerted an appreciable influence on competition.

...

The term 'concerted practice' in Article 85(1) denotes a form of coordination which, without amounting to an agreement, knowingly substitutes practical cooperation for the risks of competition.

Case 48/69 ICI Ltd v Commission ('Dyestuffs')
[1972] ECR 619; [1972] CMLR 557

ICI was among the undertakings producing aniline dyestuffs in Italy. It was the first to impose a price increase; but was shortly followed by other producers of similar products, accounting for some 85% of the market. The Commission concluded that there had been a concerted practice between the undertakings and imposed fines. The undertakings challenged the Commission's Decision, arguing *inter alia* that the price increases merely reflected parallel behaviour in an oligopolistic market, where each producer followed the price-leader.

The Court

...

Article 85 draws a distinction between the concept of 'concerted practices' and that of 'agreements between undertakings' or of 'decisions by associations of undertakings'; the object is to bring within the prohibition of that article *a form of coordination between undertakings which, without having reached the stage where an agreement properly so-called has been concluded, knowingly substitutes practical cooperation between them for the risks of competition.*

By its very nature, then, a concerted practice does not have all the elements of a contract but may *inter alia* arise out of coordination which becomes apparent from the behaviour of the participants.

Although parallel behaviour may not by itself be identified with a concerted practice, it may however amount to strong evidence of such a practice if it leads to conditions of competition which do not correspond to the normal conditions of the market, having regard to the nature of the products, the size and number of the undertakings, and the volume of the said market.

This is especially the case if the parallel conduct is such as to enable those concerned to attempt to stabilise prices at a level different from that to which competition would have led, and to consolidate established positions to the detriment of effective freedom of movement of the products in the Common Market and of the freedom of consumers to choose their suppliers.

Therefore the question whether there was a concerted action in this case can only be correctly determined if the evidence upon which the contested decision is based is considered, not in isolation, but as a whole, account being taken of the specific features of the market in the products in question.

...

The general and uniform increase on those different markets can only be explained by a common intention on the part of those undertakings, first, to adjust the level of prices and the situation resulting from competition in the form of discounts, and secondly, to avoid the risk, which is inherent in any price increase, of changing the conditions of competition.

...

In these circumstances and taking into account the nature of the market in the products in question, the conduct of the applicant, in conjunction with other undertakings against which proceedings have been taken, was designed to replace the risks of competition and the hazards of competitors' spontaneous reactions by cooperation constituting a concerted practice prohibited by Article 85(1) of the Treaty.

Joined Cases 40–48, 50, 54–56, 111, 113 and 114/73
Coöperatieve vereniging 'Suiker Unie' UA and Others v Commission
[1975] ECR 1663; [1976] 1 CMLR 295

The Commission made a decision by which it imposed fines on a number of sugar producers for engaging in concerted practices. In particular the Commission decided that Suiker Unie (S.U.) and Centrale Suiker Maatschapij (C.S.M.) had colluded with Raffinerie Tirlemontoise (R.T.) to protect the Dutch market by ensuring that R.T.'s exports to the Netherlands were channelled through C.S.M. and S.U. exclusively.

The Court

...

S.U. and C.S.M. submit that since the concept of 'concerted practices' presupposes a plan and the aim of removing in advance any doubt as to the future conduct of competitors, the reciprocal knowledge which the parties concerned could have of the parallel or complementary nature of their respective decisions cannot in itself be sufficient to establish a concerted practice; otherwise every attempt by an undertaking to react as intelligently as possible to the acts of its competitors would be an offence.

The criteria of coordination and cooperation laid down by the case-law of the Court, which in no way require the working out of an actual plan, must be understood in the light of the concept inherent in the provisions of the Treaty relating to competition that each economic operator must determine independently the policy which he intends to adopt on the Common Market including the choice of the persons and undertakings to which he makes offers or sells.

Although it is correct to say that this requirement of independence does not deprive economic operators of the right to adapt themselves intelligently to the existing and anticipated conduct of their competitors, it does however strictly preclude any direct or indirect contact between such operators, the object or effect whereof is either to influence the conduct on the market of an actual or potential competitor or to disclose to such a competitor the course of conduct which they themselves have decided to adopt or contemplate adopting on the market.

The documents quoted show that the applicants contacted each other and that they in fact pursued the aim of removing in advance any uncertainty as to the future conduct of their competitors.

Therefore the applicants' argument cannot be upheld.

S.U. and C.S.M. also submit that because their conduct on the market corresponded to the habitual attitude adopted by a producer in their situation, it does not amount to a concerted practice.

R.T. submits a similar argument but in more specific terms, namely 'that ... an important element in the legal concept of a "a concerted practice" is the causal connection which must exist between the alleged concerted action and the practices which were adopted' and which is absent 'if these practices are the natural consequence of market conditions which would have been the same even if there had been no contacts between producers'.

The documents produced are sufficient proof that S.U. and C.S.M. intended to ward off the risk of competition from R.T., to which they could by no means be certain that they would not be exposed if there was no concerted action, having regard to the considerable over-production of Belgian sugar, the short-fall of Netherlands production, the fact that Belgian prices were below Netherlands prices, that Belgian dealers wanted to export large amounts freely and also bearing in mind the opportunity which all these factors offered R.T. of at least supplying the frontier regions of the Netherlands.

Therefore the concerted action in question and the practices whereby it was implemented were likely to remove any doubts the Netherlands producers had as to their chances of maintaining – to the detriment of the effective freedom of movement of the products in the Common Market and of the freedom enjoyed by consumers to choose their suppliers – the position which they had established.

II UNDERTAKINGS

The word 'undertaking' is not defined in the Treaty but must be broadly construed, so as to embrace any natural or legal person carrying on activities of an economic or commercial nature. It includes non- profit-making organisations and public organisations carrying on economic or commercial activities.

Joined Cases 209–215 and 218/78 Heintz van Landewyck Sàrl and Others v Commission ('FEDETAB') [1980] ECR 3125; [1981] 3 CMLR 134

The Fédération Belgo-Luxembourgeoise des Industries du Tabac (FEDETAB) was a trade association comprising almost all the Belgian and Luxembourg manufacturers of tobacco. The Association Nationale des Grossistes en Produits du Tabac (AGROTAB) was also a trade association. Neither of them engaged in trade on their own account and neither was a profit-making organisation. On 1 December 1975 there entered into force a recommendation of FEDETAB dividing Belgian wholesalers and retailers into categories and allotting to the latter different profit margins. The Commission took a decision finding that the recommendation entailed a breach of Article 85(1). FEDETAB and others challenged the decision in the European Court; AGROTAB intervened in support of the applicants.

The Court

...

Certain applicants including the intervener AGROTAB complain further that the Commission wrongly treated the recommendation as a decision of an association of undertakings within the meaning of Article 85(1). The recommendation is said to have been made by FEDETAB, a non-profit-making organisation which as such does not trade.

That argument cannot be accepted... It is apparent from Article 8 of the statutes of FEDETAB that the decisions taken by it are binding on its members. Further, Article 85(1) also applies to associations in so far as their own activities or those of the undertakings belonging to them are calculated to produce the results which it aims to suppress. Since several manufacturers have expressly stated that they are complying with the provisions of the recommendation, it cannot escape Article 85 of the Treaty simply because it has been made by a non-profit-making association.

Special problems arise in the case of agreements on concerted practices between parent and subsidiary companies. Such agreements or practices are not 'between undertakings' unless the subsidiary is independent of its parent in the sense of having freedom to determine its course of action on the market.

Case 15/74 Centrafarm BV and Adriaan de Peijper v Sterling Drug Inc
[1974] ECR 1147; [1974] 2 CMLR 480

Acting on the basis of Article 177 of the EEC Treaty, the Hoge Raad referred to the Court of Justice of the European Communities a series of questions designed to assist it in resolving a dispute between Sterling Drug Inc., the holder of patents and trade mark rights in relation to a product called 'Negram', and Centrafarm, a company which had imported that product from Britain to the Netherlands without the consent of Sterling Drug Inc. Since the latter held parallel patents in different countries in the EEC, the Hoge Raad asked, among other questions, whether the case disclosed an agreement or concerted practice contrary to Article 85.

The Court

...

These questions require the Court to state whether Article 85 of the Treaty is applicable to agreements and concerted practices between the proprietor of parallel patents in various Member States and his licencees, if the objective of those agreements and concerted practices is to regulate differently for the different countries the conditions on the market in respect of the goods protected by the patents.

Although the existence of rights recognised under the industrial property legislation of a Member State is not affected by Article 85 of the Treaty, the conditions under which those rights may be exercised may nevertheless fall within the prohibitions contained in that article.

This may be the case whenever the exercise of such a right appears to be the object, the means or the consequence of an agreement.

Article 85, however, is not concerned with agreements or concerted practices between undertakings belonging to the same concern and having the status of parent company and subsidiary, if the undertakings form an economic unit within which the subsidiary has no real freedom to determine its course of action on the market, and if the agreements or practices are concerned merely with the internal allocation of tasks as between the undertakings.

III EFFECT ON TRADE BETWEEN MEMBER STATES

In order to determine whether an agreement, decision or concerted practice 'may affect trade between Member States' it is necessary to ascertain whether it is foreseeable that it may have an influence, direct or indirect, actual or potential, on the pattern of trade.

Case 42/84 Remia BV and Others v Commission [1985] ECR 2545

The Dutch company, Nutricia, a manufacturer of health and baby foods, took over two companies, Remia, a manufacturer of sauces, margarines and baking materials, and Luycks, a manufacturer of sauces and condiments. Subsequently Nutricia undertook a restructuring of its production facilities, concentrating its sauce production at Remia and its pickles and condiments production at Luycks. It then transferred Remia to its original owner (by 'the sauce agreement') and Luycks to a subsidiary of the American company, Campbell. The transfer agreements contained clauses designed to protect the purchasers from competition from the vendor on the same market immediately after the transfers. The Campbell company regarded the non-competition clause imposed on Luycks as contrary to Article 85(1) of the EEC Treaty. Campbell notified the Commission, which made a decision that the non-competition clauses were in breach of that article. Remia sought the annulment of that decision.

The Court

...

It should be stated at the outset that the Commission has rightly submitted – and the applicants have not contradicted it on that point – that the fact that non-competition clauses are included in an agreement for the sale of an undertaking is not of itself sufficient to remove such clauses from the scope of Article 85(1) of the Treaty.

In order to determine whether or not such clauses come within the prohibition in Article 85(1), it is necessary to examine what would be the state of competition if those clauses did not exist.

If that were the case, and should the vendor and the purchaser remain competitors after the transfer, it is clear that the agreement for the transfer of the undertaking could not be given effect. The vendor, with his particularly detailed knowledge of the transferred undertaking, would still be in a position to win back his former customers immediately after the transfer and thereby drive the undertaking out of business. Against that background non-competition clauses incorporated in an agreement for the transfer of an undertaking in principle have the merit of ensuring that the transfer has the effect intended. By virtue of that very fact they contribute to the promotion of competition because they lead to an increase in the number of undertakings in the market in question.

Nevertheless, in order to have that beneficial effect on competition, such clauses must be necessary to the transfer of the undertaking concerned and their duration and scope must be strictly limited to that purpose. The Commission was therefore right in holding that where those conditions are satisfied such clauses are free of the prohibition laid down in Article 85(1).

However, without denying the basic principle of that reasoning, the applicants challenge the way in which it has been applied to their case on the ground, first, that the non-competition clause contained in the sauce agreement does not affect trade between Member States within the meaning of Article 85(1) of the Treaty...

Taking first the condition with regard to the effect on trade between Member States, the Court would point out that, as it has consistently held, *in order that an agreement between undertakings may affect trade between Member States it must be possible to foresee with a sufficient degree of probability on the basis of a set of objective factors of law or fact that it may have an influence, direct or indirect, actual or potential, on the pattern of trade between Member States, such as might prejudice the realisation of the aim of a single market in all the Member States.* The Court has also held (judgment of 17 October 1972 in Case 8/72 *Cementhandelaren* [1972] ECR 977) that an agreement or practice restricting competition and extending over the whole territory of a Member State by its very nature has the effect of reinforcing the compartmentalisation of markets on a national basis, thereby holding up the economic interpenetration which the Treaty is intended to bring about.

In this case it should be pointed out that the non-competition clause at issue covers the entire territory of the Netherlands. Furthermore, the terms of clause 5 of the sauce agreement under which Nutricia, Luycks and subsequently Zuid are prohibited from engaging directly or indirectly in the production or sale of sauces on the Netherlands market do not merely affect the national production of sauces but also have the effect of prohibiting those undertakings from selling sauces previously imported from other Member States. Finally, it is not denied that Remia has the largest individual share in the Netherlands market in the sauces in question.

It must therefore be concluded that the Commission correctly assessed the facts of the case in finding that the clause at issue was likely to affect trade between Member States within the meaning of Article 85(1) of the Treaty.

For the purpose of assessing the effect of an agreement on trade between Member States, it is necessary to have regard to the whole context, including any network of similar agreements concluded between one of the parties to the contested agreement and others. In the light of that context, an agreement between two undertakings in the same Member State may well have an effect on trade between Member States.

Case 23/67 Brasserie de Haecht SA v Wilkin and Wilkin (No 1)
[1967] ECR 407; [1968] CMLR 26

The Belgian brewery de Haecht concluded three loan contracts with Wilkin, the proprietors of a café in Esnoux, by which the borrowers undertook, *inter alia*, to obtain supplies of beverages exclusively from the lender. Some years later the question arose before a Belgian tribunal whether the clause in the agreement tying Wilkin to supplies from de Haecht was compatible with Article 85(1) of the EEC Treaty. The tribunal referred questions to the European Court for a preliminary ruling. The Advocate General took the view that the agreement would have been capable of affecting trade between Member States only if it created barriers to entry at the retail level. Accordingly it was necessary to take account of sales in shops as well as cafés; and the duration of the tie had also to be considered. The Court expressed itself more generally.

Mr Advocate General Roemer

...

As we know, the purpose of the Community cartel laws is to prevent the establishment of the Common Market (which is brought about by both the application and the abolition of measures based on national sovereignty) from being impeded or delayed by agreements on competition which affect international trade and introduce private restrictions on trade when national ones are removed. To ensure that this end is fully achieved, and that no loopholes remain in the system, it may prove necessary to interpret the provisions on restrictive agreements generously, and this is one case where that should be done. The agreements which we are considering do not seem, when viewed in isolation, to be prejudicial to the Common Market in any way... It can also be stated that this assessment is hardly altered if the entire distribution network of one brewery is examined as a whole, since where many such distribution networks exist (in Belgium they number some 300) it would be difficult for a single one of them to have an *appreciable* effect on trade between countries. On the other hand it is possible for such an effect to occur as the result of the combined operation of *all* the internal beer distribution agreements in a Member State. If one takes into account their duration and the effective sanctions with which their contracts are provided, then two points are clear: first, that beer is normally sold through 'tied' houses (so that other sales are negligible), and second, that owing to the legal or factual circumstances it is difficult to establish more licensed premises. These show that the national market is widely insulated and that trade with other countries is thereby hindered, because foreign producers encounter considerable difficulties in trying to enter such a market. If one is compelled in such a situation, which, while admittedly rather hypothetical, is not inconceivable, to consider individual agreements in isolation and thus find that Article 85 of the Treaty does not apply then a dangerous loophole is revealed in the cartel laws, a loophole which the national laws on the subject may not cover (because they do not normally concern relations between countries), and one which cannot be filled by reference to Article 86 of the Treaty either, since that applies only to the abuse of a *dominant position in the market,* that is, where there is at least an oligopoly, not merely the adoption of a similar attitude by a number of separate enterprises.

...

The Court

By a judgment of 8 May 1967, received by the Court on 27 June, the Tribunal de Commerce, Liège, referred to the Court under Article 177 of the EEC Treaty for a preliminary ruling on the interpretation of Article 85(1) of the said Treaty. The Court is asked whether, 'in order to judge whether the contracts in question are prohibited by Article 85(1) of the EEC Treaty, it is necessary to take into account the economic context and the whole of the market, that is to say, in this case, the simultaneous existence of a large number of contracts of the same type imposed by a small number of Belgian breweries upon a very large proportion of liquor licensees', or whether 'consideration must be limited to an examination of the effects on the market of the said agreements considered in isolation'. According to this judgment the question refers to agreements whereby a dealer undertakes for a certain period to obtain his supplies solely from a given supplier, to the exclusion of all others.

The prohibition in Article 85(1) of the Treaty rests on three factors essential for a reply to the question referred. After stating the limits within which the prohibition is to apply, Article 85(1) mentions agreements, decisions and practices. By referring in the same sentence to agreements between undertakings, decisions by associations of undertakings and concerted practices, which may involve many parties, Article 85(1) implies that the constituent elements of those agreements, decisions and practices may be considered together as a whole.

Furthermore, by basing its application to agreements, decisions or practices not only on their subject-matter but also on their effects in relation to competition, Article 85(1) implies that regard must be had to such effects in the context in which they occur, that is to say, in the economic and legal context of such agreements, decisions or practices and where they might combine with others to have a cumulative effect on competition. In fact, it would be pointless to consider an agreement, decision or practice by reason of its effects if those effects were to be taken distinct from the market in which they are seen to operate and could only be examined apart from the body of effects, whether convergent or not, surrounding their implementation. *Thus in order to examine whether it is caught by Article 85(1) an agreement cannot be examined in isolation from the above context, that is, from the factual or legal circumstances causing it to prevent, restrict or distort competition. The existence of similar contracts may be taken into consideration for this objective to the extent to which the general body of contracts of this type is capable of restricting the freedom of trade.*

Lastly, it is only to the extent to which agreements, decisions or practices are capable of affecting trade between Member States that the alteration of competition comes under Community prohibitions. In order to satisfy this condition, it must be possible for the agreement, decision or practice, when viewed in the light of a combination of the objective, factual or legal circumstances, to appear to be capable of having some influence, direct or indirect, on trade between Member States, of being conducive to a partitioning of the market and of hampering the economic interpenetration sought by the Treaty. When this point is considered the agreement, decision or practice cannot therefore be isolated from all the others of which it is one.

The existence of similar contracts is a circumstance which, together with others, is capable of being a factor in the economic and legal context within which the contract must be judged. Accordingly, whilst such a situation must be taken into account it should not be considered as decisive by itself, but merely as one among others in judging whether trade between Member States is capable of being affected through any alteration in competition.

Equally, an agreement between undertakings outside the Community may fall within the prohibition of Article 85(1) if it is implemented within the Community. the Court has yet to state that an agreement made and implemented outside the Community is subject to Article 85 by reason only of its effects, actual or potential, in the Community.

Joined Cases 89, 104, 114, 116, 117 and 125–129/85 Ahlstrom Osakeyhtio and Others v Commission ('Wood Pulp') 27 September 1988

The applicants were forestry undertakings in Finland, Sweden and Canada. The Commission made a decision by which it declared that the applicants had committed infringements of Article 85 of the EEC Treaty, and imposed fines on them. The infringements were said to consist of concertation between various wood pulp producers on prices charged to customers in the Community. The applicants submitted that Article 85 did not extend to regulate conduct restricting competition outside the territory of the Community merely by reason of the economic repercussions of that conduct in the Community.

The Court

...

It should be noted that the main sources of supply of wood pulp are outside the Community, in Canada, the United States, Sweden and Finland and that the market therefore has global dimensions. Where wood pulp producers established in those countries sell directly to purchasers established in the Community and engage in price competition in order to win orders from those customers, that constitutes competition within the Common Market.

It follows that where those producers concert on the prices to be charged to their customers in the Community and put that concertation into effect by selling at prices which are actually coordinated, they are taking part in concertation which has the object and effect of restricting competition within the Common Market within the meaning of Article 85 of the Treaty.

Accordingly, it must be concluded that by applying the competition rules in the Treaty in the circumstances of this case to undertakings whose registered offices are situated outside the Community, the Commission has not made an incorrect assessment of the territorial scope of Article 85.

The applicants have submitted that the decision is incompatible with public international law on the grounds that the application of the competition rules in this case was founded exclusively on the economic repercussions within the Common Market of conduct restricting competition which was adopted outside the Community.

It should be observed that an infringement of Article 85, such as the conclusion of an agreement which has had the effect of restricting competition within the Common Market, consists of conduct made up of two elements: the formation of the agreement, decision or concerted practice and the implementation thereof. *If the applicability of prohibitions laid down under competition law were made to depend on the place where the agreement, decision or concerted practice was formed, the result would obviously be to give undertakings an easy means of evading these prohibitions. The decisive factor is therefore the place where it is implemented.*

The producers in this case implemented their pricing agreement within the Common Market. It is immaterial in that respect whether or not they had recourse to subsidiaries, agents, sub-agents, or branches within the Community in order to make their contacts with purchasers within the Community.

Accordingly the Community's jurisdiction to apply its competition rules to such conduct is covered by the territoriality principle as universally recognised in public international law.

...

IV MINOR AGREEMENTS

On the other hand, agreements whose effects on trade between Member States are negligible do not fall within Article 85(1). By a Notice on Agreements of Minor

Importance the Commission has intimated that as a rule it will not consider an agreement between undertakings engaged in the production or distribution of goods as one which 'may affect trade between Member States' unless it meets specific quantitative criteria.

Notice of 3 September 1986 on Agreements of Minor Importance
OJ 1986 C 231/2

...

The Commission holds the view that agreements between undertakings engaged in the production or distribution of goods or in the provision of services generally do not fall under the prohibition of Article 85(1) if:

– the goods or services which are the subject of the agreement (hereinafter referred to as 'the contract products') together with the participating undertakings' other goods or services which are considered by users to be equivalent in view of their characteristics, price and intended use, do not represent more than five per cent of the total market for such goods or services (hereinafter referred to as 'products') in the area of the Common Market affected by the agreement and

– the aggregate annual turnover of the participating undertakings does not exceed 200 million ECU.

The Commission also holds the view that the said agreements do not fall under the prohibition of Article 85(1) if the above-mentioned market share or turnover is exceeded by not more than one tenth during two successive financial years.

For the purposes of this Notice, participating undertakings are:

(a) undertakings party to the agreement;

(b) undertakings in which a party to the agreement, directly or indirectly,

– owns more than half the capital or business assets or

– has the power to exercise more than half the voting rights, or

– has the power to appoint more than half the members of the supervisory board, board of management or bodies legally representing the undertakings, or

– has the right to manage the affairs;

(c) undertakings which directly or indirectly have in or over a party to the agreement the rights or powers listed in (b);

(d) undertakings in or over which an undertaking referred to in (c) directly or indirectly has the rights or powers listed in (b).

The Notice cannot, of course, alter the scope of Article 85 nor the obligations imposed thereby on undertakings. Furthermore, an agreement which affects the market only to an insignificant extent may nevertheless fall within the prohibition laid down in Article 85(1) when it governs the distribution of a product the entire production of which is in the hands of a large undertaking: Case 30/78 *Distillers Company Ltd* v *Commission* [1980] ECR 2229; [1980] 3 CMLR 121.

V OBJECT OR EFFECT OF DISTORTING COMPETITION

The expression 'object or effect' describes requirements which are alternative rather than cumulative. An agreement, decision or concerted practice designed to prevent, restrict or distort competition infringes Article 85(1) even if detected before its implementation; equally an agreement, decision or concerted practice infringes Article 85(1) even if it has the unintended effect of preventing, restricting or distorting competition. The prohibition extends to 'vertical' agreements, decisions and concerted practices (between supplier and distributor) no less than to 'horizontal' ones (between undertakings at the same stage in the chain of manufacture or distribution).

Joined Cases 56 and 58/64 Etablissements Consten SARL and Grundig Verkaufs GmbH v Commission [1966] ECR 299; [1966] CMLR 418

The German manufacturer of electrical equipment, Grundig, came to an agreement with the French distributor, Consten, by which Consten was appointed as Grundig's sole representative in France, Corsica and the Saar. By that agreement Consten was authorised to use Grundig's name and emblem. In reliance upon that agreement, Consten registered a Grundig trade mark in France. Consten then brought proceedings for infringement of a trade mark against a French company which had attempted to sell in France Grundig products that it purchased in Germany. The Commission ultimately decided that the agreement between Consten and Grundig had the object or effect of distorting competition, notably by facilitating the partition of the Common Market.

The Court

...

The applicants submit that the prohibition in Article 85(1) applies only to so-called horizontal agreements. The Italian Government submits furthermore that sole distributorship contracts do not constitute 'agreements between undertakings' within the meaning of that provision, since the parties are not on a footing of equality. With regard to these contracts, freedom of competition may only be protected by virtue of Article 86 of the Treaty.

Neither the wording of Article 85 nor that of Article 86 gives any ground for holding that distinct areas of application are to be assigned to each of the two articles according to the level in the economy at which the contracting parties operate. Article 85 refers in a general way to all agreements which distort competition within the Common Market and does not lay down any distinction between those agreements based on whether they are made between competitors operating at the same level in the economic process or between non-competing persons operating at different levels. In principle, no distinction can be made where the Treaty does not make any distinction.

Furthermore, the possible application of Article 85 to a sole distributorship contract cannot be excluded merely because the grantor and the concessionnaire are not competitors *inter se* and not on a footing of equality. *Competition may be distorted within the meaning of Article 85(1) not only by agreements which limit it as between the parties, but also by agreements which prevent or restrict the competition which might take place between one of them and third parties. For this purpose, it is irrelevant whether the parties to the agreement are or are not on a footing of equality as regards their position and function in the economy.* This applies all the more since, by such an agreement, the parties might seek, by preventing or limiting the competition of third parties in respect of the products, to create or guarantee for their benefit an unjustified advantage at the expense of the consumer or user, contrary to the general aims of Article 85.

It is thus possible that, without involving an abuse of a dominant position, an agreement between economic operators at different levels may affect trade between Member States and at the same time have as its object or effect the prevention, restriction or distortion of competition, thus falling under the prohibition of Article 85(1).

In addition, it is pointless to compare on the one hand the situation, to which Article 85 applies, of a producer bound by a sole distributorship agreement to the distributor of his products with on the other hand that of a producer who includes within his undertaking the distribution of his own products by some means, for example, by commercial representatives, to which Article 85 does not apply. These situations are distinct in law and, moreover, need to be assessed differently, since two marketing organisations, one of which is integrated into the manufacturer's undertaking whilst the other is not, may not necessarily have the same efficiency. The wording of Article 85 causes the prohibition to apply, provided that the other conditions are met, to an agreement between several undertakings. Thus it does not apply where a sole undertaking integrates its own distribution network into its business organisation. It does not thereby follow, however, that the contractual situation based on an agreement between a manufacturing and a distributing undertaking is rendered legally acceptable by a simple process of economic analogy – which is in any case incomplete and in contradiction with the said article. Furthermore, although in the first case the Treaty intended in Article 85 to leave untouched the internal organisation of an undertaking and to render it liable to be called in question, by means of Article 86, only in cases where it reaches such a degree of seriousness as to amount to an abuse of a dominant position, the same reservation could not apply when the impediments to competition result from agreement between two different undertakings which then as a general rule simply require to be prohibited.

Finally, an agreement between producer and distributor which might tend to restore the national divisions in trade between Member States might be such as to frustrate the most fundamental objects of the Community. The Treaty, whose preamble and content aim at abolishing the barriers between States, and which in several provisions gives evidence of a stern attitude with regard to their reappearance, could not allow undertakings to reconstruct such barriers. Article 85(1) is designed to pursue this aim, even in the case of agreements between undertakings placed at different levels in the economic process.

The submissions set out above are consequently unfounded.

It is, perhaps, not finally settled whether an agreement, decision or concerted practice, capable of affecting trade between Member States, contravenes Article 85(1) whenever it restrains competition – even if only in a harmless manner. In cases involving distribution agreements, the Commission has tended to argue in favour of such an interpretation of Article 85(1); and if that argument were upheld it would follow that a relevant agreement with redeeming features could only be preserved by means of the Commission's grant of an exemption under Article 85(3). The Court's case-law suggests, however, that Article 85(1) must be read subject to a 'rule of reason': an agreement which does not have as its *object* the prevention, restriction or distortion of competition is unlawful only if its *effects* are sufficiently deleterious, having regard to all the circumstances including the market shares of the parties, the existence or absence of a network of similar agreements and the acceptance or prohibition of parallel trading.

Case 56/65 Société Technique Minière v Maschinenbau Ulm GmbH
[1966] ECR 235; [1966] CMLR 357

Machinenbau Ulm agreed to give Société Technique Minière the exclusive right to sell certain machinery in France, on the condition that Société Technique Minière should not sell competing machinery. The validity of the agreement was put in issue before a French court, which referred to the European Court questions for preliminary ruling. Before the European Court the Commission submitted that the agreement amounted to a restriction of competition and was contrary to Article 85(1) *per se*. The Court did not accept that argument.

The Court

...

For the agreement at issue to be caught by the prohibition contained in Article 85(1) it must have as its 'object or effect the prevention, restriction or distortion of competition within the Common Market'.

The fact that these are not cumulative but alternative requirements, indicated by the conjunction 'or', leads first to the need to consider the precise purpose of the agreement, in the economic context in which it is to be applied. This interference with competition referred to in Article 85(1) must result from all or some of the clauses of the agreement itself. *Where, however, an analysis of the said clauses does not reveal the effect on competition to be sufficiently deleterious, the consequences of the agreement should then be considered and for it to be caught by the prohibition it is then necessary to find that those factors are present which show that competition has in fact been prevented or restricted or distorted to an appreciable extent.*

The competition in question must be understood within the actual context in which it would occur in the absence of the agreement in dispute. In particular it may be doubted whether there is an interference with competition if the said agreement seems really necessary for the penetration of a new area by an undertaking. *Therefore, in order to decide whether an agreement containing a clause 'granting an exclusive right of sale' is to be considered as prohibited by reason of its object or of its effect, it is appropriate to take into account in particular the nature and quantity, limited or otherwise, of the products covered by the agreement, the position and importance of the grantor and the concessionnaire on the market for the products concerned, the isolated nature of the disputed agreement or, alternatively, its position in a series of agreements, the severity of the clauses intended to protect the exclusive dealership or, alternatively, the opportunities allowed for other commercial competitors in the same products by way of parallel re-exportation and importation.*

This approach appears to have been confirmed in Case 23/67 *Brasserie de Haecht* v*Wilkin* (see above p. 399).

The Court restated the 'rule of reason' in the first *Metro* case in 1977, when it held that a selective distribution system was not prohibited by Article 85(1) where resellers were chosen on the basis of objective criteria of a qualitative nature and the conditions for the application of such criteria were laid down uniformly for all potential resellers.

Case 26/76 Metro SB-Grossmärkte GmbH & Co KG v Commission and SABA (No 1) [1977] ECR 1875; [1978] 2 CMLR 1

SABA, a German manufacturer of electronic equipment, refused to supply its products to Metro, a 'cash and carry' retailer. SABA's reason for refusing was that it operated a selective distribution system whereby its goods were sold only by appointed SABA retailers. Metro did not meet SABA's conditions for appointment as a retailer. SABA had notified its arrangements to the Commission and the Commission had approved of them, in part by issuing a 'negative clearance', declaring that aspects of the arrangements fell outside Article 85(1); and in part by granting an exemption pursuant to Article 85(3). Metro challenged the Commission's decision.

The Court

...

The requirement contained in Articles 3 and 85 of the EEC Treaty that competition shall not be distorted implies the existence on the market of workable competition, that is to say the degree of competition necessary to ensure the observance of the basic requirements and the attainment of the objectives of the Treaty, in particular the creation of a single market achieving conditions similar to those of a domestic market.

In accordance with this requirement the nature and intensiveness of competition may vary to an extent dictated by the products or services in question and the economic structure of the relevant market sectors.

In the sector covering the production of high quality and technically advanced consumer durables, where a relatively small number of large- and medium-scale producers offer a varied range of items which, or so consumers may consider, are readily interchangeable, the structure of the market does not preclude the existence of a variety of channels of distribution adapted to the peculiar characteristics of the various producers and to the requirements of the various categories of consumers.

On this view the Commission was justified in recognising that *selective distribution systems constituted, together with others, an aspect of competition which accords with Article 85(1), provided that resellers are chosen on the basis of objective criteria of a qualitative nature relating to the technical qualifications of the reseller and his staff and the suitability of his trading premises and that such conditions are laid down uniformly for all potential resellers and are not applied in a discriminatory fashion.*

It is true that in such systems of distribution price competition is not generally emphasised either as an exclusive or indeed as a principal factor.

This is particularly so when, as in the present case, access to the distribution network is subject to conditions exceeding the requirements of an appropriate distribution of the products.

However, although price competition is so important that it can never be eliminated, it does not constitute the only effective form of competition or that to which absolute priority must in all circumstances be accorded.

The powers conferred upon the Commission under Article 85(3) show that the requirements for the maintenance of workable competition may be reconciled with the safeguarding of objectives of a different nature and that to this end certain restrictions on competition are permissible, provided that they are essential to the attainment of those objectives and that they do not result in the elimination of competition for a substantial part of the Common Market.

For specialist wholesalers and retailers the desire to maintain a certain price level, which corresponds to the desire to preserve, in the interests of consumers, the possibility of the continued existence of this channel of distribution in conjunction with new methods of distribution based on a different type of competition policy, forms one of the objectives which may be pursued without necessarily falling under the prohibition contained in Article 85(1), and, if it does fall thereunder, either wholly or in part, coming within the framework of Article 85(3).

This argument is strengthened if, in addition, such conditions promote improved competition inasmuch as it relates to factors other than prices.

...

Case 75/84 Metro SB-Grossmärkte GmbH & Co KG v Commission (No 2)
[1986] ECR 3021; [1987] 1 CMLR 118

The Court

...

According to Metro, there have been fundamental changes in the structure of competition on the market in consumer electronics equipment since 1975. In particular, there has been a significant increase in the number of selective distribution systems operated by the major producers both on the German market and throughout the Community. Metro claims that, in addition to the systems of which the Commission has been notified and those for which an application has been made to the Commission for exemption under Article 85(3), there is now a large number of other similar selective distribution systems which have not been notified and which also prevent self-service wholesale traders such as Metro from obtaining direct supplies.

Metro alleges that by granting a new exemption by the contested decision, the Commission failed to take those changes into account even though it was required to do so by the judgment in *Metro No 1*. It claims that the Commission ought in particular to have taken into account all the selective distribution systems, even the 'simple' systems, the sole purpose of which is to ensure that goods are supplied only to the specialised trade or to dealers with specialised departments.

The Commission points out first that, according to the judgment in *Metro No 1*, selective distribution systems constitute 'together with others, an aspect of competition which accords with Article 85(1), provided that resellers are chosen on the basis of objective criteria of a qualitative nature relating to the technical qualifications of the reseller and his staff and the suitability of his trading premises and that such conditions are laid down uniformly for all potential resellers and are not applied in a discriminatory fashion'. Consequently, the Commission has no authority to take action against the operation of such simple selective distribution systems. An increase in the number of such systems is therefore irrelevant in the context of Article 85(1). However, the existence of such systems should be taken into account in assessing whether Article 85(3) is applicable.

In that regard, the Commission contends that when it granted a renewal of the exemption to the SABA system, it was certain that no other selective distribution networks similar to the SABA network were operated on the relevant market; in particular, the cooperation agreement requiring wholesalers to sign supply estimates is a unique feature of the SABA system. Of a total number of 13 selective distribution systems operated in this sector on the territory of the Community and notified to the Commission, four involve simple obligations to supply only through specialised outlets which do not fall within the scope of Article 85(1). The remaining nine systems required exemption under Article 85(3), but none of them contained obligations pertaining to the promotion of distribution or to cooperation comparable with those in the SABA system.

It should be stated that, as Metro alleges and the Commission recognises, the Commission was obliged, when it examined SABA's application for a renewal of the exemption granted in 1975, to verify whether the competitive situation on the relevant market had changed to such an extent that the preconditions for the grant of an exemption were no longer fulfilled.

It must be borne in mind that, although the Court has held in previous decisions that 'simple' selective distribution systems are capable of constituting an aspect of competition compatible with Article 85(1) of the Treaty, there may nevertheless be a restriction or elimination of competition where the existence of a certain number of such systems does not leave any room for other forms of distribution based on a different type of competition policy or results in a rigidity in price structure which is not counterbalanced by other aspects of competition between products of the same brand and by the existence of effective competition between different brands.

Consequently, the existence of a large number of selective distribution systems for a particular product does not in itself permit the conclusion that competition is restricted or distorted. Nor is the existence of such systems decisive as regards the granting or refusal of an exemption under Article 85(3), since the only factor to be taken into consideration in that regard is the effect which such systems actually have on the competitive system. Therefore the coverage ratio of selective distribution systems for colour television sets, to which Metro refers, cannot in itself be regarded as a factor preventing an exemption from being granted.

It follows that an increase in the number of 'simple' selective distribution systems after an exemption has been granted must be taken into consideration, when an application for renewal of that exemption is being considered, only in the special situation in which the relevant market was already so rigid and structured that the element of competition inherent in 'simple' systems is not sufficient to maintain workable competition. Metro has not been able to show that a special situation of that kind exists in the present case.

More recently, the Court has indicated that an agreement which entailed restrictions on trade between Member States, without affecting the position of third parties such as parallel importers, did not infringe Article 85(1) when it was objectively justified in the interests of the dissemination of new technology and the promotion of competition in the Community between a new product and similar existing products.

Case 258/78 L.C. Nungesser KG and Kurt Eisele v Commission
[1982] ECR 2015; [1983] 1 CMLR 278

The French national agricultural research institute, INRA, reached an agreement with Mr Eisele, trading as Nungesser, assigning to the latter plant breeder's rights relating to maize seeds that it has developed after years of experimentation and granting the exclusive right to sell those seeds in Germany. Further, INRA undertook to prevent third parties from importing those seeds to Germany otherwise than through Mr Eisele. The Commission decided that these arrangements entailed a breach of Article 85(1). The Court distinguished between an 'open' exclusive general licence, whereby the licensor merely undertakes not to license anyone else for the same territory, and a 'protected' exclusive licence, under which the parties proposed to eliminate all competition from parallel importers of licensees in other territories. In relation to an open exclusive licence, the Court seems to have accepted that the protection of plant breeders' rights encouraged technical innovation. On the other hand, a protected exclusive licence was unlawful *per se*.

The Court

...

It should be observed that those two sets of considerations relate to two legal situations which are not necessarily identical. The first case concerns a so-called open exclusive licence or assignment and the exclusivity of the licence relates solely to the contractual relationship between the owner of the right and the licensee, whereby the owner merely undertakes not to grant other licences in respect of the same territory and not to compete himself with the licensee on that territory. On the other hand, the second case involves an exclusive licence or assignment with absolute territorial protection, under which the parties to the contract propose, as regards the products and the territory in question, to eliminate all competition from third parties, such as parallel importers or licensees for other territories.

...the Government of the Federal Republic of Germany emphasised that the protection of agricultural innovations by means of breeders' rights constitutes a means of encouraging such innovations, and the grant of exclusive rights for a limited period is capable of providing further incentive to innovative efforts.

From that it infers that a total prohibition of every exclusive licence, even an open one, would cause the interest of undertakings in licences to fall away, which would be prejudicial to the dissemination of knowledge and techniques in the Community.

The exclusive licence which forms the subject-matter of the contested decision concerns the cultivation and marketing of hybrid maize seeds which were developed by INRA after years of research and experimentation and were unknown to German farmers at the time when the cooperation between INRA and the applicants was taking shape. For that reason the concern shown by the interveners as regards the protection of new technology is justified.

In fact, in the case of a licence of breeders' rights over hybrid maize seeds newly developed in one Member State, an undertaking established in another Member State which was not certain that it would not encounter competition from other licencees for the territory granted to it, or from the owner of the right himself, might be deterred from accepting the risk of cultivating and marketing that product; such a result would be damaging to the dissemination of a new technology and would prejudice competition in the Community between the new product and similar existing products.

Having regard to the specific nature of the products in question, the Court concludes that, in a case such as the present, the grant of an open exclusive licence, that is to say a licence which does not affect the position of third parties such as parallel importers and licensees for other territories, is not in itself incompatible with Article 85(1) of the Treaty.

...

As regards the position of third parties, the Commission in essence criticises the parties to the contract for having extended the definition of exclusivity to importers who are not bound to the contract, in particular parallel importers. Parallel importers or exporters, such as Louis David KG in Germany and Robert Bomberault in France who offered INRA seed for sale to German buyers, had found themselves subjected to pressure and legal proceedings by INRA, Frasema and the applicants, the purpose of which was to maintain the exclusive position of the applicants on the German market.

The Court has consistently held (cf. Joined Cases 56 and 58/64 *Consten and Grundig* v *Commission* [1966] ECR 299) that absolute territorial protection granted to a licensee in order to enable parallel imports to be controlled and prevented results in the artificial maintenance of separate national markets, contrary to the Treaty.

...

It is clear from the documents in the case that the contracts in question were indeed intended to restrict competition from third parties on the German market.

...

In the event, the Commission's decision was annulled to the extent that it declared that Article 85(1) prohibited INRA from entering into an obligation not to compete with Mr Eisele. The decision was upheld, however, in so far as it declared that Article 85(1) prohibited the grant of absolute territorial protection to Mr Eisele.

More recently, in Case 161/84 *Pronuptia* [1986] ECR 353; [1986] 1 CMLR 414 (paragraphs 16–26) the Court again applied the 'rule of reason'. It concluded that distribution franchise agreements are incompatible with Article 85(1) *per se* when they contain clauses effecting a partitioning of the markets. Furthermore, to the extent that they do not contain such clauses, distribution franchise agreements must be considered to be compatible with Article 85(1) if any restrictions on competition imposed thereby are 'appropriate measures to preserve the identity and reputation of the network which is symbolised by the mark'.

VI PROVISIONAL VALIDITY

Article 85(1) imposes a clear, direct and unconditional obligation. It produces direct effects. In Case 127/73 *B.R.T.* v *SABAM* [1974] ECR 51, at paragraph 16, the Court stated that 'as the prohibitions of Articles 85(1) and 86 tend by their very nature to produce direct effects in relations between individuals, these articles create direct rights in respect of the individuals concerned which the national courts must safeguard'. The direct effectiveness of the prohibition gives rise to special problems in the case of agreements previously concluded. The Court has ruled that an agreement which was in force on 13 March 1962 (the date of entry into force of Regulation No 17) should be deemed to be provisionally valid, pending a Commission decision thereon, provided that it is duly notified or exempted from notification.

Case 48/72 Brasserie de Haecht SA v Wilkin and Wilkin (No 2)
[1973] 1 ECR 77; [1973] CMLR 287

The Court

By Article 85(2), the Treaty has, from its entry into force, rendered any agreements or decisions prohibited pursuant to to this article automatically void.

Although the prohibition set out in Article 85(1) is modified by the power of granting exemptions provided for in Article 85(3), the Treaty does not however contain any transitional provision as to the effects of Article 85(2) on agreements and decisions existing at the date of the entry into force of either the Treaty or of Regulation No 17.

This omission leads to a situation all the more ambiguous from the fact that, apart from the possible intervention by the Commission by virtue of the regulations and directives referred to in Article 87, the judiciary, by virtue of the direct effect of Article 85(2), is competent to rule against prohibited agreements and decisions by declaring them automatically void.

While the first course offers the necessary flexibility to take the peculiarities of each case into account, Article 85(2), the intention of which is to attach severe sanctions to a serious prohibition, does not of its very nature allow the Court to intervene with the same flexibility.

Whilst, in defining the powers of the Commission, Regulation No 17, and in particular Article 7 thereof, enabled the Commission to take into account the general principle of legal certainty, it did not modify – as indeed it could not – the effects of Article 85(2), but, on the contrary, by Article 1 thereof, it confirmed that, without prejudice to Articles 6,7 and 23 thereof, agreements, decisions and concerted practices of the kind described in Article 85(1) shall be prohibited, no prior decision to that effect being required.

Thus it was left entirely to the judgment of the courts to determine the lines on which the legal application of Article 85(2) should be reconciled with respect for the said general principle of legal certainty.

There is, therefore, room for distinction, in applying Article 85(2), between agreements and decisions existing before the implementation of Article 85 by Regulation No 17, hereinafter called old agreements, and agreements and decisions entered into after that date, hereinafter called new agreements.

In the case of old agreements, the general principle of contractual certainty requires, particularly when the agreement has been notified in accordance with the provisions of Regulation No 17, that the court may only declare it to be automatically void after the Commission has taken a decision by virtue of that regulation.

In the case of new agreements, as the regulation assumes that so long as the Commission has not taken a decision the agreement can only be implemented at the parties' own risk, it follows that notifications in accordance with Article 4(1) of Regulation No 17 do not have suspensive effect.

Whilst the principle of legal certainty requires that, in applying the prohibitions of Article 85, the sometimes considerable delays by the Commission in exercising its powers should be taken into account, this cannot, however, absolve the court from the obligation of deciding on the claims of interested parties who invoke the automatic nullity.

In such a case it devolves on the court to judge, subject to the possible application of Article 177, whether there is cause to suspend proceedings in order to allow the parties to obtain the Commission's standpoint, unless it establishes either that the agreement does not have any perceptible effect on competition or trade between Member States or that there is no doubt that the agreement is incompatible with Article 85.

Whilst these considerations refer particularly to agreements which must be notified in accordance with Article 4 of the regulation, they apply equally to agreements exempted from notification, such exemption merely constituting an inconclusive indication that the agreements referred to are generally less harmful to the smooth functioning of the Common Market.

When at least one of the parties to the agreement is in a new Member State, the date for distinguishing between 'old' and 'new' agreements is the date on which Regulation No 17 came into force in relation to that State.

The doctrine of provisional validity has now been qualified in one respect. When it is clear that the Commission proposes to take no further action in respect of a duly notified old agreement, national courts may apply Articles 85(1) and (2), for the purpose of declaring an agreement void. This is a necessary qualification, for otherwise third parties would be deprived of redress by the Commission's inaction.

Case 99/79 SA Lancôme and Another v ETOS BV and Another ('Perfumes')
[1980] ECR 2511; [1981] 2 CMLR 164

In the context of a dispute between the perfume manufacturer, Lancôme, and the operator of a Dutch chain of retail shops, the latter contended that the former's sales organisation in the Netherlands was based on an agreement which was partially void by reason of its incompatibility with the EEC Treaty. That agreement was an 'old' agreement. It had been notified and the Commission had written to Lancôme as follows:

'I have the honour to inform you that in these circumstances, in view of the small share in the market in perfumery, beauty products and toiletries held by your company in each of the countries of the Common Market and in view of the fairly large number of competing undertakings of comparable size on that market and because the financial links between your company and the Oréal group do not seem in this case likely to influence the volume of your turnover for the products in question, the Commission considers that there is no longer any need, on the basis of the facts known to it, for it to take actions in respect of the above-mentioned agreements under the provisions of Article 85(1) of the Treaty of Rome. The file on this case may therefore be closed.'

The Court

The court making the reference asks whether such a letter such as that of 16 December 1974 sent to Lancôme by the relevant departments of the Commission has the result of putting an end to the provisional protection which, by virtue of the case-law of the Court, is enjoyed, as from the date of notification, by old agreements which were notified within the time-limit provided for by Article 5(1) of Regulation No 17 or which are exempted from notification.

With a view to answering that question the considerations which form the basis of the case-law of the Court on 'provisional validity' should be recalled.

As the Court has observed in particular in its judgment of 9 July 1969 in Case 10/69 *Portelange* v *Smith Corona Marchant International* [1969] ECR 309, Article 85 of the Treaty is arranged in the form of a rule imposing a prohibition (paragraph 1) with a statement of its effects (paragraph 2) mitigated by the exercise of a power to grant exceptions to that rule (paragraph 3). To treat a given agreement, or certain of its clauses, as automatically void presupposes that that agreement falls within the prohibition of paragraph 1 of the said article and that it may not benefit from the provisions of paragraph 3.

The exclusive power to apply Article 85(3) which is conferred on the Commission by Article 9(1) of Regulation No 17, considered in conjunction with the provisions laid down in favour of old agreements by Articles 6(2) and 7 of that regulation, has led the Court to conclude that, in the case of those old agreements, the principle of legal certainty in contractual matters requires that, where the agreement has been notified in accordance with the provisions of Regulation No 17, a court may only declare it to be automatically void after the Commission has taken a decision by virtue of that regulation.

In the light of those considerations, it appears that the maintenance of the provisional protection from which notified old agreements benefit is no longer justified from the date on which the Commission informs the parties concerned that it has decided to close the file on the case concerning them. After the adoption of such an attitude, which indicates that the Commission does not contemplate taking an individual decision on the notified agreements in question, it is unlikely that the Commission would subsequently exercise in favour of those agreements its power to apply Article 85(3) with, where appropriate, retroactive effect for the period prior to their notification, as permitted by Article 6(2) of Regulation No 17. There is, therefore, no longer any reason to release national courts, before which the direct effect of the prohibition in Article 85(1) is relied upon, from the duty of giving judgment.

The answer to the first question should therefore be that *an administrative letter informing the person concerned that the Commission is of the opinion that there are no grounds for it to take action with regard to agreements which have been notified pursuant to the provisions of Article 85(1) has the effect of terminating the period of provisional validity accorded from the date of notification to agreements made prior to 13 March 1962 notified within the period laid down in Article 5(1) of Regulation No 17 or exempted from notification. The opinions expressed in such a letter are not binding on the national courts but constitute a factor which the latter may take into account in examining whether the agreements are in accordance with the provisions of Article 85.*

VII EXEMPTION

Agreements, decisions and concerted practices falling within paragraph 1 of Article 85 are void by reason of paragraph 2 unless exempted in pursuance of paragraph 3. An agreement, decision or concerted practice may be exempted on an individual basis or on the ground that it falls within any of four heads defined in Article 4(2) of Regulation No 17 or on the basis of a 'block exemption'.

Regulation No 17 of 6 February 1962 [implementing Articles 85 and 86 of the EEC Treaty] OJ Sp Ed 1959–62, 87

Article 4

1. Agreements, decisions and concerted practices of the kind described in Article 85(1) of the Treaty which come into existence after the entry into force of this regulation and in respect of which the parties seek application of Article 85(3) must be notified to the Commission. Until they have been notified, no decision in application of Article 85(3) may be taken.

2. Paragraph 1 shall not apply to agreements, decisions or concerted practices where:

(1) the only parties thereto are undertakings from one Member State and the agreements, decisions or practices do not relate either to imports or to exports between Member States;

(2) not more than two undertakings are party thereto, and the agreements only:

(a) restrict the freedom of one party to the contract in determining the prices or conditions of business upon which the goods which he has obtained from the other party to the contract may be resold; or

(b) impose restrictions on the exercise of the rights of the assignee or user of industrial property rights – in particular patents, utility models, designs or trade marks – or of the person entitled under a contract to the assignment, or grant, of the right to use a method of manufacture or knowledge relating to the use and to the application of industrial processes;

(3) they have as their sole object:

(a) the development or uniform application of standards or types; or

(b) joint research and development;

(c) specialisation in the manufacture of products, including agreements necessary for achieving this,

– where the products which are the subject of specialisation do not, in a substantial part of the Common Market, represent more than 15 per cent of the volume of business done in identical products or those considered by consumers to be similar by reason of their characteristics, price and use, and

– where the total annual turnover of the participating undertakings does not exceed 200 million units of account.

These agreements, decisions and practices may be notified to the Commission.

The exercise of the Commission's power to grant block exemptions is governed by Council Regulation No 19/65 of 2 March 1965 OJ Sp Ed 1965–66, 35) and Council Regulation No 2821/71 of 20 December 1971 OJ Sp Ed 1971, 1032).

In June 1983 the Commission made two regulations replacing Regulation 67/67 of 22 March 1967 on exclusive dealing agreements OJ Sp Ed 1967, 10). The first of the new regulations dealt with distribution agreements and the second with purchasing agreements.

Commission Regulation No 1983/83 of 22 June 1983 on the application of Article 85(3) of the EEC Treaty to categories of exclusive distribution agreements OJ 1983 L 173/1

Article 1

Pursuant to Article 85(3) of the Treaty and subject to the provisions of this regulation, it is hereby declared that Article 85(1) of the Treaty shall not apply to agreements to which only two undertakings are party and whereby one party agrees with the other to supply certain goods for resale within the whole or a defined area of the Common Market only to that other.

Article 2

1. Apart from the obligation referred to in Article 1 no restriction on competition shall be imposed on the supplier other than the obligation not to supply the contract goods to users in the contract territory.

2. No restriction on competition shall be imposed on the exclusive distributor other than:

(a) the obligation not to manufacture or distribute goods which compete with the contract goods;

(b) the obligation to obtain the contract goods for resale only from the other party;

(c) the obligation to refrain, outside the contract territory and in relation to the contract goods, from seeking customers, from establishing any branch, and from maintaining any distribution depot.

3. Article 1 shall apply notwithstanding that the exclusive distributor undertakes all or any of the following obligations:

(a) to purchase complete ranges of goods or minimum quantities;

(b) to sell the contract goods under trademarks, or packed and presented as specified by the other party;

(c) to take measures for promotion of sales, in particular:
- to advertise,
- to maintain a sales network or stock of goods,

- to provide customer and guarantee services,
- to employ staff having specialised or technical training.

Article 3

Article 1 shall not apply where:

(a) manufacturers of identical goods or of goods which are considered by users as equivalent in view of their characteristics, price and intended use enter into reciprocal exclusive distribution agreements between themselves in respect of such goods;

(b) manufacturers of identical goods or of goods which are considered by users as equivalent in view of their characteristics, price and intended use enter into a non-reciprocal exclusive distribution agreement between themselves in respect of such goods unless at least one of them has a total annual turnover of no more than 100 million ECU;

(c) users can obtain the contract goods in the contract territory only from the exclusive distributor and have no alternative source of supply outside the contract territory;

(d) one or both of the parties makes it difficult for intermediaries or users to obtain the contract goods from other dealers inside the Common Market or, in so far as no alternative source of supply is available there, from outside the Common Market, in particular where one or both of them:

1. exercises industrial property rights so as to prevent dealers or users from obtaining outside, or from selling in, the contract territory properly marked or otherwise properly marketed contract goods;
2. exercises other rights or takes other measures so as to prevent dealers or users from obtaining outside, or from selling in, the contract territory contract goods.

Article 4

1. Article 3(a) and (b) shall also apply where the goods there referred to are manufactured by an undertaking connected with a party to the agreement.

2. Connected undertakings are:

(a) undertakings in which a party to the agreement, directly or indirectly:
- owns more than half the capital or business assets, or
- has the power to exercise more than half the voting rights, or
- has the power to appoint more than half the members of the supervisory board, board of directors or bodies legally representing the undertaking, or
- has the right to manage the affairs;

(b) undertakings which directly or indirectly have in or over a party to the agreement the rights or powers listed in (a);

(c) undertakings in which an undertaking referred to in (b) directly or indirectly has the rights or powers listed in (a).

3. Undertakings in which the parties to the agreement or undertakings connected with them jointly have the rights or powers set out in paragraph 2(a) shall be considered to be connected with each of the parties to the agreement.

Article 5

1. For the purpose of Article 3(b), the ECU is the unit of account used for drawing up the budget of the Community pursuant to Articles 207 and 209 of the Treaty.

2. Article 1 shall remain applicable where during any period of two consecutive financial years the total turnover referred to in Article 3(b) is exceeded by no more than 10 per cent.

3. For the purpose of calculating total turnover within the meaning of Article 3(b), the turnovers achieved during the last financial year by the party to the agreement and connected undertakings in respect of all goods and services, excluding all taxes and other duties, shall be added together. For this purpose, no account shall be taken of dealings between the parties to the agreement or between these undertakings and undertakings connected with them or between the connected undertakings.

Article 6

The Commission may withdraw the benefit of this regulation, pursuant to Article 7 of Regulation No 19/65/EEC, when it finds in a particular case that an agreement which is exempted by this regulation nevertheless has certain effects which are incompatible with the conditions set out in Article 85(3) of the Treaty, and in particular where:

(a) the contract goods are not subject, in the contract territory, to effective competition from identical goods or goods considered by users as equivalent in view of their characteristics, price and intended use;

(b) access by other suppliers to the different stages of distribution within the contract territory is made difficult to a significant extent;

(c) for reasons other than those referred to in Article 3(c) and (d) it is not possible for intermediaries or users to obtain supplies of the contract goods from dealers outside the contract territory on the terms there customary;

(d) the exclusive distributor:

1. without any objectively justified reason refuses to supply in the contract territory categories of purchasers who cannot obtain contract goods elsewhere on suitable terms or applies to them differing prices or conditions of sale;
2. sells the contract goods at excessively high prices.

...

Article 8

This regulation shall not apply to agreements entered into for the resale of drinks in premises used for the sale and consumption of beer or for the resale of petroleum products in service stations.

Article 9

This regulation shall apply *mutatis mutandis* to concerted practices of the type defined in Article 1.

Commission Regulation No1984/83 of 22 June 1983 on the application of Article 85(3) of the EEC Treaty to categories of exclusive purchasing agreements OJ 1983 L 173/5

Article 1

Pursuant to Article 85(3) of the Treaty, and subject to the conditions set out in Articles 2 to 5 of this regulation, it is hereby declared that Article 85(1) of the Treaty shall not apply to agreements to which only two undertakings are party and whereby one party, the reseller, agrees with the other, the supplier, to purchase certain goods specified in the agreement for resale only from the supplier or from a connected undertaking or from another undertaking which the supplier has entrusted with the sale of his goods.

Article 2

1. No other restriction of competition shall be imposed on the supplier than the obligation not to distribute the contract goods or goods which compete with the contract goods in the reseller's principal sales area and at the reseller's level of distribution.

2. Apart from the obligation described in Article 1, no other restriction of competition shall be imposed on the reseller than the obligation not to manufacture or distribute goods which compete with the contract goods.

3. Article 1 shall apply notwithstanding that the reseller undertakes any or all of the following obligations:

(a) to purchase complete ranges of goods;

(b) to purchase minimum quantities of goods which are subject to the exclusive purchasing obligation;

(c) to sell the contract goods under trademarks, or packed and presented as specified by the supplier;

(d) to take measures for the promotion of sales, in particular:
- to advertise,
- to maintain a sales network or stock of goods,
- to provide customer and guarantee services,
- to employ staff having specialised or technical training.

Article 3

Article 1 shall not apply where:

(a) manufacturers of identical goods or of goods which are considered by users as equivalent in view of their characteristics, price and intended use enter into reciprocal exclusive purchasing agreements between themselves in respect of such goods;

(b) manufacturers of identical goods or of goods which are considered by users as equivalent in view of their characteristics, price and intended use enter into a non-reciprocal exclusive purchasing agreement between themselves in respect of such goods, unless at least one of them has a total annual turnover of no more than 100 million ECU;

(c) the exclusive purchasing obligation is agreed for more than one type of goods where these are neither by their nature nor according to commercial usage connected to each other;

(d) the agreement is concluded for an indefinite duration or for a period of more than five years.

Article 4

1. Article 3(a) and (b) shall also apply where the goods there referred to are manufactured by an undertaking connected with a party to the agreement.

2. Connected undertakings are:

(a) undertakings in which a party to the agreement, directly or indirectly:
- owns more than half the capital or business assets, or
- has the power to exercise more than half the voting rights, or
- has the power to appoint more than half the members of the supervisory board, board of directors or bodies legally representing the undertakings, or
- has the right to manage the affairs;

(b) undertakings which directly or indirectly have in or over a party to the agreement the rights or powers listed in (a);

(c) undertakings in which an undertaking referred to in (b) directly or indirectly has the rights or powers listed in (a).

3. Undertakings in which the parties to the agreement or undertakings connected with them jointly have the rights or powers set out in paragraph 2(a) shall be considered to be connected with each of the parties to the agreement.

Article 5

1. For the purpose of Article 3(b), the ECU is the unit of account used for drawing up the budget of the Community pursuant to Articles 207 and 209 of this Treaty.

2 Article 1 shall remain applicable where during any period of two consecutive financial years the total turnover referred to in Article 3(b) is exceeded by no more than 10 per cent.

3. For the purpose of calculating total turnover within the meaning of Article 3(b), the turnovers achieved during the last finanial year by the party to the agreement and connected undertakings in respect of all goods and services excluding all taxes and other duties, shall be added together. For this purpose, no account shall be taken of dealings between the parties to the agreement or between these undertakings and undertakings connected with them or between the connected undertakings.

Article 6

1. Pursuant to Article 85(3) of the Treaty, and subject to Articles 7 to 9 of this regulation, it is hereby declared that Article 85(1) of the Treaty shall not apply to agreements to which only two undertakings are party and whereby one party, the reseller, agrees with the other, the supplier, in consideration for according special commercial or financial advantages, to purchase only from the supplier, an undertaking connected with the supplier or another undertaking entrusted by the supplier with the distribution of his goods, certain beers, or certain beers and certain other drinks, specified in the agreement for resale in premises used for the sale and consumption of drinks and designated in the agreement.

2 The declaration in paragraph 1 shall also apply where exclusive purchasing obligations of the kind described in paragraph 1 are imposed on the reseller in favour of the supplier by another undertaking which is itself not a supplier.

Article 7

1. Apart from the obligation referred to in Article 6, no restriction on competition shall be imposed on the reseller other than:

(a) the obligation not to sell beers and other drinks which are supplied by other undertakings and which are of the same type as the beers or other drinks supplied under the agreement in the premises designated in the agreement;

(b) the obligation, in the event that the reseller sells in the premises designated in the agreement beers which are supplied by other undertakings and which are of a different type from the beers supplied under the agreement, to sell such beers only in bottles, cans or other small packages, unless the sale of such beers in draught form is customary or is necessary to satisfy a sufficient demand from customers;

(c) the obligation to advertise goods supplied by other undertakings within or outside the premises designated in the agreement only in proportion to the share of these goods in the total turnover realised in the premises.

2. Beers or other drinks of the same type are those which are not clearly distinguishable in view of their composition, appearance and taste.

Article 8

1. Article 6 shall not apply where:

(a) the supplier or a connected undertaking imposes on the reseller exclusive purchasing obligations for goods other than drinks or for services;

(b) the supplier restricts the freedom of the reseller to obtain from an undertaking of his choice either services or goods from which neither an exclusive purchasing obligation nor a ban on dealing in competing products may be imposed;

(c) the agreement is concluded for an indefinite duration or for a period of more than five years and the exclusive purchasing obligation relates to specified beers and other drinks;

(d) the agreement is concluded for an indefinite duration or for a period of more than 10 years and the exclusive purchasing obligation relates only to specified beers;

(e) the supplier obliges the reseller to impose the exclusive purchasing obligation on his successor for a longer period than the reseller would himself remain tied to the supplier.

2. Where the agreement relates to premises which the supplier lets to the reseller or allows the reseller to occupy on some other basis in law or in fact, the following provisions shall also apply:

(a) notwithstanding paragraphs 1(c) and (d), the exclusive purchasing obligations and bans on dealing in competing products specified in this Title may be imposed on the reseller for the whole period for which the reseller in fact operates the premises;

(b) the agreement must provide for the reseller to have the right to obtain:

- drinks, except beer, supplied under the agreement from other undertakings where these undertakings offer them on more favourable conditions which the supplier does not meet,

- drinks, except beer, which are of the same type as those supplied under the agreement but which bear different trade marks from other undertakings where the supplier does not offer them.

Article 9

Articles 2(1) and (3), 3(a) and (b), 4 and 5 shall apply *mutatis mutandis.*

Article 10

Pursuant to Article 85(3) of the Treaty and subject to Articles 11 to 13 of this regulation, it is hereby declared that Article 85(1) of the Treaty shall not apply to agreements to which only two undertakings are party and whereby one party, the reseller, agrees with the other, the supplier, in consideration for the according of special commercial or financial advantages, to purchase only from the supplier, an undertaking connected with the supplier or another undertaking entrusted by the supplier with the distribution of his goods, certain petroleum-based motor-vehicle fuels or certain petroleum-based motor-vehicle and other fuels specified in the agreement for resale in a service station designated in the agreement.

Article 11

Apart from the obligation referred to in Article 10, no restriction on competition shall be imposed on the reseller other than:

(a) the obligation not to sell motor-vehicle fuel and other fuels which are supplied by other undertakings in the service station designated in the agreement;

(b) the obligation not to use lubricants or related petroleum-based products which are supplied by other undertakings within the service station designated in the agreement where the supplier or a connected undertaking has made available to the reseller, or financed, a lubrication bay or other motor-vehicle lubrication equipment;

(c) the obligation to advertise goods supplied by other undertakings within or outside the service station designated in the agreement only in proportion to the share of these goods in the total turnover realised in the service station;

(d) the obligation to have equipment owned by the supplier or a connected undertaking or financed by the supplier or a connected undertaking serviced by the supplier or an undertaking designated by him.

Article 12

1. Article 10 shall not apply where:

(a) the supplier or a connected undertaking imposes on the reseller exclusive purchasing obligations for goods other than motor-vehicle and other fuels or for services, except in the case of the obligations referred to in Article 11(b) and (d);

(b) the supplier restricts the freedom of the reseller to obtain, from an undertaking of his choice, goods or services, for which under the provisions of this Title neither an exclusive purchasing obligation nor a ban on dealing in competing products may be imposed;

(c) the agreement is concluded for an indefinite duration or for a period of more than 10 years;

(d) the supplier obliges the reseller to impose the exclusive purchasing obligation on his successor for a longer period than the reseller would himself remain tied to the supplier.

2. Where the agreement relates to a service station which the supplier lets to the reseller, or allows the reseller to occupy on some other basis, in law or in fact, exclusive purchasing obligations or prohibitions of competition indicated in this Title may, notwithstanding paragraph 1(c), be imposed on the reseller for the whole period for which the reseller in fact operates the premises.

Article 13

Articles 2(1) and (3), and 3(a) and (b), 4 and 5 of this regulation shall apply *mutatis mutandis*.

Article 14

The Commission may withdraw the benefit of this regulation, pursuant to Article 7 of Regulation No 19/65/EEC, when it finds in a particular case that an agreement which is exempted by this regulation nevertheless has certain effects which are incompatible with the conditions set out in Article 85(3) of the Treaty, and in particular where:

(a) the contract goods are not subject, in a substantial part of the Common Market, to effective competition from identical goods or goods considered by users as equivalent in view of their characteristics, price and intended use;

(b) access by other suppliers to the different stages of distribution in a substantial part of the Common Market is made difficult to a significant extent;

(c) the supplier without any objectively justified reason:

1. refuses to supply categories of resellers who cannot obtain the contract goods elsewhere on suitable terms or applies to them differing prices or conditions of sale;
2. applies less favourable prices or conditions of sale to resellers bound by an exclusive purchasing obligation as compared with other resellers at the same level of distribution.

...

Article 16

This regulation shall not apply to agreements by which the supplier undertakes with the reseller to supply only to the reseller certain goods for resale, in the whole or in a defined part of the Community, and the reseller undertakes with the supplier to purchase these goods only from the supplier.

Article 17

This regulation shall not apply where the parties or connected undertakings, for the purpose of resale in one and the same premises used for the sale and consumption of drinks or service stations, enter into agreements both of the kind referred to in Title I and of a kind referred to in Title II or III.

Article 18

This regulation shall apply *mutatis mutandis* to the categories of concerted practices defined in Articles 1, 6 and 10.

Commission Regulation No 2349/84 of 23 July 1984 on the application of Article 85(3) of the Treaty to certain categories of patent licensing agreements (OJ 1984, L 219/15) sets out (in Article 2) a number of clauses commonly found in patent licensing agreements which are generally not restrictive of competition and therefore generally fall outside Article 85(1). The same regulation sets out in Article 3 clauses which do not benefit from Article 2. In particular, a tying obligation is not captured by Article 85(1) where it is indispensable for the exploitation of the patent.

Council Regulation No 123/85 of 12 December 1984 on the application of Article 85(3) of the EEC Treaty to certain categories of motor vehicle distribution and servicing agreements) OJ 1985, L 15/16) provides for the block exemption of selective distribution systems for motor vehicles, subject to the fulfilment of conditions designed principally to eliminate any discrimination as regards prices, conditions and availability of supplies in the several Member States.

Commission Regulation No 417/85 of 19 December 1984 on the application of Article 85(3) of the EEC Treaty to certain categories of specialisation agreements. OJ 1985, L 53/1 provides for the block exemption of agreements whereby undertakings agree to accept reciprocal obligations to manufacture certain products jointly, or to leave it to other parties to the agreement to manufacture certain products. It is a condition of exemption that no restriction of competition may be imposed other than as specified in Articles 1 and 2 of the regulation. Further, the products and the parties must fall within the limits imposed by Article 3. In particular, the aggregate turnover of the parties must not exceed 500 million ECU and the products must not represent more than 20 per cent. of the market.

Commission Regulation No 4118/85 of 19 December 1984 on the application of Article 85(3) of the EEC Treaty to categories of research and development agreements, OJ 1985, L 53/5, provides for the exemption of research and development agreements and cognate agreements, defined and listed in Article 1. The regulation lists provisions which must be included in any such agreement (Article 2) and provisions which may be included (Article 4). It also establishes a 'blacklist' of provisions which may not be included (Article 6). There is a limit to the period of validity of agreements which benefit from exemption (Article 3). An agreement which meets the conditions set out in Articles 1–6 will be treated as exempted if it has been notified to the Commission and the latter has failed to oppose the exemption within six months (Article 7).

FURTHER READING

Dashwood, A., 'A New Look at Provisional Validity' 33 CLJ (1974) 16

Forrester, I. and Norall, C., 'The Laicisation of Community Law: Self-Help and the Rule of Reason' 21 CMLRev (1984) 11

Fox, C., 'Selective Distribution Agreements: Renewal of Exemptions' 131 Sol Jo (1987) 1105

Goebel, R., 'Metro II's Confirmation of the Selective Distribution Rules' 24 CMLRev (1987) 605

Hornsby, S., 'Competition Policy for the 80s: More Policy, Less Competition' 12 E.L.Rev (1987) 79

Korah, V., *An Introductory Guide to EEC Competition Law and Practice*, 3rd edition, 1986

Korah, V., *Exclusive Dealing Agreements in the EEC: Regulation No 67/67 Replaced*, 1984

Korah, V., *Patent Licensing and EEC Competition Rules: Regulation No 2349/84*, 1985

Korah, V., *R and D and the EEC Competition Rules: Regulation No 418/85*, 1986

Korah, V. and Lasok, P., '*Philip Morris* and its Aftermath: Merger Control?' 25 CMLRev (1988) 333

Morcom, C., 'Parallel Importation of Pharmaceutical Products in the Common Market', 10 EIPR (1988) 47

Shaw, J., 'Group Exemption and Exclusive Distribution and Purchasing Agreements' 34 ICLQ (1985) 190

Sinan, R., 'Tied House Agreements and the EEC Competition Rules' 135 New LJ (1985) 1063

Toepke, U., 'EEC Law of Competition: Distribution Agreements and their Notification' 19 Int Law (1985) 117

Turner, J., 'Competition and the Common Market After *Maize Seeds*' 8 ELRev (1983) 103.

10

DOMINANT POSITIONS AND STATE INTERVENTION

INTRODUCTION

Whereas Article 85 of the EEC Treaty aspires to control those concerted practices which may affect trade between Member States, Article 86 aspires to control the abusive exercise of monopoly power which may affect such trade.

EEC Treaty

Article 86

Any abuse by one or more undertakings of a dominant position within the Common Market or in a substantial part of it shall be prohibited as incompatible with the Common Market in so far as it may affect trade between Member States. Such abuse may, in particular, consist in:

(a) directly or indirectly imposing unfair purchase or selling prices or unfair trading conditions;

(b) limiting production, markets or technical development to the prejudice of consumers;

(c) applying dissimilar conditions to equivalent transactions with other trading parties, thereby placing them at a competitive disadvantage;

(d) making the conclusion of contracts subject to acceptance by the other parties of supplementary obligations which, by their nature or according to commercial usage, have no connection with the subject of such contracts.

As in the case of Article 85(1), the illustrative list of prohibited practices is not intended to be comprehensive.

In order to identify an abuse of a dominant position it is necessary first to define the market; next, to establish dominance of that market; and finally to demonstrate conduct, amounting to an abuse, on the part of the dominant undertaking.

I THE MARKET

1. THE PRODUCT MARKET

The relevant market is defined by reference both to the product and to the geographical area. For the purpose of defining a market in a product, the Commission or Court must ask whether 'there is a sufficient degree of interchangeability between all the products forming part of the same market in so far as a specific use of such products is concerned': Case 85/76 *Hoffman-La Roche* v *Commission* [1979] ECR 461; [1979] 3 CMLR 211 (paragraph 28).

Case 27/76 United Brands Co and Another v Commission
[1978] ECR 207; [1978] 1 CMLR 429

The Commission made a decision finding that United Brands ('UBC') infringed Article 86 in the marketing in the Community of bananas grown and imported by themselves. UBC challenged that decision on the ground, among others, that it did not occupy a dominant position in the market. UBC submitted that the relevant market was not the market in bananas but that in fresh fruits generally.

The Court

...

The applicant submits in support of its argument that bananas compete with other fresh fruit in the same shops, on the same shelves, at prices which can be compared, satisfying the same needs: consumption as a dessert or between meals.

The statistics produced show that consumer expenditure on the purchase of bananas is at its lowest between June and December when there is a plentiful supply of domestic fruit on the market.

Studies carried out by the Food and Agricultural Organisation (FAO) (especially in 1975) confirm that banana prices are relatively weak during the summer months and that the price of apples for example has a statistically appreciable impact on the consumption of bananas in the Federal Republic of Germany.

Again, according to these studies, some easing of prices is noticeable at the end of the year during the 'orange season'.

The seasonal peak periods when there is a plentiful supply of other fresh fruit exert an influence not only on the prices but also on the volume of sales of bananas and consequently on the volume of imports thereof.

The applicant concludes from these findings that bananas and other fresh fruit form only one market and that UBC's operations should have been examined in this context for the purpose of any application of Article 86 of the Treaty.

The Commission maintains that there is a demand for bananas which is distinct from the demand for other fresh fruit especially as the banana is a very important part of the diet of certain sections of the community.

The specific qualities of the banana influence customer preference and induce him not to readily accept other fruits as a substitute.

The Commission draws the conclusion from the studies quoted by the applicant that the influence of the prices and availabilities of other types of fruit on the prices and availabilities of bananas on the relevant market is very ineffective and that these effects are too brief and too spasmodic for such other fruit to be regarded as forming part of the same market as bananas or as a substitute therefor.

For the banana to be regarded as forming a market which is sufficiently differentiated from other fruit markets it must be possible for it to be singled out by such special features distinguishing it from other fruits that it is only to a limited extent interchangeable with them and is only exposed to their competition in a way that is hardly perceptible.

The ripening of bananas takes place the whole year round without any season having to be taken into account.

Throughout the year production exceeds demand and can satisfy it at any time.

Owing to this particular feature the banana is a privileged fruit and its production and marketing can be adapted to the seasonal fluctuations of other fresh fruit which are known and can be computed.

There is no unavoidable seasonal substitution since the consumer can obtain this fruit all the year round.

Since the banana is a fruit which is always available in sufficient quantities the question whether it can be replaced by other fruits must be determined over the whole of the year for the purpose of ascertaining the degree of competition between it and other fresh fruit.

The studies of the banana market on the Court's file show that on the latter market there is no significant long term cross-elasticity any more than – as has been mentioned – there is any seasonal substitutability in general between the banana and all the seasonal fruits, as this only exists between the banana and two fruits (peaches and table grapes) in one of the countries (West Germany) of the relevant geographic market.

As far as concerns the two fruits available throughout the year (oranges and apples) the first are not interchangeable and in the case of the second there is only a relative degree of substitutability.

This small degree of substitutability is accounted for by the specific features of the banana and all the factors which influence consumer choice.

The banana has certain characteristics, appearance, taste, softness, seedlessness, easy handling, a constant level of production which enable it to satisfy the constant needs of an important section of the population consisting of the very young, the old and the sick.

As far as prices are concerned two FAO studies show that the banana is only affected by the prices – falling prices – of other fruits (and only of peaches and table grapes) during the summer months and mainly in July and then by an amount not exceeding 20%.

Although it cannot be denied that during these months and some weeks at the end of the year this product is exposed to competition from other fruits, the flexible way in which the volume of imports and their marketing on the relevant geographic market is adjusted means that the conditions of competition are extremely limited and that its price adapts without any serious difficulties to this situation where supplies of fruit are plentiful.

It follows from all these considerations that a very large number of consumers having a constant need for bananas are not noticeably or even appreciably enticed away from the consumption of this product by the arrival of other fresh fruit on the market and that even the personal peak periods only affect it for a limited period of time and to a very limited extent from the point of view of substitutability.

Consequently the banana market is a market which is sufficiently distinct from the other fresh fruit markets.

Where a raw material is used by manufacturers of a product sold to the public, there may be a market in the raw material which is distinct from the market in the product.

Joined Cases 6 and 7/73 Istituto Chemioterapico Italiano SpA and Commercial Solvents Corporation v Commission
[1974] ECR 223; [1974] 1 CMLR 309

An Italian chemical laboratory, Zoja, was engaged in the manufacture of ethambutol, an anti-tuberculosis drug. For this purpose it used to purchase an essential raw material called aminobutanol from the Istituto Chemioterapico Italiano SpA ('Istituto') which the Istituto obtained from Commercial Solvents Corporation ('CSC'). CSC obtained 51 per cent of the voting stock in the Istituto. CSC later refused to supply the Istituto with aminobutanol for resale to Zoja. The Commission decided that CSC and the Istituto thereby abused a dominant position. On appeal, the applicants argued *inter alia* that they did not occupy a dominant position in the market.

The Court

...

The applicants rely on the sixth recital of Section II-C of the decision in dispute for the conclusion that the Commission considers the relevant market for determining the dominant position to be that of ethambutol. Such a market, they say, does not exist since ethambutol is only a part of a larger market in anti-tuberculosis drugs, where it is in competition with other drugs which are to a large extent interchangeable. Since a market in ethambutol does not exist, it is impossible to establish a separate market in the raw material for the manufacture of this product.

The Commission replies that it has taken into account the dominant position in the Common Market in the raw material necessary for the production of ethambutol.

Both in Section II-B and in the part of Section II-C of the decision which precedes the finding that the conduct of the applicants 'therefore constitutes an abuse of a dominant position within the meaning of Article 86' (II-C, fourth recital), the decision deals only with the market in raw materials for the manufacture of ethambutol. In taking the view that 'the conduct in question limits the market in raw material as well as the production of ethambutol and thus constitutes one of the abuses expressly prohibited by the said article' the decision in dispute considers the market in ethambutol only for the purpose of determining the effects of the conduct referred to. Although such an examination may enable the effects of the alleged infringement to be better appreciated, it is nevertheless irrelevant as regards the determination of the relevant market to be considered for the purpose of a finding that a dominant position exists.

Contrary to the arguments of the applicants it is in fact possible to distinguish the market in raw material necessary for the manufacture of a product from the market on which the product is sold. An abuse of a dominant position on the market in raw materials may thus have effects restricting competition in the market on which the derivatives of the raw material are sold and these effects must be taken into account in considering the effects of an infringement, even if the market for the derivative does not constitute a self-

contained market. The arguments of the applicants in this respect and in consequence their request that an expert's report on this subject be ordered are irrelevant and must be rejected.

Moreover, the market in replacement equipment may be distinct from the market in original equipment, as is the case with tyres for vehicles.

Case 322/81 Nederlandsche Banden-Industrie Michelin NV v Commission
[1983] ECR 3461; [1985] 1 CMLR 282

By a decision taken in 1981 the Commission found that the Dutch subsidiary of the Michelin group had abused a dominant position on the market in new replacement tyres for lorries, buses and similar vehicles by applying a policy of prices and discounts which tended to prevent customers from obtaining their supplies from competing manufacturers.

The Court

...

The applicant claims that the definition of the relevant market on which the Commission based its decision is too wide, inasmuch as in the eyes of the consumer different types and sizes of tyres for heavy vehicles are not interchangeable, and at the same time too narrow inasmuch as car and van tyres are excluded from it although they occupy similar positions on the market. It further argues that the Commission's reasoning in its decision is contradictory in so far as it puts itself alternately in the shoes of the ultimate consumer and in those of the dealer. However, at the level of dealers' total sales, the average proportion of sales of Michelin heavy-vehicle tyres represents only 12 per cent, which rules out the existence of any dominant position.

The Commission defends the definition of the relevant product market used in its decision by pointing out that with a technically homogeneous product it is not possible to distinguish different markets depending on the dimensions, size or specific types of products: in that connection the elasticity of supply between different types and dimensions of tyre must be taken into account. On the other hand the criteria of interchangeability and elasticity of demand allow a distinction to be drawn between the market in tyres for heavy vehicles and the market in car tyres owing to the particular structure of demand, which, in the case of tyres for heavy vehicles, is characterised by the presence above all of experienced trade buyers.

As the Court has repeatedly emphasised, most recently in its judgment of 11 December 1980 in Case 31/80 *NV L'Oréal and SA L'Oréal* v *Pvba De Nieuwe AMCK* [1980] ECR 3775, for the purposes of investigating the possibly dominant position of an undertaking on a given market, the possibilities of competition must be judged in the context of the market comprising the totality of the products which, with respect to their characteristics, are particularly suitable for satisfying constant needs and are only to a limited extent interchangeable with other products. However, it must be noted that the determination of the relevant market is useful in assessing whether the undertaking concerned is in a position to prevent effective competition from being maintained and to behave to an appreciable extent independently of its competitors and customers and consumers. For this purpose, therefore, an examination limited to the objective characteristics only of the relevant products cannot be sufficient: the competitive conditions and the structure of supply and demand on the market must also be taken into consideration.

Moreover, it was for that reason that the Commission and Michelin NV agreed that new, original-equipment tyres should not be taken into consideration in the assessment of market shares. Owing to the particular structure of demand for such tyres characterised by direct orders from car manufacturers, competition in this sphere is in fact governed by completely different factors and rules.

As far as replacement tyres are concerned, the first point which must be made is that at the user level there is no interchangeability between car and van tyres on the one hand and heavy-vehicle tyres on the other. Car and van tyres therefore have no influence at all on competition on the market in heavy-vehicle tyres.

Furthermore, the structure of demand for each of those groups of products is different. Most buyers of heavy-vehicle tyres are trade users, particularly haulage undertakings, for whom, as the Commission explained, the purchase of replacement tyres represents an item of considerable expenditure and who constantly ask their tyre dealers for advice and long-term specialised services adapted to their specific needs. On the other hand, for the average buyer of car or van tyres the purchase of tyres is an occasional event and even if the buyer operates a business he does not expect such specialised advice and service adapted to specific needs. Hence the sale of heavy-vehicle tyres requires a particularly specialised distribution network which is not the case with the distribution of car and van tyres.

The final point which must be made is that there is no elasticity of supply between tyres for heavy vehicles and car tyres owing to significant differences in production techniques and in the plant and tools needed for their manufacture. The fact that time and considerable investment are required in order to modify production plant for the manufacture of light-vehicle tyres instead of heavy-vehicle tyres or vice versa means that there is no discernible relationship between the two categories of tyre enabling production to be adapted to demand on the market. Moreover, that was why in 1977, when the supply of tyres for heavy vehicles was insufficient, Michelin NV decided to grant an extra bonus instead of using surplus production capacity for car tyres to meet demand.

...

In establishing that Michelin NV has a dominant position the Commission was therefore right to assess its market share with reference to replacement tyres for lorries, buses and similar vehicles and to exclude consideration of car and van tyres.

2. THE BRAND MARKET

Exceptionally, a market may exist in a product or item defined by reference to a brand. This may be the case where there is a market in spare parts for products of a certain brand or in certificates legally required for the use of such products.

Case 26/75 General Motors Continental NV v Commission
[1975] ECR 1367; [1976] 1 CMLR 95

The Commission made a decision finding that General Motors had abused a dominant position by charging excessive prices for the certificates of conformity required under Belgian law for cars imported to Belgium. Under the Belgian system, the certificates could be issued only by the manufacturer. General Motors did not occupy a dominant position in the Belgian car market. It did however have a legal monopoly in the issuance of certificates of conformity for its own vehicles.

The Court

...

The applicant maintains, first, that contrary to the statement made in the decision in question, the activity involved in applications for vehicle approval and the issue of certificates of conformity could not constitute a dominant position within the meaning of Article 86.

Far from constituting a market in itself, this activity is merely ancillary to the market in motor cars, the open and highly competitive nature of which is undesirable.

Therefore, the provisions of Article 86 could not be applied to charges the imposition of which was penalised by the decision of the Commission, as the incidence of such charges can only be assessed in relation to the market in motor cars as a whole, in which the applicant does not hold a dominant position.

The approval procedure in the context of which the impositions in question were made is, by nature, a duty governed by public law which is so delegated by the Belgian State that, for each make of motor car, the performance of this duty is reserved exclusively to the manufacturer or its sole authorised agent, appointed by the public authority.

However, although it entrusted this task of inspection to private undertakings the State took no measures to fix or limit the charge imposed for the service rendered.

This legal monopoly, combined with the freedom of the manufacturer or sole authorised agent to fix the price for its service, leads to the creation of a dominant position within the meaning of Article 86 as, for any given make, the approval procedure can only be carried out in Belgium by the manufacturer or officially appointed authorised agent under conditions fixed unilaterally by that party.

It thus emerges that the submission which the applicant bases on the fact that it held no dominant position must be rejected.

Case 22/78 Hugin Kassregister AB and Hugin Cash Registers Limited v Commission [1979] ECR 1869; [1979] 3 CMLR 345

Hugin refused to supply spare parts for Hugin cash registers to Liptons, which competed with Hugin in servicing Hugin's machines. The Commission decided that in so doing Hugin abused its dominant position in the market in spare parts for Hugin cash registers. The Court upheld that decision.

The Court

...

As regards the question whether Hugin occupies a dominant position on the market the Commission takes the view that the facts of the case have shown that while Hugin has only a relatively small share of the cash register market – which is very competitive – it has a monopoly in spare parts for machines made by it and that consequently it occupies a dominant position for the maintenance and repair of Hugin cash registers in relation to independent companies which need a supply of Hugin spare parts. As regards the reconditioning of used machines and the renting out of such machines the Commission also takes the view that Hugin occupies a dominant position as regards cash registers of its own manufacture, since undertakings engaged in such activities depend on supplies of Hugin spare parts.

Hugin contests the validity of the Commission's findings on these various points. In its principal argument it states that the supply of spare parts and of maintenance services is certainly not a separate market but is an essential parameter of competition in the market for cash registers as a whole. It states that on that market after-sales service and the quality of repair and maintenance services, including the supply of spare parts, constitute such a significant competitive factor that Hugin runs those services at a loss.

To resolve the dispute it is necessary, first, to determine the relevant market. In this respect account must be taken of the fact that the conduct alleged against Hugin consists in the refusal to supply spare parts to Liptons and, generally, to any independent undertaking outside its distribution network. The question is, therefore, whether the supply of spare parts constitutes a specific market or whether it forms part of a wider market. To answer that question it is necessary to determine the category of clients who require such parts.

In this respect it is established, on the one hand, that cash registers are of such a technical nature that the user cannot fit the spare parts into the machine but requires the services of a specialised technician and, on the other, that the value of the spare parts is of little significance in relation to the cost of maintenance and repairs. That being the case, users of cash registers do not operate on the market as purchasers of spare parts, however they have their machines maintained and repaired. Whether they avail themselves of Hugin's after-sales service or whether they rely on independent undertakings engaged in maintenance and repair work, their spare part requirements are not manifested directly and independently on the market. While there certainly exists amongst users a market for maintenance and repairs which is distinct from the market in new cash registers, it is essentially a market for the provision of services and not for the sale of a product such as spare parts, the refusal to supply which forms the subject-matter of the Commission's decision.

On the other hand, *there exists a separate market for Hugin spare parts at another level, namely that of independent undertakings which specialise in the maintenance and repair of cash registers, in the reconditioning of used machines and in the sale of used machines and the renting out of machines.* The role of those undertakings on the market is that of businesses which require spare parts for their various activities. They need such parts in order to provide services for cash register users in the form of maintenance and repairs and for the reconditioning of used machines intended for re-sale or renting out. Finally, they require spare parts for the maintenance and repair of new or used machines belonging to them which are rented out to their clients. It is, moreover, established that there is a specific demand for Hugin spare parts, since those parts are not interchangeable with spare parts for cash registers of other makes.

Consequently *the market thus constituted by Hugin spare parts required by independent undertakings must be regarded as the relevant market for the purposes of the application of Article 86 to the facts of the case.* It is in fact the market on which the alleged abuse was committed.

It is necessary to examine next whether Hugin occupies a dominant position on that market. In this respect Hugin admits that it has a monopoly in new spare parts. For commercial reasons any competing production of spare parts which could be used in Hugin cash registers is not conceivable in practice. Hugin argues nevertheless that another source of supply does exist, namely the purchase and dismantling of used machines. The value of that source of supply is disputed by the parties. Although the file appears to show that the practice of dismantling used machines is current in the cash register sector it cannot be regarded as constituting a sufficient alternative source of supply. Indeed the figures relating to Liptons' turnover during the years when Hugin refused to sell spare parts to it show that Liptons' business in the selling, renting out and repairing of Hugin machines diminished considerably, not only when expressed in absolute terms but even more so in real terms, taking inflation into account.

On the market for its own spare parts, therefore, Hugin is in a position which enables it to determine its conduct without taking account of competing sources of supply. There is therefore nothing to invalidate the conclusion that it occupies, on that market, a dominant position within the meaning of Article 86.

3. THE GEOGRAPHIC MARKET

In order to determine whether the dominant position is held in a substantial part of the Common Market, within the meaning of Article 86, it is necessary to consider the pattern and volume of the production and consumption of the relevant product, as well as the habits and economic opportunities of the vendors and purchasers.

Joined Cases 40–48, 50, 54–56, 111, 113 and 114/73
Coöperatieve vereniging 'Suiker Unie' UA and Others v Commission
[1975] ECR 1663; [1976] 1 CMLR 295

For the facts see p. 395 above.

The Court

...

The Commission takes the view that RT brought economic pressure to bear on the Belgian dealers Export and Hottlet, hereinafter called 'the dealers', with the object of compelling them only to resell the sugar supplied to them to specific customers or destinations and to impose these restrictions on their own customers.

This pressure consisted 'in refusing to sell sugar to these two dealers, in particular for exporting to third countries – and such sales represent a large proportion of their turnover – if this sugar is resold for the purposes which it [RT] has not authorised'.

RT occupies a dominant position on the Belgo-Luxembourg sugar market which is a substantial part of the Common Market.

II. Examination of the Submission

RT's main submission is that the Belgo-Luxembourg market is not a substantial part of the Common Market, that it does not occupy a dominant position on this market and has not abused its position, so that the Commission infringed Article 86 of the Treaty when it applied this provision to its conduct.

1. *The question whether the Belgo-Luxembourg market is a substantial part of the Common Market*

RT considers that in view of the relatively small volume of Belgian production and the number of consumers in Belgium and Luxembourg this question must be answered in the negative.

For the purpose of determining whether a specific territory is large enough to amount to 'a substantial part of the Common Market' within the meaning of Article 86 of the

Treaty the pattern and volume of the production and consumption of the said product as well as the habits and economic opportunities of vendors and purchasers must be considered.

So far as sugar in particular is concerned it is advisable to take into consideration in addition to the high freight rates in relation to the price of the product and the habits of the processing industries and consumers the fact that Community rules have consolidated most of the special features of the former national markets.

From 1968/69 to 1971/72 Belgian production and total Community production increased respectively from 530,000 to 770,000 metric tons and from 6,800,000 to 8,100,000 metric tons (cf. contested decision, p. 18, paragraphs 3 and 5).

During these marketing years Belgian consumption was approximately 350,000 metric tons whereas Community consumption increased from 5,900,000 to 6,500,000 metric tons (cf. *loc.cit.*).

If the other criteria mentioned above are taken into account these market shares are sufficiently large for the area covered by Belgium and Luxembourg to be considered, so far as sugar is concerned, as a substantial part of the Common Market in this product.

II DOMINANCE

The EEC Treaty does not define a 'dominant position'. It is to be contrasted in this respect with the ECSC Treaty, which contains provisions designed to eliminate obstacles to competition in the coal and steel markets, and to that end authorises the Commission to address recommendations if it 'finds that public or private undertakings ... in law or in fact hold or acquire in the market ... a dominant position shielding them against effective competition' and 'are using that position contrary to the objectives of this Treaty': Article 66(7). The Court has interpreted the expression 'dominant position' in Article 86 of the EEC Treaty in a sense corresponding to that of Article 66(7) of the ECSC Treaty (although it has not construed the word 'abuse' in any such corresponding sense).

Case 27/76 United Brands Co and Another v Commission

[1978] ECR 207; [1978] 1 CMLR 429

For the facts, see above p. 428.

The Court

...

The Commission bases its view that UBC has a dominant position on the relevant market on a series of factors which, when taken together, give UBC unchallengeable ascendancy over all its competitors: its market share compared with that of its competitors, the diversity of its sources of supply, the homogeneous nature of its products, the organisation of its production and transport, its marketing system and publicity campaigns, the diversified nature of its operations and finally its vertical integration.

...

UBC does not accept this conclusion and states that it stems from an assertion unsupported by any evidence.

Article 86 is an application of the general objective of the activities of the Community laid down by Article 3(f) of the Treaty: the institution of a system ensuring that competition in the Common Market is not distorted.

...

The dominant position referred to in this article relates to a position of economic strength enjoyed by an undertaking which enables it to prevent effective competition being maintained on the relevant market by giving it the power to behave to an appreciable extent independently of its competitors, customers and ultimately of its consumers.

In general a dominant position derives from a combination of several factors which, taken separately, are not necessarily determinative.

In order to find out whether UBC is an undertaking in a dominant position on the relevant market it is necessary first of all to examine its structure and then the situation on the said market as far as competition is concerned.

...

UBC is an undertaking vertically integrated to a high degree.

This integration is evident at each of the stages from the plantation to the loading on wagons or lorries in the ports of delivery and after those stages, as far as ripening and sale prices are concerned, UBC even extends its control to ripener/distributors and wholesalers by setting up a complete network of agents.

At the production stage UBC owns large plantations in Central and South America.

...

The effects of natural disasters which could jeopardise supplies are greatly reduced by the fact that the plantations are spread over a wide geographic area and by the selection of varieties not very susceptible to diseases.

...

At the production stage UBC therefore knows that it can comply with all the requests which it receives.

At the stage of packaging and presentation on the premises UBC has at its disposal factories, manpower, plant and material which enable it to handle the goods independently.

The bananas are carried from the place of production to the port of shipment by its own means of transport including railways.

At the carriage by sea stage it has been acknowledged that UBC is the only undertaking of its kind which is capable of carrying two thirds of its exports by means of its own banana fleet.

...

In the field of technical knowledge and as a result of continual research UBC keeps on improving the productivity and yield of its plantations by improving the draining system, making good soil deficiencies and combating effectively plant disease.

It has perfected new ripening methods in which its technicians instruct the distributor/ripeners of the Chiquita banana.

...

This general quality control of a homogeneous product makes the advertising of the brand name effective.

Since 1967 UBC has based its general policy in the relevant market on the quality of its Chiquita brand banana.

...

UBC has made this product distinctive by large-scale repeated advertising and promotion campaigns which have induced the consumer to show a preference for it in spite of the difference between the price of labelled and unlabelled bananas (in the region of 30 to 40%) and also of Chiquita bananas and those which have been labelled with another brand name (in the region of 7 to 10%).

...

It has thus attained a privileged position by making Chiquita the premier banana brand name on the relevant market with the result that the distributor cannot afford not to offer it to the consumer.

...

Since UBC's supply policy consists – in spite of the production surplus – in only meeting the requests for Chiquita bananas parsimoniously and sometimes incompletely UBC is in a position of strength at the selling stage.

...

A trader can only be in a dominant position on the market for a product if he has succeeded in winning a large part of this market.

Without going into a discussion about percentages, which when fixed are bound to be to some extent approximations, it can be considered to be an established fact that UBC's share of the relevant market is always more than 40% and nearly 45%.

This percentage does not however permit the conclusion that UBC automatically controls the market.

It must be determined having regard to the strength and number of the competitors.

It is necessary first of all to establish that on the whole of the relevant market the said percentage represents *grosso modo* a share several times greater than that of its competitor Castle and Cooke which is the best placed of all the competitors, the others coming far behind.

This fact together with the others to which attention has already been drawn may be regarded as a factor which affords evidence of UBC's preponderant strength.

However an undertaking does not have to have eliminated all opportunity for competition in order to be in a dominant position.

...

UBC's economic strength has thus enabled it to adopt a flexible overall strategy directed against new competitors establishing themselves on the whole of the relevant market.

The particular barriers to competitors entering the market are the exceptionally large capital investments required for the creation and running of banana plantations, the need to increase sources of supply in order to avoid the effects of fruit diseases and bad weather (hurricanes, floods), the introduction of an essential system of logistics which the distribution of a very perishable product makes necessary, economies of scale from which newcomers to the market cannot derive any immediate benefit and the actual cost of entry made up *inter alia* of all the general expenses incurred in penetrating the market such as the setting up of an adequate commercial network, the mounting of very large-scale advertising campaigns, all those financial risks, the costs of which are irrecoverable if the attempt fails.

Thus, although, as UBC has pointed out, it is true that competitors are able to use the same methods of production and distribution as the applicant, they come up against almost insuperable practical and financial obstacles.

That is another factor peculiar to a dominant position.

However UBC takes into account the losses which its banana division made from 1971 to 1976 – whereas during this period its competitors made profits – for the purpose of inferring that, since dominance is in essence the power to fix prices, making losses is inconsistent with the existence of a dominant position.

An undertaking's economic strength is not measured by its profitability; a reduced profit margin or even losses for a time are not incompatible with a dominant position, just as large profits may be compatible with a situation where there is effective competition.

The fact that UBC's profitability is for a time moderate or non-existent must be considered in the light of the whole of its operations.

The finding that, whatever losses UBC may make, the customers continue to buy more goods from UBC which is the dearest vendor, is more significant and this fact is a particular feature of the dominant position and its verification is determinative in this case.

The cumulative effect of all the advantages enjoyed by UBC thus ensures that it has a dominant position on the relevant market.

Case 85/76 Hoffman-La Roche and Co AG v Commission
[1979] ECR 461; [1979] 3 CMLR 211

The Commission made a decision finding that Hoffman La Roche ('Roche') had abused a dominant position on the market in certain vitamins by concluding agreements with 22 purchasers whereby the latter were obliged or induced to buy all or most of their requirements of those vitamins from Roche. The Court found that Roche occupied a dominant position in the market in some of those vitamins but not in the case of others.

The Court

...

(a) *The Vitamin A Group*

The parties both concede that Roche's market share within the Common Market may be put at 47% both as to value and quantity.

According to the data produced by the Commission, which Roche does not dispute, the shares of the other producers in 1974 may be put at 27%, 18%, 7%, and 1%.

Since the relevant market thus has the particular features of a narrow oligopolistic market in which the degree of competition by its very nature has already been weakened, Roche's share, which is equal to the aggregate of the shares of its two next largest competitors, proves that it is entirely free to decide what attitude to adopt when confronted by competition.

Roche's technical lead over its competitors due to the fact that it is the proprietor of several patents relating to vitamin A, even after the expiration of these patents, is a further indication that it occupies a dominant position.

As has been indicated above the same applies to the absence of potential competition from new manufacturers, whereas the competition derived from the surplus manufacturing capacity of existing undertakings rather favours Roche as is apparent from an extract from Management Information of the middle of August 1971, which reads 'although BASF will continue to intensify its activities, we expect to achieve a further steady increase of our turnover. However, the present overcapacity of production is such that a fixing of prices cannot be expected for the next few years. Such a development would, of course, be accelerated if one of our smaller competitors ceased production'.

Therefore the Commission was right to find that the applicant occupies a dominant position on the market in vitamin A.

The fact that Roche had to obtain its supplies of raw materials for the manufacture of vitamins of group A from an undertaking of the chemical industry which also manufactured vitamin A and which was consequently its competitor is not of such a kind as to alter the Commission's conclusions, since Roche has never claimed that it was in any difficulties at all either as regards the frequency of the deliveries of its supplies or as regards prices.

...

(c) *The Vitamin B3 (Pantothenic Acid) Group*

The Commission has admitted that the figures used in the contested decision had to be corrected and the two parties agree the following evaluations of the market shares:

Vitamin B3 Roche's market share	1972 (6 Member States)	1973 (9 Member States)	1974 (9 Member States)
value	28.9%	34.9%	51.0%
quantity	18.9%	23.4%	41.2%

Market shares of this size either in value or in quantity, complemented by the statement in the document jointly prepared by the parties that the figures for 1971 were 6% lower still than those for 1972, do not in themselves constitute a factor sufficient to establish the existence of a dominant position for most of the period considered by the Commission.

On the contrary it has become apparent that the rectification which the latter had to carry out was due to its omission to take account of the imports of a Japanese competitor which in 1973 accounted for 30% of the market.

On the other hand the Commission, in the case of this particular market, has not indicated what the additional factors would be, which, together with the market share as corrected, nevertheless would be of such a kind as to admit of the existence of a dominant position.

These findings lead to the conclusion that, as far as concerns vitamin B3, there is insufficient evidence of the existence of a dominant position held by Roche for the period under consideration.

III ABUSE

An undertaking in a dominant position is said to abuse that position if as a result of its conduct the degree of competition is weakened or the maintenance or growth of the existing degree of competition is hindered. It is a conclusive but unnecessary element to show that the undertaking has exploited its position unfairly, to the detriment of actual or potential competitors.

Case 6/72 Europemballage Corporation and Continental Can Co Inc v Commission [1975] ECR 495; [1976] 1 CMLR 587

The Continental Can Company of New York ('Continental Can') were major manufacturers of metal packages with an international presence. In 1969 they acquired a German manufacturer of light metal packages, Schmalbach-Lubeca-Werke ('SLW') and in 1970 they agreed to purchase, through their subsidiary Europemballage, a controlling interest in its Dutch licensee, Thomassen-Drijver-Verblifa ('TDV'). The Commission made a decision finding that Continental Can held through SLW a dominant position on the market for metal packaging for fish and meat and on the market for metal closures for glass containers and had abused that position by the purchase of TDV. Continental Can contended that its behaviour did not amount to an abuse.

The Court

...

Article 86(1) of the Treaty says 'any abuse by one or more undertakings of a dominant position within the Common Market or in a substantial part of it shall be prohibited as incompatible with the Common Market in so far as it may affect trade between Member States'. The question is whether the word 'abuse' in Article 86 refers only to practices of undertakings which may directly affect the market and are detrimental to production or sales, to purchasers or consumers, or whether this word refers also to changes in the structure of an undertaking, which lead to competition being seriously disturbed in a substantial part of the Common Market.

The distinction between measures which concern the structure of the undertaking and practices which affect the market cannot be decisive, for any structural measure may influence market conditions, if it increases the size and the economic power of the undertaking.

In order to answer this question, one has to go back to the spirit, general scheme and wording of Article 86, as well as to the system and objectives of the Treaty. These problems thus cannot be solved by comparing this article with certain provisions of the ECSC Treaty.

Article 86 is part of the chapter devoted to the common rules on the Community's policy in the field of competition. This policy is based on Article 3(f) of the Treaty according to which the Community's activity shall include the institution of a system ensuring that competition in the Common Market is not distorted. The applicants' argument, that this provision merely contains a general programme devoid of legal effect, ignores the fact that Article 3 considers the pursuit of the objectives which it lays down to be indispensable for the achievement of the Community's tasks. As regards in particular the aim mentioned in (f), the Treaty in several provisions contains more detailed regulations for the interpretation of which this aim is decisive.

But if Article 3(f) provides for the institution of a system ensuring that competition in the Common Market is not distorted, then it requires *a fortiori* that competition must not be eliminated. This requirement is so essential that without it numerous provisions of the Treaty would be pointless. Moreover, it corresponds to the precept of Article 2 of the Treaty according to which one of the tasks of the Community is 'to promote throughout the Community a harmonious development of economic activities'. Thus the restraints on competition, which the Treaty allows under certain conditions because of the need to harmonise the various objectives of the Treaty, are limited by the requirements of Articles 2 and 3. Going beyond this limit involves the risk that the weakening of competition would conflict with the aims of the Common Market.

With a view to safeguarding the principles and attaining the objectives set out in Articles 2 and 3 of the Treaty, Articles 85 to 90 have laid down general rules applicable to undertakings. Article 85 concerns agreements between undertakings, decisions of associations of undertakings and concerted practices, while Article 86 concerns unilateral activity of one or more undertakings. Articles 85 and 86 seek to achieve the same aim on different levels, *viz.* the maintenance of effective competition within the Common Market. The restraint of competition, which is prohibited if it is the result of behaviour falling under Article 85, cannot become permissible by the fact that such behaviour succeeds under the influence of a dominant undertaking and results in the merger of the undertakings concerned. In the absence of explicit provisions one cannot assume that the Treaty, which prohibits in Article 85 certain decisions of ordinary associations of undertakings restricting competition without eliminating it, permits in Article 86 that undertakings, after merging into an organic unity, should reach such a dominant position that any serious chance of competition is practically rendered impossible. Such a diverse legal treatment would make a breach in the entire competition law which could jeopardise the proper functioning of the Common Market. If, in order to avoid the prohibitions in Article 85, it sufficed to establish such close connections between the undertakings that they escaped the prohibition of Article 85 without coming within the scope of that of Article 86, then, in contradiction to the basic principles of the Common Market, the partitioning of a substantial part of this market would be allowed. The endeavour of the authors of the Treaty to maintain in the market real or potential competition even in cases in which restraints on competition are permitted was explicitly laid down in Article 85(3)(b) of the Treaty. Article 86 does not contain the same explicit provisions, but this can be explained by the fact that the system fixed there for dominant positions, unlike Article 85(3), does not recognise any exemption from the prohibition. With such a system the obligation to observe the basic objectives of the Treaty, in particular that of Article 3(f), results from the obligatory force of these objectives. In any case Articles 85 and 86 cannot be interpreted in such a way that they contradict each other, because they serve to achieve the same aim.

It is in the light of these considerations that the condition imposed by Article 86 is to be interpreted whereby in order to come within the prohibition a dominant position must have been abused. The provision states a certain number of abusive practices which it prohibits. *The list merely gives examples, not an exhaustive enumeration of the sort of abuses of a dominant position prohibited by the Treaty.* As may further be seen from subparagraphs (c) and (d) of Article 86(2), the provision is not only aimed at practices which may cause damage to consumers directly, but also at those which are detrimental to them through their impact on an effective competition structure, such as is mentioned in Article 3(f) of the Treaty. *Abuse may therefore occur if an undertaking in a dominant position strengthens such position in such a way that the degree of dominance reached substantially fetters competition, i.e. that only undertakings remain in the market whose behaviour depends on the dominant one.*

Such being the meaning and the scope of Article 86 of the EEC Treaty, the question of the link of causality raised by the applicants which in their opinion has to exist between the dominant position and its abuse, is of no consequence, for the strengthening of the position of an undertaking may be an abuse and prohibited under Article 86 of the Treaty, regardless of the means and procedure by which it is achieved, if it has the effects mentioned above.

IV EFFECT ON TRADE BETWEEN MEMBER STATES

In the case of Article 86 as in the case of Article 85(1), the conduct falls within the Community's jurisdiction only if it may affect trade between Member States. It is not required that the effect on trade should take any particular form. Such trade would be affected, for example, if the conduct of the undertaking is such as to partition the Common Market.

Case 22/79 Greenwich Film Production, Paris v SACEM

[1979] ECR 3275; [1980] 1 CMLR 629

The Société des Auteurs, Compositeurs et Editeurs de Musique ('SACEM') brought proceedings in a French court against Greenwich Film Production ('Greenwich') for payment of royalties in respect of the public performance of the music for two films distributed in France. SACEM relied upon an assignment by two composers to itself of the exclusive right throughout the world to authorise the public performance of their works. Greenwich contended that such an assignment, made by the composers to SACEM in conformity with a requirement imposed by SACEM's articles of association, must be considered as prohibited under Article 86 of the EEC Treaty. The dispute eventually came before the Cour de Cassation which referred to the European Court a question designed to determine whether trade between Member States might be affected by an abuse of the kind imputed to SACEM by Greenwich.

The Court

...

The reply to the question thus defined may be discerned in the previous decisions of the Court of Justice. The Court of Justice, in deciding whether trade between Member States may be affected by the abuse of a dominant position in the market in question, has taken the view that it must take into consideration the consequences for the effective competitive structure in the Common Market, adding that there is no reason to distinguish between production intended for sale within the Common Market and that intended for export (judgment of 6 March 1974 in Joined Cases 6 and 7/73 *Istituto Chemioterapico Italiano and Commercial Solvents Corporation* v *Commission* [1974] ECR 223). There is no reason to restrict that interpretation to trade in goods and not to apply it to the provision of services such as the management of copyrights.

In fact, it is well known that in certain Member States the management of composers' copyrights is usually entrusted by composers to associations whose object is to supervise the exercise of such rights and to collect the corresponding royalties on behalf of any composer working within the territory of the Member State in question. *It is possible in those circumstances that the activities of such associations may be conducted in such a way that their effect is to partition the Common Market and thereby restrict the freedom to provide services which constitutes one of the objectives of the Treaty. Such activities are thus capable of affecting trade between Member States within the meaning of Article 86 of the Treaty, even if the management of copyrights, in certain cases, relates only to the performance of musical works in non-Member countries. In considering whether Article 86 is applicable the performance of certain contracts cannot be assessed in isolation but must be viewed in the light of the activities of the undertaking in question as a whole.*

It is clear from the foregoing that where an association exploiting composers' copyrights is to be regarded as an undertaking abusing a dominant position within the Common Market or in a substantial part of it, the fact that such abuse, in certain cases, relates only to the performance in non-Member countries of contracts entered into in the territory of a Member State by parties within the jurisdiction of that State does not preclude the application of Article 86 of the Treaty.

V PUBLIC UNDERTAKINGS

EEC Treaty

Article 90

1. In the case of public undertakings and undertakings to which Member States grant special or exclusive rights, Member States shall neither enact nor maintain in force any measure contrary to the rules contained in this Treaty, in particular to those rules provided for in Article 7 and Articles 85 to 94.

2. Undertakings entrusted with the operation of services of general economic interest or having the character of a revenue-producing monopoly shall be subject to the rules contained in this Treaty, in particular to the rules on competition, in so far as the application of such rules does not obstruct the performance, in law or in fact, of the particular tasks assigned to them. The development of trade must not be affected to such an extent as would be contrary to the interests of the Community.

3. The Commission shall ensure the application of the provisions of this article and shall, where necessary, address appropriate directives or decisions to Member States.

By reason of Article 90(1), the existence of a State monopoly is not as such incompatible with Article 86. The exercise of the monopoly's powers may, however, entail a breach of Article 86; and even within the framework of Article 90, the prohibitions of Article 86 produce direct effects.

Case 155/73 Giuseppe Sacchi [1974] ECR 409; [1974] 2 CMLR 177

Under Italian law, television is a monopoly granted by the State. In support of that monopoly, Italian law prohibits any other person from receiving for the purposes of retransmission television signals transmitted either from national territory of from abroad, other than on payment of a fee to the national monopoly. Sacchi, the operator of a private television relay station, was charged with breach of that law. The trial court referred to the European Court questions designed to determine whether the maintenance of the national monopoly was consistent with the EEC Treaty.

The Court

...

Article 90(1) permits Member States *inter alia* to grant special or exclusive rights to undertakings.

Nothing in the Treaty prevents Member States, for considerations of public interest of a non-economic nature from removing radio and television transmissions, including cable transmissions, from the field of competition by conferring on one or more establishments an exclusive right to conduct them.

However, for the performance of their tasks these establishments remain subject to the prohibitions against discrimination and, to the extent that this performance comprises activities of an economic nature, fall under the provisions referred to in Article 90 relating to public undertakings and undertakings to which Member States grant special or exclusive rights.

The interpretation of Articles 86 and 90 taken together leads to the conclusion that the fact that an undertaking to which a Member State grants exclusive rights has a monopoly is not as such incompatible with Article 86.

It is therefore the same as regards an extension of exclusive rights following a new intervention by this State.

Moreover, if certain Member States treat undertakings entrusted with the operation of television, even as regards their commercial activities, in particular advertising, as undertakings entrusted with the operation of services of general economic interest, the same prohibitions apply, as regards their behaviour within the market, by reason of Article 90(2), so long as it is not shown that the said prohibitions are incompatible with the performance of their tasks.

In the fourth question the national court has cited a certain number of acts capable of amounting to abuse within the meaning of Article 86.

Such would certainly be the case with an undertaking possessing a monopoly of television advertising, if it imposed unfair charges or conditions on users of its services or if it discriminated between commercial operators or national products on the one hand, and those of other Member States on the other, as regards access to television advertising.

The national court has in each case to ascertain the existence of such abuse and the Commission has to remedy it within the limits of its powers.

Even within the framework of Article 90, therefore, the prohibitions of Article 86 have a direct effect and confer on interested parties rights which the national courts must safeguard.

VI DUMPING

In the case of trade within the EEC, Article 91 authorised the Commission to investigate allegations of 'dumping' (that is, selling goods at less than the normal value of a like product) during the transitional period. Since the expiry of that period, Article 91 has ceased to apply, on the principle that the Community constitutes a single domestic market.

In the case of trade with countries outside the Community, protection against dumping is assured by action taken in accordance with Council Regulation No 2176/84 of 23 July 1984 (as amended) together with Council Decision No 2177/84 (OJ 1984 L 201/17). The decision was taken under the ECSC Treaty but in other respects it corresponds, in its principal features, with the regulation.

Council Regulation No 2176/84 of 23 July 1984 on protection against dumped or subsidised imports from countries not members of the european economic community (as amended)

OJ 1984 L 201/1

Article 1

Applicability

This regulation lays down provisions for protection against dumped or subsidised imports from countries not Members of the European Economic Community.

Article 2

Dumping

A. *Principle*

1. An anti-dumping policy may be applied to any dumped product whose release for free circulation in the Community causes injury.

2. A product shall be considered to have been dumped if its export price to the Community is less than the normal value of the like product.

B. *Normal Value*

3. For the purposes of this regulation, the normal value shall be:

(a) the comparable price actually paid or payable in the ordinary course of trade for the like product intended for consumption in the exporting country or country of origin; or

(b) when there are no sales of the like product in the ordinary course of trade on the domestic market of the exporting country or country of origin, or when such sales do not permit a proper comparison:

(i) the comparable price of the like product when exported to any third country, which may be the highest export price but should be a representative price; or

(ii) the constructed value, determined by adding cost of production and a reasonable margin of profit. The cost of production shall be computed on the basis of all costs, in the ordinary course of trade, both fixed and variable, in the country of origin, of materials and manufacture, plus a reasonable amount for selling, administrative and other general expenses. As a general rule, and provided that a profit is normally realised on sales of products of the same general category on the domestic market of the country of origin, the addition for profit shall not exceed such normal profit. In other cases, the addition shall be determined on any reasonable basis, using available information.

4. Whenever there are reasonable grounds for believing or suspecting that the price at which a product is actually sold for consumption in the country of origin is less than the cost of production as defined in paragraph 3(b)(ii), sales at such prices may be considered as not having been made in the ordinary course of trade if they:

(a) have been made over an extended period of time and in substantial quantities; and

(b) are not at prices which permit recovery of all costs within a reasonable period of time in the normal course of trade.

In such circumstances, the normal value may be determined on the basis of the remaining sales on the domestic market made at a price which is not less than the cost of production or on the basis of export sales to third countries or on the basis of the constructed value or by adjusting the sub-production-cost price referred to above in order to eliminate loss and provide for a reasonable profit. Such normal-value calculations shall be based on available information.

5. In the case of imports from non-market economy countries and, in particular, those to which Regulations (EEC) No 1765/82 and (EEC) No 1766/82 apply, normal value shall be determined in an appropriate and not unreasonable manner on the basis of one of the following criteria:

(a) the price at which the like product of a market economy third country is actually sold:

(i) for consumption on the domestic market of that country; or

(ii) to other countries, including the Community, or

(b) the constructed value of the like product in a market economy third country;

(c) if neither price nor constructed value as established under (a) or (b) provides an adequate basis, the price actually paid or payable in the Community for the like product, duly adjusted, if necessary, to include a reasonable profit margin.

6. Where a product is not imported directly from the country of origin but is exported to the Community from an intermediate country, the normal value shall be the comparable price actually paid or payable for the like product on the domestic market of either the country of export or the country of origin. The latter basis might be appropriate, *inter alia,* where the product is merely trans-shipped through the country of export, where such products are not produced in the country of export or where no comparable price for it exists in the country of export.

7. For the purpose of determining normal value, transactions between parties which appear to be associated or to have a compensatory arrangement with each other may be considered as not being in the ordinary course of trade unless the Community authorities are satisfied that the prices and costs involved are comparable to those involved in transactions between parties which have no such link.

C. *Export Price*

8. (a) The export price shall be the price actually paid or payable for the product sold for export to the Community.

(b) In cases where there is no export price or where it appears that there is an association or a compensatory arrangement between the exporter and the importer or a third party, or that for other reasons the price actually paid or payable for the product sold for export to the Community is unreliable, the export price may be constructed on the basis of the price at which the imported product is first resold to an independent buyer, or if the product is not resold to an independent buyer or not resold in the condition imported, on any reasonable basis. In such cases, allowance shall be made for all costs incurred between importation and resale, including all duties and taxes, and for a reasonable profit margin.

Such allowances shall include, in particular, the following:

(i) usual transport, insurance, handling, loading and ancillary costs;

(ii) customs duties, any anti-dumping duties and other taxes payable in the importing country by reason of the importation or sale of the goods;

(iii) a reasonable margin for overheads and profit and/or any commission usually paid or agreed.

D. *Comparison*

9. For the purpose of a fair comparison, the export price and the normal value shall be on a comparable basis as regards physical characteristics of the product, quantities and conditions and terms of sale. They shall normally be compared at the same level of trade, preferably at the ex-factory level, and as nearly as possible at the same time.

10. If the export price and the normal value are not on a comparable basis in respect of the factors mentioned in paragraph 9, due allowance shall be made in each case, on its merits, for differences affecting price comparability. Where an interested party claims such an allowance, it must prove that its claim is justified. The following guidelines shall apply in determining these allowances:

(a) differences in physical characteristics of the product: allowance for such differences shall normally be based on the effect on the market value in the country of origin or export; however, where domestic pricing data in that country are not available or do not permit a fair comparison, the calculation shall be based on those production costs accounting for such differences;

(b) differences in quantities: allowances shall be made when the amount of any price differential is wholly or partly due to either:

(i) price discounts for quantity sales which have been made freely available in the normal course of trade over a representative preceding period of time, usually not less than six months, and in respect of a substantial proportion, usually not less than 20 per cent of the total sales of the product under consideration made on the domestic market or, where applicable, on a third country market; deferred discounts may be recognised if they are based on consistent practice in prior periods, or on an undertaking to comply with the conditions required to qualify for the deferred discount, or

(ii) to savings in the cost of producing different quantities.

However, when the export price is based on quantities which are less than the smallest quantity sold on the domestic market, or, if applicable, to third countries, then the allowance shall be determined in such a manner as to reflect the higher price for which the smaller quantity would be sold on the domestic market, or, if applicable, on a third-country market;

(c) differences in conditions and terms of sale: allowances shall be limited to those differences which bear a direct relationship to the sales under consideration and include, for example, differences in credit terms, guarantees, warranties, technical assistance, servicing, commissions or salaries paid to salesmen, packing, transport, insurance, handling, loading and ancillary costs and, in so far as no account has been taken of them otherwise, differences in the level of trade; allowances generally will not be made for differences in overheads and general expenses, including research and development or advertising costs; the amount of these allowances shall normally be determined by the cost of such differences to the seller, though consideration may also be given to their effect on the value of the product;

(d) differences in import charges and indirect taxes: an allowance shall be made by reason of the exemption of a product exported to the Community from any import charges or indirect taxes, as defined in the notes to the Annex, borne by the like product and by materials physically incorporated therein, when destined for consumption in the country of origin or export, or by reason of the refund of such charges or taxes.

E. *Allocation of Costs*

11. In general, all cost calculations shall be based on available accounting data, normally allocated, where necessary, in proportion to the turnover for each product and market under consideration.

F. *Like Product*

12. For the purposes of this regulation, 'like product' means a product which is identical, i.e., alike in all respects, to the product under consideration, or, in the absence of such a product, another product which has characteristics closely resembling those of the product under consideration.

G. *Dumping Margin*

13. (a) 'Dumping margin' means the amount by which the normal exceeds the export price.

(b) Where prices vary, the dumping margin may be established on a transaction-by-transaction basis or by reference to the most frequently occurring, representative or weighted average prices.

(c) Where dumping margins vary, weighted averages may be established.

Article 3
Subsidies

1. A countervailing duty may be imposed for the purpose of offsetting any subsidy bestowed, directly or indirectly, in the country of origin or export, upon the manufacture, production, export or transport of any product whose release for free circulation in the Community causes injury.

2. Subsidies bestowed on exports include, but are not limited to, the practices listed in the Annex.

3. The exemption of a product from import charges or indirect taxes, as defined in the notes to the Annex, effectively borne by the like product and by materials physically incorporated therein, when destined for consumption in the country of origin or export, or the refund of such charges or taxes, shall not be considered as a subsidy for the purposes of this regulation.

4. (a) The amount of the subsidy shall be determined per unit of the subsidised product exported to the Community.

(b) In establishing the amount of any subsidy the following elements shall be deducted from the total subsidy:

(i) any application fee, or other costs necessarily incurred in order to qualify for, or receive benefit of, the subsidy;

(ii) export taxes, duties or other charges levied on the export of the product to the Community specifically intended to offset the subsidy.

Where an interested party claims a deduction, it must prove that the claim is justified.

(c) Where the subsidy is not granted by reference to the quantities manufactured, produced, exported or transported, the amount shall be determined by allocating the value of the subsidy as appropriate over the level of production or exports of the product concerned during a suitable period. Normally this period shall be the accounting year of the beneficiary.

Where the subsidiary is based upon the acquisition or future acquisition of fixed assets, the value of the subsidy shall be calculated by spreading the subsidy across a period which reflects the normal depreciation of such assets in the industry concerned. Where the assets are non-depreciating, the subsidy shall be valued as an interest-free loan.

(d) In the case of imports from non-market economy countries and in particular those to which Regulations (EEC) No 1765/82 and (EEC) No 1766/82 apply, the amount of any subsidy may be determined in an appropriate and not unreasonable manner, by comparing the export price, as calculated in accordance with Article 2(8), with the normal value as determined in accordance with Article 2(5). Article 2(10) shall apply to such a comparison.

(e) Where the amount of subsidisation varies, weighted averages may be established.

Article 4

Injury

1. A determination of injury shall be made only if the dumped or subsidised imports are, through the effects of dumping or subsidisation, causing injury, i.e., causing or threatening to cause material injury to an established Community industry or materially retarding the establishment of such an industry. Injuries caused by other factors, such as volume and prices of imports which are not dumped or subsidised, or contraction in demand, which, individually or in combination, also adversely affect the Community industry must not be attributed to the dumped or subsidised imports.

2. An examination of injury shall involve the following factors, no one or several of which can necessarily give decisive guidance:

(a) volume of dumped or subsidised imports, in particular whether there has been a significant increase, either in absolute terms or relative to production or consumption in the Community;

(b) the prices of dumped or subsidised imports, in particular whether there has been a significant price undercutting as compared with the price of a like product in the Community;

(c) the consequent impact on the industry concerned as indicated by actual or potential trends in the relevant economic factors such as:

- production,
- utilisation of capacity,
- stocks,
- sales,

- market share,
- prices (i.e., depression of prices or prevention of price increases which otherwise would have occurred),
- profits,
- return on investment,
- cash flow,
- employment.

3. A determination of threat of injury may only be made where a particular situation is likely to develop into actual injury. In this regard account may be taken of factors such as:

(a) rate of increase of the dumped or subsidised exports to the Community;
(b) export capacity in the country of origin or export, already in existence or which will be operational in the foreseeable future, and the likelihood that the resulting exports will be to the Community;
(c) the nature of any subsidy and the trade effects likely to arise therefrom.

4. The effect of the dumped or subsidised imports shall be assessed in relation to the Community production of the like product when available data permit its separate identification. When the Community production of the like product has no separate identity, the effect of the dumped or subsidised imports shall be assessed in relation to the production of the narrowest group or range of production which includes the like product for which the necessary information can be found.

5. The term 'Community industry' shall be interpreted as referring to the Community producers as a whole of the like product or to those of them whose collective output of the products constitutes a major proportion of the total Community production of those products except that:

- when producers are related to the exporters or importers or are themselves importers of the allegedly dumped or subsidised product the term 'Community industry' may be interpreted as referring to the rest of the producers;
- in exceptional circumstances the Community may, for the production in question, be divided into two or more competitive markets and the producers within each market regarded as a Community industry if
  (a) the producers within such market sell all or almost all their production of the product in question in that market, and
  (b) the demand in that market is not to any substantial degree supplied by producers of the product in question located elsewhere in the Community.

In such circumstances injury may be found to exist even where a major proportion of the total Community industry is not injured, provided there is a concentration of dumped or subsidised imports into such an isolated market and provided further that the dumped or subsidised products are causing injury to the producers of all or almost all of the production within such markets.

...

Subsequent articles deal with questions of procedure and with the power to impose provisional duties where a preliminary investigation shows that dumping or a subsidy exists. They also set out general provisions on duties; and provisions for review of decisions; and provisions for refunds where an importer can show that the duty collected exceeds the actual dumping margin.

VII STATE AIDS

EEC Treaty

Article 92

1. Save as otherwise provided in this Treaty, any aid granted by a Member State or through State resources in any form whatsoever which distorts or threatens to distort competition by favouring certain undertakings or the production of certain goods shall, in so far as it affects trade between Member States, be incompatible with the Common Market.
2. The following shall be compatible with the Common Market:
   (a) aid having a social character, granted to individual consumers, provided that such aid is granted without discrimination related to the origin of the products concerned;
   (b) aid to make good the damage caused by natural disasters or exceptional occurrences;
   (c) aid granted to the economy of certain areas of the Federal Republic of Germany affected by the division of Germany, in so far as such aid is required in order to compensate for the economic disadvantages caused by that division.
3. The following may be considered to be compatible with the Common Market:
   (a) aid to promote the economic development of areas where the standard of living is abnormally low or where there is serious underemployment;
   (b) aid to promote the execution of an important project of common European interest or to remedy a serious disturbance in the economy of a Member State;
   (c) aid to facilitate the development of certain economic activities or of certain economic areas, where such aid does not adversely affect trading conditions to an extent contrary to the common interest. However, the aids granted to shipbuilding as of 1 January 1957 shall, in so far as they serve only to compensate for the absence of customs protection, be progressively reduced under the same conditions as apply to the elimination of customs duties, subject to the provisions of this Treaty concerning common commercial policy towards third countries;
   (d) such other categories of aid as may be specified by decision of the Council acting by a qualified majority on a proposal from the Commission.

The procedure for the enforcement of Article 92 is governed by Article 93, the principal parts of which are set out above at p. 142.

The word 'aid' in Article 92 is broadly construed: the aim of the measure is immaterial. A measure is characterised as an 'aid' by reason of its effects.

Case 173/73 Italy v Commission

[1974] ECR 709; [1974] 2 CMLR 593

Italian law provided for the partial reduction of public charges on undertakings in the textile industry, not for the purpose of aiding the industry but for that of ensuring that the worker should receive a salary sufficient for the needs of his family. The Commission decided that the law entailed a State aid and in this respect its decision was upheld by the Court.

The Court

...

The aim of Article 92 is to prevent trade between Member States from being affected by benefits granted by the public authorities which, in various forms, distort or threaten to distort competition by favouring certain undertakings or the production of certain goods.

Accordingly, Article 92 does not distinguish between the measures of State intervention concerned by reference to their causes or aims but defines them in relation to their effects.

Consequently, the alleged fiscal nature or social aim of the measure in issue cannot suffice to shield it from the application of Article 92.

As to the argument that the contested measure has no purpose other than to rectify the amount of charges payable by the textile industry to the State insurance scheme, in this case relating to family allowances, it is clear that the Italian family allowance scheme is intended, as is the case with all similar schemes, to ensure that the worker obtains a salary which meets the needs of his family.

Since in a system of this kind employers' contributions are assessed in accordance with the wage costs of each undertaking, the fact that a relatively small number of the employees of an undertaking can, on the basis of their position as heads of household, claim actual payment of these allowances, cannot constitute either an advantage or a specific disadvantage for the undertaking in question as compared with other undertakings where a higher proportion of employees receive these allowances; the burden of payment of these allowances is rendered exactly the same for all undertakings.

...

It must be concluded that the partial reduction of social charges pertaining to family allowances devolving upon employers in the textile sector is a measure intended partially to exempt undertakings of a particular industrial sector from the financial charges arising from the normal application of the general social security system, without there being any justification for this exemption on the basis of the nature or general scheme of this system.

The argument that the contested reduction is not a 'State aid', because the loss of revenue resulting from it is made good through funds accruing from contributions paid to the unemployment insurance fund, cannot be accepted.

As the funds in question are financed through compulsory contributions imposed by State legislation and as, as this case shows, they are managed and apportioned in accordance with the provisions of that legislation, they must be regarded as State resources within the meaning of Article 92, even if they are administered by institutions distinct from public authorities.

As to the argument that the social charges devolving upon employers in the textile sector are higher in Italy than in the other Member States, it should be observed that, in the application of Article 92(1), the point of departure must necessarily be the competitive position existing within the Common Market before the adoption of the measure in issue.

This position is the result of numerous factors having varying effects on production costs in the different Member States.

Moreover, Articles 92 to 102 of the Treaty provide for detailed rules for the abolition of generic distortions resulting from differences between the tax and social security systems of the different Member States whilst taking account of structural difficulties in certain sectors of industry.

On the other hand, the unilateral modification of a particular factor of the cost of production in a given sector of the economy of a Member State may have the effect of disturbing the existing equilibrium.

Consequently, there is no point in comparing the relative proportions of total production costs which a particular category of costs represents, since the decisive factor is the reduction itself and not the category of costs to which it relates.

...

It is a distinguishing feature of a State aid that it must emanate from the State or through State resources. Aid payments made by the Caisse Nationale de Crédit Agricole, a French public body, amounted to State aid even though they were extracted from a fund built up by the management of private funds.

Case 290/83 Commission v France

[1985] ECR 439

The Court

...

It appears from the texts provided by the French Government and explanations given by its Agent in the course of the oral procedure that, according to the provisions in force of Article 1 of Decree No 53-707 of 9 August 1953 concerning State control of national public undertakings and certain bodies with economic or social aims, as amended by Decree No 78-173 of 16 February 1978, decisions concerning, *inter alia,* the allocation of the Fund's profits do not become definitive until they have been approved by the public authorities.

According to Article 92(1) of the Treaty, any aid granted by a Member State or through State resources in any form whatsoever which distorts or threatens to distort competition by favouring certain undertakings or the production of certain goods is, in so far as it affects trade between Member States, incompatible with the Common Market. By virtue of the generality of the terms employed in that provision any State measure, in so far as it has the effect of according aid in any form whatsoever, may be assessed on the basis of Article 92 for its compatibility with the Common Market.

As is clear from the actual wording of Article 92(1), *aid need not necessarily be financed from State resources to be classified as State aid.* In addition, as the Court ruled in its judgment of 22 March 1977 (Case 78/76 *Steinike und Weinlig* [1977] ECR 595) the prohibition contained in Article 92 covers all aid granted by a Member State or through State resources and *there is no necessity to draw any distinction according to whether the aid is granted directly by the State or by public or private bodies established or appointed by it to administer the aid.*

It follows that Article 92 of the Treaty covers aid which, like the solidarity grant in question, was decided and financed by a public body and the implementation of which is subject to the approval of the public authorities, the detailed rules for the grant of which correspond to those for ordinary State aid and which, moreover, was put forward by the Government as forming part of a body of measures in favour of farmers which were all notified to the Commission in pursuance of Article 93(3).

A State aid contravenes Article 92 only if it distorts or threatens to distort competition by favouring certain undertakings or the production of certain goods. This condition is fulfilled where the aid strengthens the position of the recipient in competing with other undertakings in intra-Community trade.

Case 730/79 Philip Morris Holland BV v Commission
[1980] ECR 2671; [1981] 2 CMLR 321

The Commission made a decision finding that a proposed grant of aid by the Netherlands Government to the Dutch subsidiary of a major tobacco manufacturer would entail a breach of Article 92. The proposed recipient of the aid challenged the decision on the ground that it contained an inadequate statement of reasons. According to this argument, the decision should have defined the relevant market and established how far the proposed aid would have affected competition on that market.

The Court

...

It is common ground that when the applicant has completed its planned investment it will account for nearly 50% of cigarette production in the Netherlands and that it expects to export over 80% of its production to other Member States. The 'additional premium for major schemes' which the Netherlands Government proposed to grant the applicant amounted to Hfl 6.2 million (2.3 million EUA) which is 3.8% of the capital invested.

When State financial aid strengthens the position of an undertaking compared with other undertakings competing in intra-Community trade the latter must be regarded as affected by that aid. In this case the aid which the Netherlands Government proposed to grant was for an undertaking organised for international trade and this is proved by the high percentage of its production which it intends to export to other Member States. The aid in question was to help to enlarge its production capacity and consequently to increase its capacity to maintain the flow of trade including that between Member States. On the other hand the aid is said to have reduced the cost of converting the production facilities and has thereby given the applicant a competitive advantage over manufacturers who have completed or intend to complete at their own expense a similar increase in the production capacity of their plant.

These circumstances, which have been mentioned in the recitals in the preamble to the disputed decision and which the applicant has not challenged, justify the Commission's deciding that the proposed aid would be likely to affect trade between Member States and would threaten to distort competition between undertakings established in different Member States.

...

Paragraphs 2 and 3 of Article 92 identify kinds of aid that are to be considered compatible with the Common Market. The three kinds of aid listed in paragraph 2 are apparently compatible with the Common Market even in the absence of

Commission approval; whereas the five kinds of aid listed in paragraph 3 are compatible only if approved.

Case 730/79 Philip Morris Holland BV v Commission
[1980] ECR 2671; [1981] 2 CMLR 321

For the facts, see above p. 455.

The Court

...

According to the applicant it is wrong for the Commission to lay down as a general principle that aid granted by a Member State to undertakings only falls within the derogating provisions of Article 92(3) if the Commission can establish that the aid will contribute to the attainment of one of the objectives specified in the derogations, which under normal market conditions the recipient firms would not attain by their own actions. Aid is only permissible under Article 92(3) of the Treaty if the investment plan under consideration is in conformity with the objectives mentioned in subparagraphs (a), (b) and (c).

This argument cannot be upheld. On the one hand it disregards the fact that Article 92(3), unlike Article 92(2), gives the Commission a discretion by providing that the aid which it specifies 'may' be considered to be compatible with the Common Market. On the other hand it would result in Member States' being permitted to make payments which would improve the financial situation of the recipient undertaking although they were not necessary for the attainment of the objectives specified in Article 92(3).

It should be noted in this connection that the disputed decision explicitly states that the Netherlands Government has not been able to give nor has the Commission found any grounds establishing that the proposed aid meets the conditions laid down to enforce derogations pursuant to Article 92(3) of the EEC Treaty.

The applicant maintains that the Commission was wrong to hold that the standard of living in the Bergen-op-Zoom area is not 'abnormally low' and that this area does not suffer serious 'under-employment' within the meaning of Article 92(3)(a). In fact in the Bergen-op-Zoom region the under-employment rate is higher and the *per capita* income lower than the national average in the Netherlands.

...

Finally the applicant challenges the Commission's statement in the decision that an examination of the cigarette manufacturing industry in the Community and in the Netherlands shows that market conditions alone and without State intervention seem apt to ensure a normal development and that the disputed aid cannot therefore be considered as facilitating the development within the meaning of Article 92(3)(c).

These arguments put forward by the applicant cannot be upheld. It should be borne in mind that the Commission has a discretion the exercise of which involves economic and social assessments which must be made in a Community context.

That is the context in which the Commission has with good reason assessed the standard of living and serious under-employment in the Bergen-op-Zoom area, not with reference to the national average in the Netherlands but in relation to the Community level. As far as concerns the applicant's argument based on Article 92(3)(b) of the Treaty the Commission could very well take the view, as it did, that the investment to be effected in this case was not 'an important project of common European interest' and that the proposed aid could not be likened to aid intended 'to remedy a serious disturbance in the economy of a Member State', since the proposed aid would have permitted the transfer to the Netherlands of an investment which could be effected in other Member States in a less favourable economic situation than that of the Netherlands, where the national level of unemployment is one of the lowest in the Community.

As far as concerns Article 92(3)(c) of the Treaty the arguments submitted by the applicant are not relevant. The compatibility with the Treaty of the aid in question must be determined in the context of the Community and not of a single Member State. The Commission's assessment is based for the most part on the finding that the increase in the production of cigarettes envisaged would be exported to the other Member States in a situation where the growth of consumption has slackened, and this did not permit the view that trading conditions would remain unaffected by this aid to an extent contrary to the common interest. This assessment is justified. The finding that market conditions in the cigarette manufacturing industry seem apt, without State intervention, to ensure a normal development, and that the aid cannot therefore be regarded as 'facilitating' the development is also justified when the need for aid is assessed from the standpoint of the Community rather than of a single Member State.

FURTHER READING

Cownie, F., 'State Aids in the 80s' 11 ELRev (1986) 247

Fox, D., 'The EEC Treaty: Abusive Exploitation and Provision of Discount' 130 Sol Jo (1986) 294

Gyselden, L. and Kyriazis, N., 'Article 86 EEC: The Monopoly Power Measurement Issue Revisited' 11 ELRev (1986) 134

Korah, V., 'Control of Mergers under Article 86 of the Rome Treaty' [1973] CLP 82

Korah, V. and Lasok, P., '*Philip Morris* and its Aftermath: Merger Control?' 25 CMLRev (1988) 333

Merkei, R., 'Predatory Pricing or Competitive Pricing' 7 Oxford J Legal Stud (1987) 182

Mortelmans, K., 'The Compensatory Justification Criterion in the Practice of the Commission in Decisions on State Aids' 21 CMLRev (1984) 405

Page, A., 'Member States, Public Undertakings and Article 90' 7 ELRev (1982) 19

Quigley, C., 'The Notion of a State Aid in the EEC' 13 ELRev (1988) 242

Siragusa, M., 'The Application of Article 86 to the Pricing Policy of Dominant Companies' 16 CMLRev (1979) 179

Temple Lang, J., 'Judicial Review of Trade Safeguard Measures in the European Community' Fordham Corp Law Inst 1985

11

ENFORCEMENT OF COMPETITION LAW

INTRODUCTION

The EEC Treaty authorised the Council to adopt provisions for the enforcement of Community competition law. It reserved for the Member States a significant role in regard to such enforcement.

EEC Treaty

Article 87

1. Within three years of the entry into force of this Treaty the Council shall, acting unanimously on a proposal from the Commission and after consulting the Assembly, adopt any appropriate regulations or directives to give effect to the principles set out in Articles 85 and 86.

If such provisions have not been adopted within the period mentioned, they shall be laid down by the Council, acting by a qualified majority on a proposal from the Commission and after consulting the Assembly.

2. The regulations or directives referred to in paragraph 1 shall be designed, in particular:

(a) to ensure compliance with the prohibitions laid down in Article 85(1) and in Article 86 by making provision for fines and periodic penalty payments;

(b) to lay down detailed rules for the application of Article 85(3), taking into account the need to ensure effective supervision on the one hand, and to simplify administration to the greatest possible extent on the other;

(c) to define, if need be, in the various branches of the economy, the scope of the provisions of Articles 85 and 86;

(d) to define the respective functions of the Commission and of the Court of Justice in applying the provisions laid down in this paragraph;

(e) to determine the relationship between national laws and the provisions contained in this section or adopted pursuant to this article.

Article 88

Until the entry into force of the provisions adopted in pursuance of Article 87, the authorities in Member States shall rule on the admissibility of agreements, decisions and concerted practices and on abuse of a dominant position in the Common Market in accordance with the law of their country and with the provisions of Article 85, in particular paragraph 3, and of Article 86.

On 6 February 1962 the Council made the principal regulation for the enforcement of Community competition law. Article 1 of that regulation reiterates the prohibitions contained in Articles 85(1) and 86 of the EEC Treaty. Article 2 of the regulation establishes a procedure for 'negative clearance' whereby the Commission may certify that it has no grounds for taking action in respect of an agreement, decision or practice. Article 6 establishes a procedure for exemptions pursuant to Article 85(3) of the EEC Treaty. Applications for negative clearance (under Article 2 of the regulation) and for exemption are commonly made in tandem on a single form 'A/B'.

Council Regulation No 17 of 6 February 1962 implementing Articles 85 and 86 of the EEC Treaty OJ Sp Ed 1959–62 87

Article 1
Basic Provision

Without prejudice to Articles 6, 7 and 23 of this regulation, agreements, decisions and concerted practices of the kind described in Article 85(1) of the Treaty and the abuse of a dominant position in the market, within the meaning of Article 86 of the Treaty, shall be prohibited, no prior decision to that effect being required.

Agreements falling within Article 4(2) of Regulation No 17 do not require to be notified in order to obtain an exemption. For the text of that article, see above, Chapter 9 p. 415.

I INQUIRIES AND INVESTIGATIONS

The Commission has been invested with specific powers to request information, to conduct inquiries into sectors of the economy and to exercise functions of investigation and inspection, in conjunction with national authorities. When exercising these powers the Commission must respect the confidentiality of the information it acquires and must observe legal professional privilege.

Council Regulation No 17 of 6 February 1962 implementing Articles 85 and 86 of the EEC Treaty OJ Sp Ed 1959–62 87

Article 11
Requests for Information

1. In carrying out the duties assigned to it by Article 89 and by provisions adopted under Article 87 of the Treaty, the Commission may obtain all necessary information from the Governments and competent authorities of the Member States and from undertakings and associations of undertakings.

2. When sending a request for information to an undertaking or association of undertakings, the Commission shall at the same time forward a copy of the request to the competent authority of the Member State in whose territory the seat of the undertaking or association of undertakings is situated.

3. In its request the Commission shall state the legal basis and the purpose of the request and also the penalties provided for in Article 15(1)(b) for supplying incorrect information.

4. The owners of the undertakings or their representatives and, in the case of legal persons, companies or firms, or of associations having no legal personality, the persons authorised to represent them by law or by their constitution shall supply the information requested.

5. Where an undertaking or association of undertakings does not supply the information requested within the time limit fixed by the Commission, or supplies incomplete information, the Commission shall by decision require the information to be supplied. The decision shall specify what information is required, fix an appropriate time limit within which it is to be supplied and indicate the penalties provided for in Article 15(1)(b) and Article 16(1)(c) and the right to have the decision reviewed by the Court of Justice.

6. The Commission shall at the same time forward a copy of its decision to the competent authority of the Member State in whose territory the seat of the undertaking or association of undertakings is situated.

Article 12
Inquiry into Sectors of the Economy

1. If in any sector of the economy the trend of trade between Member States, price movement, inflexibility of prices or other circumstances suggest that in the economic sector concerned competition is being restricted or distorted within the Common Market, the Commission may decide to conduct a general inquiry into that economic sector and in the course thereof may request undertakings in the sector concerned to supply the information necessary for giving effect to the principles formulated in Articles 85 and 86 of the Treaty and for carrying out the duties entrusted to the Commission.

2. The Commission may in particular request every undertaking or association of undertakings in the economic sector concerned to communicate to it all agreements, decisions and concerted practices which are exempt from notification by virtue of Article 4(2) and Article 5(2).

3. When making inquiries pursuant to paragraph 2, the Commission shall also request undertakings or groups of undertakings whose size suggests that they occupy a dominant position within the Common Market or a substantial part thereof to supply to the

Commission such particulars of the structure of the undertakings and of their behaviour as are requisite to an appraisal of their position in the light of Article 86 of the Treaty.

4. Article 10(3) to (6) and Articles 11, 13 and 14 shall apply correspondingly.

Article 13

Investigations by the Authorities of the Member States

1. At the request of the Commission, the competent authorities of the Member States shall undertake the investigations which the Commission considers to be necessary under Article 14(1), or which it has ordered by decision pursuant to Article 14(3). The officials of the competent authorities of the Member States responsible for conducting these investigations shall exercise their powers upon production of an authorisation in writing issued by the competent authority of the Member State in whose territory the investigation is to be made. Such authorisation shall specify the subject-matter and purpose of the investigation.

2. If so requested by the Commission or by the competent authority of the Member State in whose territory the investigation is to be made, the officials of the Commission may assist the officials of such authorities in carrying out their duties.

Article 14

Investigating Powers of the Commission

1. In carrying out the duties assigned to it by Article 89 and by provisions adopted under Article 87 of the Treaty, the Commission may undertake all necessary investigations into undertakings and associations of undertakings. To this end the officials authorised by the Commission are empowered:

(a) to examine the books and other business records;

(b) to take copies of or extracts from the books and business records;

(c) to ask for oral explanations on the spot;

(d) to enter any premises, land and means of transport of undertakings.

2. The officials of the Commission authorised for the purpose of these investigations shall exercise their powers upon production of an authorisation in writing specifying the subject-matter and purpose of the investigation and the penalties provided for in Article 15(1)(c) in cases where production of the required books or other business records is incomplete. In good time before the investigation, the Commission shall inform the competent authority of the Member State in whose territory the same is to be made of the investigation and of the identity of the authorised officials.

3. Undertakings and associations of undertakings shall submit to investigations ordered by decision of the Commission. The decision shall specify the subject-matter and purpose of the investigation, appoint the date on which it is to begin and indicate the penalties provided for in Article 15(1)(c) and Article 16(1)(d) and the right to have the decision reviewed by the Court of Justice.

4. The Commission shall take decisions referred to in paragraph 3 after consultation with the competent authority of the Member State in whose territory the investigation is to be made.

5. Officials of the competent authority of the Member State in whose territory the investigation is to be made may, at the request of such authority or of the Commission, assist the officials of the Commission in carrying out their duties.

6. Where an undertaking opposes an investigation ordered pursuant to this article, the Member State concerned shall afford the necessary assistance to the officials authorised by

the Commission to enable them to make their investigation. Member States shall, after consultation with the Commission, take the necessary measures to this end before 1 October 1962.

Article 20

Professional Secrecy

1. Information acquired as a result of the application of Articles 11, 12, 13 and 14 shall be used only for the purpose of the relevant request or investigation.

2. Without prejudice to the provisions of Articles 19 and 21, the Commission and the competent authorities of the Member States, their officials and other servants shall not disclose information acquired by them as a result of the application of this regulation and of the kind covered by the obligation of professional secrecy.

3. The provisions of paragraphs 1 and 2 shall not prevent publication of general information or surveys which do not contain information relating to particular undertakings or associations of undertakings.

The power to request information may be exercised in two stages. First, an informal request is made, stating the legal basis and purpose of the request and specifying a time limit for a reply; but there is no legal obligation to answer. Secondly, the Commission may make a formal decision pursuant to Article 11(5) requiring the information to be supplied, on pain of a penalty.

The Commission's power to conduct inquiries into specific sectors of the economy has been employed in particular in the brewery sector: see OJ 1969, C, 148/3.

The power to conduct investigations, unlike the power to request information, does not comprise two separate stages.

Case 136/79 National Panasonic (UK) Limited v Commission
[1980] ECR 2033; [1980] 3 CMLR 169

By a decision of 22 June 1979 the Commission decided to carry out an investigation pursuant to Article 14(3) of Regulation No 17 into the commercial activities of National Panasonic (UK) Ltd, the English subsidiary of a Japanese manufacturer of electrical goods. The decision was made on the basis of information obtained by the Commission from the German subsidiary of the same parent company, which had notified the Commission of an agreement relating to the sale in Germany of National Panasonic products and had requested negative clearance or exemption. National Panasonic (UK) Ltd had no advance warning of the decision, which was not preceded by any informal request for information. Indeed, the Commission's inspectors notified the decision to the company by handing a copy of it to the directors of National Panasonic (UK) Ltd and carried out the investigation in conjunction with officers from the Office of Fair Trading without awaiting the arrival of the company's solicitors.

The Court

...

The applicant maintains first of all that the contested decision is unlawful because it does not comply with the spirit and letter of the provisions of Article 14(3) of Regulation No 17 of the Council. To this end it maintains that on a proper construction those provisions provide for a two-stage procedure which permits the Commission to adopt a decision requiring an undertaking to submit to an investigation only after attempting to carry out that investigation on the basis of a written authorisation to its own officials. This interpretation is confirmed, according to the applicant, by Article 11 of the same regulation which is similar in structure and provides for a two-stage procedure and by Article 13(1) which makes a distinction between an investigation carried out by the Commission informally and that ordered by decision.

These arguments do not appear to be well-founded. In order to enable the Commission to accomplish its task of ensuring that the rules of competition in the Common Market are complied with, the eighth recital of the preamble to Regulation No 17 provides that it 'Must ... be empowered, throughout the Common Market, to require such information to be supplied and to undertake such investigations as are necessary to bring to light any agreement, decision or concerted practice prohibited by Article 85(1) or any abuse of a dominant position prohibited by Article 86'. For this purpose, that regulation provides for separate procedures, which shows that the exercise of the powers given to the Commission with regard to information and investigations is not subject to the same conditions.

Article 11(2), (3) and (5) ... concerns the Commission's power to request the information it considers necessary...

On the other hand, Article 14 of the same regulation on the 'investigating' powers of the Commission is different in structure...

This provision does not of course prevent the Commission from carrying out an investigation solely pursuant to a written authorisation given to its officials without adopting a decision, but in other respects it contains nothing to indicate that it may only adopt a decision within the meaning of Article 14(3) if it has previously attempted to carry out an investigation by mere authorisation. *Whereas Article 11(5) expressly makes the adoption of a Commission decision subject to the condition that the latter has previously asked for the necessary information by means of a request addressed to those concerned and specifies in Article 11(3) the essentials which such a request must contain, Article 14 makes the investigating procedure by means of a decision subject to no preliminary of this kind.*

The applicant wrongly relies in support of its argument on the wording of Article 13(1) of the same regulation which provides that, at the request of the Commission, the national authorities must undertake the investigations which the Commission considers to be necessary under Article 14(1) or which it has ordered by decision pursuant to Article 14(3). By making a distinction between the two investigatory procedures, that provision clearly shows by the use of the word 'or' that those two procedures do not necessarily overlap but constitute two alternative checks the choice of which depends upon the special features of each case.

The difference in the rules on this subject contained in Articles 11 and 14 is explained, moreover, by the diversity of the needs met by those two provisions. Whereas the information which the Commission considers necessary to know may not as a general rule be collected without the cooperation of the undertakings and associations of undertakings possessing this information, investigations, on the other hand, are not necessarily subject to the same condition. In general they aim at checking, by measures such as those listed in the second subparagraph of Article 14(1) of Regulation No 17, the actual existence and scope of information which the Commission already has and do not therefore necessarily presuppose previous cooperation by undertakings or associations of undertakings in possession of the information necessary for the check.

The applicant maintains in another connection that if it were necessary to interpret Article 14 differently from Article 11, that is, as meaning that it permits the Commission to adopt an investigation decision without previously carrying out an investigation such as that provided for in Article 14(2) the Commission might, by having recourse to the procedure laid down in the same article for requests for information, escape the conditions laid down in Article 11 and thus evade the guarantees given by the latter to the undertakings and associations of undertakings concerned.

Such arguments do not however take into account the distinction made by the regulation itself between the 'information' referred to in Article 11 and the 'investigation' referred to in Article 14. *The fact that officials authorised by the Commission, in carrying out an investigation, have the power to request during that investigation information on specific questions arising from the books and business records which they examine is not sufficient to conclude that an investigation is identical to a procedure intended only to obtain information within the meaning of Article 11 of the regulation.*

For all these reasons, it is necessary to dismiss the first submission as unfounded.

Although Article 20 of Regulation No 17 deals with professional secrecy rather than legal professional privilege, the Court has accepted that certain communications with lawyers are protected from disclosure. The privilege does not extend to communications with 'in house' lawyers; it extends only to those passing between a client and an independent lawyer entitled to practise in one of the Member States. Moreover, not all exchanges between these parties are protected. The privilege is confined to written communications passing between the parties for the purposes of the client's right of defence.

Case 155/79 AM and S Europe Limited v Commission
[1982] ECR 1575; [1982] 2 CMLR 264

A.M. and S., a company based in the United Kingdom, sought the annulment of a Commission decision requiring it to produce for examination certain documents for which legal privilege was claimed. The disputed decision was based on Article 14(3) of Regulation No 17.

The Court

...

Community law, which derives from not only the economic but also the legal interpenetration of the Member States, must take into account the principles and concepts common to the laws of those States concerning the observance of confidentiality, in particular, as regards certain communications between lawyer and client. That confidentiality serves the requirement, the importance of which is recognised in all of the Member States, that any person must be able, without constraint, to consult a lawyer whose profession entails the giving of independent legal advice to all those in need of it.

As far as the protection of written communications between lawyer and client is concerned, it is apparent from the legal systems of the Member States that, although the principle of such protection is generally recognised, its scope and the criteria for applying it vary, as has, indeed, been conceded both by the applicant and by the parties who have intervened in support of its conclusions.

Whilst in some of the Member States the protection against disclosure afforded to written communications between lawyer and client is based principally on a recognition of the very nature of the legal profession, inasmuch as it contributes towards the maintenance of the rule of law, in other Member States the same protection is justified by the more specific requirement (which, moreover, is also recognised in the first-mentioned States) that the rights of the defence must be respected.

Apart from these differences, however, there are to be found in the national laws of the Member States common criteria inasmuch as *those laws protect, in similar circumstances, the confidentiality of written communications between lawyer and client provided that, on the one hand, such communications are made for the purposes and in the interests of the client's right of defence and, on the other hand, they emanate from independent lawyers, that is to say, lawyers who are not bound to the client by a relationship of employment*.

Viewed in that context *Regulation No 17 must be interpreted as protecting, in its turn, the confidentiality of written communications between lawyer and client subject to those two conditions,* and thus incorporating such elements of that protection as are common to the laws of the Member States.

As far as the first of those two conditions is concerned, in Regulation No 17 itself, in particular in the eleventh recital in its preamble and in the provisions contained in Article 19, care is taken to ensure that the rights of the defence may be exercised to the full, and the protection of the confidentiality of written communications between lawyer and client is an essential corollary to those rights. In those circumstances, such protection must, if it is to be effective, be recognised as covering all written communications exchanged after the initiation of the administrative procedure under Regulation No 17 which may lead to a decision on the application of Articles 85 and 86 of the Treaty or to a decision imposing a pecuniary sanction on the undertaking. It must also be possible to extend it to earlier written communications which have a relationship to the subject-matter of that procedure.

As regards the second condition, it should be stated that the requirement as to the position and status as an independent lawyer, which must be fulfilled by the legal adviser from whom the written communications which may be protected emanate, is based on a conception of the lawyer's role as collaborating in the administration of justice by the courts and as being required to provide, in full independence, and in the overriding interests of that cause, such legal assistance as the client needs. The counterpart of that protection lies in the rules of professional ethics and discipline which are laid down and enforced in the general interest by institutions endowed with the requisite powers for that purpose. Such a conception reflects the legal traditions common to the Member States and is also to be found in legal order of the Community, as is demonstrated by Article 17 of the Protocols on the Statutes of the Court of Justice of the EEC and the EAEC, and also by Article 20 of the Protocol on the Statute of the Court of Justice of the ECSC.

Having regard to the principles of the Treaty concerning freedom of establishment and the freedom to provide services the protection thus afforded by Community law, in particular in the context of Regulation No 17, to written communications between lawyer and client must apply without distinction to any lawyer entitled to practise his profession in one of the Member States, regardless of the Member State in which the client lives.

Such protection may not be extended beyond those limits, which are determined by the scope of the common rules on the exercise of the legal profession as laid down in Council Directive No 77/249/EEC of 22 March 1977 (OJ L 78, p. 17), which is based in its turn on the mutual recognition by all the Member States of the national legal concepts of each of them on this subject.

In view of all these factors it must therefore be concluded that although Regulation No 17, and in particular Article 14 thereof, interpreted in the light of its wording, structure and aims, and having regard to the laws of the Member States, empowers the Commission to require, in the course of an investigation within the meaning of that article, production of the business documents the disclosure of which it considers necessary, including written communications between lawyer and client, for proceedings in respect of any infringements of Articles 85 and 86 of the Treaty, that power is, however, subject to a restriction imposed by the need to protect confidentiality, on the conditions defined above, and provided that the communications in question are exchanged between an independent lawyer, that is to say one who is not bound to his client by a relationship of employment, and his client.

Finally, it should be remarked that the principle of confidentiality does not prevent a lawyer's client from disclosing the written communications between them if he considers that it is in his interests to do so.

The Court then addressed itself to the procedures relating to the principle of confidentiality. It ruled that the Commission rather than the national courts must determine whether the production of documents is compatible with the principle of legal privilege. The Commission's decisions in this regard are, of course, subject to review by the Court of Justice.

II STATEMENTS OF OBJECTIONS AND HEARINGS

Regulation No 17 provides that the Commission is to give persons concerned the opportunity of being heard before any decision is taken. The conduct of hearings is governed by a regulation of 1963.

Council Regulation No 17 of 6 February 1962 implementing Articles 85 and 86 of the EEC Treaty OJ Sp Ed 1959–62 87

Article 19

Hearing of the Parties and of Third Persons

1. Before taking decisions as provided for in Articles 2, 3, 6, 7, 8, 15 and 16, the Commission shall give the undertakings or associations of undertakings concerned the opportunity of being heard on the matters to which the Commission has taken objection.

2. If the Commission or the competent authorities of the Member States consider it necessary, they may also hear other natural or legal persons. Applications to be heard on the part of such persons shall, where they show a sufficient interest, be granted.

3. Where the Commission intends to give negative clearance pursuant to Article 2 or take a decision in application of Article 85(3) of the Treaty, it shall publish a summary of the relevant application or notification and invite all interested third parties to submit their observations within a time limit which it shall fix being not less than one month. Publication shall have regard to the legitimate interest of undertakings in the protection of their business secrets.

Commission Regulation No 99/63 of 25 July 1963 on the hearings provided for in Article 19 of Council Regulation No 17

OJ Sp Ed 1963–64 47

Article 1

Before consulting the Advisory Committee on Restrictive Practices and Monopolies, the Commission shall hold a hearing pursuant to Article 19(1) of Regulation No 17.

Article 2

1. The Commission shall inform undertakings and associations of undertakings in writing of the objections raised against them. The communication shall be addressed to each of them or to a joint agent appointed by them.

2. The Commission may inform the parties by giving notice in the *Official Journal of the European Communities*, if from the circumstances of the case this appears appropriate, in particular where notice is to be given to a number of undertakings but no joint agent has been appointed. The notice shall have regard to the legitimate interest of the undertakings in the protection of their business secrets.

3. A fine or a periodic penalty payment may be imposed on an undertaking or association of undertakings only if the objections were notified in the manner provided for in paragraph 1.

4. The Commission shall when giving notice of objections fix a time limit up to which the undertakings and associations of undertakings may inform the Commission of their views.

Article 3

1. Undertakings and associations of undertakings shall, within the appointed time limit, make known in writing their views concerning the objections raised against them.

2. They may in their written comments set out all matters relevant to their defence.

3. They may attach any relevant documents in proof of the facts set out. They may also propose that the Commission hear persons who may corroborate those facts.

Article 4

The Commission shall in its decisions deal only with those objections raised against undertakings and associations of undertakings in respect of which they have been afforded the opportunity of making known their views.

Article 5

If natural or legal persons showing a sufficient interest apply to be heard pursuant to Article 19(2) of Regulation No 17, the Commission shall afford them the opportunity of making known their views in writing within such time limit as it shall fix.

Article 6

Where the Commission, having received an application pursuant to Article 3(2) of Regulation No 17, considers that on the basis of the information in its possession there are insufficient grounds for granting the application, it shall inform the applicants of its reasons and fix a time limit for them to submit any further comments in writing.

Article 7

1. The Commission shall afford to persons who have so requested in their written comments the opportunity to put forward their arguments orally, if those persons show a sufficient interest or if the Commission proposes to impose on them a fine or periodic penalty payment.

2. The Commission may likewise afford to any other person the opportunity of orally expressing his views.

Article 8

1. The Commission shall summon the persons to be heard to attend on such date as it shall appoint.

2. It shall forthwith transmit a copy of the summons to the competent authorities of the Member States, who may appoint an official to take part in the hearing.

Article 9

1. Hearings shall be conducted by the persons appointed by the Commission for that purpose.

2. Persons summoned to attend shall appear either in person or be represented by legal representatives or by representatives authorised by their constitution. Undertakings and associations of undertakings may moreover be represented by a duly authorised agent appointed from among their permanent staff.

Persons heard by the Commission may be assisted by lawyers or university teachers who are entitled to plead before the Court of Justice of the European Communities in accordance with Article 17 of the Protocol on the Statute of the Court, or by other qualified persons.

3. Hearings shall not be public. Persons shall be heard separately or in the presence of other persons summoned to attend. In the latter case, regard shall be had to the legitimate interest of the undertakings in the protection of their business secrets.

4. The essential content of the statements made by each person heard shall be recorded in minutes which shall be read and approved by him.

Article 10

Without prejudice to Article 2(2), information and summonses from the Commission shall be sent to the addressees by registered letter with acknowledgement of receipt, or shall be delivered by hand against receipt.

Article 11

1. In fixing the time limits provided for in Articles 2, 5 and 6, the Commission shall have regard both to the time required for preparation of comments and to the urgency of the case. The time limit shall be not less than two weeks; it may be extended.

2. Time limits shall run from the day following receipt of a communication or delivery thereof by hand.

3. Written comments must reach the Commission or be dispatched by registered letter before expiry of the time limit. Where the time limit would expire on a Sunday or public holiday, it shall be extended up to the end of the next following working day. For the purpose of calculating this extension, public holidays shall, in cases where the relevant date is the date of receipt of written comments, be those set out in the Annex to this regulation, and in cases where the relevant date is the date of dispatch, those appointed by law in the country of dispatch.

The first stage in the process of enabling the appropriate persons to be heard is the issuance of a statement of objections pursuant to Article 2(4) of Commission Regulation No 99/63. (The antecedent decision of the Commission to initiate a procedure is not an 'act' susceptible of review under Article 173 of the EEC Treaty: see Case 60/81 *IBM* v *Commission* [1981] ECR 2639; [1981] 3 CMLR 635, p. 99 above).

The statement of objections crystallises the Commission's objections. It need not set out all the facts but only those on which the Commission relies in its final decision: Case 107/82 *AEG* v *Commission* [1983] ECR 3151; [1984] 3 CMLR 325. A decision made by the Commission is void, however, if it imposes on the addressee an obligation which was not foreshadowed in the statement of objections.

Case 17/74 Transocean Marine Paint Association v Commission
[1974] ECR 1063; [1974] 2 CMLR 459

The Court

By Decision of 21 December 1973 the Commission, pursuant to Article 85(3) of the EEC Treaty, renewed, subject to new conditions, the exemption from the prohibition contained in Article 85(1), which had been granted, by Decision of 27 June 1967, to an agreement restricting competition on the market in marine paints, concluded between the undertakings constituting the Transocean Marine Paint Association (hereinafter referred to as the Association).

Inter alia, Article 3(1)(d) of the decision requires members of the Association to inform the Commission without delay of 'any links by way of common directors or managers between a member of the Association and any other company or firm in the paints sector or any financial participation by a member of the Association in such outside companies or *vice versa* including all changes in such links or participations already in existence'.

This action has been brought for the purpose of annulling that single provision.

The applicants first state that the obligation in issue was mentioned neither in the 'notice of objections' of 27 July 1973, nor at the time of the hearing on 27 September 1973, and that furthermore it was not mentioned in any letter or memorandum from the Commission, prior to the decision, so that they were never given the opportunity to make their views known on this subject. Accordingly, as regards the clause in issue, the Commission is said to have infringed rules of procedure laid down by Regulation No 99/63 of the Commission of 25 July 1963 ... on the hearings provided for in Article 19 of Regulation No 17 of the Council of 6 February 1962 ... and in particular Articles 2 and 4 of the said Regulation No 99/63.

Secondly, the applicants allege an infringement of Article 85 of the Treaty and of Article 8(1) of Regulation No 17, in that the obligation imposed upon the undertakings is wider in scope than anything which may be imposed upon them under Article 85.

In a communication of 27 July 1973 entitled 'notice of objections', drawn up in Dutch, the Commission stated that a simple renewal of the exemption could not be envisaged, since the position of the members of the Association on the marine paints market had changed as a result of the increase in the number of undertakings composing the Association, the increased size of certain of them and the links which two of the members, Astral and Urruzola, had forged with large industrial chemical concerns.

The Commission added that it was nevertheless willing to renew the exemption for a period of five years, but at the same time making it subject to fresh conditions and obligations, one of which was formulated so as to involve, for the members of the Association, apart from the obligations contained in Article 4 of the Decision of 27 June 1967, the further obligation to notify to the Commission without delay 'iedere wijziging in de deelnemingsverhoudingen van de leden' (literally: any change in the participatory relationships of the members).

The applicants claim that at no time could they infer from this statement that the Commission intended to impose on them a condition such as that contained in the provision in issue, and one to which they would not be able, by reason of its breadth, to adhere and which, without good reason, would harm their interests. If they had been in a position to realise the Commission's intentions they would not have failed to make known their objections on this matter so as to draw the Commission's attention to the inconvenience which would result from the obligation in issue and to the illegality by which it is vitiated. Since they were not given this opportunity, they allege that the decision, insofar as the obligation in issue is concerned, must be annulled since it is vitiated by a procedural defect.

...

According to Article 19 of Regulation No 17 of the Council, the Commission, before taking decisions as provided for in Articles 2, 3, 6, 7, 8, 15 and 16 of that regulation, shall give the undertakings or associations of undertakings concerned the opportunity of being heard on the matters to which the Commission has taken objection. In referring to Article 6, this provision relates to decisions taken pursuant to a request for the application of Article 85(3).

According to Article 24 of the same regulation the Commission shall have power to adopt implementing provisions in this context, which it did in Regulation No 99/63.

It is clear from both the title and from the first recital of this regulation that it is concerned with all the hearings provided for in Article 19 of Regulation No 17 of the Council and, accordingly, also applies to procedures with regard to Article 85(3). However, the obligation imposed upon the Commission by Articles 2 and 4 of Regulation No 99/63 to inform an undertaking, in writing or by giving notice in the Official Journal, of the objections raised against it and to deal, in its decisions, only with these objections, is essentially concerned with the statement of the reasons which would lead it to apply paragraph 1 of Article 85, either by ordering that an infringement be terminated or imposing a fine upon the undertakings, or by refusing to give the latter negative clearance or the benefit of paragraph 3 of the same provision.

On the other hand, the Commission cannot be expected to anticipate the conditions and obligations to which it is entitled to subject the exemption laid down in Article 85(3). In fact, the investigation of a request for exemption may bring to light various ways in which the operation of an agreement or the control of that operation may be undertaken, this prompting the Commission to withdraw the objections which it had raised against the request and justifying the grant, possibly subject to certain conditions, of the benefit of Article 85(3).

It is clear, however, both from the nature and objective of the procedure for hearings, and from Articles 5, 6 and 7 of Regulation No 99/63, that this regulation, notwithstanding the cases specifically dealt with in Articles 2 and 4, applies the general rule that a person whose interests are perceptibly affected by a decision taken by a public authority must be given the opportunity to make his point of view known. This rule requires than an undertaking be clearly informed, in good time, of the essence of conditions to which the Commission intends to subject an exemption and it must have the opportunity to submit its observations to the Commission. This is especially so in the case of conditions which, as in this case, impose considerable obligations having far-reaching effects.

Since Article 85(3) constitutes, for the benefit of undertakings, an exception to the general prohibition contained in Article 85(1) the Commission must be in a position at any moment to check whether the conditions justifying the exemption are still present. Accordingly, in relation to the detailed rules to which it may subject the exemption, the Commission enjoys a large measure of discretion, while at the same time having to act within the limits imposed upon its competence by Article 85. On the other hand, the exercise of this discretionary power is linked to a preliminary canvassing of objections which may be raised by the undertakings.

It is clear from the file that this requirement was not fulfilled in respect of the obligation in issue.

...

Accordingly, the condition stated in Article 3(1)(d) of the decision was imposed in breach of procedural requirements and the Commission must be given the opportunity to reach a fresh decision on this point after hearing the observations or suggestions of the members of the Association.

In accordance with Article 7 of Commission Regulation No 99/63, an oral hearing must be held if a request is made by a person showing a sufficient interest. Hearings are conducted in private; and in the interests of commercial secrecy, complaints and other witnesses may be heard separately. The Commission is under no obligation to disclose to the parties the whole of its file, but only those documents on which it proposes to rely.

Joined Cases 43 and 63/82 VBVB and VBBB v Commission
[1984] ECR 19; [1985] 1 CMLR 27

VBVB was a Flemish association of publishers and booksellers. VBBB was a corresponding Dutch association. They concluded an agreement involving restrictions on competition in books. They notified the agreement to the Commission, requesting a declaration of inapplicability, or alternatively exemption pursuant to Article 85(3). After delivering a statement of objections and conducting a hearing, the Commission made a decision refusing to accede to the associations' request. The associations challenged the decision on the ground, among others, that the Commission failed at the hearing to disclose its administrative file.

The Court

...the Flemish association claims that the Commission did not give it access to the administrative file and that it was therefore unable to take cognisance of certain documents or studies used by the Commission for the purposes of its decision.

It may be noted that the Flemish association was not in a position to identify any document which might have been used by the Commission as a basis for its decision but which is not accessible to the applicant. Its complaint therefore seems rather to relate to the fact that it has not had the opportunity to inspect the Commission's file with a view to determining whether it might possibly contain documents in which it might be interested.

In that connection it must be observed that although regard for the rights of the defence requires that the undertaking concerned shall have been enabled to make known effectively its point of view on the documents relied upon by the Commission in making the findings on which its decision is based, there are no provisions which require the Commission to divulge the contents of its files to the parties concerned. It does not appear in fact that the Commission has made use of any document which was not available to the parties and on which they have not had the opportunity to make their views known. This submission also must therefore be dismissed.

After hearing the views of the parties the Commission must consult the Advisory Committee on Restrictive Practices and Monopolies, which is composed of one official from each Member State. The Advisory Committee's deliberations are not made public. Having consulted the Committee, the Commission may make its decision.

III DECISIONS AND COMFORT LETTERS

The Commission's decision may take the form of a 'negative clearance' or an exemption or it may embody a requirement that one or more undertakings must terminate an infringement of the Treaty; alternatively, where circumstances permit, the decision may require parties to modify an existing agreement to ensure that it does not infringe Article 85(1). In any of these instances the decision must be published.

Council Regulation No 17 of 6 February 1962 implementing Articles 85 and 86 of the EEC Treaty OJ Sp Ed 1959–62 87

Article 2

Negative Clearance

Upon application by the undertakings or associations of undertakings concerned, the Commission may certify that, on the basis of the facts in its possession, there are no grounds under Article 85(1) or Article 86 of the Treaty for action on its part in respect of an agreement, decision or practice.

Article 3

Termination of Infringements

1. Where the Commission, upon application or upon its own initiative, finds that there is infringement of Article 85 or Article 86 of the Treaty, it may by decision require the undertakings or associations of undertakings concerned to bring such infringement to an end.

2. Those entitled to make application are:

(a) Member States;

(b) natural or legal persons who claim a legitimate interest.

3. Without prejudice to the other provisions of this regulation, the Commission may, before taking a decision under paragraph 1, address to the undertaking or associations of undertakings concerned recommendations for termination of the infringement.

...

Article 6

Decisions pursuant to Article 85(3)

1. Whenever the Commission takes a decision pursuant to Article 85(3) of the Treaty, it shall specify therein the date from which the decision shall take effect. Such date shall not be earlier than the date of notification.

2 The second sentence of paragraph 1 shall not apply to agreements, decisions or concerted practices falling within Article 4(2) and Article 5(2), nor to those falling within Article 5(1) which have been notified within the time limit specified in Article 5(1).

Article 7

Special Provisions for Existing Agreements, Decisions and Practices

1. Where agreements, decisions and concerted practices in existence at the date of entry into force of this regulation and notified before 1 August 1962 do not satisfy the requirements of Article 85(3) of the Treaty and the undertakings or associations of undertakings concerned cease to give effect to them or modify them in such manner that they no longer fall within the prohibition contained in Article 85(1) or that they satisfy the requirements of Article 85(3), the prohibition contained in Article 85(1) shall apply only for a period fixed by the Commission. A decision by the Commission pursuant to the foregoing sentence shall not apply as against undertakings and associations of undertakings which did not expressly consent to the notification.

2 Paragraph 1 shall apply to agreements, decisions and concerted practices falling within Article 4(2) which are in existence at the date of entry into force of this regulation if they are notified before 1 January 1964.

Article 8

Duration and Revocation of Decisions under Article 85(3)

1. A decision in application of Article 85(3) of the Treaty shall be issued for a specified period and conditions and obligations may be attached thereto.

2. A decision may on application be renewed if the requirements of Article 85(3) of the Treaty continue to be satisfied.

3. The Commission may revoke or amend its decision or prohibit specified acts by the parties:

(a) where there has been a change in any of the facts which were basic to the making of the decision;
(b) where the parties commit a breach of any obligation attached to the decision;
(c) where the decision is based on incorrect information or was induced by deceit;
(d) where the parties abuse the exemption from the provisions of Article 85(1) of the Treaty granted to them by the decision.

In cases to which subparagraphs (b), (c) or (d) apply, the decision may be revoked with retroactive effect.

...

Article 21
Publication of Decisions

1. The Commission shall publish the decisions which it takes pursuant to Articles 2, 3, 6, 7 and 8.

2. The publication shall state the names of the parties and the main content of the decision; it shall have regard to the legitimate interest of undertakings in the protection of their business secrets.

Instead of reaching a formal decision pursuant to Article 85(3) granting an exemption to an undertaking, the Commission may write a simple letter known as a 'comfort letter' indicating that it sees no need to take action. There is no duty to publish such a letter and most are not published. Issuance of a comfort letter does not preclude a national court from declaring the agreement in question void; but it may take account of the letter. Moreover, having issued such a letter the Commission is precluded from imposing a fine on the addressee for breach of Article 85(1); indeed, the Commission cannot alter the position to which it has committed itself in the absence of a change of circumstances.

Case 31/80 NV L'Oréal and SA L'Oréal v Pvba De Nieuwe AMCK
[1980] ECR 3775; [1981] 2 CMLR 235

L'Oréal established a selective distribution system in Belgium for their hair-care products. De Nieuwe AMCK was not part of the selective distribution system. Nevertheless it offered for sale certain of L'Oréal's hair-care products. L'Oréal brought proceedings against De Nieuwe AMCK alleging breach of Belgian fair trading law. The defendant contended that the selective distribution system was illegal as being contrary to Article 85(1). In reply L'Oréal relied upon a letter sent to that company by the Commission's Directorate-General for Competition expressing the view that there was no need to intervene under Article 85(1). The

Belgian court asked the Court of Justice to rule on the question, among others, whether such a letter is binding.

The Court

It is plain that a letter such as that sent to the L'Oréal company by the Directorate-General for Competition, which was despatched without publication as laid down in Article 19(3) of Regulation No 17 and which was not published pursuant to Article 21(1) of that regulation, constitutes neither a decision granting negative clearance nor a decision in application of Article 85(3) within the meaning of Articles 2 and 6 of Regulation No 17. As is stressed by the Commission itself it is merely an administrative letter informing the undertaking concerned of the Commission's opinion that there is no need for it to take action in respect of the contracts in question under the provisions of Article 85(1) of the Treaty and that the file on the case may therefore be closed.

Such a letter, which is based only upon the facts in the Commission's possession, and which reflects the Commission's assessment and brings to an end the procedure of examination by the department of the Commission responsible for this, does not have the effect of preventing national courts, before which the agreements in question are alleged to be incompatible with Article 85, from reaching a different finding as regards the agreements concerned on the basis of the information available to them. Whilst it does not bind the national courts, the opinion transmitted in such a letter nevertheless constitutes a factor which the national courts may take into account in considering whether the agreements or conduct in question are in accordance with the provisions of Article 85.

Consequently, it must be stated in reply to the second question that a letter signed by an official of the Commission indicating that there is no reason for the Commission to take action pursuant to Article 85(1) of the EEC Treaty against a distribution system which has been notified to it, may not be relied upon against third parties and is not binding on the national courts. It merely constitutes an element of the fact of which the national courts may take account in considering the compatibility of the system in question with Community law.

IV FINES

Council Regulation No 17 of 6 February 1962 implementing Articles 85 and 86 of the EEC Treaty OJ Sp Ed 1959–62 87

Article 15

Fines

1. The Commission may by decision impose on undertakings or associations of undertakings fines of from 100 to 5000 units of account where, intentionally or negligently:

(a) they supply incorrect or misleading information in an application pursuant to Article 2 or in a notification pursuant to Articles 4 or 5; or

(b) they supply incorrect information in response to a request made pursuant to Article 11(3) or (5) or to Article 12, or do not supply information within the time limit fixed by a decision taken under Article 11(5); or

(c) they produce the required books or other business records in incomplete form during investigations under Article 13 or 14, or refuse to submit to an investigation ordered by decision issued in implementation of Article 14(3).

2. The Commission may by decision impose on undertakings or associations of undertakings fines of from 1,000 to 1,000,000 units of account, or a sum in excess thereof but not exceeding 10% of the turnover in the preceding business year of each of the undertakings participating in the infringement where, either intentionally or negligently:

(a) they infringe Article 85(1) or Article 86 of the Treaty; or

(b) they commit a breach of any obligation imposed pursuant to Article 8(1).

In fixing the amount of the fine, regard shall be had both to the gravity and to the duration of the infringement.

3. Article 10(3) to (6) shall apply.

4. Decisions taken pursuant to paragraphs 1 and 2 shall not be of a criminal law nature.

5. The fines provided for in paragraph 2(a) shall not be imposed in respect of acts taking place:

(a) after notification to the Commission and before its decision in application of Article 85(3) of the Treaty, provided they fall within the limits of the activity described in the notification;

(b) before notification and in the course of agreements, decisions or concerted practices in existence at the date of entry into force of this regulation, provided that notification was effected within the time limits specified in Article 5(1) and Article 7(2).

6. Paragraph 5 shall not have effect where the Commission has informed the undertakings concerned that after preliminary examination it is of the opinion that Article 85(1) of the Treaty applies and that application of Article 85(3) is not justified.

Article 16

Periodic Penalty Payments

1. The Commission may by decision impose on undertakings or associations of undertakings periodic penalty payments of from 50 to 1,000 units of account per day, calculated from the date appointed by the decision, in order to compel them:

(a) to put an end to an infringement of Articles 85 or 86 of the Treaty, in accordance with a decision taken pursuant to Article 3 of this regulation;

(b) to refrain from any act prohibited under Article 8(3);

(c) to supply complete and correct information which it has requested by decision taken pursuant to Article 11(5);

(d) to submit to an investigation which it has ordered by decision taken pursuant to Article 14(3).

2. Where the undertakings or associations of undertakings have satisfied the obligation which it was the purpose of the periodic penalty payment to enforce, the Commission may fix the total amount of the periodic penalty payment at a lower figure than that which would arise under the original decision.

3. Article 10(3) to (6) shall apply.

[See below p. 482].

Article 18
Unit of Account

For the purposes of applying Articles 15 to 17 the unit of account shall be that adopted in drawing up the budget of the Community in accordance with Articles 207 and 209 of the Treaty.

The Court of Justice has unlimited jurisdiction to review decisions whereby fines or periodic penalties are imposed. Consequently it can replace the fine fixed by the Commission by a fine of a different amount.

Article 17
Review by the Court of Justice

The Court of Justice shall have unlimited jurisdiction within the meaning of Article 172 of the Treaty to review decisions whereby the Commission has fixed a fine or periodic penalty payment; it may cancel, reduce or increase the fine or periodic penalty payment imposed.

In assessing the gravity of an infringement for the purpose of imposing a fine the Commission must take into account not only the particular circumstances of the case but also the requirement of ensuring that its action has the necessary deterrent effect. The fact that it has in the past imposed relatively low rates of fine for a particular type of infringement does not preclude the Commission from imposing a significantly higher fine for an infringement of the same type, for the purposes of deterrence.

Joined Cases 100–103/80 Musique Diffusion Française SA and Others v Commission ('Pioneer') [1983] ECR 1825; [1983] 3 CMLR 221

The Commission found that Musique Diffusion Française ('MDF') and Pioneer Electronic (Europe) N.V. had engaged in two concerted practices, one with Melchers and Co., and the other with Pioneer High Fidelity (GB) Ltd, to prevent parallel imports of Pioneer high fidelity equipment to France from Germany and from the United Kingdom. The Commission imposed fines of 850,000 units of account on MDF, 4,350,000 units of account on Pioneer Electronic (Europe) N.V., 1,450,000 units of account on Melchers and 300,000 units of account on Pioneer (GB). All four companies challenged the decision. After dealing meticulously with the evidence on concerted practices, the Court concluded that this was sufficient to warrant the contested decisions, save in one respect: the Commission had erroneously concluded that there was evidence of the continuation of the practice beyond late January 1976. To that extent the decision was void. The Court then addressed the size of the fines.

The Court

...

The applicants maintain that, in fixing the amounts of the fines, the Commission failed to observe the last subparagraph of Article 15(2) of Regulation No 17, which provides that regard shall be had both to the gravity and to the duration of the infringement. According to the applicants, the Commission did not base itself on the gravity of their conduct nor on its duration.

...

In that connection it must be remembered that the Commission's power to impose fines on undertakings which, intentionally or negligently, commit an infringement of the provisions of Articles 85(1) or 86 of the Treaty is one of the means conferred on the Commission in order to enable it to carry out the task of supervision conferred on it by Community law. That task certainly includes the duty to investigate and punish individual infringements, but it also encompasses the duty to pursue a general policy designed to apply, in competition matters, the principles laid down by the Treaty and to guide the conduct of undertakings in the light of those principles.

It follows that, in assessing the gravity of an infringement for the purpose of fixing the amount of the fine, the Commission must take into consideration not only the particular circumstances of the case but also the context in which the infringement occurs and must ensure that its action has the necessary deterrent effect, especially as regards those types of infringement which are particularly harmful to the attainment of the objectives of the Community.

From that point of view, the Commission was right to classify as very serious infringements prohibitions on exports and imports seeking artificially to maintain price differences between the markets of the various Member States. Such prohibitions jeopardise the freedom of intra-Community trade, which is a fundamental principle of the Treaty, and they prevent the attainment of one of its objectives, namely the creation of a single market.

It was also open to the Commission to have regard to the fact that practices of this nature, although they were established as being unlawful at the outset of Community competition policy, are still relatively frequent on account of the profit that certain of the undertakings concerned are able to derive from them and, consequently, it was open to the Commission to consider that it was appropriate to raise the level of fines so as to reinforce their deterrent effect.

For the same reasons, the fact that the Commission, in the past, imposed fines of a certain level for certain types of infringement does not mean that it is estopped from raising that level within the limits indicated in Regulation No 17 if that is necessary to ensure the implementation of Community competition policy. On the contrary, the proper application of the Community competition rules requires that the Commission may at any time adjust the levels of fines to the needs of that policy.

The submission must therefore be rejected.

...

Melchers claims that it is unlawful to fix the fines in proportion to the undertaking's turnover, as the Commission has done in the present cases. It argues that turnover in fact gives no indication of the profitability of the undertaking or of its ability to pay a fine.

In any event, Melchers, MDF and Pioneer claim that the fine cannot be calculated, as the Commission has done in the present case, on the basis of the total turnover of the undertaking, since the goods in respect of which the infringement was committed represent only a part of that turnover.

Pioneer argues that the fine imposed on it must be reduced because the turnover on which the Commission based its calculations also related to sales of hi-fi equipment to countries not affected by the infringement.

According to Melchers, the Commission ought to have taken into consideration the fact that only about 10% of its turnover related to hi-fi products, whilst in the case of the other applicants those products accounted for the whole of their turnover. Melchers added that, in fixing the ceiling for fines at 10% of the turnover, Article 15(2) of Regulation No 17 refers to the turnover in the sector in which the infringement was committed. Because the Commission did not observe this method of calculation, the fine imposed on Melchers amounts to 18% of its turnover on the hi-fi market, thus exceeding the limit fixed by the aforementioned provision.

...

Under the terms of Article 15(2) of Regulation No 17, the Commission may impose fines of from 1,000 to 1,000,000 units of account or a sum in excess thereof but not exceeding 10% of the turnover in the preceding business year of each of the undertakings participating in the infringement. Article 15(2) provides that in fixing the amount of the fine within those limits the gravity and the duration of the infringement are to be taken into consideration.

Thus the only express reference to the turnover of the undertaking concerns the upper limit of a fine exceeding 1,000,000 units of account. In such a case the limit seeks to prevent fines from being disproportionate in relation to the size of the undertaking and, since only the total turnover can effectively give an approximate indication of that size, the aforementioned percentage must, as the Commission has argued, be understood as referring to the total turnover. It follows that the Commission did not exceed the limit laid down in Article 15 of the regulation.

In assessing the gravity of an infringement regard must be had to a large number of factors, the nature and importance of which vary according to the type of infringement in question and the particular circumstances of the case. Those factors may, depending on the circumstances, include the volume and value of the goods in respect of which the infringement was committed and the size and economic power of the undertaking and, consequently, the influence which the undertaking was able to exert on the market.

It follows that, on the one hand, it is permissible, for the purpose of fixing the fine, to have regard both to the total turnover of the undertaking, which gives an indication, albeit approximate and imperfect, of the size of the undertaking and of its economic power, and to the proportion of that turnover accounted for by the goods in respect of which the infringement was committed, which gives an indication of the scale of the infringement. On the other hand, it follows that it is important not to confer on one or the other of those figures an importance disproportionate in relation to the other factors and, consequently, that the fixing of an appropriate fine cannot be the result of a simple calculation based on the total turnover. That is particularly the case where the goods concerned account for only a small part of that figure. It is appropriate for the Court to bear in mind those considerations in its assessment, by virtue of its powers of unlimited jurisdiction, of the gravity of the infringements in question.

...

In fixing the amount of the fines regard must be had to the duration of the infringements established and to all the factors capable of affecting the assessment of the gravity of the infringements, such as conduct of each of the undertakings, the role played by each of them in the establishment of the concerted practices, the profit which they were able to derive from those practices, their size, the value of the goods concerned and the threat that infringements of that type pose to the objectives of the Community.

...

On the basis of all those considerations and regard being had to the particular circumstances of each of the undertakings, the fines should be fixed as follows.

As regards Pioneer, regard must be had particularly to the central position which that undertaking occupies in the distribution network of the products in question, which enabled it to play the role of intermediary in exerting considerable influence on the conduct of national distributors. In respect of that undertaking the fine should be fixed at 2,000,000 units of account, that is to say BFR 80,679,000.

In the case of MDF, which was the instigator and essential beneficiary of the two concerted practices, a fine of 600,000 units of account, that is to say FF 3,488,892, should be imposed.

As a result of the partial nullity of the contested decision there is no difference between the duration of the two concerted practices in which Melchers and Shriro (now Pioneer GB) were involved. To establish the relationship between the fines to be imposed on those two undertakings regard must be had in particular to the fact that Shriro was entirely dependent on Pioneer in the pursuit of its activities, whereas Melchers, as a result of the diversity of its activities, of which the sale of Pioneer products constituted only a small part, could more easily have resisted the pressure exerted upon it. Regard being had also to all the other circumstances of the cases, the fine to be imposed on Melchers should be fixed at 400,000 units of account, that is to say DM 992,184, and the fine to be imposed on Pioneer GB should be fixed at 200,000 units of account, that is to say UK£ 129,950.

V THE ROLE OF NATIONAL AUTHORITIES

Regulation No 17 deals expressly with the allocation of powers between Commission and Member States and with liaison between national and Community authorities: but it leaves untouched the question whether a breach of Articles 85 or 86 gives rise to damages in an action before a national court. That question has to be resolved by national law, in the light of the wording, function and nature of Articles 85 and 86.

Council Regulation No 17 of 6 February 1962 implementing Articles 85 and 86 of the EEC Treaty OJ Sp Ed 1959–62 87

Article 9

Powers

1. Subject to review of its decision by the Court of Justice, the Commission shall have sole power to declare Article 85(1) inapplicable pursuant to Article 85(3) of the Treaty.

2. The Commission shall have power to apply Article 85(1) and Article 86 of the Treaty; this power may be exercised notwithstanding that the time limits specified in Article 5(1) and in Article 7(2) relating to notification have not expired.

3. As long as the Commission has not initiated any procedure under Articles 2, 3 or 6, the authorities of the Member States shall remain competent to apply Article 85(1) and Article 86 in accordance with Article 88 of the Treaty; they shall remain competent in this respect notwithstanding that the time limits specified in Article 5(1) and in Article 7(2) relating to notification have not expired.

Article 10

Liaison with the Authorities of the Member States

1. The Commission shall forthwith transmit to the competent authorities of the Member States a copy of the applications and notifications together with copies of the most important documents lodged with the Commission for the purpose of establishing the existence of infringements of Articles 85 or 86 of the Treaty or of obtaining negative clearance or a decision in application of Article 85(3).

2. The Commission shall carry out the procedure set out in paragraph 1 in close and constant liaison with the competent authorities of the Member States; such authorities shall have the right to express their views upon that procedure.

3. An Advisory Committee on Restrictive Practices and Monopolies shall be consulted prior to the taking of any decision following upon a procedure under paragraph 1, and of any decision concerning the renewal, amendment or revocation of a decision pursuant to Article 85(3) of the Treaty.

4. The Advisory Committee shall be composed of officials competent in the matter of restrictive practices and monopolies. Each Member State shall appoint an official to represent it who, if prevented from attending, may be replaced by another official.

5. The consultation shall take place at a joint meeting convened by the Commission; such meeting shall be held not earlier than fourteen days after dispatch of the notice convening it. The notice shall, in respect of each case to be examined, be accompanied by a summary of the case together with an indication of the most important documents, and a preliminary draft decision.

6. The Advisory Committee may deliver an opinion notwithstanding that some of its members or their alternates are not present. A report of the outcome of the consultative proceedings shall be annexed to the draft decision. It shall not be made public.

...

Article 23

Transitional Provisions Applicable to Decisions of Authorities of the Member States

1. Agreements, decisions and concerted practices of the kind described in Article 85(1) of the Treaty to which, before the entry into force of this regulation, the competent authority of a Member State has declared Article 85(1) to be inapplicable pursuant to Article 85(3) shall not be subject to compulsory notification under Article 5. The decision of the competent authority of the Member State shall be deemed to be a decision within the meaning of Article 6; it shall cease to be valid upon expiration of the period fixed by such authority but in any event not more than three years after the entry in force of this regulation. Article 8(3) shall apply.

2. Applications for renewal of decisions of the kind described in paragraph 1 shall be decided upon by the Commission in accordance with Article 8(2).

In the *Garden Cottage Foods* case the House of Lords indicated that an abuse of a dominant position contrary to Article 86 of the EEC Treaty, which causes damage to an individual citizen, gives rise to a cause of action in English law for breach of statutory duty. Although this decision was reached only in a preliminary issue, and although Lord Wilberforce dissented, it appears to constitute very persuasive authority. (The decision is to be contrasted with that in *Bourgoin and Others* v *Ministry of Agriculture*, which turned on Article 30 of the EEC Treaty; see p. 150 above.)

Garden Cottage Foods Ltd v **Milk Marketing Board**
[1984] AC 130; [1983] 2 All ER 770

The defendants ceased supplying bulk butter to the plaintiffs, who sought an injunction to compel them to resume supplies. Parker J refused to grant the injunction on the ground (among others) that damages would be a convenient alternative remedy. His judgment was overturned by the Court of Appeal but restored by the House of Lords.

Lord Diplock

...

My Lords, in the light (a) of the uniform jurisprudence of the Court of Justice of the European Communities, of which it is sufficient to mention the *Belgische Radio* case (Case 127/73 [1974] ECR 51) and the subsequent case of *Rewe-Zentralfinanz eG* v *Landwirtschaftskammer für das Saarland* Case 33/76 [1976] ECR 1989, which was to the same effect as respects the duty of national courts to protect rights conferred on individual citizens by directly applicable provisions of the Treaty, and (b) of Sections 2(1) and 3(1) of the European Communities Act 1972, I, for my own part, find it difficult to see how it can ultimately be successfully argued, as the Board will seek to do, that a contravention of Article 86 which causes damage to an individual citizen does not give rise to a cause of action in English law of the nature of a cause of action for breach of statutory duty; but since it cannot be regarded as unarguable that is not a matter for final decision by your Lordships at the interlocutory stage that the instant case has reached. What, with great respect to those who think otherwise, I *do* regard as quite unarguable is the proposition, advanced by the Court of Appeal itself but disclaimed by both parties to the action, that, if such a contravention of Article 86 gives rise to any cause of action at all, it gives rise to a cause of action for which there is no remedy in damages to compensate for loss already caused by that contravention but only a remedy by way of injunction to prevent future loss being caused. A cause of action to which an unlawful act by the defendant causing pecuniary loss to the plaintiff gives rise, if it possessed those characteristics as respects the remedies available, would be one which, so far as my understanding goes, is unknown in English private law, at any rate since 1875 when the jurisdiction conferred on the Court of Chancery by Lord Cairns' Act, the Chancery Amendment Act 1858, passed to the High Court. I leave aside as irrelevant for present purposes injunctions granted in matrimonial causes or wardship proceedings which may have no connection with pecuniary loss. I likewise leave out of account injunctions obtainable as remedies in public law whether on application for judicial review or in an action brought by the Attorney General *ex officio* or *ex relatione* some private individual. It is private law, not public law, to which the company has had recourse. In its action it claims damages as well as an injunction. No reasons are to be found in any of the judgements of the Court of Appeal and none has been advanced at the hearing before your Lordships why in law, in logic or in justice, if contravention of Article 86 of the EEC Treaty is capable of giving rise to a cause of action in English private law at all, there is any need to invent a cause of action with characteristics that are wholly novel as respects the remedies that it attracts, in order to deal with breaches of articles of the EEC Treaty which have in the United Kingdom the same effect as statutes.

The notion that it is seriously arguable that a contravention of Article 86 may give rise to a cause of action possessing such unique characteristics appears to have been based on a misunderstanding by the Court of Appeal of a cautionary obiter dictum of Roskill LJ in *Valor International Ltd* v *Application des Gaz SA* [1978] 3 CMLR 87. In a previous decision of the Court of Appeal, *Application des Gaz SA* v *Falks Veritas Ltd* [1974] 3 All ER 51 at 58, [1974] Ch 381 at 396, Lord Denning MR had stated: 'Articles 85 and 86 are part of our law. They create new torts or wrongs'. The issue in that case, however, which was one for breach of copyright in a drawing of a tin for holding liquid gas, was whether a defendant could plead breaches by the plaintiff of Article 85 or Article 86 as a defence to the plaintiff's claim. The court was unanimous in holding that the defendant could so plead but only Lord Denning MR expressed any view whether those articles created new torts or wrongs in English law. It was unnecessary for the purposes of that case to do more than to decide that it was arguable that those articles could be used as a shield, whether or not they could also be used as a sword; and in the *Valor International* case [1978] 3 CMLR 87 at 100 Roskill LJ, who had been a member of the court in the *Falks Veritas* case, pointed this out and said that there were –

> 'many questions which will have to be argued in this Court or elsewhere in this country or at Luxembourg, before it can be stated categorically ... that Articles 85 and 86 create new torts or wrongs...'.

The concept of conduct by a plaintiff in legal proceedings that may be relied on by the defendant as a defence to the plaintiff's claim although it *does not* give rise to a cause of action on the part of the defendant against the plaintiff is one with which English law is familiar. Examples of the application of this concept are provided by estoppel and, what Roskill LJ may have had in mind as presenting the closest analogy to a contravention of Article 85 or Article 86, the application of the maxim *ex turpi causa non oritur actio*. There is nothing whatever in his observations to suggest that it had ever crossed his mind that, if Article 86 *did* give rise to a cause of action in English private law on the part of an individual citizen who suffered pecuniary loss as a result of another individual's contravention of that article, the resulting cause of action might have the unique and heterodox characteristics that it gave a remedy by injunction to prevent future pecuniary loss but none in damages for loss that had already been sustained.

To summarise, the Court of Appeal was in my view wrong in suggesting that, if it were established at the trial (a) that the Board had contravened Article 86 and (b) that such contravention had (i) caused the company pecuniary loss and (ii) thereby given rise to a cause of action in English law on the part of the company against the Board, it was a seriously arguable proposition that such a cause of action did not entitle the company to a remedy in damages although it did entitle the company to a remedy by injunction. Parker J did not misunderstand the law in this respect. He was entitled to take the view that a remedy in damages would be available and, for the reasons I have stated earlier, that such remedy would be adequate.

...

Lords Keith, Bridge and Brandon agreed. Lord Wilberforce dissented on the ground that the availability of damages for breaches of Article 86 was uncertain. In his view the House should not decide this 'difficult question of law' in the course of interlocutory proceedings.

FURTHER READING

Brearly, M., 'The Burden of Proof before the European Court' 10 ELRev (1985) 250

Davidson, J., 'Enforcing Community Competition Law in National Courts' 35 NI Legal Q (1984) 68

Forrester, I., 'Legal Profession Privilege' 20 CMLRev (1983) 75

Faull, J., '*A.M. & S*: The Commission's Practice Note' 8 ELRev (1983) 411

Holden, S., 'Notify and Justify' 5 JL and Com (1985) 644

Joshua, J. 'Information in EC Competition Law Procedures' 11 ELRev (1986) 40

Joshua, J. 'Proof in Contested EC Competition Cases: a Comparison with the Rules of Evidence in Common Law' 12 ELRev (1987) 315

Kerse, C., *EEC Antitrust Procedure*, 1981, supplemented 1984

Temple Laing, J., 'EEC Competition Actions in Member States' Courts' 7 Fordham Int LJ (1983-4) 389

Zoller, E., 'Remedies for Unfair Trade: European and United States Views' 18 Cornell Int LJ (1985) 227

12

EQUAL PAY AND TREATMENT

I THE PRINCIPLE OF EQUAL PAY

Article 119 of the EEC Treaty provides for the application of the principle that men and women should receive equal pay for equal work. The article has a two-fold object: first, to ensure that undertakings in Member States which apply such a principle should not be placed at a competitive disadvantage relative to those in Member States which fail to do so; and secondly, to meet the social aim of equality, which the Court recognises as one of the Community's goals.

EEC Treaty

Article 119

Each Member State shall during the first stage ensure and subsequently maintain the application of the principle that men and women should receive equal pay for equal work.

For the purpose of this Article, 'pay' means the ordinary basic or minimum wage or salary and any other consideration, whether in cash or in kind, which the worker receives, directly or indirectly, in respect of his employment from his employer.

Equal pay without discrimination based on sex means:

(a) that pay for the same work at piece rates shall be calculated on the basis of the same unit of measurement;

(b) that pay for work at time rates shall be the same for the same job.

The implementation of that principle is further governed by a directive of 1975, made under Article 100 of the Treaty.

Council Directive No 75/117 of 10 February 1975 on the approximation of the laws of the Member States relating to the application of the principle of equal pay for men and women OJ 1975 L 45/19

Article 1

The principle of equal pay for men and women outlined in Article 119 of the Treaty, hereinafter called 'principle of equal pay', means, for the same work or for work to which equal value is attributed, the elimination of all discrimination on grounds of sex with regard to all aspects and conditions of remuneration.

In particular, where a job classification system is used for determining pay, it must be based on the same criteria for both men and women and so drawn up as to exclude any discrimination on grounds of sex.

Article 2

Member States shall introduce into their national legal systems such measures as are necessary to enable all employees who consider themselves wronged by failure to apply the principle of equal pay to pursue their claims by judicial process after possible recourse to other competent authorities.

Article 3

Member States shall abolish all discrimination between men and women arising from laws, regulations or administrative provisions which is contrary to the principle of equal pay.

Article 4

Member States shall take the necessary measures to ensure that provisions appearing in collective agreements, wage scales, wage agreements or individual contracts of employment which are contrary to the principle of equal pay shall be, or may be declared, null and void or may be amended.

Article 5

Member States shall take the necessary measures to protect employees against dismissal by the employer as a reaction to a complaint within the undertaking or to any legal proceedings aimed at enforcing compliance with the principle of equal pay.

Article 6

Member States shall, in accordance with their national circumstances and legal systems, take the measures necessary to ensure that the principle of equal pay is applied. They shall see that effective means are available to take care that this principle is observed.

Article 7

Member States shall take care that the provisions adopted pursuant to this directive, together with the relevant provisions already in force, are brought to the attention of employees by all appropriate means, for example at their place of employment.

...

The Court has ruled that Article 119 is capable of producing direct effects; but it does so only in relation to 'direct and overt discrimination'. Furthermore, it cannot in general be relied upon to support claims concerning pay periods prior to the date of the Court's judgment in that case.

Case 43/75 Gabrielle Defrenne v Sabena (No 1)
[1976] ECR 455; [1976] 2 CMLR 98

Miss Defrenne was an air stewardess employed by the Belgian airline, Sabena. In an action before a Belgian court she claimed damages equal to the difference between the pay that she had received between 15 February 1963 and 1 February 1966 and the pay received in the same period by her male colleagues working as cabin stewards. Her action was based on Article 119 of the EEC Treaty. The Belgian court asked the European Court to rule whether that article produced direct effects.

The Court

...

The question of the direct effect of Article 119 must be considered in the light of the nature of the principle of equal pay, the aim of this provision and its place in the scheme of the Treaty.

Article 119 pursues a double aim.

First, in the light of the different stages of the development of social legislation in the various Member States, the aim of Article 119 is to avoid a situation in which undertakings established in States which have actually implemented the principle of equal pay suffer a competitive disadvantage in intra-Community competition as compared with undertakings established in States which have not yet eliminated discrimination against women workers as regards pay.

Secondly, this provision forms part of the social objectives of the Community, which is not merely an economic union, but is at the same time intended, by common action, to ensure social progress and seek the constant improvement of the living and working conditions of their peoples, as is emphasised by the preamble to the Treaty.

This aim is accentuated by the insertion of Article 119 into the body of a chapter devoted to social policy whose preliminary provision, Article 117, marks 'the need to promote improved working conditions and an improved standard of living for workers, so as to make possible their harmonisation while the improvement is being maintained'.

This double aim, which is at once economic and social, shows that the principle of equal pay forms part of the foundations of the Community.

Furthermore, this explains why the Treaty has provided for the complete implementation of this principle by the end of the first stage of the transitional period.

Therefore, in interpreting this provision, it is impossible to base any argument on the dilatoriness and resistance which have delayed the actual implementation of this basic principle in certain Member States.

In particular, since Article 229 appears in the context of the harmonisation of working conditions while the improvement is being maintained, the objection that the terms of this article may be observed in other ways than by raising the lowest salaries may be set aside.

Under the terms of the first paragraph of Article 119, the Member States are bound to ensure and maintain 'the application of the principle that men and women should receive equal pay for equal work'.

The second and third paragraphs of the same article add a certain number of details concerning the concepts of pay and work referred to in the first paragraph.

For the purposes of the implementation of these provisions a distinction must be drawn within the whole area of application of Article 119 between, first, direct and overt discrimination which may be identified solely with the aid of the criteria based on equal work and equal pay referred to by the article in question and, secondly, indirect and disguised discrimination which can only be identified by reference to more explicit implementing provisions of a Community or national character.

It is impossible not to recognise that the complete implementation of the aim pursued by Article 119, by means of the elimination of all discrimination, direct or indirect, between men and women workers, not only as regards individual undertakings but also entire branches of industry and even of the economic system as a whole, may in certain cases involve the elaboration of criteria whose implementation necessitates the taking of appropriate measures at Community and national level.

...

Among the forms of direct discrimination which may be identified solely by reference to the criteria laid down by Article 119 must be included in particular those which have their origin in legislative provisions or in collective labour agreements and which may be detected on the basis of a purely legal analysis of the situation.

This applies even more in cases where men and women receive unequal pay for equal work carried out in the same establishment or service, whether public or private.

As is shown by the very findings of the judgment making the reference, in such a situation the court is in a position to establish all the facts which enable it to decide whether a woman worker is receiving lower pay than a male worker performing the same task.

In such situation, at least, Article 119 is directly applicable and may thus give rise to individual rights which the courts must protect.

...

The Temporal Effect of this Judgment

The Governments of Ireland and the United Kingdom have drawn the Court's attention to the possible economic consequences of attributing direct effect to the provisions of Article 119, on the ground that such a decision might, in many branches of economic life, result in the introduction of claims dating back to the time at which such effect came into existence.

In view of the large number of people concerned such claims, which undertakings could not have foreseen, might seriously affect the financial situation of such undertakings and even drive some of them to bankruptcy.

Although the practical consequences of any judicial decision must be carefully taken into account, it would be impossible to go so far as to diminish the objectivity of the law and compromise its future application on the ground of the possible repercussions which might result, as regards the past, from such a judicial decision.

However, in the light of the conduct of several of the Member States and the views adopted by the Commission and repeatedly brought to the notice of the circles concerned, it is appropriate to take exceptionally into account the fact that, over a prolonged period, the parties concerned have been led to continue with practices which were contrary to Article 119, although not yet prohibited under their national law.

The fact that, in spite of the warnings given, the Commission did not initiate proceedings under Article 169 against the Member States concerned, on grounds of failure to fulfil an obligation was likely to consolidate the incorrect impression as to the effects of Article 119.

In these circumstances, it is appropriate to determine that, as the general level at which pay would have been fixed cannot be known, important considerations of legal certainty affecting all the interests involved, both public and private, make it impossible in principle to reopen the question as regards the past.

Therefore, the direct effect of Article 119 cannot be relied on in order to support claims concerning pay periods prior to the date of this judgment, except as regards those workers who have already brought legal proceedings or made an equivalent claim.

The principle of equal pay is not confined to cases like *Defrenne* where men and women are contemporaneously doing equal work for the same employer. It extends also to any case in which a woman is paid less than a man would be paid for doing the work in question.

Case 129/79 McCarthays Ltd v Wendy Smith
[1980] ECR 1275; [1980] 2 CMLR 205

Mrs Smith was employed by McCarthays Ltd., as a warehouse manageress, at a weekly salary of £50. She complained of discrimination because her predecessor, a man, whose post she took up after an interval of four months, was paid £60 a week. She brought proceedings before an industrial tribunal on the basis of the Equal Pay Act and succeeded. Her employer appealed to the Employment Appeal Tribunal and thence to the Court of Appeal, which referred to the European Court a question on the interpretation of Article 119 of the EEC Treaty.

The Court

...

According to the first paragraph of Article 119 the Member States are obliged to ensure and maintain 'the application of the principle that men and women should receive equal pay for equal work'.

As the Court indicated in the *Defrenne* judgment of 8 April 1976, that provision applies directly, and without the need for more detailed implementing measures on the part of the Community or the Member States, to all forms of direct and overt discrimination which may be identified solely with the aid of the criteria of equal work and equal pay referred to by the article in question. Among the forms of discrimination which may be thus judicially identified, the Court mentioned in particular cases where men and women receive unequal pay for equal work carried out in the same establishment or service.

In such a situation the decisive test lies in establishing whether there is a difference in treatment between a man and a woman performing 'equal work' within the meaning of Article 119. The scope of that concept, which is entirely qualitative in character in that it is exclusively concerned with the nature of the services in question, may not be restricted by the introduction of a requirement of contemporaneity.

It must be acknowledged, however, that, as the Employment Appeal Tribunal properly recognised, it cannot be ruled out that a difference in pay between two workers occupying the same post but at different periods in time may be explained by the operation of factors which are unconnected with any discrimination on grounds of sex. That is a question of fact which it is for the court or tribunal to decide.

Thus the answer to the ... question should be that the principle that men and women should receive equal pay for equal work, enshrined in Article 119 of the EEC Treaty, is not confined to situations in which men and women are contemporaneously doing equal work for the same employer.

In *MCarthays* v *Smith*, the Court acknowledged that a difference in pay between two workers occupying the same post at different times may be explained by factors unconnected with sex. The same is true in the case of a difference in pay between full-time workers, who are principally men, and part-time workers, who are principally women. Discrimination between full-time and part-time workers may amount to disguised discrimination on grounds of sex; but it will be lawful if it is attributable to factors unconnected with sex.

Case 96/80 Jeanette Pauline Jenkins v Kingsgate (Clothing Productions) Ltd
[1981] ECR 911; [1981] 2 CMLR 24

Mrs Jenkins worked part-time for Kingsgate. She received an hourly rate of pay lower than that of one of her male colleagues, employed full-time on the same work. Prior to 1975 the employer had paid different wages to men and women but the hourly rate was the same whether work was part-time or full-time. From November 1975 the pay for full-time work became the same for male and female workers but the hourly rate for part-time workers was fixed at a level lower than that for full-time workers. All of the part-time workers were women except for one male worker who had just retired and had been allowed, exceptionally, to continue working.

Mrs Jenkins brought proceedings before an industrial tribunal. On appeal to the Employment Appeal Tribunal, questions were referred to the European Court for a preliminary ruling.

The Court

...

It appears from the first three questions and the reasons stated in the order making the reference that the national court is principally concerned to know whether a difference in the level of pay for work carried out part-time and the same work carried out full-time may amount to discrimination of a kind prohibited by Article 119 of the Treaty when the category of part-time workers is exclusively or predominantly comprised of women.

The answer to the questions thus understood is that the purpose of Article 119 is to ensure the application of the principle of equal pay for men and women for the same work. The differences in pay prohibited by that provision are therefore exclusively those based on the difference of the sex of the workers. Consequently the fact that part-time work is paid at an hourly rate lower than pay for full-time work does not amount *per se* to discrimination prohibited by Article 119 provided that the hourly rates are applied to workers belonging to either category without distinction based on sex.

If there is no such distinction, therefore, *the fact that work paid at time rates is remunerated at an hourly rate which varies according to the number of hours worked per*

week does not offend against the principle of equal pay laid down in Article 119 of the Treaty in so far as the difference in pay between part-time work and full-time work is attributable to factors which are objectively justified and are in no way related to any discrimination based on sex.

Such may be the case, in particular, when by giving hourly rates of pay which are lower for part-time work than those for full-time work the employer is endeavouring, on economic grounds which may be objectively justified, to encourage full-time work irrespective of the sex of the worker.

By contrast, if it is established that a considerably smaller percentage of women than of men perform the minimum number of weekly working hours required in order to be able to claim the full-time hourly rate of pay, the inequality in pay will be contrary to Article 119 of the Treaty where, regard being had to the difficulties encountered by women in arranging to work that minimum number of hours per week, the pay policy of the undertaking in question cannot be explained by factors other than discrimination based on sex.

Where the hourly rate of pay differs according to whether the work is part-time or full-time it is for the national courts to decide in each individual case whether, regard being had to the facts of the case, its history and the employer's intention, a pay policy such as that which is at issue in the main proceedings although represented as a difference based on weekly working hours is or is not in reality discrimination based on the sex of the worker.

The reply to the first three questions must therefore be that *a difference in pay between full-time workers and part-time workers does not amount to discrimination prohibited by Article 119 of the Treaty unless it is in reality merely an indirect way of reducing the level of pay of part-time workers on the ground that that group of workers is composed exclusively or predominantly of women.*

...

II THE MEANING OF 'PAY'

The second paragraph of Article 119 defines pay broadly, to include any consideration in cash or kind which the worker receives in respect of his employment. It therefore includes special travel facilities provided by an employer for former employees after their retirement, even when they are provided without contractual obligation.

Case 12/81 Eileen Garland v British Rail Engineering Limited [1982] ECR 359; [1982] 1 CMLR 696

Mrs Garland was a former employee of British Rail Engineering Ltd. It was the employer's policy to extend free travel facilities to its former male employees and their spouses and children on the retirement of the employee. Mrs Garland complained that the employer did not follow a similar policy in regard to female employees. She pursued her complaint in the domestic courts as far as the House of Lords, which referred to the European Court questions for a preliminary ruling.

The Court

According to the order making the reference for a preliminary ruling, when male employees of the respondent undertaking retire from their employment on reaching retirement age they continue to be granted special travel facilities for themselves, their wives and their dependent children.

A feature of those facilities is that they are granted in kind by the employer to the retired male employee or his dependants directly or indirectly in respect of his employment.

Moreover, it appears from a letter sent by the British Railways Board to the trade unions on 4 December 1975 that the special travel facilities granted after retirement must be considered to be an extension of the facilities granted during the period of employment.

It follows from those considerations that rail travel facilities such as those referred to by the House of Lords fulfil the criteria enabling them to be treated as pay within the meaning of Article 119 of the EEC Treaty.

The argument that the facilities are not related to a contractual obligation is immaterial. The legal nature of the facilities is not important for the purposes of the application of Article 119 provided that they are granted in respect of the employment.

It follows that where an employer (although not bound to do so by contract) provides special travel facilities for former male employees to enjoy after their retirement this constitutes discrimination within the meaning of Article 119 against former female employees who do not receive the same facilities.

Special difficulties arise in applying Article 119 to provisions in contracts of employment governing the age of retirement and the provision of retirement pensions. So far as concerns the age of retirement, it seems clear that any discrimination practised by an employer is discrimination as regards conditions of employment and not discrimination as regards pay.

Case 149/77 Gabrielle Defrenne v Sabena (No 2)
[1978] ECR 1365; [1978] 3 CMLR 312

The Court

...

The first part of the question raised by the Cour de Cassation seeks to discover whether the principle of equal pay laid down by Article 119 may be interpreted as requiring general equality of working conditions for men and women, so that the insertion into the contract of employment of an air hostess of a clause bringing the contract to an end when she reaches the age of 40 years, it being established that no such limit is attached to the contract of male cabin attendants who carry out the same work, constitutes discrimination prohibited by the said provision.

According to the appellant in the main action Article 119 must be given a wide interpretation, inasmuch as it is only a specific statement of a general principle against discrimination which has found many expressions in the Treaty.

In particular she claims that the contested clause contained in the contract of employment of air hostesses, fixing an age limit of 40, is subject to the rule against discrimination contained in Article 119 by reason of the fact that, first, a woman worker can receive pay equal to that received by men only if the requirement regarding equal conditions of employment is first satisfied and, secondly, that the age limit imposed on air hostesses by the contract of employment has pecuniary consequences which are prejudicial as regards the allowance on termination of service and pension.

The field of application of Article 119 must be determined within the context of the system of the social provisions of the Treaty, which are set out in the chapter formed by Article 117 *et seq*.

The general features of the conditions of employment and working conditions are considered in Articles 117 and 118 from the point of view of the harmonisation of the social systems of the Member States and of the approximation of their laws in that field.

There is no doubt that the elimination of discrimination based on the sex of workers forms part of the programme for social and legislative policy which was clarified in certain respects by the Council Resolution of 21 January 1974 (Official Journal, C 13, p. 1).

The same thought also underlies Council Directive No 76/207/EEC of 9 February 1976 on the implementation of the principle of equal treatment for men and women as regards access to employment, vocational training and promotion and working conditions (Official Journal, L 39, p. 40).

In contrast to the provisions of Articles 117 and 118, which are essentially in the nature of a programme, Article 119, which is limited to the question of pay discrimination between men and women workers, constitutes a special rule, whose application is linked to precise factors.

In these circumstances it is impossible to extend the scope of that article to elements of the employment relationship other than those expressly referred to.

In particular, the fact that the fixing of certain conditions of employment – such as a special age limit – may have pecuniary consequences is not sufficient to bring such conditions within the field of application of Article 119, which is based on the close connection which exists between the nature of the services provided and the amount of remuneration.

That is *a fortiori* true since the touchstone which forms the basis of Article 119 – that is, the comparable nature of the services provided by workers of either sex – is a factor as regards which all workers are *ex hypothesi* on an equal footing, whereas in many respects an assessment of the other conditions of employment and working conditions involves factors connected with the sex of the workers, taking into account considerations affecting the special position of women in the work process.

It is, therefore, impossible to widen the terms of Article 119 to the point, first, of jeopardising the direct applicability which that provision must be acknowledged to have in its own sphere and, secondly, of intervening in an area reserved by Articles 117 and 118 to the discretion of the authorities referred to therein.

The reply to the first part of the question must therefore be that *Article 119 of the Treaty cannot be interpreted as prescribing, in addition to equal pay, equality in respect of the other working conditions applicable to men and women.*

So far as pensions are concerned, it seems that a contribution paid by an employer to an independent pension fund with which the worker is insured does not normally amount to 'pay' because it is not received by the worker. Moreover, a payment made by such a fund to a worker or to his survivors does not normally amount to 'pay' within the meaning of Article 119, because it is not made by the employer in respect of employment: rather, it is made by the fund in respect of the occurrence of an insured risk. It is otherwise, however, when the contribution made by the employer to the fund takes the form of an addition to the gross salary and therefore helps to determine the amount of the salary for the purposes of taxation, calculation of mortgage facilities and the like.

Case 69/80 Susan Jane Worringham and Margaret Humphreys v Lloyds Bank Ltd [1981] ECR 767; [1981] 2 CMLR 1

The Court

...

Lloyds applies to its staff two retirement benefits schemes, one for men and one for women. Under these retirement benefits schemes, which are the result of collective bargaining between the trade unions and Lloyds and which have been approved by the national authorities under the Finance Act 1970 and certified under the Social Security Pensions Act 1975, the member contracts out of the earnings-related part of the State pension scheme and this part is replaced by a contractual scheme.

It follows from the same order that although the two retirement benefits schemes applied by Lloyds do not essentially involve a difference in the treatment of men and women as regards the benefits relating to the retirement pension, they lay down different rules as regards other aspects not related to that pension.

The unequal pay alleged in this case before the national court originates, according to the plaintiffs in the main action, in the provisions of these two retirement benefits schemes relating to the requirement to contribute applicable to staff who have not yet attained the age of 25. In fact, it is clear from the order making the reference that men under 25 years of age are required to contribute 5% of their salary to their scheme whereas women are not required to do so. In order to cover the contribution payable by the men, Lloyds adds an additional 5% to the gross salary paid to those workers which is then deducted and paid directly to the trustees of the retirement benefits scheme in question on behalf of those workers.

The order making the reference also shows that workers leaving their employment who consent to the transfer of their accrued rights to the State pension scheme receive a 'contributions equivalent premium' which entitles them to the refund, subject to deductions in respect of a part of the cost of the premium and in respect of income tax, of their past contributions to the scheme of which they were members, with interest; that amount includes, in the case of men under the age of 25, the 5% contribution paid in their name by the employer.

Finally, as follows from the information provided by the national court, the amount of the salary in which the above-mentioned 5% contribution is included helps to determine the amount of certain benefits and social advantages such as redundancy payments, unemployment benefits and family allowances, as well as mortgage and credit facilities.

...

Under the second paragraph of Article 119 of the EEC Treaty, 'pay' means, for the purpose of that provision, 'the ordinary basic or minimum wage or salary and any other consideration, whether in cash or in kind, which the worker receives, directly or indirectly, in respect of his employment from his employer'.

Sums such as those in question which are included in the calculation of the gross salary payable to the employee and which directly determine the calculation of other advantages

linked to the salary, such as redundancy payments, unemployment benefits, family allowances and credit facilities, form part of the worker's pay within the meaning of the second paragraph of Article 119 of the Treaty even if they are immediately deducted by the employer and paid to a pension fund on behalf of the employee. This applies *a fortiori* where those sums are refunded in certain circumstances and subject to certain deductions to the employee as being repayable to him if he ceases to belong to the contractual retirement benefits scheme under which they were deducted.

III THE MEANING OF 'EQUAL WORK'

Although Article 119 refers only to 'equal work', Directive No 75/117 uses the expression 'the same work or ... work to which equal value is attributed'. Thus it is the responsibility of each Member State to guarantee the right to receive equal pay for work of equal value. In the absence of a system of job evaluation, a worker must be entitled to claim before an appropriate authority that his or her work has the same value as other work, performed by a person of the opposite sex.

Case 61/81 Commission v United Kingdom
[1982] ECR 2601; [1982] 3 CMLR 284

The Court

By application lodged at the Court Registry on 18 March 1981 the Commission of the European Communities brought an action under Article 169 of the EEC Treaty for a declaration that the United Kingdom had failed to fulfil its obligations under the Treaty by failing to adopt the laws, regulations or administrative provisions needed to comply with Council Directive No 75/117/EEC of 10 February 1975 on the approximation of the laws of the Member States relating to the application of the principle of equal pay for men and women (Official Journal L 1975, 45, p. 19), as regards the elimination of discrimination for work to which equal value is attributed.

The first article of the directive, which the Commission considers has not been applied by the United Kingdom, provides that:

'The principle of equal pay for men and women outlined in Article 119 of the Treaty, hereinafter called "principle of equal pay", means, for the same work or for work to which equal value is attributed, the elimination of all discrimination on grounds of sex with regard to all aspects and conditions of remuneration.

'In particular, where a job classification system is used for determining pay, it must be based on the same criteria for both men and women and so drawn up as to exclude any discrimination on grounds of sex'.

The reference to 'work to which equal value is attributed' is used in the United Kingdom in the Equal Pay Act 1970, as amended by the Sex Discrimination Act 1975. Section 1(5) of the Act provides that:

'A woman is to be regarded as employed on work rated as equivalent with that of any men if, but only if, her job and their job have been given an equal value, in terms of the demand made on the worker under various headings (for instance effort, skill, decision), on a study undertaken with a view to evaluating in those terms the jobs to be done by all or any of the employees in an undertaking or group of undertakings, or would have been given an equal value but for the evaluation being made on a system setting different values for men and women on the same demand under any heading'.

Comparison of those provisions reveals that the job classification system is, under the directive, merely one of several methods for determining pay for work to which equal value is attributed, whereas under the provision in the Equal Pay Act quoted above the introduction of such a system is the sole method of achieving such a result.

It is also noteworthy that, as the United Kingdom concedes, British legislation does not permit the introduction of a job classification system without the employer's consent. Workers in the United Kingdom are therefore unable to have their work rated as being of equal value with comparable work if their employer refuses to introduce a classification system.

The United Kingdom attempts to justify that state of affairs by pointing out that Article 1 of the directive says nothing about the right of an employee to insist on having pay determined by a job classification system. On that basis it concludes that the worker may not insist on a comparative evaluation of different work by the job classification method, the introduction of which is at the employer's discretion.

The United Kingdom's interpretation amounts to a denial of the very existence of a right to equal pay for work of equal value where no classification has been made. Such a position is not consonant with the general scheme and provisions of Directive No 75/117. The recitals in the preamble to that directive indicate that its essential purpose is to implement the principle that men and women should receive equal pay contained in Article 119 of the Treaty and that it is primarily the responsibility of the Member States to ensure the application of this principle by means of appropriate laws, regulations and administrative provisions in such a way that all employees in the Community can be protected in these matters.

To achieve that end the principle is defined in the first paragraph of Article 1 so as to include under the term 'the same work', the case of 'work to which equal value is attributed', and the second paragraph emphasises merely that where a job classification system is used for determining pay it is necessary to ensure that it is based on the same criteria for both men and women and so drawn up as to exclude any discrimination on grounds of sex.

It follows that where there is disagreement as to the application of that concept a worker must be entitled to claim before an appropriate authority that his work has the same value as other work and, if that is found to be the case, to have his rights under the Treaty and the directive acknowledged by a binding decision. Any method which excludes the option prevents the aims of the directive from being achieved.

...

IV THE PRINCIPLE OF EQUAL TREATMENT

No Treaty article provides expressly for the application of the principle of equal treatment of men and women, save in relation to pay. Acting on the basis of Article 235 of the EEC Treaty, therefore, the Council made a directive governing the application of that principle.

Council Directive No 76/207 of 9 February 1976 on the implementation of the principle of equal treatment for men and women as regards access to employment, vocational training and promotion, and working conditions OJ 1976 L 39/40

Article 1

1. The purpose of this directive is to put into effect in the Member States the principle of equal treatment for men and women as regards access to employment, including promotion, and to vocational training and as regards working conditions and, on the conditions referred to in paragraph 2, social security. This principle is hereinafter referred to as 'the principle of equal treatment'.

2. With a view to ensuring the progressive implementation of the principle of equal treatment in matters of social security, the Council, acting on a proposal from the Commission, will adopt provisions defining its substance, its scope and the arrangements for its application.

Article 2

1. For the purposes of the following provisions, *the principle of equal treatment shall mean that there shall be no discrimination whatsoever on grounds of sex either directly or indirectly by reference in particular to marital or family status.*

2. This directive shall be without prejudice to the right of Member States to exclude from its field of application those occupational activities and, where appropriate, the training leading thereto, for which, by reason of their nature or the context in which they are carried out, the sex of the worker constitutes a determining factor.

3. This directive shall be without prejudice to provisions concerning the protection of women, particularly as regards pregnancy and maternity.

4. This directive shall be without prejudice to measures to promote equal opportunity for men and women, in particular by removing existing inequalities which affect women's opportunities in the areas referred to in Article 1 (1).

Article 3

1. Application of the principle of equal treatment means that there shall be no discrimination whatsoever on grounds of sex in the conditions, including selection criteria, for access to all jobs or posts, whatever the sector or branch of activity, and to all levels of the occupational hierarchy.

2. To this end, Member States shall take the measures necessary to ensure that:

(a) any laws, regulations and administrative provisions contrary to the principle of equal treatment shall be abolished;

(b) any provisions contrary to the principle of equal treatment which are included in collective agreements, individual contracts of employment, internal rules of undertakings or in rules governing the independent occupations and professions shall be, or may be declared, null and void or may be amended;

(c) those laws, regulations and administrative provisions contrary to the principle of equal treatment when the concern for protection which originally inspired them is no longer well founded shall be revised; and that where similar provisions are included in collective agreements, labour and management shall be requested to undertake the desired revision.

Article 4

Application of the principle of equal treatment with regard to access to all types and to all levels of vocational guidance, vocational training, advanced vocational training and retraining, means that Member States shall take all necessary measures to ensure that:

(a) any laws, regulations and administrative provisions contrary to the principle of equal treatment shall be abolished;

(b) any provisions contrary to the principle of equal treatment which are included in collective agreements, individual contracts of employment, internal rules of undertakings or in rules governing the independent occupations and professions shall be, or may be declared, null and void or may be amended;

(c) without prejudice to the freedom granted in certain Member States to certain private training establishments, vocational guidance, vocational training, advanced vocational training and retraining shall be accessible on the basis of the same criteria and at the same levels without any discrimination on grounds of sex.

Article 5

1. Application of the principle of equal treatment with regard to working conditions, including the conditions governing dismissal, means that men and women shall be guaranteed the same conditions without discrimination on grounds of sex.

2. To this end, Member States shall take the measures necessary to ensure that:

(a) any laws, regulations and administrative provisions contrary to the principle of equal treatment shall be abolished;

(b) any provisions contrary to the principle of equal treatment which are included in collective agreements, individual contracts of employment, internal rules of undertakings or in rules governing the independent occupations and professions shall be, or may be declared, null and void or may be amended;

(c) those laws, regulations and administrative provisions contrary to the principle of equal treatment when the concern for protection which originally inspired them is no longer well founded shall be revised; and that where similar provisions are included in collective agreements labour, and management shall be requested to undertake the desired revision.

Article 6

Member States shall introduce into their national legal systems such measures as are necessary to enable all persons who consider themselves wronged by failure to apply to them the principle of equal treatment within the meaning of Articles 3, 4 and 5 to pursue their claims by judicial process after possible recourse to other competent authorities.

Article 7

Member States shall take the necessary measures to protect employees against dismissal by the employer as a reaction to a complaint within the undertaking or to any legal proceedings aimed at enforcing compliance with the principle of equal treatment.

Article 8

Member States shall take care that the provisions adopted pursuant to this directive, together with the relevant provisions already in force, are brought to the attention of employees by all appropriate means, for example at their place of employment.

Article 9

1. Member States shall put into force the laws, regulations and administrative provisions necessary in order to comply with this directive within 30 months of its notification and shall immediately inform the Commission thereof.

However, as regards the first part of Article 3(2)(c) and the first part of Article 5(2)(c), Member States shall carry out a first examination and if necessary a first revision of the laws, regulations and administrative provisions referred to therein within four years of notification of this directive.

2. Member States shall periodically assess the occupational activities referred to in Article 2(2) in order to decide, in the light of social developments, whether there is justification for maintaining the exclusions concerned. They shall notify the Commission of the results of this assessment.

3. Member States shall also communicate to the Commission the texts of laws, regulations and administrative provisions which they adopt in the field covered by this directive.

...

The principle of equal treatment has to be applied in relation to access to employment, including promotion and to vocational training and working conditions. It does not apply to social policy in general. In particular, Directive No 76/207 does not prohibit the difference in treatment that results from the application of a provision of national law to the effect that an adoptive father does not have the right given to an adoptive mother of maternity leave following the first three months following the actual entry of a child into the adoptive family: Case 163/82 *Commission* v *Italy* [1983] ECR 3273; [1984] 3 CMLR 169. Furthermore, the directive does not confer on the father of a child the same rights in respect of maternity leave as are coferred on the mother. It leaves Member States with a discretion as to the social measures which they adopt in order to guarantee the protection of women in connection with pregnancy and maternity: Case 184/83 *Hofmann* v *Barmer Ersatzkasse* [1984] ECR 3047; [1986] 1 CMLR 242.

On the other hand, Directive No 76/207 covers all collective agreements without distinction as to the nature of the legal effects that they may produce. This is because even a collective agreement which is not binding as between the parties is apt to have important consequences in fact for the employment relations to which it pertains.

Case 165/82 Commission v United Kingdom
[1983] ECR 3431; [1984] 1 CMLR 44

The Court

...

The Commission charges the United Kingdom with only partially implementing the directive in so far as it has failed to amend and supplement the Sex Discrimination Act

1975 [hereinafter referred to as 'the 1975 Act'] which, although abolishing discrimination in certain areas of employment, allows it to continue in other areas in which by virtue of the directive discrimination must be abolished by 12 August 1978 at the latest.

The Commission's complaints relate to the following points:

(a) Neither the 1975 Act nor any other provision of the legislation in force in the United Kingdom provides that provisions contrary to the principle of equal treatment contained in collective agreements, rules of undertakings and rules governing independent occupations and professions are to be, or may be declared, void or may be amended.

(b) Contrary to the provisions of the directive, section 6(3) of the 1975 Act provides that the prohibition of discrimination does not apply to employment in a private household or where the number of persons employed by an employer does not exceed five (disregarding persons employed in a private household).

(c) Finally, by virtue of Section 20 of the 1975 Act the prohibition of discrimination based on sex does not apply to the employment, promotion and training of midwives.

The First Complaint

The Government of the United Kingdom considers that this complaint is unfounded. By virtue of Section 18 of the Trade Union and Labour Relations Act 1974, any collective agreements made before 1 December 1971 or after the entry into force of that act are to be presumed not to have been intended by the parties to be legally enforceable unless they are in writing and contain a provision in which the parties express their intention that the agreements are to be legally enforceable. In fact, collective agreements are not normally legally binding. The United Kingdom Government is not aware of there being any legally binding collective agreements at present in force in the United Kingdom.

Even if collective agreements containing provisions contrary to the principle of equality of treatment do exist, those provisions, in so far as they are not capable of amendment under section 3 of the Equal Pay Act 1970, would be rendered void by section 77 of the 1975 Act.

...

These arguments are not sufficient to nullify the complaints made by the Commission. Whilst it may be admitted that the United Kingdom legislation satisfies the obligations imposed by the directive as regards any collective agreements which have legally binding effects, in so far as they are covered by Section 77 of the 1975 Act, it is to be noted on the other hand that the United Kingdom legislation contains no corresponding provision regarding either non-binding collective agreements – which the United Kingdom Government declares to be the only kind in existence – or the internal rules of undertakings or the rules governing independent occupations or professions.

The United Kingdom's argument to the effect that the non-binding character of collective agreements removes them from the field of application of that directive cannot be accepted, even if account is taken of the United Kingdom's observation that individual contracts of employment entered into within the framework of a collective agreement are rendered void by section 77 of the 1975 Act.

Article 4(b) of Directive No 76/207 provides that the application of the principle of equal treatment in the areas to which it relates means that Member States must take the necessary measures to ensure that:

...

'(b) any provisions contrary to the principle of equal treatment which are included in collective agreements, individual contracts of employment, internal rules of undertakings or in rules governing the independent occupations and professions shall be, or may be declared, null and void or may be amended'.

The directive thus covers all collective agreements without distinction as to the nature of the legal effects which they do or do not produce. The reason for that generality lies in the fact that, even if they are not legally binding as between the parties who sign them or with regard to the employment relationships which they govern, collective agreements nevertheless have important de facto *consequences for the employment relationships to which they refer, particularly in so far as they determine the rights of the workers and, in the interests of industrial harmony, give undertakings satisfy or need not satisfy.* The need to ensure that the directive is completely effective therefore requires that any clauses in such agreements which are incompatible with the obligations imposed by the directive upon the Member States may be rendered inoperative, eliminated or amended by appropriate means.

The Second Complaint

According to the United Kingdom, the exclusions from the prohibition of discrimination provided for in Section 6(3) of the 1975 Act in the case of employment in a private household or in undertakings where the number of persons employed does not exceed five are justified by the exception provided for in Article 2(2) of the directive itself, according to which:

'This directive shall be without prejudice to the right of Member States to exclude from its field of application those occupational activities and, where appropriate, the training leading thereto, for which, by reason of their nature or the context in which they are carried out, the sex of the worker constitutes a determining factor'.

It must be recognised that the provision of the 1975 Act in question is intended, in so far as it refers to employment in a private household, to reconcile the principle of equality of treatment with the principle of respect for private life, which is also fundamental. Reconciliation of that kind is one of the factors which must be taken into consideration in determining the scope of the exception provided for in Article 2(2) of the directive.

Whilst it is undeniable that, for certain kinds of employment in private households, that consideration may be decisive, that is not the case for all the kinds of employment in question.

As regards small undertakings with not more than five employees, the United Kingdom has not put forward any argument to show that in any undertaking of that size the sex of the worker would be a determining factor by reason of the nature of his activities or the context in which they are carried out.

Consequently, *by reason of its generality, the exclusion provided for in the contested provision of the 1975 Act goes beyond the objective which may be lawfully pursued within the framework of Article 2(2) of the directive.*

The Third Complaint

The Commission's third complaint relates to the fact that the 1975 Act ensures access to the occupation of midwife and to training for that occupation only within certain limits. This is said to entail discrimination based on sex.

...

It is undeniable that in the area in question, as the United Kingdom acknowledges, the Member States are under an obligation to implement the principle of equality of treatment.

It must however be recognised that at the present time personal sensitivities may play an important role in relations between midwife and patient. In those circumstances, it may be stated that by failing fully to apply the principle laid down in the directive, the United Kingdom has not exceeded the limits of the power granted to the Member States by Articles 9(2) and 2(2) of the directive. The Commission's complaint in that regard cannot therefore be upheld.

Article 6 of Directive No 76/207 requires Member States to ensure that those who consider themselves wronged by a failure to observe the principle of equal treatment shall have the means of pursuing their claims by judicial process. Member States are free to choose between the various forms of sanctions that may be imposed upon an employer who fails to observe that principle: but if the State chooses to penalise breaches by an award of compensation, the amount of compensation must not be purely nominal: Case 79/83 *Dorit Harz* v *Deutsche Tradax* [1984] ECR 1921.

V RETIREMENT

Discrimination between men and women as regards the age of compulsory retirement certainly falls within the scope of Directive No 76/207. An age limit for compulsory termination of employment pursuant to an employer's policy concerning retirement amounts to 'dismissal' within the meaning of Article 5(1) of that directive: Case 152/84 *Marshall* v *Southampton and South-West Hampshire Area Health Authority* [1986] ECR 723; [1986] 1 CMLR 688.

By similar reasoning, the conditions of access to voluntary redundancy benefit paid by an employer to a worker wishing to leave his employment falls within the scope of Directive No 76/207. It amounts to a working condition, as there defined. The Court has ruled, however, that the principle of equal treatment is not infringed when access to voluntary redundancy is made available only during the five years preceding the minimum pensionable age fixed by national social security legislation and that age is not the same for men and women.

Case 19/81 Arthur Burton v British Railways Board
[1982] ECR 555; [1982] 2 CMLR 136

Mr Burton was an employee of the British Railways Board, which made an offer of redundancy to some of its employees. The terms of the offer were such that employees could avail themselves of the scheme if they were within five years of reaching pensionable age. Pensionable age was defined by statute as 65 for men and 60 for women. Mr Burton was 58: he was therefore ineligible to avail himself of the scheme although a woman of that age would have been eligible.

He brought proceedings before an industrial tribunal. On appeal, the Employment Appeal Tribunal referred questions to the European Court.

The Court

...

The principal issue raised by those questions is whether the requirement that a male worker should have reached the age of 60 in order to be eligible for payment of a voluntary redundancy benefit whereas women workers became eligible at the age of 55 amounts to discrimination prohibited by Article 119 of the Treaty or by Article 1 of Directive No 75/117 or, at least, by Directive No 6/207 and, if so, whether the relevant provision of Community law may be relied upon in the national courts.

...

From the information supplied by the United Kingdom Government in the course of the proceedings it appears that a worker who is permitted by the Board to take voluntary early retirement must do so within the five years preceding the normal minimum age of retirement, and that he may receive the following benefits: (1) the lump sum calculated in accordance with the provisions of the Redundancy Payments Act 1965, (2) a lump sum calculated on the basis of the total length of his employment with the Board, and (3) 25% of the sum of the first two amounts. In addition he is entitled up to the minimum retiring age to an early retirement pension equal to the pension to which he would have been entitled had he attained the minimum statutory retirement age and to an advance, repayable at the minimum retiring age, equal to the sum to which he becomes entitled at that age.

Council Directive No 79/7/EEC of 19 December 1978 on the progressive implementation of the principle of equal treatment for men and women in matters of social security, which was adopted with particular reference to Article 235 of the Treaty, provides in Article 7 that the directive shall be without prejudice to the right of Member States to exclude from its scope the determination of pensionable age for the purposes of granting old-age and retirement pensions and the possible consequences thereof for other benefits.

It follows that the determination of a minimum pensionable age for social security purposes which is not the same for men as for women does not amount to discrimination prohibited by Community law.

The option given to workers by the provisions at issue in the present instance is tied to the retirement scheme governed by United Kingdom social security provisions. It enables a worker who leaves his employment at any time during the five years before he reaches normal pensionable age to receive certain allowances for a limited period. The allowances are calculated in the same manner regardless of the sex of the worker. The only difference between the benefits for men and those for women stems from the fact that the minimum pensionable age under the national legislation is not the same for men as for women.

In the circumstances the different age conditions for men and women with regard to access to voluntary redundancy cannot be regarded as discrimination within the meaning of Directive No 76/207.

VI SOCIAL SECURITY

As the Court pointed out in *Burton* v *British Railways Board*, the application of the principle of equal treatment to the field of social security is governed by a separate directive made in 1978.

Council Directive No 79/7 of 19 December 1978 on the progressive implementation of the principle of equal treatment for men and women in matters of social security OJ 1979 L 6/24

Article 1

The purpose of this directive is the progressive implementation, in the field of social security and other elements of social protection provided for in Article 3, of the principle of equal treatment for men and women in matters of social security, hereinafter referred to as 'the principle of equal treatment'.

Article 2

This directive shall apply to the working population – including self-employed persons, workers and self-employed persons whose activity is interrupted by illness, accident or involuntary unemployment and persons seeking employment – and to retired or invalided workers and self-employed persons.

Article 3

1. This directive shall apply to:

(a) statutory schemes which provide protection against the following risks:
- sickness,
- invalidity,
- old age,
- accidents at work and occupational diseases,
- unemployment;

(b) social assistance, in so far as it is intended to supplement or replace the schemes referred to in (a).

2. This directive shall not apply to the provisions concerning survivors' benefits nor to those concerning family benefits, except in the case of family benefits granted by way of increases of benefits due in respect of the risks referred to in paragraph 1(a).

3. With a view to ensuring implementation of the principle of equal treatment in occupational schemes, the Council, acting on a proposal from the Commission, will adopt provisions defining its substance, its scope and the arrangements for its application.

Article 4

1. The principle of equal treatment means that there shall be no discrimination whatsoever on ground of sex either directly, or indirectly by reference in particular to marital or family status, in particular as concerns:
- the scope of the schemes and the conditions of access thereto,
- the obligation to contribute and the calculation of contributions,

- the calculation of benefits including increases due in respect of a spouse and for dependants and the conditions governing the duration and retention of entitlements to benefits.

2. The principle of equal treatment shall be without prejudice to the provisions relating to the protection of women on the grounds of maternity.

Article 5

Member States shall take the measures necessary to ensure that any laws, regulations and administrative provisions contrary to the principle of equal treatment are abolished.

Article 6

Member States shall introduce into their national legal systems such measures as are necessary to enable all persons who consider themselves wronged by failure to apply the principle of equal treatment to pursue their claims by judicial process, possibly after recourse to other competent authorities.

Article 7

1. This directive shall be without prejudice to the right of Member States to exclude from its scope:

(a) the determination of pensionable age for the purposes of granting old-age and retirement pensions and the possible consequences thereof for other benefits;

(b) advantages in respect of old-age pension schemes granted to persons who have brought up children; the acquisition of benefit entitlements following periods of interruption of employment due to the bringing up of children;

(c) the granting of old-age or invalidity benefit entitlements by virtue of the derived entitlements of a wife;

(d) the granting of increases of long-term invalidity, old-age, accidents at work and occupational disease benefits for a dependent wife;

(e) the consequences of the exercise, before the adoption of this directive, of a right of option not to acquire rights or incur obligations under a statutory scheme.

2. Member States shall periodically examine matters excluded under paragraph 1 in order to ascertain, in the light of social developments in the matter concerned, whether there is justification for maintaining the exclusions concerned.

Article 8

1. Member States shall bring into force the laws, regulations and administrative provisions necessary to comply with this directive within six years of its notification. They shall immediately inform the Commission thereof.

2. Member States shall communicate to the Commission the text of laws, regulations and administrative provisions which they adopt in the field covered by this directive, including measures adopted pursuant to Article 7(2).

They shall inform the Commission of their reasons for maintaining any existing provisions on the matters referred to in Article 7(1) and of the possibilities for reviewing them at a later date.

Article 9

Within seven years of notification of this directive, Member States shall forward all information necessary to the Commission to enable it to draw up a report on the application of this directive for submission to the Council and to propose such further measures as may be required for the implementation of the principle of equal treatment.

...

The Court has interpreted the above directive in a broad sense, so that the term 'working population' in Article 2 includes a person who interrupts her work in order to care for a disabled relation; and the term 'statutory schemes which provide protection against ... invalidity' includes a statutory scheme providing protection against loss of earnings occasioned by a healthy person who gives up work in order to look after an invalid.

Case 150/85 Jacqueline Drake v Chief Adjudication Officer
[1986] ECR 1995; [1986] 3 CMLR 43

Mrs Drake gave up work in order to look after her mother, an invalid. The Social Security Act 1975 provided for the payment of invalid care allowance to a person who, in addition to meeting other conditions, was regularly and substantially engaged in caring for a severely disabled person. At the material time, the Act provided that the allowance should not be paid to a married woman living with her husband. Since Mrs Drake did live with her husband, the Adjudication Officer rejected an application made by Mrs Drake for payment of the allowance. On her appeal to the Chief Social Security Commissioner, questions were referred for a preliminary ruling to the European Court.

The Court

...

It must be pointed out first of all that according to the first and second recitals in the preamble to Directive No 79/7, the aim of that directive is the progressive implementation of the principle of equal treatment for men and women in matters of social security.

According to Article 3(1), Directive No 79/7 applies to statutory schemes which provide protection against, *inter alia,* the risk of invalidity (subparagraph(a)) and social assistance in so far as it is intended to supplement or replace the invalidity scheme (subparagraph (b)). In order to fall within the scope of the directive, therefore, a benefit must constitute the whole or part of a statutory scheme providing protection against one of the specified risks or a form of social assistance having the same objective.

Under Article 2, the term 'working population', which determines the scope of the directive, is defined broadly to include 'self-employed persons, workers and self-employed persons whose activity is interrupted by illness, accident or involuntary unemployment and persons seeking employment ... [and] retired or invalided workers and self-employed persons'. That provision is based on the idea that a person whose work has been interrupted by one of the risks referred to in Article 3 belongs to the working population. That is the case of Mrs Drake, who has given up work solely because of one of the risks listed in Article 3, namely the invalidity of her mother. She must therefore be regarded as a member of the working population for the purposes of the directive.

Furthermore, it is possible for the Member States to provide protection against the consequences of the risk of invalidity in various ways. For example, a Member State may, as the United Kingdom has done, provide for two separate allowances, one payable to the disabled person himself and the other payable to a person who provides care, while another Member State may arrive at the same result by paying an allowance to the disabled person at a rate equivalent to the sum of those two benefits. *In order, therefore, to ensure that the progressive implementation of the principle of equal treatment referred to in Article 1 of Directive No 97/7 and defined in Article 4 is carried out in a harmonious manner throughout the Community, Article 3(1) must be interpreted as including any benefit which in a broad sense forms part of one of the statutory schemes referred to or a social assistance provision intended to supplement or replace such a scheme.*

Moreover, the payment of the benefit to a person who provides care still depends on the existence of a situation of invalidity inasmuch as such a situation is a condition *sine qua non* for its payment, as the Adjudication Officer admitted during the oral procedure. It must also be emphasised that there is a clear economic link between the benefit and the disabled person, since the disabled person derives an advantage from the fact that an allowance is paid to the person caring for him.

It follows that the fact that a benefit which forms part of a statutory invalidity scheme is paid to a third party and not directly to the disabled person does not place it outside the scope of Directive No 79/7. Otherwise, as the Commission emphasised in its observations, it would be possible, by making formal changes to existing benefits covered by the directive, to remove them from its scope.

The Court had no difficulty in ruling thereafter that Article 4 of Directive No 79/7 is infringed when national legislation provides that a benefit falling within the directive shall not be payable to a married woman living with her husband. No similar rule applied to married men.

FURTHER READING

Arnull, A. 'Article 119 and Equal Pay for Work of Equal Value' II ELRev (1986) 200

Atkins, A. 'Equal Treatment and Retirement Age' 49 MLR (1986) 508

Brown, L. 'Air Hostesses: A Reply' 47 MLR (1984) 692

Curtin, D. 'Effective Sanctions and the Equal Treatment Directive' 23 CMLRev (1986) 505

Curtin, D. 'Occupational Pension Schemes and Article 119: Beyond the Fringe' 24 CMLRev (1987) 215

Plender, R. 'Equal Pay for Men and Women: Two Recent Decisions of the European Court' 30 Am Jo Comp L (1982) 627

Shrubsall, V. 'Sex Discrimination, Retirement and Pensions' 48 MLR (1985) 373

Steiner, J. 'Sex Discrimination under UK Law and EEC Law' 32 ICLQ (1983) 399 [illegible] ... For example, [illegible] ... [illegible]

[illegible] ... [illegible] ... [illegible]

[illegible] ... [illegible] the existence of a situation of [illegible] ... [illegible] ... as [illegible] the [illegible] ... during the oral proceedings ... [illegible] ... [illegible] ... [illegible]

[illegible] ... [illegible]

The Court has no [illegible] ... [illegible] ... [illegible] ... [illegible]

FURTHER READING

[illegible]
[illegible] (1959)
[illegible]
[illegible]
[illegible]
[illegible]

Index